I Have No Enemies

I Have No Enemies

The Life and Legacy
of Liu Xiaobo

Perry Link and Wu Dazhi

Columbia University Press

New York

Columbia University Press
Publishers Since 1893
New York   Chichester, West Sussex
cup.columbia.edu

Library of Congress Cataloging-in-Publication Data
Names: Link, Perry, 1944– author. | Wu, Dazhi, author.
Title: I have no enemies : the life and legacy of Liu Xiaobo / Perry Link, Wu Dazhi.
Description: New York : Columbia University Press, 2023. | Includes index.
Identifiers: LCCN 2022043191 (print) | LCCN 2022043192 (ebook) |
ISBN 9780231206341 (hardback) | ISBN 9780231556446 (ebook)
Subjects: LCSH: Liu, Xiaobo, 1955–2017. | Political prisoners—China—Biography. |
Dissenters—China—Biography. | Nobel Prize winners—Biography.
Classification: LCC CT1828.L595 L56 2023 (print) | LCC CT1828.L595 (ebook) |
DDC 951.05092 [B]—dc23/eng/20220907
LC record available at https://lccn.loc.gov/2022043191
LC ebook record available at https://lccn.loc.gov/2022043192

Columbia University Press books are printed on permanent and durable acid-free paper.
Printed in the United States of America

Cover design: Elliott S. Cairns
Cover image: dpa picture alliance archive / Alamy Stock Photo

Contents

Acknowledgments

We are grateful to a number of friends and acquaintances of Xiaobo who have been willing to talk or write to us about him. Some did this at risk to themselves, and for this reason we cannot name them here. Those we can mention include, alphabetically, Geremie Barmé, Jean-Philippe Béja, Peter Bernstein, Michel Bonnin, Jeremy Brown, Markus Büchler, Cai Chu, Chang Ping, Chen Jun, Chen Kuide, Chen Xiaoping, Cheng Yinghong, Donald Clarke, Gao Ertai, Gao Yu, Guo Jian, Guo Lijia, Hao Jian, Hu Ping, Hu Yong, Jiang Qisheng, Jin Zhong, Lei Yi, Li Datong, Li Jie, Li Xueguo, Liang Xiaoyan, Liao Yiwu, Liu Di, Liu Dong, Liu Hui, Liu Suli, Liu Xia, Lu Yueguang, Ma Shaofang, Tienchi Martin-Liao, Bonnie S. McDougall, Mo Shaoping, Paul Pickowicz, Pu Zhiqiang, Shang Baojun, Jon Solomon, Su Xiaokang, Sun Jin, Tang Xiaodu, Teng Biao, Tong Yi, Wang Chaohua, Wang Dongcheng, Wang Xiaoni, Wang Ya, Wei Haitian, Wen Kejian, Elizabeth Wichmann-Walczak, Wu Bin, Wu Liang, Renee Xia, Xiao Qiang, Xu Jingya, Xu Xiao, Xu Youyu, Yang Zhuo, Yu Jie, Zhang Xiaoyang, Zhang Yu, Zhang Zuhua, Zhou Duo, Zhou Zhongling, and Zou Jin.

We are grateful to the University of California, Riverside, to the Centre for Transcultural Studies at the University of Heidelberg, and to the Robert B. Silvers Grants for Work in Progress for generous support of our research.

Eight lines of Bei Dao's poem "The Answer," as translated by Bonnie S. McDougall in *The Rose of Time* (1988), are reprinted by permission of New Directions Publishing Corporation.

A Note on Names

How should a nonspeaker of Chinese pronounce the name Liu Xiaobo? The *x* used in the hanyu pinyin romanization system is something like "sh." A first pass at saying the name in English would be l'yo (rhymes with "go") shao (rhymes with "how") bo (as in "boring").

Readers unfamiliar with Chinese names should note that surnames come first in Chinese. We often refer to Liu Xiaobo only by his given name, Xiaobo, mainly to avoid ambiguity. About 67 million people in China are surnamed Liu.

Wu Dazhi is a pen name. The third syllable, "zhi," sounds almost like "Jer" in "New Jersey."

A Liu Xiaobo Chronology

December 28, 1955	Born in Changchun city, Jilin province, third of five sons to Liu Ling, a teacher at Northeast Normal University, and Zhang Suqin, a teacher at the university's nursery school
September 1962	Enters the primary school attached to Northeast Normal University
September 1968	Enters the junior high school attached to Northeast Normal University
December 1969	After China's universities are closed for the Cultural Revolution, accompanies parents and younger brothers Xiaoxuan and Xiaodong to Boulder Village, Horqin Right Front Banner, Inner Mongolia. Attends junior high school. Gets to know Tao Li, whom he later marries
Fall 1973	Returns to Changchun for high school at the Jilin Provincial Experimental School while father resumes work at Northeast Normal University
July 1974	Graduates from high school
Fall 1974	Sent to San'gang Commune in Nongan county, Jilin province, in a "sent-down youth" program
Fall 1976	Returns to Changchun and works for more than a year mixing cement for a construction company
December 1977	Passes the new national college entrance examination
March 1978	Begins study in the Chinese Department at Jilin University in Changchun

Spring 1980	Joins the student literary club, *Pure Hearts*
January 1982	Graduates with a B.A. in Chinese literature from Jilin University
February 1982	Begins graduate school in the Department of Chinese at Beijing Normal University (BNU)
October 1982	Marries Tao Li
June 1983	Son Liu Tao born
December 1983	Publishes first article, "Methods of Expression in My Country's Classical Aesthetics"
December 1984	Finishes M.A. work and is retained at BNU as a teaching assistant
September 1986	Enters Ph.D. program in Chinese at BNU
September 7–12, 1986	At national symposium on literature with famous literary figures, gives iconoclastic speech and earns the sobriquet "dark horse" on the literary scene
January 1988	*Critique of Choices* published and soon becomes a bestseller
June 1988	Before a packed house, defends Ph.D. dissertation, "Aesthetics and Human Freedom," published in September by BNU Press
August 1988	Travels as visiting scholar to universities in Oslo, Honolulu, and New York, visiting Hong Kong along the way
March 1989	*The Fog of Metaphysics* published in Shanghai
April 27, 1989	Leaves New York for Beijing to immerse himself in the democracy movement at Tiananmen
June 3–4, 1989	During the massacre in Beijing, helps to arrange the exit of several thousand students from Tiananmen Square
June 6, 1989	Sent to Qincheng Prison in Beijing as a "black hand" behind the student protests. Writes a "confession" that he later intensely regrets
September 1989	Fired from BNU
May 1990	*Contemporary Chinese Politics and Chinese Intellectuals* published in Taipei
August 1990	Tao Li serves him with divorce papers; he assents
1990 and 1996	Human Rights Watch awards him Hellman/Hammett grants for writers who have been victims of political persecution and are in financial need

January 26, 1991	Released from Qincheng Prison
September 1992	*Monologues of a Doomsday Survivor* published in Taipei
January–May, 1993	Visits Australia and the United States for seminars, lectures, and showings of the documentary film *The Gate of Heavenly Peace*
May 1995–January 1996	Sent for eight months of "monitored residence" in a courtyard in the Beijing suburbs
February 1996	Marries Liu Xia in traditional style, holding a banquet for family and friends
October 8, 1996	Arrested in Beijing; fifteen days later sent to a reeducation-through-labor camp in Dalian, Liaoning province, for "disturbing social order" by advocating dialogue with Taiwan
April 8, 1998	Marries Liu Xia officially, inside the labor camp
October 7, 1999	Released from Dalian labor camp; rejoins Liu Xia in Beijing
August 2000	*A Beauty Gave Me a Knockout Drug*, coauthored with Wang Shuo, published in Hubei
September 2000	*Selected Poems of Liu Xiaobo and Liu Xia* published in Hong Kong
July 2001	Chinese writers around the world inaugurate the Independent Chinese PEN Center. Liu Xiaobo and Liu Xia are the only two members from mainland China
2002	*A Nation That Lies to Conscience* published in Taipei. Xiaobo's thinking takes a major turn toward diving into society and focusing on rights, through 2008 in work with the Rights Defense Movement
May 2003	Receives "Outstanding Democracy Activist Award" from the Chinese Democracy Education Foundation in San Francisco
October 2003	Elected president of Independent Chinese PEN; re-elected in 2005
December 2004	Receives "Press Freedom Award" from Reporters Without Borders
2005	*The Dawn of a Free China Lies in Civil Awakening* published in Washington, D.C.; receives Hong Kong Human Rights Press Award

June 2006	*Single-Blade Poison Sword: A Critique of Contemporary Chinese Nationalism* published in California
October 2006	Becomes chief editor of U.S.-based website Democratic China
August 2007	Receives "Courage of Conscience Award" from Human Rights Foundation of Asia and the Pacific
September 2008	Joins the effort to edit and gather signatures for the democracy manifesto "Charter 08"
December 8, 2008	For his activities in support of Charter 08, taken from home by police and held under "residential surveillance" at undisclosed location
March 2009	Receives in absentia, in Prague, Homo Homini Prize for defense of human rights
April 2009	Receives PEN/Barbara Goldsmith Freedom to Write Award
December 23, 2009	Tried in Beijing intermediate court for "agitating to subvert state power"
December 25, 2009	Sentenced to eleven years in prison
May 26, 2010	Transferred to Jinzhou Prison in Liaoning province
October 4, 2010	Receives Alison Des Forges Award for Extraordinary Activism from Human Rights Watch
October 6, 2010	Receives Hermann Kesten Medal from PEN Centre Germany
October 8, 2010	Nobel Peace Prize Committee in Oslo announces that he has won for 2010
December 10, 2010	Awarded the Nobel Peace Prize in Oslo, in absentia
June 7, 2017	Transferred to First Hospital of China Medical University in Shenyang, Liaoning province; diagnosis of stage 4 liver cancer confirmed
July 13, 2017	Dies in Shenyang hospital
July 15, 2017	Ashes buried at sea

I

Arrest, Trial, and the Road to a Nobel Prize

When police took Liu Xiaobo from his home late at night on December 8, 2008, neither he nor his wife, Liu Xia, imagined that he would not return. The next morning Liu Xia found that their telephone did not work. Accompanied by Jiang Qisheng, a good friend, she went out knocking on doors in search of her husband: at the local police station, the police headquarters, the complaint department of the Beijing Public Security Bureau, and elsewhere. No help. Someone finally offered her the word "detained." Absorbing the gravity of the matter, she reached out to another friend, an experienced lawyer named Mo Shaoping. About three weeks after that, on January 1, 2009, she finally received notice that her husband's legal status was "under residential supervision"—but the "residence" was not identified.

Major media in the Western world carried the news of Xiaobo's disappearance. Did it happen because of Charter 08, the prodemocracy manifesto he had sponsored? Where had the police taken him? What were the charges? What about his friends who had also been working on Charter 08? Spokespeople for the regime, beset by such questions, at first were unsure how to respond. They needed to wait for instructions from the highest authorities about what to say. The signers of Charter 08 included some well-known names, so the official responses would need political wordsmithing approved by the very top. On December 10, International Human Rights Day, a representative of the Foreign Ministry dared say only, and incredibly, that he did not know that Xiaobo had disappeared. In the absence of clear orders from above, the standoff between liberals in society and the professional censors in the regime was at a stalemate. The liberal website Bullog was able to post Charter 08 for more than ten days before its removal was ordered.

The first signal from the top was a blanket order that police everywhere in China invite anyone who had signed Charter 08 to tea. The phrase "invite to tea" means that the invitee (the one "suffering tea drinking," *bei he cha* 被喝茶, as the popular phrase has it) is on the radar screen of the police. Tea interviews normally happen in relaxed places: a teahouse, a fast-food restaurant, perhaps a person's office. Their minimal purpose is to let a person know that he or she is being watched. That fact alone generates nervousness and maybe reluctance to continue taking risks. A second purpose—crucial in the aftermath of Charter 08—is to gather information about other people, with questions like: Did you really sign? Why? Who asked you to? Who was in charge? A third level of questioning, which more often happens in police stations, is to do "thought work" on a person. Don't you know that the people you are involved with will come to no good? Wouldn't your life be wealthier and smoother if you did something else? Transcripts are kept, and interviewees are asked to sign them. The processes are common enough that they can be pro forma. In a 2006 essay, Xiaobo writes of "the degeneration of dictatorship" that the interrogations reveal.[1] Young police simply turn wheels and check off boxes.

While enduring low-level harassment from tea invitations and surveillance, charter signers were cheered as they learned of support for their project, both inside China and overseas. On December 9, a "Proclamation by Overseas Chinese Scholars on the Release in China of Charter 08" popped up on the Internet. It was signed by Yü Ying-shih, whom many regarded as the greatest living historian of China; Fang Lizhi, the famous dissident astrophysicist who was now living in Arizona; Ha Jin, the prizewinning Chinese American novelist; Hu Ping, editor of the overseas dissident magazine *Beijing Spring*; and about fifty others. The proclamation said that Charter 08

> honors China's traditional proverb that "the fate of all depends on the actions of each"; it also honors rationality, intellectual independence, and the rights and responsibilities of modern citizens; it takes stock of history, looks squarely at the present, and peers with hope toward the future; its criticisms of China today are right on mark, its vision is objective, and its proposals are balanced and fair. We are deeply impressed and want to express our endorsement of its every provision.[2]

By signing the proclamation, these distinguished Chinese were in effect also signing Charter 08.

Another piece of good news on December 9 was that the English version of the charter had been posted on the website of *The New York Review of Books*. The world could now see a plain fact that somehow it had failed fully to appreciate before: Chinese human beings are no different from human beings anywhere—they want freedom, equality, human rights, and to live in autonomy and dignity. When China's communist rulers emphasized "Chinese characteristics," they were swimming against the tide of human civilization. Even foreigners sometimes seemed to believe them on this point. With Charter 08, that would be more difficult.

In Berlin, as part of Germany's observance on December 10 of the sixtieth anniversary of the UN Universal Declaration of Human Rights, German Foreign Minister Frank-Walter Steinmeier criticized Beijing's arrest of Liu Xiaobo and insisted that international silence on the matter was unacceptable.

On December 12, forty-two original signers of the charter signed a statement that two of them, Cui Weiping and Xu Youyu, had drafted for publication on the Internet. Xiaobo's sudden disappearance had left these supporters feeling that they too had been violated. They made clear that Xiaobo's arrest would not force them into retreat. Their statement, "We Cannot Be Separated from Liu Xiaobo," read in part:

> We share the thinking and ideals of Mr. Liu Xiaobo, and for that reason cannot be separated from him. The charter is like our soul, with each of us a part of its body. We are a composite. If Mr. Liu Xiaobo suffers harm because of the charter, then we all suffer harm. If he cannot be free, then each one of us is in prison too. . . . Each of us who has signed the charter is also an originator of it. Everything we wish to say is contained in that document, and its text is now publicly available. We hide nothing and have nothing to hide. Nothing we have done needs investigation. Each of us takes responsibility for what is written there.[3]

This statement attracted more people to sign the charter, and the more people signed, the safer it became to do so.

Also on December 12, the Dalai Lama, from exile in Dharamsala, India, announced publicly that Charter 08 "moved and encouraged me greatly." For decades, the regime in China had banned books by the Dalai Lama, blocked news of him, and denounced him as a traitor, and yet, among Chinese intellectuals who managed to stay in touch with the truth, he continued to enjoy a sterling moral reputation. His statement showed characteristic modesty: "I personally believe that President Hu Jintao's call for a harmonious society is a laudable initiative that can provide space to the viewpoints being expressed by a growing number of Chinese people. A harmonious society can only come into being when there is trust among the people, freedom from fear, freedom of expression, rule of law, justice and equality."[4]

Several groups in Hong Kong organized demonstrations at the PRC Liaison Office to protest Xiaobo's detention and the harassment of Charter 08 supporters. In Taiwan, human rights groups put statements on the Internet inviting support from all Taiwan citizens who wished to stand together with people on the mainland to work for the universal values of human rights.

The number of Chinese people both inside and outside China who wanted to sign the charter kept growing, and if anything was increased by the news that the regime was holding Xiaobo at an undisclosed location. Within six days of the charter's appearance, the number of signers leaped from 303 to 1,183. People were ready to stand up and make their voices heard even in the face of the risk involved.

The signature of the renowned artist Ai Weiwei was at the top of a list that appeared on December 13. Two days later, Ai began writing posts on the Bullog website describing what volunteers cleaning up after the Wenchuan earthquake the previous May had seen and heard during their work. He was suggesting that children would not have died if something like Charter 08 had been in place in Sichuan. Clean government would have prevented the shoddy construction that had taken their lives. Was this far-fetched? Not in the view of the regime, apparently, which moved quickly to erase Ai's blogs. Other supporters of Charter 08 began writing at Bullog, and on January 9, 2009, authorities closed the website, explaining that it contained "harmful speech." (The name Bullog came from *bull*—or *niu* in Chinese, which in current slang meant "the best, fantastic"—combined with *log*, "record," to produce "bullog," which also conjured "blog" in English.) The shutdown propelled Charter 08's reputation even further.

On December 16, the twenty-seven member nations of the European Union issued a statement demanding that Chinese authorities make public the reason for arresting Xiaobo and reveal his condition and whereabouts. On December 17, PEN International mailed an open letter signed by its president, Jiri Grusa; international secretary, Eugene Schoulgin; and the chair of its Committee on Writers in Prison, Sarah Clarke, addressed to China's President Hu Jintao, with a copy to Minister of Public Security Meng Jianzhu. The letter demanded the immediate and unconditional release of Liu Xiaobo and all other persons in China currently incarcerated for peaceful expression of their views. That same day, the U.S. Congressional-Executive Commission on China issued a statement calling upon the Chinese authorities to release Liu Xiaobo and to promise no further harassment of people who had signed Charter 08.[5]

On December 19, Vaclav Havel published an op-ed in *The Wall Street Journal* entitled "China's Human-Rights Activists Need Support." He opened by recalling Charter 77, the citizens' initiative that he had worked on in Czechoslovakia in 1977: "We wanted to create not a membership organization, but instead, as I wrote then, 'a free, informal open community of people of different convictions, different faiths, and different professions united by the will to strive, individually and collectively, for the respect of civic and human rights in our own country and throughout the world.'"[6] Havel went on to observe that China in 2008 was in some ways more open than Czechoslovakia in 1977, and that what happened in Czechoslovakia should allow China's rulers to draw an important lesson. "Only the immediate and unconditional release of Liu Xiaobo," he wrote, "will demonstrate that, for Beijing, the lesson has been learned." Xiaobo's supporters were grateful for Havel's support but not optimistic that China's rulers would see the point. In the past such suggestions had struck fear into regime leaders and thereby caused more repression.

Havel wrote his article before he could have known about the first verbal response that the Chinese authorities gave to Charter 08. On December 18, in the Great Hall of the People next to Tiananmen Square, there was a major conference called "Commemorating the Thirtieth Anniversary of the Third Plenum of the Eleventh Central Committee of the Communist Party of China." That famous Third Plenum in 1978 has been generally viewed as the inauguration of Deng Xiaoping's policies of "reform and opening" that broke from Mao Zedong's insistence on "class struggle as the key link" and emphasized economic development instead. The meeting had solidified Deng's place as the new supreme leader. Thirty years later, at the commemorative meeting in 2008, President Hu Jintao declared solemnly: "We must persist without wavering in the basic line of the Party. We must have unmovable resolve in both thought and action, absolutely not return to the old road of isolation and rigidity, but also absolutely not take an iniquitous road that changes our basic nature. We must persist without change in walking the road of socialism with Chinese characteristics."[7] The "iniquitous road that changes our basic nature" was widely understood as referring to Charter 08. Forty years earlier, Mao had fulminated against "taking the capitalist road," and Hu was ringing the same bell now.

Why would Hu want to obliterate any sign of Charter 08 but then obliquely comment on it at a major meeting? From the day the charter appeared, the names "Charter 08" and "Liu Xiaobo" were banned from all media in China; then, when comment from the top did come, it was delivered via code, "iniquitous road." Why not name the charter, denounce it, and openly explain what was wrong with it? The decision reflected a delicate balance within the regime between the need to reject the charter absolutely and the equally important need to keep it from the eyes of the public. Several times in the past, the Party had learned that denunciation of "bourgeois" things can backfire when it reveals enough detail that readers find the denounced items attractive. In 1987 Fang Lizhi became widely known and admired for his advocacy of democracy after—and because—Party propagandists produced a little book quoting his "mistaken" speeches and sent it everywhere in China. If the Chinese people could see Charter 08, they might like it. The authorities' decision to expunge the charter rather than debate it shows that they knew this to be true.

There was one spectacular exception to the public ban on mentioning the charter: the Maoist website called Realm of Nowhere (*wuyou zhi xiang*),[8] known for its strident calls for China to return to class struggle and proletarian revolution. It is not clear whether Realm of Nowhere had connections with the highest authorities, but it did have a large staff, and the fact that it could violate the ban suggests at least some level of political sponsorship. Charter 08, in its view, was a "mad attack by the bourgeoisie" that "blackened socialism"; it was backed by "enemy forces" in the West, aimed at "peaceful evolution" from communism, "split China," and was a "manifesto for color revolution." Its leaders were traitors who "should be subject to severe legal punishment." In all of this, the charter's text was not quoted.

Through early January, the charter became an increasingly dangerous topic, but people kept signing it. The characters 零八宪章 *lingba xianzhang*, "Charter 08," were added to the list of "sensitive" terms that the government's Internet filters tracked and often erased. People got around the filters by using near-homonyms. *Xiànzhāng* 宪章, "charter," for example, temporarily became *xiànzhǎng* 县长, literally "county magistrate."

For democratic-minded people, whether to sign the charter became a matter for careful personal consideration. To sign was to cross a border into a group that openly avowed a preference for freedom. That much felt good. It also felt, in a sense, definitive, something like a baptism. But the move carried obvious dangers as well. There was much discussion on the Internet about the pros and cons of signing. On January 8, one month after the charter appeared, the overseas website list of signatories reached 6,639.[9] That number cannot be taken as exact, because some would-be signers could not reach the site and certain names were false additions by provocateurs who aimed to discredit the list. (Website staff spent time winnowing these out.)

All the while, Xiaobo's physical location and condition remained unknown. Demands for transparency from both inside and outside China went unheeded. The authorities did allow Liu Xia to see him on January 1, New Year's Day, but not at his place of detention. They drove her—and him, separately—to the

Xiaotangshan Conference Center in the northern suburbs of Beijing. The two shared a meal and then were ferried, separately, back whence they had come. Xiaobo could not tell Liu Xia where he was being held because he himself did not know. He had been blindfolded during the transfer and could say only that the place was not very far away. He described the room as resembling a hotel room but with only one light bulb and no windows except for a tiny one in the bathroom. Liu Xia told friends, "When I saw him his face was pallid from lack of exposure to the sun. He said he was kept inside all day and couldn't sleep well. Every morning—sometimes all day—the authorities interrogated him. There was no television set, and he was not allowed to read. He wasn't allowed out of the room, so for exercise he paced briskly back and forth for three hours every day—like a tiger in a cage."[10] Xiaobo's friends and colleagues later figured out that the room was probably in one of the *shuanggui* 双规, "double required," detention centers used for disciplining corrupt officials. ("Double required" was jargon for stipulating that monitored people appear for interrogation at a required place at required times.) The centers were grounded in "belief in the Party," not in law, and therefore functioned extralegally. Detainees could not hire lawyers and were not allowed court procedures. (In 2012, *shuanggui* was formally adopted into law.)

At the Xiaotangshan meeting, the police told Liu Xia that Xiaobo's status with them was "residential supervision." By law that could last a maximum of six months, in his case, up to June 8, 2009, four days beyond the extremely sensitive Tiananmen anniversary date of June 4. The police did not explain why the place of supervision had to be kept secret.

In the early days of his confinement, Xiaobo was not allowed to have pen, paper, or books. When Liu Xia handed the police some books to give him, the police handed the books back. Round-the-clock surveillance of Liu Xia tightened as well. Police stopped all visitors and asked them to show IDs and to register. These procedures were designed to deter visitors, and they worked—but not always. Liu Xia's better friends showed their loyalty by defying the intimidation with frequent visits and inviting her out for meals. When Liu Xia insisted on going out, police allowed it, but required that she ride with them in police cars.

On March 11, 2009, the Czech group People in Need awarded its annual Homo Homini Prize for defense of human rights to Liu Xiaobo. The announcement praised Xiaobo and all other signers of Charter 08 for their peaceful contributions to the promotion of democracy in China. Vaclav Havel presided at the award ceremony in Prague, and three original signers of Charter 08—Xu Youyu, Mo Shaoping, and Cui Weiping—were there to receive the prize on Xiaobo's behalf.

Havel invited the three to his office the next day, asked them in detail how they were faring in the wake of the charter's repression, and encouraged them by recounting memories of his own struggles.

In mid-March, something must have happened behind the scenes within the regime, because pressure on Xiaobo and Liu Xia diminished for no visible reason. Liu Xia was allowed a special visit with Xiaobo on March 20 and this time could bring him books. She brought him Kafka.

In May, as the anniversary of the June Fourth massacre was approaching, Xiaobo's friends felt a special need to do something. Many suspected that the authorities were still detaining him because they knew about his plans for public demonstrations on June Fourth and his aim to nominate the Tiananmen Mothers for the Nobel Peace Prize. With Xiaobo incommunicado, his friends felt it doubly imperative to mark June Fourth. They decided to hold a Beijing seminar on the June Fourth democracy movement on May 10, 2009, with Xu Youyu, Hao Jian, Zhou Duo, Teng Biao, Qin Hui, Xu Xiao, Liang Xiaoyan, and twelve others in attendance. The police followed up by paying special attention to everyone who had been there. Some were invited to tea, some were summoned to police stations, and some were put under house arrest. In the days immediately before and after June 4, police pressure intensified on all "people with different political views" (the regime's euphemism for dissidents).

"Residential supervision" was to expire on June 8, but when the day came Xiaobo remained in custody even though the June Fourth date had passed. Liu Xia was told only that her husband's residential supervision had been "extended." She got no further word until 11:00 a.m. on June 24, when police presented her with a "Notice from Public Security Bureau of Beijing City of the Arrest of Liu Xiaobo." (In the formal language of the regime, what had happened so far was not "arrest" but merely supervision.) It read: "Liu Xiaobo is suspected of the crime of agitating to subvert state power. With the approval of the First Division of the People's Procuratorate of Beijing City, our bureau carried out arrest at 11:00 a.m. on June 23. He is currently being held in the Number One Beijing Municipal Detention Center." The reason the regime waited until June 23 instead of doing the formal arrest on June 8 when "residential supervision" expired is not clear. Friends speculated that it might have been to move the procedure further from the fraught date of June 4. The only two certainties were that there had to be a reason and that the regime did not want to publicize it. At least Liu Xia now knew where Xiaobo was. Again she could bring him books, daily-use items, and pocket money.

Authorities notified Liu Xia that Xiaobo's lawyer, Mo Shaoping, could no longer represent him because Mo had signed Charter 08. Mo pointed out the lack of legal basis for disqualifying a lawyer on grounds of having expressed a political opinion. That went nowhere. Mo relented and assigned his junior colleagues in the Mo Shaoping Law Firm, Shang Baojun and Ding Xikui, to Xiaobo's case.

With the formal arrest of Xiaobo, the ban on mentioning him in the state media was lifted and replaced by a requirement that he be mentioned, but in a specified way. On June 24, the daily briefing of the New China News Agency posted the prescribed words:

> In recent years Liu Xiaobo has used rumor, slander, and other means to agitate for overthrow of the socialist system, has violated *The Criminal Law of the State Council of the People's Republic of China*, and is suspected of agitating to subvert state power. Public security organs of the Beijing Municipality have, according to law, established a prosecutorial process, and on June 23 Liu Xiaobo was arrested with the approval of the relevant procuratorate. Initial investigation has revealed that Liu Xiaobo has fully confessed to the criminal facts brought forth in the charges of the public security organs.

On June 26, Shang Baojun and Ding Xikui were allowed to visit Xiaobo at the detention center. It was the first time since he had been seized on December 8, 2008, that he was allowed to see a lawyer. "Seeing" in this case happened through a glass partition, talking by telephone for about forty minutes. Xiaobo seemed in fairly good spirits. He said conditions were better than at the secret location where he had been held before. At least the room had windows. He had four roommates, so boredom was less of a problem, and he could go outdoors for half an hour every day.

He asked his lawyers if anyone else had been arrested for Charter 08 activities. When they replied that none had, he seemed relieved and, the lawyers reported, told them, "I'm willing to take responsibility and I hope that no one else will be forced to."[11] In jail and facing a hazardous future, he was ready to sacrifice his freedom to protect the freedom of others. His friends noticed this and found it especially admirable when they recalled that he had joined the Charter 08 project late.

The lawyers asked him about the New China News Agency's report that he had "confessed," and Xiaobo said yes, he had confessed to being the author of articles that he had written. Did he mind the regime's sophistry in using the word "confess" ambiguously? He did, but this was a standard tactic. Some people, at least, would see through it and not be fooled.

Before leaving, the lawyers offered to file bail papers for Xiaobo, even though they knew that approval was highly unlikely. Xiaobo agreed. A week later, notice came that the application had been rejected.

Xiaobo's next meeting with his lawyers was on July 22. He told them that since their last meeting he had been subjected to intense interrogation every day except Saturdays and Sundays. The interrogators' focus had gradually changed from Charter 08 to articles Xiaobo had written earlier. They wanted him to give summary accounts of his thinking and how it had evolved. What did he regard as the "distinctive characteristics" of his thought? What did he mean by "bottom-up change" in society? And so on. Never one to hold back, Xiaobo patiently explained his analyses to his interrogators. At the same time, he felt there was something ominous in the way their interests were shifting. Why were they digging back in time, and in more depth? It seemed odd that after arresting him, they were scouring the ground to find reasons, working from their conclusions backward. It seemed his fate had been sealed.

The letter of the law said that "investigation" of people in a detention center could last two months, extendable to three in cases that were "especially complicated." In Xiaobo's case, the three months expired on September 23. The next day, September 24, Xiaobo's lawyers received notice from the Beijing Public Security Bureau that the investigation stage was being extended again. When the lawyers asked the reason, the answers, delivered orally in nonlegal language, were vague and evasive: "it's a high-profile case," "it's very sensitive," and "it coincides with the sixtieth anniversary [of the founding of the People's Republic in 1949]."

Through the lawyers, Liu Xia learned that none of the several dozen books that she had brought to the detention center for Xiaobo ever reached his hands. He was allowed to see only premodern books, like the classic novel *Dream of the Red Chamber*, that were in the center's library. Sympathizers on the Internet had sent him countless postcards, but he received none. He was allowed to watch state television and to exercise. His food was basically potatoes and cabbage. To get better food a detainee had to pay extra, and the prices in the detention center were considerably higher than they were for the same items on the outside. Xiaobo told his lawyers that he was short on money, but every time Liu Xia brought some for him, officials brushed her off, assuring her that Xiaobo had enough. Eventually Liu Xia lost her patience and made a fuss—and after that a thousand yuan each month reached him.

On November 23, Xiaobo's lawyers received yet another notice of extension of the "investigation stage." The stated reason was "need for supplementary investigation." Xiaobo was required to sign a receipt for the notice and took the opportunity to write on it "I protest punishment for speech."

His lawyers were allowed to see him again on November 25. He reported to them that the intensive questioning he had endured during the summer had abated to practically nothing. It seemed clear that "need for supplementary investigation" had not been the real reason for postponing the case.

It occurred to Xiaobo's friends that the authorities might have been eyeing December 23–25 as the best time to hold the trial because international journalists would be busy with the Christmas holiday. There were precedents for the regime's doing its crackdowns when the world was looking elsewhere. In any case, these decisions must have been coming from the very top. Bao Tong, a chief assistant to former General Secretary of the Party Zhao Ziyang, had enough experience near the top of the regime to let his friends in the resistance movement know that only "person number one"—current General Secretary Hu Jintao—could decide such a thing. Only Hu could have made the original decision to detain Xiaobo, and only Hu could give the final nod on his trial and his sentence.

In early December 2009, the "go" signal for Xiaobo's case finally appeared, and the process hurtled forward with unseemly speed. Around 2:00 p.m. on December 8, Xiaobo's lawyers received notice that the legal file had been delivered to the No. 1 Beijing Procuratorate. They went the next morning, December 9, to read it and found that it included twenty volumes, each somewhere between a few dozen and more than two hundred pages in length. The lawyers were allowed to make photocopies, but that task alone took a full day. They were also given a copy of the prosecutorial opinion that the Beijing Public Security Bureau prepared. In the evening of December 10, the lawyers received a telephone call from a judge at the Beijing No. 1 Intermediate Court saying that the Liu Xiaobo case had already arrived there. The lawyers pointed out that for a case to go to court only two days after a defendant's lawyers had seen it was not only rare but in fact illegal. Regulations stated that a case could be at the procuratorate for one month, extendable another half-month, and that the period was to be determined in consultation with the defendant's lawyers. To expect defense lawyers to absorb such volume within two days was obviously unreasonable.

At 2:00 p.m. on December 20 Xiaobo's lawyers received a telephone call from the judge assigned to the case. He said the trial was set to open at courtroom number 23 of the Beijing No. 1 Intermediate Court at 16 Shijingshan Road. This was the same court that had released Xiaobo from prison eighteen years earlier, after he had served time as a "black hand" behind the protests that led to the June Fourth massacre. He might have reflected on his great circle route back to the same place and wondered: Where have we been? Is China any better? (Certainly civil society was.) Has the legal system improved? (Apparently not.)

The trial was set to open on Wednesday, December 23, at 9:00 a.m. Chinese law stipulated that "when a people's court decides to try a case, it shall deliver notice to defense counsel at least three days in advance." Xiaobo's lawyers pointed out that in this case the notice was only 67 hours in advance, five short of the required 72. They lost the point.

When news of Xiaobo's impending trial spread, 165 people who had signed Charter 08 joined in a declaration that said: "To put Mr. Liu Xiaobo on trial is to put the undersigned next him in the defendant's box. Whatever 'crime' he has committed, each of us has committed too. We will accept for ourselves whatever punishment is given to him."[12] After the statement was published an additional 600 people signed it. The regime said nothing.

On December 22, the day before the trial, police invited Liu Xia for a "chat." They explained that she would not be allowed to attend. Their reason was that five months earlier, after Xiaobo had been formally accused, police had given her a questionnaire asking what sources of income she and Xiaobo had, how many computers were in their apartment, what their means of getting online were, and so on. They told her at the time that the questionnaire was required. Now they told her that her decision to complete it made her a "witness for the prosecution," which meant that she could not attend the trial. On the morning of December 23, just to be sure, police barred her from leaving home.

The trial was called "public," but all the seats for the public were reserved for court-selected people. Xiaobo's supporters gathered outside the court building but could not get in. Ding Zilin, head of the Tiananmen Mothers group, had promised that she would be there. Her husband was ill and needed her home care, so she checked him into a hospital in order to keep her promise. But it was not to be. Police came the day before the trial to tell her that she would not be permitted to leave home, and early the next morning five police showed up at her door to be sure the seventy-three-year-old lady did nothing furtive. Her telephone was disconnected. Bao Tong was treated identically: first warned, then forcibly kept at home. For some of Xiaobo's other friends, house arrest continued for three days.

Gentler means were used to keep Westerners away. Dick Thornburg, U.S. Attorney General from 1988 to 1991, had written a letter in August 2009 to Wang Shengjun, President of the Supreme Court of China, asking permission to observe the Liu Xiaobo trial, but never got a reply.

The weather on December 23 was frigid. Temperatures dipped lower than they had in a decade. From about 7:00 a.m. police lined the route between the court and the Babaoshan subway station about 300 yards to the east. Police at the station interrogated people as they emerged and detained anyone who was, or seemed likely to be, headed for the trial. Police cars lined Shijingshan Road on both sides for more than half a mile. At the court itself, about one hundred police had sealed off access with cordons. A "media box" built of steel fencing held fifty or more foreigners—mostly journalists and embassy people.

The biting winter air contained stripes of brightness in the form of yellow ribbons that Xiaobo's supporters had brought with them. They wore them on their arms and chests, tied them to trees and lampposts, and even attached them to the police barriers. Plainclothes agents photographed the ribbon tiers, but that slowed no one. On Twitter, friends who could not be present took down their headshots and put up images of yellow ribbons. Gao Yu, a veteran journalist, hung a giant yellow ribbon from her balcony, where it was visible from a great distance. Other friends of Xiaobo had arisen early to hang yellow ribbons along the motor route through which, they calculated, the authorities would transport Xiaobo when they took him from the detention center to the court. Eight police cars formed the motorcade that carried him.

The courtroom was small. There were seats for only about two dozen people other than staff and lawyers. Xiaobo's brother Xiaoxuan was allowed to attend, as was Liu Xia's brother Liu Hui. The other spectators were young people— probably under thirty years old. Xiaoxuan said later that he did not recognize any of them. They were impassive, perhaps "supplied" by the authorities.

The trial opened at 9:00 a.m. with the prosecutor reading the indictment. It introduced Xiaobo as a "repeat offender": in 1991 he "had been spared criminal punishment for the crime of instigating counterrevolutionary propaganda" and in 1996 had been sentenced to three years of education through labor for "disturbing social order." In something of a surprise, the presentation of his "criminal behavior" began not with Charter 08 but with six of his articles:

"The Authoritarian Patriotism of the Communist Party of China" (October 2005)
"Who Says the Chinese People Deserve Only 'Inner-Party Democracy'?" (January 2006)
"To Change a Regime by Changing a Society" (February 2006)
"The Many Faces of Communist Party Dictatorship" (March 2006)
"How a Rising Dictatorship Hurts Democracy in the World" (April 2006)
"A Deeper Look Into Why Child Slavery in China's 'Black Kilns' Could Happen" (July 2007)

The indictment alleged that to speak of "changing a regime" was dangerous agitation. It further quoted language from the articles that it said constituted "rumor" and "slander." For example:

From the time the Chinese communists took power, what their succession of dictators has cared about most has been maintenance of their power and what they have cared about least has been the lives of people.

The official patriotism promoted by the communist dictators is sophistry that substitutes "Party" for "country"; in asking people to "love the country," it actually demands that they love a regime, love a Party, and love its dictators; it steals the name of patriotism to cover a record of disasters it has brought to the country.

All of these [above listed] techniques are stopgap measures that the dictators are using to try to patch the countless cracks in the creaky edifice of their rule, which they know cannot endure forever.

Turning to Charter 08, the indictment charged that "between September and December of 2008, the defendant Liu Xiaobo, in collusion with others, drafted and concocted slander and libel." This passage from the charter was an example: "We stand today as the only country among the major nations that remains mired in authoritarian politics. Our political system continues to produce human rights disasters and social crises, thereby not only constricting China's own development but also limiting the progress of all of human civilization." "Agitating to subvert state power" was said to be evident in this example: "We must abolish the special privilege of one party to monopolize power. We should build a federated republic of China in a framework of democratic constitutionalism." The indictment went on to say that Xiaobo's offenses involved not just the content of Charter 08 but gathering and publishing signatures. "After gathering more than 300 signatures," it alleged, "Liu Xiaobo sent the charter and the signatures by email to overseas websites [like] Democratic China and Independent Chinese PEN," who later published them.

After the indictment was read, the presiding judge issued a most unusual proclamation: because the prosecution had used only fourteen minutes for its presentation, Xiaobo and his lawyers would also be limited to fourteen minutes. Xiaobo's lawyers immediately objected, pointing out that there was no basis in either law or precedent for such a restriction. It was "an indirect way of depriving the defendant and his counsel of their rights." The judge replied, "It's my court, and what I say goes. I am not concerned with other matters." He then looked at his watch to begin counting the fourteen minutes. When Xiaobo's supporters, outside the court, heard about this, some wondered aloud whether this judge might have his tongue in his cheek. He knew, after all, that he and his court were merely turning wheels for the regime. The decision in the case had already been made—inside a room with stuffed chairs behind the great high red walls of the Zhongnanhai leadership compound. Fourteen minutes? More? Less? It would make no difference. Why not let a sliver of reality shine through in the form of some gentle satire? But there was no way to confirm or disprove such a conjecture.

Xiaobo began his self-defense by acknowledging that most, but not all, of the statements cited in the indictment were correct. "The six articles indeed are mine, and I did contribute to Charter 08," he stated. "But I was able to collect only about 70 signatures for it [not "more than 300," as the indictment alleged]. The other signatures were not collected by me."[13] He insisted, though, that he was entirely innocent of the charges of slander and spreading rumor. To say, as Charter 08 does, that dictatorship in China has led to "human rights disasters" is not "libel" but political expression well within the rights of citizens—and in this case, demonstrable fact. "Criticism is not rumor-mongering," he said, "and opposition is not slander." He further observed that "The selection of excerpts in the indictment has been made with a view to serving the preconceived goals of the prosecutors. It completely ignores the basic position of Charter 08." Then, as if addressing not a gathering of nervous functionaries but intelligent students in a lecture hall, he explained what the charter actually was about:

> Charter 08 avows certain values and advocates certain structures that are aimed at building a free and democratic federated republic in the long term. It lists nineteen specific reform measures and recommends that they be pursued gradually and peacefully. The purposes of these measures are to correct the many abuses in China's current system of crippled reforms and to press the ruling party to convert its program of crippled reforms into a healthier model in which political and economic reforms move forward in tandem. At another level the charter's aim is to bring popular pressure to bear on officialdom to return power to the people as soon as possible. Popular pressure from below can induce political reforms from above and lead to a healthful symbiosis between people and officials that can bring us nearer than ever to the dream of constitutional government that our countrymen have been cherishing now for about a hundred years.

He summarized his political position this way:

> Over the past two decades, from 1989 to 2009, I have consistently held that China's political reform should be gradual, peaceful, orderly, and under control. I have always opposed the notion of sudden radical leaps and have opposed

violent revolution even more stoutly. My preference for a gradual approach to reform is set forth in my essay "To Change a Regime by Changing a Society," where I make it clear that I look to things such as the spread of rights consciousness in society, increased numbers of rights-advocacy projects, greater autonomy at the popular level, and the gradual expansion of civil society as ways to build pressure from below and eventually to compel officialdom to make reforms.

He acknowledged that his essays occasionally contained errors or flamboyant expression: "But none of these errors has anything to do with crime, and [they] cannot be valid evidence in a criminal trial. . . . The right to free speech includes not just the right to say correct things but also the right to say incorrect things. . . . No prison walls are high enough to cut off free expression. Suppressing dissident opinion cannot buy legitimacy for a regime, and political prisons will not bring lasting peace or harmony." He concluded: "I hope that the court, by accepting my plea of 'not guilty,' will allow its ruling on this case to stand as a precedent in Chinese legal history, a precedent able not only to meet the human rights standards in the Chinese constitution and in United Nations covenants, but also to withstand moral scrutiny and the test of time." Xiaobo could not have expected this kind of Olympian perspective to be perceived, let alone adopted, within the narrow and intellectually desiccated context in which he offered it. His words were aimed at his friends, his country, and history.

His lawyers did a good job, given the laughably short time they had for preparation. Regarding the indictment's quotation from six of Xiaobo's articles, they answered:

> Liu Xiaobo has written more than 800 articles totaling more than five million characters, and since 2005 there have been 499 that come to more than 2.1 million characters in length. From this corpus the prosecution has taken 350 words from six articles and Charter 08 as its basis to judge that Liu Xiaobo meets the standard for "the crime of agitating to subvert state power." This obviously is a case of cherry-picking one's evidence.[14]

Charter 08 had used the phrase "federated republic of China," and this was deeply disturbing for communist leaders who could feel confident of their hold on power only by using the euphemistic term "people's republic." Xiaobo's lawyers pointed out that Mao Zedong himself in 1920 had written articles that suggested that China's provinces might best withdraw from the central government and operate as twenty-seven different countries—the Republic of Hunan, Republic of Guang-dong, and so on.[15] In 1922 Mao further advocated that "China be unified under a system of free association in which Mongolia, Tibet, and Huijiang [i.e., Xin-jiang] are part of a federated republic of China"[16]—using that very phrase. So, Xiaobo's lawyers asked, did the prosecution mean that Mao too was guilty of the crime of "splitting" or "subverting" the state?

On the question of Charter 08's call to "abolish the special privilege of one party to monopolize power," the lawyers pointed out many instances from the 1940s in which the Communist Party had attracted support precisely by its call to "end one-party dictatorship" by the Kuomintang. They asked: "Are we to accept that when the Communist Party of China and its prominent leaders come out in opposition to one-party dictatorship or in favor of establishing a federated repub-lic of China, it is a 'great, glorious, correct' advocacy, but when Liu Xiaobo and others do the same the appropriate response is to send them to prison for a crime?"

In addition to mounting these rebuttals, Xiaobo's lawyers compiled a long list of procedural irregularities in how the case had been initiated and investigated and how the trial had been run. Before they could finish presenting it, the judge announced that he was cutting discussion off. Next on the docket would be the "final statement" by Xiaobo. He had prepared a five-page statement that he called "I Have No Enemies," and this was his last chance to say something in public, but the judge told him that he would have only four minutes. When he began, moreover, the judge kept interrupting. When Xiaobo referred to June Fourth, for example, the judge interjected, "Let's not mention that." Xiaobo's friends specu-lated on the reasons. Was the truth too threatening? Was the judge afraid that Xiaobo's eloquence might sway people?

Xiaobo could read only part of his statement in court but later was able to get the full text to Liu Xia, who gave it to Radio Free Asia, who published it. It says in part:

> I wish to underscore something that was in my "June 2nd Hunger-Strike Decla-ration" of twenty years ago: I have no enemies and no hatred. None of the police who have watched, arrested, or interrogated me, none of the prosecutors who have indicted me, and none of the judges who will judge me are my enemies. There is no way that I can accept your surveillance, arrests, indictments, or ver-dicts, but I respect your professions and your persons. This includes Zhang Rongge and Pan Xueqing, the two prosecutors who are bringing the charges against me today. As you interrogated me on December 3, I could sense your respect and sincerity.

Hatred only eats away at a person's intelligence and conscience, and an enemy mentality can poison the spirit of an entire people (as the experience of our country during the Mao era clearly shows). It can lead to cruel and lethal internecine combat, can destroy tolerance and human feeling within a society, and can block the progress of a nation toward freedom and democracy. For these reasons I hope that I can rise above my personal fate and contribute to the progress of our country and to changes in our society. I hope that I can answer the regime's enmity with utmost benevolence, and can use love to dissipate hate.[17]

While Xiaobo was talking about "no enemies" in court, police outside the court building were busy nabbing enemies. Some friends of Xiaobo who had been ordered to stay home had snuck out anyway, and the police assigned to monitor them would have been reprimanded if they were not caught and sent back. Zhang Xianling, a cofounder of the Tiananmen Mothers; Liu Di, a famous activist for Internet freedom; and Teng Biao, a prominent human-rights lawyer, were among the recaptured that morning.

Early that morning Ai Weiwei had tweeted: "Liu Xiaobo, you haven't even gone into battle today but are already returning in glory!" A few minutes past 11:00 a.m., Ai showed up outside the court building. As a knot of reporters surrounded him, he was droll: "I came to see a friend today. Somebody said he's in court. I wonder why he was arrested." Someone in the crowd shouted a line that Ai Weiwei's father, the poet Ai Qing, had written in 1938: "Why are tears so often in my eyes? Is it because I love this piece of land too much?"[18] Someone else observed that what the regime feared most was exactly that thing—love—because love produces strength by binding people together.

The trial ended at 11:40 a.m., less than three hours after it had begun. Xiaobo's lawyers were notified that the verdict would be announced at the same court two days later, December 25, 2009, at 9:30 a.m. Liu Xia wanted to attend—not because she wanted to be the first to hear how many years the sentence would be but because it would be a chance to see Xiaobo. She had not seen him in nine months, since March 20, 2009. Her lawyers worked in advance to ensure that she could attend.

The verdict was read at the appointed hour:

Defendant Liu Xiaobo, with the goal of overthrowing the state power of the people's democratic dictatorship and the socialist system of our country, took advantage of the Internet, with its features of rapid transmission, broad reach, large influence on society, and high degree of public visibility, and chose as his means the writing of articles and posting them on the Internet to do slander and to incite others to subvert state power and the socialist system in our country. His actions have constituted the crime of incitement to subvert state power, have persisted through a long period of time, and show deep subjective malice. The articles that he posted, which spread widely through links, copying, and visits to websites, had a despicable influence. He qualifies as a criminal whose crimes are severe and deserves heavy punishment according to law.

The facts adduced by Branch No. 1 of the People's Procuratorate of Beijing in charging Defendant Liu Xiaobo with the crime of incitement to subvert state power are clear; the evidence is accurate and ample, and the charges are well-founded.... Based on the facts, nature, circumstances, and degree of social harm of the crimes of Defendant Liu Xiaobo, this court, in accordance with Section 2 of Article 105, Section 1 of Article 55, Section 1 of Article 56, and Article 64 of the *Criminal Law of the People's Republic of China*, rules as follows:

1. The Defendant Liu Xiaobo has committed the crime of incitement to subvert state power and is sentenced to eleven years in prison plus the deprivation of political rights for two years. The prison term is calculated from the day of sentencing. (Days in custody prior to sentencing reduce the sentence by one day for one day, which means the term extends from June 23, 2009 to June 21, 2020.)

2. The items submitted with this case that Liu Xiaobo used in committing his crimes are confiscated. (An itemized list is attached.)

The sentence in parentheses at the end of the first point was an error. By law, time spent under "residential supervision"—from December 8, 2008, to June 23, 2009, in Xiaobo's case—also should have been credited toward a prison sentence. Xiaobo's lawyers asked for correction of the error at the appeal stage, but the request was ignored. In the end it did not matter, because Xiaobo died in custody three years before his time was served.

A close examination of the language of the verdict shows that the regime made some minor concessions based on rebuttals Xiaobo had offered in court. Charter 08 was now called a *wenzhang* 文章, "article," whereas earlier it had been *xuanyan* 宣言, "manifesto"—a term that connotes a political program. The claim in Charter 08 that the regime had caused human-rights disasters was termed "libel" in the indictment on December 23, but after Xiaobo said in court that he was simply citing facts (meaning, for example, the Great Leap Forward famine), both the example from Charter 08 and the judgment that it was libel were omitted from the verdict. The indictment had also charged Xiaobo with "gathering more than 300 signatures" for Charter 08, but after Xiaobo said in court that he had gathered only about 70, the language in the verdict was changed to "Liu Xiaobo colluded with others" to get more than 300. This was a concession—but the gratuitously negative connotations of the term "colluded" (*huotong* 伙同) maintained the sense that the offense was serious.

The crime of "agitating to subvert state power" had been added to Chinese law in 1997, and Xiaobo's sentence was the lengthiest that had been levied for it to date. Charter 08 had opposed a one-party monopoly of power, and this was anathema to the Communist Party elite. Heavy punishment was inevitable. Xiaobo's friends and many observers have puzzled over why his sentence was so harsh when others involved with Charter 08 were spared prison sentences. This pattern is not unusual, however. The regime often selects a particular person for punishment and then broadly advertises the punishment together with the alleged offenses to warn everyone in society against similar affronts. Moreover, 303 people had signed the charter, and some of them were deeply respected figures. If even half or a third had been given prison sentences, the outcry would have been earth-shaking to the point of being risky for the regime.

One might wonder why the regime chose Xiaobo to be its main target. The fact that the indictment led with his "six articles" instead of with Charter 08 is one clue. One article refers in its title to changing a regime—*peacefully*, to be sure, but the words are still there. The titles of three of the six articles contain the word *ducai*, "dictator," a term that annoyed Hu Jintao and others at the top almost as much as "regime change" did. The word *ducai* appears a total of 69 times in the bodies of the six texts. A computer scan of Xiaobo's publications between 2000 and 2008 shows 4,526 appearances of either *ducai*, "dictatorship," or *ducaizhe*, "dictator." (A few of these refer to Saddam Hussein, Slobodan Milošević, and Kim Jong Il, but by far most are speaking of China.) Xiaobo's recurrent choice of the term cannot have made Hu Jintao and his colleagues feel good, whether or not they noticed it consciously.

Vocabulary aside, the regime's most important reason for wanting to bring Xiaobo down must have been his role in what was known as the Rights Defense Movement that had begun in the early 2000s. The movement was an essentially leaderless groundswell of activity, but Xiaobo was a conspicuous symbol of it. He offered it both theoretical underpinnings and practical tactics. He was seen as carrying the torch of the Tiananmen movement of spring 1989 and standing at the interface between the regime and society. He worked well with people both "inside the system" and "outside" and with both older and younger generations of resisters. He brought new people into the movement. He always advised that the movement downplay the roles of "leaders," but in the regime's view a leader is just what he was. To put him away would be to remove a root of "instability."

The verdict document provided a space labeled "Opinions on the Judgment of the Concerned Parties." There Xiaobo wrote: "I am innocent. History will have its own verdict on this verdict. And I will appeal."

When the reading of the sentence was over, Liu Xia was allowed ten minutes with her husband. She reported afterward that during those minutes he asked about her parents, their family, and their friends. Both of them were smiling and laughing throughout—even though, she added, both were aware of the outrageous violation of justice that had just occurred.

"He told me to live happily," she said. "I just kept laughing and he seemed relaxed and comfortable, not at all ill at ease. He said he hadn't done anything to hurt a single person—except me. He hoped that I could keep laughing. I said I hoped he could spend his days in prison with peace in his heart."[19]

On December 29, 2009, Xiaobo, back in the detention center, wrote an appeal of the court's verdict that included these words:

The sentence violates the Chinese constitution and international human rights covenants. It cannot bear moral scrutiny and will not pass the test of history. I believe that my work has been just, and that someday China will be a free and democratic country. Our people then will bathe in the sunshine of freedom from fear. I am paying a price to move us in that direction, but without the slightest regret. I have long been aware that when an independent intellectual stands up to an autocratic state, step one toward freedom is often a step into prison. Now I am taking that step; and true freedom is that much nearer.[20]

A month later, on January 28, 2010, Xiaobo's lawyers submitted to the Beijing high court a formal appeal of the verdict of the intermediate court, which, they argued, had abused its power. The subsequent hearing at the high court was not open, but the announcement of the result of the appeal was. It came on February 11, 2010, in courtroom number 3 at the Beijing high court at 10 Jianguomen South Street. Liu Xia and her brother Liu Hui were allowed to attend. As at the original trial, the other seats in the room, which held about forty people, were filled with expressionless strangers who apparently had been assigned to attend. The judge read the final ruling, which was to "uphold the original verdict." For a moment there followed pristine silence, and then Xiaobo said calmly, "I am innocent." The process took about ten minutes.

When it was over Liu Xia was ferried in a police car to the Number One Detention Center for a visit with Xiaobo that lasted about twenty minutes. They again talked about daily life, not legal matters. Xiaobo asked what Xia was going to do for Spring Festival three days hence. When they parted Xia gave Xiaobo a big hug. She thought he had lost weight.[21]

Xiaobo's heavy sentence drew strong protest both inside and outside China. Inside, Cui Weiping, beginning as early as the eve of the sentencing, used telephone, e-mail, and Twitter to survey the opinion of prominent Chinese intellectuals on the way the government was using prison to punish speech.[22] None of her 138 respondents, including people who disagreed with some of Xiaobo's substantive views, supported the prison sentence. They were willing to accept the dangers of taking a stand in plain contradiction of the government. The view of Guo Yuhua, a sociologist at Tsinghua University, was representative:

> Charter 08 asks for the most basic and the most just of citizens' rights and advocates moderate reform as the route to social progress. Where is the crime in expressing common sense? Moreover, even if the demands had been outlandish, it is wrong in principle to criminalize speech. The real act of subverting state power (i.e., state legitimacy) is not in what Liu Xiaobo says but in the act of sending Liu Xiaobo to prison. That act is a challenge to society's conscience and to human civilization.

Cui's survey spread on social media. After seventeen days the authorities suppressed it.

Around the same time, twenty senior members of the Communist Party, whose average age was about eighty and whose memberships in the Party averaged about sixty years, called upon the Party to correct its illegal and wrong conviction of Liu Xiaobo. They included Li Rui, former vice chair of the Party's Central Organization Department; Li Pu, former head of the New China News Agency; Zhang Sizhi, China's most senior rights lawyer; and Du Daozheng, former chief of the General Administration of Press and Publication, the government's central censorship organization.[23]

Outside China, on January 10, 2010, in Prague, two signatories of Charter 77, Vaclav Havel and the writer and actor Pavel Landovsky, together with Vaclav Maly, the Bishop of Prague, composed an open letter of protest to China's President Hu Jintao and carried it in person to the Chinese embassy. They went during the embassy's open hours, but repeated knocks on a closed door brought no response. They put their letter into the mailbox outside. It read in part:

> Mr. President, we would like you to know that we do not consider the [Liu Xiaobo] trial an independent judicial process in which neither you nor your government could interfere. In fact, it is just the opposite. Mr. Liu's trial was the

result of a political order for which you carry ultimate political responsibility. We are convinced that this trial and harsh sentence, levied against a respected, well-known, and prominent citizen of your country, merely for thinking and speaking critically about various political and social issues, was meant primarily to be a stern warning to others not to follow his path.

Eight days later Havel published an op-ed entitled "A Chinese Champion of Peace and Freedom" in which, speaking for himself and seven others, he broached the idea of a Nobel Peace Prize for Xiaobo:

> We are convinced that the concepts that Liu and his colleagues put down [in Charter 08] are both universal and timeless. These ideals—respect for human rights and human dignity, and the responsibility of citizens to ensure that their governments respect those rights—represent humanity's highest aspirations.
>
> Should the Nobel Committee choose to recognize Liu's courage and sacrifice in articulating these ideals, it would not only draw global attention to the injustice of Liu's 11-year sentence. It would also help to amplify within China the universal human values for which Liu has spent so much of his life fighting.[24]

Previous Nobel Peace Prize laureates Archbishop Desmond Tutu and the Dalai Lama joined in signing, as did the former Director-General of the World Trade Organization Michael Moore, the Russian democrat Grigory Yavlinsky, and others.

The impact of Havel's proposal was especially strong inside the Czech Republic and Slovakia, where veterans of the Charter 77 effort could remember only too vividly how much it had meant to them in 1977 to hear support from the outside world. The deadline for nominations for the 2010 Peace Prize was January 31, and before that date fifty-one members of the National Council of the Slovak Republic and more than forty members of the Parliament of the Czech Republic signed letters supporting Havel's proposal.

In the United States, Kwame Anthony Appiah, president of the PEN American Center, wrote on January 29 to the Nobel Peace Prize Committee in Oslo supporting the nomination. His letter read in part:

> Liu's writings express the aspirations of a growing number of China's citizens; the ideas he has articulated in his allegedly subversive writings, ideas that are commonplace in free societies around the world, are shared by a significant cross section of Chinese society . . .

If China can jail Liu Xiaobo without repercussions, it isn't just dissident voices inside China that are vulnerable. A feature of China's ascendancy on the world stage has been its implicit agreement with rights-abusing regimes in other nations that it will turn a blind eye to even the most blatant human rights violations in exchange for preferred commercial relations.... To fail to challenge the Chinese government on Liu Xiaobo's imprisonment is to concede this argument internationally, at enormous peril to peaceful advocates of progress and change not just in China but all around the world.[25]

Other prominent writers and members of PEN America, including Salman Rushdie, Philip Roth, Ha Jin, and Adrienne Rich, endorsed Appiah's letter.

On February 3, 2010, Herta Müller, the Romanian German novelist and poet, winner of the 2009 Nobel Prize in Literature, wrote to the Nobel Foundation in Stockholm that, although she was aware that literature prize winners are not technically eligible to make nominations for the peace prize, she wanted to support the idea of awarding it to Liu Xiaobo because "in the face of countless threats from the Chinese regime and great risk to his life, he has fought unerringly for the freedom of the individual."[26]

Xiaobo was still in the Beijing Number One Detention Center when his lawyers brought him the news of this domestic and international support. He replied first by asking that the lawyers relay his gratitude to all those prestigious people. Whether he got a prize, he said, was not as important as knowing that such people saw the point of what he had been trying to do. When the lawyers told him about the high-ranking octogenarian Party members who had stood up for him, Xiaobo commented that most of them had been victims of Mao Zedong's suppression of free speech in 1957 called the Anti-Rightist Campaign. They knew only too well what unfair punishment feels like, but the outside support that *they* got, back then, was minuscule compared to the support he was getting now. It was their sacrifices that laid a foundation for the modest progress China had made.

To keep his body in shape at the detention center—and to combat boredom—Xiaobo demanded of himself every day to do three hundred push-ups and at least an hour of brisk walking within the limited space available to him.[27] His fellow detainees were impressed. Here was a "thought prisoner" with drive! It was not immediately clear where he would serve his long sentence. The normal practice was to send prisoners back to their home provinces, so for Xiaobo, that would mean a return to Liaoning. Liu Xia, wanting to keep him closer to her, applied to have him serve the sentence in Beijing. This would have been good for Xiaobo's father as well. Professor Liu Ling had not been well and did not need the added psychological pressure of having a son in a nearby prison. Liu Xia waited for an answer to her application—and waited and waited—but none came. She was allowed no visits with Xiaobo in the detention center after the one on February 11, the day of the appeal verdict, and she was followed whenever she went out. Xiaobo's lawyers were allowed to see him only once, on April 19.

On May 30, Liu Xia received a special delivery express letter from Jinzhou Prison in Liaoning province informing her that Xiaobo had arrived there on May 26 to serve his sentence. Jinzhou city is in the southwest of Liaoning, 260 miles from Beijing. Its prison is one of the largest in the province and is used mostly for convicts serving terms of ten or more years. It is a gloomy place, even for a prison. High walls topped with razor wire rise on each side of its yard. Guards in towers carry rifles. At exercise time, rows of inmates respond in unison to barked commands. When Xiaobo arrived, there were many Falun Gong believers in the prison.

Liu Xia asked permission to visit Xiaobo, and a week later it was granted. Officials informed her that she could talk with him about health, food, drink, and family. Other topics were forbidden. Any disobedience would end the visit immediately.

At their first visit she and Xiaobo talked at a table, across which she could reach his hands and hold them. She later reported that he seemed in fairly good spirits but appeared a bit thinner than before. He said he had recurring stomachaches. He could go outdoors twice a day, in the mornings and the evenings, and could read books and take reading notes. There were no newspapers, but his cell had a television set that carried two channels: Liaoning Television and Central Chinese Television. He told Liu Xia that he found the programming "weird"—a poor resemblance of real life. She speculated that he might have had this reaction because he never watched television at home and wasn't used to what was normally there.

Xiaobo initially had four cellmates at Jinzhou, all of whom were ordinary criminals, not thought criminals like him. He got along fine with them after he adjusted to the very limited range of their interests. Their food was the same as his: a few boiled vegetables with rice and *mantou* (plain steamed) buns. Their routines were also the same, except that they did physical labor and Xiaobo did not. Doing labor was a way that prisoners who had confessed to their crimes could earn reductions in their sentences or parole. Xiaobo's insistence on his innocence made him ineligible for the time-reduction program. Another difference was that his cellmates, as ordinary criminals, were allowed to make telephone calls home, but Xiaobo was not. Liu Xia could visit him once a month, usually toward the end of the month. She had to call the prison in advance to fix a date.

She carried books for him. Most were history and fiction; anything political was forbidden. Xiaobo grew especially attached to a book of Paul Celan's poetry in Chinese translation. Celan, who had lost both parents in the Holocaust, wrote lines that pulled Xiaobo into dark tunnels of thought about violence and death. He found that each wall of silence in Celan, penetrated by the poet's language, revealed only broader fields of silence. The book stimulated Xiaobo to ruminate on suffering, survival, and struggles with the void. It led him to think of writing something about Celan.

He and Liu Xia exchanged letters. Depending on the efficiency of the censors who opened and read them, they could take up to ten days to arrive. At one point they noticed that two letters—one in each direction—had gone missing. Liu Xia realized that her missing letter had contained love poetry. Maybe his had too. She guessed that the censors might have decided that such intense expression might not be good for Xiaobo's "stability."

On September 20, 2010, Vaclav Havel and two Czech colleagues published an op-ed in *The New York Times* sketching Xiaobo's plight. They ended with these words:

> Next month, the Nobel Peace Prize Committee will announce the recipient of the 2010 prize. We ask the Nobel Committee to honor Liu Xiaobo's more than two decades of unflinching and peaceful advocacy for reform, and to make him the first Chinese recipient of that prestigious award. In doing so, the Nobel Committee would signal both to Liu and to the Chinese government that many inside China and around the world stand in solidarity with him and his unwavering vision of freedom and human rights for the 1.3 billion people of China.[28]

The Chinese government, of course, had sharply different views on this question and had been expressing them for some time. On February 5, 2010, shortly after the first public nominations of Xiaobo had appeared, Ma Zhaoxu, a spokesperson for China's Foreign Ministry, said at a daily press briefing that "it would be a serious mistake for the Nobel Committee to give a prize to this sort of person." During the summer, at a meeting at the Chinese embassy in Oslo, Fu Ying, a deputy foreign minister of China, warned Geir Lundestad, director of Norway's Nobel Institute, that to give a Nobel Prize to a Chinese dissident "would pull the wrong strings in relations between Norway and China [and] would be seen as an unfriendly act."[29] More warnings followed. But the prize committee's deliberations, which had been going on for years, could not be reversed in days. Lundestad later explained: "For a number of years we had been watching the field of China's dissidents, wondering who might be best to consider for the prize. On

December 25, 2009, the Chinese government answered our question for us. Their eleven-year prison sentence of Liu Xiaobo elevated him from a representative of human rights in China, maybe even its main representative, into a symbol of human rights with universal significance."[30] Later that year, Xiaobo did indeed receive the prize. For the long story of how he got there, we begin at the beginning, in the next chapter.

2

Rebel in Embryo

Liu Xiaobo was born on December 28, 1955, in the northeastern Chinese city of Changchun in Jilin province. He was the third of five siblings, all boys.

A major road runs north and south through the center of Changchun. Several other roads reach from the center like the spokes of a wheel, intersecting with circular ring roads. The great north-south road was already more than a hundred years old by the time Xiaobo was born. It had seen a lot of history, as a chronological list of its names shows. The Polish poet Czeslaw Milosz once noted that painters in Vilna, the Lithuanian city of his childhood, were kept well employed because of the need to paint new street signs every time a regime changed.[1] Painters in Changchun must have done well too.

In 1905, at the end of a war in which Russia and Japan fought each other in China's northeast, the victorious Japanese demanded that the Russians hand over railroad rights. Two years later the Japanese built a grand rail station in Changchun. In front of it they built a magnificent square, and, leading southward out of the square, a road more than a half a mile in length called Changchun Avenue. In 1922 it got the Japanese name Chūōdōri, or "Central Thoroughfare." In 1931, the Japanese military invaded all of China's northeast and set up a puppet regime it called Manchuria. Changchun was declared the capital and renamed Shinkyo ("new capital" in Japanese). A flurry of road construction followed. The axial north-south thoroughfare was extended four miles and widened to about sixty yards.[2]

In August 1945, Japan's defeat in World War II cleared the way for Soviet troops to occupy the city. The main road was renamed Stalin Avenue. Eight months later, when China's Kuomintang Nationalists took over the city, the road was reconceived as two sections and named Zhongshan (i.e., Sun Yat-sen) Avenue to the north and Zhongzheng (i.e., Chiang Kai-shek) Avenue to the south. In 1948, when the Communists wrested control of Changchun from the Kuomintang, the name reverted to Stalin Avenue. It got its present name, People's Avenue, in 1996.

Its most flourishing years were under the Japanese, between 1932 and 1945, when modern government buildings, banks, schools, and health facilities all were constructed along it. These institutions stayed in place when the Communists arrived, but now they were called "work units." The hospital in which Liu Xiaobo was born and the compound of Northeast Normal University where he grew up were both on Stalin Avenue.

The Japanese brought long-term plans to Changchun and made investments accordingly. It became the first city in China to get flush toilets, piped gas, and a system of underground electrical cable. There were plans for a subway system. The Japanese planted so many trees that by 1934 people were calling Changchun "Forest City." It was a bid to build a model international city in Asia.

In spring 2006, when Wuhan University in Hubei invited tourists to come view cherry blossoms on its campus, some supernationalist youngsters on the Internet began denouncing the cherry blossoms as a "national humiliation." They had come from Japan, after all. An online argument ensued, and Liu Xiaobo joined:

> I am from Changchun and can say that Changchun's success had a lot to do with the Japanese. It was their "new capital" and headquarters for their army, and that's why they invested in it. Had they not, it probably never would have become the capital of Jilin. In the 1950s and 1960s China's best railroads were in the northeast, as were the best natural-gas heating systems. . . . Changchun people used to say, "Little Japan really did adopt our Changchun as its home," and it's no accident that after 1949 the Communists took the northeast as their base for heavy industry.[3]

The Soviets, during their eight-month stay, did what they could to dismantle equipment in the factories, mines, and electrical stations in and around Changchun and to ship the booty to Russia. But the biggest disaster for Changchun was yet to come.

In early 1948 Communist armies laid siege to the city. Kuomintang troops were trapped inside, and the Communists tried to prevent all civilians from entering or exiting the city so that food supplies inside would steadily dwindle. Steel webs and moats—and vigilant guards—achieved this goal. Water and electricity were cut off. People inside began to eat the bark of the trees of Forest City. They also ate weeds and even leather belts. Between March and October, at least 150,000 people, including children and the elderly, starved to death. Precise numbers are unknowable—just as they are for the famous Nanjing Massacre of 1937, when Japanese armies pillaged China's capital city and a comparable number perished. Textbooks in the People's Republic of China make much of the Nanjing Massacre but do not mention the Changchun disaster at all. Children are taught instead that "Changchun was liberated without a shot."

In the same month that the siege of Changchun ended, Liu Xiaobo's father, Liu Ling, who was from a landlord family in Jilin's Huaide county, decided to support the Communist movement by applying after high school to join a "Southbound Cadre Training Group." The purpose of such groups was to recruit talent from northern areas where the Communists had already won and train them in Party ideology and policies so that as the Communists pushed southward, administrative takeovers would be smooth.

The group did its training at Northeast University, the first Communist-sponsored comprehensive university in China's northeast. It was founded in 1946 in the city of Jiamusi, Heilongjiang province, but had to move twice during the civil war with the Kuomintang—to Jilin city in July 1948 (where Liu Ling joined, in October) and then to Changchun in July 1949.[4]

Admission to the cadre training program was selective, and Liu Ling's acceptance was hardly assured, because he was only seventeen years old and from a landlord family to boot. But in those days the Communists were in dire need of talent and willing to overlook "bad class background" when recruiting it. Liu Ling's decision to join them before 1949 did pay dividends later in his life when he received the perquisites of "a prerevolutionary cadre." Timid and guarded, he seems always to have been aware of what his "bad" class background meant.

Although admitted to the program, Liu Ling was not, in the end, assigned to go south. It may have been because, although only in his late teens, he already had married and was a father. He was assigned instead to study at Northeast University, which took over the attractive Changchun campus of what under the Japanese had been New Capital Medical University. In 1950 Northeast University was relabeled Northeast Normal University; it eventually became the most important school for teacher training in northeast China.

Liu Ling's wife, Zhang Suqin, worked at the university's nursery school, and their first son, Liu Xiaoguang, was born in 1949, followed by a second, Liu

Xiaohui, in 1952. In 1953 Liu Ling finished his studies, received a degree in Chinese, and was invited to remain at the university as faculty. In 1956, a year after Liu Xiaobo was born, the school dispatched the family to Ulan Bator, in Mongolia, where Liu Ling's assignment, as a "both-red-and-expert activist in socialist construction," was to teach Chinese. The Liu family returned to Changchun in 1959, after two more sons had been born, Xiaoxuan in 1957 and Xiaodong in 1958. Xiaobo later wrote much about his childhood but apparently nothing about Ulan Bator. Only a toddler at the time, he likely remembered little.

Back in Changchun, he must have felt secure when leaving for nursery school in the mornings, because he went to school where his mother taught. He had a stutter, which his teachers and fellow students noticed, and sometimes got red in the face trying to get a sentence out. But he had zero tolerance for any teasing about it. When another child taunted, Xiaobo would come rushing forward with his little fists pumping. After a while everybody just accepted the stutter.[5] It stayed with him his whole life but never seriously inconvenienced him. His university classmates recall that his stutter-induced pauses sometimes actually added power to his rhetorical effect. Others noticed that he seldom stuttered in front of a microphone or during an intense argument. When tensions rose he could be the most fluent person in the room. The stutter would return after things had relaxed.[6]

His father, Liu Ling, built an admirable academic career in linguistics. He began at Northeast Normal University, where he taught courses and wrote textbooks and reference books. In 1985 he was invited to move to the Dalian Army Academy, where he was quickly promoted to professor, largely on the strength of his growing reputation as the founder in China of the field of military linguistics. He carried around with him a little notebook in which he jotted down bits of slang that he overheard soldiers using. His 1990 book *Military Linguistics* analyzes these as well as terms like "Attention!" and "Eyes right!" borrowed from Western languages.[7] China's leading military newspaper, *People's Liberation News*, published an article about him that claimed that this professor had a stubborn principle of refusing to repeat studies that others had done and refusing to retrace his own steps. He always wanted to break new ground.[8]

He studied China's ancient military classic *Sunzi's Art of War* and, with some others, wrote a book called *Some Captivating Applications of* Sunzi's Art of War *to Today's World*. The "applications" showed how ancient Chinese wisdom could be relevant to contemporary topics like public relations, enterprise management, and game theory. The book attracted much attention. Liu Ling retired in 1991 at the mandatory age of sixty but was "recalled" for two more years of teaching. He also did some postretirement consulting for small commercial enterprises. In 2003 the People's Publishing House came out with an authoritative book called *Twenty*

Years of Chinese Culture in which Liu Ling and Liu Xiaobo are both mentioned, sometimes side by side. The father is cited for his *Captivating Applications* book and the son for being an exemplar of antitraditionalism during the "culture fever" of the 1980s. Xiaobo is mentioned a total of six times, mostly in a negative light. His stance toward traditional culture and his father's are correctly characterized as opposite.

Liu Ling's good relations with the Communist government during the 1950s and 1960s helped to protect his sons. Compared to many of their friends, whose parents became victims of cruel political campaigns, Xiaobo and his brothers had it good. They lived in the compound of Changchun's best university, whose schooling for children from nursery school through high school was also the best in the city. Moreover, because all the important government offices and their associated residence compounds were along Stalin Avenue, all of Xiaobo's classmates were from the families of officials, civilian or military. The families differed in some ways, but not in their views of the new political regime. Their loyalty to it was absolute. No one whispered about any mistake or flaw. Memories of how Changchun's ordinary people had suffered during the 1948 siege not only were banned from expression in public; in privileged families like Xiaobo's, they were taboo in private as well. Everyone saw themselves—their ideals, their fate—at one with the Communists.

With loyalty came a sense of superiority. High officials and their families all displayed it. Xiaobo also drew confidence from knowing that his father, although not a high official, was an exemplary "red intellectual." This may help to explain why Xiaobo went through much of his life as if feeling immune from political danger. In this he resembled the Polish dissident Adam Michnik, who, noting that he had been born into a well-heeled Communist family, wrote, "I belonged during the sixties to a small circle that didn't fear the Communists. I felt that Communist Poland was my Poland. So what should I be scared of?"[9]

But eventually some hard facts of life began to puncture the social cocoons along Stalin Avenue. When China's "Great Leap" famine of 1959–1962 took more than thirty million lives nationwide, Jilin province was not the hardest hit, but nearly everyone experienced hunger. Liu Ling's salary as a university lecturer was in the middle range, but it had to feed nine people: two parents, two grandmothers, and five hungry boys. Times were tough. Xiaobo later wrote:

By 1961 the famine had reached everywhere, and food in our family was scarce. Our grandmothers would bring wild grasses home and simmer them into our sorghum congee. Each boy was limited to one bowlful. My oldest brother was twelve at the time, and second brother was nine—both at ages when boys normally are wild, or at least rowdy. But, with our hunger, it was all we boys could do after school to drag ourselves home and lie next to one another on our communal bed, waiting for dinner and that single bowl of weed-laced congee.[10]

Later things got better, but not much: "When I was young, I remember, our family could afford 'fine grain' only once a week. For us children this was a huge treat. In our family, though, 'fine grain' seldom meant fine grain alone; it meant flour with coarse grain mixed in. And whatever the mixture, a per-person limit always applied. The treats of fine grain were never enough to fill the stomach."[11]

Xiaobo had to accept a position in the family below his two older brothers. At the dinner table his parents sometimes stared at him if he reached for too much food. Nearly all his clothing and shoes were hand-me-downs. His nickname, "Little Three," said it all and stuck with him for years. In 1990, when his father, in military uniform, came to Beijing's Qincheng Prison to visit Xiaobo, who had been imprisoned for his role in the Tiananmen Square protests the year before, father addressed son as "Little Three." Using that childhood name in such an austere context signaled a mild contempt and showed that Xiaobo still was not taken very seriously in his family. Professor Liu had never had any real interest in what was going on inside his third son's head.

Xiaobo saw his father as a tyrant. As head of household, he had special privileges. His meals, called "the small fare," were prepared separately from everyone else's, called "the big fare." The inequality galled Xiaobo; years later he was still bitter when he mentioned it to friends. Moreover, his father often lost his temper and used corporal punishment. He gained a reputation within the Northeast Normal University compound for using fists to educate children, and his third son, Xiaobo, got more than his share. Over time the father's violence grew worse. Xiaobo's essays about his childhood years reveal much pain.

The only source of warmth in his childhood home was his father's mother, who lived by an unshakable intuition that all children are precious. She was illiterate but knew many traditional stories, proverbs, and myths, and liked to pass them on to her grandchildren. They were not only a buffer against the harsh "revolutionary" language outside; they also—for Xiaobo, anyway—opened another world to live in. Xiaobo spent more time with this grandmother than with his parents. When Liu Ling beat his son, the grandmother intervened. Fortunately Professor Liu, whatever his faults, believed in filial piety. He obeyed his mother.

In September 1962, at age six and a half, Xiaobo entered first grade at the primary school attached to Northeast Normal University. The school used the standard textbooks mandatory everywhere in China after 1949, whose overriding mission was to shape "correct" behavior in children. One of the stories for first-graders was "Little Cat Goes Fishing." A kitten goes fishing to "help" its mother but gets distracted by bees and butterflies and is no help at all. Lesson: be a good kitten and stay focused. Others were blood-curdling "true accounts" of adolescent martyrs. Liu Hulan, a fifteen-year-old Communist Party member, is captured and executed by the Nationalist government during China's civil war. An illustration shows her facing down some cowering, green-faced Nationalists. Another story, "Little Wang Number Two," tells of a boy of thirteen who cleverly leads a troupe of invading Japanese soldiers into a Communist ambush. When the soldiers discover the boy's perfidy they hurl him onto a rock and bayonet him to death. But he dies happy. He was doing the right thing. There were stories about adult martyrs as well. In one, Communists endure gruesome tortures in a Nationalist prison: pepper water sprinkled onto fresh wounds, bamboo needles stuck deep into fingertips. Always, though, pain and death are preferable to capitulation. The purpose of the various stories is to train "heirs of the revolution," prepared for anything, including death. The school adopted "Always Ready," the motto of the international communist pioneer movement, as its own.

Xiaobo's primary school arranged for film screenings at reduced rates. Students paid five cents—one-twentieth of a yuan—for tickets that normally cost eight (This was in an economy in which a worker was paid about 1.0 or 1.5 yuan per day.) Most of the films were about revolutionary martyrs—*Landmine War* (1963), *Little Soldier Zhang Ga* (1964), *Tunnel War* (1965), and several others. The children were told that the red scarves they wore around their necks represented the blood of martyrs. Many, especially the younger ones, left the theater not having absorbed many of the details. They could spot the villains, to be sure, and formed highly positive impressions of battlefields. The blue skies, white clouds, vast ocean, and green forests where martyrs lost their lives were all very lovely.

The school curriculum did not always produce the results the government wished. For example, the older boys, nearing puberty, sometimes liked the anti-spy movies because the female foreign spies, however evil, were sexy. This might have been their only introduction to sex. A book that seems to have influenced Xiaobo as least as much as the Communist-hero stories was *Sun Wukong Wreaks Havoc in Heaven,* which celebrates the sassy irreverence of the lovable Monkey King in the classic novel *Journey to the West.* Flexible, witty, stubborn, and quick, Wukong can disappear in a flash, if he likes, or take out his golden cudgel and beat a demon into submission. When the Emperor of Heaven tries to trick him he retaliates by ransacking the Heavenly Palace. Eventually he is captured and put into an oven to roast, but the punishment serves only to smelt "fired-metal eyes" for him. He miraculously survives and, now possessing enhanced martial powers, resumes his fantastic commotion.

Xiaobo's native character was a bit like Sun Wukong's. Moreover, he came to first grade in a sense overprepared and therefore vulnerable to boredom. He was from an intellectual's home and an especially good nursery school. His two older brothers had been to grade school and done well. He had a head start in how to learn things and deal with people. One of his friends later wrote: "The teacher's explanations were too simple for Xiaobo. He got the point within five minutes and then couldn't sit still. To attract attention, he would climb up onto the window sills and even to the rafters above, only to feel frustrated that the teacher still paid him no attention."[12] Second only to his father, Xiaobo's first-grade teacher seems to have been the person in his childhood he found most objectionable.

His surplus energy and wit did not build him a good record in school. He didn't like to study, and his unruliness earned him no extra credit. In music class one day, he and his classmates were singing while a young teacher who wore a long braid was accompanying them on the piano at the front of the classroom. Under cover of the sound of the singing, Xiaobo crept up behind the teacher, tied a string to the end of her pigtail, then tied its other end to the chair on which she was sitting. When she stood up at the end of the song, the chair was upended and she lost her balance and fell. Teachers from adjacent classrooms came to help, spotted the culprit, and chased him as he fled. Outside, as they were gaining on him, Xiaobo climbed a telephone pole and clung to it, beyond the reach of the less agile adults.[13]

Xiaobo's Northeast Normal middle school was one of the most privileged in the province. High officials sent their children there. One classmate, nicknamed "Fatty," was the son of a major-general in the People's Liberation Army. Fatty's family lived in a good neighborhood in a two-story house that had seven or eight rooms, a private entrance, and its own yard planted with a variety of flowers, shrubs, and trees. Maids did the cooking and washing, and soldier-attendants swept the courtyard and stood guard. Given the prestige of his father, Fatty could misbehave in school at will. No matter how bad the boy's behavior, when the major-general's car drove up to the school, everyone put on beaming faces.[14] Stories about Fatty recur in Xiaobo's essays. He was an early model for mischief.

When China's "Great Proletarian Cultural Revolution" erupted in summer 1966, Xiaobo was ten years old and just out of fourth grade. Mao Zedong's call to "sweep away all cow ghosts and snake spirits" fell upon very receptive ears in the city of Changchun, whose layered history contained an especially rich supply of ghostlike cows and snakes: not only Mao Zedong's recent enemies within the Communist Party but also villains from Japanese imperialism and "feudal warlords" prior to that.

An immediate task was to rename places and roads. Oppose Revisionism Road, Anti-Imperialism Street, Antifeudal Road, and Guard-the-Red Road all appeared. Northeast Normal University was renamed Maoist Education University. A scissors brigade in the city's center assisted women with cutting up or cutting off any possible signs of bourgeois thinking: long hair, skirts, the heels of high-heeled shoes. Paranoia seeped into the environment: were there Russian or Japanese agents, or Chinese traitors from the Manchurian era, crouching in the corners of the city? People scoured their homes to be sure no incriminating items—like gold or silver jewelry, Japanese currency, or documents left over from the Japanese days—could be found. Even if such things had been left behind by an earlier occupant, their discovery would mean disaster for you.

Xiaobo's first impressions of the Cultural Revolution were highly favorable. In a 1988 interview he recalled: "I felt extremely grateful to the Cultural Revolution. I was a child, and it let me do whatever I wanted. My parents were busy 'making revolution,' and my school had no classes. I could do anything! Play... fight... anything! It was great!"[15] An important divide separated Chinese youngsters who were thirteen to eighteen years old in 1966 and those only slightly younger. Anyone in junior or senior high school (seventh to twelfth grades, in the American system) was a Red Guard automatically. Anyone younger, like Xiaobo, was out of luck.

Xiaobo's eldest brother, Xiaoguang, was in the first year of senior high (tenth grade) when the Cultural Revolution arrived, and his second brother, Xiaohui, was in the first year of junior high (seventh grade). Both were Red Guards and joined the standard Red Guard activities: taunting and abusing teachers, raiding homes, doing "armed struggle," and riding the railroads free to "link up" with Red Guards elsewhere. But for Xiaobo and his younger brothers, all this was but a spectator sport. They stared wide-eyed at a carnival they did not understand but that certainly looked like fun.

When his two brothers boarded a train for Beijing to "link up," Xiaobo beseeched them to bring him along, but they refused—with scorn, he thought. He was left to regret that, just for being born a few years too late, he was missing out on the most exciting time of life.[16]

Yet there were benefits, even for the littler ones. Parents and teachers were preoccupied, and one day in the fall of 1966, Xiaobo's teacher walked into the classroom and announced, "Class is suspended to make revolution; we will resume in three months." To the students' ears, "resume in three months" meant "vacation for three months." Great! Book bags flew into the air.

The release of discipline led Xiaobo toward a habit that lasted a lifetime: smoking. Smoke caused his ten-year-old throat to gag unpleasantly, but he wanted to "grow up"—to be like his brothers and the Red Guards. And even so young, he resented his autocratic father, toward whom disobedience for its own sake may have had an allure.

Xiaobo's source of cigarettes was his privileged classmate Fatty, who had special permission to smoke. Fatty also had access to Peony brand cigarettes, the best of the best. Not just anybody could smoke them. On the very day their teacher announced the suspension of classes, after the teacher had walked out of the room, Fatty jumped up onto his desk, pulled from his pocket a bright red pack on which the Peony image was emblazoned, and waved it in the air.

"Who dares to smoke?" he barked at his classmates, the tone of his voice and the stare of his eyes allowing no doubt that he saw them all as chickens. "I stole these from my dad. They're Peonies! They cost fifty cents a pack! I'll give one free to anybody who dares!" Most of his classmates paid no attention, packed up their schoolbags, and left. The naughty ones, including Xiaobo, lingered. With aplomb, Fatty handed out one cigarette to each, pulled out a lighter, and helped them to light up.

As he later recalled it, Xiaobo felt unsure. He carefully sucked in a bit of smoke and felt a choking sensation, but nothing more. Fatty, ever the instructor, offered some demonstrations: the clutch of the cigarette, the inhale, the exhale, even how to blow a smoke ring. His big smoke rings drifted all the way to the ceiling. The little ones rolled from his mouth one by one. The observers were amazed, intrigued, daunted. Xiaobo, struggling to stifle coughs, did his best to imitate Fatty's every move. He was not the kind of child whose goal was to be second best.

Smoking became a habit. In the months that followed, Xiaobo regularly gathered with buddies—in a restroom, the corner of an empty room, an open field—to puff away. He learned to inhale. He could blow smoke rings of several kinds and knew how to smoke a cigarette to the very end so that no tobacco was wasted. His infatuation with cigarettes is also what led him (as he later wrote in a self-critical essay) into swindling money from his mother, pilfering tobacco from his father, and lying about it to both parents.

After three months, the "vacation" at Xiaobo's school was extended several times. More than a year passed before the school finally reopened. With teachers out of the picture, the only authority figures in Xiaobo's life were his parents, but even their authority dwindled as they got more and more caught up in political activity. In those harrowing times, an adult almost *had* to be a revolutionary activist, because not to be one meant almost certainly that you yourself would become a target. Aware of this danger, Xiaobo's parents both joined "rebel groups." Unfortunately, they did not join the same group, and this eventually meant that they brought political squabbles home with them.

It was only a matter of time before Liu Ling became a Cultural Revolution target because of his landlord background. He was badgered to "come clean." Xiaobo's mother had a clean political record to start with, but because of her husband's taint was required to "stand aside." This meant: for the time being you are neither approved nor disapproved.

"Study sessions" kept the parents out late, and some nights they did not come home at all. In 1967 authorities directed that Xiaobo's beloved paternal grandmother return to the countryside because of her landlord background. The pain of seeing her depart was Xiaobo's first experience of grief, but it was outweighed by the pleasures of tasting freedom. The other granny had left some time ago, the parents were often absent, and the older brothers wereout "making revolution," so Xiaobo was sometimes the senior member of the household and in charge of his two younger brothers. His warm feelings for Xiaoxuan, the older of the two, lasted all his life.

Most of the time, a little band that consisted of Xiaobo, Xiaoxuan, Xiaodong, and some other playmates just wandered around. During warm weather their favorite activity was to play at South Lake, a beautiful spot at the southern end of Stalin Avenue. There Xiaobo learned to swim. In those mad times, swimming was viewed as preparation for war, so everybody—old and young, male and female—went for it. Each year a few children drowned.

Whenever Xiaobo and his wandering buddies got wind of "armed struggle" or somebody's death (including suicides), they ran to take a look. Usually they couldn't see much, because they were the shorter ones within the encircling crowds of gawkers. If they were lucky they could climb up a nearby wall or tree where their view, if regrettably distant, was unobstructed.

Xiaobo later wrote about a scene that stuck in his memory. Some prisoners were being paraded through the streets in the backs of worn-out trucks. Their torsos were bound with rope; their hands were tied behind their backs; nooses circled their necks; their heads were shaved. White placards (diamond shaped if hung down their backs, rectangular if hung down their chests) showed their names in large, rough black characters that were crossed out with neat bright red Xs. The names of their crimes were inscribed in small characters at the bottoms of the placards. A soldier wearing a helmet and bright white gloves stood at each side of each criminal. Whenever a criminal tried to raise his head, one of the guards would press it back down. A few of the criminals had already collapsed, which meant that the guards at their sides had to hold them up while one used his white-gloved hands to tilt the shaven head up far enough to show how the criminal was so frightened that phlegm was coursing down his face. Additional helmeted soldiers, fully armed, stood in the four corners of the truck bed. Xiaobo remembered that what had impressed him most were the helmets and the white gloves.[17]

Armed struggle between rebel groups in Changchun peaked in the early summer of 1967. On June 15, an alliance of rebel groups that called itself Changchun Commune demanded the release of some of its members from police detention. When its demands were rejected, the Changchun Commune used rocks and cudgels to mount an attack on the offices of Public Security on Stalin Avenue. A rival group called Red Faction No. 2 defended the building. One night of fighting produced more than 1,500 casualties.

Red Faction No. 2 also controlled the hospital that was nearby on Stalin Avenue, and when Changchun Commune brought their wounded there, they were refused admission. This led to another battle lasting three days, from July 5 to July 8. Changchun Commune attacked the hospital and Red No. 2 defended. The attackers occupied the lower floors, trapping people upstairs without food. Somehow Red No. 2 got hold of a Soviet-made military transport aircraft from the Changchun Aviation School and dropped bread to the roof of the hospital. They also obtained a hook-and-ladder fire engine with which they tried to run ladders up the sides of the building to rescue people from balconies. The whole show was so spectacular that hordes of curious onlookers packed the streets below, freezing traffic flow at the center of Changchun. Eventually Changchun Commune attacked and burned the fire engine. The hospital suffered fire damage. In this second battle, more than 690 people were injured, 102 seriously.[18]

The preceding account is based partly on the testimony of Xiaobo's friend and college classmate Xu Jingya, who was an eyewitness. Eleven-year-old Xiaobo must have witnessed at least some of the events too, and could not have missed the frightening stories that coursed through society. Xiaobo's nursery school classmate Zhang Li recalls an incident that happened on the campus of Northeast Normal University.[19] A sophomore student wandered by mistake into a building that two opposing rebel groups were hotly contesting. One side thought she was a scout sent by the other. Loudspeakers blared, but, not comprehending, she just kept walking until she was impaled by three spears. They were primitive weapons, of the kind Mao Zedong had used in his peasant rebellions in the 1920s, but they killed her all the same.

In those days people shouted themselves hoarse with Mao quotes like "Marxism has all kinds of principles, but in the end they boil down to just one: rebellion is justified!" Children and adults alike memorized whole passages from the ubiquitous *Quotations from Chairman Mao*, nicknamed "the little red book." This one was a favorite: "A revolution is not a dinner party, or writing an essay, or painting a picture, or doing embroidery; it cannot be so refined, so leisurely and gentle, so temperate, kind, courteous, restrained and magnanimous. A revolution is an insurrection, an act of violence by which one class overthrows another."[20] People put melodies to the words and sang them lustily and in public. Xiaobo, perhaps to compensate for his inability to participate officially as a Red Guard, committed nearly a hundred of the Mao-quote songs to memory and learned the steps of the "loyalty dance" in praise of Mao. Years later, he could still produce both the songs and the dance.

Xiaobo and his underage buddies set out in search of counterrevolutionaries. They imitated the "rebel" behavior they had observed in Red Guards. Many years later Xiaobo remembered his jejune viciousness and, with characteristic honesty, traced its details.[21] He wrote of an old man named Yin Hai.

Yin Hai had been a Kuomintang soldier but wasn't very good at it. By his own account, the sound of gunfire made him quake, and eventually he went AWOL. But his shabby record with the Kuomintang was not enough to spare him the revenge of the Communists, who named him a "historical counterrevolutionary."

The label barred him from state-sponsored work, so he became an itinerant barber. He lived downstairs from the Liu Ling family, and whenever the five Liu boys needed haircuts, their grandmother turned to Yin Hai. They were partners in gossip, so he often gave the haircuts for free or at a discount. But when the Cultural Revolution arrived, the Liu family had to "draw a clear line" separating themselves from Yin Hai, who had become a target of "criticism and struggle" sessions. He was forced to live in the boiler room of the residential compound. The space, hardly larger than his bed, was dark and damp. People no longer let him cut hair; he was reduced to scavenging in refuse heaps.

Another victim of the criticism and struggle sessions was a Japanese woman whom everyone called "The East." Every morning when residents of the compound gathered to "ask instructions" before an image of Mao, and every evening when they returned to "report accomplishments," Yin Hai and The East were required to bow their heads and beg Mao's forgiveness. One day Yin Hai was beaten at a struggle session so badly that he couldn't walk. He asked the authorities for a day's respite from the routine of begging forgiveness, but they denied the request and sent a band of toughs to drag him to the scene with orders to kneel (not just bow) before the Great Leader.

Accepting his status, Yin Hai shaved his head. One day, when Xiaobo and his friends were out seeking amusement, they spotted the shiny-bald head bobbing around in a big pile of garbage. Bent at the waist, Yin Hai was poking through the trash with a prod that he had fashioned from iron wire. The brilliant sunlight made his pate shine, and Xiaobo had a sudden brainstorm. Here was fun! He gathered his playmates in a huddle. Then they tiptoed up behind Yin Hai until Xiaobo suddenly shouted, "Okay, old Yin Hai! Up with the head! Show us that forehead! We're going to thump it!"

The old man jumped in fright. What was *this*? Then, recovering, he straightened his back, stood erect, and regarded the boys.

"Little Three," he said to Xiaobo, "I'm older than your grandma. We're longtime neighbors. You and your brothers got haircuts from me. Let me off this once, can't you?"

"No way!" Xiaobo shot back. "You old counterrevolutionary—you think you can *negotiate* with us?! What nerve! We're going to thump you, you hear? No way we're not going to thump you!"

Old Yin Hai mumbled a few more pleas, but then, observing the fiendish looks on the faces of the children, realized there was no way out. He accepted the topic of how—not whether—the humiliation should proceed.

"Okay, Little Three," he said, "I'll turn around and you can thump the back of my head. All right?"

"Wow! You really are a slippery snake, aren't you?" Xiaobo answered. "No wonder you got the 'historical counterrevolutionary' label! No deal! Today I thump your forehead! No more talk!"

The other children, whooping their approval, inverted Yin Hai's bamboo basket, dumping to the ground the paltry treasures he had gathered.

"Not going to let us thump?" one shouted. "Then don't dream of doing any more garbage sifting around here!"

"You expect any more good days, old buzzard?"

There was nothing Yin Hai could do. He leaned forward, offering his forehead.

Xiaobo put his fingers through some preparatory calisthenics and then began to thump with abandon. Thump, thump, thumpity-thump! Thump, thump, thumpity-thump! There was rhythm . . . staccato . . . legato . . . a range of tempos . . . a few syncopations. When perspiration on Yin Hai's head caused Xiaobo's fingers to slip, the normal thump sound was not forthcoming. Was this resistance? Xiaobo redelivered the thumps, now doubled in number for good measure. He didn't stop when his fingers began to hurt, but did stop when they began to turn numb. The other children took their turns.

Eventually old Yin Hai gave up all manner of supplication or avoidance. He just stood inert. When the boys finally were finished, he bowed his head, turned his back, and ambled away. He knew how youngsters in those days brimmed with contrarianism: if he had begged, dodged, or fought back, they would only have enjoyed it more and attacked more exuberantly. Now, they only spat at him a few times and shouted a few final insults.

Days later, Yin Hai was still using the passive-resistance tactic on Xiaobo and his band. Whenever he caught sight of them, at whatever distance, he would raise his arm in salute and yell, "Learn from the Little Red Soldiers! Respect the Little Red Soldiers! I beg forgiveness from the little revolutionary generals!" This made them laugh, and eventually an almost friendly relationship blossomed.

Xiaobo's days of free roaming came to an end in early 1968. On October 14, 1967, the Central Committee of the Communist Party of China, the State Council of the People's Republic of China, the Central Military Commission of the Party and the State, and the Central Cultural Revolution Work Group jointly issued a "Notice Regarding University, High School, and Primary School Students Returning to Class to Make Revolution." It wasn't clear exactly what that was supposed to mean, and because the risk to school administrators of getting the politics wrong could be disastrous, implementation around the country was tentative and slow. A "return to classes" did not always mean a return to the same teachers (some of whom had disappeared) or the same curriculum, since subjects like history, literature, art, and music were still politically dangerous. Most of the former textbooks remained "feudal-bourgeois-revisionist poisonous weeds," so something else had to be used. At Xiaobo's school, like many, the solution was to have students sit in classrooms and "study" newspapers or political documents. The goals were to divine Party Central's "spirit" (meaning new nuances in its political direction) and to study the conditions of the current "struggle" as well as the exemplary behavior of newly discovered heroes.

But this did get Xiaobo officially through to the end of elementary school. In July 1968 he received a certificate of graduation from sixth grade, and in September he entered the Attached High School of Northeast Normal University for junior high study.

Yet the return to school brought unanticipated trouble. Xiaobo and some others had acquired the designation "naughty boys on Stalin Avenue," and the label began to cost him. He later wrote: "We young smokers were viewed as little hoodlums. We did all the bad stuff: cutting class, getting into fights, making fun of teachers, stealing military hats, stealing Mao badges, and blocking girls."[22] "Blocking girls" meant a string of boys jumping out in front of girls as they walked down the street, swaying back and forth in a threatening manner, and then finding mirth in their frightened reactions. The reputation of Xiaobo and his buddies for this practice went so far that parents began to counsel their daughters in how to avoid them. In later essays Xiaobo expressed disgust with himself.

What he did not foresee was how politically dangerous his bad behavior was. In the jargon of the time, smoking by children was a key manifestation of the intense class struggle between the proletariat and the bourgeoisie for control of the next generation. Xiaobo had been "corrupted and used" by the bourgeoisie, "shot by the bourgeoisie's sugar-coated bullets," and had fallen into its dissolute lifestyle. He had "slid to the brink of the bourgeois mud pit," and if he didn't change fast, would pass a tipping point and become the bourgeoisie's prisoner and eventually its heir.

In fall 1968, a Worker Propaganda Team for Mao Zedong Thought appeared at Xiaobo's school. The team established a military-style regimen that called for examining every student as he or she entered the building. First, a student's appearance had to be right: buttons buttoned, hat worn properly, book bag slung across the shoulder at the proper angle, and so on. There were also full-body searches for knives, slingshots, pornography, cigarettes, and other items that, if discovered, were sent to the school's Never, Ever Forget the Class Struggle exhibition hall, where they were displayed alongside contraband like poisonous-weed reading material and alternate-regime records (i.e., documents that people had secretly saved in case the Kuomintang returned) confiscated from capitalist roaders, landlords, rich peasants, counterrevolutionaries, rightists, and bad elements.

Students caught with illicit items were evaluated for "attitude." If their attitude was good, the punishment was to write a self-criticism and read it aloud before one's class. If their attitude was not good, the punishment was to undergo a session of criticism and struggle whose size depended on the severity of the offense. There were four sizes: criticism in one's own class, in a joint session of all classes at one's grade level, in a meeting of the entire school, and in a special event for all schools in the area. Whatever the level, the guilty person had to stand with head bowed while the accusers assumed fierce demeanors. People shouted slogans after each speech.

Recidivists for whom these methods were insufficient were subjected to "the dictatorship of the proletariat." A squad of "proledicts," as they were called for short, detained and interrogated the offender, then held him or her in a "proledict jail" where interrogators worked in shifts to maintain a nearly continuous bombardment of questions, taunts, and sometimes beatings. Delivery of meals was the responsibility of the family. The length of confinement depended, again, on "attitude."

In Xiaobo's retrospective essays he does not recall the number of times he was investigated for smoking, fighting, or cutting classes. He remembers undergoing "criticism and struggle" sessions at class level, grade level, and school level. He was sent to proledict jail at least once for not admitting a crime or because a self-criticism was not deep enough. In his case the jail was his own classroom. Tables and chairs were pulled together to form a makeshift bed on which he slept when he wasn't allowed to go home.

He was only twelve and thirteen at the time but got no sympathy at home. His parents were adamantly opposed to his smoking. His father smoked, but that was an adult's right; Xiaobo's smoking was a serious character flaw. His parents did not use class-struggle arguments on him. Their punishments were nonideological: berate and beat. His father sometimes tied him to heating pipes or bed legs in order to deliver good beatings. Hardest to take, for Xiaobo, was his parents' interminable badgering about where he got his cigarettes. When they didn't like an answer, an inquisition ensued. They used all kinds of carrots and sticks until they finally got an answer they liked.

Xiaobo later wrote an essay about the first time his mother discovered his smoking:

> She noticed the odor of tobacco on my body. Then she found half a cigarette in my box of school supplies. I'll never forget what happened next. She shouted questions at me nonstop. Hearing no answer, she grabbed a broom and started pounding me. When that too got nothing out of me, she threw the broom to the floor and grabbed her wire-mesh cooking spoon. I panicked, hurtled toward her—knocking her down—and rushed out of the house. It was winter. I knew I had made a colossal mistake and would be in for a ferocious thrashing if I went home. So I decided not to go home. I wandered around in the cold until dark, so chilled that I could hardly stand it, and finally hid inside a vegetable cellar for storing cabbages, potatoes, and turnips through the winter. Mother later told me that when she and Father found me inside that cellar I looked like a puppy, body curled up under a gunny sack, head pillowed on a large cabbage, sound asleep.
>
> From then on, every day when I came home from school Mother would search my clothing and book bag and make me open my mouth so that she could smell my breath. I had my countermeasures, though. I would gargle vigorously before going home or eat a few cloves of garlic. I still hid my cigarettes.[23]

In short, Xiaobo had an eventful childhood. His sensitivity to cruelty and his strong rejection of it, which became very visible in his mature writing, were rooted in his Cultural Revolution years. So, perhaps, was his personal mettle. Demands to "bow your head and ask forgiveness" would be made of him later in life with greater force. While most people seek to escape pressure, for Xiaobo the normal mode was resisting pressure. Through a lifetime of battle he eventually got good at it. He could endure things others could not. A few days before he died in July 2017, in a text message to a friend, he used an idiom from northeastern Mandarin to call himself "an iron-egg embryo."[24] "Iron egg" means a child tough as iron; by "iron-egg embryo" Xiaobo meant someone who was destined from the start to be battered and would endure.

3

Puppy Love and Serious Reading

Record-setting cold seized Changchun in the winter of 1969–70. In early December temperatures were already dipping below zero degrees Fahrenheit, and yet the Liu Ling family was busily preparing to move to a place in Inner Mongolia that was even colder. Its name in Mongolian, Khorchin Baruun Garyn Ömnöd Khoshuu, was hard for Han Chinese to pronounce, so it was given the Chinese name Keerqin Youyi Qianqi, or, in English, Mongolian Horqin Right Front Banner. It is located on the eastern edge of Inner Mongolia, about 300 miles northwest of Changchun. In winter, the temperature can plummet to minus 40 degrees—a point where the Fahrenheit and Centigrade scales converge.

At the end of 1969 the most violent convulsions of the Cultural Revolution had passed. "Authorities," both intellectual and political, had been largely driven from their posts. Local governance was now in the hands of "three-in-one revolutionary committees" made up of military people, workers, and "revolutionary officers." The military were the first among equals. In the cities, one of the first duties of the revolutionary committees was to give work assignments to young people who had been busy "making revolution" for two years or more and now, with that activity winding down, often had nothing to do. The solution was to send them in large numbers to villages for farm work. Xiaobo's two older brothers, Xiaoguang and Xiaohui, fell into this category and were sent to the Yanbian Korean Autonomous Prefecture, 270 miles east of Changchun.

A few months later, intellectuals and state officials whom the Cultural Revolution had disgraced and demoted were sent to the countryside as well. Some went to rural reform camps called "May Seventh Cadre Schools." The name derived from a letter that Mao Zedong had written to Lin Biao on May 7, 1966, in which he recommended that people of every occupation take up farming, at least as a secondary line of work, while simultaneously learning rural values as armaments against the bourgeoisie. Living conditions at the camps were primitive, but inmates could generally tolerate them, in part because they expected that they could go home to the city someday. There was a related program, though, that relocated entire families to rural areas with the goal that they take root there. It was on this program that Liu Ling, his wife, and two of their sons, Xiaobo and Xiaodong, went to Inner Mongolia in late 1969. Xiaoxuan, the fourth son, went to live with his beloved paternal grandmother in Huaide for a time and joined the others in Inner Mongolia later.

A blizzard was blowing in Changchun on December 4, 1969, but inside the main auditorium of Northeast Normal University, 440 teaching staff were receiving a roasty-warm sendoff by worker-soldier propaganda teams. Amid a hubbub of drums and gongs, the departing "volunteers" and their heroic families were led to the railway station where they embarked "under the skies of the broad earth to receive re-education from the poor, lower, and middle peasants." They were the first group from Northeast Normal to head out; another 392 families would follow later, for a total of 832, which represented 70 percent of the university's teaching staff.[1] Their departures brought the university essentially to a halt.

People in the jostling crowds were wearing smiles despite apprehension that the unpredictable venture was generating. Xiaobo, not quite fourteen years old, felt uneasy. He did not want to leave Fatty and the other buddies with whom he had cruised up and down Stalin Avenue. He suddenly realized he might never see them again. They had done everything together. They had rescued him from his alienation. They had taught him to smoke. Images from his years in Changchun, sweet and bitter, flitted through his mind: those "struggle" sessions at school had been disgusting and funny at the same time; the romping around South Lake had been exhilarating. Was he losing everything?

After jerking to a start, the train kept stopping at countless little stations and took more than ten hours to reach Baicheng, a city 120 miles northwest of Changchun on the border between Jilin and Inner Mongolia. There the families changed trains and rode another hundred miles to their destination at Dashizhai or "Boulder Village." Local officials met them at the train station with horse carts, in frigid air. Xiaobo felt reassured to think of the railroad as staying in place—a possible reconnection to civilization from this almost unimaginably remote place. The Japanese had built the railroad in 1937.

The full name of his new home was Boulder Village Commune, Horqin Right Front Banner, Xing'an League, Inner Mongolia. Each word was packed with history. "Horqin" in Mongolian means archer. The area was a nomadic grazing plain that had been ruled, seven centuries earlier, by Habtuhasar, a younger brother of Genghis Khan. Wide open and favored with ample water and rich grass, it bordered the plains of the Xilingol League to the west and was not far south of the plains of the Hulunbuir League.

The terms "banner" and "league" were legacies of Qing times (1644–1912) when the Manchus ruled China, including its Mongol areas. "Banner" at first referred to a hunting area, later to a military unit, and still later to an administrative division within the government. A "league" was a loose alliance of "banners." Normally a league brought its banners together every one to three years for a big meeting. The authoritarian Qing dynasty imposed the banner-and-league system on Mongol tribes to control them. When the Communists took over in the late 1940s they left the Qing arrangements intact and then, in 1958, added the "people's commune" system on top of it. This layered history can help explain the quaint address, Boulder Village, Horqin Banner, Xing'an League.

The Communists adopted more than place names from their predecessors. They inherited problems and policies as well. In the middle of the eighteenth century, the Qing had had to deal with population pressure in China's heartland. Scarcity of land was leading to social unrest. Under a policy called "borrowing land to support the people," Qing rulers had encouraged large numbers of Han from the provinces of Shandong, Liaoning (called Fengtian at the time), and Jilin to move their agriculture to the Mongolian grasslands. The word "borrowing" was a tacit admission that Han people were now living on Mongolian land. In the early twentieth century, when China's northeastern warlords revived and intensified the land-borrowing policy, Mongolians resisted. A famous Mongolian martyr, Gada Meiren (1892–1931), hailed from the Horqin grasslands. Even Han schoolchildren knew the song about "the rebellion of Gada Meiren . . . all for Mongolian land." But despite the resistance, Han people came to outnumber Mongolians in the Horqin Right Front Banner area. The nomadic lifestyle gave way to a mixed economy of animal husbandry and agriculture. Grasslands were turning into croplands—or, drained of water, deserts.

The most recent influx of Han people had happened in 1968 when nearly 13,000 "sent-down youth" arrived from Beijing, Tianjin, Shanghai, and elsewhere. Before that, the population of the town had been about 100,000; afterward, sent-down youth comprised more than 10 percent of residents. Han immigration continued in ensuing decades until, by 2017, the Han were 47.4 percent of the population. Mongols were 47.3 percent, and the remaining 7 percent were ethnic minorities: Manchus, Koreans, Daurs, Evenks, Oroqens, Sibes, Uyghurs, and others.[2] Horqin Banner was and is a cultural potpourri.

In the late 1960s, though, it was viewed as a Mongolian place. It therefore seemed strange to residents when, just a few months before the Liu Ling family arrived, maps of the area were suddenly redrawn and Horqin Banner became part of the neighboring district of Baicheng in Jilin province. The change meant that technically, the migrant families from Northeast Normal University were being "sent down" to another part of their home province.

The reason for redrawing maps lay in Cultural Revolution violence, which had been especially severe in Inner Mongolia. By 1968 Inner Mongolia exceeded all Chinese provinces[3] in the fraction of its population that had become victims during the Cultural Revolution. This happened because in 1967, when a craze to "grab traitors and spies" spread across China, a "rebel group" of zealous Maoists in Inner Mongolia uncovered materials from 1925 on the activities of an Inner Mongolian People's Revolutionary Party. They used this discovery to make up a story about a "New Mongolian Party" that was operating underground in the present day. During 1967–69, as many as 700,000 people, mostly Mongolians, were tortured, many to death, in search of information on the New Mongolian Party.[4]

In July 1969, central government officials in Beijing held an emergency meeting on "the Inner Mongolia question." Their stated purpose was to end the violence, but the deeper fear was that something like a New Mongolian Party might really exist and that the Chinese Communist Party might lose control in the area. Following the defeat of Japan in 1945, some Mongolians in the eastern part of Inner Mongolia had had thoughts of unifying with Outer Mongolia, and Beijing was worried that such thinking might now return. Officials at the July 1969 meeting drew up a plan to disaggregate Inner Mongolia by reassigning some of its banners and counties to neighboring Chinese provinces. The very next month, in August, Horqin Right Front Banner, Zhelim Banner, and Tuquan county in Hulunbuir Banner were declared to be part of Jilin province. Other parts of Inner Mongolia were remapped to be in Heilongjiang, Liaoning, and Gansu provinces and in the Ningxia Autonomous Region. The original boundaries of Inner Mongolia were restored in 1979, during the post-Mao thaw.

The bloody repression in Inner Mongolia tapered off toward the end of 1969, and, in a pattern that was common around the country, ordinary people moved quickly to restore the status quo ante. Officially the Cultural Revolution was not over until 1976, but in fact life became considerably more tolerable after 1969. People in Horqin Banner, both the original residents and the sent-down people, could say good-bye to the interminable struggle sessions and required study of the 1966–69 years.

Physically, Horqin Banner was a lovely area featuring rolling hills and gentle streams that ranged between 1,300 and 3,100 feet above sea level. Its four seasons were distinct, animals of many kinds filled the mountains, and rich foliage covered the hills. Flowers and birdsong were everywhere during spring and summer. The Han people had brought domesticated animals to the area and introduced a sophisticated silkworm industry. The sky was often crystal clear and the sunlight brilliant and bold. At night the stars were a splendid spread, and the black outlines of the mountains at the edge of the moonlight caused reverie in a person—even reverence, almost to the edge of fear. The position of the Milky Way in the sky varied with the season, but the Herd Boy and the Weaving Girl on its two sides remained steadfast.[5] On winter nights, glancing at Orion's belt, which the locals called the Three Stars, was how, without wristwatches, they told time.

There were good reasons the Liu Ling family could be happy at Boulder Village. The many languages and dialects heard on the streets made it a wonderful laboratory for scholars of linguistics like Professor Liu. Materially too their lives were not as difficult as one might imagine. They still drew their salaries: Liu Ling got 90 *yuan* per month, and his wife, Zhang Suqin, got about 35 *yuan* even though she could not do the nursery-school duties in her job description. The family income of about 125 *yuan* per month put them well above the local average and did not vary with farming output as others' income did. The state, hoping to get sent-down intellectuals to sink permanent roots into the countryside, offered grants for materials with which sent-down families could build their own houses. The Lius did not pursue this, though. They hoped to return to Changchun. As sent-down intellectuals being "re-educated," they were obliged to "participate in farm work." Essentially this meant getting familiar with the various tasks that farmers perform. In practice, they and most of the migrant-intellectuals did various kinds of office work.

Daily life in Horqin Banner brought the Liu Ling family members closer together physically than they had been in Changchun. For Xiaobo this was difficult. His father continued to hold himself above the rest and to domineer. "His word was law," Xiaobo later wrote. "He never chatted casually with his children or shared what was on his mind,"[6] and he was still using corporal punishment on Xiaobo, whose continued smoking only exacerbated the conflict. It finally destroyed whatever mutual trust they ever had. Many years later Xiaobo was still describing his father as an example of "Party culture," meaning that he treated his children the way superiors treat inferiors in a communist system: the only role for the inferiors is to obey. Xiaobo's mother played a role that resembled his grandmother's back in Changchun. She loved Xiaobo, and the worse the father's abuse, the greater her care. But she too was a underling in the Party-culture household. It never occurred to Liu Ling that his wife's opinions should soften his severity toward Xiaobo.

Now in his mid-teens, Xiaobo began to think about his place in life. His two older brothers were out in Yanbian near Korea, doing who knows what—but anyway independent of the family. He, in Boulder Village, had no worries about livelihood but did feel, as he later put it, like an uprooted turnip plunked down on indifferent soil. What should he do now? Continue fighting with his father? What was the point? Continue smoking? That would require continuing to steal money from his parents, and this made him feel pulled in two directions inside. It was an early example of his lifetime pattern of struggling with inner dilemmas.

In this mood he began to notice a girl who eventually became an important part of his life. She was Tao Li, the eldest daughter of Tao Dezhen and Pu Manting, two professors who had taught with Liu Ling in the Linguistics Department at Northeast Normal University. The Tao family had come to Boulder Village in the same "to the countryside" project as the Liu Ling family. As youngsters Tao Li and Liu Xiaobo had grown up in the same university housing compound and on the same playgrounds. But they hadn't interacted much, because boys played only with boys and girls with girls. They differed considerably in behavior too. Tao Li was a model student. Her grades were good, her reputation was excellent, and she practiced empathy. Xiaobo had a mixed record in school, was a known rule breaker, and cared little about his poor-to-fair social reputation. The two seemed, to borrow an idiom from northeast Mandarin, "carts with wheels in the ruts of different roads." That was not to be, however.

Tao Li was nearly a year older than Xiaobo, but they were put into the same class at Boulder Junior High School. They both lived at the school, in separate girls' and boys' dormitories and came home on weekends.

Their two families had been growing closer. In Changchun they had known each other as colleagues and neighbors. Together they had witnessed the plotting, backstabbing, and general unraveling of human decency that the Cultural Revolution caused within their campus community. Now co-survivors of that trauma and sharing a fate in the countryside, they were ready for deeper familiarity and more trust. There was a difference in their political status, though. Liu Ling had been recruited into the Communist Party to be a future official, whereas the two Taos were but ordinary intellectuals—viewed by the Party as "progressive," but not leadership material.

While scoldings and beatings were common in the Liu household, in the Tao family scoldings were rare and beatings unimaginable. Tao Li's mother discussed important issues like schooling or careers with the children; the shy father stood aside, beaming in silence. The parents focused especially on Tao Li, the older daughter, because she was brilliant in school. They did whatever they could for her, and she emulated them, especially the father. The younger sister, Tao Ning, referred to Tao Li as her father's "ace student" and "prize product." Physically, though, Tao Li was frail and often ill. Her health was a perennial worry for the parents.

Boulder Junior High was a new school, founded in 1960 and the fortunate recipient in the early 1970s of an influx of idealistic college graduates "sent down" from the cities. The bright newcomers playfully dubbed their school "the most exalted seat of learning in the Boulder area" and were eager to get things right. They came from all over China and spoke in many different accents, but they shared a destiny in their assignments to Boulder Junior High and on that foundation built camaraderie. They looked for ways to avoid politically stilted teaching materials by searching for new offerings. The oft-heard generalization that Chinese education collapsed during Mao's Cultural Revolution in fact has many larger and smaller exceptions, where teachers, students, and parents persisted through the maelstrom.

Horqin Banner was sufficiently remote that it was less upset than other places by the political ups and downs that undulated from Party Central, and thanks to idealistic sent-down teachers, the school curricula often had solid content. Language arts class introduced Lu Xun (1881–1936), the great writer from China's Republican era, as well as some classical texts. Mathematics class taught logarithms, geometry, and parabolas. There were no science laboratories, but the teachers of chemistry and physics did manage to find combustion cups and electrolysis cells that somehow had survived the Cultural Revolution. The school library reopened and although certain books had been removed, a number of interesting ones were still there, like translations of Jules Verne's novels *The Mysterious Island, Twenty Thousand Leagues Under the Sea,* and *The Children of Captain Grant.*[7] Russian novels, including Leo Tolstoy's *Resurrection* and *Anna Karenina,* and Maxim Gorky's *Mother,* were available as well. So were some works from Eastern Europe, such as *Notes from the Gallows* by the Czechoslovakian anti-Nazi hero Julius Fučík. *The Gadfly* by Ethel Voynich, a socialist from New Jersey who later moved to England, was well known and deeply influential all across China, including at Horqin Banner.

None of Xiaobo's classmates remotely resembled his privileged friend Fatty in Changchun. They were all bumpkins, farmers' kids. They were about his age, but many were already shouldering responsibilities in their families. They seemed more mature, or anyway more worried, than the still-mischievous Xiaobo. He couldn't tell from looking at them which were Mongolians and which were Han, but at meal times the difference was obvious. The Mongolians always had their milk tea and homemade cheese. To each other they spoke Mongolian and to the Han or any other ethnicity spoke Mandarin with a Mongolian accent. Their different habits and ways of seeing the world left impressions on Xiaobo. The ethnic diversity he experienced during childhood (Changchun was multiethnic too) probably helps to explain his lifelong antipathy for Han chauvinism.

At the Boulder school, just as in Changchun, Tao Li inspired people's trust. She had large bright eyes that seemed to talk. She had been classroom representative in her Changchun school and was selected again for that role at Boulder Junior High. Xiaobo, alas, also maintained his Changchun traditions: smoking, cutting class, playing tricks.

He later recalled how, one day as he was leaving school, there were two girls walking in front of him, laughing and chatting. One of them suddenly let out a peal of laughter so full of unrestrained joy that he had to ask himself, *Can there really be a person in this world so free of worry and concern? I should get to know her.* He caught up with the two only to discover that the ebullient laughter had come from none other than the older sister of the Tao family, whom he had known in Changchun.[8] He began to watch Tao Li. Years later he told friends how he had become entranced by her hair, which she kept in two pigtails of gleaming black. Once he saw her outside the girls' dormitory drying her just-washed hair in the brilliant Mongolian sunshine. He was smitten. How could a girl's hair be as enchanting as this?[9]

Tao Li began to sense that a pair of eyes were trained on the back of her head as she walked around. Simultaneously Xiaobo's attendance at school began to improve. He responded better to his teachers, and his grades went up. Tao Li was in charge of the "blackboard news" for their class, which meant she had to gather and post the political "trends" handed down from Beijing and also write accounts of "good people and good deeds" in their own classroom. The blackboard news was also supposed to include art. That was fine, because Tao Li could draw. Xiaobo, enthralled, volunteered to be her assistant.

The similarities in Tao Li's and Xiaobo's backgrounds and school situations provided them with plenty to talk about, yet neither felt confident about how to interact. Xiaobo, from a family of all boys, had never observed girls at close range, let alone understood crushes. But here was Tao Li, right in front of him, good at all kinds of things that he admired. For her part, the composed and circumspect Tao Li had never encountered a bright, rebellious person like Xiaobo; his contrarian thinking and mischief took her by surprise. For both, the other person arose as if from a different place, in some ways an opposite place. That feeling of strangeness and curiosity added spice to the normal feelings that give rise to red faces and quicker heartbeats in newly pubescent girls and boys.

Xiaobo and Tao Li became reading partners. Horqin Right Front Banner was about as far from Paris, Brussels, or London as one could get, yet there the two young people came together under the intellectual spell of Karl Marx. On November 6, 1970, Party Central in Beijing issued a "Notice on the Question of Study by High-Ranking Officials Everywhere in the Country." It recommended six classics:

Karl Marx and Friedrich Engels, *The Communist Manifesto*
Karl Marx, *Critique of the Gotha Program*
Karl Marx, *The Civil War in France* (selections)
Friedrich Engels, *Anti-Dühring* (selections)
Vladimir Lenin, *Materialism and Empirio-criticism* (selections)
Vladimir Lenin, *The State and Revolution* (selections)

To intellectuals like the Taos and the Lius, the list was very welcome. Compared to *Quotations of Chairman Mao*, these books offered access to the world outside China, to trends in thinking in the West, and to a field upon which the intellect could practice something other than blind obedience. China was so tightly sealed from the outside world during the late-Mao years that the works of Marx were one of the best available windows onto many topics in Western culture. Classical Greek drama, the Renaissance, Shakespeare, the Enlightenment, the English enclosure movement, utopian socialism, and German idealist philosophy all were mentioned in Marx but, in China, hardly anywhere else. Xiaobo wrote that his strong avocation in reading European philosophy in college and graduate school had its origins in reading the early Marx.[10]

The Tao parents organized a family salon: after dinner on certain days, the two professors and their brilliant eldest daughter, whom they treated as an intellectual equal, gathered under a kerosene lantern to discuss their views of the readings. Tao Li made astonishing intellectual progress at these salons. When Xiaobo noticed how she could read such abstruse texts, his awe redoubled.

So he decided to try it himself. The most straightforward way to start was to borrow books by "the bearded gurus" directly from Tao Li, whom he wanted to see in any case. Borrowing and returning books among classmates, of either sex, was unremarkable and nothing to hide from either parents or teachers. When he returned her books, he appended his "reading harvests" for her reference. He wrote notes on little slips of paper that he inserted between pages or sometimes directly in the margins. Wondering if he had gotten this or that point right, he would politely ask Tao Li to "help out."[11]

The exchange with Tao Li allowed Xiaobo to discover a gift that he had not known he had: a prodigious ability to memorize texts. He had already noticed, during the Cultural Revolution, that when Mao quotes, political slogans, or revolutionary songs floated into his ears, they seemed to take root in his brain—from where he could spit them back out almost word for word. But now he was learning that the gift also worked for written texts, even fairly long ones. If he saw something he wanted to remember—or even if he just liked it, not meaning to memorize it—it would stick, and later he could produce it almost verbatim. The ability was doubly useful because he could use it to impress Tao Li. He could stand in front of her and recite paragraph after paragraph that he had read the night before in *The Communist Manifesto* or *Critique of the Gotha Program*. How much he understood was a different question, but it probably was at least some. When Tao Li first observed his performances she didn't know whether to laugh or to cry but, with time, came to view this "younger brother" (beneath her in both age and learning) as conscientious. She felt she was at least partly responsible for his progress, and the thought made her happy.

Later in his life Xiaobo became a fierce and relentless opponent of the communist system that Marxism had brought to China. But he remained honest enough to recall that "when I was about fifteen I was infatuated with Marxism-Leninism, and even today I can recite lengthy passages from the early Marx."[12] In a 1989 essay called "At the Gateway to Hell," he wrote:

> It's hard to forget the excitement I felt when I first read *The Communist Manifesto*. The author's passion and self-confidence struck me powerfully. In high school I read *Selected Works of Marx and Engels* and later, in college, the *Complete Works of Marx and Engels*. I always preferred Marx's early works, though. They had a richer philosophical flavor and were more uncompromising in their spirit of rebellion. That spirit had a huge influence on me. In addition, Marx's works were full of references to other European philosophy, and those leads became important for me when I went on to study philosophy seriously. One could say the works of Marx have run through my whole life—first as texts I accepted uncritically and finally as texts that I studied in order to refute.[13]

In the same essay he wrote: "In his day, Marx stood alone in opposition to the entirety of capitalist society. He issued his challenge, without hesitating, on a principle of thoroughgoing and uncompromising rebellion." Xiaobo's own astonishing courage to challenge a status quo came in part from this early reading.

Reading Marx was also Xiaobo's introduction to reasoning about society in theoretical terms. He quoted snippets from Marx even long after he had begun to oppose communism as a system. In 1988, for example, when journalists asked him why he had said certain things that "sold out his country," he was ready. "Sold out my country?" he answered. "Let me quote Marx in *The Communist Manifesto*: 'The workers have no country. We cannot take from them what they have not got.'"[14]

Marx occupied a similar place in Tao Li's mind. She often quoted Marx and Engels, and the quotes were not ornaments of the kind that other scholars used merely to stay safe politically. They were natural and fitting intellectual observations.

Lu Xun too had a major impact on both Tao Li and Xiaobo. Often called the father of modern Chinese fiction, Lu Xun was sharply critical of traditional Chinese culture, of the character of his fellow Chinese, and of himself. After he died, he was claimed politically by Mao Zedong, who called him a "resolute revolutionary hero" in a way that he would have cringed to hear. But Mao's apotheosis of Lu Xun did have the happy consequence that his works remained on the shelves of bookstores and libraries throughout China, including at Boulder Junior High, during the late-Mao years. In 1973 the People's Publishing House in Beijing came out with twenty-four little booklets of Lu Xun stories and essays. For Xiaobo and Tao Li, these were a gold mine. They raised topics that went well beyond Marx and class analysis: existential theory, the liberation of the individual, the meaning of life. The allure was overwhelming. For Xiaobo, it became almost a sacred mission to inhabit Lu Xun's spirit and carry on his legacy. He went through some major intellectual shifts during his life, but through them all never really left Lu Xun.

Xiaobo and Tao Li also explored the natural world around them at Horqin Banner. As children growing up in Changchun, they knew that the sun shone overhead, but they had not asked where it arose. They knew about rain, but not how raindrops are formed. Now, in Horqin Banner, to see the red sun rise in the east was a step forward in understanding the world. Looking to the sky for not only clouds but also sheets of rain, falling in the distance, was their introduction to meteorology. They saw how rainbows appeared in Boulder Valley and how, as sunlight illuminated the grasses on its two sides, the rainbow might form an overhead bridge under which people could walk.[15] One could observe how whirlwinds formed inside the distensions of low-lying clouds and how the air at their centers turned faster than at their peripheries, forming funnels that drilled downward toward the earth. In certain conditions, "bolts from the blue" appeared in a literal sense. A few clouds, low and white, floating against a blue sky could, without warning, suddenly generate a dazzling bolt of lightning that would flash down to earth, immediately delivering a sharp clap of thunder. The event could come and go in an instant—without a drop of rain.

In springtime wildflowers covered the low hills around Boulder Village. Wild apricot was the local pride. Its bright, fresh blossoms, white with red flecks, grew on nude branches, and their fragrance spread through the air to a considerable distance. Farther from town, a wealth of animals lurked in the woods. Among mammals there were wild boar, deer, roe deer, foxes, squirrels, voles, moles, and marmots; the birds included pheasants, sand grouse, hawks, larks, and cuckoos. Snakes were represented by the poisonous copperhead.

In short, Horqin Banner basked in sunlight and brimmed with life. It was the kind of glorious natural world that could move people to song and dance. Later in life, Xiaobo often said that he was a "sense-based" person. He thought that to be sense-based, a person needed to have had a grounding in sensual experience early in life and that he was lucky to have had it. The striking beauty of the environment sharpened the sensitivities of Tao Li as well and led her to form what felt like a secret channel with Xiaobo. It had to be secret because in those days it was forbidden to have boyfriends or girlfriends at school. The rules were more relaxed in rural areas than in cities, but even in Horqin Banner it was not acceptable to behave like lovers in public. Doing so could bring the serious charge of "incorrect conduct." Tao Li was especially attentive to propriety. There was no way she would allow herself to become the object of gossip. She was one of those people who could feel surging passion inside but show no sign of it on the surface. Her feelings for Xiaobo stayed buried deep down. They probably never used the word "love" at Horqin Banner. That would come later.

The content that flowed through their secret channel was mostly books and thoughts about books. These were becoming very important to Xiaobo, and the volume of the traffic began to absorb most of his time. That meant he was running out of time for mischief. Tao Li enjoyed observing the changes. He was learning how not to be her naughty little brother, and that was fine with her.

In January 1972, Tao Li and Xiaobo, after two years as classmates, graduated together from Boulder Junior High School. In June 1972, Tao Li's parents were sent back to Northeast Normal University in Changchun, and Tao Li and her siblings went with them. (The Tao children were classified as "family of sent-down officials," which meant that their legal residence followed their parents.' This made them luckier than "sent-down youth," who had been assigned to the countryside as individuals and were allowed to return, if at all, only as individuals.) Liu Ling's family could not return to Changchun until late 1973, so Xiaobo and Tao Li endured more than a year of separation.[16] There was no Boulder Senior High to match Boulder Junior High, so for the year following graduation Xiaobo transferred as a boarding student to the Soren Railway High School, about twenty-five miles from Boulder Village. By then his brother Xiaoxuan, who had been living with their grandmother in Huaide since 1968, had rejoined the family at Horqin Banner. Xiaoxuan joined Xiaobo in attending Soren Railway High[17] but was no substitute for Tao Li as an intellectual partner.

When Tao Li returned to Changchun she went to the Jilin Provincial Experimental School, a premier school known for its high quality. When Xiaobo returned he too went to that school, but there was not much chance for the two to see each other. They had no classes in common, and the culture said that male and female students should stay separate.

In 1974, after they graduated, Xiaobo was almost immediately sent to the countryside again. This was in the "sent-down youth" program, so he knew that this time it might not be so easy to get back to the city. He also realized that from now on, his future was in his own hands.

Fortunately, a new national policy was being implemented right at that time. In 1972 a schoolteacher in Fujian province named Li Qinglin had taken the risky step of writing a letter to Mao Zedong complaining that his sent-down son was hungry and homeless. No letter from such a person would ever change government policy, but apparently Mao and others at the top had their own reasons for wanting to soften the program, so used the Li Qinglin letter to advertise a change. Food and shelter were to be improved, and sent-down youth should not be sent too far from home. Xiaobo's assignment was to the Lin Family Store Production Team in the Victory Brigade of San'gang Commune in Nongan county, Jilin province, about seventy miles northeast of Changchun.

He set out with no sense of adventure of the kind he had felt when heading for Inner Mongolia five years earlier. He had, moreover, not the slightest intention of setting down any roots in San'gang Commune. He and the twelve others in his group saw themselves as earning a credential that was necessary for eventually getting a good urban reassignment. They were going to the countryside to "gold-plate" themselves, as they put it. At San'gang Commune they lived in two adjacent rooms—seven males in one and six females in the other. The rooms had no beds. Each contained a large *kang* bed platform, which was heated in winter. But there was no privacy. And the work was boring.

His deepest impression was of the poverty he saw. The first year he was there, full-time pay for a male worker was thirty cents a day (about ten cents U.S. at the official exchange rate), and the next year, when the harvests were poor, that went down. Men of middle age or older had trouble affording wives. Xiaobo could also see, more clearly than ever before, how inequality in power led to inequality in living standards. The leaders lived in red brick houses with tiled roofs; the farmers lived in mud brick huts with thatched roofs.

Meanwhile, the political heavens were rumbling with power struggles, and ideological lightning bolts flashed intermittently to earth. The people were exhorted to hate one or another leading comrade and to join in propaganda work—intoning slogans, composing doggerel, writing stories—whether or not they understood the reasons. In 1974 there was the "Criticize Lin and Criticize Kong" campaign. "Lin" meant Lin Biao, formerly Mao Zedong's "closest comrade in arms," who died after allegedly plotting a coup against Mao, and "Kong" meant Confucius, a code word for China's Premier Zhou Enlai, whom Mao also wanted to attack but couldn't risk doing so by name. (Most ordinary people at the time did not know the Confucius = Zhou code, but that didn't matter. So long as the masses were denouncing "Confucius," Mao's purposes at the elite level were being fulfilled.) In late 1975 another bolt from the heavens demanded that people "Criticize Deng and Counterattack Against the Right-Leaning Tendency to Reverse Verdicts." Stripped of jargon, this meant that Mao, influenced by his wife, Jiang Qing, and others who later were excoriated as the "Gang of Four," was aiming to depose the reformist-in-waiting Deng Xiaoping. Mao had only recently re-elevated Deng from the disgrace of former association with Liu Shaoqi, who twenty years earlier had been Mao's number two man at the top but ten years after that, as mortal enemy number one, had died in prison.

Xiaobo comprehended none of this at the time. Years later, reflecting on his youthful innocence, he wrote: "My literary life began when I was an 'educated youth' in the 1970s. It was an era of revolutionary fervor when empty slogans and blind passions, including the lies in *Quotations of Chairman Mao*, ran rampant. As a young man I embraced all of them as the absolute truth."[18] During those years, sent-down youth in some parts of China were able to obtain and surreptitiously pass around so-called "yellow cover" or "gray cover" books. These books were not sold in public bookstores; only officials of certain ranks were allowed to buy them. They included works by Americans Jack Kerouac and J. D. Salinger and by Soviets Ilya Ehrenburg, Vasily Aksyonov, and others. Such books leaked into underground trading networks and for many young people became eye-openers to a whole new world. Not for Xiaobo, though. The places to which he was sent down were too remote to access such pleasures. Xiaobo cut his intellectual teeth entirely within what he and others called "Party culture"—at first accepting it and later, through the power of his own reasoning, seeing through it.

By 1976 it had become less difficult for sent-down youth to get permission to return home. By November, two months after Mao Zedong died, Xiaobo had been at San'gang Commune more than two years and was allowed to return to

Changchun. His work assignment there was to mix cement for a construction company. He did this for a bit more than a year.

His relationship with Tao Li—from 1972, when her family left Boulder Village, until 1982, when the two were married—survived even though they did not see much of each other in person. Their contact was mostly by exchange of letters about reading experiences. When Xiaobo was sent to the San'gang Commune and many other people their age were "sent down" as well, Tao Li was spared because of her fragile health. She had long had eye trouble and was beginning to experience mild heart trouble as well.

In spring 1978, she and Xiaobo both went to college in Changchun, but to different schools. Tao Li entered the Chinese Department at Northeast Normal University, where her parents were on the faculty. Xiaobo went to the Chinese Department at Jilin University, nine miles away. With this physical proximity their relationship warmed to the point where they began discussing marriage. They had endured many setbacks, but the result, in Xiaobo's view, had been well worth the effort. He was fond of telling his friends how amazing Tao Li was and how he had been a naughty boy until she turned him around. He adored her. In 1980 he published the following poem about how he felt upon returning to Changchun from the countryside:

This Place

I believe . . . this place

Has something special.
I lived a long time in this place.
I hovered much near this place.
I left this place with resentment in the heart.
I returned from far away with love in the heart.

I believe . . . this place
Has something special.[19]

"Love in the heart" likely meant Tao Li.

4

College Years, and the
Mask of Mao Falls

After the death of Mao in 1976, China began to uncurl itself from a great knot. Slowly, cautiously, society relaxed into the more customary patterns of what were called the "seventeen years" of 1949–66 and then ventured toward an exciting but only vaguely understood goal that people with a variety of viewpoints all agreed to call "modernization." For Xiaobo and millions of other young people, the change meant that they now had much better chances of going to college.

This happy prospect reversed the sudden shift in the summer of 1966, when postsecondary education in China had screeched to a halt. In 1970, tentative programs for "worker-peasant-soldier" students were set up at Peking University and Tsinghua University, and two years later were imitated elsewhere. Admission was by "recommendation." To be recommended a student had to have served at least two years as a "worker, peasant, or soldier" and had to be "reliable"—meaning politically reliable. There were entrance exams, but they were used only "for reference." The surest route into college was to be born to parents in the Communist elite, to be sent out for two years to get the worker-peasant-soldier credential, and then to await "recommendation." This was the path taken by Xi Jinping, who became China's paramount ruler in 2012. Xi had only a junior high education when, in 1976, he was recommended for admission as a worker-peasant-soldier to the Department of Chemical Engineering at Tsinghua University. Many students with better academic records but from less politically favored backgrounds could not even apply.

In 1977 a dramatic change arrived as Deng Xiaoping worked his way toward the pinnacle of political power in China. A year earlier Mao Zedong, as he lay dying and considering a successor, had looked past Deng, whom he had purged during the Cultural Revolution as the "number two renegade taking the capitalist road," and handed the baton of supreme power to a colorless bureaucrat named Hua Guofeng. By early 1977, though, the far more talented and experienced Deng was already maneuvering to replace Hua. One of Deng's first moves while Hua was formally in charge was to offer to handle matters in education, and in that capacity he oversaw the first major social change of the post-Mao era—the restoration of a national college entrance examination.

The announcement was made to the Chinese people on October 21, 1977, when the *People's Daily* published an article entitled "National Conference on College Admissions Makes Suggestions on Student Recruitment for the Coming Year." The "suggestions," which were Deng's, actually were mandatory. They made it clear that, effective immediately, any high school graduate in China could apply for college admission, and decisions would be made primarily on academic merit and only secondarily on the applicant's politics. The first of the restored exams were held in December.

A backlog of millions of would-be college students had accumulated between 1966 and 1976. So many registered for the exam that the printing of exam materials literally created paper shortages. Deng took the extraordinary step of reallocating paper that originally had been earmarked for printing volume 5 of the *Selected Works of Mao Zedong*.[1] Such a decision would have been unthinkable two years earlier.

Of the 5.7 million aspirants who took the exam, only 0.27 million, or 4.8 percent, were successful. Xiaobo was one. He was admitted to the Chinese Department of Jilin University. He and others in the class of 1977 arrived on campuses in March 1978, right after the New Year's Festival. All the testing and other necessary administrative work had meant that they had to begin a few months late.

People in Xiaobo's neighborhood started gossiping about what a great educator Professor Liu Ling must be: he had five sons, and by fall 1978 all five were in college. The oldest, Xiaoguang, had been admitted to the politics department at Northeast Normal University; the second, Xiaohui, was in a college-level worker-peasant-soldier program; Xiaobo's younger brother Xiaoxuan was in the polymer major at Dalian University of Technology; and the youngest, Xiaodong, was in the Biology Department at Northeast Normal.

Xiaobo's classmates at Jilin University ranged in age from sixteen to thirty-two. (This was largely because of the ten-year backlog.) One-fifth were women. Xiaobo and nine bunkmates were assigned to room 202 in Jilin University's Dormitory Number Seven. Their room resembled a railroad sleeping car with upper and lower berths. Xiaobo's father was sufficiently proud of Xiaobo that he came to visit.I It was the first time he had shown any real sign of moral support for this particular son.

One of Xiaobo's roommates was Zhang Xiaoyang, whose father was a colleague of Xiaobo's father at Northeast Normal University. Xiaoyang's father had been labeled a "rightist" in 1957, and the stigma had barred Xiaoyang from attending a regular high school despite his excellent grades. He went instead to a technical high school that did not prepare students for college. During the Cultural Revolution, when he was only nineteen years old and primarily because of his father's taint, he was labeled an "active counterrevolutionary" and tortured. He was beaten unconscious several times and "sat on the tiger bench" (in which the legs of a reclining person are tied down and the knees bent backward) so often that his legs suffered permanent damage. Later he was assigned to factory work that exposed him to toxic chemicals. When, despite all, he passed the college entrance exam, he was already twenty-eight years old. A younger sister and brother, also part of the backlog, passed also.

On their first night together the bunkmates of room 202, even though they were strangers, started talking and could not stop until deep into the night. They talked about where life had brought them so far, and their stories were extremely varied. Classmate Qifu was from the army and talked about nothing but guns, bombs, and ammunition. Classmate Wenlong was a calligrapher who described how he made elegant name cards for himself. Classmate Mingyi had worked on overhead electrical lines and explained all the hazards of climbing power poles. Classmate Laofan, experienced as a store clerk, boasted about the many ways he had mastered for short-changing customers. Xiaobo, in his turn, drew peals of laughter when he explained what a bore it was to be a cement mixer. After 1:00 a.m., as things began to quiet down, a classmate with a thick Sichuan accent asked timidly, "Can anybody tell me . . . is . . . is it okay in Changchun to wear tight-bottomed pants?" He was afraid that the city had not yet lifted its Cultural Revolution ban. The question stunned the group, who a moment later began chuckling at their naive bunkmate. Yes, they assured him, in Changchun you may wear the pants you choose.[2]

Xiaobo's own choice of pants—and all his clothing—was supremely undiscriminating. Others called him the earthiest student in the class—so earthy, in fact, that he brought the label "earthiest" to his entire dormitory. He was 5'8" tall, had ragged hair and rough skin, and simply didn't care about looks. He spoke bluntly and used local brogue. Wang Dongcheng, a classmate who became a lifelong friend, says he showed up for college looking like a bandit—or someone you might imagine throwing bricks on Stalin Avenue during the Cultural Revolution.[3]

In the 1950s, when China embraced the education system of the Soviet Union as its model, the training of engineers took precedence over training in the arts and sciences, including the social sciences and law. Every private or religious college in the country was closed. This was disastrous, of course, for those schools, but for the newly established ones like Jilin University, which the Communists had created in 1946 after they moved into China's northeast following World War II, it was a windfall. Top-flight professors from Beijing, Shanghai, and elsewhere came to Jilin and established nationally famous departments in fields like mathematics and chemistry. Humanists and libraries came as well. Xiaobo noticed that when he borrowed books from the humanities library at his school, many bore imprints from famous universities in the heartland.

Yang Zhensheng, a famous literary scholar and former provost at Tsinghua University and president of Qingdao University, moved to Jilin University to head its program in the history of Chinese literature. Faculty of this caliber brought a liberal-minded atmosphere to the university. Even the intellectuals who came up through the Communist movement were of the more free-thinking kind. Professor Gong Mu was a poet from the Communist base at Yan'an, where, in 1939, he had penned the lyrics for "The Song of the Eighth Route Army" (later "The Song of the Chinese People's Liberation Army"). In 1957, during the Anti-Rightist movement, he was labeled a rightist and restricted to teaching only classical Chinese literature, but after 1979 he came back as professor, department chair, and then vice president of the university. He provided political protection and even a bit of funding to Xiaobo and some of his classmates when they wanted to launch a literary magazine during years when the Communist Party, despite asking intellectuals to "liberate their thought," was still deeply suspicious of anything it did not control.

Jilin University formally reopened with a ceremony on March 20, 1978. A renowned chemist named Tang Aoqing was the featured speaker, and that fact itself was momentous. Tang, known as China's "father of quantum chemistry," had finished a Ph.D. at Princeton University in 1949, the year of the Communist revolution, and had returned immediately to China, to Peking University, to support the new society. In 1952 he moved to Jilin University to found its chemistry department, and in 1956 he was promoted to university vice president. This whole record meant nothing, though, when the Cultural Revolution arrived and most professors were deposed and denounced. Tang was sent to work in a factory.

In 1978, here he was again, just returned from a "National Symposium on Science" in Beijing where Deng Xiaoping had announced that China was going to "return to the road of modernization." In a stunning departure from Maoist policy, Deng had declared that science and technology were "forces of production" and that "intellectuals are part of the proletariat." With that, weights that had hung on the necks of Chinese intellectuals since 1957 or even earlier seemed to disappear overnight. Professor Tang became a campus legend again, now all the more glorious for having survived the Cultural Revolution ordeal. In July 1978, he was named university president.

The faculty in the Chinese Department at first were a bit unsure what to do with Xiaobo and their other lively charges, who not only were supertalented and diverse in age and background but also had arrived on campus with an urgency to speed things up because of the time they had lost. Curricular structure was useful in imposing some discipline. All students had to take Introduction to Literature, Introduction to Linguistics, History of the Chinese Communist Party, and Japanese language. The legacy of Japanese rule in Changchun, even three decades after it ended, had left its imprint on the city.

Xiaobo felt frustrated with his classes in literary theory. He loved the topic but hated the lectures. The professors were still using Russian readings left over from the 1950s—Vissarion Belinsky, Nikolay Chernyshevsky, and others.[4] From the writings of Nikolai Dobrolyubov, he and his classmates were asked to learn about literature and "people-ness" (*renminxing*), which did not mean human nature or humanism but "people" in the Marxist sense of the masses who support and are led by the Party. The Chinese literary histories, like You Guoen's *History of Chinese Literature* and Wang Yao's *History of New Chinese Literature*, were, to Xiaobo, dull: all material came in the same three boring lumps: historical background, main theme, artistic features.[5]

The questions on the minds of Xiaobo and his classmates, which produced bristling debate both inside and outside class, were quite different: "Do literature and art really have class nature?" "How can [the Maoist model opera] *The White-Haired Girl* have appeal in capitalist countries?" "Is there an imbalance in China between literary development and material development?" "Can proletarian literature inherit non-proletarian literary legacies?" On issues such as these, the students ran circles around their intellectually less flexible teachers.

Meanwhile, on campus and in society, a startling series of political surprises arrived.

In the afternoon of April 29, students were summoned to the library auditorium on campus to listen to a reading of a report from Party Central on "Removal of All Hats from Rightist Elements." ("Hat" was the widely understood metaphor for "arbitrary political label." The phrase as a whole meant "forgiveness of people who were labeled 'rightist' during the 1957 Anti-Rightist movement.") The father of Zhang Xiaoyang, one of Xiaobo's roommates, was among the de-hatted. No longer a rightist, he was transferred to Jilin University to teach Shakespeare in Chinese translation to students in the Chinese Department. Soon thereafter, Party Central announced and began to promote a nationwide discussion of the principle that "practice is the sole criterion for testing truth." The unspoken but widely understood purpose was to dismantle the position of "Mao Zedong Thought" as the final arbiter of every question. Three months later, in October, another ruling from the top brought an end to the "send-down" program that ordered young people "to the mountains and the countryside" to rusticate their thinking. Next, at the end of 1978, farmers in sixteen households in a village in Anhui province all but risked their lives to announce that they were forming a "household responsibility system" to grow and market their crops outside the system of people's communes that had been imposed in 1958 and had led to famine and profound bitterness. As their idea spread, the rulers in Beijing saw that they would have to accept it and call it "reform," or face major trouble. Xiaobo, from his experience of living in the countryside, reflexively sympathized with the farmers.

As these and other reforms arrived, a feeling of goodwill suffused society. Energy that had lain dormant for years now gushed forth. At least for the time being, there was societywide consensus, from top to bottom and both inside and outside the ruling system, that a new, modernized nation could arise on the Eastern side of the globe and join the rest of the modern world in striding toward the future. Accounts of suffering during the late-Mao years—at least some of them—could now be written. In November 1978, Xiaobo and his classmates discussed a story called "Scar" that had appeared in the *Wenhui Daily* newspaper in Shanghai.[6] The author was a first-year student at Fudan University, and the story tells of a young woman whose relationships with both her parents and her boyfriend are destroyed because political labels like "traitor" and "counterrevolutionary" imposed stigmas and induced shame that could not be overcome. "Scar" was a simple story but like a champagne cork popping from a bottle: it released an effusion of emotion that produced many similar works—about corruption, violence, bullying, political privilege, falsity in language, a generation gap, and other topics that for years had been forbidden. These stories, appearing from 1978 through 1980, were known collectively as "scar literature."

During the same years a group of talented writers who had been born in the 1930s, labeled "rightists" in 1957, and then repressed for two decades re-emerged. Called the "returnees," they included Wang Meng, Liu Binyan, Shao Yanxiang, Bai Hua, Zhang Xianliang, Gao Xiaosheng, and many others. They had much to say about recent Chinese history and were eager to say it. A cascade of their works, one following close upon another, shook readers and stirred discussion.

Xiaobo was their avid reader (even though, a few years later, in deeper perspective, he assailed many of them for conformity of a new kind).

With "reform and opening" after Mao, cultural influences from Hong Kong and Taiwan, including the languid tones of Hong Kong and Taiwan music (so radically different from Maoist music!) began to seep into the mainland. The music had an especially large effect on Xiaobo's generation of university students. It arrived gently—not outdoors or in auditoriums but secretly, among trusted friends, through furtive exchanges of cassette tapes inside dormitories. Xiaobo later remembered the rush he felt, mixed with an awkward sense of guilt, when he first heard the Taiwan crooner Teresa Teng in 1977:

> [Her songs] were like interior monologue in music, brimming with human feeling. The lyrics, pouring pain and grief out from the heart, were nevertheless fraught with nuance, at times almost whispered, and they delivered a jolt to my soul. My generation had grown up with strident revolutionary songs that were as towering and torrential as mountains and rivers. Our orthodox communist education had taught us slogans like "never fear hardship, never fear death" and had infused class-struggle ideas that lacked even a silhouette of human feeling. Education like that taught us how to spout violent language and how to hate people. There was scant attention to the things of daily life or to human feeling, or to showing respect toward others. Teresa Teng's songs struck a primal chord. I can recall that exciting atmosphere as if it happened yesterday.
>
> However, I can also recall struggling with conflicted feelings about those songs. They were immediately, instinctually attractive, but on the other hand, from the habits of thought left over from my education, I was afraid that listening to sappy bourgeois songs was a sign of moral degeneration. Was I falling into the bourgeois quagmire?[7]

Xiaobo's reference to "bourgeois quagmire" shows that ordeals he suffered during elementary school—being isolated as a "little heir of the bourgeoisie," for example—remained with him however much, consciously, he might by now have rejected them.

Films also helped him to discover the contemporary world outside China. He later wrote about his sense of revelation in watching Japanese films like Jinyo Satō's *Pursuit*: "When I saw two lovers galloping on horseback, the woman's long hair trailing in the wind, rising and falling in rhythm with the galloping horse, I felt overwhelmed. I had never imagined there could be such a beautiful woman or such an exhilarating scene."[8] Xiaobo's relationship with Tao Li had earned him the label, in the jargon of the times, of suffering "early love," but now he was enthralled to imagine how much more about love and beauty still awaited his exploration. He noted that an "invisible Great Wall" inside his mind was waiting to be knocked down. He wrote that "Teresa Teng's soothing love songs washed those steel structures of my wolf-milk education into total collapse, and the flying hair of that woman in *Pursuit* replaced the 'iron heroine' image of femininity that I had grown up with."[9]

In Chinese universities at the time, students entered departments from day one and followed set courses of study. But Xiaobo, less interested in academic rules than in new learning wherever he could find it, ventured outside his home department of literature and into the philosophy department, where Professor Che Wenbo was teaching Freud and Professor Zou Huazheng was teaching classical German philosophers. Xiaobo went to classes in both departments. He later estimated that during his four years of college he read more philosophy, especially Kant and Hegel, than literature. Several of his classmates remembered how he enjoyed reciting Hegel on aesthetics. The lines were arcane, but Xiaobo could chant them word for word. Other classmates could recite poetry, ancient or modern—but only Xiaobo could do Hegel.[10]

After classes Xiaobo did not go directly to his homework. He had a habit of first making the rounds of the dormitories offering his views on both schoolwork and current events. His classmates sometimes objected that his visits distracted them from their own work. Eventually he would go back to his dormitory and in an hour or so write out many pages about his galloping thoughts.[11]

His care for grades, which had improved under Tao Li's influence at Boulder High, grew stronger. He now demanded straight As from himself. His weakness was Japanese, mostly because he found homework tedious. One day he resorted to copying a classmate's exercise. The teacher noticed and, deciding to expose the cheating in front of the whole class, announced that he was giving zeroes to the papers of both students involved. Xiaobo stood up and said, "I did the copying, sir. You should punish only me, not him." Luckily Japanese was an elective that did not count in Xiaobo's major, so his departmental record was unaffected. He finished with straight As in his major for all four of his undergraduate years. Such records were rare.[12]

Some of Xiaobo's college classmates left impressions that were deep and had lasting influence. Wei Haitian was one. Wei and Xiaobo shared the fate of having had cruel fathers. They found that Franz Kafka did as well, and when they read Kafka's "Letter to Father" together, they bonded at a deep level. Wei had a sharp mind and a withering pen; he later became a noted journalist. At college exams he was always first to hand in his paper: he answered questions with terse precision and then just stopped. He had a personal magnetism that survived his refusal to suffer fools. In 1979, when China went to war with Vietnam, calling it a "War of Defensive Counterattack," college students were required to listen to broadcasts about China's military advances and war heroes. During the broadcasts Wei lay in his dormitory bunk and shouted, "I oppose this war!" He also had an analysis of China's nineteenth-century Opium Wars that began in dormitory debates and later spread to the whole campus. "Those wars may have been humiliating," he argued, "but they did knock China's door open."[13] Xiaobo found this a novel and interesting view. Could there be a good side to what the nasty imperialists had done? He and Wei later had many talks about the "double nature" of the Opium Wars and the larger problem of China's relation to the outside world more generally.[14] In 2009, when Xiaobo was given his eleven-year prison sentence for "subversion of the state," Wei Haitian wrote, "I have always felt both pride in having been one of Xiaobo's classmates and shame for not joining his opposition to violent government. Beginning today, I stand with him."[15]

Another classmate who had a deep influence on Xiaobo was Zhang Xiaoyang, the one who had been tortured because his father was a "rightist." In a controversial speech in 1986, Xiaobo argued that in order for a culture to grow it needs the challenge of an entirely different culture against which to measure itself, and it needs to interact with that other culture. He mentioned Zhang Xiaoyang, but not by name: "A classmate of mine has observed that only a person who can take in two kinds of value systems and use each to refer to the other can truly stand outside of absurdity and perceive what absurdity really is. There is much truth in this."[16] Zhang knew Russian, English, and Japanese, and later went to England to do a Ph.D. on Shakespeare. He stayed in England to teach comparative literature.

At one point in their college years, Zhang translated Katherine Mansfield's story "A Cup of Tea" and posted it on a bulletin board in the humanities building of the university. The story tells of an upper-class young woman who, taking pity on a beggar girl who asks for money to buy a cup of tea, brings her home and is thinking of adopting her, but then, when the wealthy woman's husband comes home and comments that the beggar girl is beautiful, changes her mind and returns the girl to the street. Xiaobo read the posted story, was smitten, and went back to their dormitory able to recite long passages from it verbatim. His classmates, including Zhang Xiaoyang, listened in awe. After Xiaobo died, Zhang wrote that Xiaobo "began by loathing Zeus [meaning Mao] and ended by spreading the sparks of democracy across China's vast land. He died defending truth."[17]

Political criticism during Xiaobo's college years was encouraged at one level but forbidden at another. The Deng Xiaoping regime was urging people to denounce the "Gang of Four"—Mao's widow and three others who were close to Mao—while Mao himself remained untouchable. The distinction was the result of a careful calibration by Deng: popular denunciation of the Gang of Four served his purposes, because it helped to legitimize the major policy changes that he was planning, but to go as far as to denounce Mao himself would shake the foundation of the Communist edifice, and that of course would not be good for Deng. (Well into the twenty-first century, Deng's successors have continued to shield Mao for the same reason.) For Xiaobo and his classmates, any discussion that seriously questioned the core principle of Communist rule had to be kept out of public places, including classrooms. But in dormitory rooms, debates about Mao-era martyrs who had challenged Communist rule left Xiaobo with very deep impressions.

As a boy, he had admired the Communist heroes and martyrs in his grade-school textbooks. He venerated them especially when they were selfless. The martyrs who were now emerging from his dormitory bull sessions resembled those earlier heroes except, of course, that now they were anti-Mao, not pro-Mao, and for one other important reason: they thought for themselves and died for their own, not the government's, ideals. Xiaobo and his friends got their information about the anti-Mao martyrs almost entirely from the state-run press, although sometimes this required reading between the lines. For example, on May 25, 1979, the *People's Daily* published a long article on Zhang Zhixin, a mother of two small children who had been executed in 1975 for political offenses. The Deng government, blaming the Gang of Four, was using her story to seek popular support.[18]

Born in 1930, Zhang Zhixin was a Russian-speaking official in the Communist Party Committee of Liaoning province before she was arrested in 1969. The initial charge against her was "opposing the Great Proletarian Cultural Revolution," but in 1970 a new charge, the one for which she eventually was executed, was "opposing Chairman Mao, opposing Comrade Jiang Qing, and reversing the verdict on Liu Shaoqi [whom Mao viewed as a rival]." The specific evidence for her crimes was not put into print. People said she had shouted "Down with Mao Zedong!"—but that was after she had already been sent to prison. Inside prison she was persecuted to the brink of insanity and then, on April 4, 1975, executed by a bullet to the head. To ensure that she did not shout any slogans on the way to the execution grounds, her captors took the precaution of cutting her throat. The *People's Daily*, in addition to reporting these details, accompanied its article with photographs of her with her daughter and son. The boy had been three when she was arrested, nine when she was shot.

More photos and reports on Zhang Zhixin were released in the ensuing days and were posted on the roadside bulletin board outside the main gate of Jilin University. The photos showed that Zhang had been a beauty. She was talented too—she could play the violin. A poem called "Weight," by Han Han, spread across China:

> She places her bloodied head
> Onto the scales of life
> And lets us careless others
> Lose all weight

Zhang Xiaoyang recalls that in the dormitory debates that he and Xiaobo joined, opinions on her were of basically two kinds. One was that she was opposing Mao, not just the Cultural Revolution, and therefore was going too far. Moreover, she was a loose woman with too many male friends, so to arrest and execute her was proper. The other view was that to cut a person's throat in that way was unspeakably cruel and should be banned forever—and it was only one among countless cruelties perpetrated during the Cultural Revolution. Xiaobo held the second view.[19]

The reports on Zhang Zhixin raised a tide of popular emotion that went far beyond what the Deng regime had anticipated. Chary of eliciting another such reaction, authorities decided to suspend plans to reveal a second case, that of Lin Zhao, who was executed for political crimes on April 29, 1968. The Lin Zhao report had already been written but was kept under wraps for a year and a half until the Zhang Zhixin story had faded. On January 27, 1981, *People's Daily* published an article on the sentencing of the Gang of Four, whose show trial had just been completed and whose historic iniquity, in the view of the Deng regime, needed some examples. Lin Zhao's case could be one. Readers were told that "details of Lin Zhao's martyrdom remain unclear," but one was mentioned, and it stuck with Xiaobo for life: in the early morning of May 1, 1968, representatives of "the relevant offices" came looking for Lin Zhao's elderly mother, informed her that her daughter had been shot two days earlier, and said that, since a "counter-revolutionary element" had cost the state one bullet, the family was required to pay a bullet fee of five cents.[20]

Born in 1932 and a devout Christian during her school years, Lin Zhao was an enthusiastic Communist in her late teens but later, while a student in the Journalism Department at Peking University, turned into an inveterate protester of the Mao regime's suppression of free speech. She was labeled a "rightist" in 1957 and three years later was sent to prison for her work on *Sparks*, an unofficial magazine that exposed starvation during the enormous famine of 1959–1962 that Mao Zedong's Great Leap Forward policies had caused. In prison she went on many hunger strikes. Denied access to ink, she wrote poems and letters using her own blood.[21]

After Lin Zhao's story came to light, following a 2002 documentary film by Hu Jie, people began paying respects at her grave in Suzhou. So many came that the authorities designated the graveyard a "key site for surveillance." On Grave-Sweeping Day in spring, rows of soldiers stood guard. Xiaobo, in a 2004 essay called "Lin Zhao Used Her Life to Write Down Last Words That Were the Only Free Voice in China," turned poetic: "Any person's memorial, whatever the arrangement of the tomb, will appear mediocre next to that of a person like you, who gave your life for freedom. The misty rain on Grave-Sweeping Day can moisten the dry earth but cannot soften your lost soul, and those many stars that still light the rainy night cannot retrieve your beauty. You may be the only truly noble one in China today."[22] When Xiaobo himself died in July 2017, it was plain to his friends that the authorities were in a rush to cremate his remains and bury the ashes at sea in order to avoid another Lin Zhao result. They knew it was best to leave no spot on the earth where such people could be remembered.

A third Mao-era martyr who ranked with Zhang Zhixin and Lin Zhao in Xiaobo's veneration was Yu Luoke. At age twenty-seven Yu was executed before a crowd in a large stadium for his public criticisms of school-admission policies that favored the children of Communist Party members. Yu's case had come to light on wall posters and in unofficial magazines in Beijing in late 1978. Authorities in the Deng regime noticed the story and saw how it could be useful to them in indicting the Gang of Four but decided, as in the Lin Zhao case, to keep it temporarily out of the official press. Two years later, in July 1980, while Xiaobo and his friends were still deep in their dormitory debates, the *Guangming Daily*, a national newspaper pitched to intellectuals, published an unusually long piece called "A Meteorite Tearing Through the Night Sky: Remembering Yu Luoke, Pioneer in the Liberation of Thought."[23]

Yu Luoke's father was a senior engineer in China's Ministry of Water Resources and Electric Power, but in communist social categories the family history before 1949 counted as "bourgeois," and in 1957 both parents were labeled "rightists." In the 1950s Yu Luoke took China's university entrance exam three times and scored well each time but was barred from college for political reasons. At the beginning of the Cultural Revolution in August 1966, a rhymed couplet appeared:

> Sons of the revolution, be you well!
> Sons of reactionaries, go to hell!

As it spread, the insult moved Yu Luoke to write a spate of articles under the pen name "Small Group for the Study of the Family-Background Problem." He published them in *High School Students' Cultural Revolution News,* an unofficial periodical that he himself edited. The most famous article in the series, "Class-Background Theory," eventually rocked the entire nation. He accused the Communist government of establishing a "new caste system" and called for it to be replaced by equality and universal human rights. He was arrested and sent to prison in January 1968, and on March 5, 1970, was executed as an "active counterrevolutionary."

In later years Xiaobo wrote two essays on Yu Luoke: "The Lost Soul of Yu Luoke Is Still Weeping Blood: Written at the Thirty-Fifth Anniversary of the Cultural Revolution" (2001) and "In Sincere Humility, I Salute Yu Luoke: Remembering the Cultural Revolution After Forty Years" (2006).[24] He calls Yu "a rare pathbreaker in the fight against violent government" and argues that the passage of decades hardly diminishes his relevance: "The fact that today we see, time and again, how red princelings get privileged head starts in the political and cultural spheres shows us that the 'bloodline theory' and 'political privilege' that Yu Luoke decried has never really disappeared."[25] He told filmmaker Hao Jian in 2008, "In my view, [Yu's] long essay 'Class-Background Theory' is China's first human rights manifesto."[26]

One more Mao-era case that struck Xiaobo hard was that of Wang Shenyou, a staff worker at East China Normal University in Shanghai who was executed on April 27, 1977, for expressing politically unapproved opinions. Xiaobo wrote in 2006:

> In the fifty-some years the Communists have ruled China, the great heroes, in my view, have been people like Lin Zhao in the Anti-Rightist times and Yu Luoke, Zhang Zhixin, and Wang Shenyou during the Cultural Revolution. They lost their lives insisting on personal conscience and defending aspirations that are intrinsic to human nature. But their actions were rejected not only by the authorities; even the great majority of the populace found it hard to follow their lead. Determination of their kind stood well above the crowd—so lonely, so noble![27]

Xiaobo found himself small by comparison, merely a rock within the comet tail of those pioneers whose examples inspired him: "Compared to the determination of the Lin Zhaos and Yu Luokes of the Mao years, my self-assigned heroism seems light as a feather. . . . I feel both pride and shame to think of myself as inheriting the unfinished work of Yu Luoke, but the shame outweighs the pride. . . .

Yu Luoke was a thinker as well as a hero. He wrote to himself in his diary, 'Be strong at the start, and still strong at the end.' He did that. Can I?"[28]

Xiaobo was not immediately aware of the effects that these Mao-era martyrs were having on him. It wasn't until his release from labor camp in 1999 that he was able finally to digest the harsh episodes in his youth and to see them as the origins of the intellectual maturity that by then he had achieved.

Xiaobo's natural interests were in the humanities, but in the late 1970s in China it was dangerous to call oneself a humanist. Mao had viewed "humanism" and "the bourgeois theory of human nature" as evils that needed to be fought against because they spoke of universal human values, contradicted "class nature," and undermined "class struggle." He insisted that humanism be ferreted out wherever it lurked, and its most obvious lair was in literature. Mao's "literary critics" were assigned the job of digging humanism out, and no amount of digging was enough because humanism was insidious.

"Literary theory" and "aesthetics" were both acceptable topics, however, and they became popular fields on Chinese campuses in part because they could serve as rubrics under which other fields—like politics, economics, law, and sociology—could go forward during years when they were still officially banned. The topic of "freedom" could be couched as an issue in aesthetics. Statements in the early Marx writings about the "complete development of the person" and of "alienation" were borrowed as turf upon which to discuss contemporary problems that were quite different from what Marx had meant. Marx had analyzed the "alienation" of factory workers from capitalist means of production, but now Chinese thinkers were pointing out that alienation—of ordinary people from the state—existed in communist systems as well. These currents of thinking bore a resemblance to the Soviet and Eastern European humanism in the 1950s that was sometimes called "Marxism with a human face." With thoughts like these, Xiaobo declared aesthetics and literary theory to be his primary fields.

For some who thought along these lines, the word "alienation" was too weak for what they wanted to say. The painter and art critic Gao Ertai went right to the edge of denouncing the entire political system. Imitating the abstruse style of Marx's "Economic and Philosophic Manuscripts of 1844," Gao concluded that China's system, "in the name of the nation and of class, demands and forces people continually to make sacrifices for it. It turns every person into a tool that it can exploit and manipulate at will. . . . In the abstract, the people are a god, but actual people are objectified and made into sacrificial offerings to the god."[29] Xiaobo saw Gao Ertai as an ace among the thinkers of the day. Later, in Beijing in the mid-1980s, the two became friends and frequent conversation partners.

During the final two years of Xiaobo's undergraduate studies, his interests in literature, aesthetics, and individual liberation converged in his enthusiastic support of a student-run literary magazine called *Pure Hearts*.

Literary journals had proliferated in China in the first half of the twentieth century, when they were lifeblood for groups of young writers, but in the communist era such groups were not possible. After 1949 any publication in mainland China that was not government controlled was formally illegal. So it took courage for Xiaobo's classmates to launch *Pure Hearts*. It helped that they had strong support from their department chair, Professor Gong Mu, whose pedigree in the Communist movement protected him. It helped too that "unofficial publications" had sprung up elsewhere in China and—for a time, anyway—were surviving.

Deng Xiaoping had made a decision to allow unofficial student magazines for essentially the same reason he tolerated "Democracy Wall" in winter 1978–79, when courageous people put up posters expressing their views about government policies on a long brick wall in Beijing, and allowed stories like Zhang Zhixin's to appear: his plans for turning away from Mao needed popular support. Unofficial journals associated with Democracy Wall like *April Fifth Forum*, *Explorations*, *Fertile Earth*, and *Beijing Spring* had asked openly for freedom of expression and assembly. Wei Jingsheng, an electrician at the Beijing zoo, became famous when he called for democracy as a "fifth modernization" to add to Deng's stated four (agriculture, industry, national defense, and science and technology). A number of the new unofficial magazines were specifically literary in nature. *Today*, launched in 1978, was an early exemplar. *Pure Hearts* soon followed, as did *Unnamed Lake* and *Morning* at Peking University, *Mount Luojia* at Wuhan University, *Red Beans* at Sun Yat-sen University in Guangzhou, and a number of others.

Pure Hearts was founded by Xiaobo's classmate Xu Jingya, who later became a well-known poetry critic. In a memoir, Xu recalls that the idea of beginning a journal arose when the university's course in modern Chinese literature began discussing the literary journals of the 1910s through 1930s—*New Youth*, *Creation Quarterly*, *Literary Threads*, and others.[30] Students began to ask, "If *they* could, why can't we?" Campus journals seemed a good way to answer the government's call to "liberate thought." Perhaps a new day was dawning. There were eighty students in Xiaobo's class in the Chinese Department at Jilin University, and within that small population alone three different literary clubs sprang up. At its peak, *Pure Hearts* had twenty-four members. Its first issue, in spring 1979, included works by Wang Xiaoni and Lü Guipin, both of whom later became well-known poets.

FIGURE 4.1 The *Pure Hearts* group, 1980. In front from left: Liu Xiaobo, Qu Youyuan, Lan Yaming. Standing behind: Zou Jin, Wang Xiaoni, Bai Guang, Xu Jingya, Lü Guipin

Xu Jingya

The traffic light from the top did not stay green for long, however. Once Deng's goal of showing popular support had been achieved, he reversed course on unofficial publications. Wei Jingsheng was detained in March 1979, and in October was sentenced to fifteen years in prison. In December that year Democracy Wall was ordered to leave its location at Xidan in downtown Beijing and to move across town to Moon Altar Park, where anyone contributing opinions had to sign in with police before writing anything. Across the country, campus literary magazines withered and died. The *Pure Hearts* group dwindled to a mere six people. At the beginning of 1981, Party leaders at Jilin University laid down two conditions on which they could continue their magazine. First, they would have to publish some poems that praised the Party. Second, they would have to publish poems by students who were not members of the *Pure Hearts* group. They complied. Their issue no. 9 in spring 1981 published

FIGURE 4.2   *Pure Hearts* no. 6, 1980

Anonymous (with permission)

some poems by nonmembers, and each of the six regular members contributed a poem that praised the Party. How others may have read those poems is hard to say; but in the minds of the young poets themselves, they were satirical.[31] The group produced no issue in fall 1981, and they graduated in January 1982. That was the end of *Pure Hearts*.

Xiaobo joined *Pure Hearts* at low ebb, and largely by chance. He had decided to stay on campus during the winter break in 1979–80 in order to prepare his application to graduate school; Xu Jingya was also staying on campus to work on a manuscript. The two carried their meals from the school kitchen back to their otherwise-deserted dormitory, where they ate together, chatted, and became good friends. Each discovered unexpected depth in the other. Xu invited Xiaobo to join *Pure Hearts* for their issue no. 4. Xiaobo accepted and became the seventh member of the core group. They all remained fast friends until they graduated—and in some cases, beyond.

The young poets would pass their poems to one another during class. They were apprehensive about doing this, because to ask other students to pass slips of paper back and forth could be distracting and possibly annoying. (As it turned out, the furtive poeticizing often amused their classmates, and even teachers tended to look the other way.) Their criticism of one another's work took many forms. Some of them were consistently thoughtful and precise; others were playful or sarcastic; others were eager to stir emotion. Xiaobo's trademark contribution was to offer scholarly annotation—citing Marx, Hegel, Lu Xun, or others whom he had read or memorized.

Issue no. 6 of *Pure Hearts* included a poem by Wang Xiaoni called "I Can Feel the Sunshine." It was later republished in *Poetry*, China's foremost state-sponsored poetry journal. The poem became famous nationwide as an expression of the mood of the younger generation.

I Can Feel the Sunshine

I walk down a long, long corridor . . .
　　—Ah! An eye-piercing window at the end casts sunlight onto the
　　walls at the two sides
I, I stand with the sunlight!
　　—Ah! The sunlight is so strong, warm enough to stop one's feet,
　　bright enough to halt one's breath
The sunlight of the entire universe is concentrated at this spot.
　　—I don't know what exists other than myself
Leaning on the sunlight, standing for ten seconds, ten seconds
Sometimes longer than a quarter century.
In the end, I rush downstairs,
Push open the door,
And race into the sunlight of spring

Wang Xiaoni later married her friend and coeditor Xu Jingya.

Xiaobo contributed a poem to issue no. 6. In March 1979, a special issue of *Today* devoted exclusively to poetry had appeared. It contained a piece by Mang Ke called "On My Mind" that jolted Xiaobo and his friends into an entirely new way of seeing poetry. Before then, "poetry" had meant a voice that spoke for the public, expressing fixed goals and firm resolve; it did not venture into individual minds or mention anything like bewilderment or doubt. But Mang Ke had written lines like:

> The great earth, a misty gray
> As I look at you for a long, long time
> There is nothing that I want to say
> But even if your clothes are made in Heaven
> Want to undo the button-stars

Such words sent Xiaobo's imagination soaring. He borrowed Mang Ke's title "On My Mind" and wrote a poem of his own. He had written many at Boulder Village and San'gang Commune, but this was his first effort at the radically new way of writing that Mang Ke had introduced. It was also the first poem he ever published. He wrote it in three sections that he called "Waiting," "Little Paths," and "Little Boats." The focus is on things close at hand, but near the end he raises his gaze toward the horizon:

> My life belongs to the open sea
> To its surging billows
> Life is a white sail fluttering upon it
> Death a worn-out shuttle.

Years later he may have found the poem embarrassing. It seemed pathbreaking at the time but was not authentically creative so much as a borrowing from Mang Ke.

The youngest person in the *Pure Hearts* group was Xiaobo's exceptionally bright and hard-working classmate Zou Jin. Zou and Xiaobo were assigned to edit issue no. 7. They wrote in its epilogue: "Here in north China, where the sky and the plains seem open and endless, we have turned our attention the other way—toward smaller things, toward the innumerable particular feelings that infuse the ragged tapestries of daily life. When we were finished with the last text of this issue and had handed it to the classmates in charge of printing, we suddenly felt a burst of euphoria. Yes, this is us! There will be more magazines in our futures!" Within a few years, Zou Jin did become the working editor of a major literary journal called *China*. Xiaobo was a regular contributor, and Zou and Xiaobo had a strong lifetime friendship.

Xiaobo published a few more poems in issue no. 7, and they showed a remarkable advance over what he had done for issue 6. One of the new ones, "Believe!"

was a reply to famous lines in a poem called "The Answer" that Bei Dao, of the *Today* group, had published in 1976. Bei Dao's lines were:

> Let me tell you, world,
> I—do—not—believe!
> If a thousand challengers lie beneath your feet,
> Count me as number thousand and one.
>
> I don't believe the sky is blue;
> I don't believe in thunder's echoes;
> I don't believe that dreams are false;
> I don't believe that death has no revenge.[32]

Xiaobo's response was:

> Believe!
> Believe your own spirit!
> Just as you believe in the earth, in high mountains, in the open sea
> Just as sincerely as when kneeling before altars to gods.
>
> In a dark night as heavy as lead
> Here too is a cloudless sky
> Where moon and stars stand watch
> Ten million pairs of eyes look toward dawn.
>
> In a winter cold as steel
> Here a warm breeze of early spring dances through
> A myriad of flowers and plants stir in their time
> Bees and farmers awake to their diligent work.
>
> In times when truth must stay quiet
> Here the objections of Bruno sound
> Lives are incinerated in the wild blaze
> Ghosts linger in the mists of gunfire
>
> Even in life that has passed into death
> Here will appear dreams that are pure
> Look at the rose-colored haloes
> They are love, longings that drip with dew

Stand up!
Undaunted as a towering mountain
Dither no more
Treasure those feelings, be they all that you have.

The words in the poem reflect a duality in Xiaobo's mind. On one side are "lead," "heavy," "dark night," "steel," "cold," "winter," "wild blaze," "gunfire," "ghosts," "death"; on the other are "cloudless sky," "dawn," "cradle," "warm breeze," "rose," "love," "longings," "towering mountain." Powerful forces seemed to be pulling him in opposite directions, causing strife within. Struggle inside was a hallmark of his life. It began in elementary school, where he was one of the brightest students yet one of the naughtiest. He had been through "criticism and struggle" sessions and had been to "proledict jail." As a child he probably did not notice the "I am good, but I am bad" duality, but in college he seems to have begun to see it. In later years, when he went to prison because he thought it was the right thing to do, the duality had become a fully conscious part of his thinking.

One of Xiaobo's poems in issue no. 7 of *Pure Hearts*, called "Myself," reveals his awareness of his inner struggle and shows a budding capacity for self-analysis, one of the more important fruits of his college years:

Yes, self,
You are
An ocean and a droplet
A mountain and a granule
The universe and an atom
Eternity and a split second
Tiny yet a magnificent whole
Your life is independence!

Later in the poem he struggles with the mutual implication of opposites: "there may be no dawn, but the black night does hold twinkling stars; there may be no joy, but lament itself carries the message of life." Such negotiation, and the tensions it generated, was an intellectual habit throughout his life.

His college years were his best ones with Tao Li. The two shared the excitement of the post-Mao thaw on their campuses, she at Northeast Normal and he at Jilin University, and this gave them much to talk about. Tao Li's expressive eyes and warm smile continued to win friends. She earned top grades, and her serious approach to scholarship impressed people. Xiaobo was among them, and his own turn toward taking academics seriously had much to do with her. Unfortunately neither family really approved of their tie. Xiaobo's parents worried that Tao Li's health was poor, and Tao Li's parents felt the scholarly atmosphere in the Liu Ling family was subpar. It rattled with five boisterous boys, after all, and the mother didn't have much education. At one point Tao Li felt despondent about their prospects and even suggested that they consider a breakup.[33]

Through it all, though, that special channel that Xiaobo and Tao Li had built at Boulder Village remained sturdy. For more than a decade the couple had encountered problems and together figured out ways to solve them. Xiaobo did not involve Tao Li in activities with his *Pure Hearts* friends, but at one point he did invite them to visit his family home when Tao Li was present. That was his way of introducing them to his fiancée. When Xiaobo learned that Tao Li's parents would move to Beijing in May 1979 to teach at Beijing Normal University, he began thinking about applying to graduate school in Beijing. He was feeling increasingly attracted to academic life—and also wanted to follow Tao Li. He applied only to universities in Beijing. He was sure that Tao Li, because of her fragile health, would follow her parents there.

Xiaobo's friend Wang Dongcheng, who had once remarked on Xiaobo's ragtag appearance, later observed that he never saw a person change more during four years in college, in both appearance and temperament.[34] At Jilin University Xiaobo grew more intellectual, more civil toward others, more deeply aware of morality in history, more keen toward literary art, and more self-critical. His attention to dress also improved, but not much.

His mind was opening in several ways, but he was still far short of the political clarity he later achieved. At the end of 1981, just before he graduated, he wrote a "self-appraisal." This kind of exercise was all but required at the time, the last and probably most important thing one did in college. Everyone knew that your self-appraisal went straight into a government-held "personnel file." The file followed you for life, wherever you went (except overseas). You were not allowed to see its contents; it was only for the political leadership, the people who would be making decisions about your employment, where you lived, and how much you were to be trusted. To make a mistake in your self-appraisal could hamper or even ruin your life. Intellectuals at the time were expected to address the two matters of "red" and "expert." "Red" meant correct political views and was crucial. Xiaobo's self-appraisal included these lines:

- From studying the Party's Sixth Plenum, especially its "Decision," I have become clear on the spirit of the complete system of Mao Zedong Thought. From the beginning I have been unswerving about the historic position of Comrade Mao Zedong, have studied every word and every sentence of the

"Decision" and of Hu Yaobang's speech, and have come to understand Comrade Mao Zedong's great contributions. His mistakes were but the mistakes of a great man.

- On bourgeois liberalism, I have gone through a process of moving from being influenced by it to conscious resistance of it and am now actively relying on the Party organization.

- I have taken initiatives to resist attacks from bourgeois liberal thought and to cultivate communist morality, and have volunteered to help classmates repair a floor and to establish in themselves proletarian worldviews and philosophies of life.[35]

Considering that Xiaobo knew the eyes of a Big Brother were watching, and considering what he stood to lose if he got something wrong, it is hard to know whether he meant these sentences literally, in part, or not at all. In any case, during his college years his thoughts about freedom were in an embryonic stage, not absent but also not clearly formed. He had perceived the challenge of choosing between pursuit of ideals and seeking personal benefits but had yet to decide what to do about it.

5

Aesthetics and Human Freedom

Xiaobo's plan to follow Tao Li to Beijing succeeded. Her parents had lived there since 1979, when they both took positions at Beijing Normal University, and in February 1982, when Tao Li and Xiaobo graduated from their separate universities in Changchun, they both headed there as well. Xiaobo had been admitted to Beijing Normal for graduate study. Tao Li had not applied to graduate school but had been given a work assignment (in those days, officials at universities assigned graduating seniors to jobs) at the Writing and Research Office of the Children's Section of the Ministry of Culture. The reason for that particular assignment might have been that her mother, Pu Manting, was well known in the field of children's literature.

At Beijing Normal, Xiaobo was assigned a room with two roommates in the graduate student dormitory. Each roommate was supplied with a bed, a bookcase, a minidesk, and a small closet. The furniture nearly filled the room, which was only about 130 square feet. The toilet was outside, down the hall. One of the roommates had a family home in Beijing and stayed there, so in practice Xiaobo had only one roommate. He was Yang Jidong, a student of ancient Chinese who entered graduate school with Xiaobo in 1982 and, after finishing an M.A., went home to Taiyuan in Shanxi province to edit a magazine called *Appreciating Famous Works* (*Mingzuo xinshang*). He later headed the Beiyue Literary Arts Publishing House, also in Taiyuan. Yang and Xiaobo got along very well.[1]

Things were good with Tao Li too. She and Xiaobo married on October 1, 1982, which was National Day. Their ceremony was simple in the extreme—Tao Li's parents just invited some friends, including Xiaobo's new friend Yang Jidong, to a special meal at their apartment. The Taos lived in university faculty housing, and for a wedding present they moved out of one of their rooms so that the new couple could use it. From then on Xiaobo basically lived with his parents-in-law. One of his friends recalls how Xiaobo would hug his wife in front of others, intoning "Li! ... Li! ... " in a manner that was highly unusual among the generally inhibited Chinese youth of that era. His classmates were impressed with how harmonious the couple seemed to be.[2] Xiaobo still had his dorm room, which he used as a hideaway for study. It was especially useful when he stayed up late and did not want to disturb Tao Li's sleep, or when he wanted to gather a group of classmates to argue about some topic.

In June 1983, Tao Li gave birth to a son. They named him Liu Tao, using Tao Li's surname as the boy's given name. The infant naturally brought an extra burden of work to the household, where the four adults—Tao Li, her parents, and Xiaobo—all had duties outside the home, so they arranged for day care from a service that Beijing Normal provided in the residential courtyard. Xiaobo guarded his study time tightly. When he was under pressure he sometimes retreated to his dorm room and stayed all night. The room was only a few minutes' walk from the Tao apartment, so he was never too far away.

In the early 1980s, the Soviet education system that had been imported in the 1950s (and was suspended during the Cultural Revolution) was still basically in

FIGURE 5.1 Liu Xiaobo, Tao Li, and their son, Liu Tao, in 1983

place. The M.A. was a terminal degree, not a stepping-stone to a Ph.D. It was taken very seriously, required a thesis, and needed three or more years to complete. Xiaobo had applied to work for the M.A. with Professor Zhong Zi'ao in the ancient literature section of the Chinese Department. He began in February 1982 and finished at the end of 1984. Later in his life he rejected much of Chinese tradition, but he certainly did not begin that way. He dove deep into classical poetics. Students of his generation had seen how Maoist political campaigns had hurt the generation of intellectuals before them, and they wanted to make something of themselves as classical scholars so that—whatever else might happen—they at least could claim some solid learning.

Zhong Zi'ao was from Anhui. He had come to study at Beijing Normal in 1947 at age twenty-four and was on campus for the historic changeover in 1949, when a "bourgeois" education system was "proletarianized." In 1957 he finished a book called *A Survey of the Study of Literature and Art.* Beijing Normal University Press published it for "internal circulation," a label used for publications restricted to certain types of readers. The book was on the Marxist literary theory of "reflection," a politically welcome theme under the new regime, and this helped Professor Zhong to qualify as a "new-style intellectual, both red and expert." (Xiaobo's father, Liu Ling, achieved the same status.) Zhong remained primarily interested in classical poetics, however, and with his political bona fides secure, he returned to that field. In 1984 he published a book, *Liu Xie on the Ways of Writing,*[3] which stands as his most important scholarly achievement.

In 1979, during the post-Mao thaw, he published a widely noticed article, "On Shared Aesthetics," the point of which was to rebut the Maoist view, unchallengeable until then, that because different social classes are unalterably opposed they cannot possibly share aesthetic values. Zhong's position was that farmers, miners, and professors might all appreciate the same lovely sunset. He was willing not only to "break into forbidden zones" but to tolerate, and even to encourage, his students to do so as well.

Xiaobo did not get along well with Professor Zhong, however. The professor had quirks. Perhaps because he had been only thirty-five when he wrote—or felt that he had to write—politically saturated nonsense in his first book, he came up with a watchword for his graduate students: "Publish nothing till you're fifty, when you've really got something to say." Some took these words to heart. Others, like Xiaobo, did not. Some turned it into a joke about a dotty old professor.

Xiaobo was also irritated by Professor Zhong's frequent editing of the wording in his papers. The two worked on closely related topics, so there was plenty of room for conflict. Professor Zhong studied Liu Xie (465–532 CE), one of China's earliest and most important theorists of literature, and Xiaobo studied Sikong Tu (837–908 CE), whose theory of twenty-four poetic styles rivaled Liu Xie's in both substance and elegance of style. Xiaobo's M.A. thesis was titled "A Tentative Discussion of the Aesthetic Significance of Sikong Tu's 'On Poetic Feeling.'" He wrote it in sections, handing them to Professor Zhong one by one. The teacher read them with pen in hand, correcting liberally as he went, then returned them to Xiaobo, who, according to his dorm mates, often wailed, "THAT'S NOT WHAT I MEANT!!" and used his own pen to make restorations before handing the manuscript back to his teacher—who, undaunted, crossed out Xiaobo's emendations and wrote his own meanings back in. In the final version of the thesis, there are sentences in which it is impossible to say which words originated from Xiaobo and which from Professor Zhong.

The back-and-forth exhausted both parties and was devastating to their relationship. They stood on its head the Chinese ideal that the passing of the Way between teacher and student be gently enveloped by trust and respect on both sides. The two argued their way to a truce, the harshest condition of which was that Xiaobo was prohibited from publishing his M.A. paper. Xiaobo agreed.

Despite the strife from which it sprang, the thesis is an excellent source for his intellectual values at the time. He thought highly of Sikong Tu, whom he saw as blazing a new trail, different both from the ornate, ostentatious poetry of the imperial court and from the Confucian tradition of serious poetry in which a poet "absorbs a scene and expresses a moral feeling." Xiaobo saw Sikong as advocating a less burdened art in which the poet can transcend the world, especially its material concerns, and focus on an inner self that is self-sufficient, pure, and free. The poet absorbs impressions from the outside while remaining aware that deeper truths lie beneath the surface. In a poem, the impressions from the world should be expressed with vitality, and the deeper truths should evoke a sense of limitlessness. The spirits of the writer and the reader of a poem should be able to meet in a place that exists beyond the words. They must not linger at the level of words, however elegant those may be. A good poet both "enters" (into the natural world, to grasp forms) and "exits" (transcends the world, to reach spiritual freedom). In "exiting" the natural world, a person does not leave it behind. The goal is that "the world and I are one, until both sides forget the distinction." The ultimate goal is a state in which one "enters" without noticing and "exits" without trace.[4]

Xiaobo recognized that the language of his paper was somewhat mystical and, characteristically, asked himself to justify his way of writing. He wonders whether the appeal of mystical language might be that it offers escape from the chaos of recent Chinese history.[5] He also notes that he enjoys the challenge of writing about meanings that "can only be grasped intuitively, not conveyed in words." What words can one use, in the end, to get beyond words? He had tried using the vocabulary of Soviet aesthetic theory that filled the textbooks of the time— terms like "artistic form," "aesthetic subject," "aesthetic object," "aesthetic conditions," "aesthetic process," "the laws of aesthetics," and "appearance versus essence"—but such words did not blend well with traditional Chinese terms. The two vocabularies seemed to be twisting around each other like the dough of a multicolored Chinese fried breadstick—colors intertwining without blending.

At a minimum Xiaobo's M.A. thesis shows that he became broadly conversant in the abstruse language of traditional Chinese literary studies. He read an immense number of classical poems and ancient texts, both related to Sikong Tu and not. He also read widely in the history of Chinese painting. He had a habit of ending his work with a sentence or two about his personal feelings on what he had done. At the end of his master's thesis he wrote, "Worth it!"

Xiaobo found a connection between Sikong's key concept of "reaching transcendence by departing forms" and the thinking of the ancient Daoists Laozi (d. 533 BCE?) and Zhuangzi (369–268? BCE). Laozi held that "the best music has no sound, the greatest objects have no form," and Zhuangzi famously said, "When you catch the fish you can forget the net; when you catch the meaning you can forget the words." To Xiaobo, these philosophers, in their claim that "the Way" of the universe fills everything, including human beings, with vitality, saw freedom as an intrinsic principle of nature. Xiaobo especially loved Zhuangzi and said so often. He loved, for example, Zhuangzi's description of the earth's surface: its tree branches, forests, gorges and crags, and towering peaks, all harboring innumerable cavities that wait to produce many sounds when the wind blows over them. Each sound is different because the feature that creates it is different. These are "nature sounds," and each is "self-selected"—meaning sufficient to itself and able to stand on its own. Xiaobo took Zhuangzi to be saying that in order to have a free and ideal human life one needs to find and to express one's own "nature sound" and "follow one's own pattern." Doing so releases power that is immanent in a person. Zhuangzi's notions of original nature, the primacy of feeling, and intuitive cognition conditioned Xiaobo's approach to other ideas that he encountered in life. In a 1987 interview he said, "I perceive things through the senses; it doesn't matter if it's abstract philosophy or vivid literature, I perceive it through the senses. I read Wittgenstein's thoughts and Kafka's stories in quite the same mood."[6]

His first publication on aesthetics, "Modes of Expression in Classical Chinese Aesthetics," appeared at the end of 1983 in a nonspecialist magazine called *Knowledge of Every Kind.*[7] He argued in it that "imagistic thinking" in Chinese aesthetics is superior to "conceptual thinking" in Western aesthetics. Classical poetry criticism in China, he observed, is itself written in poetry; it draws the reader into a realm where the poem it discusses touches readers' hearts as well as their senses. He wrote:

> A person who has grasped what Sikong Tu, in his *Twenty-four Poetic Styles*, means by "stalwart," "grieving," "ethereal," "marvelous," and other poetic moods might not be able to answer a Westerner's question about what "beauty" or "the sublime" *is*. These poetic moods are things that Kant in *Critique of Judgment* and Chernyshevsky in *Aesthetic Relations of Art to Reality*—both of whom pursue an aesthetics based in the structure of concepts—have no way of conveying.

Xiaobo followed this article with three others, "Subjective and Objective in Classical Chinese Aesthetics,"[8] "An Exploration of Artistic Intuition,"[9] and "On Ubiquitous Natural Beauty in the Zhuangzi."[10]

In November 1984, he wrote a "self-appraisal" of the kind he had done at the close of his undergraduate years. He reflected that he was happy with China and his place in it. He wrote about his recent travels to Luoyang, Dunhuang, Mount Emei, Mount Jiuhua, and the Yangtze River, and how the experience "made me appreciate our great rivers and mountains and the brilliant ancient culture of our ancestral land; my personal confidence and my pride in our nation were strengthened."[11] He also wrote about "the benefits that reform policies have brought":

> They appear in the rich variety of commercial products that are available and in the ways people everywhere now talk about the importance of efficiency, time, speed, and money. All of this brings me to the heart-warming recognition of how wise and correct were the decisions at the Twelfth Plenum of the Third Party Congress [in October 1984, where it was resolved to deepen economic reforms]. The hope of the Chinese nation lies in reform, which will bring this great dragon of the East to soar once again.

He reflected that during his three years of M.A. study he had not only read systematically in classical Chinese aesthetics and Western aesthetics but also read the complete works of Marx and Engels, which had just been reprinted in a new edition.[12] He had "explored widely through fields of philosophy, history, economics, religion, psychology, and elsewhere . . . and there have been changes in the structure of my knowledge." His self-appraisal concludes: "Now I am preparing to graduate. I am determined to make the most of my time, to study hard, and to be ready to throw myself at any time into the great tide of educational reform.

Society has given me three years of valuable support, and I am determined to transform the harvest into benefits that I can offer back to society. The people, the motherland, and the Party are all full of confidence and strength; so am I." One might wonder how these protestations of oneness with Party are part of the road he eventually traveled. For all his avowed zeal, his final grade in the mandatory "politics" course was "fail." He had to go to his teacher to talk his way into a passing grade.

Despite the frictions that had arisen between Xiaobo and his main professor, Zhong Zi'ao, Zhong gave Xiaobo high marks in a final report:

> Liu Xiaobo worked very diligently for three years for his M.A. His thinking was lively, his eyes were open, his learning was unusually broad, and his analytic abilities were strong. His test results in all fields were superior. His Japanese is sufficient for reading most books and for translating most articles. Because of deficiencies in his prior training, his thinking is sometimes not rigorous and his writing and attitude are unrefined. With some strict and systematic training, he has the potential to become an outstanding scholar. I recommend that he be retained at the university to do work in research and teaching.[13]

Xiaobo was indeed retained by Beijing Normal. He was appointed a teaching assistant in the Research Section on Literary Theory in the Chinese Department. This made him a colleague of Tao Li's father, although the two were in different sections.

Around this time Tao Li also began to publish. Continuing to take her father as a model, she pursued a specialization in Japanese literature and performed brilliantly. Her natural talents and hard work were both well above the norm for her peers. In 1983, she published a penetrating and elegantly written article, "Kawabata Yasunari's Nihilist Thought as Seen in His Novel *Snow Country*." It appeared in *Research on Foreign Literature*, China's leading journal in the field. She contributed a companion piece to the same journal three years later (the delay caused by the birth of her son Liu Tao) under the title "Kawabata Yasunari's Positive Tendencies as Seen in the Novel *The Old Capital*." In fall 1985, the government approved her request to transfer from the Ministry of Culture to the Department of Foreign Languages at the Beijing Languages Institute, where she became a teaching assistant in Japanese literature. She and Xiaobo now held comparable junior-faculty positions. Tao Li was assigned a room in a faculty dormitory at the Languages Institute, so for the first time the little family had a nest of its own. They continued to rely on Beijing Normal for day care of Liu Tao.

To observers, it seemed that Tao Li and Xiaobo were headed for an enviable reputation as a young husband-and-wife scholarly team. In 1985 Xiaobo published a translation of a Kawabata short story, "Of Birds and Beasts,"[14] about a lonely middle-aged man who is obsessed by his pet birds and recalls a past affair with a dancer. It includes fine psychological detail and what Xiaobo later often referred to as the distinctive "disillusionment" that writers feel. In the same journal issue, Tao Li published an appreciation of the story that she called "Between Reality and Emptiness: My Shallow Reading of 'Of Birds and Beasts.'" That, though, was as far as the spousal scholarly cooperation ever went.

In the mid-1980s a malaise was rising among Chinese intellectuals. Their exuberance at the "smashing of the Gang of Four" after Mao's death in 1976 had been deflated by the closing of Democracy Wall and the imprisonment of Wei Jingsheng in 1979. Yet many were still hoping at the beginning of the 1980s that the trend toward openness would continue. Then new disappointments arrived. In 1981 the official press attacked the writer Bai Hua for "bourgeois liberalism," and two years later it unleashed a broader and deeper attack on "spiritual pollution."

To most people, the latter term meant little more than new Western influences that the authorities did not like: bell-bottom trousers, permed hair, flirting in public, organizing unofficial clubs, talking about democracy, and things like that. "Rock 'n' roll," in some of the official warnings, was conceived as rolling around on the floor during dance. No one knew exactly what counted, or did not count, as "spiritual pollution." (Long hair for males clearly was not good, but at what length did it become "pollution"?) Whatever the illness, the regime's prescription was to "strike hard." Young people accused of illicit sexual relations—even as mild as dancing cheek to cheek—could be executed. No one knows how many people were punished in the "Strike Hard" campaign, but many stories of mistaken or grossly unfair treatment surfaced later. In 2013, Chinese journalists found an official record of 861,000 court cases, of which 24,000 ended in death sentences—and that did not account for extrajudicial punishments.[15]

Very few ordinary people in China were aware that the "Eliminate Spiritual Pollution" campaign, in its origins, had little to do with things like clothing, hair, or dance. It sprang from a struggle between two factions at the top level of the Party. One was the "Marxist humanists"—people who had concluded from the brutal record of the years since 1949 that their society needed a reaffirmation of human dignity and humane values. These included Wang Ruoshui, deputy editor of the *People's Daily*, and Zhou Yang, a literary hatchet man for Mao who had later turned remorseful. The other group, called "conservatives," feared any such rocking of the boat. (The term "conservative" here inverts the way it is used in Western democracies, where it means right-leaning. In China the term has meant doctrinaire communist—conservative in the sense of protecting the status quo.)

To the conservatives, bell-bottom trousers and kissing in the park were nothing compared to the poison of the humanists' "revisionism," which aimed at changing the nature of Marxism. To them, the only solution was to remove the Marxist humanists from power. After twenty-eight days of intense campaigning in October and November 1983, the conservatives won the struggle and the humanists lost their posts. Society felt a major shock when news arrived that Wang Ruoshui had been fired from the *People's Daily*. If the closing of Democracy Wall in 1979 was the crucial blow against democratic forces "outside the Party," this purge in 1983 was the fateful stroke "inside the Party."

The coup was a turning point for many of China's intellectuals—writers, artists, professors, and their students. The years since 1978 had been a kind of honeymoon during which intellectuals and the Communist Party could come together under the banner of jettisoning radical Maoism and pursuing "modernization." Now the common ground was ruined. Intellectuals reverted to their more customary position of feeling separate from, and often opposed to, the government. But their passions for a better China still surged and could not be blocked, any more than a human hand can block a gushing garden hose. If they could not work with the government, they would work around it. They began looking not just to Marxist humanism but to humanism generally, and not just to reform of the Communist system but to alternatives.

Their major difficulty in trying to reason within a Marxist framework was the lack of vocabulary for dealing with some obvious problems: hero worship of a great leader, trampling on human rights, and strict hierarchy in power relations. In the wake of the Cultural Revolution, even the regime leaders realized that these phenomena needed labels, and they chose the term "feudal (*fengjian*) remnants." In August 1980, Deng Xiaoping had given a major speech in which he stressed "the duty to purge the influence of the remnants of feudalism in the fields of ideology and politics."[16] In Marx, feudalism is the stage of human history that falls between slave society and capitalism. The European Middle Ages are its main example. But when the Chinese communists adopted the term, they used it to cover about two thousand years of imperial Chinese history from the Han to the Qing—for which the European model of serfs, lords, and theocracy was a very poor match. In Chinese communist language, "feudalism" has meant essentially the deplorable aspects of premodern tradition.

For intellectuals in the 1980s, the richest resource for exploring ways to extricate China from "feudalism" was the great May Fourth Movement of the late

1910s and early 1920s.[17] People looked back at those years of "Chinese Enlightenment" with their contemporary worries in mind. The Republican revolution of 1911 had abolished the "feudal" imperial system, but after a few chaotic years, President Yuan Shikai proclaimed himself another emperor. In addition to feeling disappointment and anger, intellectuals realized that merely changing a political system was not enough—China needed basic cultural change. "Tear down the house of Confucius" became a May Fourth slogan. China was to be rebuilt from the ground up, and "Mr. Science and Mr. Democracy" would inhabit the new building. People were fascinated with many new "-isms" that drifted in from the West. Marxism was one, and the Communist Party's own tag for the May Fourth Movement came to be "antifeudal." For the intellectuals, this label provided convenient ambiguity: the Communist Party approved it, so no one could be faulted for using it, and yet its meaning—conservative authoritarianism—referred to Communist Party rule in a way that everyone understood.

The crackdown on the Marxist humanists led people to wonder whether China needed a "second enlightenment" to follow May Fourth. Bao Zunxin—a writer, editor, and later close friend of Xiaobo's—coined the term "new enlightenment" (*xin qimeng*), and others adopted it.[18]

Translations of Western writing—fiction, drama, poetry, social science, and history—had been tremendously important in May Fourth times. Could they revive that tradition? Under Mao, nearly all writing from the modern West had been viewed as degenerate, pernicious, and to be kept out of the minds of young people at all costs. A slight reprieve in this policy happened in the early 1960s when Mao split with the Soviets and briefly supported anti-Soviet dissidents in the communist world. Translations of Leon Trotsky's *The Revolution Betrayed* and Milovan Djilas's *The New Class: An Analysis of the Communist System* were published. A few translations from the "bourgeois world"—J. D. Salinger, *The Catcher in the Rye*; Jack Kerouac, *On the Road*; and Jean-Paul Sartre, *La Nausée and Other Stories*—were allowed as well, to illustrate alienation and decadence under capitalism. (The names of most of the translators are unknown, because they were intellectuals sent to the countryside as rightists in 1957 and therefore viewed as unfit to be credited in print.) Such books were available in unmarked bookstores to which only officials of a certain rank or above were allowed access. During the Cultural Revolution, these books began to spread more widely when Red Guards, after raiding home libraries, began sharing their booty hand to hand. Reading the contraband changed some young people forever.

By the mid-1980s, the translation floodgates had opened more widely. Books that previously were for "internal use only" now could be sold openly, and a cascade of new translations appeared. In 1983 the People's Publishing House in

Shanghai came out with a series it called Selected Works of Western Modernism. Jean-Paul Sartre, Franz Kafka, T. S. Eliot, Albert Camus, Ezra Pound, Maurice Maeterlinck, August Strindberg, and Eugene O'Neill, among others, were published in Chinese translation. Readers began talking about things like "theater of the absurd" and "black humor."

For a young university literature teacher like Xiaobo, this Shanghai series was a treasure trove. Xiaobo's favorites were Kafka and Eliot, and his passion for Kafka lasted a lifetime. He discovered Luther John Binkley's *Conflict of Ideals: Changing Values in Western Society* and devoured its chapters on Sigmund Freud, Erich Fromm, Søren Kierkegaard, Friedrich Nietzsche, and others. All this reading overwhelmed the Marxist framework and led Xiaobo to step outside it. The next year, 1984, another stream of translations called Striding Toward the Future appeared. The series was officially published by the Sichuan People's Publishing House in Chengdu, but it was edited in Beijing, where independent editorial boards composed of prominent younger scholars in history, literature, economics, sociology, and philosophy were in charge. (One of them was Wang Qishan, who thirty years later was Secretary of the Central Commission for Discipline Inspection under President Xi Jinping and arguably the second most powerful man in China.) The youngsters in Beijing did the work of identifying works to be translated, assigning translators, and reviewing and editing manuscripts, while officials in Sichuan maintained rights of final approval and took political responsibility. The Sichuan people seldom intervened; they supported the young editors and in a sense had no choice but to trust them, because the material was over their heads intellectually. The editors had ambitious goals. They aimed at encyclopedic scope and made an initial plan to publish one hundred books. When forced to close in 1989, they had produced seventy-six.

They published Max Weber, *The Protestant Ethic and the Spirit of Capitalism*; Dennis Meadows et al., *The Limits to Growth*; and works of John Maynard Keynes as reprinted in Yang Junchang, ed., *Macroeconomics: The Keynesian Revolution*. Readers were enthusiastic, and circulations reached into the hundreds of thousands. Douglas Hofstadter's *Gödel, Escher, Bach: An Eternal Golden Braid*—a book that intertwines mathematical logic, genetic inheritance, the workings of the cerebrum, artificial intelligence, and even topics in painting and music—made an especially big splash, selling 700,000 copies. It seemed that every serious young intellectual owned or had read it, and everyone claimed to understand it.

Spreading excitement about the books in the Striding Toward the Future series led to a subtle but important change among intellectuals—the sense of a public sphere arose. The Communist Party had long used the principle of divide and rule as a technique of control; in the Mao era, urban people lived, worked, and did nearly everything in "work units"—factories, schools, government organs, and so on—that were controlled by Party committees. These committees were the bottom level of a Party-run hierarchy. Activities that bridged work units could happen only by arrangement of the Party. The Striding Toward the Future books, however, began to produce an intellectual community that spanned work units, cities, and disciplines. Physicists, sociologists, botanists, poets—people in many fields—were raising common questions: What did we miss during the years our doors to the world were closed? What's to be done now? Jin Guantao, the successor to Bao Zunxin as chief editor, illustrated the bridging of disciplines in his own person: he had been a natural scientist but during the 1980s turned to the social sciences and humanities. He consciously pursued what he saw as French Enlightenment ideals.

In 1986, yet another book series, Culture: China and the World, appeared. Its chief editor, Gan Yang, and most of his colleagues were young scholars from the elite departments of philosophy at Peking University and the Chinese Academy of Social Sciences. They translated and published Sartre, *Beijing and Nothingness*; Heidegger, *Being and Time*; and Nietzsche, *The Birth of Tragedy*. These books, elite as they were, sold well. The translator of Nietzsche's book, Zhou Guoping, wrote his own book to explain Nietzsche—and it sold 90,000 copies within in six months. The same group published a thick journal, also called *Culture: China and the World*, packed with lively, pathbreaking articles on philosophy, values, and society. Its first issue was printed in 30,000 copies in June 1987, and four more issues appeared until November 1988. In spring 1989 its editors were caught up in the democracy movement of the season, and the massacre on June 4, 1989, ended any possibility of its continuing further.

Gan Yang and Culture: China and the World became famous for "opposing tradition" and promoting "modernization" of Chinese culture. In the hundred years between the Opium Wars of the mid-nineteenth century and the Communist accession in the mid-twentieth, Chinese thinkers had grappled with two major dilemmas: tradition versus modernity and China versus the West. The Communists had closed China's doors to the West in 1949, and debate of the two questions atrophied. Now they were returning.

The regime's position in the 1980s was that it opposed only Westernization, not modernization. But young intellectuals (including the gradually awakening Liu Xiaobo) were puzzled: how could the Communists denounce every strand of Western thought *except one* (Marxism) and then claim that that single strand was the reason for ruling out all the others? It seemed odd too that while claiming to be new and modern, Communist culture was highly traditional in the way it enforced rules like "subordinates are to obey superiors."

Not all reexamination of tradition was negative. In 1984 a group called the Academy of Chinese Culture, led by Peking University philosophers Feng You-lan, Zhang Dainian, and Tang Yijie, combed China's past—in public lectures and a book series—in search of resources that contemporary China might use. There was a sense that China might reattach to what it had had before the disastrous Mao interlude intervened. Cultural resources—Confucian, Daoist, Buddhist, and others—might, at least in some ways, reanchor the ethically battered society. The group was eclectic. The noted cultural historian Li Zehou was a member, as was Bao Zunxin, inventor of the "new enlightenment" phrase. The search for value in traditional culture contradicted much that had been done during the Mao years but was not antithetical to May Fourth, when there had been efforts to "organize the national heritage" (*zhengli guogu*). Chinese fiction in the mid-1980s was known for a "roots-seeking" trend, but the roots were of two kinds: valuable resources, such as the transcendent detachment that was suggested in A Cheng's story "Chessmaster," and sources of intractable disease, like the confusion in Han Shaogong's story "Ba, ba, ba."[19]

The term "culture fever" (*wenhua re*) came to be used to refer to all sides of the debate about what to do with Chinese tradition and how much of it to replace with the culture of the West. The government could tolerate "culture fever" because it took a step back from the political challenge that was implicit in terms like "antifeudal" and "new enlightenment," where authoritarian abuses were more clearly the focus.

Young readers like Xiaobo felt as if they were emerging from uncorked champagne bottles. Once out and free to explore, they felt the most curiosity about precisely those aspects of "the West" that had been denied them. Then when they tasted those things and appreciated that there were other ways to run societies than the ways of emperors and the Communist Party—that freedom, equality, and democracy were also possible—they had more reasons to continue reading.

Xiaobo followed the contemporary ferment even as he wrote his thesis on a poet who had lived eleven centuries earlier. In early 1985, when his M.A. was finished and he had begun to teach, he had more time for contemporary thoughts. He was enchanted by Gabriel García Márquez's *One Hundred Years of Solitude*, which had been published in Chinese translation the year before. The novel's "magical realism" suggested exciting new possibilities for liberating the imagination, and its inspired reexamination of traditional folk culture resonated with China's root-seeking trends. Xiaobo was so taken by *Solitude* that he decided to read it aloud at home—start to finish—with Tao Li and the three-year-old Liu Tao as his audience. He did not demand that mother and son sit to listen. They could go about their activities while he declaimed.

Then, in 1986, the Chinese writer Mo Yan published a short novel—perhaps inspired by García Márquez—called *The Transparent Radish*. It tells of an abused farm boy who exhibits uncomprehending responses to human interactions yet has super sensitivity in touch and hearing. Xiaobo loved it. A friend recalls how, at a publisher's meeting in late 1986, he was moved to tears as he recited passages of it from memory. Tong Qingbing, with whom Xiaobo later did Ph.D. work, also noticed Xiaobo's prodigious reading speed and memory. Tong recalls that in 1985 Xiaobo went to the library, checked out volumes of the *Compendium of Famous Works of World Scholarship in Chinese Translation*, edited by Beijing's Commercial Press, and read through them one by one: Plato, Aristotle, Augustine, Kant, Wittgenstein . . . with what seemed like total recall.[20]

At Beijing Normal Xiaobo was assigned, at his own request, to a new subfield in the literary theory section called "literary psychology." This was close to what the Western academy came to call "reception theory," which investigates how "appreciation" happens when a person reads or hears a literary work. What psychological processes—sense perception, illusion, imagination, intuition, and so on—are involved? In Marxist "reflection theory," the only constituents of a work of art are the objective historical conditions that surround it. Neither the intentions in an author's mind nor the responses in a reader's are relevant. Xiaobo and his colleagues in literary psychology, young and old alike, found this framework seriously inadequate.

In a burst of productivity between April 1985 and April 1986, Xiaobo published six articles on aesthetic reception theory. The six cohere almost like a book. The demure tone of his thesis on classical poetry was gone, but the swashbuckling approach he used later in the 1980s was yet to appear. The titles of the six pieces suggests their range:

"Heavens as Red as La Marseillaise: Aesthetic Sense and Artistic Appreciation" (April 1985)
"Look at the Distant Horizon: Illusion, Imagination, and Aesthetic Appreciation" (May 1985)
"Aesthetics and Human Freedom" (January 1986)
"Heaven and Earth Are Born with Me, All of Creation Is One with Me: Shifting Emotion and Aesthetic Sympathy" (February 1986)
"Breaking Through a Fog to Find Rosy Clouds on the Other Side: Intuition and Aesthetic Appreciation" (March 1986)
"Naked and Exposed, Moving Toward God: Aesthetics and the Subconscious, (I)" (April 1986)

The articles were published in *Appreciating Famous Works*, where Xiaobo's former roommate Yang Jidong was an editor.

The six pieces are more about philosophy than about literature or politics. Xiaobo had always liked philosophy, ever since he audited courses in European philosophy in college. The translations from "the new enlightenment" of the mid-1980s revived that interest. The third article, "Aesthetics and Human Freedom," is especially important in the evolution of his thinking. In college he had studied concepts of aesthetics in Immanuel Kant's *Critique of Judgment* and Friedrich Schiller's "Kallias Letters." He saw in Kant and Schiller a connection between aesthetic reception and human freedom because, for those two thinkers, art appreciation entails setting aside fixed goals and utilitarian calculations. In observing beauty one becomes as free as a child playing a game, and only in that utterly disinterested mood can one exercise pure human freedom. For Xiaobo, Schiller's description of the Good Samaritan who "forgot himself" to help another shows how freedom and beauty are linked. The concept was consistent with what he had taken from passages in the early Marx, where divisions of labor were said to block possibilities of unfettered action—by which, according to Marx, one might hunt in the morning, fish in the afternoon, raise cattle in the evening, and criticize after dinner.[21]

The word "aesthetics" had played an important role in the debates about "Marxist humanism" in the early 1980s. For people who had been conditioned to believe that literature and art must serve politics, the notion of a pure independence from politics arrived like a gust of fresh air. In time, "aesthetics" became a code word for freedom. When it was dangerous to say "freedom," one could say "aesthetics." Xiaobo accepted this code, but for him aesthetics was much more than that. He writes in "Aesthetics and Human Freedom": "aesthetics are freedom in action. Beauty and aesthetics make possible a complete fulfillment of basic human nature, a comprehensive release of human creativity, and a thorough liberation of human life."[22] Xiaobo noticed that Kant and Schiller had something in common with Zhuangzi, who similarly had stressed the need to transcend material interests in order to set the spirit free. The text of *Zhuangzi* (the man and his text have the same name) opens with a story that impressed Xiaobo deeply. He took it as an allegory of reaching a state where the human spirit is free. It tells how a fish from the Great Northern Darkness, who was called Kun and whose body was so wide that no one could measure it, changed into a great bird called Peng, whose back was so broad that no one could say how broad it was. When Peng took flight, its wings were like clouds that blocked the entire sky. Xiaobo comments:

Here we can see why Zhuangzi was so adamant in his rejection of material pursuits and his advocacy of a disinterested worldview. His reason was similar to the reasons Schiller, Hegel, Marx, and others disdained the moneyed world. Only through the pursuit of beauty can we human beings, in our brief time on earth, correctly see fame and fortune as the floating clouds that they are, fundamentally cast off the fetters with which material pursuits tie us down, and enter a world where the spirit is free.[23]

Quoting Rousseau—"man is born free; and everywhere he is in chains"—Xiaobo holds that art can be an escape. When art triumphs, it is a triumph of the subjective over the objective, of sense perception over the rules of reason, of spiritual enjoyment over material desire, and of the individual life over pressures from society. The aesthetic realm is a peach-blossom spring outside the world, a utopia in which humanity might be saved. He continues: "What surprises me is that human beings actually have been able to locate this thin crack called aesthetics, this moment that, however mysterious and fleeting it might be, however incorporeal or illusory—arriving like a dream, without a trace—can somehow transcend everything. Geniuses the world over see in it the eternal, the limitless, and the only passage to freedom that is available to human beings."[24]

Xiaobo's six essays on aesthetics came out within a period of slightly more than a year. One can see in them a gradual shift from his original interests in classical Chinese poetry to an exploration of the cornucopia of translations from the West that were coming into view. In the last essay, "Naked and Exposed, Moving Toward God," not one classic Chinese poet is mentioned—only European thinkers. Xiaobo also retreats from his ambition to find a way "upward," toward transcendence. He prefers to peer downward, toward the abyss of the fundaments of human nature. "Since no one can escape the abyss," he writes, "we might as well just sink into it, the deeper the better, until our hearts feel the terror and pain of that most worthy of aesthetic experiences—tragedy." Later he adds, "I must say, from this point of view, that aesthetics is a version of profanity."[25] These words might have been inspired, whether he was conscious of it or not, by T. S. Eliot, whom Xiaobo revered, and who opens his "Four Quartets" poems with a fragment from Heraclitus: "The way upward and the way downward is one and the same."

Xiaobo's research section in the Chinese Department launched a project on comparing Eastern and Western aesthetics. Finding the topic fascinating, Xiaobo wrote two articles. The first compared angels in the European Christian tradition with "flying nymphs" (*feitian* or, in Buddhist tradition, *apsara*).[26] For Xiaobo both represented freedom from human bonds. They could fly. But angels were still more concrete, because they had wings like birds. Apsara were even freer. They had no clear physical features—were more like soaring abstractions, fairies who could appear and please people as they chose. Xiaobo did not draw any important cultural conclusions from the difference between angels and apsara.

In the second piece, though, he did. In "Conflict and Harmony: The Basic Differences Between Chinese and Western Aesthetic Consciousness," he argues that

> Westerners emphasize tragedy, human labor, and the individual. They want to dig into the prerational levels of the human mind. They dare to oppose tradition. They value innovation and are willing to go to extremes. Chinese people emphasize comedy, naturalness, and social groups. They stay at the rational level of the human mind, and they seek to uphold tradition. They stick to established patterns and stop before going too far. Chinese aesthetics avoids the disillusionment, despondency, and extreme individualism in Western aesthetics, as well as its need to blame itself for narcissism or pointless innovation for its own sake. But it has also left the Chinese people hobbled with the most disgraceful of blights: servility and inertia.[27]

During 1986 Xiaobo was finding that the fields of ancient poetry and literary psychology were not enough to satisfy his voracious intellect. He began to work on the contemporary Chinese literature that was at the center of many of the culture-fever debates. His general appraisal of that writing had fallen sharply since his college years. He had once "sung the praises of the new literature from the bottom of my heart."[28] Later he looked back at that praise and felt a bit embarrassed. He wrote a piece called "An Unavoidable Reappraisal" in which he argues that suffering intellectuals—a recurrent trope in "scar" literature—are not the tragic figures they pretend to be.[29] Yes, Mao had treated them terribly. But scar literature goes too far: it portrays them as stoutly high-minded and devoted to their missions even as they endure denunciation and ostracism in silence, without complaint or regret, and often without anyone else even knowing how much they are suffering—all the while remaining loyal to communist ideals and to the men who rule, even though those same men run the system that is humiliating them. They remain optimistic about the future, expecting that someday they will be able to return to their political and social environments and all will be well. Among other examples, Xiaobo offered Xu Chi, "The Goldbach Conjecture" (1978), about the genius Chinese mathematician Chen Jingrun, who shows how, under the banner of the Four Modernizations, China can join the world in

mathematics;[30] Chen Rong, "At Middle Age" (1980), about an idealistic ophthalmologist devoted to serving her patients, her husband and son, her
society—everyone!—until she literally collapses;[31] and several autobiographical
works by Zhang Xianliang about a disgraced rightist suffering in the countryside—
through famine, stigmatization, labor camps, hordes of mosquitoes, and more—
but always seeking redemption in the eyes of the Party.[32] These are famous
examples, but Xiaobo was critiquing an entire category of stories whose stereo-
typical heroes, as he saw it, are not tragic figures so much as bit players in a kind
of comedy. They fall far short of the genuinely tragic figures in May Fourth fiction. For Xiaobo, the work of Lu Xun evoked the deep despair and isolation of
people who could see further than the crowd and for that reason were fated to be
misunderstood and rejected. Zhang Xianliang's protagonist, by comparison, is
banished to the remote countryside but there finds an unlettered rural woman,
marries her, starts a family, and comes to feel healthful and fulfilled. No isolation, no anomie—no authentic tragedy.

The breakthrough in Xiaobo's "Unavoidable Reappraisal" article was deeper
than just a contrast between two kinds of protagonist. Scar literature arrived in
the wake of the state-sponsored slogan "Liberate Thought," and some authors and
many eager readers supposed that an entirely new day might be arriving. But,
Xiaobo argues, the horizons never opened fully, as they had during May Fourth.
Lu Xun and others had explored world literature, and their criticisms of their current environment could be as profound as they cared to make them; scar writers
were writing on the tether of state policy. Some were more conscious of the limits than others, but all were aware at some level that the principles of "love the
country" and "love the people" (and further, unspoken but unmistakable, "love
the Party") could not be violated. Suffering could be noble, so long as it was
couched in fundamental loyalty to the political status quo. To Xiaobo, the
aggrieved paragons in scar literature were radically different from Lin Zhao, Yu
Luoke, and Zhang Zhixin.

Xiaobo saw the mentality of scar literature paragons as highly traditional in
certain ways. In the *Analects,* Confucius praises Yan Hui, one of his favorite disciples, by saying that "a bowl of food, a ladle of drink, and a lowly hut" are enough.
"Others might find such conditions unbearable, but Hui is happy with them."
Xiaobo wondered if this was exactly how the heroes in scar literature wished
to be seen and exactly how the state wanted their "nobility" to be seen. He saw
that scar literature would not—could not—lead to a genuine modern Chinese
literature.

But a genuine literature is what he wanted, and he had an important companion in that quest. Wang Furen (1941–2017) was fourteen years older than

Xiaobo, but they both arrived at the Chinese Department at Beijing Normal University for graduate school in 1982, Wang to pursue a Ph.D., Xiaobo an M.A. Wang's field was modern Chinese literature, and he specialized in Lu Xun. Xiaobo admired and imitated Wang's free and easy literary style. Neither of them was fond of footnotes. When they finished their degrees both were retained by the university to teach, Wang as a lecturer and Xiaobo as a teaching assistant, and both were assigned rooms in the dormitory for young faculty. Xiaobo used his room only occasionally because he spent most of his time at the Taos', but it was important as a place where he and Wang Furen debated literary and cultural questions. In a society where film and television were still only occasional treats and computer games far in the future, a common form of entertainment was to drop in on friends and join bull sessions (in Chinese, *kan dashan*—"bloviate the great mountain"). Xiaobo and Wang Furen liked to *kan*. When Wang died in 2017, his classmates reminisced about how he and Xiaobo sometimes carried on until dawn.[33]

Wang Furen was adamant that China should be looking back at May Fourth for inspiration. In 1983 he published an influential article, "A Mirror for China's Revolution Against Feudalism: On the Intellectual Significance of *Outcry* and *Hesitation*."[34] *Outcry* (1923) and *Hesitation* (1925) are collections of Lu Xun's most important short stories. Wang argued that Lu Xun understood in the early twentieth century that China needed more than a political revolution; it needed a thorough reworking of its values and thinking. The nation's slave mentality needed to be replaced by respect for individual dignity. For many years the Communists claimed to agree and called Lu Xun "antifeudal." But now, with the record of the Communists' massive trampling of human rights during the Cultural Revolution, there was an even greater need to respect the individual and to oppose "feudalism"—to return, in short, to May Fourth. "*Outcry* and *Hesitation*," Wang Furen wrote, "have indelible significance for us today in our struggle against feudalism under new historical conditions."[35]

Wang's article had much to do with Xiaobo's embrace of "the new enlightenment," as Bao Zunxin had called it. Xiaobo wrote: "Today's resurgence of the traditional feudal mentality—to unprecedented heights—is like an ancient beast reawakening and coming to attack the modern Chinese people. . . . To support the enlightenment movement against feudal thought should be the highest duty of contemporary Chinese intellectuals and writers."[36] Xiaobo often used the polar terms "awoken" and "ignorant" in his writing. Many in the "new enlightenment" movement did that, but Xiaobo stood out because he found benighted thinking not only in ordinary people but also in intellectuals. Indeed, he tended to find it *especially* among intellectuals, who were badly in need of reflection on themselves. He wrote:

> In all of those instances of wild cheering at Tiananmen Square during the Cultural Revolution, are we to believe that none of the people waving *Quotations of Chairman Mao* were intellectuals? Could it be that all of those big-character posters [i.e., politically combative wall posters] that intellectuals wrote were written only because they were forced? The reason the Cultural Revolution could happen all across the vast land of China has a lot to do with the fact that all its citizens, and especially its intellectuals, were mired in turbidity—were not prepared, as their May Fourth predecessors had been, to declare thoroughgoing opposition to feudal patterns of thought.[37]

This sharp view is admirable for challenging a common and too-convenient response to the Mao era, which was to point fingers at others but never at oneself. Still, in historical perspective, his opinion was not fair. Beginning at the communist base in Yan'an in the early 1940s and extending until he died in 1976, Mao Zedong persecuted intellectuals far more fiercely than either Stalin or Hitler had. Mao acted as if using a scythe on a vegetable garden. It was fine for people to grow to his specifications, but any further? Slash, whack, slash! A "rectification movement" in Yan'an beginning in 1942, destruction of the "Hu Feng clique" in 1955, a nationwide "Anti-Rightist movement" in 1957, and the tumultuous "Great Proletarian Cultural Revolution" of 1966–69 touched nearly all Chinese intellectuals. Those who were not direct victims—humiliated, beaten, imprisoned, forced to divorce, or killed—became obsessed by what they had to do to avoid such fates, for so long that it came to feel normal. People hardly noticed their own conformity. In short, there were forces at work on their minds far more powerful than the "feudal thought" they might have inherited—and if they understood those lethal pressures, they were not at liberty to mention them; that would have been far too dangerous. Even in China today, it is dangerous.

A month after Xiaobo's "Unavoidable Reappraisal" article, he published another, "A New Kind of Aesthetic Thought: On Works by Xu Xing, Chen Cun, and Liu Suola."[38] The two pieces drew much more attention than all of his previous publications combined. They established him as a leading literary critic who produced distinctive and penetrating views.

The second article highlighted a Bohemian strand that was growing in contemporary Chinese writing. This was not new to the world and had predecessors in precommunist China, but it was certainly new in the People's Republic. Xu Xing,

Liu Suola, and Chen Cun created characters whose lackadaisical and irreverent attitudes undermined, even ridiculed, the "sacred and exalted" values of the time. To match their themes, the three authors wrote sentences that were chaotic, sometimes even ungrammatical. Xiaobo analyzed and compared the three of them.

Xu Xing's "Variations on No Theme" tells of a worker at a Peking duck restaurant (Xu himself, in real life) who, identifying himself as "lower class," has nothing but derision for what most people regard as "success"—such as a college degree. People called Xu's story "the Chinese *Catcher in the Rye*," but Xu said he had never seen J. D. Salinger's book. (He did own a translation of Jack Kerouac's *On the Road*.) The critical response to "Variations on No Theme" was mixed. It included some blistering attacks, but Xiaobo defended Xu Xing stalwartly.

Xiaobo and Xu Xing later became good friends. They shared a native rebelliousness. Their wives were good friends too, and the families saw much of each other. Their homes were at opposite ends of Beijing, one in the north and one in the south, so they did a lot of bicycling back and forth. The Xu home had for some time been a meeting place for young literature lovers, and soon the Xiaobo-Tao Li home became one as well. People gathered to *kan dashan* about everything under the sun. Xu Xing remained contemptuous of nearly all of contemporary Chinese literature and literary criticism, but he continued to publish. He and Xiaobo both contributed to an important but short-lived magazine called *China*.

China produced only eighteen issues, in 1985 and 1986. Its chief editor was Ding Ling (1904–1986), a renowned writer who began writing about feminine subjectivity in the late 1920s, joined the communist movement out of political idealism in the 1930s, clashed with Mao Zedong at the communist base in Yan'an over corruption and unequal treatment of women in the early 1940s, was immediately punished by Mao, submitted, and after 1949 was rewarded with the editorship of *The Literary Gazette*, the regime's major literary-political magazine. In 1956 she was again ostracized politically, and in 1957 was sent to the "great northern wasteland" in Heilongjiang province until 1978, when she was "exonerated" and allowed to return to Beijing. In 1983, she surprised many of her fellow writers by supporting the regime's drive to "eliminate spiritual pollution." That show of submission to authority might have been useful, though, in allowing the regime to trust her as editor of *China*, in which role she did her best, at age eighty, to create a lively and open publication devoted to "a new era in literature."[39] She enlisted Niu Han, a sixty-one-year-old poet who had been denounced as part of the "Hu Feng clique" in 1955 and imprisoned for two years, to be her founding coeditor.

The two needed younger talent to staff the magazine. For day-to-day work they recruited Zou Jin, who had been Xiaobo's classmate and colleague at *Pure Hearts* at Jilin University, to be poetry editor, and Wu Bin, a fiction writer who had worked on a student literary magazine at Shandong University, to handle fiction. Like Xiaobo and Tao Li, Wu Bin was part of the "class of '77" who were the first in a decade to enter university by merit-based examination. After graduation Wu went to work in Beijing, from 1982 to 1984, at the China Financial Publishing House. Wu had a co-worker named Liu Xia, a budding artist he fell in love with and married in 1984. Zou Jin, from 1982 to 1985, worked for the China People's Insurance Company, which shared a cafeteria with the Financial Publishing House. Hence it happened that Xiaobo, his close friend Zou Jin, and Zou's friends Wu Bin and Liu Xia all became acquainted. In 1985 Zou Jin resigned his post at the Financial Publishing House and went to teach for a year at the Beijing Languages Institute, where he was a colleague of Tao Li. Near the end of 1985, Zou Jin and Wu Bin both went to their editing jobs at *China*. Each was twenty-seven years old, had a shaved head, and brimmed with energy and new ideas. They got along well too. Together they published many new young writers, poets, and theorists, of whom Xiaobo was one. They were just what Ding Ling needed.

When Ding Ling died in 1986, conservatives in the Party used the occasion to move against the magazine and force it to close. Cofounder Niu Han wrote: "We will succumb, but we are innocent." When Xiaobo was taken from his home by police in 2008, Niu Han made this public statement: "*China* published several of Xiaobo's essays. They were always wickedly sharp and showed extraordinary intelligence. I know his character well enough to predict that the huge system that has now consumed him will show him no mercy."[40] Niu Han may have gotten his impressions of Xiaobo's character from observing him at the editorial offices of *China*, where young writers and editors often got into heated debates. Zou Jin recalls Xiaobo's signature approach: he actually did not *want* people to agree with him. If you said "Good point," he would push the point deeper to bring out complexities you hadn't thought of or would turn the matter to view it from a different vantage—in any case, would make it so that he again would stand alone against everybody else.[41]

Xiaobo's methods of winning an argument could be brutal. Once, in a debate with the young investigative journalist Lu Yuegang, whose nickname was "Live Tiger" because of his fearlessness, Xiaobo, feeling cornered, blurted out, "I've read more books than you!" The claim was probably true, and it did end the debate, but not because Lu Yuegang felt defeated. Lu just didn't know what to do with someone who argued like that.

The first six months of 1986 were a golden age in Xiaobo's professional career. His "Reappraisal" and "New Aesthetic" articles had brought him fame, he was getting numerous invitations to lecture, students on the Beijing Normal campus loved him, and he had also found time to translate 70,000 characters of works by Imamichi Tomonobu and other Japanese scholars of aesthetics. (He and some friends translated a collection of articles by Japanese scholars called *Methods of Aesthetics* that was published in 1990 when Xiaobo was already in prison for supporting democracy. The name "Liu Xiaobo" could not appear on the book; only "Xiaobo" was permitted.)[42]

Signs began to appear that his academic success was going to his head. In college in Changchun he had been "the earthiest student in the class" and gave the impression that he could not care less about dress. He walked around in a T-shirt and shorts that looked like baggy underpants. Now, though, his look remained casual, but *studiedly* casual. He paid attention to brand names.[43] As a well-known intellectual, he may have wanted to look the part. His friend Xu Xing, who had always shared his indifference to dress, tells of a chance encounter with Xiaobo around this time. The two had not seen each other for a while, and Xiaobo had grown famous in the interim. Xu Xing was no longer working at the Peking duck restaurant because too many reporters had come to ask him about his fiction, and his boss, irritated, had fired him. He was reduced to plying the streets with a pedicab, selling magazines. Xiaobo was not expecting to meet this street vendor. Xu writes: "Xiaobo was wearing a spiffy dress shirt and leather shoes—not fancy shoes, but certainly leather. He was wearing intellectual-looking glasses. I, facing him, had a dirty pullover, plastic slippers that were falling apart, and a shining shaved head. I looked like a shiftless hooligan—I admit that. In any case, I got the impression that Xiaobo felt embarrassed to be standing there with me. The free-and-easy bearing of earlier times was gone."[44] Not much earlier, Xiaobo had been poking fun at intellectuals who cared for their appearance. Guo Lijia, a poet who had known Xiaobo since Changchun days, found the speed of the changes startling.[45] It was also around that time that Xiaobo began boasting about smoking marijuana. Tobacco was his lifetime vice, and he only dabbled in marijuana. But he did want to brag about it.

In June 1986, Beijing Normal considered Xiaobo for a promotion from teaching assistant to lecturer. As part of the process, the Literary Theory Section of the Chinese Department had to write a comprehensive (and confidential) evaluation of his work. Its summary stated:

> From the time comrade Liu Xiaobo was retained at Beijing Normal as a teacher, he has diligently studied Marxism-Leninism, supported the Communist Party, and supported socialism.

In the last two years, Mr. Liu Xiaobo has taught Introduction to Litera-ture in the undergraduate curriculum, night school, and university extension, and has been able to renovate and enrich the content of this course by including his own distinctive views. His attitude toward teaching is conscientious. He has shown that he can design an Introduction to Literature course independently.

He has published more than ten articles since 1983. Some explore fundamen-tal theory, others do research in comparative poetics and reception theory. His superior research ability shows in his breadth of learning and fluent writing.

We support Liu Xiaobo's promotion to lecturer.[46]

This recommendation for promotion ran into problems, however.

In those days one could begin a Ph.D. while simultaneously serving on a uni-versity's teaching staff. Xiaobo was offered a Ph.D. slot studying with the distin-guished Professor Huang Yaomian (1903–1987), a poet and aesthetician who also carried the impressive credential of having joined the Communist Party of China as early as 1928. Huang came to Beijing Normal in the 1950s as a professor of aes-thetics and department chair. He also worked with China's "democratic parties" (eight very small political parties that were formed before 1949 and allowed to continue existing afterward on condition of unquestioned fealty to the Commu-nist Party of China). Declared a "rightist" in 1957, Huang should have been exonerated, as other rightists were, in 1978 or 1979, but because of his sharp expres-sions of anger at the Cultural Revolution, school authorities disapproved, and the question had to go all the way to paramount leader Deng Xiaoping before Huang got a reprieve. He then became the first professor in China to be allowed to accept Ph.D. students in the field of literary theory, and his first group of them arrived in 1985. Xiaobo, in 1986, was in the second group.

His acceptance as Professor Huang's student may have been, along with his attention-grabbing articles, another accolade that went to his head. Looking around him at the temptations in the city of Beijing, Xiaobo saw how other peo-ple of his age were making names for themselves. His competitive juices were stim-ulated, and he can be seen as reverting, in a sense, to the hubris that had made him "a naughty boy on Stalin Avenue" twenty years earlier.

When his teacher Zhong Zi'ao died in September 1986, Xiaobo declined to bow to the body at the memorial service and did not shake the widow's hand. These actions became costly to Xiaobo's reputation.

His relationship with Tao Li deteriorated. New sounds, scenes, and people had come into his life, and Tao Li shared them only partly. She was understand-ably bitter, and they quarreled. Sometimes, after quarrels, Xiaobo rolled up his bedding and escaped to his dormitory room at Beijing Normal for a few nights. Once there, though, he would tell his dorm mates how he and Tao Li understood and loved each other.

For years his wife Tao Li had helped him, taken good care of him, and tried to corral him as she could. Now, though, he was starting to view her as a kind of obstacle, and she began to feel frustrated about how to cope with this obstreperous young man.

6

Mutiny! A Dark Horse Soars

The impact of Xiaobo's article on "new aesthetic thought" was powerful enough to earn him an invitation to an important conference. Sponsored by the Literature Research Institute of the Chinese Academy of Social Sciences and held in Beijing from September 7 to 13, 1986, the conference was entitled "Ten Years of Literature in the New Era: Changes and Tendencies in Literary Thought." It was where Xiaobo became a public figure.

Mao Zedong had died on September 9, 1976, so the timing of this conference exactly ten years later was significant. Calling it a "new" era meant, without saying so directly, ten years out from under Mao. The decade had seen remarkable progress, not just in literary art but in intellectual and social life of many kinds. People were arriving at the conference hoping to sort things out and take stock.

A number of eminent literary figures sat on a dais at the opening ceremony. Nearly every one of them could be viewed as both pioneer and survivor—responsible for one or another literary milestone but also a victim of Maoist rule. Qian Zhongshu (1910–1998), the erudite scholar and author of the famous novel *Fortress Besieged*, published in 1947, who during the Cultural Revolution was derided and assigned to work as a janitor, was there. So were Zhong Dianfei (1919–1987), a distinguished film critic, persecuted as a "rightist" in 1957; Li Zehou (1930–2021), a leading philosopher who used his years in a Maoist "cowshed" for disgraced intellectuals to read voraciously; and Wang Meng (1934–), a famous novelist and another "'57 rightist" who, just four months earlier, had been named Minister of Culture in the government.

Away from the dais, Xiaobo sat with a group of young literary critics, most of whom he was meeting for the first time. They came from all over China but resembled one another in distinctive ways. All were talented, energetic, and—perhaps most important—intensely motivated to depart the ruins of Cultural Revolution China and try to make something of themselves.

Professor Liu Zaifu, director of the Literature Research Institute, delivered an opening speech that affirmed the value of the past ten years and emphasized that literary works were now beginning to prioritize "subjectivity," a concept that Liu had been advocating for some time. He called for more respect for the individual person and for a balance between pursuing literature for its own sake and consideration of the needs of society. He spoke also of the need for "repentance," not only as a nation that needed to look back squarely at its "ten years of catastrophe" but also at the individual level—asking oneself, How was *I* complicit? Intellectuals needed more "consciousness of self-examination."[1] Xiaobo agreed with this critique.

Liu Zaifu did not reveal—and Xiaobo did not know then—that he was walking a dangerous political tightrope at the time he was making these comments. Two months earlier he had published a book called *On Composite Character*,[2] whose point was to oppose the Maoist dogma that literary characters be either plainly good or plainly bad. Liu took the position—still a bold one, even though Mao had been dead ten years—that human nature is a mix of the good and the bad. Intellectuals had been wanting to hear such a message, and Liu's book had had a considerable impact. People in Beijing queued up around the block to buy it at bookstores. Its very success, though, brought special attention from political conservatives. In August, just before the "ten years" conference began, a long article appeared in *Red Flag*, the Communist Party's most authoritative theoretical journal, entitled "The Problem of Method in Studying Literature." Its main point was to denounce Liu Zaifu and "subjectivity." Liu, the article said, was casting aside Marx's "reflection theory," and the affront was nothing less than a challenge to socialism and to Marxism in China. *Red Flag* seldom published articles of such length and seldom criticized people by name, so this attack clearly was serious. Its author, Chen Yong (1919–2015), was a Marxist literary critic who had begun publishing as early as 1938 at the Communist base at Yan'an. He was now a researcher in the Literature Research Institute and therefore, bureaucratically, a subordinate to Liu Zaifu. But in Communist pedigree he far outranked Liu. Chen's article drew criticism from intellectuals, but that reaction only led conservatives at *Red Flag* to organize a conference on the topic of "Deepening the Debate on Literary Theory." They scheduled that conference at the same time as the "ten years" conference—in obvious competition with it.

If Xiaobo had appreciated the political pressures that Liu Zaifu was under, he might not have done what he did next. But something about the opening scene irritated him. Was the panoply too pretentious? Did he think Liu Zaifu was mincing words too much? Was he resentful that Li Zehou, whose views on culture were too conservative for his taste, was up on the dais? Whatever the reason, Xiaobo was in no mood to sit and listen. Linda Jaivin, an Australian Sinologist and friend of Xiaobo's, once commented that he "was never a great audience."[3]

He decided to take action. He leaned toward Tang Xiaodu, a young poetry critic sitting next to him. He had known Tang for several years. Looking at Liu Zaifu, Xiaobo asked, "Who is this guy? Let's give him a hard time!"

Tang shook his head. "Let's listen. Maybe he's right."

So Xiaobo leaned the other way, where Li Jie, a young teacher from East China Normal University, whom he had just met, was sitting.

"Let's give them a rollicking good time!"

Li Jie wasn't sure whom Xiaobo meant by "them." But the next afternoon, in a discussion session where Liu Zaifu was present, Li commented that, from a scholarly point of view, he could not entirely accept Liu's explanation of humanism. The two then had a debate. When Xiaobo heard about this he was thrilled.

"I hear you're already taking it to Liu Zaifu," he said to Li. "Good! Great!"

On the third day, Li Jie and Xiaobo were elected as delegates of their respective discussion groups to represent the group opinions to the larger assembly. Comments did not have to be written out in advance, which meant that delegates were free to ad lib if they liked. This was their chance to make a splash.

Li Jie had gotten wind of the political pressure that Liu Zaifu was suffering and decided not to follow through. "When a humanitarian is face to face with a bunch of antihumanitarians," he later commented, "it's not the right time to step on the toes of the humanitarian."[4]

So if there were to be a revolt, Xiaobo would have to do it himself, and he did. No recording of what he actually said to the assembly has survived, but he later published a written version. It opens:

> I am not famous, but I offer you something that famous people can't offer. When famous people speak, they have to look in every direction before deciding what to say. And Chinese people, who feel comfortable not using their own brains, look up to famous people. That's why we're always seeing mindless fads in society. When somebody stands up and shouts a truly new idea, people are mesmerized. There aren't enough people with their own brains and ideals.[5]

Xiaobo the brash upstart, seemingly dropped into the meeting from the sky, went on to criticize nearly every notable contemporary Chinese writer, some of whom were sitting in the audience before him: the generation born in the 1930s, persecuted as rightists in 1957, and "rehabilitated" after Mao died (including Wang Meng and others) as well as stars of his own generation, who had been sent-down youth during the Cultural Revolution (Han Shaogong, Wang Anyi, A Cheng, Jia Pingwa, and others). He even took swipes at Jiang He, Yang Lian, and others of the "misty" poets whom he had so admired during his college years.

His basic argument was an extension of his "Unavoidable Reappraisal" article. Chinese national character had been formed by a thousand-year-old "feudalism" that was still alive and well.[6] He complained that contemporary Chinese writers of all generations were not carrying on the pioneering spirit of May Fourth but doing the opposite. Their consciousness was "backward-looking" and caused people "to retreat." Some of their works were not modern at all but only clumsy recyclings of classical culture. In a later recap of his speech, he wrote:

> Deng Youmei's "Snuff Bottles"[7] and Liu Xinwu's "Drum Tower"[8] both paint the life of old Beijing in luscious colors and call for a revival of a pure, uncompetitive kind of interpersonal relations that once supposedly infused the city. Jia Pingwa's series of stories called *Shangzhou*[9] is a study in how to resist the onslaught of modern life by holding on to the simple, pure past, with its warm interpersonal relations. Liu Shaotang is an admirer of pastoral songs about herd boys and weaving girls that are so ancient as to be downright moldy.[10] Han Shaogong's "Ba, Ba, Ba"[11] goes all the way back to the mythical Emperors Yan and Huang and even to Pangu, creator of the universe. Wang Anyi's *Baotown*[12] begins from the prehistoric Yu the Great, tamer of floods, and makes Confucius's ancient words "benevolence and righteousness" the moral backbone of the town. Zhang Xinxin, in her *Chinese Profiles*,[13] does come down to earth to look at people today, but focuses on their display of traditional virtues and can only lavish rhapsodic praise on it.[14]

This assessment is not entirely fair. The reversion of these writers to China's ancient roots was not as pervasive as Xiaobo suggests, and he seems unsympathetic to some of the defensible reasons for root-seeking. China had just been through the catastrophe of late Maoism. With Mao's death there was a chance—indeed a pressing need—to repair, recover, and find values that might bring China back to some kind of even keel. Writers often saw themselves as digging into China's past not in retreat but as a search for resources with which to move forward.

Later in his ad lib address to the conference, Xiaobo described his personal view of literature:

To put my point in extreme form, there should be no "rationality" in literature. Any addition of rational intent to a literary work at least to some extent diminishes the purity of its aesthetic effect.... Humanity is eternally suspended between incompatible opposites—sensibility and rationality, "spirit and flesh," instinct and civilization, natural man and social man. It is imperative that when we interact with traditional culture we stress sensibility, nonrationality, instinct, and flesh. By "flesh" I mean primarily two things—sex and money. Money is considered a good thing; anybody's eyes glow when they look at it. And sex of course is not a bad thing, even though gentle folk pretend to sneer at it.[15]

If Xiaobo's goal was to transfix his listeners, he succeeded. There was no denying his rhetorical talents. Behind a microphone, his stutter disappeared. His eloquence flowed like a stream, gushing through the room and enlivening it. Word of his performance buzzed through the conference and eventually seeped into the whole Chinese literary world.

As it spread, an anecdote about him spread with it. Liu Zaifu had missed Xiaobo's ad lib talk. He had been summoned to that other conference, "Deepening the Debate on Literary Theory," that the *Red Flag* editors had organized and had had no choice but to go listen to the scoldings the elderly conservatives had prepared for him. When he returned to the literature conference and heard about Xiaobo's brilliant talk, he went looking for Xiaobo at dinnertime. "Thank you for giving such a good talk!" he is said to have said to Xiaobo, who then, according to the anecdote, tilted his ear in Liu Zaifu's direction and pretended he couldn't hear clearly.

"Your . . . your name again?" Xiaobo's stutter was at full pitch. "Liu . . .? Liu . . .? Liu . . . Zai . . .? Liu Zaifu . . .?" He was pretending he couldn't even recognize the name.

Later he felt he had gone too far. He went to Liu Zaifu's hotel room the next day and apologized, saying his stunt had been inspired by a sense that it was his only route to fame.

A friend of Xiaobo's named Li Qingxi, who was at the conference, looked for a chance to pull Xiaobo aside and ask him if he could acknowledge that his views were a bit extreme. Xiaobo's reply, Li recalls, was to chuckle and say, "Lu Xun told us that that's the problem with the godforsaken Chinese! If you want to open a window for fresh air, nobody pays attention. You have to take down the whole house in order to get anywhere!"[16] A year or two later, Xiaobo came to see that the main problem with his approach was not that it was too extreme but that it identified the wrong adversary. That literature conference in 1986 was one of the freest and most open events the Communist Party of China had ever organized. Xiaobo's resistance of Party repression was still in the future.

It was only by a stroke of luck that his conference speech was ever published. It appeared in *Shenzhen Youth News*, where one of the editors was Xu Jingya, his old friend and classmate from days of working together on *Pure Hearts* at Jilin University. When Xu graduated in 1982 he was already recognized as a leading critic of the new "misty poetry" of Bei Dao, Yang Lian, Gu Cheng, and others, who were called "misty" because of their allusive language. The next year, when Xu published his undergraduate thesis under the title *Towering New Poems*, it drew sharp attacks from conservatives who were angered by the idea that any writing should be misty. For them, every statement had to be clear enough that the Communist Party of China could, if it wanted, determine it to be officially "correct" or "incorrect." Those were the only two categories into which statements could fall. Misty? Purposefully misty? A third category in between "correct" and "incorrect"? Nonsense! Dangerous! Out with it! Xu was required to write a "self-criticism," which was later published all across China in *People's Daily* without Xu's knowledge or permission. After that Xu left home and traveled far to the south, to Shenzhen, just north of Hong Kong, which was perhaps the only place in China free enough to allow him to continue his work. He and some friends launched *Shenzhen Youth News*.

In mid-September, right after the "ten years" conference, Xu happened to be returning to Shenzhen from Lanzhou in Gansu province and stopped off in Beijing to see classmates and friends. Xiaobo told him about the conference—how things had built up gradually until, at a big plenary session, his cannon fire had shocked all those "dogfart experts"—professors, theorists, and what have you. He also mentioned poverty: how some classmates had no money, how he himself was too damn poor, how he wished some money fountain would spout. Listening, Xu Jingya turned to Huo Yongling, another of their classmates who was present, and made a proposal: "Go find a tape recorder, get Xiaobo to repeat his speech into it, make a transcript, edit it, send it to me, and I'll publish it in *Shenzhen Youth News*. You and Xiaobo can split the payment. Okay?" Everyone agreed.[17]

When the edited transcript was ready, it was obvious that its length of about 15,000 characters—enough to fill two full pages in a newspaper—was going to be a problem. To devote even one full page to a single article was highly unusual and normally done only for big-name writers. Xiaobo was but a Ph.D. student. *Shenzhen Youth News* came out twice a week, on Tuesdays and Fridays, and Xu Jingya considered splitting the article between two issues. That, though, would make it harder to spread around the country, and spreading it was the whole point. So he took out his editor's pencil and cut the piece by nearly half. He chose the title "Crisis! Literature in the New Period in Crisis!" and added a laudatory "editor's note" in which he referred to Xiaobo as a "dark horse," surging from obscurity and into prominence in the intellectual world. The "dark horse" label stuck for many years.

Shenzhen Youth News published the piece on October 3, 1986. Xu Jingya mailed two hundred copies to Xiaobo in Beijing, where Xiaobo handed them out and they spread quickly. Later in the month, on October 21, *Shenzhen Youth News* was forced to shut down, but not because of that article. Another piece, "I Second the Idea That Comrade Deng Xiaoping Should Retire," had angered Party Central.

The "Crisis!" article delivered a jolt but was not the main factor in Xiaobo's rise to prominence in the late 1980s. A long article that he published in the October issue of *China*, "Sensibility, the Individual, and My Choice: A Dialogue with Li Zehou," was a more substantial piece of work and, together with his follow-up book called *Critique of Choices*, really launched his reputation. Li Zehou was a major intellectual figure, and Xiaobo was able to contend with him on a more or less equal footing.

Li had graduated from Peking University in 1954 and been assigned to the respected post of researcher at the Institute of Philosophy in the Chinese Academy of Sciences. During the Cultural Revolution, he was sent to a "cowshed" (where "cow ghosts and snake spirits" were held) but used his time there to read extensively and, after Mao died, emerged to publish a series of hefty books on art and philosophy.[18]

In the late 1970s Li Zehou became a hero among young intellectuals. Students in the humanities devoured his books, and Xiaobo himself once compared him to "the midday sun." "Like everybody else," Xiaobo wrote, "I loved his writing and read everything I could find."[19] An article of Li's that had an especially big impact appeared in August 1986 under the title "The Duet of Enlightenment and National Salvation."[20] It argued that China's May Fourth enlightenment had been snuffed out by a "national salvation" mentality that took over when the Japanese invaded China beginning in the 1930s. In the 1920s, "enlightenment" had meant science, democracy, rights, dignity, freedom, and independence. But "saving the nation" in the 1930s had required very different virtues: unity of will, collective strength, iron discipline. Japan left in 1945, but after 1949, under Mao, the suppression of enlightenment only grew stronger. The article concluded that:

> Beginning in the mid-1950s and extending into the "Cultural Revolution," feudalism in the guise of socialism attacked capitalism ever more fiercely and promoted an artificial morality that celebrated a spirit of sacrifice. It proclaimed that

"individualism is the source of all evil" and asked that everyone "fight selfish-ness and criticize [Soviet-style] revisionism." Every citizen was supposed to become a shining moral example like the sage-kings Yao and Shun. The result was to push China into a quagmire that became a total restoration of feudalism.

It was bold, to say the least, to be so frank about the effects of Communist rule.

Xiaobo's decision to challenge Li—about not this idea but others—originated in discussions with two young friends, Wu Bin and Wang Zhongchen, who had been colleagues of Xiaobo's on the editorial board of the magazine *China*. The three young thinkers wanted to stir up the literary scene in China—somehow give it more life—and they thought of highlighting, and perhaps arguing with, that great shining sun Li Zehou. Wang Zhongchen wanted Xiaobo to take the lead, and Xiaobo agreed. He took a few days to read everything he could find by Li that he had not already read, and by the end had arrived at a critical perspec-tive. Wu Bin and Wang Zhongchen helped with edits.

They decided to take aim at the "accumulation theory" that Li develops in his 1981 history of Chinese art called *The Path of Beauty*. Li observes in that work that the ancient earthenware uncovered by Chinese archeologists is decorated with images of birds, frogs, fish, snakes, and geometric shapes, all of which seem to have been related to ancient religious beliefs and shamanist rituals. Li calls these "natural forms of accumulated social content."[21] "Accumulation" continues, he argues, and Confucius plays a crucial role in it. Confucius helps to shape the struc-ture of Chinese culture and the character of Chinese people by making "rational morality" the guide in daily life as well as the framework for family relations and for basic concepts in political life. After Confucius, Li argues, art and propriety in ancient China consistently stressed control of emotions and avoidance of wild behavior.

Xiaobo took strong objection to this. His distaste was grounded in his study of classical poetry, where emotions were at the heart of things, and in his love of Zhuangzi, who had had unconventional, even "wild" ideas. But his opposition to the "accumulation theory" had also been primed by a bitter debate that his friend the aesthetician Gao Ertai had already had with Li Zehou.

The history between Gao and Li had long been sour. In the 1950s they had pub-licly squabbled over aesthetics. Li had gone along with Marxist aesthetic theory during years when Gao had the misfortune of being labeled a "rightist" on the grounds that he was a "bourgeois idealist." Gao was banished to rural Gansu and almost died during the Great Leap famine of 1959–62. Exonerated in the late 1970s, he published an article in 1983, "Pursuing Beauty and Liberating Humanity," in which he distinguishes between "rational structures" and "the power of sensibility."[22] Genuine beauty in art, he argues, results only from the latter. It is precisely people who do *not* repress their senses and their emotions who can be forward-looking, open, and creative. Li Zehou's "accumulation theory," in Gao's view, might help to explain certain phenomena in art history, but to would-be artists it is poison. It only stifles imagination and creative expression.

Xiaobo had long been a keen reader of Gao Ertai; he had especially admired Gao's views on "alienation" during the national debate on Marxist humanism. In the 1985–86 academic year, when Gao took a leave from Sichuan Normal University and came to Beijing to revise a manuscript and to court a girlfriend, he lived for a time in the graduate dorm at Beijing Normal, where Xiaobo had many opportunities for face-to-face contact with him.

Xiaobo's article rebutting Li Zehou was published in October 1986 in *China*. Its title was "A Dialogue with Li Zehou: Sensibility, the Individual, and My Choice."[23] In it Xiaobo endorses Gao Ertai's argument in favor of the senses and pushes it further. Influenced by Freud, he explores unconscious impulses and counterposes ideas of "rationality" (standard, society, tradition, entirety, essence) and "sensibility" (breakthrough, creation, individual, adventure, ephemerality). The rational is collective, stable, traditional, confined, hard, pale, cold, and inhibited. The sensible is individual, set in flesh and blood, open, profound, indistinct, mysterious, authentic, bountiful, creative, and rebellious. While Li Zehou sees people as rationally conforming to the environment and to received tradition, Xiaobo stresses their sensory impulses: "The life of the sensing individual can be developed and realized only through constant critical examination and sometimes negation of rational society. . . . The readiness to rebel, intrinsic to sensory life, is the eternal and limitless force by which sensory life deals fatal blows to rationalist dogmas, which by nature are limited in both time and place."[24] Xiaobo's essay sees the history of aesthetic expression as an unending procession of skirmishes. It measures "freedom" by how well a person makes worthwhile breakthroughs. Using Nietzschean language, Xiaobo sketches an arc of human history:

If the shackles of "rational accumulation" were to fall asunder, humanity would come face to face with an entirely new universe, filled with life force, where the wild god of wine has become spectacularly inebriate. But the rationalism in our world would again very soon produce a system of prohibitions against which we would again have to make breakthroughs—and we would do so again, for sure, until inebriate freedom again could be ours.[25]

Here Xiaobo was thinking beyond aesthetics alone—he was challenging Li Zehou's entire worldview. Xiaobo believed that China needed an enlightenment of the kind Lu Xun had sought during May Fourth, when it was precisely cultural "accumulation" that needed to be dug out and discarded. He saw Li Zehou as approving and even in some ways nostalgic for accumulation. Hegel had accepted that "what exists is rational," Xiaobo wrote, and Li was doing the same. Beneath the surface of Li's writing lay conservatism, weakness, servility. It was the opposite of the radical break with the past that Lu Xun had called for in the late 1910s and that Xiaobo wanted now.[26]

Was Xiaobo's advocacy too one-sided, too extreme? Some people called him a "cultural nihilist." Some approached him with well-intentioned advice that he be more balanced and even-handed. Xiaobo understood but declined. He wrote: "At the junctures in human history where societies have improved, the differences have been made precisely *not* by people with balanced views but by ones who are passionate about moving in radically new directions. This is especially true when the barrier to progress is a deeply entrenched tradition."[27] He was afraid that, when confronting Chinese tradition, "the consequence of a balanced approach inevitably will be compromise that leads to assimilation." In pursuing radical change, Xiaobo's voice comes to resemble Lu Xun's: "When I reflect on how tradition works inside me, and how I might be rid of it, I see nothing before me but darkness. Tradition gives me nothing but feelings of despair."[28] On its face, "tradition" here would have to include Xiaobo's own graduate studies in classical poetry and philosophy. It seems that in a sense he was seeking self-incineration for the sake of rebirth.

And perhaps he was, to an extent, but he was not opposing the whole of tradition. He had a particular target within it: the strong hierarchical bias in Confucian political culture. This for centuries had been the backbone of Chinese authoritarianism. Xiaobo called it "feudalism,"[29] as many others did, even though he knew it was not the same as European feudalism.

However named, the pernicious tradition he saw in China was that of a rank-ordered social order that demanded everyone stay in his or her designated place and, as Confucius said in the *Analects,* "subdue self and observe proprieties" (*keji fuli*). Xiaobo saw this rule as creating the "self-induced slave character" of the Chinese, especially intellectuals. It led people to "obey destiny, be content with what one has, and accept manipulation by others."[30] This was the point on which Xiaobo disagreed most sharply with Li Zehou: "[Li's] theories offer far too much support for Confucian hierarchy and propriety. He holds that contemporary Chinese still need certain things from Confucian doctrine, and my view is that we need to bury them."[31] For Xiaobo, getting rid of the inequality implicit in

Confucianism was a prerequisite to any transition to democracy and the modern world. In a retrospective essay in 2002 (when he was more ready to be politically confrontational), he wrote that he had picked the quarrel with Li Zehou not for cultural reasons so much as a way to comment on politics. "We were borrowing culture to talk about political systems," he wrote.[32]

The use of euphemisms for unpleasant facts has been common in the People's Republic, and the regime itself has invented or approved many of them. There was no huge famine in the early 1960s, only "three years of difficulty." When the Cultural Revolution was over one could not refer to tyranny or idol worship but only to "unhealthy tendencies" that had arisen under a "Gang of Four." The term "People's Republic" itself can easily be seen as a euphemism. Words like "authoritarian" or "dictatorship" could apply only to foreign countries or to premodern China. Li Zehou's use of the word "feudalism" in his 1986 "Duet of Enlightenment and Salvation" article was significant because before then "feudal," like "authoritarian," could not apply to the Communist era. In the "culture fever" of the late 1980s, however, "feudal" was widely used to mean "politically backward"—even, perhaps especially, when it was referring to government behavior. The opposite term in the code, equally arbitrary, was "Western" to mean open, modern, or democratic.

As of 1986 the code was common only among elite intellectuals, who were but a tiny part of the Chinese populace. In 1988, however, the binary of "feudal versus Western" spread to a far larger audience—countless millions—when China Central Television broadcast a six-part series of programs called *River Elegy*.[33] The premise of the series was that China hangs in a dilemma, on one side of which is Chinese "Yellow River civilization" (land-based, inward-looking, hidebound, authoritarian) and on the other Western "azure ocean civilization" (seafaring, open, free, democratic). Although it could not be said explicitly, the Communist Party was identified with Yellow River civilization. *River Elegy* captured the mixture of worry and hope that pervaded urban China at the end of the 1980s and made it more tangible.

The reverberations of Xiaobo's challenge to Li Zehou were many and various. Wu Liang, a brilliant young literary critic in Shanghai, coined the phrase "Liu Xiaobo tornado." Wu had attended the "ten years" conference in Beijing, had witnessed Xiaobo's "dark horse" outburst, and had kept a certain distance from it. But when Xiaobo's piece lambasting Li Zehou appeared, he wrote an article in *Wenhui Reader's Weekly* praising Xiaobo for "showing the intrepid will of a true intellectual warrior right when such will was dwindling in our literary circles."[34] The "misty" poet Yang Lian and the poetry critic Tang Xiaodu published a dialogue about the matter, explaining that "the entire cultural world has felt a jolt from Liu Xiaobo." Tang wrote that Xiaobo "has focused on vital issues that have lurked since May Fourth and that still bedevil contemporary culture; their significance far exceeds the criticism of any particular literary phenomenon or particular theoretical system."[35] A story spread that an assistant to the famed filmmaker Zhang Yimou, while working on the film *Red Sorghum* (later to become a big hit), passed out copies of Xiaobo's article to the film crew in hopes that it would inspire them to absorb Xiaobo's already-famous "human sensory surge."[36]

Both scholarly journals and general-interest magazines organized special sections or columns on "the Liu Xiaobo phenomenon." Points of view appeared both supporting and opposing Xiaobo. In its first issue of 1987, the *Journal of Shanghai Normal University* published short articles by eight scholars who took Xiaobo to task. With titles like "Some Questions for a Badly One-Sided View" and "More One-Sidedness," the essays took a toll on Xiaobo's reputation. Yet the tornado kept spinning. Even specialized journals in remote places were drawn in. In February 1987, the *Journal of the Changsha Water and Electricity Teachers Institute*, in a special edition on the "social sciences," published a collection of articles on how Liu Xiaobo viewed traditional Chinese culture.

Xiaobo's critique of Li Zehou made something of a straw man of Li, conceiving of his thinking as narrower than it actually was. Xiaobo was correct to point out the difference between Li's preference for the "rational" and his own for the "sensory," and also to show how Li's approach harbors a conservatism that can lead to servility (even if he didn't mean it to). But on issues like seeing "feudalism" grow within the Communist Party, there was little difference between Li Zehou and Liu Xiaobo. They were in substantial agreement too on the thesis of Li's "Duet" article that the Japanese attacks on China had stifled May Fourth "enlightenment." But Xiaobo did not see Japan as the only reason May Fourth enlightenment withered. Another reason, in his view, was the failure of May Fourth to address the root of China's problem:

> The great majority of intellectuals who threw themselves into the May Fourth Movement could never rid themselves entirely of the mediocre national character [accumulated from Confucianism] and so could never see the essence of feudal culture clearly.... [They] adopted certain parts of Western culture that could be grafted onto their existing foundation and used these in order to resist the deeper spirit of Western culture, which to them was indigestible.[37]

Li Zehou did not see May Fourth as being this weak but was gracious in all his responses to Xiaobo. Li did not answer all of his criticisms and later explained that one reason for his forbearance was his sense that Xiaobo was "expressing the anger, discontent, and frustration that young people feel toward many things—as if wishing they could tear everything down and start afresh."[38] Good-naturedly, he noted that Xiaobo's article was "selling like hotcakes."[39]

Xiaobo reciprocated Li's generosity, and mutual respect between the two lasted many years. When the government announced its eleven-year sentence of Xiaobo in 2009, Li Zehou took the courageous step of opposing the regime in public. He announced, "I'm against sending people to prison for what they write."[40]

But although Li Zehou was temperate in his response to Xiaobo, some of Li's graduate students were not. A group of seven threw down a gauntlet to Xiaobo: would he debate them, the graduate students, in public? The leader of the group, Liu Dong, was the same age as Xiaobo but had already served on the editorial boards of both Striding Toward the Future and Culture: China and the World. When Xiaobo told his friend Wang Furen about the graduate students' challenge, Wang was worried. One against seven? He asked if Xiaobo needed his help, afraid that his stutter would be a handicap. Xiaobo himself wasn't worried. "No problem!" he answered.

So a debate between Liu Dong and Liu Xiaobo took place near the end of December 1986,[41] in the graduate school dining room at the Chinese Academy of Social Sciences. This was home turf for Liu Dong, and the audience, mostly other graduate students from the Academy of Social Sciences, was a home crowd. As the debate unfolded, though, sympathy in the room tilted toward the dark-horse rebel.

In round one, each participant chose a topic for an opening statement. Xiaobo chose "The Differences Between Chinese and Western Culture." It was an area in which he could talk fluently about all kinds of things, from Hegel's logic to Chinese versus Western medicine. He said Western medicine uses X-rays to diagnose and surgery to fix a problem, while Chinese medicine has the patient drink bitter liquids one after another and not get anywhere. The audience chuckled its appreciation. Liu Dong, whose opening topic was "Husserl's Intersubjectivity," got a much cooler reception. People said later that he seemed only to be passing along—stiffly—some book learning that he himself had not digested very well. Xiaobo's final triumph in bonding with his audience came during a singing competition held in the evening. Liu Dong offered a song by Felix Mendelssohn, far too elite for the audience to follow, let alone to resonate with. Xiaobo then stood up and belted out Cui Jian's popular moan-from-the-streets "Nothing to My Name." Everyone joined in, and soon the whole room was rocking. That evening some M.A. students put up posters bemoaning the "loss of face" that Li Zehou's

Ph.D. student had brought to the graduate school of the Academy of Social Sciences.[42] Li Zehou was surprised to hear about the unfortunate results but gentle with Liu Dong: "You're a good debater and Xiaobo stutters. What happened?"[43]

It was around this time that Xiaobo discovered he had a talent for public speaking. His unusual powers of memory allowed him to quote texts, Eastern and Western, seemingly at will and across a broad range. His analyses, always sharp, unconventional, and expressed with passion, kept audiences spellbound. As "culture fever" spread, Xiaobo began getting invitations from universities to give lectures. He usually accepted, not least because of the honoraria. (The salaries of university teaching assistants were low; Xiaobo and Tao Li together were paid only about 200 yuan—U.S. $63 at the official exchange rate—per month.) As his fame spread, invitations began coming from outside Beijing—from Hebei, Shanxi, Hubei, and elsewhere. He packed auditoriums, often to standing room only. Students would sit or stand on the metal-grate platforms outside of windows. Xiaobo relished applause; it made him feel he must be doing something right and strengthened his confidence in his opinions. It fed a personal swagger, which in turn became part of his rhetorical performance. Audience expectations that he would be outlandish encouraged his penchant to be outlandish.

His lectures left behind a trail of overstatements that others could—and did—use against him. At Tsinghua University in mid-December 1986 he said: "Don't divide tradition into essence and dregs. . . . If you're going to knock it down, knock it *all* down. Don't look for theories of balance and harmony. Vital force shows its brilliance only at extremes. The intellectual leaders who made great breakthroughs were all, in this sense, extremists: Rousseau, Marx, Freud, Nietzsche—all of them."[44] And this:

> A first responsibility of you university students today is to change yourselves from the bone marrow outward, to remove the thinking that has been instilled in you since elementary school and replace it with thinking of your own. I'm famous now, but I was not made famous by any outside force. I did it entirely on my own. I don't think you need a grand "sense of duty" or "sense of mission" [phrases that others in literary circles were pushing]; you just need to be loyal to yourself, to try to perfect yourself, to pursue your own beliefs with the same ardor that a religious believer feels in pursuing a religion, without layers of moral "righteousness." Each person should become one's own self; one's self should be one's God.[45]

At the end of 1986, Peking University organized an "arts festival" to which it invited a number of famous cultural figures. The renowned misty poet Bei Dao was there, but Xiaobo somehow drew more attention. He told his audience that his wife Tao Li had noticed how he liked to say the words "I am Liu Xiaobo" when he met people. "Do you feel a sudden rush of joy in doing that?" she had asked him. He told his audience that he answered "yes" to this question and then spent quite a bit of time dissecting what the psychological roots of the joy were.[46] After the lecture, he took questions by inviting people to pass slips of paper forward. One slip read, "I'd like to beat you up, Liu Xiaobo!" Xiaobo read the message aloud, then stuttered, "Who . . . who . . . who is this? Come . . . come on up!" The audience roared.[47]

Several times in those months, he told a story about "a bottle of foreign whiskey." At Beijing's "Friendship Store" (which offered rare goods to foreigners and denied entry to Chinese), he had once seen a bottle of foreign whiskey for sale for 160 "foreign exchange certificates" (a special currency for foreigners). He told his audiences, "I stood in front of that whiskey bottle feeling like a weakling, feeling completely beaten. But why should I?"[48] The story spread, and the whiskey acquired the nickname "Louie the Thirteenth." Xiaobo's message was that it's all right to have material desires. One of Xiaobo's college classmates, the poet Yisha, wrote, "I felt that this story fit all the rest of what he was saying in those days. His were revolutionary words, words that could reignite natural desires in people, that could get them to see material things in a new way."[49]

It may seem odd that Xiaobo's advocacy of material interests came to be symbolized by a whiskey bottle, because he did not drink. He was allergic to alcohol. His other main example of benign materialism was sex, which he discussed as both analyst and practitioner. Students liked to hear him talk about the topic, and he obliged with characteristic frankness (but sometimes with insufficient consideration that he was talking also about Tao Li). Xiaobo's arrogance extended to the question of his speaking fees. At one talk he stopped halfway and renegotiated his pay for the second half. At another, when he received his honorarium after the lecture and saw how small it was, he gave it to two students from the audience and asked them to go to a nearby tavern and have a couple of drinks.[50]

News of Xiaobo's antics reached the ears of his distinguished Ph.D. adviser, Professor Huang Yaomian, but at age eighty-three he found himself lacking the energy to take the problem on and handed it to his colleague Tong Qingbing (1936–2015), vice chair of Xiaobo's Ph.D. committee. Professor Tong, like Xiaobo's father, was from the "new generation" of intellectuals trained after the 1949 revolution. Disgraced, like others, during the Cultural Revolution, he returned afterward and became known for his hard work, warmth, and tolerance toward others. He looked for Xiaobo, counseled him to heed his reputation, and urged him to return to scholarship. One day near the end of 1986, the two had a long talk at Professor Tong's home. It dragged on for three hours, mostly because

Xiaobo was not ready to sit and listen. He kept arguing back. Finally the professor's wife grew irritated. "Why don't you two go outside to talk? Not in the
house—okay?" The two obeyed. They went to an athletic field at Beijing Normal
and walked around for four more hours. That made seven hours all together.[51]

Whichever was more impressive—the teacher's undying patience or the student's feisty spirit—Professor Tong failed to win the argument and had to report
that fact to the elderly Professor Huang, who then summoned Xiaobo to his
home.

"Money? Sex? You can't just talk about anything you like," Professor Huang
warned. "Students should use their energies studying. Don't pull them so far
afield." On the question of whether "vital force shows its brilliance only at
extremes," the professor had this to say: "Debate with others is a good thing. Do
it. But you have to be reasonable. You shouldn't keep saying that 'one-sidedness
has depth.' It is *not* good to be one-sided—you know that, right?"[52]

Professor Huang had golden intentions—Xiaobo could see that. But still he
didn't listen. He told friends later that the professor had not convinced him.

A staff member at *China Youth News*, who for protection chose to write under
the pen name Zhuge Man of the Mountains, later recalled an episode with Xiaobo
that includes a rare account of Tao Li and Xiaobo at home.[53] One day in December 1986, some of Zhuge's colleagues visited room 408 in dormitory building 12
at the Beijing Languages Institute, where Tao Li and Liu Xiaobo lived. Xiaobo's
criticism of Li Zehou had stirred up such a storm that the reporters were very keen
on getting an essay from Xiaobo. They knocked on the door but heard no "Come
in" or "Who is it?" in reply. Then the door suddenly opened and a striking figure
appeared.

"I am Liu Xiaobo!"

The reporters described him as "gallant, unpretentious, about five feet nine
inches in height. High cheekbones, piercing eyes, and hair that somehow stood
up even though it was disheveled."

They were invited into a rectangular room of about 130 square feet. Against
the wall on the left a simple three-drawer desk was covered in books and papers.
On the right was a small loveseat. Down the middle of the room, dividing it in
half, was a bookshelf about six feet long, behind which there was a double bed
and no room for anything else.

"Please have a seat, have a seat!" said Tao Li, at the same time, as if by magic,
causing some fruit and snacks to appear. "You've come from so far, you must not
have eaten, right? Just make do with these." Seeming embarrassed at the paucity
of her offerings, Tao Li made explanations. "Xiaobo and I are so busy that we

seldom get around to cooking . . . we just make do like this. When we do buy food we buy a big supply."

While Tao Li busied herself, Xiaobo merely watched, as if an outsider. When she went out to the corridor to call to their son Taotao, Xiaobo pointed casually to the food and said, "Have some." He then answered the reporters' questions, using calm, measured tones and tight logic. The reporters noted that when he spoke he seemed to stare at a point about three feet in front of him, as if there were something there. Every now and then the curse words "his mother's!" escaped his lips, and as soon as they did, Tao Li snapped at him: "Xiaobo!" Her rebukes brought him to a halt and caused him to stare blankly for a few seconds, but were not enough to prevent another "his mother's!" from popping out again before long.

Xiaobo agreed to give them a manuscript. Later, though, authorities told *China Youth News* that works by Xiaobo had been banned. As a stopgap, the reporters who had visited him rewrote one of his essays as an interview and brought it back to him for approval. When they arrived, Xiaobo was amusing his son by playing with a pigeon. When they told him about their publishing plan, he exploded.

"No way! The whole tone is ruined! I understand why you want to do this, but the bite of my style is completely gone. No way! Absolutely not!"

A moment later he continued. "I don't write articles just for you, you know; I write them for myself. Look at my writing and you'll see there are no wasted words—that's because the writing is part of me, part of my life. If other people want or don't want to publish my work, that's their business, not mine!"

Later a reporter went back to the Tao-Liu home hoping that Xiaobo on second thought would compromise. He was away lecturing, but Tao Li was at home, and the reporter took the opportunity to ask her some questions. "We've read Xiaobo's articles and have interviewed him, and we think that he's not really as radical as his reputation has him."

"That's what I think too," Tao Li answered. "He probably felt he had to make a splash, because this thing 'tradition' is just too big and heavy! I didn't entirely agree with some of the things he wrote, and we used to argue about them. But later I decided not to disturb him. Just think of it—trying to do something like this! How hard it must be! Especially when you're still just working out what your worldview is . . . there can't be perfection at every turn. A person's energies have limits . . . it could be that a person's tide of inspiration comes only during youth. So I think I should give him a wide berth, let him get all his thoughts out, and then see where we are. How could I dump a basin of cold water on a spark of life that has just begun to burn?"

In the end, Xiaobo's article did not appear in *China Youth News*.

In late 1986, a major student democracy movement erupted in Hefei, Anhui province, at the Chinese University of Science and Technology, and spread to university campuses in Shanghai. Fang Lizhi, a brilliant astrophysicist and vice president of the University of Science and Technology, had been encouraging students to "think for yourselves." Together with the university president, Guan Weiyan, Fang instituted policies that promoted that goal and gave speeches extolling transparency, freedom, and democracy. The speeches had two kinds of national impact. Students and intellectuals were delighted; the men who ruled in Beijing were frightened.

On January 28, 1987, Party Central issued a "Notice on Several Matters Relating to the Opposition of Bourgeois Liberalism in the Present Day." Shortly thereafter Hu Yaobang, the general secretary of the Communist Party of China, was forced to resign. (Hu was nominally the highest-ranking person in the Communist Party but in fact served at the pleasure of the "paramount leader," Deng Xiaoping.) Three prominent intellectuals—Fang Lizhi, Liu Binyan (beloved for his muckraking journalism), and Wang Ruowang (an outspoken writer and critic)—were expelled from the Communist Party. Wu Zuguang (a dramatist and articulate humanist) and Wang Ruoshui (the "humanist Marxist" former deputy editor of the *People's Daily*) were "advised to resign" from the Party. (Wang refused but was removed anyway.)

Officials in the academic world felt pressure to "coordinate" with Party Central by identifying bourgeois liberals and subjecting them to discipline. At one meeting, He Dongchang, the state commissioner of education, commented that Liu Xiaobo was not fit to be a Ph.D. candidate. He recommended rescinding Xiaobo's student status and sought to block Beijing Normal's plan to promote him from teaching assistant to lecturer.

When the commissioner's recommendations arrived at Beijing Normal, the school's Party secretary asked Professor Tong Qingbing to compile and submit a collection of politically inappropriate things that Xiaobo had said and done. Tong resisted. During the Cultural Revolution he had witnessed far too much of this kind of political harassment, informally called *zhengren*, "repairing people," and he found the Party secretary's request disgusting. Tong later wrote about what happened next:

> "You're asking a teacher to supply black materials on his own student?" I asked.
> "Are you crazy?"
> The Party secretary grew incensed and was about to slap the table. Wanting to beat him to it, I slapped the table first and left.[54]

Professor Huang Yaomian was equally adamant in refusing to send "materials" to Party Central. At an impasse, the Education Commission referred the Liu Xiaobo question to Zhu Houze, chief of the Communist Party's Department of Propaganda. Zhu was a relatively open-minded Party official, and he thought that there was no need to gather materials to send to the center. Instead Liu Xiaobo should be "educated" by his academic adviser Huang Yaomian. The Education Commission dropped its demand for materials but sent an official to press Professor Huang on the "re-education" plan. Huang responded that Xiaobo's articles fell into the category of scholarly debate. Before Xiaobo wrote them, Huang said, the atmosphere at Beijing Normal had been dreary; Xiaobo had stirred things up and injected the literary field with new vitality, and that had been good for broadening horizons and stimulating literature and the arts.

Word of Professor Huang's enlightened response spread, and when it reached *Wenhuibao*, the major daily newspaper in Shanghai, the paper sent reporters to interview him. The professor saw an important opportunity. He spent more than a week reading Xiaobo's work. At the interview, he said that new thinking and new viewpoints are the lifeblood of "reform and opening"; if everyone stayed stuck in the old ruts, the road to reform and opening would only get narrower. At the same time, he did point out some places where Xiaobo had gone too far.[55]

Wenhuibao came out with an article, and after it appeared Xiaobo visited Professor Huang several times to express both thanks and contrition. Many years later he was still thanking both professors, Huang and Tong. In 2006, he wrote that "it was only the protection of my two professors that kept the Education Commission off my back."[56]

In early 1987, Xiaobo made some important new acquaintances. His friend Xu Xing brought him to meet Liu Binyan, recently expelled from the Communist Party as a "bourgeois liberal." Liu said nothing of his own mistreatment but showed a broad mind and an optimism about what Chinese freedom seekers should be doing next. The ever-candid Xiaobo criticized him for being insufficiently radical. Liu Binyan listened respectfully to the critique; he took out a notebook and took notes.

It was also in these months that Xiaobo became friends with Wang Shuo, the prolific writer of satire and master of Beijing brogue, whose works the establishment called "hooligan literature." He also befriended the famous film star Liu Xiaoqing, the first two characters of whose name were identical to his, suggesting, if one didn't know better, that they might be siblings. She did call him "little brother."

His friendship with the Australian Sinologist Geremie Barmé began during the same months. In 1986 Xiaobo and Barmé were both working on Ph.D.

dissertations, and in December Barmé went to Beijing Normal looking for Xiaobo, rightly suspecting that he would discover a kindred spirit. The two shared skeptical, often cynical, views on many issues in Chinese culture and society. At the time, Barmé was writing on contemporary cultural issues for the magazine *Emancipation Monthly* in Hong Kong, and he decided to publish a dialogue with Xiaobo there. It was politically "sensitive" (i.e., risky) for Chinese writers to publish "across the border," but that didn't bother Xiaobo. The kindred spirits went ahead and poked their fun at Liu Zaifu and the Chinese literature of the day. Xiaobo repeated his views that contemporary Chinese writers were superficial, derivative, and lacking in creativity and in contrast, the new translations of foreign works in China were very worthwhile. He expressed disdain for the recent student protests in Hefei and Shanghai. "Chinese students sometimes want to get into politics—higgledy-piggledy, march on the streets, whatever—but those are just superficial symptoms."[57]

Xiaobo's indifferent attitude toward political protest was actually shared fairly widely among Chinese intellectuals who had been through the Cultural Revolution. It was a common feeling that political action gets you nowhere; only culture or art repays effort. In just two or three years, this view of Xiaobo's would change.

Barmé introduced Xiaobo to Linda Jaivin, an Australian writer and Sinologist. Jaivin was a good friend of the well-known Taiwan singer Hou Dejian and introduced him to Xiaobo. Hou's most famous song at the time was "Heirs of the Dragon." Xiaobo did not like the song—or at least its name—and frankly said so. Bragging about Chinese heritage was quite the opposite of what China needed, in Xiaobo's view. Other than that, though, Xiaobo felt a strong intuitive bond with Hou. Listening to him sing was a whole lot better than listening to the pontifications of an intellectual. Linda Jaivin later described Xiaobo, a "Beijing literary critic, scholar and fan of Nietzsche,"[58] this way:

A skinny chain-smoker with acne-ravaged skin, with a severe stutter and wearing thick glasses, he nonetheless possessed a strange charisma and was an irrepressible raconteur. His written output was prodigious and he could recite everything he'd written word for word—and frequently did. Though I enjoyed the style with which Xiaobo blasted nearly all of Chinese culture's sacred cows, and admired his essays, I thought him intolerably full of himself. He also had the worst table manners I'd ever seen in my whole life. Once, when I was staying with the Yangs [Yang Xianyi and Gladys Yang, famous translators of Chinese literature into English], he came to visit after dinner. Xiaobo fetched a pair of chopsticks from the kitchen and hoed into the leftovers, scarcely pausing to swallow or even chew, all the while delivering a monologue on the subject of why women didn't make great mathematicians or philosophers. I was so appalled by the whole performance I think I may even have yelled at him.[59]

As of early 1987 the well-intended admonitions of Xiaobo's wife, professors, and others appear to have had little effect on his personal style. If anyone was going to slow down this galloping dark horse, it would likely have to be the horse himself. He wanted fame, but did he really care how others were seeing him? Amid all the raging controversy that he stimulated, he never deigned to write a word in answer to his critics. He sometimes revised his opinions, but only in obedience to his own mind, not as a compromise with others.

In the first months of 1987 Xiaobo concentrated on revising his dialogues with Li Zehou into *Critique of Choices*,[60] where he calls for a new Chinese enlightenment that extends much more deeply and broadly than May Fourth. "I personally would feel honored to pour myself into the antifeudal torrent," he wrote.[61] China, in his view, was still trapped in its "accumulated" habits:

> The West, for the most part, has entered the stage of development where individual consciousness is primary, while Eastern culture remains stuck in the stage where collective consciousness dominates. *Chinese tradition is a typical example of stubborn hierarchical collectivism, although it does differ a bit because of its many layers of accumulated habit.* The key question in the current debates about culture is the opposition between collective consciousness and the sprouts of individual consciousness that have appeared.[62]

Nietzsche looms large in the book. Lu Xun, whom Xiaobo greatly admired, had written that it might take a Nietzschean superman to knock open hermetically sealed China. When a "Nietzsche rage" came to China in 1985 and 1986, Xiaobo read whatever he could find on Nietzsche, whose views on the individual versus the group; on genius versus mediocrity; on isolation, tragedy, and human transcendence; and on confronting "rationality" appear liberally in *Critique of Choices*. So does a parallel between the ways Confucianism in the East and Christianity in the West had stultifying effects. Xiaobo borrows Nietzschean views of Christian culture to see Confucian culture as suppressing individuality for the sake of groups, "bloodline ethics," and "harmony." Both of these blanketing belief systems opposed the spirit of skepticism and caused human beings to be repressed, frail, and untrue to themselves.

When *Critique of Choices* appeared in January 1988 it sold well and sparked much conversation, especially among the young. In early 1989 an unconventional

professor at Peking University named Kong Qingdong wrote an article specifically on the distribution and sales of the book.[63] Kong tells how, in an experiment,
he asked the proprietor of a bookstall outside the Peking University gate to stock
eighty copies (a very large number for a bookstall) and see what would happen.
They were gone within a day. Between January 1988 and June 1989, when the June
Fourth massacre forced the book from the shelves of bookstores, it had sold 50,000
copies.

The book is 202 pages long (nearly 300 pages if translated to English) and
makes hundreds of literary references but contains only three footnotes. Even
those three do not cite sources but are expansions of arguments in the body of
the text. Xiaobo had always enjoyed declaiming his views aloud to friends, classmates, and his wife—as if his making the air reverberate might strengthen his
points—and much of *Critique of Choices* reads as if he imagines himself doing
that. What keeps it from being a self-indulgent monologue is that it presents a
kaleidoscope of other voices. He quotes not only Nietzsche but also Rousseau,
Sartre, Freud, Fromm, and others, and not only once but as part of a tapestry in
which those thinkers appear and reappear. Xia Zhongyi, a professor of Chinese
at East China Normal University in Shanghai, compared the book to musical
improvisation:

> [Liu Xiaobo] is like a jazz artist. He grabs a trumpet and blows it a while, then
> tosses it away and turns around to beat the tar out of a kettle drum—unrehearsed.
> What his dialogue [with Li Zehou] offers the scholarly world is not well-
> considered propositions backed by carefully discovered and presented evidence
> but "thought rock" in which you say something first without wondering whether
> you can defend it, attack here without asking the implications for over there, say
> something cool and assume it applies everywhere, and mix bon mots and plain
> language at will.[64]

Xia was not being wholly sarcastic. He had a fair point and was observing, not
scolding. Xiaobo never answered.

Powerful though it was, *Critique of Choices* represents only a transitional stage
in Xiaobo's thinking. He struggles in it to pull himself free from the communist
worldview that he had grown up with, introducing terms like "personal consciousness," "individual subjectivity," "internal freedom of the person," and "the
creative power of the individual." But he does not yet reach the concept of individual rights. Fifteen years later, in the mature stage of his thinking, political
rights have moved front and center, and he sees that to make political progress it

is not enough to be a lone radical; one needs to bring people together. He eventually became very good at this.

Close on the heels of *Critique of Choices*, Xiaobo's next book project was a history of Western philosophy that he wrote between May and December 1987. (The seven months were actually five, he notes in a preface, because of an arm injury that prevented him from writing for two months.) Called *The Fog of Metaphysics,* it is a bold survey from a distinctive point of view of classic Western thinkers from Socrates to the Frankfurt School.[65]

It opens with a conundrum: why would immensely talented Western thinkers, beginning long ago and extending to the present, spend so much time and energy on metaphysics, trying to find eternal principles behind the universe, society, and human life? Xiaobo sees metaphysics as a pursuit of finished-ness, closed-ness, or perfection—in his words, "using 'one' to encompass all, using a single factor to explain everything within a closed system."[66] Then he announces a "discovery": beneath the gleaming surfaces of metaphysical systems, "noise" in the mental life of actual human metaphysicians. They have fears, pains, fights, self-consolations, escapes, and various passions—to conquer, to occupy, to rule, and more. He argues that the ragged landscapes of their minds are relevant to their fine finished thoughts because the one explains the need for the other. Metaphysicians seek "unity, completeness, order, simplicity, and the exalted" in order to answer the human thirst for perfection.[67] Xiaobo's two-leveled analysis of psychology owes much to Freud. If Nietzsche was the sage behind the curtain *Criticism of Choice*, then Freud was that person for *The Fog of Metaphysics.*

As he surveys Western philosophers, Xiaobo finds some who record fears, pains, and desires from their daily lives. He calls these "the anti-metaphysicians." The others—the metaphysicians—ignore the potholes in human life and search for a fissure-free universal order that, if it addresses humanity at all, steers clear of the messy subconscious. Structured to imitate a history of rational thought in the West, *The Fog of Metaphysics* is an idiosyncratic tour of the nonrational thinking of rational thinkers. Xiaobo often told friends that it was his favorite among his books.

In Xiaobo's terms, Plato was an anti-metaphysician and Aristotle a metaphysician:

> Plato is well known for metaphysics, but, compared to Aristotle, is also the West's first major anti-metaphysician. He was a *life-based* philosopher; the foundation of his philosophy is not rationality but his perception of the fragility of human beings. His metaphysics grows out of the direct perception

that arises from impulse, and out of the insight that imagination provides. By contrast, Aristotle was a *knowledge-based* philosopher; the foundations of his philosophy are speculative rationality that takes no account of nonrational impulses.[68]

Xiaobo's favorite Western philosopher was Augustine, whose character he saw as "acerbic and unsparing." "On the surface he confesses to God, but deeper down he is delivering a deadly challenge to humanity."[69] The challenge is his view that sins of the flesh are not the only sources of evil; evil resides also in that lofty thing called the soul. Augustine's confession of stealing pears as a boy left Xiaobo with a deep impression:

> The problem wasn't that Augustine was hungry or gluttonous—his theft had no basis in the flesh. He tells us that his own home had better pears anyway. The transgression *came from inside the soul itself, where an element of adventure, an instinctual partiality for wrongdoing,* was lurking. . . . Human beings harbor a frightful instinct: when something is despicable, evil, dangerous, or frightful, they sometimes want all the more to cling to it, pursue it, crazily love it, and sacrifice anything to get it. Their consciences see such behavior as shameful, but they ignore the warnings of conscience and are carried away by the joy of misbehaving. This, if anything, is humanity's true original sin.[70]

The notion that human nature includes the impulse to break rules may have reminded Xiaobo of his smoking as a ten-year-old, when he gagged on those first puffs while loving the sense of disobedience. As a boy he himself had stolen grapes from a neighbor's backyard—not from hunger so much as avarice, plus that Augustinian "joy of misbehaving."[71] In 2006 he wrote a poem for his wife Liu Xia called "To St. Augustine," which includes the lines:

> . . . in my neighbor's pear garden
> I met you
> I spied a thieving child
> And knew the joy of risk[72]

Thomas Aquinas, in Xiaobo's view, fell far short of Augustine. Aquinas had introduced Aristotelian philosophy into the church, and his thought resembled Aristotle's: "If Aristotle was the major metaphysician of ancient Greece as well as its most mediocre philosopher, then Aquinas was the major metaphysician and most mediocre philosopher of the Middle Ages."[73]

Among Enlightenment thinkers, Rousseau was Xiaobo's favorite. Like Augustine, if not to the same extent, Rousseau could expose his sinful thoughts and actions to the world. His confessions were sometimes frivolous, crotchety, or even self-promoting, but still, on the whole, he deserved praise:

> Rousseau's spirit is an example of humanity's quest for adventure and for extremes. When he criticizes or opposes something he does so completely. When he praises or supports something he does it with passion, eloquence, and high idealism. He seems never to look back or to worry about how people see him. By nature he seeks powerful stimulation and pursues a turbulent life. He finds conflict and even destruction, where necessary, to be attractive.[74]

If this description departs somewhat from the historical Rousseau, it can be read in part as a self-portrait of Rousseau's avid reader, the thirty-three-year-old Xiaobo. In the late 1980s he was struggling not only with conflicts in the world but also with conflicts within himself. His interpretation of Immanuel Kant also reflects his inner struggle. He sees in Kant "a stiff exterior covering an agitated mind."[75] Kant's "antinomies" are valuable precisely because "they upend the principle of noncontradiction that Aristotelian logic had laid down and that later thinkers had continually held to be inviolable, and they demonstrate that accommodation of contradiction is built into human thought, where it is not a flaw but an advantage."[76] Xiaobo was becoming ready to accept the "split" nature of the human condition, or at least of himself, in that he had "no way to transcend even while wanting to." Whether gazing at the sky or toward an ideal realm, it seemed to him that he could only drop further down.

The Fog of Metaphysics appeared at an inopportune time. When it reached bookstores in March 1989, the democracy movement of that spring was about to erupt, and soon the great massacre of June 4 utterly annihilated the market prospects for any book by Liu Xiaobo. The rich context of "culture fever" was over. Su Xiaokang, author of *River Elegy*, said culture fever "has 'fevered' its way to malaria."[77] Government publicity declared Xiaobo to be "a black hand behind the counterrevolutionary riot" and an advocate of "all-out Westernization." Intellectually these were feeble tags, easy to refute, but intellectual accuracy was not the point. The political aim was to link Xiaobo with all-out Westernization and, in one swoop, to stigmatize both. The massacre left the Party so short on popular legitimacy that it could no longer appeal to social ideals like "serve the people" but had to reach for baser passions, like chauvinistic nationalism.

The decade of the 1980s is one of the more complex in recent Chinese intellectual history. Years later, scholars are still sorting it out. In 2009, Wang

Xuedian, an historian at Shandong University, published an article, "How Have the 1980s Been Interpreted?,"[78] asking whether the decade had seen a "new enlightenment." For people emerging from the "new ignorance" of the Cultural Revolution, Wang writes, all of the 1980s was enlightenment of a sort. But the decade can be further analyzed in three major phases: opposing the Cultural Revolution, opposing feudalism, and opposing tradition. In the third stage, which Wang dates as 1986–1988, he points to the crucial influence of Xiaobo's "antitraditionalism." Xiaobo's article "Sensibility, the Individual, and My Choice" and his book *Criticism of Choice* focused an entire debate and should have established him as a major figure in contemporary Chinese intellectual history. Writing under severe censorship, and thus needing to pretend a political distance from Xiaobo, Wang mixes his citation of Xiaobo's name with references to "the madman."

Xiaobo's respect for sensual and instinctual life may have originated during his adolescent years within the natural beauty around Big Boulder in Inner Mongolia. It appears to have matured during his college and graduate school years through his immersion in poetry, both as a poet himself and as a scholar of classical poetry, and in his almost compulsive attraction to philosophy both East and West. His first ideas about the value of freedom emerged from a deep humanism. He wrote in 1988, "To choose freedom is to choose pain and adventure. Freedom like Rousseau's or Nietzsche's requires not just intellectual valor but a gift of instinct that one is born with. A person who has theory or knowledge but lacks tenacity that comes from the body will find it very hard to reach levels of freedom like theirs."[79] Fifteen years later, Xiaobo had changed. He had begun writing tightly reasoned, dagger-like political essays, such rationality eplacing the sensual, nonrational tendencies in his earlier thinking. But the new emphasis was not so much a displacement of what had gone before as an outgrowth of it. The humanistic grounding remained deep in Xiaobo's character. In 2002 he wrote to a friend, "In matters of scholarship and intellectual creativity, I learned much humility during graduate school. Those towering minds in the humanities were monuments I knew I never could match. My hope for myself was only that I might absorb their discoveries into my own flesh and blood and do my best, on this troubled earth that we share, to live in truth and with dignity."[80] Zhuangzi can in some ways be viewed as his model in these regards. Zhuangzi puts special emphasis on the body, the senses, and the freedom of spirit that arises from sensate life. His phrase "eyes see the presence of Dao" means that Dao (the Way, the occult truth) requires the corroboration of the senses, and only the body can supply that. For Xiaobo, just as truth and the body depend on each other, so freedom is tested and measured by what happens to the body. In the 1980s, when he used phrases like "sensual individual" and "stark naked body," the words were not casual or, as it might seem, meretricious; they were seeds of what later became his willingness to sacrifice his body for political freedom. He was aware that when the state imprisons or kills a person, what it imprisons or kills is the body. And indeed, his ideas about freedom always shone most brightly when his body was in prison.

7

Gods and Demons Wrestle

After Professor Huang Yaomian died on September 3, 1987, Xiaobo and two other graduate students were reassigned to Professor Tong Qingbing, who until then had been deputy chair of their Ph.D. committees. Professor Tong announced two requirements for finishing their dissertations: one, that there be no gross errors; and two, that the writing be free of the modish academic jargon that always obscured more than it clarified. The dissertations would require final defense examinations, but there would be no "prospectus examinations" (where two or three designated faculty—plus anyone else who wanted to—could offer criticisms). Xiaobo felt relaxed about the whole matter. The contrast with his M.A. ordeal was great.

In fall 1987, Professor Tong was also running a writing workshop for talented young writers who had missed their education because of the Cultural Revolution. One of them was Mo Yan, who later became famous as the 2012 recipient of the Nobel Prize in Literature. After the workshop, Mo Yan enrolled for an M.A. with Professor Tong, so people later said that Tong had "hatched" two Nobel laureates. The professor made it clear at the time that of the two, Xiaobo was the more difficult to work with. He said neither he nor Professor Huang Yaomian had been able to "train" Xiaobo, but that was all right, because Xiaobo was neither trainable nor in need of training. "In both speech and writing, he frees himself from customary patterns," the professor wrote. "Were he to purge himself of what others call his extremism or one-sidedness, and walk steadily forward in conventional ways, he would lose all of his incisiveness, depth, and brilliance."[1]

The genesis of Xiaobo's Ph.D. dissertation was unconventional. One evening in early 1988 he went to see his classmate Sun Jin to borrow some milk powder. People on campus generally viewed Sun Jin as a genius. In the early 1980s, with only a junior high education, he had already been accepted as an apprentice researcher at the Jiangsu Academy of Social Sciences in Nanjing. When he arrived in Beijing for graduate study, he was already married and had an infant child, so he wanted to finish his degree and find a job as soon as possible. In barely a year and a half he had written a dissertation, a recondite work entitled "A Bright Spot in the Dark Ages: Theoretical Aesthetics in the European Middle Ages." Sun asked Professor Tong for permission to defend the dissertation earlier than normal, and after a bit of hesitation, the professor agreed.

Sun Jin's dissertation was finished—printed and ready to submit—when Xiaobo arrived that evening. Sun later recalled how Xiaobo's eyes gleamed when he saw the stack of paper. He asked if he could borrow it, got Sun's permission, and took it away. The next day he brought it back in high excitement, as if a wonderful new thought had occurred to him. He told Sun he had not slept all night and then blurted out, "Wait for me! We'll defend together!" Convinced that Xiaobo would indeed be fast, Sun Jin said, "Fine." Professor Tong agreed too.[2]

What had animated Xiaobo was the sudden realization that the six articles he had written two years earlier for *Appreciating Famous Works* were already close to a dissertation. With a bit more work he could be finished! Within about a month, he revised the essays, stitched them together in a different order, cited specific works and page numbers for all the quotations, and added footnotes. He named the result "Naked and Exposed, Moving Toward God." Before his oral defense in June, however, he changed the title to "Aesthetics and Human Freedom," the title of the third piece he had published in 1986. Now that essay was the dissertation's introduction. It analyzes ways aesthetics can transcend four kinds of limitation: objective law, rational dogma, selfish interest, and social pressure.

The introduction adds a section on how "aesthetic freedom transcends the divided nature of the individual person." This was necessary because Xiaobo's thinking about the individual and society had undergone an important shift. Always before he had thought of the two as opposed: society constricts the individual while the individual thirsts to break free. Now he saw society and its rules as beneficial human inventions that were necessary if individuals were to protect and develop themselves. The unpleasant truth, he now argued, is that human desires are unlimited and, if fully released, would lead to murder and mayhem. So restrictions are necessary and are self-imposed by society. Ultimately, the opposition between the individual and society is an opposition between two forces, both of which arise within the self. Since the human self is split in this way, the escape offered by aesthetics is only "a limited and temporary transcendence of the divided self."[3]

Xiaobo added a new chapter to the dissertation that he called "The Eternal Allure of Myth: On Aesthetics and the Subconscious." This may have been the seventh essay that he had originally planned for *Appreciating Famous Works* in 1986. At the end of the title of the sixth, which was about Freud, he had added a (I); the new piece, about Jung, seems to have been the (II) that was to have followed. The Freud essay explores the individual subconscious; its conclusion is that art, because it inquires into the evil in human nature, turns aesthetics into a kind of blasphemy. The Jung piece on the collective subconscious addresses "primal human nature" and uses the American film *Apocalypse Now*, which Xiaobo calls "the zenith of art that portrays war," as an illustration. The message of the film, he says, is that

> War is human nature. In war there is only kill or be killed. Any kind of moral teaching or charitable impulse is either hypocrisy or utopianism. The world is a giant battlefield; war is in its every corner at every moment. The will to possess, the readiness to attack, and the ability even to feel pleasure in inflicting suffering on others spring from inherited human nature. . . . Works like this are not for the weak to watch; they are for the strong to watch.[4]

A "Concluding Remarks" chapter was also new. It seemed, albeit abstractly, to augur the course of Xiaobo's own life to come. One section is called "The Heavy Burdens a Life Must Bear"; another is "Even if in Vain, One Must Stand and Fight."

As Xiaobo's interest in the murky depths of the human mind grew, he tended to stand at a middle position where he was vulnerable to powerful pulls from two opposing sides. When he thought about freedom, he considered its drawbacks: "Freedom is not the beautiful, poetic state that people often take it to be. It has its cruel side as well; it imposes huge costs on people who pursue it. The road to reach it is fraught with strife and storm. In humanity's current condition, freedom has ties on the one hand with independence, autonomy, and self-realization, and on the other with isolation, suffering, and risk."[5] Similarly, as he considered how the human spirit can soar, he remained aware of the body, whose weight inhibits soaring: "Nature has provided that human beings live in a space midway between Heaven and Hell. We are given two legs to accommodate the fact that we are forever bound to the surface of the earth. We are also given free spirits that seek to transcend and to aim for Heaven. The soaring of the spirit and the downward pull of the flesh provide human life with its unique tension and generate a pervasive sense of tragedy."[6]

Beginning in fall 1986, many people saw Xiaobo as a fanatic "dark horse" in pursuit of fame. There were good reasons for this perception, but it was shallow. Beneath the veneer, Xiaobo was in anguish. He was desperately looking for ways to rise above the world but—more than at any time before or after—felt the weight of his body, that earthbound frame that seemed to obey him only awkwardly. He was seeking great fame but disparaged the kind he already had. He had no patience for what he regarded as superficial fame.

He returned in part to conceptions of heroism that he had learned in school, although now the heroes were not revolutionary martyrs but tragic figures torn between their upward-gazing spirits and their downward-pulling flesh. He saw tragedy—conflict, division, mixed results, futility—as "intrinsic to the human condition"[7] and very much worth reflecting upon. Reminiscent of Camus, whom Xiaobo admired, he wrote:

> Human life is absurd. People die, the future is unknowable, and gray clouds loom and do not disperse. But can we flee? No. We are born with freedom but have no choice but to live with absurdity, death, and unknowability. We should expect no ultimate miracles: there are no endpoints, only process. Whether the results are disappointing or entirely in vain, every person, in isolation, tries as hard as possible to achieve self-creation even while knowing it cannot be done.[8]

Xiaobo's dissertation concludes with the observation that, since ultimate objectives are beyond reach, tragedy is the only reality. It follows that awareness of tragedy is a heightened form of awareness. "It allows . . . an appreciation of the breadth and the depth of life."[9]

Xiaobo's understanding of the scale of the human predicament led him to see that the West too was deep in crisis. When God was displaced from center stage in European history, people began to hold high the banners of science and democracy instead. But these two were hardly a panacea. Some of science went to making war, and war became ever more destructive. Even worse: "Science called for unification, rationalization, and mechanization. It turned the triangle, ruler, and calculator into masters of everything. Modern authoritarians have based their power in social structures formed by unified technological systems. But democracy is different. It calls for diversity, feelings, and life. The incompatibility of science and democracy is intrinsic."[10] Some people have viewed Xiaobo as advocating "all-out Westernization," and the Communist Party of China derided him for it, but his deep worries about the West are plain to see in his dissertation. They came primarily from his reading of Western thinkers who themselves were critical of the West. "Most modern people are enchanted with the myths of science and democracy," he writes, "and very few can see the impending crisis that the myths contain."[11] Those "very few," for Xiaobo, included Theodor Adorno and the Frankfurt School, whom Xiaobo singles out. He was also inspired by criticisms of the West that he found in Rousseau, Marx, Freud, Camus, and Sartre.

In short, Xiaobo's dissertation shows some profound shifts in his thinking that occurred between 1986 and 1988: from viewing aesthetics as a peach-blossom garden outside the world to seeing it as a means of access to the murky depths of human nature; from seeing freedom as a person's thrusts against society to seeing it as two sides of an intrinsic dilemma; and from celebration of the life of the mind to descent into a mood of despair. He was aware of these changes in himself and willing to be critical of them. A few months later, when the dissertation was published, he added an epilogue in which he confesses, "Some of the passages where I was trying to be poetic are overwrought . . . they reveal an arrogance that lacks self-awareness. Worse, they occasionally exude a traditional scholar-official flavor that is an all-too-perfect example of the kind of 'rotten national characteristic' I have often deplored."[12] His disparagement of "scholar-official flavor" shows his fear of backsliding in his critique of Confucian conservatism. An inner struggle was now in full swing. The rising, Shangri-La-seeking Liu Xiaobo was battling the falling, anguished Liu Xiaobo. Juxtaposed, they left him no peace.

When Xiaobo's dissertation was finished, the question of how to conduct the customary oral defense became a political headache for his adviser Professor Tong. Xiaobo was already under watchful eyes at both the State Education Commission and the Communist Party Committee of Beijing city, so a few "relevant comrades" would certainly be attending. Moreover, Professor Tong, who was standing in for the deceased Professor Huang Yaomian, had yet to receive formal credentials as a Ph.D. dissertation adviser. His challenge was considerable.

He asked Professor Xie Mian of the Chinese Department at Peking University, a well-known expert in the field of contemporary Chinese poetry, to join the dissertation defense as an outside examiner. Xie had sided with Xu Jingya in the controversy over misty poetry and for that reason had endured some withering attacks from political conservatives. But he accepted Tong's invitation.

In his written report, the ebullient Professor Xie heaped praise upon Xiaobo's language. It was "gorgeous" and "a pleasure to read." Its chapters contained well-written analyses of Zhuangzi, Tao Yuanming, Du Fu, Wang Guowei—and even Confucius, whom Xiaobo elsewhere had been roundly scolding in recent years. Professor Xie was delighted to find Xiaobo now "respectful and sincere" toward traditional Chinese culture. Xie's praise was obviously more than ceremonial politeness, because he delivered a very different verdict on Sun Jin's dissertation, for which he was also serving as an outside examiner. Sun's methodical and meticulously documented tome was "all but unreadable," in Xie's view. It was "torture."[13]

Professor Tong's next hurdle was to arrange an oral defense for Xiaobo's politically sensitive case. Who could chair it? This was a tricky question. In order to protect Xiaobo, the person should have good political credentials. But it could not be a conservative; it had to be a reform-minded person. And of course, it should be someone who knew Chinese literature. Professor Tong approached Professor Wang Yuanhua (1920–2008) of Shanghai Normal University, who met all three criteria. Wang had published on Liu Xie's *The Literary Mind and the Carving of Dragons* (fifth century CE), which Xiaobo had studied closely in researching his M.A. thesis. So he and Professor Wang shared a field. Wang also had wonderful political credentials. He had joined the Communist Party in 1938, which was very early. In 1955 he was silenced for his association with the purged literary critic Hu Feng and remained in disgrace for more than twenty years. But in 1983, after his political return, he was appointed Communist Party propaganda chief in Shanghai. In 1985, finding that government work did not suit him, he returned to teaching. He knew about Xiaobo's troubles with the Education Commission and was on his side, so he said yes. Even for him, though, the move involved a certain risk.

Next, a full examination committee needed to be formed. In addition to Professors Wang, Xie, and himself, Professor Tong secured commitments from Professor Jiang Peikun of the Literature Department of People's University in Beijing;[14] Professor Gao Ertai, the aesthetician from Sichuan;[15] the poet Niu Han, cofounder of *China* magazine;[16] and one more. That made seven, which was certainly enough. The Education Commission, though, was still worried about politics and insisted on adding four more who were known to be politically "reliable." No one before had heard of a committee of eleven, but there it was.

The defense, which was held on June 25, 1988, on the Beijing Normal campus, drew a much larger audience than anyone anticipated. Some students may have come because they knew the famous Professor Wang Yuanhua would be there and wanted to see what he looked like. Xiaobo's own fame drew people too, including foreign journalists. Reuters, Associated Press, and Agence France-Presse sent reporters. The State Education Commission sent two mid-level officials. Soon the small room that had been assigned for the event was overflowing, so they had to move to another, larger room. When that one proved too small, the meeting was moved again, this time to the eighth floor of the main instructional building,

FIGURE 7.1 At the Ph.D. defense, June 1988. Front row, left to right: Zhang Zichen, Wang Yuanhua, Jiang Peikun, Xie Mian, Deng Guoquan. Back row: Sun Jin, Tong Qingbing, Wu Yuanmai, Gao Ertai, Liu Xiaobo, Niu Han

Anonymous (with permission)

FIGURE 7.2 At the Ph.D. defense, June 1988

Anonymous (with permission)

which had an auditorium that could hold five or six hundred people. There the defense began, more than an hour behind schedule.[17]

Everything went smoothly. Xiaobo spoke clearly and fluently, with no sign of a stutter. Occasionally his performance waxed to where it resembled one of his audience-entrancing lectures. After Gao Ertai delivered his prepared remarks, he ad libbed two sentences: "Our cultural movement needs more Liu Xiaobos. The more of this kind of independent thinker we have, the better."[18]

During the intermission Professor Tong drafted a summary of the committee's evaluations and read it to the other eight examiners. One of the State Education Commission officials, who was listening in, intervened: "Isn't that evaluation too high?"

The underlying political threat was clear, and Professor Wang Yuanhua pushed back. "What do you mean too *high*? In my opinion, some of the ratings are too *low*! May I ask Professor Tong to raise them?"

The question put Tong in a bind. Listen to the distinguished professor or to the State Education Commission? He compromised. He raised one of the evaluations as Professor Wang wished, but not the other two. He lowered nothing.[19] In the end, the examiners unanimously recommended Xiaobo for the Ph.D., and ten days after that the school formally granted the degree.

Xiaobo naturally was pleased with the morning's result, but he stayed for the afternoon session where Sun Jin would defend his dissertation. That went well too. After the chief examiner announced that Sun had also passed unanimously, he invited questions or comments from the floor. Xiaobo raised his hand. The examiners chuckled but agreed to let him speak.

"Sun . . . Sun . . . Sun Jin . . ." Xiaobo began, his stutter returning. "Sun Jin's dissertation, only two . . . two people in all . . . all of China can understand. One is Sun . . . Sun Jin himself. The other is Liu . . . Liu Xiaobo, *me*!" He paused here, allowing time for the audience laughter and applause that he knew from past experience he could expect when he said such things.

Wang Yuanhua and Gao Ertai had traveled all the way from Shanghai and Sichuan, respectively, to attend Xiaobo's oral defense, and both men were staying at the Beijing Normal guest house. Taking advantage of this unusual opportunity, Wang invited Gao to his room for a chat, and Gao later summarized it in a penetrating essay.[20] The two talked about how China's "culture fever" in recent years compared with the May Fourth Movement of sixty years earlier, and some of what they said amounted to criticism of Xiaobo's views, which they had supported at his dissertation defense. Wang said: "Pursuing enlightenment is not just a question of courage. It matters which 'light' one is pursuing and how one goes about it . . . some people [meaning Xiaobo] seem to think that freedom entails revolt against rationality and logic. They miss the point that human freedom survives only when these regularities are respected." "Antilogical" and "the irrational" were indeed two of Xiaobo's favorite terms. But Gao Ertai held that Xiaobo's skepticism of rationality should be a point only of philosophy, not of politics:

> To hold that individual demands—including existential ones—are "rational," you need to acknowledge that conflicts among demands do occur and that there is a need to limit and balance them. Civilization needs a universality, even if it is conceived only at the metaphysical level. [Xiaobo's] opposition to "logic" and "rationality" means a denial of universality. To go that far is to undo the structure of civilization. It is to use the cause of political freedom in the outside world as a way to understand an internal search for meaning. It turns a political challenge to authoritarian rule into a philosophical challenge to nihilism.[21]

Wang's and Gao's insights applied not only to Xiaobo but also to young Chinese intellectuals generally. To be rebellious and yet advocate a rule-governed society was, and would remain, a challenge for them.

A few days after the oral defense, Xiaobo accompanied Wang Yuanhua to meet Wang Ruoshui, the former deputy editor of *People's Daily* whose contributions in the early stages of the post-Mao liberation of thought had been tremendous. Later, on the evening before Wang Yuanhua returned to Shanghai, he invited Gao Ertai, Wang Ruoshui, and their spouses to dinner to talk about establishing a new magazine. The "reform" press was turning increasingly toward entertainment, and they wanted to found a serious journal. They would call it *The New Enlightenment*. That phrase—new enlightenment—had been widely used in the 1980s. Now it would have a home.

But individuals—even ones with good political bona fides, like the two Wangs—could not just go out and found a magazine. They needed a state license, and such things belonged only to state work units. One way around this problem was to say that a periodical was in fact a series of books, and that is the route *The New Enlightenment* took. Formally published by the Hunan Education Press, it came out in four "books" between October 1988 and April 1989. The first one included an essay by Xiaobo, "Metaphysics and Chinese Culture." Later topics addressed by other writers—"The Choices We Face Today," "Reform and Crisis," "The Concept of Alienation," and others—eventually became too much for the authorities. The order to close the series down came from the very top.

Beijing Normal University Press published Xiaobo's *Aesthetics and Human Freedom* in September 1988, having produced it in almost record time. Xiaobo's insatiable mind had led him seamlessly from poetry to aesthetics to existential philosophy to the edge of politics. For him, aesthetics was still at the heart of everything; it was never "marginal." Fang Lizhi, the famous astrophysicist and democrat, tells of an unannounced visit that Xiaobo and another young scholar made to his home during the summer of 1988:

> The two of them studied literature, which was far from the physics that my wife Shuxian and I worked on, and they were both from China's northeast, so we didn't share any regional roots, either. That meant there wasn't much to talk about. Happily, my book *Philosophy as a Tool for Physics* had just come out, and some copies were resting on my shelf. Liu picked one up and started reading. His just-finished Ph.D. dissertation was on aesthetics, a branch of philosophy. Apparently he wasn't yet familiar with things like Kepler's *Harmonices Mundi* or Paul Dirac's famous dictum that "an equation that is not beautiful is sure to be wrong." Anyway, my book intrigued him. He dove into it and stopped chatting with us— his friend took over the chatting. Until then, I hadn't known he had a severe stutter. "So . . ." he said as he was leaving, "So . . . so for you . . . you physicists, philosophy is at best a tool; when it's useful, you grab it and use it; when you're finished, you toss it out. I . . . I'm going to have to cite this in my lectures." (Cite unfavorably, I surmised.) Then he picked a copy of the book and left. I await its return still.[22]

Xiaobo's haughtiness in the late 1980s was fed by the intellectual stardom he had acquired. People were constantly asking him for lectures and articles. Even editors at *Contemporary Cinema*, China's leading film magazine, asked him to write. He gave them a piece called "Philosophy and Reflection." It contained not one sentence that had anything to do with film, but the editors were glad to take it.

But Xiaobo's spectacular success in the spring and summer of 1988 still did not settle him internally, where conflicting pulls and pushes were only intensifying. In June 1988 he wrote a "self-appraisal" upon receiving the Ph.D.—just as he had earlier for his B.A. and his M.A. Those documents had been largely pro forma, though, and included boilerplate like "the Party and the people," whereas the one for the Ph.D. was seriously introspective. He wrote:

> I have a sense of awe about the mysteries of the universe and human life, and this stimulates my appetite to explore. I enjoy reading on my own and daydreaming. I feel a rush of enthusiasm and inspiration whenever I am at a lectern or a writing desk.

My natural inclination is to trust intuition wherever it leads. I value authenticity and do my best to be an authentic person.

I like soccer and swimming and am a sports fan.

I am suspicious of anything that is fixed. I am discontent with the way things are. I like innovation.

All of this makes it hard for me, whether in my behavior or my scholarship, to avoid going to extremes. This is a limitation, and I should try to get beyond it. I want to be a free person within the oceans of philosophy, art, and religion and will aim to stay free as well as I can, whatever my limitations. Even if I have to pay prices for trying things that turn out to be impossible, I am quite willing.

I am never content with myself. This motivates me.[23]

When he refers to himself as an authentic and free person, he clearly means to imply that he is different from others. When he mentions limitations like "going to extremes," he does not elaborate. Most people, in acknowledging their faults, seek to "correct" them, but Xiaobo speaks of "getting beyond" them—not correcting but outgrowing. Will he try to change old habits? He makes no promises.

The goals he sets for himself, such as to be "a free person within the oceans of philosophy, art, and religion," are goals for his inner world. He seems to be saying to the political world on the outside, "I'm going to be free in my own mind—what are you going to do about it?" He says nothing about acting freely in the outside world. But that very question would soon impinge on him with great force.

In September he published an article, "My View of Aesthetics," that pushed his self-appraisal deeper.[24] He apparently felt that the conclusions he reached at the end of his dissertation were insufficiently explicit and needed a comprehensive review. He writes: "Everyone says aesthetics is a kind of transcendence, and I myself have said this many times, unreflectively. But thinking about it again, aesthetics precisely disproves the possibility of transcendence." With this sentence he effectively disavows the whole first half of the dissertation he defended only three months before. The "possibility of transcendence" had been one of his basic tenets ever since he began working on literary theory. Now, it turned out, what he had transcended was his own former view.

For two years following his appearance as "dark horse" he had developed some intellectual themes: instinct versus civilization, repression and release, division and tragedy, modernity and tradition. In "My View of Aesthetics," he drew together eleven summary points:

1. The things that ethics and rationality identify as "evil" are precisely the focal points of aesthetics.

2. Human life cannot be subjected to any essential rules. It is an eternally unsatisfied field of forces, a great ocean filled with every sort of desire.

3. The progress of history is civilization's step-by-step compromise with instinct.

4. Human civilization is but a loincloth that aesthetics exposes and tears up.

5. Philosophy of life . . . returns people to the state of facing desire directly.

6. Human limitations make transcendence impossible.

7. The source of Nietzsche's spirit is despair about both himself and humanity generally, because people cannot become God.

8. Aesthetic feeling has layers. Sex in *The Golden Lotus* is an animal sense, in *Dream of the Red Chamber* a human sense, and in *Lady Chatterley's Lover* an untargeted sense. Eros that produces a religious feeling is probably the zenith of human experience.

9. Human nature harbors a destructive impulse. It will not allow the universe to be stable or humanity to enjoy a secure mooring.

10. The tragedy of humanity is inside humanity itself. To attribute tragedy to causes outside of humanity is only to obscure the truth of human existence.

11. To remake oneself means this: die once, be reborn once; collapse once, rebuild once.[25]

Lines such as these—filled with words like "unsatisfied," "destructive," "impossible," and "despair"—revealed his inner self. In the outside world he was leaping from pinnacle to pinnacle—Ph.D., fame, invitations—but an inner voice was pulling the other direction, making him feel that to exult in these things would to be to fail. "Success" as the world saw it was a frill. His hero Lu Xun had distinguished between "killing by attack" and "killing by praise." He had been attacked in recent times, but death by praise was the greater danger. He concludes "My View of Aesthetics" with a warning that "people who have been propelled to the top and are unaware of the abyss beneath their feet will end up only with broken selves, or even imaginary selves, whereas those who climb out of the ruins of disillusionment will possess the whole world."[26] The two inner Xiaobos were competing: one was tempted by the joys of celebrity while the other feared the loss of a clear head.

Meanwhile, Xiaobo's publications on aesthetics were offering powerful new perspectives. It mattered little "which Xiaobo" the writing was coming from or whether his allusive and sometimes aphoristic language was well understood. He was inducing people to think for themselves. In a Soviet-influenced society, where individuals are not supposed to be autonomous but only, in Lenin's famous phrase, "screws and cogs" in a machine, Xiaobo was leading his Chinese readers to look within themselves, to contemplate the dilemmas and crises of the human condition and adopt their own positions. To do that, and to hold that "human life cannot be subjected to any essential rules," was to obstruct the Leninist machine at the level of its most basic gears. In a sense it did not really matter what people's particular positions were; what mattered was that the contemplation, the power to decide, and responsibility for decisions made all were individual. Each person's consciousness belonged to each person, not to an abstraction in whose name an outside authority presumed to speak. Each person was the only one who could judge how acceptable the life one was presently living was. And in terms of action in the world, each person's own conscience was to be the guide. Havel had called this "living in truth." Nothing threatened authoritarianism more profoundly.

Xiaobo's claim of power over his own consciousness was an internal act, but it was also the indispensable foundation for the external action that would soon become so important to him. His explorations in aesthetics had led him to close familiarity with his inner self and had begun to forge a durable base of psychic and moral resources that would help him through trials to come.

Throughout these crucial months and all of the 1980s, Tao Li was Xiaobo's wife as well as his most loyal critic. In his epilogue to *Aesthetics and Human Freedom*, Xiaobo notes that "my wife once warned me, 'Xiaobo, some of your candor is concocted.' "[27] Six months later, when Xiaobo was publishing his fourth book, *Contemporary Chinese Politics and Chinese Intellectuals*, he again quoted Tao Li in the epilogue:

> Xiaobo, on the surface you seem to be a rebel in this society, but in fact you have a deep identification with it. The system takes you as an opponent, and in so doing it accommodates you, tolerates you, even flatters and encourages you. In a sense you are its oppositional ornament. Me, on the other hand? I'm invisible; I disdain even to demand anything of this society and don't lose sleep over how I am going to denounce it. It is I, not you, who am fundamentally incompatible with it. My profound indifference is something not even you can comprehend or "accommodate."[28]

Xiaobo accepted Tao Li's criticism. "When I first read these words they went right past me, but now, thinking back, I can see that they were uncannily accurate. I am grateful to my wife. She is not only my wife but also my most perceptive critic, and her criticisms leave me nowhere to hide." But their marital relationship was having problems. Cracks had been appearing in it for several years.

Their living conditions had never been ideal. After marriage they lived at first with Tao Li's parents, where they had no private space. Moreover, Xiaobo was in the same academic department as the parents, so he was never far beyond their gaze either at home or at work. He and Tao Li did locate a room elsewhere that they could have rented, but it was new and had no heating, which in Beijing winters would have been hard to endure. Both were later assigned rooms through their universities, but these were only single rooms, too cramped for their small family of three.

Tensions arose between Xiaobo and Tao Li's parents. The Taos were mild people whose experience of Mao Zedong's jarring political campaigns had taught them to be cautious above all else. Watching their feisty son-in-law run around saying what he thought caused them to fear for their daughter. They had seen too many cases where a single political misstep, even an inadvertent one, had ruined the life of a person or even a whole family. They tried to counsel Xiaobo, and he resented being counseled.

Tao Li felt stuck in the middle. She respected her parents' caution but also enjoyed her husband's irreverent spirit. He was like Sun Wukong, the monkey king in *Journey to the West*, jumping out of rock crevices to create ruckuses and wreak havoc.[29] Her own life stayed the course: rigorous, constant, going one step at a time. As Xiaobo's circles of friends and acquaintances expanded, she for the most part stayed out of them, and this added to their growing separateness, even though Xiaobo continued to idolize her. But as his fame grew, his focus shifted from her to himself.

The fissures in their relationship became a major crack when Xiaobo began liaisons with other women. Rumors spread and he did not deny them. In an essay in 1992, he called the late 1980s his "licentious days."[30] Friends have defended him by conjuring the context in Chinese cities. In the heady atmosphere of "culture fever," the sense of release from political and sexual fetters alike grew strong, and promiscuity was common, especially in elite circles in art and culture. A star like Xiaobo was especially susceptible. In any case, the problem was severe. Friends report that Xiaobo did not even introduce some of the girlfriends who followed him into and out of their homes. Asked to explain his behavior, Xiaobo would come up with high-sounding talk about "modernity." To the icy intelligence of Tao Li, the verbal fluff amounted to nothing. She was hurt.

She was also surprised. She had seen no sign in Xiaobo, ever since they had met in Big Boulder, that he might jump the rails like this. He had been loyal when she knew him in high school and college; why was this happening when he was over thirty years old? Six years earlier, when she was considering whether to marry him, she had thought about a few things that might go wrong, but not this. This struck her out of the blue.

A few years later, in the early 1990s, Xiaobo felt remorse. He wrote: "I was not a good husband. I was irresponsible. I helped around the house, but that was beside the point. All she asked from me was loyalty. . . . If I was disloyal, then I meant nothing but pain to her. I was truly a ghoul."[31] By 1988 the people around Xiaobo, including his professor Tong Qingbing, were aware of the problem. They heard the word "divorce." Old friends tried to help.

Tao Li was not the kind of person to complain to third parties. But Yang Jidong, Xiaobo's M.A. classmate, does remember her once saying, "From the height of happiness I've fallen to the depths of misery."[32] One way Tao Li sought to dull her pain was to plunge into scholarship. She wrote a book called *Murasaki Shikibu and Her* Tale of Genji. She finished in the late 1980s but couldn't publish it until 1994. In an epilogue dated August 1993, she writes, "This book should have appeared four years ago, but, for reasons that have nothing to do with it, was sidelined as it was about to go to print."[33] "Four years ago" was the point at which Xiaobo had just been sent to prison as a "black hand" behind the democracy movement of spring 1989. Postponement of publication was collateral damage. The book was written during the last months she and Xiaobo lived under one roof. Always reserved, she said little about that life but wrote in her epilogue, "others say their works are born of pen and ink; but this book comes right from my life."[34]

Tao Li had long suffered eye and heart trouble, and after Xiaobo was sent to prison in June 1989, her general health declined severely. He was still in prison in August 1990, when she asked him for a divorce, and her own condition, both physical and spiritual, was at least as bad. He left prison in 1991; she remained bedridden until August 1993.

What exactly had she meant by writing "this book comes right out of my life"? Her book on Genji is rigorous scholarship, the first full treatment of the tenth-century Japanese classic to appear in the Chinese scholarly world, and it won the prize for the best book of 1994 in the East Asian Division of China's Foreign Literature Association. Its distinctive contribution was to view the novel as an account of not just the capers of a dissolute young aristocrat but also the suffering and insult dealt to the women around him. Tao Li's sympathies clearly lie with the women. The fluent and detailed language of her book reflects confidence in her mastery of her subject. She shows how rich and powerful families sought influence over the imperial court, and one way they did this was to compete to get their daughters inside the palace, where they might produce offspring who would bind their families to the emperor. The constant offerings of women were one reason princes were so easily led astray.

It is also not hard to sense that Tao Li's experience with Xiaobo animates her analysis. Genji, in her telling, turns out to have a conscience. He is flirtatious, promiscuous, and treacherous, but he feels guilty and regretful and blames himself. When he recalls how he has brought anger and pain to the women he has loved, he feels not only regret but also anguish at how far his spirit has diverged from his flesh. As these two sides of him go their separate ways, pursuit of pleasure and generation of self-blame become interlocked. Tao Li presents the inner world of Genji's troubled psychology in fluent, almost casual language:

> With splendid sincerity he plucked his flowers of love and made of them a gorgeous world that could last in lingering memory. But with his other hand he crushed the same flowers. He loved Jiji—to lose her would be like losing his own life. But he also could not restrain his wandering eye for others, and time after time his unfaithful behavior hurt her. . . . He swore many times to become a better person, and most of his oaths were utterly sincere, but then, when he found himself again in an actual situation, they dissolved into nothing. . . . Genji was a god in one aspect and a devil in another, but always the same animal—vacillating and wobbling between his two sides.[35]

Genji here is Xiaobo. Tao Li's conclusion is that "Genji's romantic history had three stages: abandonment to desire, attempts at control, and depths of remorse."[36] But in Xiaobo's case, the remorse stage arrived too late to help Tao Li. His second wife, Liu Xia, was the main beneficiary.

Tao Li's depictions of the Genji-Xiaobo foibles are notable for their restraint. Her theme is not the iniquity of a prince but his loss of self-control. The coolness allows comprehension, precision, and remarkably, even a kind of tolerance. In the end it cuts more deeply and is harder to dismiss than vituperation could have been. Reaching the core of things, she finds a power that leaves a man nowhere to hide and no argument to make. From early in their relationship, Tao Li was able to see Xiaobo more clearly than he saw her. From their time in Boulder Village, her example had led Xiaobo from being a mischievous boy to a serious young scholar.

At more than one point in his life, Xiaobo's problem of self-control exhibited a pattern. He would try something, later see it as a mistake, resolve to stop, keep doing it despite his resolve, confess, blame himself severely, and then try again to stop. The problem was not that he couldn't see the difference between right and wrong or didn't care about it. He was ready to change his views when he got new information or insights and had an unusually strong inborn tendency to doubt himself, reflect on himself, and criticize himself—sometimes harshly.

Friends attest that even when he drifted furthest from his moorings he never had a negative word for Tao Li. No part of their split was her fault at all, in his view. He wanted to preserve the ideal image of her that he held in his mind, and he blamed only himself. In April 1989, when his book *The Fog of Metaphysics* was published, it featured a photo of him and Tao Li on the cover. That was unusual. When he chose words for the flyleaf of his book *Contemporary Chinese Politics and Chinese Intellectuals*, which was being published in Taiwan that same year, he wrote:

> This book is for my wife Tao Li!
> But still I know, it
> Cannot possibly repay all that she has done for me.[37]

One might read these words as hypocritical cover for a wayward husband. But they likely were a cry from the heart of a man wrestling with his own demons.

8

Out Into the World

On August 24, 1988, Xiaobo flew to Norway to be a visiting scholar at the University of Oslo. His reputation in China studies had spread overseas. The State Education Commission in China approved his trip, but only after Chinese Communist Party (CCP) officials at Beijing Normal had approached Xiaobo's teacher Tong Qingbing to extract a promise from him that Xiaobo would return to China afterward and not seek to remain abroad. Tong gave the promise, and the departure went smoothly. Xiaobo left carrying a case filled with translations of his favorite Western philosophers—Augustine, Rousseau, Kant, and others. This was his intellectual arsenal.

His host in Oslo was Bonnie McDougall, a famous Australian Sinologist and translator whose father had once been a leading member of the Communist Party of Australia. In 1958, when she was only seventeen years old, McDougall had left Sydney for Beijing to study Chinese. After she returned, she took B.A., M.A., and Ph.D. degrees at the University of Sydney and published a book on the introduction of Western literary theories during China's May Fourth years. Later she translated the poetry and a novel by the famous *Today* poet Bei Dao.[1] After teaching briefly at Harvard and then working for the Foreign Languages Press in Beijing, she joined the Department of East Asian Studies at the University of Oslo in 1986. That department had a fund that allowed young Chinese writers or scholars, one at a time, to visit Oslo. Xiaobo was the first.

Living in the outside world was new to Xiaobo, and Professor McDougall invited him to stay at her house. It was a generous gesture, but it put two strong-willed people under the same roof and led to some friction. Xiaobo complained to his friends that the professor set forth "residence regulations" such as how to use kitchen equipment, how to share in chores like washing dishes, and even what time to be home at night. Norwegians—and many Chinese too—might have taken this as normal, but for a wild horse like Xiaobo it was highly irritating.

An explosion erupted one evening. Xiaobo went visiting at the home of Mi Qiu, a Chinese artist, and was having a great time until he suddenly realized that he should call Professor McDougall to tell her he wouldn't be home that night. He would sleep at Mi Qiu's place. Xiaobo later wrote that McDougall reacted with anger, telling him to get into a taxi and come straight home. She would pay. McDougall, for her part, felt that Xiaobo was in Norway at her invitation and that therefore she was responsible for him. Xiaobo reluctantly obeyed and returned to her house, where a heated argument ensued. At one point, according to Xiaobo, McDougall asked, "How can you speak to me that way?! Do you want to stay here?" Xiaobo then exploded: "*Your* words are what make me feel like I never left China. It feels like you just had me packed into a suitcase and put on a plane, and now you are displaying me here as you like. I'm not a person but a material object."[2] According to Xiaobo, the professor then said, "You're the first person I've invited from China who has come here and then not taken advice."

The imbroglio shows, at a minimum, the silliness of the claims the Chinese government soon would be making that Xiaobo was a blind worshiper of the West who liked to prostrate himself before foreigners. Quite the opposite: he was quick to defend his dignity as a Chinese.

He later referred to the "shock" of encountering daily life in Europe. Before he arrived, his impressions of the West were ideal images that had come from books. Now, on the scene, the hurly-burly of ordinary life did not match. A second reason for the shock was that he had imagined that by living in a Western society he would in a sense become a temporary Westerner, and he was disappointed when people always viewed him as a "Chinese person."

> The biggest discovery of my trip outside China has been that foreigners view people as this or that nationality. My own habits in looking at other people have always been to assess the person, not the nationality or ethnicity. Everyone is equal, in my view. I know that many Chinese don't see things this way, and now I am learning that many Westerners don't, either. Some of them view other kinds of people as slaves. It's just lucky that the West's value systems and social systems prevent those would-be Western masters from doing whatever they want.[3]

This passage, which includes what might be the first use of the word "equality" in Xiaobo's writing, sprang from his new realization that *inequality* is a problem. Westerners were classifying him, unequally, as a Chinese. His sense of demotion might also have come in part from the sudden loss of the elevated position he had enjoyed in China. There he had been a well-known intellectual; here he was one housemate among others. In any case, he drew a lesson. He wrote that to be an authentic person "demands courage and intelligence—whether you are in China or the West."[4]

His appointment at University of Oslo was for six months, but he stayed only three. This happened in part because of a medical emergency for Bonnie McDougall. She had long had a mild eye ailment, but a sudden turn for the worse now led her ophthalmologist to see the danger of a permanent loss of eyesight and to recommend that she cease work immediately. The diagnosis later turned out to be mistaken, but in the moment there was no choice but to obey. McDougall asked Xiaobo if he could cut his stay short. Xiaobo was startled and even suspected that their conflict had played a part. Where could he go?

Soon after his arrival in Norway he had attended a conference on Chinese film and performing arts and there had met Elizabeth Wichmann-Walczak, a young professor from the University of Hawaii. They had gotten along well, and she now popped into his mind.

In 1979 Wichmann-Walczak had gone to the Chinese Department of Nanjing University to work on a Ph.D. dissertation on Peking opera. Wanting to learn to sing Peking opera herself, she had found her way into rehearsals at the Jiangsu Institute of Peking Opera and into practice rooms at the Jiangsu Provincial Drama School. Soon she was singing the part of the famous beauty Yang Guifei (CE 719–756). The Chinese press, punning on *yang*, which can mean "foreign," began touting the Foreign Guifei. In the early 1980s, after she revealed that she wanted to marry a Chinese artist, the Chinese government put her under house arrest

FIGURE 8.1   In Norway, fall 1988

Zhang Yu

for a week but in the end allowed it. Her spoken Chinese was remarkably good. The Chinese writer Gao Xingjian, winner of the Nobel Prize in Literature in 2000, was at the 1988 conference that she and Xiaobo attended. The three bonded, shared meals, and talked about many things.

Xiaobo asked Wichmann-Walczak if he might visit Hawaii. She answered quickly, and Xiaobo soon received an invitation from the Center of Chinese Studies of the School of Pacific and Asian Studies at the University of Hawaii at Manoa. His itinerary from Oslo to Hawaii involved a change of planes in Hong Kong, and he decided to plan the stop for five days so that he could take a look at the city. While in Norway, he had begun writing for the Hong Kong magazine *Emancipation Monthly* that specialized in politics and culture. In its November 1988 issue he published a piece called "Devil Incarnate Mao Zedong" that went far beyond anything that could have been published inside China.[5] Xiaobo notes that after 1978 Mao's surrogates, the "Gang of Four," could be called "all evil," but Mao himself could be no worse than "30 percent mistaken." From there he asks what, in the end, Mao's actual achievements were. His only real successes, in Xiaobo's view, were toward his personal goal of attaining absolute power inside China. He did not succeed in attaining international influence and failed completely to lead China into the modern world. He had merely perpetuated the dynastic cycle that left China in mire many times before. For Chinese writers to submit articles "outside the border" was highly risky at the time; it could bring severe punishment. To submit *this* kind of article was especially unheard of. Only writers living in exile, who had cut ties with the mainland, dared write in this way. The Hong Kong editor of *Emancipation Monthly*, Jin Zhong, loved Xiaobo's article and published it twice, in November 1988 and again in August 1989.

Xiaobo's five-day stopover in Hong Kong brought "a sudden tremble to my life." Soon after he left the city, he wrote: "During three months in Norway, I never felt the slightest desire to write travel notes or casual essays. But in only five days in Hong Kong, I was overwhelmed with a desire to write about how the city made me feel."[6] He felt a surge of energy that contradicted the oft-heard judgment that Hong Kong is "a cultural desert." He was full of hope that "Hong Kong will always be a free port in the world," because "All kinds of beautiful but inexpensive objects in the shops exude a charm that is hard to resist. Exchanging them has become people's primary mode of living. . . . Products from all over the world move in and out, and each import and export brings wealth to Hong Kong people."[7] He put these observations side by side with the dogmas in the Chinese state media, where "China" and "the West" are always opposed, the word "conflict" dominates, and China, grandly if artificially, "contends with" the modern West, refusing in key ways to change. It was exciting that Hong Kong was a *Chinese* place but with a very different way to be Chinese: "There

FIGURE 8.2 In Hong Kong, November 1988

Jin Zhong

can be no doubt that commodification is an important feature of the modern world. . . . The free exchange of commodities opens every corner of the world to every other. Commodity exchange, the mechanization of production, and the democratization of politics are interlocking components of modern culture."[8] Hong Kong popular culture—television drama, film, and song—also enchanted Xiaobo.[9]

These thoughts about Hong Kong, China, and modernity were in Xiaobo's mind on November 27, 1988, when Jin Zhong, with audio and video equipment at the ready, asked him to do an interview that he had promised. Having stifled himself for three months in Oslo, Xiaobo felt like stirring things up again now that he was back in a Chinese-speaking environment. He decided to be his usual provocative self. So he bemoaned the shallow understanding of China that he found among Sinologists in northern Europe. He mercilessly criticized astrophysicist Fang Lizhi and writer Su Xiaokang, even though their political views much resembled his own. (After the June Fourth massacre, official denunciations tied Fang, Su, and Xiaobo together. Fang and Su later both forgave Xiaobo for the interview language.) But his most famous line was one about China perhaps needing "three hundred years of colonization" in order to get out of its traditions. It appeared in this context:

JIN ZHONG: What in your view is the developmental stage of today's Chinese society?

XIAOBO: It has yet to emerge from agricultural society.

JZ: Does China need to go through the capitalist stage [before, in Marxist theory, it can enter socialism]?

XB: Yes, it must.

JZ: So you mean that China is still living by modes of agricultural society?

XB: Yes. But it's adjusting the ways of its dictatorship in response to crises.

JZ: Can China today remold itself fundamentally?

XB: No. Even if one or two rulers were to resolve sincerely to do this, it wouldn't
work. The conditions aren't ripe yet.

JZ: Then what conditions would allow a true historic transformation in
China?

XB: Three hundred years of colonization. Hong Kong took a hundred years of
colonizing to get where it is today, so the mainland, huge as it is, would need
three hundred to reach Hong Kong's level. I don't even know if three hundred would be enough.

JZ: That's pretty thick "treason," isn't it?

XB: Let me quote Karl Marx, in *The Communist Manifesto*: "The workers have
no country. We cannot take from them what they have not got." I'm not
thinking in terms of "loving" or "betraying" any particular country. If you
want to call me a traitor, go ahead! I'm digging up the tombs of the ances-
tors? Fine! I'm proud of it!

JZ: You're saying China should follow Hong Kong's example?

XB: History can't give China that option. The colonial age is gone. There's no
one now ready to take up the burden of transforming China.[10]

The Chinese government has repeatedly taken that "three hundred years of
colonization" line out of context and used it to stoke Chinese nationalism and
to tag Xiaobo as a traitor. Many people in mainland China have known nothing
about Liu Xiaobo except for that one sentence. The Deng regime had come to
realize in the 1980s that patriotism was the only ideological card left to it to play.
Mao's Great Leap Forward and Cultural Revolution had sapped socialist ideals
of whatever appeal they originally had had, so patriotism now needed to be played
to the hilt. No distinction was allowed between loving the country and loving
the Party. Patriotism demanded that one love both, and disobedience was a third
rail; any touch of "treason" was disastrous.

Xiaobo was aware of all of this when he gave his interview to Jin Zhong. But
when had he ever shied away from controversy or fear of angering someone? During his "dark horse" days he had advocated making points by going to extremes.
This interview came on the cusp of a transition from cultural critic to political
critic, and he had yet to appreciate that a political critic must be more careful about

anticipating how people will interpret one's words. In a 2007 article, he explained why he had declined several times to retract the statement:

> I am not going to make excuses for an ill-considered line that I tossed out in an interview in order to get people to think—and especially not when rabid nationalism is running wild as it is in China today. That sentence is nothing but an extreme version of a view that I continue to hold today: China's modernization will require an extended process of Westernization before it can be realized. So never mind the denunciations of the state or the rain of spittle from angry young nationalists; every time I think of that interview I always feel grateful for the opportunity it gave me.[11]

Moreover, and more importantly, there was some rich intellectual background to his statement. Xiaobo's earliest understandings of colonialism had come from reading Karl Marx in his junior high years at Boulder Village in Inner Mongolia. Volume 2 of a four-volume edition of *Selected Works of Marx and Engels* that he had avidly consumed opens with *The Communist Manifesto*, which he more or less memorized. The same volume ends with Marx's 1853 writings on India, and Xiaobo could not have missed them. In one of those pieces Marx writes about how the British ordered that railroads be built in India and how this helped to tie countless tiny villages together. The web of railroads promoted exchange of commodities that brought the villages into the mainstream economy. In his essay about commodity exchange in Hong Kong, Xiaobo uses language almost identical to Marx's. Marx writes of it connecting "every village" of India, Xiaobo of it connecting "every corner" of Hong Kong.[12]

Marx denounces the predatory capitalism that lies behind colonialism, and Xiaobo, in an article written around the same time as his Jin Zhong interview, writes of how the oppressive and exploitative elements in colonialism made a mockery of "equality" and caused "humankind to pay a huge price."[13] But Marx's articles on India also go into considerable detail about the "undignified, stagnatory, and vegetative life" in Indian villages, where caste and superstition rule and "murder itself [is] a religious rite." Marx continues: "The question is, can mankind fulfill its destiny without a fundamental revolution in the social state of Asia? If not, whatever may have been the crimes of England, she was the unconscious tool of history in bringing about that revolution."[14] A few days later, in another piece, Marx writes: "England has to fulfill a double mission in India: one destructive, the other regenerating the annihilation of old Asiatic society, and then laying the material foundations of Western society in Asia."[15] In short, Marx on India and Xiaobo on China are not very far apart. Xiaobo does not cite Marx directly, and it is impossible to say whether he was aware of borrowing from him or simply drawing on language and concepts stored in his prodigious memory after rereading all of Marx during his M.A. years. It is also possible, of course, that no borrowing was involved, simply coincidence. But in any case, the similarity creates a stark dilemma for the Chinese Communist Party's Propaganda Department: Is Marx also wrong? Or Xiaobo not wrong after all?

One month after his interview with Jin Zhong, Xiaobo published an article, "The Tragedy of Enlightenment," in which he raises the topic of colonialism again and pushes his analysis further. Despite its violence and inequality, colonization:

> did advance the world toward modernization. It opened up one after another area that formerly had been closed off and established new commodity markets and cultural markets. It also made parts of the world no longer as separate and isolated from other places as they had been. Even more important, it brought to the whole world concepts like human rights, equality, freedom, and democracy that formerly had belonged only to Westerners.... Without colonization it is hard to see globalization and internationalization arriving as soon as they did. In these respects, the prices paid for colonization must be weighed against the prices of even longer-lived despotism and dictatorship.[16]

Leaving Hong Kong, Xiaobo proceeded to Hawaii, where Elizabeth Wichmann-Walczak was the welcoming host that she had promised to be. Chinese government authorities had approved Xiaobo's visit to Oslo, but not to Hawaii or to New York, where he went next. When he returned to China they blamed him for the unauthorized parts of his travel.[17]

Xiaobo was happy in Hawaii. He enjoyed the lovely weather, the natural scenery, the banyan trees, and the laid-back lifestyle. He was fascinated to learn about Mormon missionaries after meeting a few of them there. The lush environment seemed to elicit a surge in his creative inspirations. He wrote to his friend Geremie Barmé, who was in Beijing, "I even surprise myself... I'm writing at an almost terrifying rate; sometimes I get scared that it's all a shoddy mess."[18] He was writing a series of articles for the Hong Kong magazine *Contending* and later brought them together in his book *Contemporary Chinese Politics and Chinese Intellectuals*.[19]

This book was an expansion of his "dark horse" critique of Chinese intellectuals since 1949: "[They] have been a component of the dictatorship. They not only produce cultural tools that support dictatorial rule; they offer their persons to the bureaucracy as human resources. Their main political role has been to help the emperor do evil."[20] More specifically, he contends that Chinese intellectuals since "reform and opening" in 1978 have cowered behind "know-nothing loyalty" and been far too gentle in describing the Cultural Revolution. He notes their claims about doing "critical reflection on the Cultural Revolution" (a cliché in which "reflection on" actually means "rejection of") and asks if that is what China really needs. The Cultural Revolution's "spirit of rebellion," in his contrarian view, might be precisely what today's antidictatorial struggle needs most.

The book confronts Liu Binyan, the investigative journalist whose well-documented exposés of government wrongdoing had brought him a towering reputation among readers in the 1980s. Liu had joined the communist underground in his home province of Heilongjiang in 1943 and had learned the techniques of politically engaged reporting from the Soviet writer Valentin Ovechkin in the early 1950s. After he wrote two stories in 1956 exposing corruption and censorship in the New China, Mao Zedong personally named him a rightist in 1957, and for two decades afterward he lived in labor camps and was barred from publishing. His reputation in the 1980s grew from pieces that he published after 1978, but one of these, "A Second Kind of Loyalty" (1986), drew criticism from writers a generation his junior, Xiaobo chief among them. The story tells of two young men who, in separate cases, are so devoted to building the socialist motherland that they take the extraordinary step of writing letters to Mao Zedong telling him that he has made mistakes. One didn't do that to Mao. The young idealists are persecuted and imprisoned but continue to insist that what they did was right. They had been protecting truth, honesty, and freedom. They had been loyal to ideals, which was something higher than loyalty to any human being. Liu Binyan saw himself as exemplifying this pattern. Mao had gone wrong, and the post-Mao leaders were going wrong too. But that did not mean the ideals of socialism that he had embraced in the 1940s were wrong. He admired the phrase "socialism with a human face" that Alexander Dubcek, Communist Party chair of Czechoslovakia in 1968, had announced during the "Prague Spring" of that year. Whatever his kind of loyalty, Liu Binyan was stripped of his Communist Party membership by Deng Xiaoping in 1987. By the time Xiaobo was writing about him, he was a Nieman Fellow at Harvard University, and after denouncing the June Fourth massacre in 1989, had to live in exile until he died in 2005.

In Xiaobo's view, the theme of "A Second Kind of Loyalty" was "ignorant in the extreme.... Such loyalty is built on a master-slave relationship; it can be loyalty only to authoritarianism and can only intensify the master-slave relationship."[21] A few weeks later, when Xiaobo and Liu Binyan met in New York,

Xiaobo's impulse to criticize the "second kind of loyalty" only grew stronger. He and some friends went so far as to plan a conference on "the Liu Binyan phenomenon" for the coming June. Soon the events of spring 1989 overtook them, though, and it never happened.

Xiaobo eventually outgrew the kinds of attack he had directed at Liu Binyan and others in *Contemporary Chinese Politics and Chinese Intellectuals*, though the analysis was still there. When Liu Binyan died in New Jersey in December 2005, Xiaobo wrote from Beijing a long and very warm tribute, bemoaning the exile that had been forced upon him during the last sixteen years of his life and encouraging friends to join a committee that was planning a memorial. By then Xiaobo had become more critical of himself. In a remarkable passage that he wrote upon receiving the Outstanding Democracy Activist Award in San Francisco in 2003, he recounted:

> Looking back carefully, I realize that my entire youth was spent in a cultural desert and that my early writings had all been nurtured in hatred, violence, and arrogance—or, alternatively, in lies, cynicism, and loutish sarcasm. These poisons of "Party culture" had been soaked into several generations of Chinese and into me too. Even in the liberal tides of the 1980s, I had not been able to purge myself of them entirely. I knew at the time that Mao-style thinking and Cultural Revolution-style language had become ingrained in me, and my goal had been to transform myself from the bone marrow out. Ha! Easier said than done. It may take me a lifetime to rid myself of the poison.[22]

In any case, *Contemporary Chinese Politics and Chinese Intellectuals* marked an important turning point in Xiaobo's intellectual life. He no longer used the special vocabulary with which he had discussed Nietzsche, Sartre, and Freud, and he turned from fields like aesthetics, human consciousness, and existential philosophy to topics like authoritarianism, law, and Communist Party rule. His longstanding interests in "instinct versus civilization" and "the individual versus society" receded as he now found that "no matter what I begin to analyze, the topic seems, one way or another, to migrate toward questions of official ideology and authoritarian political systems."[23]

Observation of daily life outside China brought new dimensions to his thinking about democracy. He was struck by the ways people treated one another and felt that their habits were connected to the political systems they lived under:

> Living outside China for eight months has changed me. It has let me understand that democracy is not just principles or the features of a system; it is not just

choice of system, or a separation of powers, or freedom of the press. It is also ways of behaving both in public affairs and in daily life personal relations. Democracy is not firm and settled until democratic principles have seeped into daily life— until, in any situation, a person knows how to preserve his or her own rights as well as to respect the rights of others. Without that condition, democracy is abstract and might collapse at a simple touch.[24]

His impressions were confirmed when he went back to China a few weeks later. Even in the democracy movement he joined, he found that people were "overbearing" in addressing each other. They "did not respect the other party, interrupted at will, and showed strong desires to vanquish or destroy the aims of others."[25] He realized that he himself had sometimes behaved this way.

If democratic systems foster civilized behavior in their citizens, it is an error, he held, to expect the reverse. Democratic systems are not good because the politicians who inhabit them are good people. They are good because of the systems of rules within which politicians have to work. To rely on the moral quality of leaders is classic Confucian theory, and many people in contemporary China, including elite intellectuals, tended to accept such a premise unreflectively. That, for Xiaobo, was a mistake. In *Contemporary Chinese Politics and Chinese Intellectuals* he reviews examples of unconstrained power struggles in Chinese history, including ones between Mao Zedong and his rivals in recent Chinese history, and concludes that "the real power struggle" that should concern us is "the competition between two kinds of system. In this kind of struggle, moral character cannot make a difference in a fundamental sense. A democratic system replacing a dictatorship is not a matter of an enlightened ruler taking over from a muddle-headed tyrant; it is rule of law replacing rule by humans and separation of powers replacing autocracy."[26] Xiaobo no longer emphasized the virtues of instinct in producing sincere expression. In order to avoid moral and political rot in government (he cited Nixon and Watergate), "the key is to have governing rules that are established by a legal authority that stands above all the contending political forces."[27]

Xiaobo's epiphany about rule of law led him to want to bridle himself. His impulses to be a wild horse or a bouncing Sun Wukong would now have to observe the principle that no one is outside the law. This might seem simple enough, he thought, but to a person who grows up under inequality enforced by arbitrary power it is somehow not an easy lesson to learn and, once grasped, becomes hugely important in one's self-education. Xiaobo writes: "The relations among people in [democratic] society, especially the crucial relations of economics and politics, cannot happen without the mediation of law. Law has nothing to say about power, rank, sentiment, face, or morality; it is a mechanism that applies to everyone. The rules of the game in democracy are both open and universal; they eliminate the space in which autocrats can get their ways using hidden rules."[28] Xiaobo's first references to Communist China as "autocratic" (*zhuanzhi*) appear in *Contemporary Chinese Politics and Chinese Intellectuals,* as do his first comparative analyses of "democratic systems" and "autocratic systems" and his first assertions that democratic systems are superior. When he left China in 1988 he had not yet arrived at these views.

Chinese intellectuals, he now thought, should be "an independent force in society." Their social position, their values, and their roles must all be independent,[29] which means, above all, separate from the autocratic political system. Intellectuals must not be vassals to the powerful. Anticipating the views of his friends who twenty years later wrote the manifesto for democracy called Charter 08, he wrote that intellectuals should "put human rights, equality, freedom, and other concepts of democracy in the place of imperial authority, hierarchy, autocracy, and authoritarian concepts; put rule of law in place of rule by man; put free markets in place of state ownership and planned economy; and let diversity in culture replace exclusive reverence for Marxism-Leninism."[30]

Then, in a turnaround that resembles the epilogue he wrote for his Ph.D. thesis and shows again his tough-minded habit of continually reexamining himself, Xiaobo adds an epilogue to *Contemporary Chinese Politics* in which he seems to undermine most of what he wrote in the book. He refers to his earlier "arrogance." He asks himself to stop, take stock, and rethink certain things from the ground up. He finds his just-finished book too Sinocentric. It "uses Western culture to try to shake the Chinese people awake, but that's not the same thing as taking a square look at the West itself. . . . If we stand at a higher point and worry about the fate of the world and all of humankind, then [this book] might not be worth a penny."[31] Xiaobo realizes that he needs to do critical reflection on the West, not just on China. This means returning to beginnings and thinking anew. He starts the rethinking, he says, with very little to go on. He can see only as much sky as the proverbial frog at the bottom of the well. He worries, moreover, that his upholding of the West in the past has been, in an indirect way, self-serving:

> Prettifying the West in an exaggerated way was just a way of prettifying myself. It was as if Western civilization were not only a shining model for China but also the ultimate destination for the whole of humankind—and I was relying on this illusory idealism in order to cast myself in the role of savior. I have said many times that I loathe "saviors." But by that I always meant other people; when

it came to me, I began, intentionally or not, to slip into that despicable savior pose.[32]

Few people can criticize themselves as mercilessly as this. Xiaobo's ability to do so may have come in part from the practice he had in writing self-criticisms as a naughty schoolboy. But it was more than that; it was a fundamental feature of his character.

He was also afraid that he lacked the "higher view" that would let him look upon humankind as a whole. He thought this was a problem not only for himself but also for his idol Lu Xun, who was always preoccupied with worldly worries. In the late 1920s Lu Xun had wanted to reach toward transcendent values but largely failed, so he went back to the squalor of the world and settled for alliance with the Communist Party, at the time China's best chance for a "savior." Xiaobo vowed not to make the same mistake. He would not look to saviors but move forward thinking for himself, even if it meant constantly being on the brink of peril. "There's no road back for me," he wrote. "I'll either leap across the chasm or pulverize my body with the try. If you want freedom, that's what you face."[33] Some people have observed that this tendency to see challenges as all-or-nothing risks and to be willing, if necessary, to go all in was another distinctive trait in Xiaobo's character.

During his time in Hawaii, Xiaobo was also trying to rethink Marxism from the ground up.[34] He had been conditioned in youth to accept Marxism as absolute truth, but what should he think of it now? He had originally been attracted to the spirited attitude in its critique of capitalism, but in practice in China it had become more like a tool in the hands of Eastern autocracy. Marxism's monistic thought structure, projection of an egalitarian utopia, and advocacy of violent revolution reinforced certain deep currents in popular Chinese thought and left Marxism no longer critical but in an important sense conservative. He wrote that "Eastern peoples, in their benighted backwardness, do not understand that social progress can emerge by means that are entirely peaceful and democratic. Only violent revolution [such as one finds in Marx] makes sense to them."[35] This is one of the earliest passages in which Xiaobo mentions democratization through peaceful means. Fifteen years later it would become one of his most prominent themes.

The term of Xiaobo's visit to Hawaii ended in February 1989. Where should he go next? He chose New York because he had been invited to give talks at some universities on the American East Coast—Cornell, Harvard, and Columbia— and because he knew some people in New York. From times in China he knew the poet Huang Beiling, who wrote under the pen name Bei Ling. Xiaobo made Bei Ling's apartment in Flushing his first destination, and Bei Ling later wrote the following about his arrival:

> It was Xiaobo, my good friend Xiaobo. What a character! Constantly fidgeting, walking around the room, a cigarette hanging from his lips. He was rolling a little ball of clay between his fingers, wearing a look of blank innocence on his face and asking the simplest of questions about daily life. It occurred to me that he might be spoofing me. My suspicions must have caused some twitches on my face, and these might have shown him that his little act was working. He kept stuttering questions at me. I tried to interrupt and to infuse some of my gloom into the room. I thought too of perhaps changing the subject to a topic in metaphysics that would set him off into a soliloquy that at least would be more interesting. If that happened, though, there might have been no end to it. The role of listener to a Xiaobo soliloquy is to follow where his mind wanders, one moment to Kant, the next to Camus, the next wherever. He had repeated to me more than once the famous line in Camus' *The Myth of Sisyphus*, "I have never seen anyone die for the ontological argument."[36]

For several nights after Xiaobo arrived, he and Bei Ling stayed up all night talking. The following days, in the afternoons, they went to Greenwich Village, the East Village, or Little Italy and wandered around until late at night. They sometimes stopped at Ai Weiwei's basement apartment on Fourth Street between Second and Third Avenues to see how Weiwei was doing with his current business, reselling small appliances and cameras that he had picked up from street vendors. Bei Ling remembers that Xiaobo bought a black leather jacket for three hundred U.S. dollars and then wore it every day. In most of his photos from New York he is wearing that jacket.

The two went to see the poet Jiang He, whose poems had appeared in *Today* in 1978 during the Democracy Wall ferment. Jiang had been in the United States less than a year and was applying for political asylum. The three—Jiang, Bei Ling, and Xiaobo—spent an entire night in conversation, the upshots of which were that they would found a Chinese literary magazine together and—all three—apply for political asylum. They went to see a lawyer about asylum, but, walking down the street afterward, Xiaobo suddenly turned sour on the idea and abandoned it.[37] This pattern of behavior recurred several times during those years: he would be curious about something, get excited, and perhaps try it, but then, listening to the voices deepest inside himself, back off. There were still two

Xiaobos in dialogue, and sometimes conflict: an extroverted and sometimes playful one and an introverted, deeply serious one.

In his epilogue to *Contemporary Chinese Politics and Chinese Intellectuals,* Xiaobo thanks "my friend Jon Solomon for discussing this book with me."[38] Solomon was a graduate student at Cornell who had met Xiaobo in Beijing in 1986. His mother, an artist, had a loft in New York, and Xiaobo lived there for a number of days while he finished the book.

Yan Li, a Chinese poet and painter, brought Xiaobo to the Metropolitan Museum of Art, and that experience seems to have jolted him profoundly. For years he had given lectures on aesthetics and "the power of perception," but not until he was face to face with the tremendous force of great paintings did he feel he had truly understood creativity. He claimed that his earlier lectures, by comparison, were "utterly meaningless":

> Looking at those masterworks, I was struck with how superficial my thinking was, and how atrophied my vitality, after so many years of being cooped up in a benighted environment of what was, essentially, a cultural desert. Eyes kept too long in the darkness do not easily adapt to dazzling sunlight when it suddenly pours through a window. How could I, all of a sudden, face my own situation squarely, much less engage in dialogue with world-class intellects?[39]

Bei Ling brought Xiaobo to Queens to meet Hu Ping, a champion of free speech in China in the late 1970s who had been living in exile since 1987. Hu played an important role in Xiaobo's transition from cultural critic to political critic, starting in China and continuing in New York.

A brilliant political philosopher, Hu Ping graduated from high school in 1966 and was sent to the countryside during the Cultural Revolution. He missed college but was able to get into a Ph.D. program at Peking University on the strength of his high school education and his own independent reading. During Beijing's Democracy Wall interlude in 1978 he was editor of the unofficial magazine *Fertile Earth,* for which he wrote a stunning, and later very famous, essay, "On Freedom of Speech." That essay and Wei Jingsheng's "The Fifth Modernization," which was also published at Democracy Wall, were the first appeals for democracy to appear openly in China since 1949. Xiaobo, who was in college in Changchun when Hu's essay appeared, had been entranced by its words almost as if they were poetry. In his notebook he wrote: "Having the right to speak is not to have everything, but losing the right to speak does lead to the loss of everything."[40] In 1980, when a door was briefly opened to allow people who had not been nominated by the Communist Party to run for local representative positions, Hu Ping competed to represent Beijing's Haidian district and won a five-year term. In 1987 he went to study politics at Harvard University but dropped out in order to devote himself full time to the overseas Chinese democracy movement. In response the Chinese government canceled his passport, and that meant permanent exile. By the time he and Xiaobo met in New York in 1989, Xiaobo was already looking up to him as a veteran political activist—an "enlightener," in Xiaobo's words. Later he wrote that Hu was "one of a tiny minority of early prophets in the Chinese movement for freedom, and I was just one of the many, many followers."[41]

In 1983, before Hu Ping left China, a group of Chinese graduate students and visiting scholars in the United States founded a group called the Alliance for Chinese Democracy and began publishing a magazine called *China Spring*. (The first director of the alliance, Wang Bingzhang, was abducted by CCP agents in Vietnam in 2002, taken illegally to China, and put in prison, where he remains, serving a life term on false charges of espionage and terrorism.) Beginning in 1988, Hu Ping became the second director of the Alliance for Chinese Democracy and second editor of *China Spring*. The Chinese government viewed both as "hostile foreign organizations," and visitors from China, even ones who were critical of the government, usually kept their distance, at least in public. Xiaobo was well aware of the risks of publishing in *China Spring* but before he left Hawaii had already decided to send his article "The Tragedy of Enlightenment" to Hu Ping. He compromised slightly by submitting it under the pen name "Dark Horse." This was his first use of a pseudonym. He allowed it be an open secret among his friends.

Hu Ping's political experience and sharp analytical mind attracted Xiaobo immensely—so much, in fact, that he eventually decided to gather up his things and move into Hu's apartment. When propaganda workers in Beijing learned of this, they came out with a headline—"Liu Crashes at Hu's Place"—that they used in several contexts to support their larger argument that the entire overseas democracy movement sprang from a plot hatched by hostile overseas forces. The Alliance for Chinese Democracy was the hub.[42]

In fact, Xiaobo was not very interested in the alliance. But *China Spring* appealed to him greatly, and he asked Hu Ping if he could volunteer. Hu Ping was delighted, so for about two weeks Xiaobo went to the magazine office every day, mainly doing solicitation of manuscripts on the phone. He liked it so much that he suggested he himself take over as chief editor and *China Spring* be formally separated from the Alliance for Democracy so that the editorship would not be subject to change every time a director of the alliance changed. Hu Ping was amenable but said the new arrangements would require a process; they could not just be made on Hu Ping's say-so. But before the proposals could be properly considered, the democracy movement in Beijing heated up and wrote a different script for Xiaobo's future.[43]

Even before it arrived, the year 1989 carried a sense of foreboding in China. Important anniversaries were approaching. It would be forty years since the founding of the People's Republic, seventy years from "China's enlightenment" in the May Fourth Movement, and two hundred years since the great French Revolution, which loomed large in part because it had figured so prominently in the writings of Marx. "History" in China, a country so rich in it, can claim the right to reveal or to augur things, somewhat the way "religion" does in Western cultures. In the name of history one might allow oneself to say things usually kept unsaid. Entering 1989, the political atmosphere in Beijing was different from the usual.

On January 6, Fang Lizhi, the famous astrophysicist, sent an open letter to Deng Xiaoping calling for a general amnesty for prisoners and specifically for the release of Wei Jingsheng and other political prisoners. The letter of course could not be published inside China, but it circulated widely in the international press and leaked back into China, where it sparked further activity.

On February 13, thirty-three prominent writers, poets, scholars, and others in cultural fields released a statement that echoed Fang Lizhi in calling for an amnesty for Wei Jingsheng and others. Bing Xin, a writer from the May Fourth era, then eighty-eight years old, signed, as did Wu Zuguang, seventy-one, a playwright whose fame dated from China's war years with Japan. There were many from the "reform and opening" years of the 1980s: fiction writers Zhang Jie and Zong Pu, poet Bei Dao, Peking University professors Tang Yijie and Yue Daiyun, and the distinguished historian Li Zehou, with whom Xiaobo had recently locked horns. Two additional declarations followed this one, signed by scientists and by social scientists respectively. Nothing like this had happened since 1949.

The thirty-third signature on the writers' petition was that of Chen Jun, a graduate of the philosophy department at Fudan University in Shanghai. Chen was not as well known as the other thirty-two, but it was he and Bei Dao who did the work of going around to gather signatures. Chen was married to an American and had a green card. In Beijing he ran a bar that foreign news correspondents liked to visit, so when the statement of the thirty-three writers was ready, people from the Associated Press, Reuters, *The New York Times*, and elsewhere knew about it right away.[44]

On April 6, the Chinese government intercepted Chen Jun at the Shanghai rail station, confiscated his passport, and returned it only after he agreed to leave

China and go back to the United States. Chen submitted and went to New York. He knew Hu Ping well and, through Hu, met Xiaobo. The two hit it off immediately. Both liked to say exactly what they thought, and both had backgrounds in philosophy and literature, so they had much to talk about: fiction, poetry, personal ethics, aesthetic pursuits, even metaphysics. They moved easily from topic to topic. Hu Ping joined, and the three became good—and lifelong—friends.

On April 15, Hu Yaobang, former General Secretary of the Communist Party of China, died of a heart attack. Two years earlier Deng Xiaoping, with the approval of a group of elderly Party conservatives, had forced Hu to resign on grounds that he had been "tolerant of all-out Westernization" and "weak in opposing bourgeois liberalization." The latter charge referred to his refusal to repress student prodemocracy demonstrations in Hefei and Shanghai in late 1986. Before that, in 1978 and 1979, Hu had taken a lead in "reversing the verdicts" on "unjust, false, or mistaken cases." (This was Party jargon for making things right with victims of Maoist purges from the Anti-Rightist movement in 1957 to the end of the Cultural Revolution in 1976.) This work had earned him a good reputation among intellectuals, some of whom saw his sacking in January 1987 as a recrudescence of the kind of persecution he himself had worked so hard to erase. Hu's heart attack came while he was attending a meeting of the Politburo of the CCP, and this unfortunate detail helped to feed a rumor that he died in political torment.

The public mood in urban China was already delicate at the moment Hu died. "Reform" was flagging, and political reform in particular seemed ever more remote. The conservatives in the leadership were gaining the upper hand. In the economy, prices had been rising for a few years, and Party Central, ever fearful that economic woes might lead to political instability, decided it must do something. In September 1988, the government imposed austerity measures that included retracting the rights of individuals and many small enterprises to do business freely; that, in turn, led to an economic slowdown. At the same time, popular indignation at the mode of gross corruption called "official turnaround"—in which a holder of political power used that power to control resources that benefited his or her own private enterprise—was growing steadily stronger. In sum, the overall situation was far short of what people had expected at the outset of reform a decade earlier. Chinese urban society was a tinderbox upon which Hu Yaobang's death was a spark.

In New York, on the day Hu Yaobang died, Xiaobo was attending a major event to mark the seventieth anniversary of the May Fourth Movement. At one point the master of ceremonies, Du Nianzhong, who was a U.S. correspondent for the Taiwan newspaper *China Times* and had become a good friend of

Xiaobo's, was called out of the meeting room. He returned a few minutes later, visibly agitated, to announce Hu Yaobang's death. The news did not shock Xiaobo; his initial reaction was mild indifference. But he noticed that his much-respected elders at the meeting—Liu Binyan, Wang Ruoshui, Ruan Ming, and others—were all upset. They shared their shock with one another and immediately looked for telephones to call Hu Yaobang's son to express their sympathy. It was their response, more than Hu's death itself, that set Xiaobo to thinking. Wasn't this more evidence of the inability of intellectuals to stand independent from political authority? Why should they be *that* upset?

Back in Beijing, people were gathering at Tiananmen Square to place wreaths honoring Hu Yaobang at the Monument to the People's Heroes. In the afternoon of April 17, six or seven hundred students and young teachers from the Chinese University of Politics and Law appeared carrying a huge wreath. They were also holding up their school flag and a number of banners bearing elegiac couplets. Admiring crowds followed them through busy streets to the square, and gradually the procession turned into a large, unplanned public demonstration. The news spread through the city. That same evening at Peking University a giant banner, about thirty feet by twelve feet, bearing the words "China's Spirit" was draped from one of the student dormitory buildings. The students took it down and marched it around their campus, and then about a thousand of them accompanied it to Tiananmen Square. Nearly a thousand others joined from nearby Tsinghua University.

The ferment continued the next day. Students at Tiananmen Square decided upon a list of demands to present to the government. They included: reevaluate Hu Yaobang; allow unofficial publications to exist; and publicize the private wealth of government leaders. These demands have been seen as the beginning of the "1989 Tiananmen Democracy Movement." It felt at the time as if a volcano were beginning to rumble. There was no physical violence, but something was in motion.

Xiaobo, as he sat in New York, watched what he could on television. The rising emotion at Tiananmen Square moved him. He remained skeptical of lionizing Hu Yaobang personally, but it was becoming ever more obvious that the underlying issues ran deep and that this was turning into a societywide movement against authoritarianism. He was restless.

On April 18, he joined Hu Ping, Chen Jun, and seven others in signing "A Proposal for Reform: Urging the Chinese Communists to Reflect on Their Mistakes and to Correct Them," which they published two days later in Hong Kong.[45] The statement called for freedom of the press and for deletion from China's constitution of Deng Xiaoping's "Four Cardinal Principles" (insistence on the leadership of the Communist Party, the dictatorship of the proletariat, the socialist road, and Marxism-Leninism-Mao Zedong Thought). Two days later, Xiaobo and Hu Ping jointly published "An Open Letter to Chinese University Students" in which they recommended that students consolidate the organizational gains they had made, begin publishing their own magazine, strengthen their ties with other sectors of society, maintain their dialogue with the government and their university administrations, and work hard to bring freedom to their campuses.[46] They faxed both the statement and the open letter to Xiaobo's friend Zhou Duo at Peking University to relay to the demonstrating students.

Zhou Duo played an important part in the next forty days of Xiaobo's life. Zhou was a lecturer in sociology at Peking University until 1988. He resigned that year to work as head of general planning and deputy chief of public relations for the Stone Group, China's most successful information technology company at the time. Stone had just taken over a state-run enterprise in Kunming, Yunnan province. The business cultures were so different, though, that Stone decided to set up a Stone Institute of Management to retrain local staff who were too inured to the command culture of state enterprises. Zhou Duo was tasked with starting the institute, which meant both structuring curricula and hiring teachers. He had the inspired thought that there should be lectures on aesthetics; someone recommended Xiaobo; Xiaobo went to Kunming; things went well; and Zhou Duo and Xiaobo became good friends—even though their personalities were very different. Zhou Duo was reserved by nature.

Zhou informed Xiaobo that the open letter he and Hu Ping had written to the demonstrating students in Beijing had not gone down very well. The students felt they did not need such simple advice, and the fact that they had received a letter signed by the head of the Alliance for Chinese Democracy, a group that the government had branded a "hostile organization," created a problem for them that they could have done without. Xiaobo and Hu Ping telephoned Fang Lizhi for his impressions, and Fang said that the students were behaving better than any demonstrating students he had ever seen. They were well organized, their actions were planned, and they were remarkably rational and mature. Fang's report left Xiaobo feeling much more optimistic about the movement than he had at first.[47] His patronizing advice might indeed have been unnecessary.

On April 21 he wrote a long article, "Thoughts on the Death of Hu Yaobang," that was published the next day in the *World Daily News* in New York. It presented sharp criticism of a double standard among Chinese intellectuals: on the one hand, they bemoaned the unfair political treatment that Hu Yaobang had suffered and used the occasion of his passing to vent their feelings; on the other, they said not a word to support Wei Jingsheng, who was still languishing in prison, and indeed avoided the topic however they could. Hu Yaobang had been disgraced because he lost out in a power struggle; Wei Jingsheng had been worse than disgraced because he called for ending one-party dictatorship. Xiaobo's article raised a furor. Liu Binyan called him to say, "I won't ask that you have a sense of justice, Xiaobo, but you do need a bit of common sympathy."[48] The responses led Xiaobo to read the article once more on the evening it came out in the print newspaper. He suddenly felt hollow inside. How often had he criticized intellectuals for being armchair activists? But wasn't he himself doing that right now? How could he sit in New York and send remote-control instructions halfway around the world?

Until that moment he had never considered cutting short his stay in New York. On April 23, when he met with friends to wrestle once again with issues the student movement was raising, he could hardly contain himself. "That's it," he said at one point. "Either I go back and join the movement or swear off any more talk about it." But to swear off talk was a pipe dream. He would have to go back. He would try to make it by May 4, the seventieth anniversary of the May Fourth Movement. May Fourth's "enlightenment" had loomed in his mind in recent years with increasing intensity, like a beam from a lone lighthouse in China's dark history. At such a crucial anniversary, he would have things to say.

At the end of April there was to be a conference in California on the ferment brewing in China, and he wanted to wait and go to that first. Checking flight availability, though, he found that tickets to Beijing were sold out until mid-May—except for one ticket on April 26, just three days away. He bought it.

Before leaving he collected his thoughts one more time on "the Hu Yaobang death" and put them into a trilogy of articles: "I. The Tragedy of a Tragic Hero"; "II. Perfect a System—or Merely Create the Image of a Perfect Leader?"; and "III. The Aims and Procedures of Chinese Democratization."[49] All address contentious questions, but the tone is circumspect and generally lacks the brashness of much of Xiaobo's earlier writing. The second article anticipates a point that, a few weeks later, he would write into his famous "June 2nd Hunger Strike Declaration": "In pursuing democracy . . . one must not base oneself in hate. Too often, the Chinese people respond to the hate that pervades their dictatorial system not with wisdom but with more hate and ignorance. Hate rots a person's wisdom."[50] The third article holds that the "procedures" of democracy, in addition to protests and demonstrations, must include "democratization in those tiny, particular, and concrete parts of life that arise in small political contexts like group sessions in school, in student clubs or editorial boards, and in families."[51] A few years earlier his thinking had galloped through the skies like a heavenly horse; now he was focused on the texture of ordinary life.

His political thinking had also changed during the brief eight months he had been outside China. From a romantic young littérateur with some fairly impractical illusions, he had turned into a political dissident. From a critic who stood "inside the system" yet occasionally took potshots at it, he had come to stand outside his country's dictatorial system and to compare it with democratic political systems. Rejecting the "hatred" that Chinese Communist education instills in young people, he was becoming more interested in nonviolence, not only as a political tactic but also as a way of living.

9

In Tiananmen Square

Xiaobo's trip from New York to Beijing (leaving April 26, arriving April 27) called for a change of aircraft in Tokyo. While waiting in the Tokyo airport, he met a Chinese student who had come from Beijing that very morning. The student told him that the *People's Daily* on April 26 had carried a frightening headline: "Be Bold and Direct in Opposing Turmoil." The political atmosphere in Beijing had turned suddenly rancid, the student said.

The article was a front-page editorial. That kind of position in the *People's Daily* meant that the message came from the very highest level in the Communist Party. Its purpose was to announce an authoritative decision on the "nature" (a momentous term in Communist jargon) of the protests: "a tiny minority" of "people with ulterior motives" were using the student movement to "create turmoil." "Their actual motive," the piece declared, "is to negate the leadership of the Communist Party of China and the socialist system."

It later became clear that the word *dongluan* ("turmoil" or, more literally, "producing chaos") had come from Deng Xiaoping himself. Using a distinction that Mao Zedong had invented, Deng was defining the student movement as a "conflict with our enemies," not a "conflict among ourselves." The Chinese people knew from bitter experience what this sort of distinction could lead to. When the regime's pretenses of equanimity wear thin, the hard rock of its underlying paranoia can emerge and smash anything that even looks like a challenge. That point apparently had been reached. Publication of the editorial meant that the student movement would be suppressed.

April 26 was only eleven days after Hu Yaobang's death. The student movement had frightened the top leaders very quickly. On April 18, some student leaders had asked for dialogue with officials and been rebuffed. The next day, April 19, students at Peking University formed a "preparatory committee for a united association of Peking University students," and similar groups popped up on other campuses in the next few days. On the night of April 19 students began a sit-in at Xinhuamen, the entrance to the cloistered compound where nearly all the top leaders reside, still demanding dialogue. The gate remained closed, students continued to sit in, and at around 3:00 a.m. on April 20, police drove them off with billy clubs.

The beatings outraged students and led to the formation of independent student associations on several campuses. Such groups were unwelcome to the regime, because they cast the preexisting Party-controlled student associations into near irrelevance. Worse, from the regime's point of view, was that the independent associations began to talk with one another. On April 23 they formed an inter-campus organization, the Association of Autonomous University Student Organizations, in Beijing. Such bridging was politically taboo. It contradicted the divide-and-rule principle that the Party had relied on for decades, all across society. The students came up with the idea of boycotting classes, and on Monday, April 24, a city-wide strike began. Sixty thousand students from thirty-eight campuses participated, protesting the Xinhuamen beatings and demanding that the authorities stop ignoring student requests for dialogue. The next day, April 25, the Autonomous Association of Beijing Student Organizations held its first meeting.

In New York, Xiaobo had followed these events closely. What he now heard at the Tokyo airport on the morning of April 27 raised a number of questions in his mind. What if the student movement were instantly crushed? If that happened, there would be nothing for him to do in Beijing. If the movement somehow staggered on, would his return help it or hurt it? The highest authorities had just proclaimed that a "tiny minority" from "outside the country" was causing the trouble. Might the regime use his return to try to substantiate this ridiculous charge? Moreover, there was his own fate to consider. During his stay outside China he had written a number of articles, including "Devil Incarnate Mao Zedong," that obviously had crossed a line. Where would that leave him? The "relevant comrades" might already be heading for the Beijing airport to meet him.

Such thoughts were troubling. Unsure what to do, Xiaobo went to the airline counter to ask if there were any seats on flights back to the United States. There were not. Soon the boarding of his flight to Beijing was announced. He boarded. What would be, would be.

As the airplane ascended, he chided himself for hesitating. Wasn't this a rare opportunity? How often does history give a person such an opportunity?

Would he have the courage and intelligence to make a difference in China's history? He told himself, *If I'm going to do this, I'd better do it right.*[1] When the airplane landed in Beijing, Xiaobo did not leave his seat immediately. His friends in New York had made him promise to call them if he were arrested at the airport. It was a depressing thought. He stood up only after everyone else had left.

After exiting customs, he saw his wife, Tao Li; her younger sister, Tao Ning; and their friend Zhou Duo waiting for him. Xiaobo's friends in New York had made Zhou Duo promise to be there. Tao Li looked haggard and worried. "You really shouldn't have come back," she said. This was the same advice his professor Tong Qingbing had given him during their last phone call before he left New York. Tong advised him to remain abroad. To do so would violate the guarantee Tong had given to the authorities that Xiaobo would return. One reason he was glad to be coming back was to spare his professor that price.

Not until they were all inside a taxi heading to the city did Xiaobo finally feel comfortable. Tao Li and Tao Ning began regaling him with happy news that he had not known until then. Beijing students had mounted a huge demonstration that very day to express their rejection of the April 26 editorial. In the morning of April 27, about 50,000 students from the northwest of Beijing, where a number of university campuses were located, had defied a decree that they stay off the streets. Passing through police barricades and ignoring uniformed personnel, they marched southward to Xidan, then turned east on Chang'an Boulevard and marched through Tiananmen Square. When they reached the Second Ring Road they followed it to march a circle around the city. They arrayed themselves in rows of about a dozen students each; at each side of the marching column a line of student monitors kept order. The strict discipline was living rebuttal of the charge of "chaos." They held aloft school flags and homemade banners that offered other rebuttals: "Peaceful Petition Is Not Turmoil"; "Be Bold and Direct in Opposing Corruption" (echoing the *People's Daily* headline "Be Bold and Direct in Opposing Turmoil"); "If Official Corruption Stands, Public Morale Falls." As many as a million ordinary citizens who shared the students' ideals cheered them along their route and opened their purses to buy them water, bread, and other things they needed. The morale of the entire city soared; it seemed a spiritual baptism had occurred.

Xiaobo had arrived too late to witness all of this, but he saw the tail end of the demonstration. Around midnight on April 27, as their taxi neared Beijing Normal, clutches of students returning from the march were still cheering and singing as they approached the university gate. An ocean of people was there to welcome them. The taxi had to make a detour.

The glorious student march was not the only event on April 27, 1989, that had a major impact on the democracy movement. In Shanghai, state agents entered the offices of the newspaper *World Economic Herald*, relieved the editor, Qin Benli, of his position, and shut the paper down. This happened because four days earlier the paper had published a lengthy collection of the speeches at a conference commemorating Hu Yaobang, some of which had asked for too much democracy. Yan Jiaqi, a political scientist at the Chinese Academy of Social Sciences, had observed that Hu Yaobang's sacking had not been done according to prescribed procedures and that more generally, transitions in China's political leadership are not done democratically.

The closing of the *World Economic Herald* turned out to have a powerful counterproductive effect. It became a clarion call for Chinese reporters, editors, and intellectuals of many kinds to join the democracy movement. "Freedom of the press" became one of the movement's strongest demands.

Xiaobo's friends in New York had viewed him as a hero when he decided to risk all and head back to Beijing. He wondered if some of that hero's aura would stick with him as he arrived, but the intellectual stardom that he had achieved in the summer of 1988 had largely disappeared. People had become riveted on the current democracy movement. At Beijing Normal in particular, a new star had risen. Born in Beijing to a Uyghur family, Uerkesh Davlet (known as Wuerkaixi in transliterated Chinese) was a first-year undergraduate in the Education Department. He had delivered a spectacular speech on April 17 at a spontaneous student assembly to mourn Hu Yaobang's death. Two days later, in the evening of April 19, he showed remarkable courage and talent in leading the student protests at Xinhuamen. On the evening of April 21 he presided at a meeting of 40,000 students from twenty colleges and universities in Beijing as they prepared for a march to Tiananmen the next day for Hu Yaobang's memorial service. He was the leader of the autonomous student association at Beijing Normal and one of the organizers, as well as briefly the president, of the Association of Autonomous University Student Organizations in Beijing. In short, he was the main reason Beijing Normal was viewed as a bustling hive of activity during the spring protests.

In high school Wuerkaixi had admired Xiaobo. A "dark horse" ready to bombard an establishment figure like Li Zehou was just the kind of person he liked. He applied to Beijing Normal, he later wrote, because he wanted to study with such teachers. By the time Xiaobo returned from New York, though, Wuerkaixi had been catapulted to the center of a historical stage and was far too busy to go looking for his admired professor.

Xiaobo felt a vague sense of estrangement from the student movement during the first few days after his return, and that feeling grew sharper one morning as he walked across the Beijing Normal campus and noticed a wall poster. It said that he, Liu Binyan, and others had met in the United States and exhorted Chinese students to support Qin Benli, the just-fired editor of the *World Economic Herald*. It went on to say that when Xiaobo returned to Beijing he was carrying $9,700 or more in U.S. dollars to support the student movement. This was hardly true, and the rumor made Xiaobo angry. He looked for someone to complain to and couldn't find anyone, so decided to rip the poster down with his own hands. Students saw him and began to berate him. One grabbed his hands and wouldn't let go. "But *I* am Liu Xiaobo!" he shouted. A crowd gathered, and the ruckus wasn't settled until some students from the Chinese Department came along to testify, "Yes, that's him."

Another incident left him feeling sour. An admiring student came to visit and happened to notice, lying on Xiaobo's desk, a copy of the *World Journal*, a newspaper published in North America and owned by the *United Daily News* in Taiwan. The paper contained an article by Xiaobo, "Reflecting on the Phenomenon of the Hu Yaobang Death," in which he exhorts people to look not for saviors but for practical ways to reform China's political system. The student loved the piece and carried the newspaper away, and soon the article was being broadcast on loudspeakers across the Beijing Normal campus. Xiaobo felt a bit uneasy, because the customary language of the Taiwan-based *World Journal* was different from that on the mainland—to say nothing of the content of the piece! For a few minutes the whole campus was hushed as the loudspeakers continued.[2] Later Xiaobo heard complaints from nearly everyone close to him—Tao Li, her parents, his professors, and others. *Why had he been so rash?*[3]

He looked for ways to fit better into the current scene. The long-anticipated anniversary of May Fourth was about to arrive. What should he do? His habitual role of loner was not the right answer. He sought out a former student of his, Cheng Zhen, who was a member of the leading group in the autonomous student association at Beijing Normal. The students have already done much, he told her; if I don't do something to help, I can no longer be called their teacher. On May 3, Cheng invited him to a meeting of students from around Beijing that evening to agree on how to word a "Declaration on May Fourth." Xiaobo had met a Hong Kong journalist that day and invited her to come along too.

The meeting was in a dormitory at Peking University. When Xiaobo and the journalist arrived they were barred at the door. "This is a confidential meeting." Xiaobo gave his name, and that did some good, but not much. He was allowed in, but the Hong Kong journalist was not. Inside, there were no admiring eyes like those that would have greeted him a year earlier; the faces in the room showed only tension and suspicion. As Cheng Zhen was introducing him, Wuerkaixi interrupted: "Why wasn't I consulted before people were invited?" Xiaobo stayed only a few minutes, said a few words, and went home. He mumbled something about the matter to Tao Li.

Later that night, about 1:00 a.m., the telephone rang. It was Cheng Zhen, who said that she had spoken with Wuerkaixi on the way back from the meeting and that he realized he had been impolite to Xiaobo and would like to talk with him—right now, if possible. They fixed a place to meet outdoors on the Beijing Normal campus, where Wuerkaixi retraced the entire course of the student movement for Xiaobo. Xiaobo asked him how it felt to be a student leader.

"You have to be dictatorial," Wuerkaixi said.

"What?"

"Given the way China is these days," he continued, "you have to establish personal authority. The students don't get it about democracy."[4]

The words startled Xiaobo, but it was clear that Wuerkaixi was speaking honestly. There was work to be done in teaching democracy. Xiaobo and Wuerkaixi stayed in close touch from then on. They saw each other nearly every day.

On May 4 student demonstrations happened all around the country. Beijing saw another large and well-organized student march like the one on April 27. Xiaobo and Tao Li rode bicycles alongside the Beijing Normal contingent, at the center of which Wuerkaixi was surrounded by seven or eight guards while he held the school flag aloft. Two hundred journalists and editors at the front of the march chanted, "The news must tell the truth!" The police assigned to block the march retreated when pressured and let it pass. Every time such a "breakthrough" occurred, Wuerkaixi's guards hoisted him onto their shoulders and the school flag flew high.

By chance it was also that day, May 4, when Communist Party General Secretary Zhao Ziyang gave a speech in Beijing to representatives from the Asian Development Bank and in passing commented on the student movement. He took a much softer line than the April 26 editorial had. He said the students were not opposed to China's fundamental system but wanted only to correct its flaws. He saw no danger of major turmoil and hoped that issues could be resolved democratically and by rule of law. He favored more and broader dialogue between the government and people in all sectors of society.[5] Zhao's speech was printed the next day in *People's Daily,* and students and many others praised it. The day after that, May 6, student spirits rose even higher when *China Youth News* reported at length, with photos, on the demonstrations of May 4. Students at some schools considered ending their strike of classes.

On May 7, Xiaobo put up a wall poster at Beijing Normal. It was a critical reflection on the slogans of the May 4 demonstrations. He had found them too simple and sometimes empty. "We mustn't save every issue for dialogue with the top leaders," he wrote. "We need dialogue right now, from the bottom up, starting in daily life." He offered some concrete proposals: the Beijing Normal campus could set up a "Freedom Forum" where people could express their opinions—especially their opinions on the school's administration. A faculty group "to study the democratization of China" could be formed and investigate topics like "human rights in China" and "the current condition of China's legal system." He raised again his recurring theme of dispelling hatred and enmity:

> Chinese democracy must be grounded in ridding ourselves of the "enemy mentality." In a functioning democracy, there are no enemies; there is only political balance among different interest groups in a democratic system. It is better that ten devils be working within a system of checks and balances than that one angel be ruling with unchecked power. To struggle for democracy means to forbid hatred from poisoning one's wisdom.[6]

This was a lesson he had learned from the Cultural Revolution. Much of his thinking during his adult life can be read as a response to his memories of the cruelty of that time, when the phrase "class struggle" meant that one's opponent was a devil, not a human like oneself. In 1989 the term "class struggle" was no longer used, but mental habits that went with it were still in place. It is a measure of the distance between Xiaobo's thinking and that of the top leader, Deng Xiaoping, that Deng was afraid the student movement might turn into a Cultural Revolution while Xiaobo dearly hoped that the movement might bring an end to that whole way of thinking.

Xiaobo's phrase "political balance" stuck out as strange in the linguistic environment of the time. Wuerkaixi later wrote: "There I was, charging through enemy lines, but at the time I didn't really appreciate what was at stake. It was Xiaobo who taught me the concept of 'civil society' and helped me to see that the student movement was 'society checking political power.' Without that kind of guidance, I might have become a major detriment to the student movement."[7] Wuerkaixi was not the only person slow to see what Xiaobo was trying to express. Beneath his wall poster at Beijing Normal Xiaobo wrote, "If you agree with what I say, please sign your name below." He expected that others might sign. When he went back the next day, the poster itself had been torn down. Nobody had come looking for him to talk about it, either. He needed disciples but had none. In the summer of the previous year he had been admired as a cutting-edge radical; now he seemed a pilgrim of cool-headed rationality. Maybe that was the problem.

In any case, the protesting students were in no mood to be diverted from their standoff with the top leaders. They felt a crisis looming. Were the warmer tone of the Zhao Ziyang speech and their better treatment in the press part of a new trend? Or were the ominous threats in the April 26 editorial still going to be carried out? Seeking to press the issue, some students thought about doing a hunger strike. Chai Ling, a graduate student in psychology at Beijing Normal, was all for this, and she, Wuerkaixi, and Wang Dan, a prominent student leader at Peking University, formed a "hunger strike group." They knew the tactic would have added leverage with the government because Soviet leader Mikhail Gorbachev was due to arrive in Beijing on May 15 for the first meeting of Chinese and Soviet heads of state since Sino-Soviet relations had soured three decades earlier. There was to be a welcoming ceremony in Tiananmen Square. How could it happen if the square were filled with fasting students?

Moderates within the Communist Party feared that a hunger strike and a threat to complicate the Gorbachev visit could hurt Zhao Ziyang and the reform wing of the Party. Conservatives might seize on such events to attack the moderates, and the results could be disastrous. Years of reform might be lost. Yan Mingfu, head of the Party's United Front Department (a bureaucracy charged with keeping groups and prominent people in society in a "united front" with the Communist Party), who had built up considerable goodwill with Chinese intellectuals in recent years, wanted to head off this kind of calamity. In the morning of May 13, just a few hours before tens of thousands of students—the hunger strikers and their supporters—were planning to go to Tiananmen Square, Yan convened a meeting of mostly young intellectuals to discuss ways a hunger strike might be averted or shortened. Zhou Duo and others at that meeting proposed that the United Front Department itself initiate dialogue with student leaders. Yan agreed, and Zhou Duo immediately telephoned Xiaobo to see if he could persuade Wuerkaixi and other leaders to come to a meeting that evening at the United Front Department.

When Xiaobo got this message he knew the stakes were high. Wuerkaixi had already been busy that morning on the campus of Beijing Normal posting a "Declaration of a Hunger Strike" that said students would go to Tiananmen Square at 2:00 p.m. that day to begin fasting. How could Xiaobo find Wuerkaixi *right now*? The only hope was to broadcast a message on the students' loudspeaker system. That worked, and soon Wuerkaixi was in front of him, a white headband bearing the red characters "Hunger Strike" tied around his forehead and a diagonal sash across his chest boldly bearing his name. He was willing to go to the United Front Department that evening but first had to lead the hunger strikers to the square.

Xiaobo then went in search of other student leaders who might be willing to attend. At the broadcasting stand he found Wang Chaohua, a graduate student at the Academy of Social Sciences. Wang, older and more mature than most of the other protesters, was not in favor of the hunger strike. She agreed with the Autonomous Association, which a few days earlier had passed a resolution to put city-wide protests on hold and instead return to schools to "build campus democracy" by giving speeches, putting out newspapers, and holding campus-level demonstrations. She told Xiaobo and Zhou Duo about another student group, the Dialogue Delegation, that was also seeking to meet with state leaders. "If there's to be a meeting," Wang said, "then all three groups [the Autonomous Association, the hunger strike group, and the Dialogue Delegation] should be there." Xiaobo and Zhou Duo agreed.

That evening Zhou Duo came to Beijing Normal to pick up Wuerkaixi for the meeting. Because it was an official government meeting of the United Front Department, Zhou was assigned a government sedan. Xiaobo was standing with Wuerkaixi when it arrived, and Zhou asked Xiaobo, using the kind of Chinese politeness that normally is politely turned down, if he would like to come along. Xiaobo said yes, and that was that. Zhou Duo knew that Yan Mingfu might not feel comfortable with this addition, given Xiaobo's reputation for extremism during his dark horse days. And sure enough, when they entered the meeting room, Yan's face "abruptly darkened."[8] Zhou Duo noticed the glare; Xiaobo did not. He felt as welcome as anyone.

Tension was in the air when Yan Mingfu, chair of the meeting, opened it at 8:00 p.m. Students sat according to the groups they belonged to: the hunger strike group (Wang Dan, Chai Ling, Wuerkaixi, and others), the Autonomous Association (Wang Chaohua and others), and the Dialogue Delegation (Xiang Xiaoji, Shen Tong, and others). Two other "student" groups—the government-sponsored student association and the Communist Youth League—were represented as a formality. A number of young intellectuals who were seen as possible mediators between the government and the students were there as well. They included Zheng Yefu of Peking University, Chen Xiaoping of the Chinese University of Politics and Law, and Wang Juntao, who led an unofficial think tank called the Beijing Institute of Economics and Social Sciences.

Yan opened in a modest, sincere tone. He said he hoped the students could understand how important a Sino-Soviet summit was and why it would be best not to disrupt one by occupying the city's central square. He told about a meeting he had witnessed that afternoon in which Zhao Ziyang and other members of the ruling Politburo met with representatives of workers. "Dialogue" had happened. Perhaps the students could be next. He invited students to express their concerns and promised to pass them to the top. Wuerkaixi said that the "root of the problem" was the April 26 editorial and that if this remained unsolved, there was no way the student movement could end, with or without a Gorbachev complication. Other students followed in the same vein. They stressed that their movement was propelled from below: if the causes were not addressed, the student leaders could not end it even if they wanted to.

When it was Xiaobo's turn to speak he addressed three topics, sharply and tersely. First, the government should renounce the attitude of its April 26 editorial; the longer the delay in doing so, the greater would be the price. The government should also recognize the legitimacy of the autonomous student organizations; they did not violate China's constitution. Second, the hunger striking students should leave Tiananmen Square by May 15 so that the Sino-Soviet summit could go forward smoothly. Third, democratic government is an art of compromise. The students had to learn how to compromise and make concessions. An enemy mentality or pursuit of face at all costs could ruin mutual understanding even after it had begun to emerge. If the students wouldn't compromise—couldn't make concessions—they would gradually lose the sympathy and support of people inside the Party and the government. The students should stay away from the power struggles there but also look for the broadest support they could get from all quarters, especially inside the Party.[9]

The response to Xiaobo's comments was generally favorable. Yan Mingfu changed his attitude on the spot. "Deftly done," he commented to Xiaobo later. Wang Juntao, surprised that someone as feisty as Xiaobo would counsel students to leave the square, commented that "the spirit of Yan Mingfu seems to have moved God."[10] By the time the meeting was over, Wang Dan and Wuerkaixi, leaders of the hunger strike group, had come to the view that to accommodate a reception of Gorbachev by emptying the square, or at least part of it, was something they could consider. But then Chai Ling and her husband, Feng Congde, who had emerged as important leaders of the student movement, left the meeting before it ended, without a word. The message was, "We're not interested in negotiating."

Xiaobo went straight from that meeting to Tiananmen Square, even though the hour was approaching midnight. Students from around the city had gone there in the afternoon, and he wanted to be with them. From then until the fateful night of June 3–4, he basically lived at the square.

He looked for the Beijing Normal students. The evening was cool, and there were not yet tents to shield people from the night air. Xiaobo asked students individually why they were hunger striking. He got all kinds of answers. Some said they were protesting the April 26 editorial. Some said they did not want to miss out on a historic event. Some said they wanted to experience all the flavors that life offered, including hunger and, if need be, prison. Others said, "Prison? There are *too many* of us! Where would they put us all?" Some female students said they were accompanying their boyfriends to "look after them." Most students felt it would be better if Xiaobo and other teachers stayed away. Their presence would give the government an excuse to say that the students were being manipulated from behind the scenes by "graybeards."

At about 2:30 a.m. on May 14, when things seemed to have quieted down a bit, suddenly there was a commotion. Three high officials—Commissioner of Education Li Tieying, Vice Chair of the Beijing Party Committee Li Ximing, and Beijing Mayor Chen Xitong—had arrived at the square in an attempt to persuade the students to end their strike and leave. Xiaobo sidled his way to where he could see the action and watched Li Tieying take a bullhorn and start shouting through it: "Good students, we represent the government in coming to see you! We hope you will guard your health!" His words drowned in an ocean of hooting: "Don't listen!" "We won't listen!" "Why don't you say something that matters?!" Li Ximing and Chen Xitong took turns trying to be heard, but it was useless. Xiaobo was annoyed by both sides. How could these officials be so dumb? How could the students be so brazen?

He found it hard to contain himself. Standing next to a flatbed cart, he jumped up onto it and started giving a speech. Because he was in the Beijing Normal part of the crowd, when he shouted out his name the students recognized him and listened. He praised them for their idealism—risking their health and their futures to try to make the world better. But if they were going to do it this way— not even letting Li Tieying and the others speak—then "This isn't democracy, it's hatred. . . . Hatred can lead only to violence and dictatorship, hatred only sees straw men. . . . What Chinese democracy needs most is to rid itself of hatred and of the enemy mentality; what we need most is calm, reasoned dialogue— consultation—what we need above all is tolerance!"[11] He urged the students to go back to their campuses and begin building campus-level democracy. "Right now we need to be sure that Gorbachev's visit to China goes smoothly."

When he began his speech the students listened quietly. There was occasional applause and a few cheers. But as he continued some hisses and whistling emerged, and by the end some students were mocking him: "Coward! Get down from there!" "Fake scholar, down!" "When did the dark horse turn into a sheep?!!"

Xiaobo was miserable. Public speaking had always been his forte. This was his first taste of audience ridicule. Was this what he had come all the way back from New York for? The next day friends from New York telephoned him. They had seen media reports about his running into this stone wall, and they teased him about it. He hadn't been arrested by the Chinese government, as he had feared, but he might be hooted back to the United States by the Chinese students he had set out to help.

In the afternoon of May 14, a group of twelve intellectuals led by Dai Qing, a writer close to the moderates within the Communist Party, went to the square to try to persuade the students to end their hunger strike. Yan Jiaqi, Bao Zunxin, Liu Zaifu, Su Xiaokang, and other very well-known figures were among them. Dai Qing read aloud "Our Emergency Appeal on the Current Situation," which all of them had signed. It called upon the government to recognize the legitimacy of the student organizations and pledge not to repress them with violence. It called upon the students to withdraw from the square at least long enough to allow the Gorbachev reception to proceed. In the view of these liberal intellectuals, the students had already made important progress, but it was fragile. A tactical error at this point could trigger a crackdown that would put them back to square one. Some of the students who listened agreed, but many did not. When Dai Qing suggested that she ask Zhao Ziyang and Li Peng to come to the square for a visit with everybody, following which the students would all retreat to their campuses, a huge chorus of "No . . . o . . . o!" was the answer. Finally a thin, bespectacled student edged his way to the front, grabbed the megaphone from Dai Qing, and shouted, "Classmates! Classmates! We need to read the hunger strike declaration together again!" He did, and stunning words rang out: "blood . . . life . . . democracy."

The event ended there. The well-intentioned intellectuals, would-be mediators, were all but jeered away. Xiaobo, observing, thought that Dai Qing was doing the right and rational thing, yet after spending the last twenty hours among the students he had been so taken by their earnest and selfless spirit that his allegiance was drifting to their side. He realized that there was no way the students would accept any instructions from outside the square or any moves by mediators. The only way to join the movement was to "get into the trenches with it; pontificating from above just wouldn't do."[12] It was then that his judgment changed from opposing to supporting a hunger strike.[13]

The square was continuously tense. The students were afraid that police would arrest them and cart them away, but that did not happen. The government abandoned the plan to welcome Gorbachev in Tiananmen Square and moved the ceremony to the airport. Meanwhile the number of hunger strikers kept increasing, from a few hundred to more than three thousand. Some students, feeling that refusing food was not getting enough attention, decided to refuse water as well, and this heightened the tension and sense of emergency even more. Fearing that a hunger striker might die, the Beijing city government deployed teams of doctors and nurses and about a hundred ambulances. Amid the hordes of students holding aloft their flags and banners, the white ambulances, sirens wailing, ferried weakened or fainting strikers to hospitals. They were like singing white threads weaving through the living tapestry that the square had become.

Images, both real and imagined, of students exposed to the elements and risking their lives while the central leaders remained impassive attracted more and more popular support for the movement. On May 15, students established a "Tiananmen Square Hunger Strike Command" with Chai Ling in charge. Mikhail Gorbachev arrived in Beijing the same day, but the thoroughfares were so crowded that the Soviet leader's motorcade had to find alternate routes. A march of more than 30,000 intellectuals—writers, reporters, editors, professors— was taking place. No mass march of intellectuals like this had ever happened before in the Communist era. It startled people. The purpose was not just to support the students but to debunk the government's claim that a "tiny number" of

FIGURE 9.1 In Tiananmen Square, spring 1989

Scott Savitt

intellectuals—"black hands" who were "behind the scenes" with "ulterior motives"—were manipulating the students. That rhetoric was meant to plant fear in people who might want to support the students, because they might be singling themselves out as targets if they did so. The march was to show that nobody was hiding.

Also on May 15, Xiaobo heard that students from Beijing Normal wanted to publish a *Hunger Strike Bulletin* and needed equipment—a mimeograph machine, stencil paper, printer paper, and some other things—and volunteered to solicit funds. He found a cardboard box, wrote "Contributions" on it, and approached people on the streets. A young woman leading a child made one of the first contributions: a fifty-yuan note. A vegetable farmer from Shunyi, a Beijing suburb, said he didn't understand politics but really admired the students and handed over a hundred yuan. Two young men came along with a flatbed cart piled high with comforters and clothing—donations from their neighbors, they said. Everyone knew it got chilly at night on the square. The same two youngsters said their mothers were at home simmering mung bean soup; they would be back soon to deliver it.[14] Xiaobo had always been vulnerable to surges of sentiment, and what he heard from these citizens was almost too much for him:

> I was stunned by the warmth, courage, and daring—the self-awareness and the optimism—that Beijing citizens were displaying. It was like nothing I had seen before. A repressed, atomized populace suddenly seemed to meld into a single organism. All of Beijing was acting as if it had one brain, one goal, one motive, one voice: oppose bureaucratic dictatorship, establish a democratic order.
>
> For the first time I doubted my pessimism about Chinese national character, for the first time could shed my disdain for the "the mediocre crowd," and for the first time felt the power that could flow if people woke up.[15]

Xiaobo enlisted a few students to join him, and in three afternoons they had gathered more than four thousand yuan, enough to buy not only mimeograph equipment but also flashlights, megaphones, sun umbrellas, toiletries, and—for the students who were volunteering as monitors—box lunches, drinks, chocolates, and cigarettes. Xiaobo asked students if he was forgetting anything. He wrote later about a female student who approached him about a "special need." "Sure," he answered, "anything," but still was surprised when she approached his ear and said: "Contraceptives." He took a fifty-yuan note from his wallet and asked, "That enough?" She laughed and said, "Way too much! Enough for a few years."[16]

The demonstrations peaked on May 17, when a crowd estimated at around a million gathered in and around Tiananmen Square. It included workers from a variety of government offices, journalists from the *People's Daily* and other state media (one banner read "Don't Force Us to Lie!"), and even trainees at a police school. Demonstrations of ten thousand or more people supporting the Beijing students erupted in Shanghai, Harbin, Xi'an, Wuhan, Changsha, Nanjing, Shijiazhuang, Lanzhou, and other cities. By now Deng Xiaoping had become one of the targets. Some demonstrators held up posters showing Mao Zedong and Zhou Enlai as a way of expressing opposition to Deng.

Xiaobo was far from the only observer to attest that life on the streets of Beijing during those days was uncharacteristically civil. People were polite to strangers. After a collision of bicycles the riders jumped up to ask if the other party was all right. People said that street vendors stopped haggling over prices. They joked that pickpockets and purse snatchers followed the students in going on strike. When troops gathered at the edges of the city, poised to enter it, citizens brought them food, drink, and even flowers. They sang songs, cried "Soldiers won't attack their own flesh and blood," and appeared to believe it. Soldiers often reciprocated the warmth.

This kind of goodwill filled the atmosphere even though few police were visible to monitor behavior. How many police of the less visible kind were active in the crowds was another question. Xiaobo had a puzzling experience when two young men volunteered to install a telephone in the tent he was living in on the square. "It's our contribution," they said, "better than donating money." Xiaobo agreed and used the phone to call Tao Li, Wuerkaixi, Professor Tong Qingbing, and others. But later he and some of his friends wondered: Who were those two? They hadn't given their names. Why give a phone to Xiaobo? Was someone seeking evidence of "overseas backing" of the student movement? It didn't help that everyone knew that state agents, for security reasons, standardly work in pairs. Were two people needed to install a phone?

The *Hunger Strike Bulletin* was filled with all kinds of news about the movement, and the mimeograph machine that cranked it out ran day and night. Students said they wanted its "seeds of fire" to spread throughout Beijing and to other cities in China. Xiaobo himself wrote a few pieces. In one, "To Overseas Chinese and All Foreign Persons Concerned About China," his argument anticipated principles of universal human rights that he would come to embrace explicitly a few years later: "Humanism and human rights are the business of all of humanity." Another piece, "Our Proposals," appeared on May 23. Martial law had been declared in Beijing on May 20, so he omitted his name and signed it "Autonomous Committee of Beijing University Students." It called upon "people in all sectors of society, based on their own group interests, to press for democracy in any way they can." Workers should organize independent unions that genuinely supported their interests. Nonstate commercial enterprises should demand rights of private ownership and freedom from state interference. The eight "democratic parties" should stop serving as "political ornaments" and demand genuine participation in government. Their leaders should be allowed to build their own followings as a basis for becoming an authentic political opposition. The piece closes with another appeal to everyone—protesters and the government alike—to shed the "enemies mentality" because it was "antithetical to democracy and can lead only to violence and dictatorship."[17]

The authorities condemned this article as a document that "certain people" were putting forward as a "working program."[18] Among the students, though, the proposals didn't get much traction. The words that got the most attention were brave declarations about readiness to risk all, to die for the cause, and so on. After Wuerkaixi read Xiaobo's essay, he commented on the recommendation to "establish political leaders outside the Party-state." He said that if he ever played such a role he would invite Xiaobo to be his adviser.[19]

Xiaobo was regaining respect among the Beijing Normal students after losing some of it at his impromptu flatbed speech a few days earlier. He of course welcomed the new esteem but found that it sometimes went too far. The students gave him a special bench to sit on, for example. This was a big honor, because the norm was to sit on the ground on mats. The students added the condition that no one else could use the bench even if Xiaobo wasn't there. That was too much. When Xiaobo saw a student being shooed from the bench at one point, he reflexively ran over, apologized, and escorted the student back to it.

There were other aspects of the students' behavior that disappointed him, even angered him. Monitors who controlled entry to the center of the square began to enjoy their power too much and addressed strangers harshly. Some leaders had their own "bodyguards" and were becoming too proud of that fact. Litter was everywhere, and some students seemed to urinate wherever they liked. Xiaobo organized a few students to help sweep up, and they did, but within minutes the same ground would be relittered. Once, after Tao Li brought Xiaobo some cigarettes and a change of clean clothes, he was startled to see a student grab the offerings for herself. She lit a cigarette, put on some of the clean clothes, and started strutting around as if no one else were there. In short, some students seemed to think "democracy" meant "do whatever you like."

A question of integrity bothered him as well. The striking students had pledged not to eat, and people in the city were crediting them for that, but some were eating secretly. Originally Xiaobo had advised against fasting: better to protect your health, he said. He would have supported an end to the hunger strike. But breaking a promise? Pretending to fast? That was unsettling. Part of extricating oneself from the "enemies mentality" in communist education was to be honest to both sides—all sides—in any encounter. This became a principle that ran throughout the second half of Xiaobo's life.

A disturbing event occurred in the very early morning of May 19. General Secretary of the Communist Party Zhao Ziyang and a few subordinates suddenly appeared among the students at Tiananmen Square. Zhao looked haggard. He spoke through a megaphone in his heavy Sichuan accent: "We have come too late. . . . The situation is very complicated. . . . You should protect your health. . . . Your situation is different from ours. We are old, so it doesn't matter so much to us."[20] He paused and seemed on the verge of tears. The students who were listening could not fully grasp the import of what he was saying. They did not realize a power struggle at the top of the Communist Party had taken a decisive turn. Zhao had been removed from his top positions in the Party and the government, and this, in chilly air at 4:00 a.m., would be his last public appearance ever. He and his reformist colleagues were headed for purge; their hardline opponents had won decisive victory, at least for now. Where would the country go from here? How would the drama of the student protests end? Perhaps only Deng Xiaoping knew.

On May 20, just a few hours before martial law was declared, the Tiananmen Square Hunger Strike Command announced that the strike was over and was being replaced with a sit-in. The main issue then became whether to withdraw from the square or not. One side said yes, they should reap the harvest they had won and go home to build democracy on campuses. The other side said no, the only way to keep pressure on the government was to remain in the square. Another question was how to rename the Hunger Strike Command, since there no longer was a hunger strike. Personnel changes might also be appropriate.

On May 23, Chen Ziming and Wang Juntao, cochairs of the nongovernmental Beijing Institute of Economics and Social Sciences, convened a broadly based meeting at the Academy of Social Sciences, with an unwieldy but carefully crafted name: Conference of Patriotic Supporters of the Constitution from All Quarters in the Capital. Participants included prominent student leaders—Wang Dan, Wuerkaixi, Chai Ling, Li Lu, and others—and intellectuals who were supporting the protesters—political scientist Yan Jiaqi, publisher Bao Zunxin, novelist Zheng Yi, editor Gan Yang, professors Liu Suli and Chen Xiaoping, and others. By this time the Autonomous Association of Beijing Student Organizations and the group called the Dialogue Delegation both had faded, and the convocation gave its blessing to a new student organization, the Defend Tiananmen Square Command, that would replace the Hunger Strike Command. Chai Ling was named "commander in chief" of the new group.

The Conference of Patriotic Supporters continued to meet almost daily, either at the Academy of Social Sciences or at a semi-independent institution called the Institute of Chinese Culture. Wang Dan chaired the meetings and Wang Juntao was a key organizer. On May 27 the group held an expanded session that Xiaobo attended. Chai Ling made a surprising report that the square had descended into wrangling, both among different Beijing groups and between Beijing groups and groups from other cities. Fewer students were in the square than before, and a higher percentage were from outside Beijing. Morale was very low. The litter and mess showed no improvement. A week into martial law, Beijing citizens were doing a good job of cajoling and resisting the troops stationed at the outskirts of the city, but popular support for the students had cooled.

At the same meeting, Gan Yang and Bao Zunxin presented a "Ten-Point Declaration on the Present Situation" that called on the government to vacate its martial law order, to renounce its April 26 editorial, and to convene an emergency meeting of the National People's Congress to consider removing Premier Li Peng from office, all within a few days; otherwise the large-scale peaceful petitioning in Tiananmen Square would likely extend at least until June 20, the date of the next regular session of the National People's Congress.

Feng Congde, deputy commander in-chief of the Defend Tiananmen Square Command, presented a financial report revealing that the organization's funds could last only one or two more days. For the students who favored withdrawal from the square, this was an opportunity to press their case. Xiaobo continued to be in favor as well. The shabby condition of the square was depressing, and he feared that the mess would reduce the enthusiasm of the Beijing people. To leave the square would not be a defeat; it would open an opportunity for the newly established autonomous student groups to return to campuses and establish permanent presences there, from which they could aim to make longer-term democratic progress.[21] The sense of the meeting drifted in this direction, and at its end there was a vote to leave the square on May 30. Chai Ling and Feng Congde were among those who raised their hands to approve.

But before the meeting ended, another twist arrived. Xiaobo made the comment that Lech Walesa was an important unifying voice in Poland's Solidarity movement. China would do well to have a similar "voice of the people"—someone who would monitor the Communist Party of China and continuously express a view from civil society. Xiaobo commented that Wuerkaixi might be able to play such a role. He was well known by now because of the democracy movement, and older intellectuals could serve as his advisers and consultants.[22] When Wuerkaixi responded that he thought he could, with the advice of a teacher like Liu Xiaobo, take such a responsibility, Chai Ling and Feng Congde immediately objected and listed several reasons Wuerkaixi was unsuitable. They left the room in anger, after announcing that from that day on the Defend Tiananmen Square Command, as a student group, would have nothing to do with this Conference of Patriotic Supporters, which was an intellectuals' group.

Back at the square that evening, there was a press conference in front of the Monument to the People's Heroes. Wang Dan announced the plan to leave on May 30 and Chai Ling contradicted him. She repeated the view that the resolution had not come from her student group. Li Lu, a deputy commander of that group, had done much to sway her opinion. Li was from Nanjing, had traveled to Beijing expressly to join the students at Tiananmen Square, and was firmly against withdrawal. He saw the intellectuals' group as intruders. A decision on whether to withdraw or not should be made by democratic vote among the occupiers themselves, he said.

Xiaobo was troubled by the looming split between the students and the intellectuals. They vitally needed each other, he felt.[23] What could he do? How could he gain credibility with the students? Strangely, perhaps, for someone who had argued against hunger striking, he concluded that he should do a hunger strike himself. He would limit it to three days, but that would be enough to make a point: "We intellectuals want to influence the students through reason, but the students won't believe us unless we can match them in actions. It's hard to go down to the headquarters of the Defend Tiananmen Square Command and make speeches about what to do if you have done nothing yourself."[24] He was as eager as ever to get his political philosophy across to the students. "A personal fast could earn me the right to speak at the square," he wrote. "I can use it to get my main points out, then hope they will sink in."[25] He also began to see a spiritual component to fasting. It could add significance to his life. "There is no route from here to divinity," he later wrote, "but that doesn't mean that an effort in that direction is wrong."[26]

If he were to do a hunger strike, he thought, wouldn't it be better if others participated? He thought first of Zhou Duo, knowing that he shared his views about the role intellectuals could play in bringing reason to popular movements. He asked Zhou, who hesitated, but then agreed. Tao Li had been opposed to the risky idea of a hunger strike but softened when she heard that Zhou Duo would be joining Xiaobo. Zhou's judgment was sound, and Xiaobo respected Zhou enough that he would probably listen to his counsel. Tao Li's trust added to the weight of the responsibility that Zhou felt. In any case, Xiaobo and his friend discussed what to put into a "Hunger Strike Declaration," and then Xiaobo sat down to write it.

The declaration revisits his ideas about "no enemies, no hatred." It draws sentences from the reflections on Hu Yaobang's death that he had written in New York in April, from the wall poster he had put up on the Beijing Normal campus on May 7, and from "Our Proposals," published in the students' *Hunger Strike Bulletin* a week earlier. He wanted finally to move beyond the ideology that he and other Chinese children of his generation had learned in school. Where in their teaching materials had they ever encountered heroes, either historical or fictional, who were good at compromise? No, all heroes struggled to the end, even to death, unbending. Xiaobo now saw that kind of mentality as weakness, not strength. A truly independent person is one who has the strength to decide when to make concessions and whose confidence remains the same before and after a concession is made. His goal was to write the clearest possible statement of this new political philosophy. He wanted it to be deeper than a mere denunciation of the Cultural Revolution or even of all of Communist rule in China. He wanted it to address Chinese political culture at its root.

"For several thousand years," he wrote, "Chinese society has been caught in the vicious cycle of tearing down an old dynasty in order to set up a similar new one."[27] This is why "thousands of years of Chinese history are filled with instances of hatred between adversaries and the use of violence to fight violence." The pattern had lasted to the present day, without any fundamental changes. When the modern era comes, any nation should be allowed to modernize its politics along with other things. Political modernization need not arrive simultaneously with economic modernization, but it is bound to happen when society reaches a certain level. China's Republican years (1912–1949) were but a new turn of the old cycle. They helped to establish a modern industrial base for the country but did not bring about a modern political transition. Mao Zedong was only another sovereign of the ancient kind, not a modern political leader.

The declaration recommends a new starting point: "What we need is not an ideal savior but to pursue an ideal democratic system [that includes] checks and balances, which are the heart of democracy." It then repeats a line from his May 7 poster: "It is better that ten devils be working within a system of checks and balances than that one angel be ruling with unchecked power." Democratic balance lies in structures and procedures. The declaration calls, accordingly:

First, for the establishment throughout society of self-governing organizations that can gradually give shape to popular political forces that will serve as counterbalances to the central governing authority.... Second, for the gradual establishment of a system of recall of officials who have seriously abused power. The questions of who enters office and who leaves it are not as important as the questions of how enterings and leavings are determined. Undemocratic procedures lead inevitably to dictatorship.

Xiaobo's new ability to explicate the rules and procedures of democratic government much impressed his teacher Professor Tong Qingbing. Tong saw the intellectual breakthroughs that Xiaobo was making as the fruit of the same determination to study and to improve himself that he had always shown. His analysis of Chinese tradition, moreover, was not glib generalization but rooted in the conscientious study of classical literature and philosophy that he had done in graduate school. Yet, in some ways, Xiaobo's intellectual orientation had seemed to reverse. Then, he had favored the spontaneous, the unplanned, the "irrational." Now, he was a champion of rationality and rule observation. The change seems to have come about largely because of an inversion of the angle from which he was viewing "rules." When they were authoritarian strictures that limited and controlled people from above, he opposed them. When they were tools of democratic governance agreed upon among the people below, they were necessary and good.

One trait that remained constant in Xiaobo was his bent for critical reflection: on himself, on Chinese intellectuals, and on all of Chinese culture. He writes further in the hunger strike declaration: "Intellectuals must end our thousands-of-years-old traditions of standing in docility before power. We can no longer use words alone, without actions. We must, through actions, resist martial law, declare the birth of a new political culture, and repent the mistakes to which our long-term weakness has given rise." Amid the current crisis at Tiananmen, he had criticisms for both the students and the government, although the government's responsibility was by far the heavier:

> The main mistake of the government has been to cling to the "class struggle" mentality in how it views the protesting students and citizens; this mentality casts the protesters as enemies and has led to continual escalation. Instead, the government could learn something valuable by asking itself why such a large democracy movement has arisen. It could learn to listen to what people are saying, to accept their constitutional rights to express themselves, and to adopt techniques of democratic rule. The democracy movement could actually help to teach the government how to govern a society using democracy and rule of law.

The students' mistakes

> have been mostly in the less-than-ideal internal workings of their organizations. Their efforts to build an edifice of democracy have used too many undemocratic

bricks. There have been three kinds of problems: 1) theory is democratic but the handling of problems is not; 2) the ends are democratic but procedures are not; and 3) effort is wasted because cooperation is poor. These problems have led to confusion in policy, jumble in finances, and material waste. Too many decisions are based in sentiment, not reason, and there is too much emphasis on special privilege rather than on equality.

He called on the students to work on their procedures so that democratic goals would be pursued through democratic means. Civic consciousness is not only about right and wrong or about sympathy; it requires a sense of political responsibility:

> We should recognize that all Chinese citizens are strangers to the matter of running a country on democratic principles. All the Chinese people, including the top leaders of the Party and state, need to learn these principles from the beginning. As the learning happens, there are bound to be many mistakes among the populace and officialdom alike. The key will be to recognize mistakes when they happen, to correct them, and to learn from them. If we proceed this way, mistakes can be turned into good things. Through continual correction of errors we can learn, step by step, how to govern our country democratically.

The declaration ends with four summary points:

1. We have no enemies. We must not let hatred or violence poison our thinking or the progress of democratization in China.
2. We must reflect on our ways. China's backwardness is everyone's responsibility.
3. We are citizens before we are anything else.
4. We are not seeking death. We are seeking authentic lives.

In retrospect, this hunger strike declaration should be viewed as a rare and important document in China's pursuit of modern government. A few days after he wrote it, Xiaobo said, "I was not just criticizing the government. I was addressing everyone."[28] He certainly meant to include the protesting students, most of whom had been born in the 1960s and who therefore had grown up with the enmity training in Communist schools. They had (in a phrase that was common at the time) "been raised on wolf's milk." Xiaobo wanted all sides—rulers, students, citizens—to perceive their commonalities, to look for common language, and to realize the need for a new beginning in their political culture.

Even while assuming an Olympian height from which to make his observations, Xiaobo took care to rebut the government's charges that he and others were "black hands" behind the protests. The declaration confronts those charges directly: "We in this so-called 'tiny minority' are citizens who feel a political responsibility and who have joined a broad social movement in which students have taken the lead. Everything that we have done is rational and legal." On the evening of June 1, in a speech at the main gate of Beijing Normal, even as a helicopter of the martial law troops was circling overhead, Xiaobo put it even more bluntly: "I am not afraid of being a black hand; in the context of the democracy movement, I actually take the label as a badge of honor."[29]

Xiaobo and the popular Taiwan singer Hou Dejian had seen each other several times during the demonstrations. By then Hou was widely known in China, and Xiaobo thought it would raise the profile of his and Zhou Duo's hunger strike if Hou could be persuaded to join. Hou was in Hong Kong at time, having just participated there with dozens of other performing artists in a huge "Concert for Democracy in China" at which three hundred thousand people raised thirteen million Hong Kong dollars for the students in Beijing. Hou answered yes, he would join the strike. The line at the end of the "June Second Declaration" that read "We are not seeking death, we are seeking genuine lives" was Hou's suggestion.

Another line in the declaration—"Li Peng is not our enemy"—was the contribution of Gao Xin, who became its fourth signatory. Gao was another member of the brilliant "class of 1977" who had passed the newly reinstated university examinations that year. He had earned his B.A. in the Chinese Department at Beijing Normal University, where he was hired upon graduation as editor of the school newspaper. He wanted to join Xiaobo's hunger strike because he was a Communist Party member and wanted to make the point that the declaration was important to people both inside and outside the Party. Xiaobo welcomed this. Gao wanted to add the line about Li Peng not being an enemy because some demonstrators had been shouting not only "Down with Li Peng" but things like "Burn Li Peng" and "Fry Li Peng." He wanted people to notice that here too were the continuing ripples of Cultural Revolution hate language.[30]

When Xiaobo brought his idea of a hunger strike to the Conference of Patriotic Supporters he met with some resistance. Wang Juntao at first was puzzled. But when he thought more about the lines "We have no enemies. We must not let hatred or violence poison our thinking," he thought, *Yes, that's Xiaobo, and it comes from his heart.*[31] Wang arranged for Chen Xiaoping from the University of Politics and Law to be the spokesperson for the "four gentlemen" who would do the fasting. Wang also drafted a plan for a "relay team" of others who, three at

a time, would carry on with the strike after the three-day period Xiaobo was planning had expired. The team would maintain the strike until the National People's Congress met on June 20.

About 3:00 p.m. on June 2, Xiaobo and his three companions went to the base
of the Monument to the People's Heroes in Tiananmen Square to begin their fast.
Hou Dejian needed to rush back to Hong Kong for a concert in two days, so his
fasting time was set at forty-eight hours, but for the other three it was set at
seventy-two. Wang Juntao presided over a press conference that began with intro-
ductions of the four, after which each was to make his own statement. When the
megaphone was passed to Hou Dejian, the gathered crowd shouted for him to
sing, not speak. People crushed forward seeking autographs or just wanted to be
near the singer's pretty face. Hou's only rival in attracting attention on the square
was a magnificent statue, about thirty-five feet tall, of a "goddess of democracy"
that about two dozen students from the Central Academy of Art and the Beijing Film Academy had built in only two days. A ditty surfaced in the square:
"First see the goddess, then see the star."

The four hunger strikers set up camp on the top level of the monument's base,
facing north. The base was tall enough that they were looking down on crowds
as they passed by below. Faces beamed up at them. Their tent contained four cots,
each with brand-new pillows and blankets, and volunteer doctors were present.
Xiaobo later wrote that he actually felt pampered. The people below shouted,
cheered, waved their banners and their arms, and chanted slogans. The ones close
by held out pens and notebooks, seeking autographs. Flashbulbs kept going off
and video cameras rolled. People reached out with cassette recorders, hoping to
catch fragments of the strikers' conversation.[32] The hubbub exceeded anything
that Xiaobo had expected and was a bit more than he could take. He'd always
been at home in front of crowds, but in this case was so excited that all he could
do was say, "Thank you! Thank you!" over and over.

The carnivalesque atmosphere was exhilarating but detracted from Xiaobo's
original, very serious purpose. It seemed perhaps that the dramatic student hunger strike just concluded had drained the public appeal of such. When the "four
gentlemen" announced their own strike, it might have seemed even a bit playful.
Few people read Xiaobo's "June Second Declaration" carefully. One who did
was Wu Renhua—a professor at Chinese University of Politics and Law and a
member of the Patriotic Supporters group—and he did not entirely like it. "I
couldn't understand how they could lay blame equally on the students and
the Communist regime," Wu later wrote.[33] But he remained in awe of Xiaobo's
moral courage.

FIGURE 9.2 The "Four Gentlemen"—Zhou Duo, Liu Xiaobo, Hou Dejian, and Gao Xin—at Tiananmen Square, June 2, 1988

S. F. Choi

Ever self-critical, Xiaobo later wrote about gaps between his high-minded principles and his actual behavior on the square. He had proclaimed, "We have no enemies," but also found himself joining a student chant, "Have it out with Li Peng to the end!" He had criticized Wuerkaixi for using bodyguards, but now student monitors were tightly controlling access to himself as well. He sometimes held grudges: the poet Mang Ke and the poetry critic Tang Xiaodu came to see him with a proposal to organize a poetry reading at the square, and Xiaobo said, "Mang Ke can come in—but not that other one." He was still blaming Tang for an incident in 1987 when Tang had compared Xiaobo, in his attacks on Li Zehou, to Xing Tian, a mythical headless giant who roars in vain at Heaven using his navel for a mouth. How could such a grudge pass the "no enemies" test? And what about his repeated urging that students return to their campuses, and people in general to their daily lives, to "do democracy" at the micro level? Wasn't he himself ignoring that advice? He had come to Tiananmen Square to be in the spotlight and to joust with those at the top. The first time he addressed students at Tiananmen he began by shouting, "I am Liu Xiaobo! Liu Xiaobo! Liu Xiaobo!"

over and over. Later he reflected, with disapproval, on "the special joy that came from shouting my own name."[34]

He noticed some intellectual inconsistencies in himself as well. He despaired that Chinese intellectuals were too "utilitarian" in their motives, looking for material advantages instead of pursuing truth for its own sake.[35] But he found himself also being utilitarian. "I can't shake off the tradition of seeking practical advantage. . . . Where can you find me pursuing 'learning for the sake of learning'?"[36] He criticized Chinese intellectuals for worshiping power and bragging about their connections with high officials but recalled how he himself had pulled Yan Mingfu's telephone number out of his pocket to show to his teacher Tong Qingbing. Wasn't that showing off?

He also chastised himself for his marital infidelities, which reached even into the hunger strike tent. Tao Li came to see him there, hugged him, and said she wished he would come home. Later, when his fellow gentleman Hou Dejian observed him flirting with a girlfriend inside the same tent, Hou finally couldn't take it anymore. "Xiaobo, you jerk, did you drag me here to do a hunger strike or as a plot to torture me? I'd love to lift my foot and kick you off the bed."[37]

At the famous Tiananmen Square, which within a few hours would become the focus of the entire world's horrified attention, and with Xiaobo courageously struggling at its center, it is painful to see this behavior as part of the picture—written there by the culprit himself.

10

A "Black Hand" Goes to Prison, Feels Deep Remorse

Seeing that the hunger strike of the "four gentlemen" had stimulated an unusually boisterous atmosphere on the square, the Conference of Patriotic Supporters decided to dispatch two professors to assist them: Wu Renhua to be in charge of the student monitors and Liu Suli, a colleague of Wu's at the University of Politics and Law, to be press secretary. They arrived on the afternoon of June 3, bringing forty students ready to serve as monitors.

Meanwhile, quietly at first, a more ominous trend was afoot. The government was using civilian vehicles to move military equipment into the city. Citizens first noticed this by chance when at about 11:00 p.m. on June 2, a Mitsubishi jeep driving at a place called Muxidi ("alfalfa land," so called because, in imperial times, it was a feeding spot for camels), 3.5 miles due west of the city center, suddenly veered onto a sidewalk and killed three people. It had no license plate. Witnesses were naturally perplexed. Looking inside the jeep's cargo space, they found maps, walkie-talkies, and other equipment that showed this was no ordinary vehicle. Word spread through the city. Tensions rose. Hoping to stop any further military intrusion, people rushed to about thirty main intersections, where they blocked and surrounded other military vehicles.

About 1:00 p.m. on June 3, citizens blocked a suspicious-looking bus at Liubukou, about a mile west of Tiananmen, and found it packed with guns and ammunition. A protester climbed on top of the bus and brandished weapons he had "captured." About 2:30 p.m., armed police released tear gas at the scene until an area about a mile in diameter reeked. The mood on the square tightened abruptly when news of these events was broadcast over the students' public address system. People began teaching one another how to defend against tear gas. Xiaobo overheard them also talking about disabling tanks and making Molotov cocktails.

The army's plan for clearing Tiananmen Square had been made well in advance.[1] The choreography merely had to unfold. About 6:30 p.m., the Beijing City government and the Martial Law Command jointly issued an "Emergency Notice" instructing people to stay in their homes and stay away from Tiananmen Square. It warned that "officers of Public Security have been authorized to deploy any and all means of enforcement."[2]

Many ordinary citizens who heard the announcement did the opposite and came to the streets. If the students needed help, they wanted to help. The phrase "any and all means of enforcement" did not frighten them as much as it should have. This was not because of lionhearted courage so much as a failure to imagine that the People's Liberation Army might really open fire. Even after the shooting began and people began to fall to the ground, some were shouting, "Rubber bullets! Rubber bullets!" Only real blood and real death forced the conclusion: no, *real bullets*.

The thrust of the army's assault on Tiananmen Square arrived from the west and was approaching Muxidi in the late hours of June 3. As word spread, thousands of people armed only with rocks and pieces of concrete gathered at the flyover bridge there. Tanks led the military's approach, and behind them came a long column of vehicles carrying fully armed soldiers. The angry protesters maneuvered three large public buses transversely across the avenue that led toward Tiananmen. Hundreds of people pressed their bodies against the buses to resist the tanks, which had to ram several times before breaking through. When the soldiers released tear gas and followed it with bullets, the protesters were forced into retreat. They looked for trees or other obstacles to hide behind.

The apartment home of Professor Jiang Peikun, who had been one of the examiners at Xiaobo's Ph.D. dissertation defense a year earlier, was nearby. Jiang was in the Chinese Department at People's University, and his wife, Ding Zilin, also at People's University, was a professor of aesthetics in the Philosophy Department. They had a seventeen-year-old son, Jiang Jielian, in high school, and an excited supporter of the democracy movement. The parents, fearful of what their son might do, told him he had to stay at home. When he resisted they locked him in his room. Willful adolescent that he was, he exited through a window about 10:30 p.m. and went to Muxidi. About 11:10 p.m., he and some of his classmates were crouching beneath a low brick wall that bordered one of the flower beds at the center of the avenue when Jielian said to a classmate, "I think I've been hit." He collapsed and never stood again. In the space of about two hours, about a hundred others fell at Muxidi. Some, screaming "Fascist!" risked their lives to reach the wounded and carry or drag them to the nearby Fuxing Hospital.

At Tiananmen Square, students had gathered at 10:00 p.m. at the statue of the Goddess of Democracy to observe the opening ceremonies for "Tiananmen Square Democracy University." A different distinguished professor was to be invited every night to lecture on a topic related to "freedom, democracy, rule of law, or human rights." Professor Yan Jiaqi, a political scientist and honorary president of the university, was to give the first lecture, to be followed by free discussion. This activity ended abruptly when sounds of guns and the glint of fire impinged from the west. The students' broadcasting stand became the focal point of the square as students and citizens came, one by one, to tell what they had witnessed: how the "people's army" was indeed firing on the people, who were falling.

The first report of a student death arrived about midnight. It happened in front of the Military Museum of the Chinese People's Revolution, about four miles west of Tiananmen. The news had a sharp and immediate impact. Some students, recklessly brave as they shouted things like "Fight to the end!" began rushing up Chang'an Avenue toward spots where the fighting was said to be the fiercest: the Xidan intersection and the overpass at Fuxingmen. Citizens emerged from their homes with bicycles, flatbed carts, and simple medical equipment and headed to the danger zones to help ferry people to hospitals. Students who remained in the square looked for funeral music to play at their broadcasting stand, but no one had brought any—why would they? One student went to the microphone and sang a dirge set to Chopin. The student leaders of Defend Tiananmen Square asked the protesters to gather peacefully at the Monument to the People's Heroes to prepare a nonviolent response to the attacks. Eventually a crowd of about ten thousand, including both students and nonstudents, assembled.

The burning question was whether to stay or withdraw, and opinions were strong. Chai Ling recalls in a memoir how she was confronted with two directly opposing threats. A citizen who had captured some guns and bayonets from the army shouted at her: "So many people have already died for you students. If you dare withdraw, I'll execute you right here!" But another student, who had been in the movement from the beginning, shouted: "So many have died over there [to the west]. If you're going to let even more die you'll go down in history as a criminal. We should save the lives in front of us. If you don't give the order to withdraw, I'll do it myself—but will kill you first."[3] Immobilized for the moment, Chai Ling gave neither order.

Around midnight Wu Renhua noticed Xiaobo sitting and leaning against the Heroes Monument with a young woman who was leaning against him. The two were frozen in silence, wearing grave expressions. Wu felt an impulse to go ask Xiaobo for his thoughts on the looming crisis, but he held back. He didn't want to disturb that solemn and quiet moment, which might be the last they would have for a long time.[4]

The first military arrivals in the square were two armored cars that emerged from Chang'an Avenue at the northwest corner and traversed its north edge eastward at breakneck speed. When people tried to stop them, they did not even slow down. Then two more armored cars entered at the southern edge, one from the east and one from the west, and raced around the square at the same speed. It was a choreographed show of force. One of the cars, after crashing into a concrete road divider and a steel fence, came to a stop. Angry protesters ran to it and set it afire, and the heat drove three soldiers to evacuate. A tide of people surrounded them, assailed them with insults, and escorted them to a first aid station at the northeast corner of the square.[5] The next step in the choreography came about 12:50 a.m. when the military shot bright flares into the sky in such numbers that it could have seemed bright as daybreak. News came of more deaths. People in the square grew frantic.

Some continued to leave in the direction of the fighting, hoping somehow to halt the approach of the tanks. Wu Renhua recalls a group of about thirty workers who had originally volunteered as monitors but headed west when they heard the crackle of gunfire. About 1:30 a.m. one of them came back—alone. His clothes were stained with blood, and he said his brothers had been "sacrificed." Two women in the group, who originally had not rushed to the front, now insisted on doing so. They could not be stopped, Wu writes. They headed off with their bloodstained co-worker, and they too did not return.[6] This almost unimaginable behavior among Beijing commoners—accepting their own deaths to preserve life for the students—became a hallowed leitmotif in later accounts of the massacre.

The troops who had been killing their way eastward arrived at the northwest corner of the square about 1:30 a.m. Their vanguard was an especially vicious group whose gunfire seemed incessant. Around the same time, another contingent of troops arrived at the southern edge of the square. Next, doors of the Great Hall of the People, on the west side, opened wide and about ten thousand more troops emerged. They had entered the hall through tunnels built more than two decades earlier as emergency escape routes for state leaders. Troops now completely surrounded the square. Civilians were allowed to exit but not to enter. Another emergency "Notice" blared from a high-amplitude speaker atop the Great Hall. It used the term "counterrevolutionary riot" to describe the student movement— and ever since, that has been the Communist Party's "correct" term for the events.

The notice exhorted people to "cooperate with the People's Liberation Army . . . we cannot guarantee the safety of anyone who disobeys this advice . . . [and who] will themselves bear responsibility for all the consequences."[7] It was broadcast at high volume over and over.

Xiaobo, Hou Dejian, Zhou Duo, and Gao Xin, who were more than thirty hours into their fast, listened intently to reports as the troops approached. When gunfire became audible they emerged from their tent, but student monitors, fearing stray bullets, would not let them leave the monument. When a new contingent of monitors arrived, its leader handed them a note: "Dear four teachers: If anything dangerous happens, we will protect you for sure. If we die, we all die together." The four strikers wrote a note in reply promising that under no circumstances would they leave the square before the students did; everyone was in this together. When one of the monitors took that outside the tent and read it aloud, it brought applause. The monitors brought the strikers food and drink, urging them to end their fast. They did. The dramatic events had made fasting moot.

Nonviolence had been a firm principle of the protest movement from its beginning, not least because, given the huge inequality in firepower, violence would have been suicidal. But the worry that the regime might use violence had been growing among the protesters ever since martial law was declared on May 20, and they had begun to cache weapons and even potential weapons, such as vegetable cleavers, that supportive citizens had brought them. At 2:30 a.m. Feng Congde, deputy commander of Defend Tiananmen Square, made a speech reaffirming the principle of nonviolence, after which Xiaobo, Hou Dejian, Zhou Duo, and Gao Xin all made similar speeches, pleading with the students not to answer regime violence with violence of their own. Xiaobo said that those gathered at the base of the monument were the precious elite of a whole generation—so they should not make any stupid sacrifices.

Word arrived that a "captured machine gun" had appeared on the south side of the monument. Xiaobo, Hou Dejian, and Wu Renhua rushed to the spot and saw that two young workers indeed had such a gun, had wrapped it in a bed comforter, and weren't letting anyone else get near it. The two had already been to massacre sites in the city and seen friends die, and were planning revenge. They had lifted the machine gun from an armored car. Hou Dejian went over to one of them and wrapped his arms around him, using a single embrace both to hug and to confine him, and said, "I am Hou Dejian."

"Big brother Hou!" the young man wailed, breaking into tears.

Xiaobo also went over to give hugs but was more discursive than Hou. Fighting back tears, he approached the two workers, bowing and clasping his hands in front of his chest in the traditional Chinese gesture of entreaty, and said: "I completely understand how you feel, but just think, if you can—the moment a gun goes off from our side, blood will flow like a river! You can let fly and kill a few martial law troops, yes, but there are a few thousand defenseless lives sitting here in the square. You can look for your revenge, but this is not the time!"[8] The two young workers handed the machine gun over. Reflecting on this incident four years later, Xiaobo wrote:

> I'm eternally grateful to those two, whose names I do not know and whose faces I barely remember. They did a tremendous service in the cause of peace that night. I'm sure their fate has been worse than mine. They must have been detained as "rioters" and may still be in prison now. When I was released from prison in January 1991, the judge read out their "confessions" on the matter of the machine gun, and those statements had a lot to do with my getting a reduced sentence.[9]

In 1991 the court that released Xiaobo attributed his relatively light sentence to "merit" he had earned in the eyes of the regime, likely due to this incident.

Soon there came another shout, this time from the north side of the Monument to the People's Heroes. A semiautomatic rifle had turned up. Xiaobo rushed to the spot and, with the help of two monitors, captured the weapon. It was smaller than the machine gun, and Xiaobo realized he might actually be able to destroy it. He raised it above his head and thrust it full force onto the stone fence that lines the base of the monument. It did not bend on first impact, so he repeated the action continually until his arms were weary and his hands were going numb. Finally the thing did bend. He accompanied his performance with these words: "I am smashing this gun! I am doing it to confirm our principle of nonviolence and to show that the government's violent repression is fascist behavior!" Then he handed the gun to the monitors, who continued whacking it against the stone fence until it fell in two parts. A foreign journalist saw Xiaobo smashing the gun and took a photo that later became an iconic illustration of nonviolence on the square. It is also likely that the act saved many lives that morning.

Violence was imminent and everyone knew it. Should the students withdraw? Chai Ling, as leader of Defend Tiananmen Square, went to the student broadcasting stand and announced that each student should decide for him- or herself. She was near exhaustion, and her voice was hoarse. "If you choose to leave," she called out, "then leave; if you want to stay—as I am choosing—then stay." To Xiaobo and his colleagues, this guideline seemed dangerous. Might students who were genuinely fearful be afraid to say so? Wouldn't there be conflicts if some left and some stayed? And how could they know that the ones leaving would really be safe? They tried to think about how a collective retreat could be achieved.[10]

Around that time, Shao Jiang, a Peking University student who was on the steering committee of the students' Autonomous Association, found his teacher Zhou Duo amid the chaos. Shao was trembling. He had just come from the combat zones to the west. His words tumbled out: "It's awful, Teacher Zhou! Nothing like anything we ever imagined! Blood is everywhere! Those soldiers have gone crazy, just crazy—like mad dogs! When they see somebody, they fire! Anyone—male, female, young, old . . . it doesn't matter who! They just fire! . . . Teacher Zhou, *please, please*! The only ones who can save the students here are you four teachers! You *have* to think of something! *Please!*"[11] Shao Jiang's passion caused something inside Zhou Duo to snap. He now *had* to act. Was there a way to get the students out of the square? He couldn't go to their leaders by himself, because he, Xiaobo, Hou Dejian, and Gao Xin had agreed that they would act jointly on any important questions. Guessing that Xiaobo would have powerful opinions, Zhou Duo went to Gao Xin and Hou Dejian first. Both agreed that a retreat was best. All three then went to Xiaobo to see if they could persuade him. It wasn't easy.

"Now?!" Xiaobo objected. "You want to withdraw *now*?" The square was surrounded by armed troops; why would going now be safer than staying put? Besides, he argued, hadn't the students who wanted to leave already done so? To persuade the remaining students would be well-nigh impossible. Xiaobo thought too of the people at Liubukou, Muxidi, and elsewhere who had already given their lives to "protect the students at the square." Was that so the rest could retreat? Moreover, the four of them were not in the students' organization. They could not decide this question; at most they could only advise the students.

Xiaobo's view seemed to have changed within an hour. He had just smashed a rifle lest "blood flow like a river" and thousands of lives be lost. Now he seemed to be arguing against protection of those same lives. Wasn't that contradictory? It may not have been. Xiaobo's principle of pacifism, drawn from his reading, was "non-violent non-cooperation."[12] To grab a machine gun and start shooting was violent and would have triggered much more, indeed disastrous, violence. So nonviolence was called for. But the "noncooperation" part of the formula was just as important. The government's blaring loudspeakers had for hours been exhorting people to leave the square. It was important to the government that people obey, because then it could claim that in the end everyone had accepted its authority as legitimate. What those who remained sitting peacefully in the square were doing was precisely "noncooperation" with a political goal. Asking them to get up and leave would be siding with the government. (In the days following the massacre, the state media did indeed claim repeatedly that students in the square had "cooperated" with the military.)

Moreover, another of Xiaobo's deep-seated principles, rooted in his admiration of Zhuangzi and his study of aesthetics, was to respect the autonomy of human beings. Hundreds, perhaps thousands, of students on the square had chosen to stay even if the price were their own lives. They had had time to consider the decision—from 11:00 p.m., when the first reports of the killings came in, until now, about 3:00 a.m. Xiaobo thought: *Even if I disagree with a person's judgment, don't I need to respect it?* Later, when Zhou Duo and Hou Dejian went to negotiate with the military, a number of students were irate for exactly that reason: it was their decision—who were the teachers to intervene?

In the end, though, Xiaobo relented and accepted Zhou Duo's proposal. The argument that saving three to five thousand lives should outweigh other factors was powerful. Moreover, there was the principle of democracy—within their group of four, Xiaobo was being outvoted three to one.

But agreement among the four still left the question of what exactly to do. At that critical juncture a surgeon named Song Song, who worked at the Peking Union Medical College Hospital and had been assigned in the afternoon of June 3 to work at Tiananmen Square, came looking for the "four gentlemen" to get them to persuade the students to heed the government's warnings and leave. Song wrote later that he had heard ominous words like "bloody fight to the end" on the students' loudspeaker and thought he should do something. People who saw him at the square noted how unusually calm he seemed.[13] He proposed that he and another doctor accompany two representatives from among Hou, Zhou, Gao, and Liu to negotiate with the military about terms for a withdrawal. He said he could arrange an ambulance to ensure safe passage for such a delegation.

The four were ready to give negotiation a try. Obviously, though, they could not do so without the students' approval, so they went as a group to the tent of the Defend Tiananmen Square Command, not far from their own tent, and shared their plans with Chai Ling, Li Lu, and Feng Congde. The three rebuffed them. Chai Ling said that she could not leave the leadership tent at a crucial moment like this. Feng Congde said that the hunger strikers could go negotiate but couldn't represent the students. The fact that others had already died to protect them, he said, made it hard to up and leave. According to Hou Dejian's account of the meeting, Chai Ling also said that Zhao Ziyang, Yan Mingfu, and other moderates in the Party elite were hoping that the students could hold out until dawn, when they, the moderate leaders, might be able to do something. Xiaobo was contemptuous of letting state leaders of any stripe gamble with student lives in this way.[14]

The student leaders were unwilling to endorse a delegation, but the hour was late—3:00 a.m. already—and the protesters remaining in the square seemed like a skiff tossing on storm waves. Delay could be disastrous. The four teachers decided to negotiate even without license from the students. But which two should go? Xiaobo thought he should. The hunger strike had been his idea, and "the hunger strikers" was the label under which they were going to present themselves. He thought the other representative should be Hou Dejian, because his fame would provide an additional layer of safety. Zhou and Gao agreed on Hou but not on Xiaobo because of his peppery character. They thought the steady, careful Zhou Duo should be the second delegate. They further pointed out that Xiaobo's prestige with the students was the greatest among the four of them; he would be the best person to stay behind to persuade them to leave.

So Hou and Zhou set off with the two doctors while Xiaobo and Gao Xin took up megaphones and, guarded by monitors and fighting back tears, circled the base of the Monument to the People's Heroes, calling upon the students to set down their "weapons" (stone slabs, glass bottles, etc.) and to organize by school into groups, in preparation to leave. A student held up a homemade fire bomb and asked what to do with it. "Destroy it!" Xiaobo answered. "And whatever you do, keep it away from both the fanatical students and the soldiers!"[15]

Around 3:30 a.m. Zhou Duo and Hou Dejian began talking with a colonel in the People's Liberation Army named Ji Xinguo. The negotiations were preceded by some mutual denunciations. "You're intellectuals," the colonel said. "How can you support a riot?" Zhou Duo answered by asking how the "people's" army could kill so many people and said they had come to see if further bloodshed could be avoided. Ji Xinguo replied, "I would like that too, but it's not up to me." He stepped away to consult electronically with higher authorities.

Right at that moment all the lights in the square went out at once, and soldiers on every side, as if taking a cue, began shouting, hooting, and moving guns into position. Colonel Ji returned to the negotiation. He said the army command had agreed and that the safe route out of the square would be to the southeast. He also said that if Hou and Zhou could persuade the students to leave, the government would view them as having "earned great merit."[16]

After the lights went out, a few protesters left the square, but somewhere between three and five thousand remained. Many were from outside Beijing. They huddled at the four sides of the Heroes Monument—perhaps more at the north side, the side closest to the threatening troops. To ward off darkness and perhaps fear as well, some had used their bedding and tents to start bonfires. In the murky background of the still unlit square, the passing of armored cars and the grinding of tank treads were audible. The light from the fires was just enough that people could descry the majestic crash to the ground of the statue of the Goddess of

Democracy as tanks pushed it over. The tanks went on to crush student tents in the square. How many students were inside? No one knew then or knows today.

Hou Dejian and Zhou Duo, now nearly in panic, rushed through the gloom back to the monument, specifically to the student broadcasting stand at its southwest corner, where Hou shouted the result of their meeting with the army: the authorities had agreed to permit a peaceful withdrawal through the southeast corner of the square. The sounds of rifle fire and the stench of tear gas were drawing ever closer from the west, but those menacing portents did not prevent some students from shouting that Hou, the negotiator, was a lily-livered ghost. The everbookish Zhou Duo was explaining to the crowd that "whatever drop of blood we can save tonight will make our democratization that much stronger starting tomorrow."[17]

Xiaobo spoke too, and reserved time to address the nonstudent protesters: "Please don't get carried away! Try to stay calm. This student movement would be nowhere without your support. Sticking with the students right to the final moment shows your courage and your faith! I hope you can keep your cool. You have already made huge sacrifices for the students—we don't want to see you make any more! At this point, saving yourselves will be the biggest gift you can give to Chinese democracy." He then addressed students and nonstudents together: "Let's not burn any more garbage or make more messes. What we need now is to get organized in an orderly and safe way and to leave the square."[18] Xiaobo and Hou Dejian announced that neither of them would go until the very last protester had.

Around 4:30 a.m. the lights in the square came back on and showed in one vile glare how the military had advanced from every side. The government's giant speaker at the Great Hall of the People to the west bellowed the message, "The clearing of the square will commence. We accept the students' call for leaving the square."[19] Most of the students could not have known at that point that their Defend Tiananmen Square Command had in fact not agreed to leave the square. In any case, it was clear that the government was issuing its final ultimatum.

The troops began to move. On the east, from in front of the Museum of Chinese History, rows of armored cars and tanks rumbled toward the square. The army at the south approached as well. Around the Monument to the People's Heroes on all four sides, scarcely 35 feet distant, a dense assemblage of soldiers and armed police stood ready. Wu Renhua's overall description would be humorous if it were not horrific: a knot of unarmed students, sitting in peaceful protest, watching the approach of a military force at whose front were special forces troops (the "scouts") wearing camouflage suits and metal helmets, each supplied with a submachine gun and, tightly gripping its bolt, creeping forward bent at the waist in classic assault posture. Behind them was a huge array—hundreds, if not thousands—of supporting soldiers and armed police. In case all these were not enough, uniformed riot police, carrying shields and billy clubs, were at the ready. In the very back, as if supervising, were more tanks and armored cars.[20] Students flashed the V sign in the direction of this military jungle, as if they had not considered whether such a gesture might cost them their lives. Even at this point, they were divided over whether to withdraw or not.

The atmosphere of looming disaster made Zhou Duo and Hou Dejian frantic with worry. Was their deal with the army going to fall through? Again accompanied by the two doctors, they rushed to ask Colonel Ji Xinguo, who by now had moved with the advancing troops toward the middle of the square, if there were any possibility of slowing the strangling approach a bit while the students got better organized.

"None whatever," was the reply. Colonel Ji did not reveal that his own instructions, which came from the highest level in the government, were to "resolutely" clear the square by 6:00 a.m., with "absolutely no delays permitted."[21] But he did advise that Zhou, Hou, and the others leave right away even if the students didn't. "We can't promise your lives will be safe if you don't," he said.[22]

Rushing back to the monument, Zhou and Hou found that its top level, where the student headquarters and the hunger strikers' tent both had been located, was now occupied by a dense crowd of helmeted soldiers.

A few minutes earlier, a commando squad of about forty soldiers had rushed onto the monument, firing bullets into the air and thrusting rifle butts against the sitting students. They knocked down the students' broadcasting stand by slinging their submachine guns as wrecking tools. Luckily, a decision by the student leaders to withdraw had just gone out over that very broadcasting system ten minutes earlier.

In the years since then, Feng Congde has written several times that it was the advice of the four teachers that swayed student opinion and led eventually to a voice vote on whether to leave the square.[23] At the crucial moment Feng used the loudspeaker to ask that all who favored withdrawal shout "Withdraw!" and then all who favored staying shout "Hold on!" It was not easy to say which was the louder sound, but Feng declared that the "withdraws" had it. He, Chai Ling, and Li Lu then joined the flow of students that soon began moving slowly toward the southeast corner of the square. Soldiers in camouflage lined their route at a distance of about fifty feet. The deal that Hou Dejian and Zhou Duo had negotiated did not work perfectly, but it did work.

The troops did not keep Colonel Ji's promise that the students could withdraw "safely." They beat students wherever they found them, with no regard for whether they were moving out of the square or not. Victims fell to the ground, many with bloodied heads.[24] Zhou Duo, whose habitual demeanor was about as far from "rioter" as one could get, bears a permanent scar from being struck across the chest. When the students arrived at the southeast corner, where the safe exit was supposed to have been assured, troops and riot police were waiting to give them more beatings.

The army's plan to remove the students—both techniques and timing—clearly had been set in advance. Someday, when military archives are opened, perhaps the original plans will be accessible. One problem was that Zhou Duo and Hou Dejian's intervention with Colonel Ji was not originally in the plan, and a machine like the People's Liberation Army is very poor at accommodating unexpected events. So, although the students carried out their "peaceful retreat" as negotiated (there were no Molotov cocktails, perhaps not even a thrown stone), it was a different matter to get the military to play its agreed part.

Xiaobo did not witness the commando assault on the monument. He and Gao Xin had been elsewhere, exhorting students to leave. When he returned, he went to see if Chai Ling and other leaders were still in their tent. He bent to look inside and saw that it was empty. Straightening up to leave, he suddenly felt the cold, hard muzzle of a gun pressed into his back. "Still not leaving?!" a voice barked. "Time's up!" He staggered forward, down the monument steps, the gun muzzle still pressed into his ribs. Three soldiers at the bottom shouted, "Hurry up!"

Suddenly he remembered that he had left his book bag inside the hunger strike tent. His passport and other documents were in it. So were his address books. He turned and jogged back up the monument base but was shouted to a halt by a soldier with a rifle. "Still want your *passport*?! *Now*?! Get back down if you know what's good for you!" His student Wang Yuehong and a young lecturer from People's University named Yu Shuo stepped forward to try to negotiate with the soldier, who blurted, "Don't need your *life*?!"[25]

Xiaobo gave up on the book bag. He urged the two young women to leave while they could. He spotted Gao Xin, who was already receding with the crowd, which he joined himself. Sheerly by chance, he ran across a shocked and disoriented Hou Dejian, who apparently had been hurt. He and another friend helped Hou to the Red Cross station at the northeast corner of the square.

Dawn was breaking. Inside the Red Cross station Xiaobo could see two or three hundred injured people surrounded by soldiers and riot police. A chilling scene. Eight medical staff raised Hou Dejian aloft to carry him to the nearby Peking Union Medical College Hospital. Xiaobo went along. In the afternoon, he and Hou Dejian left the hospital and headed for the diplomatic quarter, where they hoped to find shelter beyond the reach of the army. They stayed in the home of Nicolas Jose, cultural attaché of the Australian embassy.

During the morning of June 4, word spread through Beijing that the Chinese Red Cross had estimated the death toll from the night of killing at 2,600 or more. There has never been a way to confirm this number. On June 6, China State Council spokesperson Yuan Mu announced that the death toll was about 300.[26] That number too is impossible to confirm but certainly too low. The number of wounded is even harder to estimate, in part because the survivors have been afraid to come forward. In the sullen terror that followed the massacre, to show a wound would reveal having been a "rioter" or a "counterrevolutionary," and such a label could bring even more suffering to oneself and one's family.

Throughout the day a sense of guilt weighed ever more heavily on Xiaobo's traumatized mind. Later he wrote: "If I had not begun the hunger strike, the protest movement would not have gained its second wind; had that new energy not come, the government might have just waited for the movement to peter out on its own; there might have been no confrontation between populace and military and no violent massacre at the end."[27] His friends assured him that this fear was largely a mirage. The government machine had constructed its strategy for clearing the square many days in advance, and those plans had nothing to do with the comings and goings of one Liu Xiaobo. (*The Tiananmen Papers* shows that the friends were right. Troops on the outskirts of Beijing were declared "ready both spiritually and physically" for the order to clear the square on June 1, 1989, the day before Xiaobo declared his hunger strike.)[28] Still, he continued to feel guilty.

In the evening of June 5, at Nicholas Jose's home, Hou Dejian suggested that the four hunger strikers write "An Appeal to the World Community." Xiaobo agreed and drafted a statement, and then he and Hou reached out to Zhou Duo and Gao Xin for their approval. The text condemned the government for "mobilizing armored cars, tanks, military trucks, and fully armed troops to repress unarmed students and Beijing citizens" and appealed to the international community "to impose economic, political, diplomatic, and moral sanctions on the fascist Chinese government and to give the democratic movement of the Chinese people and the victims of 'June Fourth' every possible sort of aid and support."[29] To put the statement out in their own names would have been forbiddingly dangerous, so they gave it to the writer Linda Jaivin, who was with them at Nicholas Jose's home, and she got it published in Australia as authored by "Beijing citizens."

Tao Li suffered the massacre in her own way. From the time bullets started flying on the night of June 3, she wandered through the streets around Beijing Normal looking for students who were returning from the square and asking if they had seen Xiaobo. When she saw the bloodstains on their clothing, she feared he was either dead or wounded. She wept. Her chronic eye disease flared up. Around noon on June 4, Gao Xin went to find Tao Li on the Beijing Normal campus to explain where Xiaobo was and to comfort her. She gave Gao Xin three thousand yuan and asked him to try to get the money to Xiaobo. She also sent the message that Xiaobo should hide or leave the country, if possible, and not worry about her and Liu Tao.

During the two days Xiaobo stayed with Nicolas Jose, Linda Jaivin asked him more than once if he would like to take refuge in the Australian embassy, and he said no. About 11:00 p.m. on June 6, he decided to get on his bicycle and head back home to Beijing Normal. He was about a quarter of the way there when a van suddenly veered in front of him, forcing him off the road. Its doors flew open and some ruffians emerged, covered his mouth and eyes, bundled him into the van, and drove off. For about fifteen minutes he could only sit and quiver, wondering, *Where are they taking me? To an empty place to do an execution?*[30]

They brought him directly to Qincheng Prison, where he stayed for the next twenty months. Gradually he learned what had happened to the other three hunger strikers: Hou Dejian accepted the offer of refuge in the Australian embassy and stayed there for seventy-two days. Gao Xin was arrested at home on June 14. Zhou Duo was arrested in Yantai, Shandong province, on June 30.

Qincheng is a special prison. Most of the workers and other common citizens who were rounded up after the massacre were sent to the Beijing No. 2 Prison, a maximum-security facility for serious offenders. Students and intellectuals were sent to the more comfortable Qincheng. Years later, following two other confinements, Xiaobo wrote a letter to his friend Liao Yiwu, who had also been detained after the massacre, but in a prison for ordinary people in Sichuan. Xiaobo wrote: "Compared with your years in prison, my three prison stints were pretty mild. During the first, at Qincheng, I had my own room, and my living conditions were better than what you had to endure. Sometimes I was deathly bored, but that's about it."[31] Liao's memoir of his experience in Sichuan is shocking. Inmates were cursed, spat at, kicked in the head, and subjected to endless and almost pointless drudgery that was cynically labeled "socialist labor." Special tortures for the disobedient had nicknames ("Stewed Ox Nose" meant a guard rammed two fingers up an inmate's nose until it bled; "Sichuan-Style Smoked Duck" meant he burned the inmate's pubic hair, pulled back his foreskin, and blackened the head of the penis with fire [the prison houses only men]). Liao records the full "menu" of thirty-eight "dishes."[32]

But Qincheng, established under Mao in 1960, was a prison for the upper class in China's classless society—for elite people who had lost in power struggles. Mao's widow and her confederates, known in the late 1970s as the "all-evil" Gang of Four, charged with visiting "ten years of catastrophe" on China, were sent there. Their "monstrous" crimes dictated that they go to prison, but their royalty kept them out of the nasty ones.

Relatively comfortable though it was, Qincheng had almost absurdly tight security. At least three layers of cable netting separated the exterior prison walls from the courtyard. To enter any interior building, one had to go through three heavy metal doors.

At first Xiaobo was held with a group of students in Qincheng's Building No. 204, but he soon was transferred to the intellectuals' building, No. 203. Chen Ziming, Wang Juntao, Liu Suli, and Chen Xiaoping were there as well. The students in 204 playfully called 203 "the high officials' quarters" because each person had a private room of more than 250 square feet plus a curtained porch area of another hundred or so square feet. The food too was considerably better. Inmates were given Party newspapers, so Xiaobo could read, among other things, the official denunciations of himself as they came out over the summer. Building 203 also had a lending library that inmates could use if they showed good behavior.

The psychological engineering was impressive. Each inmate, upon arrival, was body searched and stripped of anything that resembled string or rope. Xiaobo had to turn over his belt and shoelaces, and the drawstrings for his cotton trousers and even for his undershorts, including those he was currently wearing. He had to watch, in front of others, as a prison guard began snipping the strings off. He later wrote that he felt a new kind of humiliation. When he shrieked at the guard, "Don't worry," came the reply, "take it easy. There's nothing to be afraid of—no way we're going to hurt you. It's just a prison regulation. Routine. Mostly for your own safety." If "safety" were the only reason, then the snipping of underwear strings could have been done in private. Afterward, Xiaobo had to hold up his pants with one hand to keep from being exposed. Later he wrote: "What was I? A human being? How could they make a person feel so helpless? In an instant, my dignity was all gone. Words like 'weak,' 'powerless,' 'depressed,' and 'dispirited' aren't enough to describe the feeling. It was more like a head-to-toe numbness, a disconnection from my own self, from other people, and from the world, a feeling beyond despair."[33] The guard's phrase "just a prison regulation" may have come from his training. This most unusual place, Qincheng Prison, was charged with a difficult task: to handle the most important kind of offender entirely without physical violence. This put a great premium on psychological methods: how to dismantle people's dignity, lead them into mental traps, and even induce psychological collapse. Prison personnel—likely including this guard—received special training in such things.

During the ensuing days a haunting anxiety, born of having no idea what might happen next, grew inside Xiaobo. He did not have the right to a lawyer. No one in the prison did. The regime gathered evidence on its own and didn't tell prisoners anything until the day of their trial, when it assigned a lawyer not to argue their case but to see that the wheels of the court turned smoothly.

The "single room" that the Building No. 204 inmates admired was in fact a pretty name for solitary confinement. The lower edge of its windows was above eye level, and the glass was frosted slats that could be turned up or down but at most left only a "line in the sky" visible. Other inmates of Qincheng have written about that line, which occasionally allowed the glimpse of a passing sparrow. The only human contact was the blank-faced orderly who came thrice daily to deliver food but never gave a name, making it impossible to address the person, and the human eye that occasionally peered in silence through the half-inch peephole in the door, which showed the inmate only a black dot inside a while circle.

The authorities made no announcement of their abduction of Xiaobo at the time it happened. After seventeen days the Xinhua (New China) News Agency published a short item, "Liu Xiaobo, Who Participated in the Turmoil, Is Detained." It said that Xiaobo "while in New York was in close touch with people like Hu Ping, the head of the 'Alliance for Chinese Democracy.'" This fit the government's line that the student movement had been plotted by "reactionary forces" outside the country. To acknowledge the homegrown roots of the movement would be to accord it a certain legitimacy, and the authorities were not ready to do that, so any arguable evidence of "foreign connections" became their most important tool. American connections were the easiest to portray as toxic because, ever since the Korean War and especially during the Cultural Revolution, the United States had been cast as the vanguard of imperialism in the world. And Xiaobo had been *right there,* in the den of the predators, immediately before the democracy movement began.

Xinhua's announcement was not news in the conventional sense so much as a signal that the Party's highest authorities had, between the massacre date and June 23, selected Xiaobo to be a primary vehicle in their campaign to tarnish the student movement. A blizzard of denunciations followed quickly in the state press. Xiaobo, inside Qincheng, caught up with them after about a month's delay.

The next day, June 24, *Beijing Daily* published an article four thousand characters in length, "Grab Liu Xiaobo's Black Hands." The purpose of the unsigned piece was to "define the nature" of the "Liu Xiaobo question." In a contemptuous tone, it described the days before and after Xiaobo's return to China in April. His "systematic, overarching program" was to "use a bourgeois republic to overthrow a socialist republic." His contacts with Hu Ping and others in New York, and the joint declaration he wrote with them, were clear evidence of "collusion with foreign forces." The article further claimed that Xiaobo had rushed to Beijing on April 27 on the direct orders of the Chinese Alliance for Democracy and that he was carrying with him "several thousand U.S. dollars and more than ten thousand Chinese yuan" that the alliance and other foreign reactionary organizations had donated for use in China. In fact, the Alliance for Chinese Democracy had not assigned Xiaobo to do anything. He was not even a member of the group. The charge about his carrying money was so easy to refute that the government stopped mentioning it.

A more interesting but equally false charge was that he had said to an unnamed democracy movement leader, "We must organize a people's military force."[34] Chen Xitong, the mayor of Beijing, gave a widely distributed speech on June 28 in which he put a sharper point on this claim. He said, "On June 2, in a 'dialogue' with a so-called 'leader of the mainland democracy movement,' [Liu Xiaobo] openly shouted, 'We hope for a return of Zhao Ziyang and we must organize a people's military force.'"[35]

The comment came about because on June 2, before Xiaobo began his hunger strike, he did a telephone interview with Chen Jun in New York. Chen Jun had the interview translated into English for the Western media, and the *Independent Evening News* in Taiwan used the English version to translate the article back into Chinese and publish it on June 17. The back translator apparently had interpreted Xiaobo's reference to popular "forces" in China as military forces, because the result was *wuzhuang liliang*, "armed forces." This misunderstanding should have been avoidable, because in the context of the interview Xiaobo and Chen Jun were clearly discussing popular political forces. But the mistake was reprinted in the June 21 issue of the Hong Kong *Ming Pao*, which is where the Beijing authorities saw it.

This "evidence" that the democracy movement had military aspirations was especially valuable to the regime because it could be used to support the charge that the democracy movement was "counterrevolutionary," whether the regime actually believed it or not. If the democracy movement had wanted armed forces, then the decision to use military troops to repress it could be made to seem more normal. Using hollow-point "dumdum" bullets (which cause more severe flesh wounds than normal bullets) is outlawed internationally, but against a domestic "counterrevolutionary" rebellion perhaps could be allowed. The army did use such bullets.

The label "counterrevolutionary" was useful to the regime for another reason. It was vague enough to be an open hunting license for anyone the government wanted to sweep up. Beijing citizens who had risked (and sometimes lost) their lives trying to block tanks or pull wounded victims from the street now could be arrested as counterrevolutionary hoodlums. Careful research by Wu Renhua has identified twenty-two cases of "rioters" who were executed by firing squad after show trials or no trials shortly after the massacre.[36] Seven of them were trussed up and placed before Xinhua cameras before execution, to serve as warnings to others. Li Hai, a graduate student in philosophy at Peking University, compiled a list of more than 500 people who were given prison sentences of more than ten years for their parts in the counterrevolutionary riot. A few were well-known intellectuals like Chen Ziming and Wang Juntao, but the great majority were factory workers. Many were labeled "counterrevolutionary arsonist" to fit a propaganda theme about setting fires. Their sentences were long: up to eighteen years in prison, life in prison, or "commuted death," meaning a death sentence that was postponed while the person worked in a labor camp awaiting appeal. For his efforts in compiling the list, Li Hai himself was given a nine-year prison sentence. Hardly any of the names are of people who were ever known to the world. "The tank man," who blocked a row of tanks in central Beijing, is a highly unusual case of someone who did become famous, although not by name. On state television in China he was called the "mantis-armed traffic-obstructing hoodlum."

In the months and years that followed, the regime seems to have realized that its terminology had a credibility problem and opted to shrink the massacre, hoping it eventually would disappear from public consciousness. "Counterrevolutionary riot" became "turmoil" (*dongluan*, Deng Xiaoping's word), then "tempest" (*fengbo*), then "incident" (*shijian*), until, decades later, the policy was to expunge the matter entirely from every context—media, books, schools, and, as far as possible, personal conversations.

Through July and August 1989, the campaign against Xiaobo continued. Newspapers reprinted "Grab Liu Xiaobo's Black Hands." Central Chinese Television broadcast a narration of it in prime time. Seeing the sentences that were being handed to others, Xiaobo's friends began to fear for his life. Claudia Rosett wrote in *The Wall Street Journal* that "he might face the death penalty."[37] In New York, Hu Ping put Xiaobo's face on the cover of the August issue of *China Spring* and voiced his own fear that execution was possible. Scholars at Columbia

University wrote to China expressing concern for Xiaobo, and the school's provost telexed the president of Beijing Normal saying that Columbia would like to have Xiaobo back as a visiting scholar as soon as possible.[38] Linda Jaivin organized a petition of prominent Australians emphasizing that Xiaobo had at no point advocated use of violence. A number of private appeals went to the United Nations. A group of prominent Norwegian scholars wrote to the Nobel Peace Prize Committee recommending Xiaobo for the prize.[39]

But foreign opinion did not stay the tide of propaganda inside China. National publications like *Guangming Daily, Workers' Daily*, and *Study and Research* as well as prominent local papers like the *Beijing Evening News* were unrelenting in their attacks on Xiaobo. No one connected with June Fourth was attacked more, save perhaps Fang Lizhi or Su Xiaokang. In September, only three months after the massacre (and just a year after Xiaobo's Ph.D. dissertation had been published), China Youth Publishing House came out with a 154-page book, *Liu Xiaobo: Who He Is and What He Has Done*. The first part is a collection of published articles that denounce Xiaobo. The second is a selection of Xiaobo's own writings, mostly from what he published or said during his eight months outside China during 1988–89.

On August 16, Hou Dejian left the Australian embassy and went to his home in Twin Elms in northwest Beijing. That very afternoon he got a visit from an officer of Beijing Public Security and an official in the government's United Front Department who worked in the section on "liaison with Taiwan compatriots." They wanted Hou to do an interview with state media telling what he had seen at Tiananmen. They subtly threatened him by revealing that they knew he and his three hunger-striking friends were the authors of the "Appeal to the World Community" that Linda Jaivin had published in Australia. Qincheng Prison officials had confiscated a cassette tape found in a pocket of Xiaobo's jacket. Hou was trapped. He agreed to be interviewed.

The next day, reporters from Xinhua, Central Television, and *People's Daily* crowded at Hou's door. After the interview, Hou telephoned Linda Jaivin to describe it. She later wrote:

When one [of them] asked, "Was anyone killed on the square?," Hou sensed that in this question lay the whole point of the interview. Carefully, he phrased his answer to say that while he had not "personally" seen anyone killed, he had heard many reports about the number of citizens killed on roads leading into the square. He related how he'd been carried out on a stretcher with a coat over his head and therefore hadn't seen much himself.[40]

This testimony, after editing by Xinhua, turned into the following for nationwide broadcast the same evening: "Hou Dejian Talks About What He Saw and Heard in the Early Morning of 'June Fourth': In the Process of Withdrawal Not One Person Was Killed and He Saw No Tank Run Over a Person."[41]

The regime wanted a similar statement from Xiaobo, and police at Qincheng Prison twice approached him for an interview. Leery of becoming a government tool, he refused. They showed him Hou's interview as published in *People's Daily* and went to work on his psychology: "You didn't in fact see anyone killed, so what's wrong with making that true statement? This isn't the Liu Xiaobo everyone knows!" And so on.

Xiaobo had always been contrarian, especially when telling the truth was at stake, so this tactic carried some weight with him. The police followed up with the argument that to lead students safely out of the square was a good deed, from whatever point of view. This too seemed right to Xiaobo. Should he agree to an interview? In the end he did, after giving himself three reasons:

1. When many people are repeating that "Tiananmen Square was a river of blood," it takes courage to stand up and say that, in fact, that was not the case.
2. Hou Dejian was only reporting what he saw. He should not have to shoulder all of the abuse that will certainly fall on him.
3. Saying that no people were killed in Tiananmen Square is not the same as saying no people were killed anywhere in Beijing.[42]

Qincheng authorities allowed Xiaobo forty minutes outside the prison to do the interview. Central Television edited the videotape to the regime's needs and broadcast it in prime time. On September 18, 1989, the *People's Daily* reported Xiaobo as saying: "I did not see the troops fire their rifles at the masses. They fired only into the air or at loudspeakers. I did not see a single person die, and still less did I see rivers of blood in Tiananmen Square."[43] Until that point Xiaobo had been a prime target for the regime's slings and arrows, but now it was using his words to support its case. His public image suffered a major blow.

He began to feel depressed about what he had done even before the first criticisms appeared. As he walked back into the prison, he "had not felt dissatisfied with how he had put things, but was already heavyhearted about how others would see it." He worried about the morality of what he had done. He felt that Hou Dejian had been like the child in "The Emperor's New Clothes": he had "said facts are facts," that was all.[44] In early 1992 Xiaobo wrote, "Even now, I do not second-guess my decision to go on state television to say what the facts were. I was able to set aside the question of public image and be responsible to history, to friends, and to myself."[45] The habit of obliging himself to call a spade a spade recurred. It sometimes led to misunderstandings with friends—to say nothing of confrontations with political authorities.

In September, Beijing Normal notified him of the decision—no doubt made at a higher level—that he had been fired from his job. The regime had squeezed its interview with him for every possible drop of advantage to itself and now was ready to turn around and claim that all—or all the rest—of Liu Xiaobo's thought was poisonous. On November 7 *People's Daily* ran an article called "From Nihilist to Traitor: The Bourgeois Liberal Absurdities of Liu Xiaobo." Someone had done some superficial research into Xiaobo's intellectual history. The piece opens:

> "Crazy man" Liu Xiaobo, by meddling in the student movement and inciting turmoil and counterrevolutionary rioting, has turned himself into a historic anti-Party antisocialist offender. His arrival in this position is not accidental. It is the natural result of his extreme individualism, cognitive idealism, metaphysical worldview, and deep-seated bourgeois-liberal thinking. The goal of the present article is to repudiate the absurdities of his national nihilism and his treason and to wash away all of his poisonous influences.[46]

Xiaobo was hardly a disciple of cognitive idealism; he was always skeptical of it, favoring the concrete. Far from embracing metaphysics, he published a whole book attacking it. But the authorities again were hardly concerned about such things. What mattered to them was that the verbiage they were using could be useful in discrediting Xiaobo and eliminating him as a possible challenge to their authority.

In early 1990, two events unrelated to Xiaobo's case led to a relaxation of pressure on him. One was that martial law was lifted on January 10. The second was Spring Festival, China's biggest holiday and a time when families come together. People were allowed into prisons to see close relatives, so Tao Li and her parents could come to visit Xiaobo. The reunion was a mixed blessing, however. Tao Li's parents had witnessed the Anti-Rightist movement of 1957, when colleagues around them had been driven to divorce, suicide, and family dissolution, and ever since had been skittish about anything political. When Xiaobo was active at Tiananmen Square in spring 1989, they sent Sun Jin, one of his Ph.D. students at Beijing Normal, to counsel him to withdraw and come home.[47] They had raised Tao Li to keep her distance from politics, to lie low, and to concentrate on scholarship. They were extremely concerned to keep her and the little boy Liu Tao out of trouble. Now, visiting Xiaobo in prison, they gave him their message directly. They said that his behavior had already brought worry and pain to the family and could harm the future of Liu Tao, to say nothing of Xiaobo himself. They advised him not to be so stubborn, to cooperate with the regime and earn reprieve.

Tao Li said little during the meeting, but her tears and facial expression cut Xiaobo like a knife. She did not mention that ever since he went on television to say no one had been killed in the square, people in her school dining hall would not line up next to her. Her book *Murasaki Shikibu* was finished but had been blocked from publication because of her status as the wife of a black hand criminal. Worse, Liu Tao's first-grade teachers, responding to the government's propaganda, were mistreating the boy. A small infraction on his part would bring a quip like, "You're on course to be like your hoodlum father." Tao Li was deeply worried that the child's self-respect could be injured. Xiaobo had to weigh these heartbreaking facts even as he tried to guess what his own fate might be. A sentence of fifteen years or more? If it were that bad, what would be the gain in any compromise at all with the brutish government? In the end he told Tao Li, "I might die here, but so long as I'm living I'm not going to compromise with them."[48] The Tao family left in despair.

Solitary confinement was boring to Xiaobo, so he always anticipated his daily opportunity to be "released in the wind"—prison argot for exercise in the courtyard. It was a space formed of buildings on three sides. An aerial walkway spanned the two sides that faced each other, and guards patrolled there, watching the prisoners below. Even in this activity, the inmates were separated. Walls ten feet high partitioned the courtyard into subdivisions. Prisoners could look for moments when the guards seemed inattentive and quickly exchange a word or two of news over the walls, but that was dangerous. Liu Suli at one point was in a space next to Xiaobo's, and the two communicated by writing on slips of paper, rolling the slips into little balls, and tossing the balls over the wall. A guard discovered them and they were summoned—separately—for interrogation. Later Chen Xiaoping was in a space adjacent to Liu's, and he and Xiaobo communicated by disguising their talk as English language practice. That too was discovered, and they were relocated at a distance. Yang Guansan, who before the June Fourth repression had worked for a prominent think tank in the State Council, was another neighbor whom Xiaobo tried to reach. He found a tree twig and wrote "Liu Xiaobo" on a cement slab, then tossed the slab over the wall when he heard Yang jogging by. The slab cracked in half on impact, so Yang had to piece it back together in order to read the message. Months later, when the two met outside prison, Yang said, "Great, Xiaobo, just great! Here I am jogging along when a cement slab falls from the sky, grazes my head, and smashes to the ground. The Communist Party didn't kill me, but *you* almost did!"[49]

In the early 1990s the Chinese government, apparently in an effort to persuade foreign governments to lift economic sanctions placed on China after the massacre, decided to release some political prisoners. Xiaobo was elated when he heard on the Qincheng broadcasting system on May 10, 1990, that Zhou Duo and Dai Qing were to be released without charges. Might there be hope for his own case? Its criminal investigation stage was finished, and the signals he was getting were that lenience was possible in return for repentance. There were even suggestions between the lines that because Xiaobo was a number one black hand, his repentance would be especially valuable and the reduction in his sentence could be large.[50] At least in part, his fate was back in his own hands. He had not had such a feeling for nearly a year.

In August 1990, he and Tao Li divorced. Tao Li sent legal papers to the prison, where Xiaobo signed without question. Later he wrote:

> Both before our divorce and after it, I have always felt guilty toward my former wife, the mother of my son Liu Tao. The pain and despair that my degenerate lifestyle forced upon her mind and body are inexcusable. That was in addition to all the storms of the "'89 protest movement," which left her in perpetual anxiety, day and night, from the day I returned from abroad. I suffered too—suffered deeply—from the ghastly way the protest movement ended, but that was pain that I brought entirely on myself. Tao Li had nothing to do with it. They were my decisions alone to come back from New York, to get involved, and to hunger strike. Out there in public I had plenty of stimulation. I had a voice and an audience, and when I suffered I got rewards for the suffering. Even if I died it would have been my own choice, my own responsibility. But Tao Li? What did she get? Anything besides pain, shock, worry, and anxiety? Anything but the torment of illness and burdens of raising a child alone? She lay in bed battling a disease for two years and got nothing. I never thought of her once when I was out there listening to cheers from crowds of protesters. When I faced reporters, their flashbulbs popping, feeling very good about myself, Tao Li's suffering never crossed my mind. Still less did I ever think about her suffering spirit and bleeding heart as I flirted with other women, right there on the square. Tao Li had every reason to ask me for a divorce at any time. Someone like me, dissolute by nature and infatuated with personal fame, is basically unqualified to have a family, unqualified to be a husband or father, unqualified for the love of Tao Li. The pain I felt in receiving the divorce papers was entirely deserved, and it was far, far less than Tao Li's pain.[51]

More than a decade later, Xiaobo revealed what he understood to be the more pressing reason for Tao Li's request for a divorce: to protect Liu Tao from the debilitating consequences of having a father in prison.[52]

In October, the prison authorities arranged for Xiaobo's father, Liu Ling, to visit. They met outside Qincheng, at a detention center in the Xuanwu district of Beijing. This was after Professor Liu had been transferred from Northeast Normal University to the Dalian Army Academy, and he showed up in full military garb. He was carrying two large suitcases filled with clothing, fruit, and cigarettes. (Qincheng Prison banned cigarettes, but Professor Liu, who years earlier had tried to enforce his own ban on Xiaobo's smoking, did not know that.) His political attitude had not changed. Still a "good son of the Party," he advised Xiaobo, "Just admit what you're supposed to admit; the Party and the government will handle your problem correctly."[53]

But the father had also turned a corner that was new to Xiaobo. Liu Ling had always ruled his household like a tyrant. He had constantly berated Xiaobo and often beat him. That day at the prison, though, he used Xiaobo's toddler name, Little Three, to tell him how his actions affected his mother. "You were always her favorite, you know," Liu Ling said. "Now she cries almost every day. She can't sleep at night and sometimes cries until dawn." Xiaobo noticed that his father's hand, holding a cigarette, was trembling as he spoke, and that the old man's eyes were tearing up. "Do something to corral your stubborn impulses," Liu Ling pleaded. "You're charging down a blind alley." Xiaobo felt himself begin to crumble inside. He had a penchant for self-criticism, and now it was rising again. When his father left he sat down to write a "Repentance."[54]

We do not have the text of what he wrote, but a summary appears in his memoir *Monologue of a Doomsday Survivor*. He allowed himself to be guided in some ways by the article in *People's Daily* on November 7, 1989, that had denounced him. He also fell back on techniques he had learned in writing confessions of his naughty behavior as a schoolboy in Changchun. One trick was to highlight not what he had done wrong but what had caused him to do wrong. He did not have to confess to smoking, fighting, or pulling pranks if he wrote about "falling victim to bourgeois thinking and to the poison of Liu Shaoqi's revisionist line in education." He wrote his "Repentance" quickly, in only about two hours. Later he came to consider it one of his worst mistakes ever.

He began by admitting that in the turmoil and rioting in spring 1989, he had done a number of illegal deeds. The reasons were by no means incidental; they were deeply rooted in his thought. He went on to organize his misbehavior, as the *People's Daily* had done, under four headings: political, cultural, moral, and intellectual.

Politically, I stood on the opposite side from the Party and the people and opposed the Party's leadership and the socialist system. I advocated a multiparty system over one-party dictatorship, private ownership over public ownership, and multiplicity in thought over guidance by Marxism-Leninism. In sum, I wanted capitalism to replace socialism.

Culturally, I favored national nihilism and "complete Westernization," holding that everything Western is good, that everything Chinese is bad, and even that Chinese people are naturally inferior to others. I have been to the West, but gathered only some superficial impressions. I have read many Western books, but that's all that they are—just books. Even though I don't know the West very well, I took it as my ideal against which to denigrate China, both traditional and contemporary. I have really not been good to the motherland that raised me.

Morally, I advocated extreme individualism, believing that "whether I ascend to the skies or fall to the earth depends entirely on my own effort."[55] Solely for my personal satisfaction, and in defiance of the advice of friends and relatives, I charged bull-headed into turmoil. I stirred things up at Tiananmen with another hunger strike right when they were beginning to settle down. I turned ebbing turmoil into a counterrevolutionary riot.

Intellectually, I was stuck in metaphysics [here Xiaobo compromises by using the Chinese Communist Party's sense of the term "metaphysics" to mean something like "extreme one-sidedness"], in two different ways. One was my moral extremism—anything was either all good or all bad. The other was my departure from Chinese realities; truth came only from Western book learning. This could lead only to severe bias and to proposal of unrealistic and extremely mistaken solutions for Chinese problems.

The roots of my taking the road of committing crime lie in the four areas listed above. I will view the court's judgments in my case as correct and will accept them entirely.[56]

"Repentance" gave the government just what it needed, saying that he confessed guilt and would accept punishment. To the authorities his statement was far more satisfying than those of Wang Dan and others. He had not merely confessed to crimes but had dug into "the depths of the soul."[57]

A case against Xiaobo for "spreading propaganda to incite counterrevolution" was sent to the Beijing People's Intermediate Court on January 26, 1991. The proceedings were secret. The "Repentance" document was used as his "Final Statement." Xiaobo read from it in court in the morning. In the afternoon the court announced its judgment:

The court finds that the accused Liu Xiaobo used writing articles, publishing articles, joining a hunger strike, and other means to fan incitement in all directions, that he carried out resistance and broke laws and regulations in his attempts to overturn the people's government and the socialist system, that his crimes meet the standard of spreading propaganda to incite counterrevolution, and that the crimes are serious and should be punished according to law. However, because Liu Xiaobo made important meritorious contributions by exhorting and organizing students and masses to leave Tiananmen Square before the entry of the martial law troops and by dissuading rioters from using weapons, and because he provided a confession and has acted in accordance with it, he can be treated with lenience according to law. Based on the facts of the criminal behavior of Liu Xiaobo, on the record that connects them, and on the damage to society as well as Liu's positive contributions and repentance behavior, and based on provisions number 102 and 59 of the *Criminal Law of the People's Republic of China*, this court determines that the crimes of the accused Liu Xiaobo of spreading propaganda to incite counterrevolution will be exempt from criminal punishment.[58]

The court did not explain how "exempt from criminal punishment" squared with Xiaobo's service, already completed, of twenty months in prison.

Still, the reprieve startled Xiaobo and sparked in him a surge of feeling that he could not easily control. On his way out the courtroom door he leaped into the air, snapped his fingers, and shouted, "Won again!" A guard told him to quiet down.[59] Outside the room, an official warned him that even though his "major merit" had spared him a heavy sentence this time, if he failed to show that he was continuing in repentance there was no way he would be spared; next time he would face at least a few years in prison.[60]

That evening Central Television, in broadcasting the news of Xiaobo's release, put special emphasis on his "important meritorious contributions." Neither then nor at any other time did the government specify what those were, and this ambiguity was costly to Xiaobo's reputation among supporters of democracy. Some speculated that he had cooperated much more than he actually had. Within only twenty months, his image had turned from a semiheroic "number one black hand" to a "self-remade, leniently treated" model that the regime was using for its purposes.

Soon the sentences of other intellectuals and students who had been prominent in the 1989 movement were announced. On January 27 Wang Dan was sentenced to four years in prison. On February 12, Chen Ziming and Wang Juntao were sentenced to thirteen years each for "counterrevolutionary incitement and plotting to overthrow the government." Wuerkaixi, Chai Ling, Feng Congde, Li Lu, and other student leaders fled abroad.

Xiaobo became painfully aware of how he had been used. The government was ordering universities in Beijing to mobilize students and young faculty to "learn from" his repentance document. At his home campus, Beijing Normal University, a vice chair of the Chinese Department complied by reading it at a meeting of the entire teaching staff. He added, at the end, his own arch comment: "It shows he's a real Ph.D.—even his repentance has literary flair. What a waste!"[61]

11

Picking Up and Starting Over

As Xiaobo left the courtroom on January 26, 1991, two policemen, all smiles, ushered him into an adjacent room and offered him a cigarette. Then the judge entered, accompanied by three of Xiaobo's former colleagues at Beijing Normal University, including his department chair, Liu Qingfu. Xiaobo was required to sign or put his thumbprint on four documents: the court ruling, an assignment to custody, a guarantor's letter signed by Liu Qingfu (which was odd, because Xiaobo had been fired from Beijing Normal), and a certificate of release. The judge then read from legal boilerplate informing Xiaobo that he would need to register with Beijing police and could not leave the city for ten days. He also read a policy statement informing Xiaobo that, as a "June Fourth rioter . . . you cannot remain in Beijing but will need to return immediately to your parents' home in Dalian." People in the room listened with straight faces. The contradiction between law and policy was accepted as a matter of course. Everyone knew that policy trumped law and that Xiaobo would leave for Dalian. He asked if he could first go see his former wife, Tao Li, and their eight-year-old son, Liu Tao.[1]

"No. Leave directly."

The court had arranged that a clerk bring Xiaobo straight from the courtroom to dinner. As they ate, the clerk observed that he had worked many years for the court and this was the first time he had gotten a meal out of it. After dinner an official car delivered the two to the Beijing Rail Station, where Xiaobo boarded train no. 229 leaving at 11:37 p.m. for Dalian. Two young teachers from the Chinese Department at Beijing Normal had been sent to the train station to accompany him. Their assignment was to watch him all the way until he entered the door of his parents' residence inside the compound of the Dalian Army Academy, then return to Beijing to report this fact to their superiors.

Xiaobo's family welcomed him warmly. Over the years he had caused them much worry—marrying, becoming a father, divorcing; rising as a famous "dark horse" in 1986 and a hunger-striking hero in 1989, then plummeting to be a "number one black hand," imprisoned and almost executed; then rising again (at least, in the family's view) to be touted on national television as a model of "confessing crime and submitting to law." Now he was finally home, and bygones could be bygones. To him Dalian wasn't really "home," though, because his memories were of Changchun. Still, it was home in the sense of family. As the Spring Festival neared, his four brothers all came home from where they were living in Changchun and in Shantou, in Guangdong province. The family all thought Xiaobo had made a good bargain by trading a confession for his freedom. In return for their congratulations, he regaled them with stories about his naughty behavior while in prison.

He wrote to Tao Li, hoping that she and Liu Tao could come to Dalian for a visit during the holidays. She did not reply.

The regime had an unpublished policy of trying to get "June Fourth elements" to settle down permanently outside of Beijing. Perhaps for this reason, the public library in Dalian suddenly offered Xiaobo a job, which he declined.[2] Sedentary work did not appeal to him. In mid-March he returned to Beijing to be what people called at the time a "three no" person—no job, no income, no registration. City residents in China needed legal registration in order to access housing, health care, education, and anything that was rationed. Xiaobo's registration had been canceled when he went to prison. Where could he live now?

It turned out that Hou Dejian, whom the authorities had unceremoniously shipped back to Taiwan ten months earlier, still had rights to his apartment at Twin Elms in Beijing, and Xiaobo, still in touch with Hou through friends, went there to live. (That the authorities had "shipped" Hou Dejian away is not purely a metaphor. In June 1990 Hou was packed onto a navy patrol boat in Fuzhou and deposited onto a Taiwan fishing boat in the Taiwan Strait.) The government had given the Twin Elms apartment to Hou rent free back in 1983, at a time when it viewed him as a target for "United Front" work in Taiwan. (Offering rent-free space to famous figures from Taiwan was not only a commerical gift but a way of saying, "You are welcome here anytime.") The luxurious apartment had three bedrooms. Xiaobo moved into the smallest, which faced southwest. Two young couples lived in the other two, although one of the couples was usually absent. The group chipped in to hire a maid to do the cooking.

Xiaobo began reconnecting with Beijing friends. Tao Li and Liu Tao were first on his list. He visited them weekly and tried to help with housework whenever he could. Tao Li's health, which had worsened since 1989, eventually reached a point where she could hardly get out of bed. She began to get better only in 1993. Xiaobo also went to see his old teacher Tong Qingbing. He knew that Tong had suffered for having been the mentor of a "black hand"; at one point Beijing Normal was thinking of canceling his classes. For his part, Professor Tong was worried about how the unemployed Xiaobo would support himself. Xiaobo simply grinned at the question and said "Independent writer—I'll live on my manuscripts." But that, they both knew, was only a stiff upper lip. Xiaobo's political record would keep people from daring to publish him.

Liu Xiaoqing, a famous film actress from the 1980s, was at the time romantically involved with the actor Jiang Wen, who later became a famous film director. The two had both befriended Xiaobo before 1989. They had starred in the 1987 film *Hibiscus Town*, based on a novel by the Hunan writer Gu Hua and directed by the famous Xie Jin from Shanghai. The film, which bemoaned the fate of intellectuals under senseless and repeated assault by Mao, was a classic of post-Mao "scar" culture and did very well at the box office. Because of this, Liu Xiaoqing and Jiang Wen had plenty of money. When they heard that Xiaobo had been released from prison and was in financial straits, they decided to give him ten thousand yuan (about $1,900 in U.S. dollars at the time). If he had not been fired from Beijing Normal, it would have taken him seven or eight years to have earned that amount in salary. When he had brushed off Professor Tong's question about how he would make ends meet, he was facing a dire emergency. Now there was no emergency.

Linda Jaivin and her husband, Geremie Barmé, were still in Beijing, and Xiaobo reconnected with this Australian couple as well. Barmé was unusual among Westerners who study China because he carried none of the centuries-old Western habit of viewing the country as unique and mystical. He criticized Chinese intellectuals as squarely as he would if they were Australians. In 1990, when Xiaobo was still in prison, Barmé wrote an essay, "Confession, Redemption, and Death," about Xiaobo and the Tiananmen movement.[3] The piece captures Xiaobo's prickly independence and shows how he maintained critical distance from intellectuals and students as well as from the government. It also shows how the internal workings of the movement fell short of the democratic ideals it claimed to pursue.

Barmé was ready to criticize hypocrisy when he found it in Chinese intellectuals. As Xiaobo recalls it, his message was: "Many of China's elite intellectuals want to be seen as suffering Jesus Christs, as momentous moral heroes. But they also don't want to be nailed to the cross forever. They want to spend a bit of time there and then be helped down, to a sea of plaudits from admiring crowds. You might call this "crucifixion with Chinese characteristics."[4] The criticism struck home for Xiaobo. Wasn't this exactly himself? A moral hero in the square, he had gone to crucifixion in Qincheng but then had confessed his way out and was looking for the limelight again. Ordinary life bored him. Banality sapped a person's will.

From Tong Qingbing, Xiaobo heard that Jiang Jielian, the seventeen-year-old son of Ding Zilin and Jiang Peikun, had been killed by gunfire late on June 3, 1989. Xiaobo had a mental impression of the young Jielian because they had met a few times during Xiaobo's visits to the Jiang-Ding household in 1988 when he was consulting Professor Jiang about his Ph.D. dissertation. Now, hearing of the death, he decided to go offer his sympathy. He did not anticipate the impact the visit would have on him.

It was June 1, 1991. He showed up in a casual T-shirt and colorfully patterned knee-length shorts. The son's ashes had not been buried; they were in a jar inside a special wooden cabinet placed where his boyhood bed had been. Professor Jiang related the story of how Jielian had joined the protest movement and the details of what had led to, and then followed, the horrid killing. Stunned, Xiaobo turned abruptly and left the room. He returned a half-hour later holding a bouquet of flowers, placed them in front of the boy's urn, and fell to the floor, sobbing.[5]

It was this experience more than anything Xiaobo saw on the square on the night of the massacre that brought him starkly face to face with the horror of June 3–4, 1989. It haunted him to think of the immeasurable distance between this pain and the sea of cheering crowds that he had enjoyed. Two days later, on the second anniversary of Jiang Jielian's death, he returned to the Jiang home carrying a poem, called "Your Seventeen Years," and asked if he could read it in front of the boy's ashes. He began:

> I, alive
> and with my share of infamy
> have not the courage, nor the right
> to come bearing flowers or words
> before your seventeen year-old smile . . .[6]

Professor Jiang did not allow him to finish. Those few words were enough. He was afraid his wife would not be able to hold up.

The poem had a subtitle: "Two Years after June Fourth." Xiaobo had written a poem a year earlier, on the first anniversary, while he was in Qincheng

Prison—and later he wrote another on every anniversary, wherever he was, in prison or not.[7] (We do not have any poems from 2009 on, when he was in Jinzhou Prison in Liaoning. But it is hard to imagine that he did not continue to write them.)

Xiaobo developed something of a complex about Tiananmen Square. His first impulse on getting out of Qincheng Prison was to head straight there, but somehow he couldn't do it. Twice he set out and twice got only as far as Xidan, about a mile and a half short. The first time he re-entered the square was by accident. He was riding with friends in a car and not really paying attention to where they were until he noticed the Monument to the People's Heroes outside the window. Immediately his body trembled and his eyes moistened. He broke down and wept. Next he felt something resembling nausea and "a mood of self-loathing that I had never experienced before": "Today I am alive. My reputation half stinks, but at least I am free and have the concern and protection of my friends and a few strangers. But what about those others, who died or are still in prison? What about their relatives and friends? What about that young guy who spread his arms out to block a row of tanks?"[8] Later, in Xiaobo's "Final Statement" at his trial for subversion on December 23, 2009, he wrote, "June 1989 has been the major turning point in my life, which now is just over one half century in length, [and is what] put me on the road to political dissidence."[9] Elsewhere he describes his memory of the massacre as like a needle that moves inside his flesh; it is "always causing pain, never dissolving, always repeating its moral principle."[10] He believed the needle would stay inside him for the rest of his life, never letting him rest. In this sense there were two June Fourths for Xiaobo: one was a memory of a massacre in the past and the other a beacon that constantly urged him forward. Over the years he wrote dozens of articles, open letters, and appeals about the massacre, a total of more than 120,000 characters.

The months after Xiaobo's release from Qincheng were difficult for him emotionally. He needed time to deal with his mental turmoil and to listen to his inner voice. *Why did I write that "Repentance," and what should I think about it now?* As he had felt two years earlier in New York, he felt again, only more strongly, that he needed to rethink himself "from zero." In this effort the counsel of his long-standing friends was more useful than that of his recent, more activist friends. Yang Jidong, his dormitory mate from his M.A. years, listened patiently to his self-flagellations about "Repentance."[11] Wei Haitian, his friend from undergraduate years in Changchun, was his sounding board in reaching the conclusion that "it was true, after all, that I had avoided a possible bloodbath at the square, so on that question I feel no need for regret and can endure the scoldings of others."[12]

It was hard to answer the unending and often accusatory questions about what the government meant by the "great meritorious service" he had rendered. Had he betrayed the movement? Had he leaked names to the government? Good friends told him flat out that he had paid too high a price. These were painful arrows, and they rained down even while he was struggling mightily inside.

The strain showed in occasional flares of temper. An embarrassing example happened during a group trip led by Zhou Duo to Baiyang Lake in Hebei. Zhou had been a "sent-down youth" there during the Cultural Revolution. A young man in the group kept flattering Xiaobo, saying how great his writing was, and finally asked, "Will you give me a book?" Irritated, Xiaobo shot back, "If you want a book, why don't you go buy one?" Things got worse later, when the group was eating at a restaurant. The local Baiyang Lake people were volunteering to host the group, but the guests decided that no, each of them would chip in ten yuan. When it came time to pay Xiaobo put down twenty yuan, saying he was covering for one of the young reporters who had come along. But then the same young man who had wanted a free book decided he wanted a free dinner too. He just stood up and left. Xiaobo was incensed. "Wipe your mouth and leave? Eat for free? The Baiyang Lake people owe you something, do they?" Inspired by his own words, Xiaobo went over and starting punching the young man. Others had to pull him away.[13] His pacifism, so splendidly in evidence at Tiananmen, frayed under the mental pressures he was now experiencing.

He needed a life partner but had lost Tao Li. In his writings he refers several times to "a girlfriend I was in love with" at the time but does not give her name, apparently out of respect for her wishes.[14] Here we will call her Apple.[15] A gentle and agreeable person seven years younger than Xiaobo, Apple had graduated from Beijing Normal's History Department and in the early 1990s was working in the field of American studies at a research institute. She knew Xiaobo from before the spring '89 events. When he came out of prison in 1991, she harbored no suspicions that his "great meritorious service" to the government had been anything nefarious. Few people were as confident in this as she, and to Xiaobo her attitude was immensely consoling. For more than a year, Apple stayed with him on weekends at the Hou Dejian apartment. On one occasion, when Xiaobo didn't come home on time, Apple became so worried that she picked up the telephone and called the home of Tao Li's parents to see if they knew anything. That call was not, understandably, very welcome, but Xiaobo later told friends he felt moved that Apple would do such a thing. The other two couples who lived in Hou Dejian's apartment viewed the two as a model pair—"they never quarrel." Xiaobo brought Apple to meet his friends, and they remained a couple until 1993 when Xiaobo left to study and lecture in Australia.

Xiaobo began to study English during the months Apple was with him. Her English was good, and she probably helped him. An Australian friend sent Xiaobo a copy of I. F. Stone's *The Trial of Socrates*, which, he wrote later, he read "in a daze," laboriously using a dictionary. (Stone's book later came out in a Chinese translation, which Xiaobo read with great interest during his stay in a labor camp at Dalian from 1996 to 1999.)

It is a gentle irony that Xiaobo's comforting respite with Apple seems to have made it possible to improve his relations with Tao Li. Divorced, they now had less to argue about. Xiaobo also realized that the bedridden Tao Li and their son, Liu Tao, really did need his help. He appreciated the responsibilities of fatherhood better than before and never missed his weekly visit. His friends learned the schedule and were careful not to interfere with it. Although short on money himself, Xiaobo strained to help Tao Li financially.

As a means both to work out his inner turmoil and to answer the questions of others, Xiaobo arrived at the idea of putting his inner life onto paper. After the Cultural Revolution many Chinese intellectuals had become painfully aware that they had been victimizers, not just victims. They had hurt others in order to save themselves. Scholar Liu Zaifu noted a trend that he called "repentance consciousness." In Xiaobo's mind, Augustine and Rousseau remained models of how to be introspective and seek redemption by facing wrongdoing. "The only route to liberating the spirit," he wrote, "is to repent and to hold oneself responsible."[16] Accordingly, during the second half of 1991, he began writing *Monologue of a Doomsday Survivor*, which he published in Taiwan in September 1992. The book was read more widely overseas than inside China, where it was officially banned.

Monologue created a stir, not all of it favorable. It is a brutally frank record of Xiaobo's subjective life during the forty days after he returned from New York in April 1989. It is not, and was not intended to be, a properly considered history but a meticulous transcription of his inner world—indeed, of both his inner worlds, because he acknowledges two Xiaobos:

One, the rational and clear-headed me, wanted only to observe, not to get involved. This was the me who aspired to be that free and supertalented person who disdains the activities of large crowds and feels that China's penchant for mass movements is regrettable. The other me was emotional, blind, and eager not only to reach into every nook of the movement but also to hold a special position in it. That second me greedily observed every wrinkle and could not tolerate the notion that such an historic movement would not the bear the stamp of Liu Xiaobo.[17]

He is similarly self-analytical about his decision to return to Beijing from New York. He was aware, he writes, of the "commodification of dissidence" in the West. To return to China, to enter the cauldron of the movement, would be seen as moral capital: "I was confident that my going back to China at this juncture would pave the way for an easy return to the West if I ever wanted one. It could be a credential in extending a visa or getting a green card."[18] At the square, he carried his passport day and night. He also had his invitation letter from Columbia University and an exit visa issued by Beijing Public Security, in case things got bad and he needed to leave quickly.[19]

He writes in *Monologue* about his thoughts on the evening when he decided to begin a hunger strike and his personal infatuation with self-sacrifice: "I saw the world as a closed, black stage. I stood at its center as one beam of light shined on me and the eyes of observers followed the beam. I suddenly felt that the most beautiful image in the world was Jesus nailed to the cross, the sufferings of all humanity weighing on his shoulders. . . . A hunger strike might turn into a self-sacrifice, but it would be the chance of a thousand years. If I didn't do self-sacrifice, who would?!"[20] If here the reader thinks of Hamlet ("The time is out of joint; O curs'd spite, That ever I was born to set it right!") it would not be the only moment in *Monologue* where Xiaobo seems to pose as Prince of Denmark.

His dissection of himself in *Monologue* is accompanied by an equally severe dissection of the 1989 student movement. His friend Geremie Barmé had always called it a "protest movement," not a "democracy movement," and Xiaobo agreed.[21] He regrets that student leaders liked to show off and be officious. They couldn't tolerate opposing opinions and had no sense for political compromise. In this they resembled their adversary the Communist Party. Reverting to his tendency of going to extremes, Xiaobo writes that all players on the scene—officials and nonofficials, students and intellectuals—were both believers and manufacturers of lies. An effusion of unreliable rumors kept coursing among the protesters: "Li Peng died," "Deng Xiaoping resigned," and so on. Times were exciting and reliable news sources were absent, so "lies flying through the skies became the main fuel for the whole movement."[22] When *Monologue* was published, its flyleaf carried the spectacular message: "China, you have nothing but lies!"[23]

Lies were not the only problem, in Xiaobo's view. In both *Monologue* and an article called "We Were Defeated by Our Own 'Righteousness,'" which he published in Taiwan on the fourth anniversary of the massacre,[24] he argues that the Chinese democracy movement did not evolve beyond the undemocratic mental habits that lie deep in Chinese political thinking. He warned about the word "revolution." Protesters in 1989 saw themselves as a second wave of revolution—but that was a very undemocratic idea. Participants in a revolution know that it is right and the other side is wrong, that they needn't give freedom of speech to the other side as long as their own side has it, that unitary leadership makes for the strongest force, that one's righteous ends justify any means, and can believe falsities or even spread lies, as long as it is done for a righteous cause. His article uses the word "we" to make clear that he includes himself in the group holding these unfortunate views.[25] And he goes a step further to argue that the noisy and self-righteous 1989 movement may even have slowed China's progress toward democracy by frightening to a halt the gradual changes that had been happening within the ruling party.[26]

The publication of "Our Own 'Righteousness'" and *Monologue* elicited a flood of criticism from China's prodemocracy ranks, including some of Xiaobo's allies and old friends. Liu Binyan, Wang Ruowang (a Shanghai novelist expelled from the Communist Party together with Liu Binyan and Fang Lizhi in 1987), Zheng Yi (a prizewinning novelist who had been close with the students on the square and was currently underground), and Xiaobo's old friend Xu Xing all wrote indignant and sharply critical responses. Liu Binyan wrote that if the protesting students showed extreme egoism or disrespect for the "lower ranks" of the common people, there might be roots of these attitudes in their teachers like Liu Xiaobo.[27] Wang Ruowang said that to blame the students was to invert the proper assignment of responsibility for the bloody massacre.[28] Zheng Yi and Xu Xing were both indignant over factual errors in the book and suggested it was not reliable. In April 1994, when Bao Zunxin, who had been an important figure in the "culture fever" of the 1980s, wrote a preface to Wang Dan's prison memoir, he gave it a name that pointedly rebutted Xiaobo: "We Are Spurred on by Our Righteousness."

It was especially painful for Ding Zilin and Jiang Peikun to read the Taiwan article. In a retrospective in 2010, they wrote:

> Viewed from today, Xiaobo's reflections on the '89 movement may have some merit, but the writing is too sharp and extreme. As June Fourth bereaved, we have always felt outrage in our hearts, and at the time found it extremely difficult to read such an article. We just couldn't accept it. We remembered how Xiaobo, when he visited us after he got out of prison, fell to the ground in tears over the fate of our son, and then how he wrote that poem "Your Seventeen Years." Still, we respected the principle that every person is entitled to an opinion, so we never criticized him in private and still less were moved to write anything in public. We just went through his teacher and some close friends to let

him know that he needn't come to our apartment again, lest there be any deepening of the wound.[29]

Xiaobo of course complied but later, in 1996, reconciled with the couple.

When the student leader Wang Chaohua saw *Monologue,* her impression was that it was likely colored by the interrogations that Xiaobo was made to endure in Qincheng Prison. The points he selected to highlight and the way he pieced events together both showed signs of influence from the regime's agenda, she felt.[30]

But there was also praise for *Monologue.* Zha Jianying, a Chinese writer who witnessed the June Fourth massacre and later settled in New York, wrote that in the book Xiaobo "is perhaps the only one among the Tiananmen leaders to expose moral frailties, including his own."[31]

Some of the musings in *Monologue* run very deep. One, for example, is about the regime's decision to call Xiaobo a "number one black hand." Of course there was an obvious political motive: he had just returned from the United States, and the authorities wanted to show that "foreign forces" were behind the "turmoil." But they did not foresee other effects of this move, Xiaobo reasoned. For one, it elevated his status. He had never been "number one" before, in anything. No one on the square—no student leader, no intellectual supporter—remotely had the powers that the regime attributed to the "Liu Xiaobo" it had invented.[32] A careful look at what actually caused the escalation of tensions during the spring events shows that in every case it was an action of the government, not the protesters, that was crucial. And among the protesters, Xiaobo's was only one small voice among many. Casting him as "number one" was a regime-built myth.

Then he presses harder: Had he too been deceived by the myth? Had it brought him to suppose—and to enjoy the idea—that yes, I *am* a number one in this movement?[33] Had he, on one level, felt grateful to the regime for conferring this status?[34] Next he wonders if this pattern might hold for other dissidents:

All of the heroes of the Chinese opposition in recent times are heroes because of the regime. If the Communist authorities knew what they were doing, dissident heroes would not exist today. But in fact, they do not know what they are doing. Their inane puffery is the papier-mâché from which dissident heroes are formed. It would be lovely if all us dissidents were aware of this and did not overestimate ourselves. But we are seldom aware. We do not see that our shining names are generated by the regime, not by ourselves.[35]

Analysis of "dissident heroism" as penetrating as this is truly rare. No one else in the democracy movement (including Xiaobo, at the time) had said or written anything close to it; nor have Chinese dissidents in other times. Are dissident heroes by-products (perhaps *necessary* by-products?) of the way a Communist Party represses a population: by constructing a model dissident to show people what not to do, then leaving the model to history as a "hero"? Is the model chosen less for what he or she actually did than to fit the needs of the regime's "political situation" of the moment? And does the regime make the "dissident" label so strong that people in China—and outside—are seduced into thinking, *Yes, this is a hero*? The reputations of Soviet and Eastern European dissidents could have been products of a similar process, but there too, no one seems to have put the matter as incisively as Xiaobo does in *Monologue*.

Xiaobo digs further into himself to find, still there, the fatuous notion that "degree of punishment" equals "degree of heroism." He notices that Chen Ziming and Wang Juntao were both sentenced to thirteen years in prison, whereas he was released with no sentence after only twenty months. Before the massacre, the three had been on a par. The big discrepancy in sentencing was no doubt because Xiaobo had written a "Repentance" and Chen and Wang had not. They insisted that everything they had done was within the rights of a citizen, and this effrontery had angered the authorities. Now their heavy sentences exalted them in the eyes of many. They were thus more heroic than Xiaobo, but not because they had done more on the square than he had. That is wrong, Xiaobo thinks. But isn't it selfish of him, in this context, to point such a thing out? Xiaobo finds within himself "all kinds of jumbled feelings" about Chen's and Wang's long sentences[36] and confesses that one of the feelings might be envy. *Couldn't the authorities have given me at least a two-year sentence? Then I might feel better.* He does not spare himself in writing all these thoughts down in *Monologue*.

He blames himself harshly for writing "Repentance." In the past, hadn't he criticized Chinese intellectuals for having "weak knees" in the face of power? So what about his own knees? He writes that in the past, "I thought that too much comfort and praise poison a person's spirit; now I realize that fear and anxiety can destroy a person's will."[37] He finds within himself two different kinds of regret for "Repentance." One is that his public image has suffered: the government's decision to recognize his "merit" and not to punish him pulverized his reputation. The other, now coming more clearly into view, is that he did indeed sell out his conscience. He wrote down words that did not originate from inside himself. To face that fact is extremely difficult and painful. His decision to give the regime what it wanted was, he writes, "a choice to lie and to betray. It was a huge debt to incur. I will need to spend the rest of my life paying it back, and even that will not be enough."[38]

The many admirers whom Xiaobo attracted later in life, especially after he won the Nobel Peace Prize, seldom saw the side of him that labored under guilt feelings and, when they did, found it hard to understand. To close friends, though, he often commented that he might need to go back to prison, perhaps several times, if he was ever to atone for what he did. His repentance for having written "Repentance," together with his acts of self-preservation immediately following the June Fourth massacre, are keys to understanding the second half of his adult life. His writing about Tao Li shows that he felt deeply guilty about his failures as a husband and a father. Two brief passages in *Monologue* seem to be the only places where, in the many thousands of pages he wrote, he ever mentions his son, Liu Tao.[39]

While struggling inwardly, Xiaobo needed something to do with his daily life. He no longer had a job at Beijing Normal. He had a financial cushion thanks to Liu Xiaoqing and Jiang Wen, and he had a place to stay thanks to Hou Dejian. But what should he *do*?

Many of his peers, including those who had been involved in the protest movement, turned to money making. Deng Xiaoping, the helmsman at the top, had opened that door. Wanting to break the mood of depressed immobility that had seized China after the massacre—and not wanting personally to go down in history with the tag "butcher of '89"—Deng made a "southern tour" to Shenzhen, Zhuhai, Guangzhou, Shanghai, and other places that were among China's closest to the outside world, stressing that the country should continue with "reform and opening." It was clear that he meant only economic, not political reform. The essential message was, "Go make money but keep your mouths shut." To many Chinese, including intellectuals, this was a deal worth making. One might as well take advantage of the one sphere of life in which freedom was allowed. In large numbers, people left government offices, scientific institutes, and universities to pursue profit. It was called "jumping into the sea," and many 1989 protesters were doing it.

But Xiaobo could not. It just wasn't him. He was among a minority who still wanted to talk about philosophy, art, ideals, and other impracticalities. In Shanghai, when some professors announced a "discussion of the spirit of humanism," its impact was tiny. By contrast, in Beijing, when the novelist Wang Shuo satirized the self-elevation of intellectuals, the response was huge.

Xiaobo's explorations of where to turn led him to the topic of popular culture. He had long been aware of a confrontation between natural, authentic expression of human life at one level of society and a ruling authority that pressed down on it from another. He recalled how, in college, the soft voice of Deng Lijun had undermined the iron-willed dare-to-die Communist ideology that had filled his grade-school textbooks; he also remembered how, in graduate school, his love for Zhuangzi and Sikong Tu had come from the way those thinkers supported authentic, untrammeled human expression. The Communist government periodically launched campaigns to repress "low culture," but somehow the underside kept pushing back.

During twenty months in Qincheng Prison, Xiaobo had read so much in *People's Daily* about how the Party was "wiping out low culture" that it made him very curious to see what this low culture looked like. On his way home to Dalian in January 1991, he took a moment to browse at the book stalls near the rail station, and an eye-catching magazine cover grabbed his attention. It showed a curvaceous nude woman, semireclined, above a caption that read "Hot Enough to Wake the Dead." Headlines on some other covers read "Exposé of China's Biggest Sex Abuse Cases," "Secrets of the Oral Fixation," and "I'll Tell You the Secrets of Enjoying Sex." He was astonished. Not only had the vaunted "wiping out" apparently achieved nothing; the sex and violence were more pronounced than before the Tiananmen movement.[40]

He wanted to learn more. What were ordinary people actually thinking? During the Tiananmen movement he and a friend who studied social psychology had done some surveys of popular opinion about the protests. Why not look for that friend and try something similar now? Xiaobo did find him, and the friend was willing. So Xiaobo drafted a series of questions. What did people do in their free time? What entertainment equipment did they own—televisions, cameras, stereo speakers, and so on? What films and TV programs did they watch? Which were their favorites? What did they do for exercise? Did they care about fashion? What did they think about sex and violence in popular culture? Did they believe in the special effects of *qigong* (breath exercises)? Fortune-telling? There were questions about the differences between popular culture and Party culture and between new Western ideas and Chinese traditions. The friend formatted the questions into a list of forty-five, with eight possible responses to each. They distributed 1,500 copies of the questionnaire at eight locations in Beijing and nearby suburbs. The response rate was high. All but ten questionnaires were returned.

Xiaobo financed the initial stages of the project from his own pocket, but later the *China Times Weekly* in Taiwan purchased their research and published the results in three parts during February and March 1993.[41] In a summary analysis, Xiaobo wrote:

> Three items recur in what the respondents say about their life contexts: one, my area is a manic building site, where heavy construction is going on constantly,

and where most of the activities are for pleasure—restaurants, luxury apartments, vacation villages, gaming arcades, and so on. Two, my area is a major banquet table—eating and drinking goes on like crazy, everywhere. Mao Zedong once said, "Revolution is not a banquet," and today one would need to switch but one word: "Revolution is *only* a banquet." Three, my area is a big amusement park—frivolity and vulgar garishness are everywhere.[42]

Popular culture, Xiaobo concluded, was once a wellspring of resistance to state ideology but now had become a playground for the leisured. He saw irony in the fact that he was using phrases like "frivolity and garishness" to describe popular attitudes. Only a few years earlier he had been lecturing to large audiences about the need to liberate "material values and sex" from Communist austerity and criticizing intellectuals for their hypocritical high-mindedness. Now, what he had called for had come to be, and the deluge far exceeded what he had anticipated or ever would have wanted.

Originally Xiaobo had thought his surveys might be a foundation for a book on Chinese popular culture. The results, though, made that project seem less palatable than the somewhat related idea of doing a series of taped interviews with influential cultural figures. He would avoid people like Bao Zunxin or Jiang Qisheng, whom the regime would view as too "sensitive." But he looked for, and eventually secured, interviews with writers Wang Shuo and Zhong Acheng; film directors Chen Kaige, Zhang Yimou, and Jiang Wen; musicians Cui Jian, Liu Huan, and Na Ying; and others. He went through friends to be in touch with mainstream state publishers and hoped his book might become a best-seller.

At the time, Wang Shuo was the only Chinese writer whose works circulated in more than a million copies. Interviewing Wang, Xiaobo calls him "the spokesperson for the rebellious spirit of youth" because his "hooligan literature" makes great fun of the pompous self-righteousness of both political authorities and intellectual luminaries. With characteristic candor, Xiaobo reminds Wang Shuo that his writing feeds off politics, whereas "in real literature, an author avoids political halos."[43] Xiaobo wanted to move away from politics and write more about culture and society.

He then ran into a wall. He hadn't realized that the authorities had banned the name Liu Xiaobo from any mention in any publication anywhere in China. Absorbing that hard fact, he concluded that his only route to writing for a living was to send articles to media outside the People's Republic—to Hong Kong, Taiwan, and the United States.[44] This meant that readers on the mainland would find it harder to see his essays, but that was still better than total silence, and the modest payments he could receive from the outside at least would help to keep food on the table.

The shift to writing for overseas publications required shifts in his topics. Editors outside China were less interested in philosophy and literature than in political commentary. In 2008, shortly before Xiaobo was sent to prison, he stated publicly that the change in his themes should be viewed primarily as his response to forces set in motion by a less-than-rational government.[45]

In early 1992 he embarked upon the difficult task of passport renewal. Not easy under any circumstances, the process was especially difficult for a "black hand." It took him eight months. This meant that he could leave for Australia in January 1993 to be a visiting scholar at Australian National University, where he gave lectures on three topics: popular culture and its relation to Communist Party culture; Chinese democracy in the wake of all the mendacity surrounding Tiananmen; and the problem of exile for Chinese intellectuals.

Two months later, in March, he traveled to Boston to do interviews for the film *The Gate of Heavenly Peace* that Carma Hinton and Richard Gordon (and Geremie Barmé, as an associate director) were producing. The film sought to document the 1989 protests from start to finish, and it included some criticisms of the student protesters that Xiaobo agreed with: their understanding of democracy was shallow, and they exhibited some of the very traits of Communist culture that they were protesting. Xiaobo himself appeared in the film, where he criticized himself for contradictory behavior: he had advised students against a hunger strike but in the end had done one himself; he had started out rationally but, amid the thrill of attention from crowds, had let rationality slip away.

Gao Xin and Zhou Duo were also in Boston at the time, both having been invited by Harvard University as visiting scholars, so they and Xiaobo had a little reunion. Hou Dejian was in New Zealand, but they reached him by telephone and raised the question of whether the four of them might again try to do something. Hou was unenthusiastic, though, and the idea withered. The "four gentlemen" never came together again. Gao stayed in the United States, Zhou went back to China, and Hou remained in New Zealand until 2006, when he quietly moved to Beijing.

While in Boston, Xiaobo gave a lecture at Harvard on the relationship between popular culture and Party culture in China.[46] He argued that popular culture cuts two ways politically. It undermines the worldview that the Party tries to impose, but it also can serve the Party's interests by distracting people from more important things, like memory of massacres and continuing injustices in society. Xiaobo was reading Vaclav Havel at the time, and Havel had pointed out how post-totalitarian governments encourage people to focus on things like interior decorating and washing machines in order to keep their minds out of politics.[47] Xiaobo went further, though, in writing that the effusion of insipid popular culture in China gave cover to the pernicious thought that "Chinese people have no souls."

All the while Xiaobo was, once again, struggling with his own soul. He made the trip from New York to Boston by car. His old friend Chen Jun drove, and Hu Ping was riding along. They got lost looking for Carma Hinton's house and during the extra driving time fell into a deep discussion. Criticisms of Xiaobo's *Monologue* were continuing to surface. The three friends disagreed about how he should respond, and that discussion led to debate over what the ultimate value of fighting for human dignity is. We do not have a record of the conversation, but later, from Australia, Xiaobo wrote to Hu Ping: "When I had to submit to all those regulations in [Qincheng] prison, I began to wonder: why keep going? What's the value of holding to a political position? There in prison, the disappointment and disgust I felt in observing the total collapse of my dignity seemed enough to annihilate all tenacity and resistance."[48] So a political prison can cause a person who pursues freedom and dignity to lose both.

Perhaps because Chen Jun was trained in philosophy, he was able, in a memoir of his own, to abstract *Monologue* from its political context and to view Xiaobo as a philosopher. To Chen, Xiaobo resembled Rousseau in his *Confessions*; he was exploring ethics and aesthetics as they arise from human nature in daily life. Chen approves of Xiaobo's tendency to introspection but finds that it can go too far. Xiaobo sometimes seems actually to enjoy criticizing himself, even to show some zeal for it. That zeal can turn into a kind of self-regard, even vanity, that puts readers off and might explain some of the criticism of *Monologue*. Chen recalls going to Xiaobo to tell him, as a friend, that this might be occurring.[49] He believes that Xiaobo heard the message and took it to heart. Some of the clear changes for the better in his character a few years later were likely the results not only of his self-examination but also of counsel from his friends.

Some of the criticisms of *Monologue* irritated Xiaobo. Certain intellectuals who had fled China and settled in the United States after the 1989 massacre said he was too hard on the students. In an interview with *China Spring*, Xiaobo struck back.[50] He faulted these "June Fourth people" for profligate spending of the moral capital that the massacre had earned. "They have pretty well divided the June Fourth cake until there is nothing left," he said. He went on to bemoan that overseas dissident groups were at each other's throats and then argued: "In fact everybody realizes that the route forward of lowest cost for Chinese society would be to improve the Communist Party itself. People in all stations in society can see this point; it spans social divides. So we should all work, in every way and from every angle, to bring about positive change in the Communist Party." These were not words that exiles wanted to hear. Was Liu Xiaobo forgiving the Party's crimes? Signaling that he was ready to cooperate with it? In his view he was doing neither. He was just offering practical—one might even say cynically practical—advice.

In the same interview, he reflected on the nonviolence principle that he and others had invoked at the square. He said that very few in the protest movement understood nonviolence as a principle in democratic theory or a means for advancing rationality during confrontations. Nonviolence was a principle at Tiananmen only because the other side had overwhelmingly superior armament. He recalled that he himself, at the time, was thinking only at this simple level. If the arms imbalance had not been so lopsided, there would have been no talk of refraining from violence at the square.[51]

Reporters at the interview asked if Xiaobo was considering staying in the United States on this, his second visit. He said no—the question had never even occurred to him.

"After you had all those troubles in China," a reporter asked, "did you ever reflect that if you had not gone back in '89 you would have been spared them?"

"No," Xiaobo answered. "It never crossed my mind. I guess my attitude is that if I am going to hell, I can't complain that it's dark."[52]

From New York, Xiaobo went back to Australia and then, in May 1993, returned to China and never left again. His departure from Australia seems to have coincided with a cooling of his relationship with his old friend Geremie Barmé. Linda Jaivin, married to Barmé at the time, refers in a 2010 essay to "what happened between Xiaobo and myself" in 1991, when Xiaobo was released from Qincheng. She praises Barmé for being "big-hearted" about the affair.[53]

Back in Beijing, Xiaobo reconnected with old friends who shared his political leanings. Gradually they formed an informal group. A key member was Chen Xiaoping, whose recent experience had paralleled Xiaobo's closely: the two had met at Yan Mingfu's United Front meeting on May 13, 1989; cooperated in efforts on the square; gone to Qincheng Prison about the same time; and together had "caused trouble" there by disguising their communication as English practice. When Xiaobo returned to Beijing he heard that his friend Xiaoping was out of prison. He set out by bicycle one night to look for Chen and, after considerable searching, found him. He was recovering from hepatitis B contracted in prison. (Wang Juntao also contracted hepatitis B in Qincheng Prison. Xiaobo, later found to be an asymptomatic carrier, also got it somewhere unknown.)

Xiaobo learned that the parallels between his life and Chen Xiaoping's had continued after prison: both were fired from their university positions, both were charged with "spreading propaganda to incite counterrevolution," and at trial both were released "without punishment." Chen, like Xiaobo, had "confessed" in prison. Both felt remorse. Others viewed them as "the twin cowards."

Bao Zunxin, editor in the late 1980s of the hugely influential Striding Toward the Future book series as well as deputy editor of the leading intellectual magazine *Reading,* was in the group as well. Bao was another "black hand" of 1989 and had been to Qincheng Prison too. He went to trial the same day as Xiaobo and was sentenced to five years in prison but released in November 1992. Like Xiaobo and Chen Xiaoping, he emerged to find himself fired from his posts. Common fate was a magnet drawing such people together. Another in the group was Liu Weihua, who had worked in Chen Ziming's Beijing Institute for Social and Economic Research and also had been arrested after the massacre. The student protest leader Wang Dan, who was released from prison in February 1993, joined them. In 1994 Zhou Duo joined, as did Liu Xia, Xiaobo's new girlfriend, later to be his wife. The group dined together nearly every weekend, sharing not only food but also recollections, both the sweet and the sour.

Chen Ziming played an especially important role. In 1994, under pressure from the U.S. Congress to make concessions in return for "most favored nation" trading status, Beijing authorities released Chen, together with Wang Juntao, on the face-saving pretext of "medical parole." (Wang did carry the hepatitis B virus; Chen, without examination, was declared to have "chronic itchy skin." Wang chose to leave for the United States and went directly from prison to the airport, but Chen stayed in China.) By now their group was a significant fragment of the larger group that in May 1989 had called itself the Conference of Patriotic Supporters of the Students in Tiananmen. Could they regain that energy?

Chen advocated a position that he called "constructive opposition" and persuaded others to embrace it. He felt it was important that the group not spin off into a "dissident" orbit but stay within mainstream society, commenting on important issues and working to get oppositional thinking accepted as a normal part of intellectual discourse. This meant staying in constructive dialogue with people in universities, research institutes, and government. Chen proposed that the group organize projects on selected topics and suggested these six:

The Post-Deng Era
Reform and Development of the Chinese Economy
Constitutionalism in China
The Study of Local Autonomy
The Structure of the Former Soviet Union and Eastern Europe
Political and Economic Corruption

It was agreed that six members of the group—Chen Ziming, Bao Zunxin, Chen Xiaoping, Liu Weihua, Zhou Duo, and Liu Xiaobo—would each take the lead on one of the topics.[54]

Xiaobo took the corruption topic. Consulting with others, he drafted a paper, "A Proposal for Opposing Corruption," that the group released on February 20, 1995.[55] A week later another paper appeared, drafted by Chen Xiaoping, titled "Abolish Detention for Investigation and Protect Personal Freedom."[56] The group submitted both papers to the National People's Congress. They were the first examples since 1989 of intellectuals publicly offering policy suggestions to the government.

Xiaobo's work on corruption obliged him to do tedious research far different from the literary and philosophical essay writing he was accustomed to. Day after day he went to the periodicals room of the Beijing Library to gather statistics. His draft opened with a review of the years 1982 to 1993, during which he identified four major "anticorruption" campaigns. The National People's Congress and the State Council had both issued numerous anticorruption regulations, many anti-corruption conferences had been held, and more than 3,000 centers for reporting corruption had been established. And the results? Between 1982 and 1993, corruption (understood as embezzlement, bribery, and use of public funds for eating, drinking, or travel) serious enough to be investigated by prosecutors nationwide—whether measured in number of cases, number of people involved, or rank of the people involved—had doubled, tripled, or worse.

Xiaobo focused on an item in the records called "largest bribe discovered to have been made in a given year." In 1982 the figure was 69,700 yuan and by 1993 it was 25,300,000 yuan; that amounted, he pointed out, to a 366-fold increase in eleven years. Moreover, about three-quarters of the 1993 amount was paid in U.S. dollars. Why, he then asked, did corruption get worse and worse even as anticorruption measures became more and more common? He argued that it was time for new proposals and offered some in two categories, short-term and long-term. A key short-term proposal was "accountings of the personal wealth and property of public officials should be made public." The long-term proposals were essentially political, because they aimed at the underlying structures that generated corruption: "end the ban on forming political parties," "end the ban on an independent press," "establish separation of powers in government," "make a constitution the supreme authority and establish independent courts," and so on.

Arbitrary detention, the topic of Chen Xiaoping's draft, was an extralegal device used against all kinds of people—vagrants, people lacking IDs, violators of family-planning policies, people cohabiting outside marriage, and others. Sometimes the charges were simply pretexts for detaining a person whom someone powerful wanted to see locked up. Chen was a constitutional scholar, and he knew his field thoroughly. The appearance of his article in tandem with Xiaobo's corruption piece deepened the friendship and sense of solidarity between the two.

In May 1995, Xiaobo and his friend Xiaoping jointly drafted a statement called "Lessons Written in Blood Press Us Toward Democracy: An Appeal on the Sixth Anniversary of 'June Fourth.'"[57] It was a sober, carefully worded reflection that placed the blame for the democracy movement's tragic result squarely on the government: "China's ruling authority failed to recognize and to adjust to the worldwide trend toward more openness, diversity, and democracy and could not turn to democracy and law to address China's social problems. Instead it answered the efforts of citizens to participate in politics with its time-tested mentality of enmity and an authoritarian attitude." The appeal went on to call for using law to address society's many conflicts and problems, including the rifts caused by June Fourth. Only adherence to law—in particular press law, assembly law, constitutional and judicial law, and protection of human rights—could prevent a continuing vicious cycle. In an essay written seven years later, Xiaobo was still recalling how much his and Chen Xiaoping's appeal in 1995 had benefited from Chen's legal acuity.[58]

Xiaobo wanted to present this joint appeal as an open letter signed by a broadly representative group of people. In a later reminiscence, he recalls how difficult collecting signatures had been in 1995, before the age of the Internet.[59] Former student leaders like Wang Dan and Ma Shaofang were quick to sign, but to reach others he could not use the telephone, because lines were tapped. He had to go around by bicycle to find people who might be getting involved for the first time, like the poet Mang Ke, the art critic Li Xianting, and the independent filmmaker Jiang Yue, all of whom signed. Xiaobo's friend Liao Yiwu, who was just out of prison for "counterrevolutionary incitement," signed. Xiaobo was disappointed—but not resentful—when a few people who signed later asked to have their names removed when they learned that Xiaobo had spent time in prison. They were afraid his political taint might spread to themselves. In the end Xiaobo gathered fifty-six signatures.

Another open appeal, organized by the distinguished physicist Xu Liangying, translator of Albert Einstein into Chinese, appeared around the same time. In 1993 the United Nations had named 1995 a "Year for Tolerance," and Xu titled his statement "Let's Greet the United Nations' Year for Tolerance by Calling for the Reality of Tolerance in Our Country." Signed by members of China's Academy of Sciences and some well-known cultural figures, it called for the "release of all persons imprisoned for what they think, say, or believe" and for an effort, throughout society, "to cultivate the spirit of tolerating others and to advocate rational and fair attitudes." The first signature on the list was that of eighty-eight-year-old Wang Ganchang, a distinguished physicist and honorary director of the China Institute of Atomic Energy. Yang Xianyi, the illustrious translator of Chinese literature into English, who had denounced the June Fourth massacre on British radio the day it happened, signed as well, as did the famous playwright Wu Zuguang, who had recently been expelled from the Communist Party. Wang Furen, Xiaobo's nighttime conversation partner during his M.A. years and now a professor at Beijing Normal, also signed.[60]

The tones of the two open appeals were different—one more challenging, the other more sedate—and the credentials of the signatories differed too: one group comprised newer activists and the other were well-established intellectuals. In any case, the two letters together seem to have shocked the regime. Six years after the massacre, here was a recrudescence of human rights activity. The authorities decided to take action. They began with vulnerable targets. Wang Dan was detained and five months later sentenced to eleven years in prison. Xiaobo was taken from his home on May 18 and held under house arrest for eight months in a traditional-style courtyard near the Fragrant Hills Botanical Garden on the western outskirts of Beijing. Chen Ziming, who was on parole from prison when the appeal on June Fourth came out, decided not to risk signing it, but his wife Wang Zhihong did, and that was enough to send Chen Ziming back to prison on June 25. When the authorities learned that Chen had cancer, they asked that he consider leaving for the United States, accepting the U.S. offer as Chen's colleague Wang Juntao had. But Chen declined and went back to prison.

Xiaobo's detention in the courtyard was handled entirely outside the law: no charges, no paperwork, no procedures, no sentence. It went forward under the euphemism "monitored residence." For the first few days, the two policemen assigned to watch him shared a room with him, but later they moved into a different room in the courtyard and allowed him a bit of private space. So as long as he did nothing to confront his minders, he could live his life reading and writing. His girlfriend, Liu Xia, could visit him once every two weeks, and she always brought him a big stack of books. "Except for my freedom," he wrote later, "I had just about everything."[61] Moreover, he had a secret way of expanding his freedom. He would wait until after dark, after the courtyard had settled down, and then steal out and climb over the courtyard wall, get on a bus, ride into the city, and find Liu Xia—and Chen Xiaoping, Bao Zunxin, or others—and eat and play mahjong until dawn neared, then head back, jump the wall again, and "continue" sleeping. He did this several times without being caught.

From the beginning of the 1990s Xiaobo often suffered abdominal pain. His firing from Beijing Normal had left him without state-sponsored medical care, so he usually just pressed his thumbs where it hurt. During his 1995 detention he was diagnosed as suffering stomach ulcers.

Upon release in February 1996, he was again delivered in a police car to his parents' home in Dalian. This was protocol. He soon returned to Beijing, though, and joined Bao Zunxin in organizing a petition asking that Chen Ziming be released from prison on medical parole. This mission sent him out by bicycle once more, looking for as many signatures as he could find.[62] In these kinds of human rights causes, Xiaobo always preferred to go into society looking for broad support rather than staying within a small circle of "dissidents." For Chen's case he got signatures from his Beijing Normal Ph.D. mentor Tong Qingbing, his old dorm mate Wang Furen, the famous Peking University Sanskrit scholar Ji Xianlin (author of *Notes from a Cowshed*, about his persecution during the Cultural Revolution),[63] as well as Tang Yijie, the philosopher, and Yue Daiyun, the literature scholar, a married couple from Peking University. He and Liu Xia, together with Chen Xiaoping and Liu Weihua and their spouses, often had meals with Wang Zhihong, wife of the imprisoned Chen Ziming, in an effort to cheer her up. The months of 1996 from February until October, when Xiaobo was incarcerated again, were also when Xiaobo and Liu Xia grew closer and decided to marry.

12

Love That Jumps Walls

The earliest poems that Liu Xia and Liu Xiaobo exchanged were private and have never been published. The earliest one publicly available was written by Liu Xia on June 2, 1989, the day Xiaobo and his three hunger-striking friends were standing amid a sea of admirers on the Monument to the People's Heroes at Tiananmen:

> There's no way I can say a word to you.
> You're a celebrity now.
> I can only hide in the crowd's fringe
> smoke a cigarette, and look at the sky.[1]

The next day, June 3, as conditions in the city became ever more menacing, a group of Xiaobo's friends, deeply worried, headed to the square by bicycle. They invited Liu Xia to go with them, but, unable to ride a bicycle, she could not. Instead she wrote a note for them to carry to Xiaobo: "Please be careful!" After the shooting began, in the wee hours of June 4, her friends carried a voice message back to her on a cassette recorder. The elevators in her building had stopped for the night, but the friends carried the recorder up sixteen flights of stairs to let her hear the message: "Don't weep, Liu Xia. Live well!"

Eight years later, in a labor camp in Dalian, Xiaobo wrote a poem that seemed to reply to Liu Xia's poem of June 2:

> A seething, cheering crowd
> elevated me to an imaginary height.

Shining foreheads pierced the cold
and the fast-talking me
never saw
in that churning sea
the tranquil you.

You raised your head to look at me
while your mind was hidden in its own corner.
Blinded by the gaze of so many eyes
I could not see you, but could sense
your back, on its lonely stroll.[2]

These two oppositely directed people—one who rushed toward crowds and the other who walked the other way—also had much in common.

Liu Xia was born in Beijing in 1961. She grew up with two brothers, Liu Tong, three years her elder, and Liu Hui, eight years younger. Her father, Liu Zhihua, was born in 1927 and joined the Communist Party at age seventeen to fight Japan. Wounded in the war, he returned to his home in Shenzhou in central Hebei province. With the Communist revolution in 1949, he was transferred first to Tianjin and then to Beijing, where for many years he did "political work" (meaning control of ideology and personnel) in the central government's Ministry of Finance. From 1972 to 1977 he was sent to work in Hong Kong—an assignment that only a very politically reliable person could be given—and from 1987 to 1991 he served as Communist Party secretary at the Central College of Finance and Economics.[3] In short, it would be hard to have a career more "red" than his.

In private he was hardly a straitlaced Communist, however. He brought Western-flavored things from Hong Kong to his family and friends in Beijing—even a Bible at one point. He doted on Liu Xia. He once brought her a picture album of sketches of famous Westerners, which in Beijing of the 1970s was an extremely rare and attractive book. When word leaked out, a stream of visitors descended on the Liu home to take a look.

There were times when both parents were away on work assignments and the older brother, Liu Tong, was out at his job. The teenaged Liu Xia was left in charge of Liu Hui, who was too young to be left alone. She became an apprentice mother—cooked for him, supervised his homework, and played games with him. The two bonded.

The family had one serious problem, however. It came from Liu Xia's mother, Xiang Bihua, although it was not at all her fault. It was inherited from her father,

Xiang Daguang—although it's hard to say it was his fault, either. Xiang Daguang had a "bad class background"—a label that was sufficiently negative in the 1950s to send him to prison and to make it difficult for his family members to get good job assignments. When Liu Xia was a child, no one spoke about her tainted grandfather. The topic was taboo; even her mother said nothing.

To the Communists, Xiang Daguang was an odd mixture of hero and villain. Born to a poor family in Hunan in the 1890s,[4] the gifted youngster could afford college in Beijing only with funds from the Xiang Family Ancestral Hall in his hometown. He attended National Peking Teachers College, the forerunner of Beijing Normal University,[5] where he became a student leader in the May Fourth movement. An interesting parallel between Xiang Daguang and Liu Xiaobo is that, based at the same campus, the two were prominent in the student movements of their times: May Fourth and, seventy years later, June Fourth.

May Fourth happened in the wake of World War I, when leaders of the victorious nations at the Paris Peace Conference transferred German suzerainty over China's Shandong peninsula to Japan instead of allowing it to revert to China. News of this affront to Chinese dignity spread quickly on college campuses across China, and on May 4, 1919, students in Beijing took to the streets to protest the Chinese government's weak response. They surrounded and then burned down the residence of Cao Rulin, the Chinese government official who had signed the treaty. The government responded by sending armed police to disperse the students. Thirty-two were arrested, one of whom was Xiang Daguang. Within three days a sharp public outcry forced the government to release the students to their campuses. When Xiang and seven others went back to National Peking Teachers College, fellow students lifted them into the air to carry them through the main gate. They were heroes!

After graduation, Xiang immersed himself in the modernizing tides of the times. He headed for Shanghai, center of the liveliest new thinking, where he met the essayist Zhu Ziqing, the fiction writer Ye Shengtao, and other leading intellectuals. Xiang was hired to teach at China Public College (Zhongguo gongxue), founded in 1906 and famous as China's first modern university. Later, from October 1937 to August 1938, he served as county magistrate of Wenling county in Zhejiang province. The governor of Zhejiang at the time was Zhu Jianhua, and nine years later, in 1947, Daguang used his status as a former subordinate to write a letter to Zhu, who was now minister of education in the central government. On May 20, 1947, students in Nanjing, Shanghai, Suzhou, Hangzhou and elsewhere had taken to the streets to protest government policies of underfunding education and famine relief while pursuing civil war with the Communists.

Police answered the demonstrators with clubs and sticks, injuring nineteen and arresting many others. Daguang invoked his status as a veteran of the "foul drama" of burning Cao Rulin's house during the May Fourth movement to advise Zhu to "give the students tolerant guidance and strictly avoid provocations that could lead to harmful reactions."[6]

Meanwhile he had raised a family. He had four daughters and one son and, in keeping with his progressive ideals, made sure that the girls had the same opportunities the boy had. One by one, all four daughters joined the Communists' People's Liberation Army and took self-supporting jobs afterward. Liu Xia's mother, Bihua, born in 1933, went to Beijing in 1949 to study at the Logistical Engineering College of the People's Liberation Army and then went to work at the Ministry of Finance. But in the 1950s, the problem of her father's "bad class background" suddenly raised its head. Because he had been a county magistrate under the Nationalists, Xiang Daguang now counted as a "historical counterrevolutionary." It didn't matter that he had been a hero of May Fourth. Bihua was transferred from the Ministry of Finance to work as an accountant at the China Grain, Oil, and Food Import and Export Corporation. Daguang himself was sent to prison, was never released, and died there in the 1960s, alone. His family, whether fearing further association with him or perhaps themselves too caught up in "revolutionary" tides, turned its back on him.

Xiang Bihua felt so ashamed of her counterrevolutionary father that she went to extremes to tilt the other way. She demanded her children do "political study" beyond what they did in school. She fed them "remember-the-bitter" dinners. These were skimpy, flavorless meals intended to mimic "life before the revolution" so that the younger generation would "appreciate the sweet" the Communists had brought.

One year when Liu Xia was in her early teens, her father brought her a brightly colored set of clothes from Hong Kong. She was crazy about them. But even before she could try them on, her mother confiscated them, packed them into a clothing chest, and summoned her and her elder brother to a study session in politics. Liu Xia cried all night, but her mother was not moved. Indeed, the tears were counterproductive. The mother saw Liu Xia's emotional attachment to the clothing as a bad sign and redoubled her efforts to arrest the bourgeois rot in her daughter's character. Years later, Liu Xia found that set of pretty clothing, still pressed at the bottom of one of her mother's storage chests.

Her mother began watching Liu Xia's every move. She even scheduled exams at intervals to check on the girl's virginity. Liu Xia began to resent her mother intensely. She would not even sleep near her. In 1997, Xiaobo wrote that he understood Liu Xia's not wanting to have children as grounded in her fear and hatred of her mother.[7]

Liu Xia's rebellious spirit seems at least in part to have been the result of her mother's severity. After Liu Xia learned that her grandfather was a black sheep in the family, she sometimes mentioned him on purpose, as if lighting a fuse and waiting to hear the firecracker explode. Her family began to accept that Liu Xia was a troublemaker. As an adult she recalled, "I was one of those children whom adults gave up on."[8] In school she didn't do well in math, and her solution to the problem was not to try. When the hour for math class arrived, she would, as she saw fit, choose between going to class and going outside to play. She didn't like physical education, either. The other children rode bicycles and swam, but not Liu Xia.

When she was in tenth grade news came that the national college-entrance examination would be revived. Her classmates started concentrating on getting into college, but Liu Xia remained indifferent. She just read contemporary literature and whatever else she felt like reading. She took up painting. She failed the exam, which confirmed her self-conception as someone who did not follow the crowd as well as her resolve to stay that way.

Instead of going to college Liu Xia took an editorial job in 1981 with *Finance* magazine. Her father's connections in the financial world no doubt helped her get it. The next year she met and fell in love with a young editor named Wu Bin, who had just graduated from the Chinese Department at Shandong University. They married in 1984. Wu Bin was at the center of a group of young writers, editors, and critics who shared many a convivial meal at which virtually every topic under the sun got good coverage. Liu Xia was chef and did a good job of it. Zou Jin, Xiaobo's friend from Jilin University, was a member of the group, and through him Xiaobo was introduced to it as well. Xiaobo and Liu Xia first met in that group in 1982.[9] On the day in 1986 when Xiaobo and Li Jie gave their bombshell speeches at the conference on "Ten Years of Literature in the New Era," Xiaobo brought Li Jie to meet the group, and the informal seminar that he stimulated lasted nearly all night. Well-known creative writers made visits as well. The novelist Yu Hua recalls an evening in 1988 when he rode public buses, transferring several times; found the building where Wu Bin and Liu Xia lived; then squeezed into a cramped elevator to ride up to their apartment, knocked on the door, and went in to watch a videotape of Ingmar Bergman's film *Wild Strawberries*. The later-renowned author and screenwriter Wang Shuo was also a visitor. He and Wu Bin worked on drama scripts together and in 1988 founded a film company.

Liu Xia began writing poetry and fiction within this context. She developed some strong preferences among world poets, but her own name was made with a long poem, "A Bird, and Again a Bird," that appeared in 1983. Her literary friends could attribute it to nothing but her own creativity. It opens:

> Long ago,
> we often mentioned
> that bird.
> We didn't know where it came from
> but were enthralled.
> It brought us joy.
>
> One night in winter
> yes, winter—it came to us.
> We were sound asleep.
> Neither of us saw it,
> but when the sun rose in the morning
> we could see its little shadow
> on the window pane.
> The shadow stayed a long time
> unwilling to leave.
>
> Winter bored us
> with its long, long sleeps.
> We wanted to leave a red lamp outside
> for a long, long time
> to tell the bird
> that we were waiting.

Near the poem's end,

> [One gray day]
> The red lamp in the courtyard was flashing on and off.
> A bunch of green grapes had fallen on the steps.
> Our footsteps stopped.
> We looked up at the sky
> then quickly back down.
> It had visited
> but we didn't dare say so.
> We kept our thoughts private
> lest it never come again.

Liu Xia's readers imagined the possible meanings of a bird that isn't there and of people thinking of something, perhaps hoping for something, but not willing to say so.

Liao Yiwu noticed Liu Xia's published poems and began a correspondence with her that grew into a close friendship lasting thirty years. On one visit to Beijing, Liao noticed that a portrait of the American poet Sylvia Plath (1932–1963) rested above Liu Xia's bed. Works by Plath, famous as a "freedom poet" in art circles in China in the early 1980s, had begun to appear in Chinese poetry magazines and were leaving deep impressions on Chinese poets, especially women poets. Plath became to Liu Xia roughly what Nietzsche was to Xiaobo. Liu Xia did not consciously imitate Plath, as some young Chinese poets did, but resemblances are discernible. The final lines of Plath's poem "Words" are:

> Words dry and riderless,
> The indefatigable hoof-taps.
> While
> From the bottom of the pool, fixed stars
> Govern a life.

A Liu Xia poem from 1995, "A Word," ends:

> I truly admire this word
> It invades and occupies me
> And then gushes vitality[10]

In another poem, Liu Xia makes Plath her subject:

> She is so graceful and soft
> but cutting and wild too.
> You can never keep up with her.
> Your words cannot touch her soul.
> Her vital spirit
> floats outside the skies.[11]

"You" in this poem refers to Plath's husband, the poet Ted Hughes. The two married in 1956 but separated in 1962, and Plath took her own life in February 1963 at their London home. It was her third suicide attempt. Liao Yiwu remembers a visit with Liu Xia in the 1980s when the two discussed those three suicide attempts and, strangely, both burst into laughter.[12] Liao could not explain the laughter except to note that he and Liu Xia at one level shared an alienated, mocking view of the world.

After the June 4, 1989, massacre, Liao Yiwu wrote a poem, "Massacre," that he later made into a video called "Requiem." He and about twenty of his friends were detained for helping to make it. One was an especially close friend, a poet and fiction writer from Chongqing named Zhou Zhongling, with whom, years earlier, Liao had edited an underground poetry journal. Zhou's nickname was Zhongzhong, "the loyal one." He had a lame left leg from childhood polio, and perhaps for that reason the government held him for only a month and then released him. Liao was sent to prison for four years for "the crime of inciting counterrevolution."

Zhongzhong later met Liu Xia (who also was questioned in the "Requiem" case but not detained) and they too became tight friends. After Zhongzhong's first visit to her home in Beijing, he wrote: "From the moment I walked through her door to the moment I left, she did nothing but giggle and grin. Enveloped in a cloud of smoke, this chain-smoker struck me as vacuous—as a person who completely lacked a subjective life. I couldn't imagine why a man of any caliber would be attracted to her. Later on, though, it was this very quality of Liu Xia's that became the foundation of our friendship. I had been wrong."[13] Liu Xia's natural effervescence grew on people. She was sensitive, sharp-witted, always frank, and famous for her irrepressible laughter. She laughed with people even before she had decided what, if anything, she wanted to say. She loved books and wine, composed poetry, painted, and wrote fiction. *China* magazine published two of her short stories, but she did not rush to publish sequels. She didn't care about the world's opinions. She had her own standards, and they were tough.

The events of 1989 affected Liu Xia's marriage to Wu Bin. Strains had appeared earlier, and Wu had already raised the possibility of their going separate ways. Then the cataclysm of '89 shook both of them profoundly. Both needed to rethink the world and their places in it. They realized they would have to work on their marriage, and did, but finally divorced in 1994. The marriage had lasted ten years.

Xiaobo looked to reconnect with old friends after he was released from Qincheng Prison, including Zou Jin, Wu Bin, and Liu Xia. Hou Dejian's apartment in Twin Elms in northwest Beijing, where Xiaobo lived, by chance was only a fifteen-minute walk from Wu Bin and Liu Xia's apartment, so it was easy to revive friendships with them. Xiaobo wrote three poems in the summer of 1991 that he designated "to Xia," but they were not love poems. Entitled "The Me That's in the Rain," "Astonishment," and "That Man Sits," they were about random scenes on the street and his fragmented, subjective responses to them. They were difficult poems—"poets' poems"—and Xia was the other serious poet in his neighborhood. In Xia's poem "June 2, 1989," written two years earlier, a flicker of flirtation is involved. But that, for the moment, was minor.

In December 1992, when Xiaobo was about to leave for Australia, Liu Xia wrote a poem called "The Wind—for Xiaobo."[14] It revealed some feelings that had been hidden until then:

> Your life is fated to be like the wind
> blowing here, blowing there
> playing games in the clouds.
> I have thought of going with you,
> but what kind of base
> would ever hold you?
> Walls would choke you.
> You can be only the wind, and the wind
> never tells me
> when it will come and when it will go.

Zhou Zhongling recalls that it was around the same time that words about Xiaobo seemed to flow steadily from Liu Xia's lips in a way that "left no doubt in the mind of an observer that their love story had begun,"[15] even though Xiaobo was overseas at the time.

In early 1993 Liu Xia resigned from her job in the publicity department of the State Revenue Service. The work was tiresome, and she felt she was wasting her life in it. The resignation left her without the financial security of employment in the state system, and she never re-entered it. To mark her new freedom, she set out alone on a trip to Tibet. It was a bold move for her, because she had barely ever left Beijing before and by nature was physically timid. She seldom even crossed streets alone. But she stayed in Tibet three months and loved it. The remoteness and wide, open spaces were just what her spirit needed.

Xiaobo wrote three more poems "for Xia" in June and July 1993, after he returned from Australia. These, unlike the three written in 1991, were "electric." The first, "Praise in Five Minutes—for Xia," was written at Xia's behest.[16] She went to the kitchen to make congee and said she would return in five minutes, within which time Xiaobo would have to write a poem praising her. The next two, "Dangerous Merriment"[17] and "One Morning,"[18] were about Xia's trip to Tibet that began in the second week of July. "One Morning" includes these lines:

When you left
I was calm.
When your receding figure disappeared
my longing was born, off in the distance
like how inside the lines of a child's palm another person walks
passing through my body, circuitously
looking for a unique word.

The three poems clearly set their relationship in a new direction. Not long afterward, Xiaobo headed to Tibet as well. He was accompanying a writer from Taiwan but stayed a few days after the writer left, asking around for Xia and eventually finding her. She was living at the home of a painter friend who worked for Tibet state television. Xiaobo stayed a few more days before returning to Beijing. Xia returned in October.

After Xia's divorce from Wu Bin in 1994, Xiaobo pursued her purposefully. The meetings of the informal political group he founded with Chen Xiaoping did not include her at first, but Xiaobo regularly went to see her when they were over. Chen noticed that when he asked Xiaobo where he was going as the meetings ended, Xiaobo seemed ill at ease, as if embarrassed. He didn't want to say he was going straight to Liu Xia's place, but to a good friend like Chen Xiaoping his intentions were as plain as day.

Xiaobo intended to be a proper suitor if he could. Aware of his reputation for unreliability in romantic matters, he felt handicapped, and deservedly so, in pursuing the affections of a young woman like Liu Xia. He resolved to cherish her fastidiously if he could have the chance. As if by magic, women of every kind, whether romantically attached or not, disappeared from his environment. Liu Xia had cast a spell over him that others could not. A number of years later, the poet Bei Ling observed, "I have never elsewhere seen a person try so determinedly to change nearly everything about himself, become a new person, and do it through a process that so went against the grain and required such immense effort."[19] Pursuit of Liu Xia was the first field upon which Xiaobo undertook this herculean kind of effort, but others were to come.

Xiaobo became very careful with money. He moved in with Liu Xia and took to heart what he saw as a duty, in the traditional male role, to be the provider. But it wasn't easy. His work writing position papers with Chen Xiaoping and the others didn't bring in any money. He tried to be frugal and never asked friends for loans. Despite his public image of being "bold and uninhibited," in daily life he pinched pennies. Smoking was his only indulgence, and he kept it under control. His income came from selling articles to overseas magazines and newspapers, and he milked those sources well. No one in his group of friends who came out of prison after June Fourth wrote more in volume than he. Some actually criticized him for writing too much. Manuscript payments were calculated by number of characters, and Xiaobo, they felt, was sometimes padding his essays by recycling content.

When Liu Xia joined the Chen Xiaoping discussion group, she came basically as an auditor. She followed Xiaobo's lead but didn't talk much. Others in the group eventually realized that this attitude came less from weakness than from a quiet self-confidence. The conventional values of "success," "status," and "honor" held no attraction for Liu Xia; she felt no need to "show" anything. But it was equally true that she felt little need to hide things. Her attitude toward the plain-clothes police who followed her was: So what? I have nothing to hide; if you want to watch, then watch.

When Xiaobo was released from "monitored residence" in February 1996, he and Liu Xia discussed getting married and decided to do it. There was a barrier, though. One of Xiaobo's punishments for having been a "black hand" was revocation of his residence permit. Without one, he had no legal grounds for asking authorities to do anything official. The couple's fallback was to arrange a "do-it-yourself" wedding.

In premodern China people could marry by just inviting relatives and friends to a banquet and announcing the marriage to everyone. Liu Xia's parents approved of Xiaobo and were pleased that their daughter was remarrying. Her mother gave the couple the very substantial wedding gift of the right to live in the quarters to which her work unit had assigned her. It was a two-bedroom apartment on South Cuiwei Lane off Wanshou Road in Beijing. Xiaobo's parents also approved of the marriage and traveled from Dalian to attend the wedding banquet. The meeting of the two sets of parents was the most important stamp of approval. Xiaobo presented Liu Xia with a diamond ring that cost eight thousand yuan (about US $1,200). He had squeezed every possible penny to buy it.

Some time after the formal banquet there was a lively, less formal dinner that included Chen Xiaoping, Zou Jin, and other friends. Wu Bin hesitated about attending, but after repeated pleas from both Liu Xia and Xiaobo, he came and brought his new girlfriend with him.

Xiaobo felt that Xia should have a chance to go abroad, and in summer 1996 he and his friend Chen Jun in New York figured out how to make that happen. Chen was organizing an exhibition of work by women artists in New York and added Liu Xia's name to an invitation list. When she arrived, though, she could speak of nothing but her husband, Xiaobo. All she ever wanted was to get on the telephone with him and tell him, sometimes through tears, how painful it was to be apart. Chen Jun's long-distance phone bills were ballooning. Liu Xia cut short her stay and flew back to China after only a month. Xiaobo met her at the airport clutching a huge bouquet of flowers. When they got home Xia saw that the entire apartment had been festooned in flowers.[20]

Meanwhile, for his recidivism in talking about political change, Xiaobo had been elevated on government surveillance lists. He learned this when he went on a trip to visit friends in south China while Liu Xia was in New York. Police monitored him the whole way, and they did it in teams. When he left any location, the team that had been watching him there would recede while another from the new location took over. Friends he visited were watched too. He visited a college classmate named Wen Yujie in Zhuhai, Guangdong province, and five days later police came knocking on Wen's door, asking: What work do you do? Who was that friend of yours? Why did he come to Zhuhai? The police left, but the taint on Wen did not. Even three years later, when nearby Macao reverted to China after 442 years of Portuguese rule, Wen got a phone call from the police notifying him that he must not leave his home. If he wanted to see the reversion ceremonies, he should watch on television. Wen was puzzled. What was this about? Then he recalled Xiaobo's visit in 1996.[21]

The trip caused other political ripples. In Shenzhen, Xiaobo met with Shao Jiang, Zhou Duo's student who had been active in Tiananmen Square the night of June 3–4, 1989. Xiaobo asked Shao who else it would be worth talking with in the area, and Shao recommended Wang Xizhe in Guangzhou.[22] Xiaobo had never met Wang but had known about him for more than a decade. In November 1974 Wang and two friends, Li Zhengtian and Chen Yiyang, had put up a poster in downtown Guangzhou two months before the opening of the Fourth People's Congress. Drawing one syllable from each of their names, they signed it Li Yizhe. The poster called for political reforms such as making legal guarantees of the democratic rights of citizens, putting limits on the privileged class, and ending the use of torture and other tools of "fascist dictatorship." Large crowds of people gathered to read it. From his college days, Xiaobo had admired people in the Mao era who were able to see through the dictatorship and courageous enough to speak honestly. Li, Chen, and Wang were tracked down and in 1977 sent to prison. This happened, ironically, *after* Mao had died and a political thaw was setting in.

Xiaobo went to Guangzhou and found Wang Xizhe. The summer heat was oppressive, and Guangzhou did not yet have air conditioning, so the two met outdoors at Yuexiu Park and elsewhere. They felt an immediate and strong affinity. The eighty-first anniversary of the founding of the Republic of China in 1912 was coming up, and Wang had drafted a declaration on relations between mainland

China and Taiwan. He proposed that the rival governments in Beijing and Tai-pei return, as a basis for negotiating their differences, to the "Double Ten Agreement" they had made in 1945, in which each party recognized the other as a legitimate entity. Xiaobo was impressed. Wang Xizhe's statement encouraged respect for people's freedom and rights. Moreover, it used an approach that resembled what Xiaobo had been advocating for years: the settling of differences through reasoned dialogue and compromise rather than you-die-and-I-live confrontation. Apart from the Taiwan issue itself, the precedent of settling things in this way would be a valuable precedent in Chinese politics. It might even help to lay a foundation for multiparty government someday. Xiaobo agreed to cosign the statement.[23]

In September Xiaobo took another trip, with Liu Xia and with no aim but to enjoy life. They headed for Sichuan to see their friend Liao Yiwu, who had long been urging them to visit. Liao had been released from prison in 1994, but his wife and child had left him. He lived at his parents' home with his new girlfriend, Song Yu. Their mutual close friend Zhou Zhongling was there too, and everyone had a great time despite the sweltering heat that afflicts Chengdu well into September. Xiaobo and Liao Yiwu played Chinese chess, and they played for money. The loser of a game had to give the winner ten yuan, and Liao kept losing. Suddenly he jumped up and bolted. Xiaobo gave hot pursuit, and the two went screaming and careening through a nearby woods. Finally Liao Yiwu, exhausted, turned to face Xiaobo and shouted that he'd sooner pull down his pants than pay. He then stripped buck naked, and Xiaobo, not to be outdone, did the same. The two then ran off, streaking in the moonlight, whooping at the top of their lungs. The plainclothes police charged with watching them suddenly were nowhere to be seen.

After Xiaobo and Liu Xia had left, Yiwu discovered that he couldn't find his copy of *Selections from Vaclav Havel*. As he was frantically looking for it, the telephone rang. It was Xiaobo, quacking in laughter, saying that he was happily sipping Sichuan tea and reading Havel's "The Power of the Powerless."

"How . . . how . . . how about I re . . . re . . . read you a passage?" Xiaobo asked his friend.[24]

Xia and Xiaobo went next to Shanxi, where their friend the journalist Wang Ya, who loved photography, brought them to see the famous tourist site called Qiao's Grand Courtyard in Qi county. Built in 1756, it is typical of well-to-do residences in north China during the Qing period. It was the harvest season in Shanxi, the air brimmed with pleasant aromas, and the poplars and sunflowers along the roadside gleamed in the sunlight. Xiaobo was not especially interested in ancient architecture, but the natural scenery captivated him, and at one point

FIGURE 12.1   With Liu Xia in Shanxi, 1996

Wang Ya

he suggested that they just park their borrowed car at the roadside and run around outside. The two went prancing and chatting through the sunflowers and sunlight, their spirits as warm and lively as could be. Wang Ya busied herself taking photos of them.

But there was a shadow across the joy as well. The authorities still had their eyes on Xiaobo, and he, Liu Xia, and their hosts were all aware of the monitoring. After they left Shanxi, police invited Wang Ya "for tea"—a euphemism for preliminary interrogation. The move angered Wang Ya, who brusquely rejected the invitation (at the risk of receiving a note in her police file). Xiaobo and Xia noticed that other friends they met on their trip were keeping a studied distance. One whom Xiaobo had invited to come see them showed up at their door very nervous. After knocking, he pushed quickly inside and laughed stiffly. "Hi, hi," he said. "Can't you tell things are sensitive these days . . . pretty *inconvenient*?" After a few sentences of routine talk, he turned and left. The behavior surprised Xiaobo.

Although the police could not have known it, Xiaobo had already written two articles that were published later in the fall and only added to his "offenses." Entitled "Political Conservatism in China in the 1990s"[25] and "Extreme Nationalism in China in the 1990s," [26] they presented an analysis of contemporary thinking at both the elite and popular levels. Xiaobo argues that intellectuals—including Li Zehou and Liu Zaifu in their book *Farewell to Revolution*—had retreated after the debacle at Tiananmen to embrace a conservatism that in some ways undermined the tradition of May Fourth enlightenment, which they now saw as "too radical." The government, meanwhile, had marshaled the full power of state media to present the ordinary people who were struggling in the breathless new world of "money is everything"—and especially the angry people at the lower end of the ever-widening divide between rich and poor—with the new elixir of "patriotism" at home and "nationalism" abroad.

But by the time the two articles appeared, Xiaobo was behind bars again. Xiaobo and Xia had barely arrived home from their travels when, early in the morning on October 8, 1996, they were awakened by a pounding on their door. Two policemen were there. One was Ju Xiaofei, their regular local cop, whom they knew well and actually had a cordial relationship with, and the other was someone they had never seen before. Officer Ju normally wore plain clothes but today was in uniform. So was the other. Something serious was afoot.[27]

They brought Xiaobo to the local Wanshou police station and directly upstairs to the second-floor meeting room. This was where he had had a great many "chats" with section 1 (the political protection section) of Beijing Public Security and "staying in touch" sessions with the local security people. Despite the informality of those labels, both sides always knew that the real purpose was to remind Xiaobo, "We're watching you, always." But this time the atmosphere was different. Seven or eight police officers were already there despite the early hour. Some were in uniform, some not. Three were sitting in formal position behind a long table.

Xiaobo was seated on a chair facing the table. Unruffled, he asked for a glass of water and lit a cigarette. Then, before he could even ask what this was all about, the officer in the middle began a formal interrogation, asking for his surname, given name, age, residence, ethnicity, and so on. Xiaobo noticed a man in one corner of the room holding up a video recorder that was trained on him. A clerk presented him with "An Agreement on Reform Through Labor" on which the titles of two of his articles were listed under the heading "Crimes." They were "Deaths Forgotten and Profaned," published in 1994 in the *United Daily News* in Taiwan and republished in the June 1996 issue of *Kaifang* magazine in Hong Kong; and the 1995 piece coauthored with Chen Xiaoping, "Lessons Written in Blood Press Us Toward Democracy: An Appeal on the Sixth Anniversary of 'June Fourth.'" Xiaobo had already served time for the latter piece (albeit informally) in the courtyard in the Fragrant Hills. But never mind: here it was as the basis for more punishment.

The message that day was: You're not allowed to mention the June Fourth massacre. At a deeper level it was: Stop writing and doing things that depart from Party policy. We already have warned you, with your eight-month detention, but you have not learned. You still run around linking up with others and writing unapproved statements. So now we must immobilize you.

Xiaobo's joint statement with Wang Xizhe on Taiwan had not yet been published. It appeared in Taiwan two days later, on October 10. State security on the mainland already knew about it, though, and it clearly was a proximate cause for the current detention. When Wang Xizhe heard that Xiaobo had been detained, he slipped out of Guangzhou to Hong Kong, went to America, and stayed there.

The police interrogator asked Xiaobo if he recognized the two articles cited in the agreement, and Xiaobo of course said yes. The police took that to mean "I confess." The interrogator then read a "Decision by the Labor Education Committee of the People's Government of Beijing City." Xiaobo was sentenced to three years of "education through labor" (*laodong jiaoyang*) for "rumor-mongering, slander, and disturbing social order." That was it. The elegance of labor education sentencing, as opposed to criminal sentencing, is that there is no need for a prosecutor, lawyers, a court, or other time-consuming window dressing. The whole process took about fifteen minutes. The practical result was the same: being held behind bars, separated from society.

The Chinese Communist Party's program of "reform through labor" was built in the 1950s. Its original function was to coerce people who might become political opponents of the new post-1949 Communist regime into accepting the new system. In 1957 the government announced a "Decision on Questions of Labor Education" that explained that its labor camps were for "vagrants and idlers, unruly people, and people who are able to labor but have no job." That last category—able-bodied people who are jobless—was a euphemism for intellectuals and officials who were victims of Mao Zedong's 1957 Anti-Rightist movement, in which intellectual "work units" were obliged to report 5 percent of their staff as political "rightists" unfit for their current jobs. (Mao had commented in a speech that about 5 percent of intellectuals were rightists, and as a result there was pressure on every newspaper, university, hospital, museum, and other intellectual "work unit" to designate those people among their staff.) A parallel system called "labor reform" (*laodong gaizao*, or *laogai* for short) involved more severe punishment than did "labor education" (*laodong jiaoyang*, or *laojiao* for short). *Laogai* required trials; *laojiao* could be done by administrative decree.

Perhaps because Xiaobo had been sent to confinement twice before, he did not feel shock when his sentence was read. He knew his rights better this time too. When the police asked him to sign the sentencing document, he declined. They asked him repeatedly to consider the consequences of refusing to sign. These were standard threats, he knew, and continued to refuse. What weighed more heavily on his mind was his guilt over having bent to pressure in Qincheng Prison. Here, he thought, might be a chance to atone for that mistake. He would not retreat an inch. In the end the police asked him to write the sentence "I refuse to sign" so that they could close their file. He obliged.

Punishment commenced immediately. Xiaobo asked if he could go say good-bye to his wife, and the answer was no. "We will notify her." That morning, while putting on his clothes, he had been reassuring to Liu Xia. "No big deal," he had said. Now he couldn't bear to imagine what her reaction would be. Shouting? Tears? That much for sure. As he walked outside with the police and past the building where their little apartment was, he noticed that the window was open a crack. He looked through it, hoping perhaps to glimpse Xia's face. He wanted to carry one last image with him to the labor camp. But he didn't see her.

The police brought him to the Beijing Public Security Detention Center at no. 44, Banbuqiao, in the city's Xuanwu district. Yu Luoke, whom Xiaobo had revered since college days, had once been held there. It was also where Xiaobo had been allowed to meet briefly with his father in October 1990, while serving his sentence at Qincheng Prison. Xiaobo now requested pen and paper. He wanted to write a legal power of attorney and a formal appeal of his sentence. Ju Xiaofei, the local policeman, slipped him a pack of Marlboro cigarettes when no one was looking and asked if there was any message he might relay to Liu Xia. Xiaobo accepted Ju's sympathy and took out his wallet and keys for him to give her, but he couldn't think of any right words to send. Ju delivered the wallet and keys and explained to Liu Xia where Xiaobo was. Ju was punished when the authorities learned that he had done these unauthorized favors.

From Banbuqiao, Xiaobo was delivered on October 23, 1996, to the Dalian Labor Education Camp in Liaoning province, about 585 miles from Beijing and not far from where his parents lived. The trip took ten hours. Sending people to do labor education at locations near to their family homes was a principle of the system. This was meant to make a prisoner feel embarrassed before his or her family and the family feel embarrassed before their neighbors; both kinds of embarrassment applied pressure to the prisoner to accept "education." When

Xiaobo arrived at the camp, his parents were notified that he was there but not immediately allowed to see him. Camp authorities reported to his father that Xiaobo's behavior was not ideal.

For Liu Xia, this marked the beginning of a protracted ordeal of trying to visit her imprisoned husband and supply him with things he needed, especially books. For her, this project would occupy eleven and a half of the twenty-one years that remained in Xiaobo's life.

During the early months of Xiaobo's confinement at the Dalian camp he learned about Liu Xia's grandfather Xiang Daguang. Xiaobo was gripped first by curiosity and then by a deep respect. Although he had never met Xiang—Liu Xia herself had never met him—he felt an immediate bond because of what they had in common: Beijing Normal University, imprisonment, and a connection with Liu Xia. But their deepest bond was May Fourth "enlightenment," in which much of Xiaobo's thinking now was grounded. In 1997, Xiaobo wrote to Liu Xia, "Your grandfather has become my grandfather—not by inheritance or genes but spiritually. Here in prison I've often written to you about him. His departed spirit has become an ancestor of my own."[28]

The spirit of Xiang Daguang had a staying power. During the Cultural Revolution a remarkable photograph had turned up. Someone had taken it on May 7, 1919; it showed a triumphant Xiang Daguang and a few others being hoisted aloft by their fellow students at the gate of National Peking Teachers College after their release from jail. A precious relic of the great May Fourth Movement, to which the Communist Party itself traced its origins, the photo was exhibited in the Museum of Chinese History near Tiananmen Square after the Cultural Revolution passed. In 2009, when the ninetieth anniversary of May Fourth was observed, the photo was put on display at the old city campus of Peking University at Shatan, and Xiang Bihua and the other daughters of Xiang Daguang were invited to attend an opening ceremony. At the time, Liu Xiaobo had been detained on charges of inciting subversion of state power, and a rule had been put in place that no relative of his should be acknowledged (let alone honored) in public. Xiang Bihua was Xiaobo's mother-in-law. No one noticed—or one eye was open and one eye closed, pretending not to notice.

At the labor camp in fall 1996, a first big hurdle for Liu Xia was that camp officials denied her spousal visiting rights on grounds that she was not a spouse. They did not recognize the banquet-wedding that the couple's family and friends had accepted. They needed government documentation. For now, Liu Xia could deliver books and supplies to Xiaobo but could not see him. She turned for help to Mo Shaoping, a lawyer whom Xiaobo knew and trusted.

Mo, thirty-eight years old at the time, was a graduate of the Chinese University of Politics and Law. He was already famous in China for his defense of victims of political persecution, notably Liu Nianchun, an activist at Democracy Wall in 1978 who was sent to prison for three years in the 1980s. After his release Liu Nianchun continued with his political advocacy and just recently, in July 1996, had been sentenced to another three years of servitude, this time at a labor education camp, as Xiaobo had been. Mo Shaoping's principle in taking dissident cases was that any person charged with any crime, whatever it might be, had the right to a legal defense. His small Mo Shaoping Law Firm included a few other idealistic young lawyers.

Mo's first move in Xiaobo's case, in December 1996, was to appeal the decision to the local Xuanwu District People's Court in Beijing. He argued that the "Decision by the Labor Education Committee of the People's Government of Beijing City," in which Xiaobo had been sentenced to three years of labor education, was illegal because there had been no trial. Mo wrote, in the name of Xiaobo, that "the reason for my appeal is not that I am afraid of losing my freedom; it is to exercise my rights as a citizen to have the protection of legal guarantees." The court agreed to review the case.[29]

A trial on the appeal was held three months later, on March 5, 1997, inside the labor camp in Dalian where Xiaobo was being held. The ruling upheld the "Decision by the Labor Education Committee."[30] Xiaobo had lost, but the trial did provide the first chance for Liu Xia to lay eyes on her husband since October 8 of the previous year when he had been plucked from their home early in the morning. The two were allowed to chat for about ten minutes after the proceedings. Then Xiaobo was ushered away.

If they were to meet again in the next two and a half years, they would have to secure official recognition of their marriage. For that, Xiaobo would need an official residence permit. Luckily his father cooperated, and Xiaobo's residence was declared to be his parents' home in Dalian. But the official marriage problem was more complicated. The law stated that both parties must be physically present at a wedding, but Liu Xiaobo could not exit the labor camp because he was an inmate and Liu Xia could not enter because she was not. It was a puzzle for lawyer Mo Shaoping. He wrote to the Ministry of Justice citing law that specifies which rights in civil affairs continue to belong to *laojiao* inmates, and he attached Liu Xia's application for a marriage license. For the regime, what to say about marriages of political prisoners was a new and thorny question. There had been plenty of cases of people wanting to divorce prisoners, but not to marry them. Many administrative bucks were passed in both the Ministry of Justice and the Ministry of Public Security. In the end, the two ministries issued a joint statement approving the marriage of Liu Xia and Liu Xiaobo. An exception could be made to allow Liu Xia to enter the camp.[31]

Officials chose April 8, 1998, for the wedding day because of the lucky number 8. (The superstition arose because the word for "eight" in some Chinese dialects is a near homonym for the verb in "get rich.") After formal papers were signed, the couple was allowed to go outside the camp for a meal with Xiaobo's parents. Then the two were ushered back into the camp for one "newlyweds' night."[32]

Part of newlyweds' night was a party with selected inmates—selected by the authorities, not by Xiaobo. Not everyone who wanted to attend was allowed to. But word spread through the whole camp and raised the spirits of nearly everyone, whether invited to the party or not. Like the authorities, inmates were accustomed to seeing divorces, and it was exhilarating to hear news of a wedding. Liu Xia was a heroine not just for marrying an inmate but for leaping numerous barriers in order to do so. Even the normally stony-faced prison guards joined in the celebration.[33]

Reflecting on weddings and divorces in prisons, Xiaobo must have recalled August 1990, when Tao Li presented him with divorce papers while he was in Qincheng Prison. His failure to treat her properly had firmed his resolve, no matter what, to do right by Liu Xia. After the marriage to Liu Xia, his relationship with Tao Li naturally faded. His son, Liu Tao, continued to live at the Beijing Normal campus with Tao Li's parents, who essentially adopted him as a fourth child of their own. In the late 1990s Tao Li moved to the United States and took Liu Tao with her. In the months before she left, she gradually began cutting off connections with friends she and Xiaobo had shared. She clearly wanted a final break with him. Later, as he received his eleven-year sentence, won the Nobel Peace Prize, and died in prison, Tao Li stayed apart consistently, not revealing her whereabouts and offering no comment. She returned to China in 2000 when her father died and again in 2012 when her mother passed.

There were four inmates per room in the camp dormitory. Xiaobo was allowed out in the mornings to run and (at least sometimes) to play basketball. His first labor assignment was making toothpicks, and next was picking beans. "Picking beans" meant sifting through mounds of gravel and dirt that had been swept from workplaces and still contained several kinds of beans—soybeans, mung beans, azuki beans—and sorting the beans into separate piles. It was tiring work, in part because it was so tedious, and it took place inside damp, dark sheds.[34] Later, thanks primarily to legal pressure that Mo Shaoping was able to exert, Xiaobo was allowed increased time for reading.

In November 1997, after a visit to the camp, Liu Xia reported that "a recent blood test has revealed that Xiaobo carries the active hepatitis B virus."[35] This meant that if he became too tired or his nutrition were inadequate, there was a risk of developing hepatitis B or cirrhosis of the liver. Unrelated to the hepatitis, Xiaobo's stomach problems began to recur in summer 1998, sometimes so painfully that he couldn't eat. In August the camp authorities arranged for a gastroscopic exam that revealed ulcers of the stomach and duodenum. With this news, added to the hepatitis, Liu Xia feared the worst and through Mo Shaoping applied for medical parole for Xiaobo. The authorities replied that the illness was "occasional incidence of a chronic condition" that did not warrant outside medical treatment.

In total Liu Xia made thirty-eight visits to the Dalian camp. The rule for visits by spouses was one per month, and she went each of the thirty-six months of his incarceration even though, as a not-yet-official spouse, she couldn't see him the first eighteen times. She just brought books and supplies. The other two "special" visits were for the trial of the appeal and for the wedding. She usually traveled by train, which was about 1,170 miles round trip, around the Bohai Sea, but sometimes she went by air. She and Xiaobo exchanged hundreds of letters. Xia sent hers by registered mail and kept every receipt. She strung the receipts together and taped the string to her window, as a kind of installation art.

On each visit she carried two packages, a "small package" and a "big package." The small package contained medicines, powdered milk, sugar cubes, and other daily use items. The big package held books—everything from Chinese history to autobiographies of film directors to scholarship on contemporary Western thought. Liu Xia had a special interest in the fate of the Jewish people in World War II and brought him books by Elie Wiesel and other Holocaust survivors. Signs of mettle and courage in the human spirit under extremity attracted her. "I am a Jew," she once said.[36]

Liu Xia did not want martyrdom for Xiaobo but did feel attracted to the spirit of sacrifice for principle that he also admired, and she wanted to stand with him. When Xiaobo's head was shaved in the camp, she shaved her own, as if to say Xiaobo was in a small prison and she was in a large one—and kept it shaved afterward. Friends started calling her "the Chinese Decembrist wife," referring to the wives of the Russian rebels who in 1825 had sought to end serfdom and promote democracy only to be slaughtered by Czar Nicholas I—or to be banished to Siberia, where many of the loyal wives followed them. But in a letter to Hu Ping in New York, written June 5, 1997, she retreated a step from that identity:

> I feel I have never understood this society, this kind of reality. I have my own ways of rejecting it.
>
> In this society I become, quite consciously, a useless thing.

I am eternally on the side of the minority—or the dead.

I cannot possibly become the wife of a "revolutionary" as most people understand that idea. Things that the majority accepts are, in my eyes, frightening.

The only item about which I feel fully confident is that Xiaobo will be proud of me.[37]

Liu Xia led a simple life during Xiaobo's three years in *laojiao*. It was necessarily a frugal life, since her only sources of income were intermittent payments from outside China for Xiaobo's articles plus some help from her younger brother, Liu Hui. She occasionally went out for meals with friends, but for the most part stayed at home reading books and writing letters to Xiaobo. She wrote more than three hundred letters in the three years, and he wrote about as many back. His included reading notes and many poems, totaling, she calculated, more than two million characters.

In a letter to Liu Xia in January 1997, Xiaobo wrote:

Dear one: The first and constant staple of our love is the durable, almost religious sense of our mutual trust and our undying hope for the future. The meaning of our lives—in their entireties, one end to the other—comes from our love. With our love, we will survive any trial: when we waver, our love will give us confidence; when we fear, it will give us courage; when we are depressed, it will raise our spirits; when rattled, it will bring peace; when listless, it will bring us energy; if despondent, it will bring us hope. Our love lets us live full spiritual lives wrapped in the warmth of rich feeling. It also gives us the courage and confidence to uphold justice for human beings, to challenge bullies, and to guard human dignity, honesty, and freedom.[38]

Most of the letters between Xiaobo and Liu Xia have been lost.[39] Police probably confiscated some or all of them when they raided the couple's home on December 13, 2004. It is not impossible that someday they will be recovered.

Letters to and from a prison or labor camp are valuable for more than their specific content. For a political prisoner, letter writing was vital for maintaining intellectual balance and acuity. Letters going into or out of Xiaobo's camp had to get past censors and so could not comment on politics. But topics in art, philosophy, and other fields—even political theory, if the language was abstruse— were let through. Through letters, the prisoner, although banished physically from the outside world, could maintain a sense of connection and belonging to it .

Xiaobo, recalling how he had written poems for *Pure Hearts* in his college days, turned to poetry. Combining his loves for poetry and for Liu Xia, he began writing poems on many topics—but always "to Xia" or "for Xia." Sometimes he used nicknames: "Little Eye," "Finger," "Toe," or "Nutty Sister." In the single month of December 1996 he wrote twenty-three poems for Xia. After full days of labor, he called them his "spiritual push-ups."[40]

Most of the poems involved poets, artists, or thinkers whom he or Xia or both found interesting. There were, for example, "To Saint Augustine—For Xia, Who Likes *The Confessions*,"[41] and "The Will of the Grand Historian—For Xia," about China's famous historian Sima Qian (145–186[?] BCE). In other cases, where Xiaobo knew about someone but Liu Xia didn't, he would make an introduction. So there were "Wittgenstein's Portrait—For My Wife, Who Doesn't Do Philosophy," "The Unforgettable Zhuangzi—For Xia, Who Indulges My Talk About Zhuangzi," and "Hats Off to Kant—For Xia, Who Has Never Read Kant."[42] For artists beloved to Xia, he would pretend to their positions and write poems to her. There was, for example, "To Liu Xia from [filmmaker] Marguerite Duras" and "To Liu Xia from [poet] Marina Tsvetaeva."

Xiaobo's poems during these years played a role in his gradual but decisive turn away from the "enemies" mentality that Maoist education originally had given him. Leaving thoughts of battle behind, he wrote poems about utterly ordinary things—teacups, gravel, ants, dust—and developed a modesty and gentleness that stayed with him for the rest of his life. To Liu Xia, his absolute confidante, he could allow himself to be vulnerable in a new and unaccustomed way and could offer strong empathy as well. Liu Xia enjoyed smoking, for example. She tried several times to quit but could not, and this made her unhappy when smoking and unhappy when not smoking. Xiaobo wrote a poem called "Smoking Feeling—For Younger Sister, Who Is Smoking Right Now":

> Smoking is nearly a faith for you.
> Both of us feel this way.
> When smoking we feel so close
> like water merging into water.

The prison environment was harsh, though. Xiaobo's poems often depicted desperate situations. For example:

As Your Explosion—For Xia

> It's time to get up, dear one.
> The bridge over the abyss is about to collapse . . .
> I hand all my terror, all my hatreds

to you, to you alone
and allow my head once more
to try to look upward, until
the darkest hour descends.[43]

Or even more painfully:

To Liu Xia, from Camille Claudel —For My Wife

I implore you
not to write poems for my wounds.
If you have the nerve
just toss on some sharp-angled salt
and let me, clear-headed, in burning pain
finish the unfinished sacrifice.[44]

Liu Xia, who preferred to write letters, wrote fewer poems than Xiaobo did, but on the eighth anniversary of the June Fourth massacre, she wrote for the victims:

Black Night

Those eyes will come back tonight
Those ghosts will come back tonight
in the posture of gravestones . . .
All of the ghosts all of the eyes
assembling next to this little candle flame
using silence to converse with me.[45]

Xiaobo replied:

You • Ghosts • The Defeated—For My Wife (excerpt)

My dear
all day you wander among tombs
and spirits of the dead in the wind
facing them in silence.
You peer deep into each other
freezing the other's blood.

These, the completely defeated
have left no name, no history.

And you
this woman infatuated with the defeated
are yourself never defeated
because from the grins of corpses
you've learned
that it is only death
that never fails.[46]

Identifying with underdogs and losers was a habit of Liu Xia's. As she saw it, within the raucous jamboree of China's spiritually lost society, she and Xiaobo huddled, largely out of sight, together with the dead and the defeated.

Emily Brontë's *Wuthering Heights* appears three times in Xiaobo's prison poetry. He compares his and Xia's intimate access to each other's inner worlds to the fusing of the untamed souls of Catherine and Heathcliff in Brontë's novel. Xiaobo writes in one poem, "You are the woman who has shaped me, and been shaped by me."[47] He felt that in the exploration of his love for Liu Xia, a deeper, truer version of himself came into view. Liu Xia, the utterly unornamented one, was a mirror for him by which to cleanse his inner self.

Xiaobo's reflections during his *laojiao* years were deepened considerably by newly available reading—and that was made possible, in part, by fortuitous events in international politics. In early 1997, the Chinese and American governments were negotiating the arrangements under which U.S. President Bill Clinton would visit China. In this the United States had considerable leverage. No president had come to China since February 1989, when George H.W. Bush visited. After the June Fourth killings that year, domestic opinion in the United States turned so sharply against the Chinese Communist Party that Bush had to keep his "old friend" contacts with Beijing a tight secret. Later it became a considerable concession on the U.S. side to invite Chinese President Jiang Zemin to the country in October 1997, and it was a further concession to agree that President Clinton would visit China in June 1998 and even be welcomed at Tiananmen Square, the site and symbol of the massacre. These concessions left the U.S. side able to ask some things in return, one of which was reprieve for prisoners of conscience. Wang Dan and Wei Jingsheng were released and went straight from prison to the United States, where Xiaobo's friend Chen Xiaoping had also gone. Had Xiaobo wanted, he likely could have gotten out too. The labor camp officials all but said so. They contacted Liu Xia and asked her to advise him to agree to medical parole and release to America.

"Go ask Liu Xiaobo yourself," was Liu Xia's reply. "This is not my decision."

When the officials asked Xiaobo, he refused. In a later interview he recalled saying that if he still had ten years or more on his sentence, he might consider it. "But it's a only a three-year sentence, and it's now already half over; I'll get through the other half somehow."[48]

The crowning achievements of the minithaw came on October 27, 1997, when the Chinese government agreed to sign the United Nations' International Covenant on Economic, Social and Cultural Rights. A year later it also signed the UN's International Covenant on Civil and Political Rights, the more political of the two agreements, but kept a distance from the latter by not "ratifying" it. The temporary relaxation showed up in Chinese publishing. Works that had been suppressed for years could now appear. Liu Xia was astute in spotting them and carrying them to Xiaobo in the labor camp. She brought him, for example, Yu Luoke's *Reminiscences*. Xiaobo knew Yu's story from his college years but now was smitten again by the extraordinary integrity and courage of this man who had spoken against Mao's "blood-line theory" and paid for it with his life.

Other books that hit Xiaobo with great force were accounts by intellectuals who had joined the Communist Party out of idealism and then later, under conditions that betrayed their ideals, toiled on because they had little choice. Gu Zhun, born in 1915, was a child genius who taught himself accounting, joined the Communist Party, and after 1949 became the chief financial officer of the city of Shanghai. Repeatedly attacked in the Mao campaigns of the 1950s, Gu watched as his wife committed suicide and his children turned against him. He wrote in his books *Diary* and *Seeking Thoughts* about his route from youthful idealism to life under a vicious tyranny. He dared to mention "superstition about a person" (i.e., adulation of Mao) while Mao was still alive.[49]

Wei Junyi, born in 1917, reached the high position of editor-in-chief at the People's Literature Publishing House in Beijing. Her new book *Painful to Think About*—which detailed the persecution of intellectuals from the Party's Yan'an years in the 1940s through the Cultural Revolution of the 1970s—caused a literary earthquake, coming from a person so far "inside the system." Wei explains how the Party initially viewed her as "different," how she gradually got caught up in its machine, later found herself powerless to alter it, and in the end herself turned into a victimizer.[50]

Zhu Zheng's book *Summer 1957: From a Hundred Flowers Down to Two*, about the 1957 Anti-Rightist movement, offered plainspoken accounts of how intellectuals had been cowardly under pressure: they caved, they betrayed one another, they abandoned dignity. The book struck Xiaobo with tremendous force, as it led him once again to examine his own behavior:

> I remembered writing my "Repentance" in Qincheng Prison in 1989. How did I compare with those intellectuals back in 1957 who were under attack as "rightists"? Considering the society-wide pressure they were under, one perhaps can understand their decisions to debase themselves. But for me to write that political self-criticism in 1990 was inexcusable—beyond pardon! It stands as my permanent offense, my eternal shame. I cannot wash it clean even if I spend the entire rest of my life trying to. . . . My two imprisonments following Qincheng alleviate at least some of the remorse that I feel, but even if I were to remain in prison for the rest of my life, the shame would not be fully washed away. It will follow me forever, right until it is carved upon my gravestone (assuming that I will have a gravestone).[51]

This reading note on Zhu Zheng's book might explain more about Xiaobo's motivations during the second half of his life than anything else he wrote.

Xiaobo's interest in reading about integrity in Chinese intellectuals extended back in history. He read Sima Qian's *Record of History* in the camp.[52] Sima, who wrote in the second century BCE, is a revered figure in Chinese intellectual history not only for his meticulous records but also for his principle of presenting historical figures accurately, free from flattery or bias—in contrast, for example, to the *Spring and Autumn Annals* of Confucius. Sima persisted in his mission despite suffering castration and imprisonment by his emperor. Xiaobo deplored the practice in Chinese historical writing of flattering the famous and the powerful, because this left later generations with distorted and inauthentic impressions. He admired the May Fourth historian Gu Jiegang (1893–1980) for his premise of "doubting antiquity." In his reading notes on Gu's *Outline History of Scholarship in the Han*, Xiaobo writes:

> If freedom's resistance to dictatorship is, in part, the resistance of memory against forgetting, then the continuation of despotism for thousands of years in China owes much to the emptiness of national memory. Whether the emptiness is a result of obliteration or of distortion, it leaves almost no way for people to learn from the past. From dynasty to dynasty, the purges of national memory meant that the same historical tragedies were replayed over and over. A new autocrat in every era could rise from the material and spiritual ruins left behind by the predecessor.[53]

Xiaobo's examination of his values and behavior led him toward transcendent concerns. Seven years earlier he had published a book opposing metaphysics, but now, in prison, found it not so far-fetched. He and Liu Xia had read Simone Weil's *Waiting for God* together. Now he began reading more about Christianity. He went back to his favorite Saint Augustine, reread *The Confessions*, and now added *The City of God*. He read works by Thomas Aquinas on political thought and Hans Küng's *On Being a Christian*. His reading notes include this passage: "Xiaobo, you have to remember: to be a pure person in a thoroughgoing way, the first and most important quality is religious awareness—not Buddhist, Daoist, or Islamist, but Christian. I may never become a follower and may never join an organized church. But Jesus Christ is my moral model. I know I cannot hope ever to achieve his kind of saintly character, but at least I can pour my life into striving in that direction."[54] In August 1998 Liu Xia brought him Dietrich Bonhoeffer's *Letters and Papers from Prison*. She had been reading it herself and writing to Xiaobo about it, so he had built up a considerable appetite before it reached his hands. Through Liu Xia's descriptions, he had already sensed Bonhoeffer's gravitas and humility. When she handed him the book he said, "This is great, a political prisoner really needs the sustenance of ones who've gone before." It would be going too far to say that Bonhoeffer gave Xiaobo an enthusiasm for prison. But he did impart an enthusiasm for how to have the right attitude about it.

Bonhoeffer had gone to America in 1939 to give lectures and could have stayed there but chose to return to his Nazi-ruled homeland. He was arrested in March 1943 for his part in a plot to assassinate Hitler and on April 9, 1945, was hanged at the concentration camp at Flossenburg where he had been held. A few days later the camp was liberated by Allied armies. In Bonhoeffer, Xiaobo saw "a readiness to share the burdens of his compatriots even at the cost of his life . . . and to participate in rebuilding the spirit and the faith of humankind." He wrote to Liu Xia that "living in prison is one way of sharing the suffering of the secular world; we cannot give up the sharing, no matter what." At the same time he reminded himself again to beware the pose of martyrdom, which is an outgrowth of the "enemy mentality." He wrote: "Maintaining enthusiasm behind bars is fundamentally different from romanticizing death and suffering. To exaggerate suffering is even stupider and more superficial than to exaggerate joy. Equanimity in the face of danger is impossible to fake. Bonhoeffer warns that 'the most important thing is not to give in to self-pity.' We must remember that."[55]

The contemporary Chinese philosopher Xu Youyu has observed that in the mid-1990s humanist scholars in China made a broad turn in the direction of political science. People who had studied philosophy, literature, aesthetics, religion, and related fields directed their interests and attention more toward political theory and political philosophy. Xiaobo, who was isolated physically—but not intellectually, thanks to Liu Xia—joined this trend. His wife brought him books on political and social theory by Benjamin Constant, Max Weber, Friedrich Hayek, Isaiah Berlin, John Rawls, Ronald Dworkin, Robert Nozick, and others. Works by these writers could pass prison censorship because their language was beyond what the censors could comprehend; it helped too that the pages contained no Chinese names and therefore, to the censors, could not be criticisms of current Communist Party leaders. Xiaobo took copious notes.

Xiaobo was released from the labor camp on October 7, 1999, having served his three-year sentence in full. Liu Xia was there to meet him. The next day, by chance, Xiaobo's mother entered a hospital for a liver ailment. Xiaobo spent time with her there, and his visits were a relief to the elderly lady, who had spent many years worrying about her third son. She left the hospital but never recovered from the illness and died within a year.

FIGURE 12.2   After leaving the labor camp, 1999

Liu Xia

FIGURE 12.3 After leaving the labor camp, 1999

Liu Xia

Xiaobo was physically weak when he left the camp, but a medical exam found nothing seriously wrong. In a telephone interview with Radio Free Asia he said his concerns now were simply to live by conscience and normal standards of human dignity. His immediate question, he said, was what to read to Liu Xia at bedtime. She suffered insomnia. If he had really good books to read to her, she could fall asleep. He mentioned the poetry of Rainer Rilke and Jorge Borges and the stories of Marguerite Duras as particularly effective in getting her to sleep.[56]

13

In the Service of Underdogs

In the years following his release from *laojiao* in 1999, Xiaobo devoted himself increasingly to the defense of people and groups whom the government was persecuting. His abstract ideas about fairness and justice came down to earth, as it were, in a realization that he had to do actual good for actual people or none of it would matter. This was, in a sense, a recognition that the prodemocracy efforts in the 1980s, which had focused on engagement with the top leadership, had failed. It was time to focus on underdogs and to work from the bottom up.

In November 1999, Xiaobo was invited to a scholarly conference in London on "Prospects for the Twenty-First Century." He applied for a passport to the Public Security bureaus in Beijing and also in Dalian (which was still his official residence), but both turned him down without explanation. He was out of *laojiao*, but it was clear that the regime still wanted to control him. And from the regime's point of view, there was indeed reason to be wary. The society that Xiaobo was reentering in 1999 was significantly different from the one he had left in 1996. The media had been changing, and intellectuals were beginning to speak out again. The Internet would soon play an unprecedented role in relations between state and society. The sense of leavening in the air in some ways recalled what Deng Xiaoping had fostered during the post-Mao thaw years of the late 1970s, but with the important difference that this time there were no blessings from the top. The ferment was coming from below.

Changes in the media came partly for economic reasons. After the 1989 debacle, the prestige of the Communist Party had sunk so low that Party newspapers did not sell well. Under the new watchword of "Take responsibility for your own profits and losses," most newspapers were on their own financially. They had two things they could sell: copies and advertisements. To sell either they had to attract readers, and to do that, many came out with subsidiary editions called "evening papers," "weekend papers," or "city papers" that carried stories about movie stars, crime, police, sports, travel, and the like. It became a recognized pattern that "big newspapers hatch little ones, and the little ones pay for the big ones." Before long, it emerged that readers of the little newspapers were interested not only in entertainment but also in serious stories about economic inequality and political corruption, especially when the reports touched on readers' own problems with employment, health care, children's schooling, or environmental safety. This development opened a door for liberal-minded editors, who now could let the little newspapers play the classic role of the press as monitor of political behavior and voice for public opinion. But the little papers were never fully free. Always registered through their parent newspapers, they were still within the state system and could be closed down if they went too far.

Southern Weekend, a little newspaper that eventually was not so little, was the leader in the trend. Founded in 1984 as the offspring of *Southern Daily*, the Communist Party's flagship newspaper in Guangdong province, for years it carried stories on topics like planting flowers, raising goldfish, and the rumored activities of entertainers from Hong Kong and Taiwan. Circulation was about 7,000. A major turn came in 1995, when a group of idealistic young reporters began writing deep background stories on topics like fake liquor, bridge safety, the underworld, unjust convictions, and abuse of power. *Southern Weekend* always took the side of victims in cases of human trafficking, bias against HIV carriers, workers stiffed by their bosses, and other such problems. Its editors observed a principle of "no local reporting." As long as the muckraking was about *other* places, not Guangdong, publication was generally allowed. But this very point made *Southern Weekend* much sought after in all those other places—indeed nationwide. By 1998 the paper was being printed in nineteen cities across China, and its circulation had soared to 1.3 million.

The success of *Southern Weekend* caused lights to go on in the minds of editors elsewhere. In Beijing, *Beijing Youth News* and *China Industry and Commerce* were born; in Xi'an, there was *China Business News*; in Chengdu, *West China City News* and *Chengdu Commerce*. A sibling of *Southern Weekend* called *Southern Metropolitan Daily* popped up in Guangzhou. Words like "commerce" and "business" were often used in the titles of the new papers, but this was largely for political cover; the real purpose was to report on problems in society and to reflect popular opinion. For analysis and comment the papers turned to intellectuals, who usually were happy, even eager, to oblige. Their opinions, once confined to salons or dinner tables, now could reach tens of thousands of readers. It was a happy symbiosis. "Liberal" thought was spreading.

From 1949 until the late 1990s, the word "liberal" and the idea that went with it were hard to find in China. In the 1980s the government denounced a few prominent intellectuals (Bai Hua in 1981 and Liu Binyan, Fang Lizhi, and Wang Ruowang in 1987) as "bourgeois liberals," but in that usage "liberal" was derogatory and meant something like "wayward" or "self-interested." In the late 1990s, however, more and more people, mostly intellectuals, were identifying themselves in a positive sense as *ziyoupai*, "liberal." The term now meant something like "pro-freedom." An anecdote about this new use became well known. The Chinese writer Wang Xiaobo, famous for his novels about Chinese youth during the Cultural Revolution as well as for the blistering satires of thought control that he published in newspapers, died suddenly of a heart attack on April 21, 1997. Five hours before he died, Wang wrote an e-mail to a friend in which he said: "A trip of a thousand miles begins with a single step. China needs 'liberals.' So let's start right now—us! Is that too crazy?" Wang saw himself at the cusp of a long-overdue arrival of liberalism in Chinese political life. He had not seen himself on the cusp of death, but his passing immortalized his call for liberalism. Liu Xiaobo had been a personal friend of Wang Xiaobo.

A year and a half later, Zhu Xueqin, a respected historian of modern Chinese thought and an adherent of the new liberalism, wrote a defining statement of what he took liberalism to be. Its implied contrast with communist ideology was hard to miss:

> [Liberalism] is both intellectual theory and practical advocacy. It reaches conclusions empirically, not *a priori*. It sees history as moving in fits and starts and does not accept historical determinism in any form. It sees change as arriving through natural and gradual evolution and is opposed to planned social systems. In politics it calls for representative democracy, constitutional authority, and rule of law. It opposes any dictatorship whether by one person or by a small group; it also opposes the dictatorship of majorities over minorities. In ethics it calls for protection of the individual person and holds that while many values can be disaggregated, the value of the individual cannot be; an individual cannot be made into a tool and sacrificed for an abstract idea.[1]

Zhu's call for liberalism in fact went further than the demands for political change that had appeared in China in the 1980s. No student leaders at Tiananmen in 1989 had called for anything beyond what the regime on paper claimed its system already included: democracy, constitutionalism, and rule of law. By contrast, the liberal demands of the late 1990s (for example, Zhu's "oppose any dictatorship whether by one person or by a small group") did imply a change of system.

When Xiaobo got out of the labor camp, he became an avid reader of the feisty articles published in *Southern Weekend*. One piece, "Old Soldiers Go to Court," had appeared the previous year from the pen of Peking University law professor He Weifang.[2] It complained that the government was appointing retired military officers to serve as judges in courts—no legal training needed. With blistering irony, the professor asked why some of those old soldiers weren't assigned to be doctors in hospitals as well. His point was not just that judges need training; it was the larger principle that law should be independent of politics. Military newspapers fired back with a fusillade of comment that ended only when *Southern Weekend* (with its existence now threatened) issued a stilted apology.

At the end of 1999, the political scientist Liu Junning published a piece in *Southern Weekend* called "Rulers."[3] He had originally called it "Taming Rulers," but editors at the newspaper thought it safer to remove "taming." The idea remained quite plain in the content of the piece, however. Liu wrote: "The measure of the civility of a political system is the degree to which its rulers have been tamed. In a democratic system the taming of rulers is maximized." Readers of *Southern Weekend* were getting used to a new understanding of the term "democracy." The Communist system had long employed the word, in phrases like "democratic centralism" and "people's democratic dictatorship," but in those uses the point was that the Party knows and implements what is best for all the people. Now there was a new notion. The new press called it "constitutional democracy," which meant not only that the people as a whole decide but also that individual people have rights. "Law" is not just a tool that rulers use on citizens; it is a principle that governs everyone, citizen and ruler alike.

Some of the first and most eager to drink from *Southern Weekend*'s intellectual fountain were editors and reporters at other newspapers. Even if not daring to be as bold, they borrowed *Southern Weekend* concepts and applied them in their own environments. The notion of "rights" spread quickly.

Xiaobo was eager to join the ferment but could not because of the ban on publishing his writings inside China. Knowing of his frustration, Zhou Zhongling, the Sichuan poet referred to as Zhongzhong, came up with a proposal. Zhou had a business as a "book merchant" doing "second-channel publishing"—a gray area that the government could see but usually pretended not to. In this system, state-run publishers sold "book numbers" to "book merchants" for 10,000 to 30,000 yuan or so. The book merchant then did all the work of finding, editing, producing, and marketing books, while the publisher took political but no financial responsibility. For the book merchant, therefore, it was very important to find manuscripts that would sell.

Zhou Zhongling had noticed a durable friendship between Xiaobo and the satiric novelist Wang Shuo. When Xiaobo emerged from the labor camp, many people, for safety, distanced themselves from him. Wang Shuo did not. By then Wang was famous for his films and television shows. His TV series *The Story of the Editorial Department*—packed with dry humor, sarcasm, and Beijing brogue—had made him a household name. And his name glowed with a special light because of his reputation for staying entirely clear of the government. He often joined Xiaobo for meals, where the two traded witty comments on all kinds of topics. Zhou Zhongling, watching, came up with the idea of collecting this repartee in a book. It would likely sell well.

Wang Shuo agreed to the plan immediately, but Xiaobo surprised his friends by saying no. The problem was that second-channel books still had to go through censorship at the official publisher, and the government was still banning his name. This meant that he would have to use a pen name, and he reacted viscerally against that idea. A few days later, however, he had second thoughts. He knew that Zhou Zhongling and Wang Shuo's intentions were, in part, to help him financially. His gut reaction had sprung from pride—perhaps too much pride. He also understood that Zhou needed the money. The project would be a big help to an old friend who had given money to Liu Xia to help her while Xiaobo was in the camp. So he relented. For a pen name he took Lao Xia—*lao* meaning "old" and *xia* the righteous knight-errant of Chinese *gong-fu* stories. *Xia*, moreover, was a homonym of Liu Xia's name. Everybody thought it was a good choice.

Zhou Zhongling rented a room at the nearby Wanshou Hotel and put Xiaobo, Wang Shuo, and a recording machine into it for three days and three nights. They took breaks only for meals and sleep. Liu Xia was there too, with her close friend Gan Qi, a founder of the All Saints Book Grove, one of the most beloved of Beijing's independent bookstores at the time. Gan Qi helped to raise questions that kept the Wang-Liu banter more or less on track. The subjects included the latest "new wave" fiction, trench warfare in the poetry world, the frankly sexual female "body writers" who had recently emerged, the great May Fourth writer Lu Xun, the Hong Kong master of knight-errant fiction Jin Yong, and the famous cultural critic Yu Qiuyu. These were all hot topics at the time.

Surprisingly, the conversation wandered into moral reflection. Wang Shuo was so known for his sarcasm and cat-and-mouse games in interviews that it seemed out of character for him to reveal an inner self, but he did. He said that during his youth the mainstream political culture had misled him; when he grew older he fought back using sharp satire; later, though, his satire itself became a commodity, and when that happened, the original bite in his barbs melted away. This analysis elated Xiaobo, who immediately drew a parallel to how protest had become commodified in American culture: "The protests of a bold pioneer can turn into items of consumption and enjoyment for the mainstream. No howl of resistance, no matter how loud, can maintain its original power once it has been commodified and made a fashion in popular culture."[4] Besides the moral seriousness, something else seemed strange: Liu Xiaobo and Wang Shuo, both known for their sympathy with commoners, were both complaining about popular culture. They were talking about ideals, specifically about whether any ideals at all could grow out of a society in ruins like the one that lay before them. Wang Shuo asked: "Can intellectuals supply us with the ideals we now need? Or will these have to emerge from conversation among ordinary people all across society? I think only the latter will do."[5] Xiaobo answered: "The function of human ideals . . . is to provide a system of reference and measurement for examining human behavior. Ideals arise because of reality's inadequacies; they stimulate people to feel discontent with both their environments and themselves, and that leads to distrust and criticism of both."[6] He shared with Wang Shuo some of the thinking on the transcendent to which his reading in the labor camp had led. Augustine's *The City of God*, for example, had helped him realize that:

Ideals—like God or freedom—are not comforts, not congratulatory halos. They are more like whips, like demons that whip you into staying clear-headed even as you suffer, into guarding your independent mind and your abilities to criticize and to resist. Only when tempered in this way can an ideal become a transcendent shining halo. The brighter ideals shine the more they illuminate the darkness of reality and the breakdown of lives. What their light illuminates is not the high peaks of the future but the abyss of the present. "Reverence" refers to our humility in the face of ideals, our dissatisfaction with ourselves.[7]

Such thoughts were largely new to Wang Shuo, who had pondered the transcendent about as often as a honeybee ponders moonlight. Gamely, though, Wang held his own. He found ways to steer the conversation back toward familiar turf—until Xiaobo, more circuitously still, would steer it back toward topics like the devils in human nature and how to repent. The two interlocutors were like sumo wrestlers maneuvering for position to control the dialogue: one looking at the world, the other peering beyond it; one ignoring the transcendent, the other seeking it.

Xiaobo's pursuit of the transcendent was never an effort to achieve a "saved" state. The goal was not to find God, hand over one's mind and will, and then relax. Quite the opposite. He pursued transcendent values for their use in secular life. In January 2000, shortly after his dialogues with Wang Shuo, he wrote to Liao Yiwu:

> Compared to people in other nations that have lived under the dreary pall of communism, we resisters in China have not measured up very well. Even after so many years of tremendous tragedies, we still don't have a moral leader like Václav Havel. It seems ironic that in order to win the right of ordinary people to pursue self-interest, a society needs a moral giant to make a selfless sacrifice. In order to secure "passive freedom"—freedom from state oppression— there needs to be a will to do *active* resistance. History is not fated. The appearance of a single martyr can fundamentally turn the spirit of a nation and strengthen its moral fiber. Gandhi was such a figure. So was Havel. So, even more, was that humble boy born in a manger two thousand years ago. Human progress is the result of the accident of birth of people such as these.[8]

From his early adulthood, Xiaobo had struggled with two-sided problems in which both sides made sense to him. How to seek transcendence on the one hand and be worldly on the other was one more example.

Most of the second half of his book with Wang Shuo contains short perorations by Xiaobo on a variety of topics. He had mellowed in recent years but still was harsh when he got excited. He berated Confucius. He called Liu Zaifu a "theory pope" despite Liu's exile to the United States after the June Fourth massacre and patent inability to be anyone's pope. He was also harsh on writers of his own generation, including Zhang Chengzhi and Liang Xiaosheng, for their pursuit of what he saw as apocryphal purity and emotional righteousness. He chastised Yu Jie, with whom he later became good friends (and who later wrote a biography of him), for a sophomoric sycophancy.[9]

Zhou Zhongling hired people to transcribe the taped dialogues and then showed the results to both Xiaobo and Wang Shuo, who edited them carefully. The manuscript was ready in December 1999, and in January at the annual Beijing book fair, Zhou displayed a model book cover using the title *Finding Truth from the People*. He received more than 100,000 yuan in orders even before he had secured a second-channel "book number" from a publisher. He eventually signed with the Changjiang Literary Publishing House in Hubei. When the book appeared in August 2000, it bore the mischievous title *A Beauty Gave Me a*

Knockout Drug. The poet and essayist Ye Fu, a friend of Xiaobo and Wang Shuo, had proposed it to them.

Word spread among Xiaobo's friends that he was now back in print, albeit under a pen name. Friends bought the book and gave copies to others. Among the larger public who had no idea who "Lao Xia" was, there was much speculation. People kept asking Wang Shuo, who improvised answers so many times that he began to stumble when trying to remember what he had said the time before. Sometimes he said, "an old friend who is even more famous than I am." Other times it was "somebody who came back from overseas." The most common reply— "an old teacher of mine, returned from the hills"—did not satisfy Wang Shuo's fans, who saw him as too smart to have needed any teachers. If reporters calling on the telephone pressed Wang too hard, he just hung up.

Xiaobo and Wang Shuo had originally agreed to split the royalties fifty-fifty, but when it came time for the publisher to make the payments, which totaled 270,000 yuan, Wang Shuo said, "Give it all to Xiaobo." News of Wang's gallantry spread among their friends. When the money arrived, Zhou Zhongling mentioned that he would like to borrow 90,000 yuan of it to buy copies of the book from the publisher for later resale on his own. To that Xiaobo and Wang Shuo said, "No loan—just keep the 90,000." So in the end Xiaobo took home 180,000 yuan. He spent it on his and Liu Xia's move from their 540-square-foot two-room apartment on Cuiwei Lane to a three-room apartment twice that size at Seven Sages Village near the Purple Bamboo Park.

Two events later that year weighed on Xiaobo's spirits: his mother died, and his father—rather too quickly, he thought—took a second wife. So he turned his attention to writing political and social commentary. The Internet made it much easier to submit and edit articles. He wrote about the magical feeling he had when sending manuscripts overseas with the click of a computer mouse and getting responses within hours.[10] At the ends of many pieces he added the date of composition and wrote "at home." The two words seemed to be notes of appreciation that home could now be his publishing base. He was able to send out two or three essays per week. "The Internet is like a magic engine," he wrote. "It has helped my writing to erupt like a geyser. Now I can even live off what I write."[11]

Writing for overseas publications liberated Xiaobo from worry about censorship. He could refer to past and present Communist leaders—Mao Zedong, Hu Jintao, and others—by name and could call them *ducai*, "dictators," a term that they seemed to detest more than the word "authoritarian." He could excoriate the pervasive corruption that concentration of political power had created. He could castigate the Chinese government for ignoring, indeed selling out, the interests of Chinese farmers. He could criticize George W. Bush for coming meekly to China to ask the Communists for help with his "war on terror"—as if he had forgotten that his father, George H.W. Bush, had already shown far more meekness than necessary by sending emissaries to express "friendship" to Deng Xiaoping right after the June Fourth massacre.[12]

He directed criticisms at his fellow citizens as well: how they immersed themselves in mah-jongg all day; how they watched interminable costume TV shows that depicted ancient times without any regard for realism; how comedians at the annual New Year's television gala failed to say anything actually funny; and how intellectuals were so weak and indifferent. Borrowing the spirit of Socrates's question about whether it is better to be a pig satisfied or a human being dissatisfied, Xiaobo invented the phrase "porcine philosophy" to describe the attitude of peering barely beyond the end of one's nose, staying numb and forgetful, making self-interest the criterion for evaluating everything, and preferring to surrender to intimidation rather than to risk anything for conscience or justice.

In deploring the "national character," as his idol Lu Xun had done before him, Xiaobo felt frustrated that, banned in China, he could not address his compatriots directly. His dream, like Lu Xun's, was to inspire people, not to reject them. He missed the give-and-take that he had enjoyed with live audiences when he gave lectures in the 1980s. People would clap and hoot, ask questions, make comments, and keep him well aware of what they were thinking and how he was doing. But now? His essays, peppery though they were, were like stones tossed into the sea. His writing was considered "dissident" and he a leader in dissident thought, but that was not the same as being engaged with society. He wanted a way back in.

He began to appreciate, more deeply than before, the viewpoints of those whom the regime had rejected. The interests of the mistreated, the downtrodden, and the forgotten became a priority. He defended people who were in detention centers, prisons, or labor camps for their thought crimes. (A "thought crime" in theory was an expression of an unauthorized political or religious view; but in practice it could also be almost anything that a power holder considered a challenge to his or her power.) Thought prisoners existed at all levels in society, and they numbered far more than any one person in any one location could know about—let alone what the outside world could know about. Countless other victims, although not in prison, carried political taints that interfered with employment, children's education, access to medical care, the right to travel, and more. An underclass that lay in China's belly—almost entirely invisible and silent—became Xiaobo's first concern in "speaking for victims."

He remembered these people most clearly at times when the favored strata of the populace were celebrating. When people danced in the streets in July 2001 after Beijing won the bid to host the 2008 summer Olympics, Xiaobo wrote a piece called "Welcome the Olympics, Release Political Prisoners." China would look better both at home and abroad, he argued, if "as a first step, controls on the media are gradually loosened and every person who is being held for reasons of thought, speech, or belief is released."[13] In late 2002, as Chinese families everywhere were coming together to welcome a new year, Xiaobo wrote "On New Year's Eve, Let's Not Forget the Broken Families," pointing out how high-level state leaders liked to appear on television at New Year's and make political shows of sharing in the happiness of the people and how wonderful and joyful everything was. Xiaobo reminds readers not to forget the families who cannot unite because loved ones are in prison, and "the people who have suffered terribly because of abuses of power or dereliction of duty in government, or whose lives are barren because of protracted unemployment, or who even have set fire to themselves to protest nonpayment of wages.... Whoever remembers such people, even if it is only to stop for a moment to say a silent prayer for them, is honoring the fundamental human condition."[14] Xiaobo often reached into his own pocket to help people, with hundreds of or even a thousand yuan, when they ran into unexpected medical or legal emergencies.

Between 2000 and 2003 Xiaobo wrote a series of articles that deplored the cruel repression of Falun Gong, a semireligious health-exercise regimen that had spread widely during the 1990s. In the post-Mao years, general disillusionment with Communist ideology had left people searching for something to believe in. They turned to religions old and new, domestic and foreign, to help fill the void, and *qigong*, "breath exercise," was an important part of that search. *Qigong* combined physical exercise with metaphysical beliefs—Daoist, Buddhist, and folk traditions—about how to connect with energy currents in the body, the natural world, and the universe. Originally the Communist Party tolerated *qigong* and even preferred it to other belief systems, like Christianity (which was also spreading rapidly) because *qigong* was thoroughly Chinese. It posed no foreign threat.

Falun Gong, founded in 1992, grew to be one of the larger *qigong* groups. In addition to health benefits and intercourse with the ultimate, it offered a moral code of "truth, goodness, and tolerance." Most adherents were commoners, but some distinguished intellectuals, wealthy entrepreneurs, Communist Party members, and retired military officers joined as well. The government's attitude toward Falun Gong changed abruptly after April 25, 1999, when members in Beijing staged a peaceful sit-in outside the government's office for receiving complaints, on the western side of Zhongnanhai, the compound in which many of the top leaders resided. The protesters were there because of a newspaper article that had described Falun Gong as unscientific superstition. What frightened the regime, though, was not the issue of superstition but how numerous the protesters were, and that someone other than the Communist Party had organized them. They were peaceful and orderly, moved with precision, and left behind no litter. To President Jiang Zemin and other leaders of the regime, their autonomy was precisely the reason to repress them. China had a long history of charismatic leaders who used millenarian ideologies to grow popular movements that became large enough to overthrow dynasties. The Communist movement itself largely fit this pattern. Falun Gong had to be extirpated! The regime referred to the Falun Gong sit-in as "the siege of Zhongnanhai incident."

When the all-out government campaign against Falun Gong was launched on July 20, 1999, Xiaobo was still in the *laojiao* camp in Dalian. He could see on state television frightening images of billy clubs in action, but only later, after his release, did he learn the full extent of the repression. People who refused to renounce their beliefs—thousands, and eventually hundreds of thousands—were sent to labor camps and prisons where many were tortured and some killed. Those who avoided such fates went underground, fled the country, or, after weighing their options, renounced their beliefs.

In less than a year, what had begun as an apolitical group turned into a mortal enemy of the Communist Party and was losing a war on a steeply tilted battlefield. The government's steady drone that Falun Gong was an "evil cult" intimidated people to a point where scarcely anyone dared say a word for the victims in public. A few distinguished intellectuals, including the writer Wang Meng, compromised themselves by going on television to denounce Falun Gong. Xiaobo could hardly restrain his anger at the herd mentality that had taken over. It was not that he endorsed *qigong*. In the 1980s he had written criticisms of it as superficial and lacking in intellectual weight. Later he had difficulty with some of Falun Gong's factual claims.

But none of that weighed much compared to the brutal repression. Falun Gong was being annihilated, and no one was speaking up for it. He would. Articles between 2000 and 2003 bore titles like "The Costs of Repressing Falun Gong," "Brilliance Under Repression," "Twice-Strangled Children," "Falun Gong and Diversity in Values," and "The New Crime of Persecuting Falun Gong."[15] Reacting to the cowardice of his compatriots who remained silent, he wrote "How Terror and Self-Interest Teach Shamelessness," "Falun Gong and the Spread of Human-Rights Consciousness," and "A Nation That Lies to Its Conscience."[16]

Xiaobo borrowed that last title as the name for a collection of essays he published in Taiwan in 2002.

He saw the Falun Gong episode as "a new human-rights disaster"—not only for what it did to the Falun Gong faithful but also for what it was doing to the thinking of the populace as a whole. The strictly enforced unanimity—in every newspaper, on every airwave, from top to bottom in every school, and with woe to anyone who would stray in the slightest—reminded Xiaobo of the Cultural Revolution. But then he realized that this was *not* the same as the Cultural Revolution. People then had believed what they were saying. The unanimity in that era, however deplorable, was for the most part genuine. Now people were just manipulating words for their own safety. Sincerity was not the point. It was all right to lie to your conscience. If there was indeed a genuine unanimity, it was not on Falun Gong itself but on the belief that the best way to get through life was to adjust to unanimity of thought—whatever the thought. *What is more frightening?* Xiaobo asked himself. *Uniform belief or uniform lying to conscience? And which government is worse—one that demands the former or one that induces the latter?* It was not easy to answer.

Shortly after coming to the defense of Falun Gong, Xiaobo turned his efforts to the aid of another group, the Tiananmen Mothers. He had defended Falun Gong's right to be free from persecution but had never endorsed its beliefs. The Tiananmen Mothers were a different case. That group came to exert a profound influence not only on Xiaobo's political tactics but also on his whole philosophy of life.

The Mothers movement arose after the massacre of June 3–4, 1989, when Jiang Jielian, the seventeen-year-old son of Ding Zilin and Jiang Peikun, disobeyed his parents and stole away from home to go to Muxidi, where he was shot and killed. Another young man, Wang Nan, nineteen years old, went out that same night to take photos. About 3:30 a.m., at the northern side of the Great Hall of the People, just west of Tiananmen Square, he was shot though the head. Someone tossed his body into a makeshift grave at a nearby high school, and it was only discovered when a rainstorm a few days later washed away the thin covering of dirt. Wang Nan's father was an expert on the *pipa*, the Chinese lute, at the Central Academy of Music. His mother, Zhang Xianling (a cousin of the eminent China historian Yü Ying-shih), felt an immediate deep bond with Ding Zilin when they met, and the two mothers decided to search for others who had lost children or husbands in the massacre. For each case, they sought to determine a time and location of the murder and where the bullet had entered the body. They invited the families of victims to join their group.

Finding such families and getting them to join was not easy, because the Communist Party viewed the Tiananmen Mothers as another organization that threatened its grip on power. Ding Zilin, Zhang Xianling, and others had their telephones tapped and were monitored closely. They were followed and in "sensitive times" (like anniversaries of June Fourth or the presence in Beijing of important foreign leaders) placed under house arrest. The people they were looking for had to defy government intimidation in order to speak with them. In the government's view, the fact that a person had been shot on the night of June 3–4, 1989, was reason to categorize them as a "counterrevolutionary hoodlum"; this meant that claiming to be a victim was almost tantamount to pleading guilty as a perpetrator. Families did not need to add that burden to what they were already suffering.

Nevertheless, in 1995, twenty-seven representatives of bereaved families dared to write a joint letter to the Standing Committee of the National People's Congress asking for an investigation of the massacre. In a gesture of conciliation toward the government, they referred to it as an "incident." But they got no response. In June 1999, on the tenth anniversary of the massacre, the Tiananmen Mothers organized a June Fourth Dialogue Delegation and requested a "sincere dialogue" with the government on equal footing. They wrote also to the Supreme People's Procuratorate (i.e., prosecutor's office) asking that Li Peng, the premier of the State Council at the time of the massacre, be investigated for his responsibility in it. By 2000, one hundred and eight people had signed on as members of the Tiananmen Mothers.

In the years after 2000, the Mothers soldiered on despite increasing repression from the regime. As in the case of Falun Gong, the repression itself forced the group into a dissident posture. In the 1990s the Mothers had hoped that the government could use exoneration, apology, and reparation to heal the wounds of June Fourth and thereby lead to a broader reconciliation within society. But when their appeals were repeatedly rebuffed or ignored and they themselves came to be viewed by the regime as its enemies, they accepted the posture of out-and-out dissidence. Although punctiliously nonviolent, they began issuing a barrage of public statements—not only on June Fourth anniversaries but on occasions such as Tomb Sweeping Day, the annual opening of the National People's Congress, and the arrival in Beijing of foreign dignitaries.

Xiaobo's deep involvement with the Mothers might be marked as beginning on December 31, 1999. It was the eve of the new millennium, and there were many parties that he and Liu Xia could have gone to that night, but instead they went quietly to pay their respects to Professors Ding Zilin and Jiang Peikun. Xiaobo hadn't seen the elderly couple since early 1996. Now, keen to reconcile with them,

FIGURE 13.1 Liu Xia and Liu Xiaobo, 2000

Li Hong

he was startled to see how their hair had grayed and their faces had wrinkled. The effects of pain, he thought. The two received the younger couple as if they were parents to them. They counseled Xiaobo to take good care of Liu Xia. *Laojiao* had deprived her of his company, and it was now his duty to be sure she never felt lonely again. They made this point several times, and Xiaobo, who at a deep level still felt guilty about how he had treated Tao Li, took the words to heart. He heard Ding Zilin's instructions not as a scolding but "as genuine concern for me personally, as pure concern of one human being for another."[17]

The two professors presented Xiaobo and Liu Xia with a collection of accounts they had gathered from the families of 155 victims of the June Fourth assault. They called it "Witness to Massacre: In Search of Justice."[18] Xiaobo took the stack of papers home with him, began to read it, and, he later reported, was so stunned that he could not even pause for tea. He read the accounts aloud to Liu Xia, page by page, interrupted only by constriction in his own throat and sobs, followed by brief, pure silences that sat in the room until he could recover. He was struck that Ding Zilin and the others had been searching not only for family, friends, students, and famous people. They looked with the same diligence and respect for strangers and ordinary workers. To them, every human being was equally valuable. Did it take a massacre for people to see this?

Reading "Witness" became a turning point in Xiaobo's life. It shook him profoundly to see the massacre victims not as an abstraction but as real people.

"How," he asked, "could those bloodthirsty people be so casual about taking away the lives of ordinary people, who were not elites of any kind, but people who wanted only to live life normally, in pursuit of pleasures that human beings normally pursue."[19] He vowed "to learn to care, on an equal basis, for the actual sufferings of ordinary people [and] to live in the wealth that dignity and noble character can bring to human beings."[20]

He recalled again the embarrassment of having written "Repentance" inside Qincheng Prison in 1990 and how people later were willing to "understand" why he had compromised with his jailers. How could such a shabby performance compare with the people who now lay beneath the earth? Or the ones still rotting in nondescript prisons, whom the government called "hooligans"? He began to feel that it was only in a bookish sense that he had ever stood for human rights, freedom, and justice. He had not seen these ideals embodied in flesh-and-blood human beings. In the past, when people had expressed concern for his personal safety, he had thought such worries to be a retreat from ideals, a descent from the lofty plane at which he operated. But was he just playing a lofty game? He remembered Tao Li's withering comment that he was but "an oppositional ornament for an antihuman system." He had been arrested, then released, then rearrested, then rereleased, and then . . . how many times? Was it just show? In this mood, he took profound new inspiration from the way the Tiananmen Mothers were doing their work.[21]

By 2001 the Tiananmen Mothers had moved to the center of Xiaobo's consciousness. When people who had known him in the 1980s saw him as less arrogant and more gentle than before, he credited "the principles of the Tiananmen Mothers," which he summarized as:

> Using love to dissolve grudges, using reason to control rage, using benevolence to dispel ill intentions, using conciliation to narrow differences, using courage to summon conscience, and relying on tenacity to earn respect. Never take excessively radical action, never make excessively radical demands, and never direct teeth-grinding language at others. . . . [The Mothers'] version of noble love, their brand of sober rationality, and their never-ending toughness and courage are all models for the exercise of social conscience in daily life and the most valuable moral resources that exist in Chinese society today. Such principles can play a key role in China's eventual transition out of dictatorship.[22]

Xiaobo was aware that these principles were ideals; it would not be easy to put them into practice, especially for his generation, who had grown up in the Mao-era hatred mentality.

Around the same time, Xiaobo did much to protect people who were under attack for their online expression. When the Internet arrived in China in the late 1990s, few people thought the Communist Party could repress such a decentralized medium. As early as the 1940s, the Party had mastered techniques of controlling print media and radio, and in the 1950s, when film became widespread, and in the late 1970s, when television appeared, it found ways to control those media as well. But control in all these cases depended on the same model: messages originated at the top of a power pyramid and were beamed downward. The Internet was different because messages now could originate from below—from literally millions of places. It seemed a potent antidote to the Party's classic propaganda model in which "leaders" send messages to "the people," who remain atomized and mute. It opened a vast new space for people both to share news and to express opinions. The number of Internet users in China quickly led the world—not only because the Chinese population was the largest in the world but also because hundreds of millions of people who had been kept in boxes could now spring out of them.

Xiaobo was thrilled. It was as if muzzles everywhere were suddenly falling from mouths. Lively discussions reached far beyond anything that had been possible before. In early 2001, people online were discussing China's entry into the WTO; in March, the collision of Chinese and U.S. aircraft over Hainan Island; in summer, Beijing's bid for the 2008 Olympic Games; then in September, the 9/11 attacks in the United States. Each new topic mushroomed with debate. The government's flagship newspaper, *People's Daily*, fearing it might fall behind in the general bustle, opened an online People's Web. It included a forum, "Strengthening the Nation," that allowed much more latitude for expression than the parent newspaper had ever had. Xiaobo began surfing the web. This allowed him to monitor public opinion much more efficiently than before, and he used what he found in his writing.

He especially liked the "thought pages" that young people were setting up. The word "thought" (*sixiang*) was operating somewhat the way "culture" (*wenhua*) had operated in the late 1980s—as code for "politics," which was still too sensitive to use directly. One website that Xiaobo especially admired, Thought and Boundaries, was set up in September 1999 by a young man named Li Yonggang, a teacher at the School of Management at Nanjing University. Similarly to what *Southern Weekend* had done for newspaper supplements, Thought and Boundaries set an inspiring example for other thought pages.

Li's strategy was to raise important contemporary questions, including political questions, by presenting them as scholarship. He invited contributions not only from the emergent "liberals" but also from the "new left," an offshoot of contemporary academic leftism in the West. Dai Qing, who had been generally shunned by state media ever since she emerged from Qincheng Prison after June Fourth, was one of the early voices on Thought and Boundaries. When Cui Weiping, a professor at the Beijing Film Academy, completed a translation of the works of Václav Havel, no state media would touch it, but in spring 2000 it appeared on the site in full. Havel's emphasis on individual conscience and personal resolve to obey it were an inspiration to many and provided a new foundation for the modest resistance movement that was forming. Li Yonggang set up two discussion boards, "the sharp one" and "the mild one." "Sharp" meant politically sharp, and young readers flocked to it. Soon it had received more than three hundred thousand visits. Xiaobo's name was banned from online appearance, but he used the pseudonym Little Shrimp on the Water Surface to contribute to a thought page called Freedom and Democracy run by the activist Ye Du. "Water surface" meant *bo*, "wave," as in Xiao*bo*, and "little shrimp" was code for *xiaoxia*, referring to Liu Xia.

The authorities were slow to perceive the significance of thought pages but quick to react when they did. They began with a standard approach: try to intimidate a whole field by making an example of a particular case. They chose a page called Thought Garden of the Goat Child, run by a young scientist named Yang Zili. Yang had an MA in mechanical engineering from Peking University and was part of a group of young intellectuals who met to discuss issues in society. They followed no particular ideological line. Yang called himself a liberal, but his close friend Xu Wei, also in the group, counted himself a Marxist. An activist as well as a thinker, he was a recent MA in philosophy from Beijing Normal, where he had founded a student group called The Children of Farmers who went to rural areas to volunteer as teachers, donate teaching materials, and train local teaching staff.

In May 2000, Yang Zili's friends began to call themselves the New Youth Study Association. In the ensuing weeks the association met five times, and that little move toward organization may have been fatal. It was likely the reason the group was charged with subversion. In 1997, the government had amended its *Criminal Law* to replace the Mao-era crime of "counterrevolution" with the more modern-sounding crime of "subverting state power"; the crime of "instigating counterrevolutionary propaganda" was changed to "agitating to subvert state power." The latter kind of crime referred to words alone while the former, the heavier crime, referred to actions. Organization was an "action," and the New Youth Study Association had done it. So the charge was counterrevolution. It did not matter that the association had no charter and only eight members (one of whom, the rest of the group learned later, was working for the police as an infor-mant and provocateur).

The arrest in March 2001 of all eight members of the New Youth Study Asso-ciation threw down a gauntlet to all Internet thought pages. Xiaobo's first impulse, when he heard the news, was to reach out to Yang Zili's wife, Lu Kun, whom he had already met. He remembered how Liu Xia had suffered so terribly when he himself had been hauled away, so what must Lu Kun be feeling? As if a mes-sage had gone out telepathically, Lu Kun telephoned at that very moment. Xiaobo invited her to come to his and Liu Xia's place right away. She came and told her story, sobbing throughout. Xiaobo and Liu Xia half succeeded in comforting her, but after she left, her sobs reverberated in their memories. Xiaobo sat down and, in an essay called "Yang Zili and Lu Kun as I Have Known Them," wrote: "Lu Kun is weeping. She suffers. She feels pressure. She will endure a night nursing a broken heart. She needs to face, alone, a story whose ending she cannot predict. . . . In China today, how many Lu Kuns are there? How many wives and mothers suf-fer sudden disaster?"[23] Elsewhere in the essay, Xiaobo recorded his personal his-tory with Yang Zili. Yang was good with computers and had taught Xiaobo much of what he knew about them, making house calls whenever a computer caused a problem. Now Xiaobo was helping when the government was causing Yang Zili a problem. None of the young people in the newly criminalized group had any experience with the police or the legal system. They had no understanding of how "house arrest," "detention," and "arrest" differed and not even much grasp of what distinguished police stations, detention centers, labor camps, and prisons. Xiaobo knew all this turf well and could help them analyze their particular situations.

State media did not carry the story of the repression of the New Youth Study Association, but word of the prison sentences—eight years for Yang Zili and Zhang Honghai, ten for Xu Wei and one other member, Jin Haike—spread quickly on the Internet. When Li Yuzhou, the government informer, heard about the heavy sentences he was devastated; he went on the Internet to confess and to apologize, then fled to Thailand. Xiaobo remained loyal to everyone in the group through the months, and then years, of their ordeal. He comforted their families.

From the outset Lu Kun faced the problem of whether to speak out about what had happened to her husband. She wanted to and felt that she ought to, but doing so would carry risk of further punishment. She eventually decided to go ahead. Xiaobo introduced her to his lawyer, Mo Shaoping, and Mo accepted the case. In his defense brief, Mo pointed out that the New Youth Study Association's trea-sury never held more than 200 yuan. "After a meal used up some of that," Mo wrote, "about 100 yuan remained. Is that enough to 'overthrow the state'?"[24] Mo's rhetorical gesture laid bare the flimsiness of the state's case even as it revealed a solid fact about the authoritarian regime: it had zero tolerance for groups it did not control or could not easily control if it wanted.

When Xu Wei's girlfriend, Wang Li, learned that Xu had been confined behind the big red gates of the Public Security Detention Center in an eastern suburb of Beijing, she went almost daily and walked around the periphery of the walled compound calling "Xu Wei!" as loudly as she could. She sometimes persisted until 1:00 or 2:00 a.m., when police would chase her away, threatening to have her sent out of Beijing if she did not stop. She consulted often with Xiaobo, and after a few months he noticed growth in her political maturity. In a letter to him she wrote, "I was under twenty-two when Xu Wei was detained. I feel as if I understood nothing during my first twenty-one years. But I feel that in the last six months I have suddenly grown up. I can behave like a twenty-two-year-old now!"[25]

On October 13, 2001, Xiaobo and his old friends Bao Zunxin and Liao Yiwu published an "Open Letter to the Beijing People's Court, Procuratorate, and Public Security Bureau" about the case against the New Youth Study Association. They laid bare ways the state's "evidence" was full of ambiguities and doubtful assertions and how its "interrogations" were in fact forced confessions. The prosecutor's charge that the defendants had sought to "overthrow the socialist system and the dictatorship of the proletariat" was absurdly far-fetched—and untrue to boot. One mark of a civilized society, the letter said, is that thought is no crime; to make it so now would move China back into its ultraleftist years. Despite the letter, the prisoners remained jailed, and their health deteriorated. Six years later Xiaobo pressed for medical parole for them.[26] That was in late 2007, a year before Xiaobo himself went to prison.

This open letter marked the first time since leaving the *laojiao* camp that Xiaobo had written a public statement. There would be many more to come—by Xiaobo as well as others inspired by his example. The open letter as a technique for defending the defenseless was about to spread.

Among families of political prisoners in particular, Xiaobo had built a reputation by the end of 2001 as the go-to person for advice and support. The people who sought him out were not just intellectuals but migrant workers and "petitioners," who travel to Beijing or to provincial capitals, often living on the streets, waiting to air their grievances and to plead for justice. People visited Xiaobo and Liu Xia's apartment in the evenings and sometimes stayed late into the night. The hosts turned down no one. A night owl in any case, Xiaobo welcomed them to stay as long as they liked and turned to his writing only after they had left. Many visitors were women seeking help for their husbands or boyfriends. Liu Xia teased

Xiaobo that he had been promoted to "director for women." In one sense Xiaobo's role had come to parallel Ding Zilin's: Ding had her following among families of June Fourth victims, and Liu had his among families of political prisoners. Ding Zilin herself noticed the parallel; from time to time she sent Xiaobo
humanitarian aid funds that people overseas had donated to her group.

Xiaobo felt good about his new role as advocate and adviser for people who
had fallen into political trouble. But from another point of view, it felt like Band-
Aid work. The larger ambition that he and his friends had had in the mid-1990s
was to move the whole of society closer to democracy, and prospects for that
seemed to be dimming. Some of those friends—Chen Xiaoping, Liu Nianchun,
Wang Dan, and others—had left for the United States or elsewhere. One night
in late autumn 2001, in a glum mood, Xiaobo telephoned his friend Zhang Zuhua,
who lived nearby. Zhang originally had been a government official but in 1989
had supported the protesters at Tiananmen; for that he had been fired from his
posts and banned from publishing in the state-run press (except for a few short
pieces in 2004). He maintained a strong interest in democracy and human rights.
Xiaobo told Zhang that he felt depressed, and Zhang proposed that they go to a
nearby teahouse. They met and talked deep into the night.

In talking with Zuhua, Xiaobo began realizing that to pin hope for China's
transformation on marginalized dissidents was far-fetched. However admirable
they might be, and however unmarginal in what they had to offer, they were both
few in number and beleaguered. Out in society there clearly were untapped sources
that could support an opposition movement—if only they could be reached and
people could be made less fearful of speaking out.

So Xiaobo headed outward. The market economy and the Internet had brought
a new diversity in people's activities and their visible interests and values. Freedoms were creeping into their daily lives, and they were more willing than before
to defend those freedoms. They did not want to do battle with the Communist
Party and certainly did not seek glory or martyrdom; but, so long as their basic
survival was not threatened, they were willing, as Xiaobo put it, to "nibble at the
system's edges." Such activity could proceed without any obvious leaders or
organization.

Xiaobo explored the philosophy and tactics of edge nibbling in an essay that
proved pivotal in his thinking: "In the Gray Area: Resisting While Surviving."[27]
The phrase "resisting while surviving" meant that, when faced with a political
threat or attack, one does not necessarily confront it. Confrontation produces
leaders and organization, playing into the hands of the regime, whose favorite tactics are punishing leaders and crushing organizations. Moreover, to argue back
explicitly can lead to exposure of details that can serve as evidence for further

attack from above. So it was better just to nibble leaderlessly, bide time, and prepare for another day. A saying at the time was "The top has its policies and the bottom its counterpolicies." In the "resisting while surviving" philosophy, it was best to keep counterpolicies out of sight.

For example, Xiaobo admired the way thirty-eight journalists at *Southern Weekend* conducted a protest. Three liberal editors had been fired in the spring and summer of 2001, and intellectuals who supported the newspaper were angry.[28] They decided against writing a joint statement, however. Instead they formed a kind of leaderless tide by each writing a letter individually. The letters had no unity except in their topic and their use of similar tactics. Some cited classical texts. One protester wrote that *The Book of Rites* (ca. 200 BCE) advises, "In facing difficulties, don't just hide." Another quoted the *Huainanzi* (ca. 139 BCE): "The cock crows before the dawn, and the crane whoops at darkest night, but neither escapes slaughter when sacrifice comes." Another drew on a poetic essay by Fan Zhongyan (989–1052): "Better to speak and live than to be silent and die."[29] Yet another invoked the modern Indian poet Rabindranath Tagore (1861–1941): "I thank thee that I am none of the wheels of power but I am one with the living creatures that are crushed by it."[30] This kind of literary guerilla attack fit well what Xiaobo meant by "resisting while surviving." These people were having their say without staking everything on a single dramatic (and perhaps suicidal) gesture.

For another example, Xiaobo pointed to the way editors at *Southern Weekend* responded when summoned to Beijing to hear criticism and receive "central guidance." They brought notebooks, looked very sincere, took copious notes, and then returned to Guangzhou to continue what they had been doing before. The trip's only effect on their work, if any, was that afterward they enjoyed the comfort of feeling that they had bought some time. Xiaobo admired this little game but worried that "over time it could lead to a pride in petty cleverness of a kind that can erode one's spirit." He preferred the leaderless-guerilla technique of the thirty-eight letter writers. "Their words were mild," he wrote, "but amounted to a unique kind of collective resistance."[31]

Managers of state media "work units" (publishers, television stations, and the like) were themselves sometimes liberal minded and willing to protect people who worked for them. They had to answer to the regime's higher levels, though, so needed to be circumspect. They could "open one eye and close the other" when an employee chose to step "outside" the state system to make a critical comment. If a television station invited a "sensitive" guest or a magazine published an edgy article, a generous-minded unit leader could write a self-criticism on behalf of the whole unit so that the individual perpetrator could be spared. People fired from one work unit for speaking too freely might be picked up by another. (This happened to Xiaobo's friend Liu Junning, who in 2002 was fired from the Institute of Political Science at the Chinese Academy of Social Sciences and then hired at Chinese National Academy of Arts.)

To Xiaobo these deft, low-key tactics were an important change from the style of resistance in the 1980s. He called the latter a "reformist era filled with moral passion,"[32] when emotions were expressed in high-sounding and sometimes self-promoting language that carried the same flavor of reverence for sacrifice that Maoist ideology had lived on. Today's tactics were superior. Now people who chose to resist could balance their risk against the limits of what they could reasonably endure. They avoided letting their idealism land them in a place where, like the beleaguered dissidents, they had little and could do even less.

As these thoughts turned in Xiaobo's mind, he pieced together his own understanding of "liberalism." In the same "gray area" article, he wrote:

> Liberal politics is humane. It is low-key. The reason a liberal political system can get the most out of people, can call forth their creativity, is that it does not ask for cruel sacrifice or seek to produce saints. The preservation of life is its highest priority, and it quite respects the ordinary human desires that appear in daily life. It evaluates a person's behavior by whether it accords with common rules of civility. . . . Even in the rough and tumble of nasty politics, a true liberal does not surrender to bursts of blind passion that impose pointless costs on self or society.[33]

"Cruel sacrifice" here is yet another example of Xiaobo's antipathy toward his Maoist schooling. No one in Changchun had ever taught him that life is long and that he should educate himself broadly, for an unknown future, and learn to handle life's problems and how to act in good conscience.

Xiaobo then asks in the essay, what *would* be worth sacrificing one's life for? Characteristically, he turns the question starkly on himself. What would he say to the Hungarian poet Sandor Petofi, who famously wrote:

> Liberty, love! These two I need.
> For my love I will sacrifice life,
> For liberty I will sacrifice my love.

Xiaobo asked himself: *In what order would I rank liberty, love, and life?* His first thought was that, in this day when human rights (should, anyway) outweigh sovereign rights, anyone's answer to the question must be only his or her own; no one has the right to tell someone else what to do. He wrote: "For me, were I in an extreme circumstance where I was absolutely forced to choose between love of my wife and love of freedom, then I would have to choose my wife and sell freedom out. I just can't imagine it the other way around."[34] It was only a thought experiment. But it showed his devotion to Liu Xia as well as his lifelong penchant for juxtaposing abstract ideals and worldly values—and struggling for answers.

Four months later, on July 27, 2002, Xiaobo and seventeen others announced a "Declaration of the Rights of Internet Citizens." Their purpose was to make a clear and unified stand against the practice of arresting people for what they wrote on the Internet. Under his new principle of moving into society, Xiaobo made it a point to reach beyond the circle of personal friends and reliable dissidents who certainly would sign. He was sure many others would in their hearts agree with the idea of free expression and perhaps need only a friendly nudge in order to join. The first-time statement signers whom he was able to attract included some notable people.

Yang Xiaokai had been jailed for ten years during the Cultural Revolution for writing a wall poster entitled, "Where Is China Going?" He used his prison time to learn English and calculus from college professors with whom he was incarcerated. After his release he distinguished himself in the field of economics and once was even nominated for a Nobel Prize.

Mao Yushi, well known as an "outside the system" economist, with some friends in 1993 set up an unofficial think tank, the Research Institute on the Natural Economy. Its motto was, "Speak for the ones who have wealth, act for the ones who do not." The first part meant taking the side of independent businesses against state-owned enterprises, and the second part meant doing practical things for poverty-stricken people. He pushed for miniloans for farmers and ran "nanny-training schools" for migrants to the cities.

Wu Si was the editor of the journal *Yanhuang Chunqiu* (Annals of [the emperors] Yan and Huang; the official name in English was *China Through the Ages*). Its mission was to revisit episodes in the early history of the Chinese Communist movement that don't appear in contemporary media or textbooks. Contributors were mostly elderly Party members who could recall the ideals of freedom, justice, and democracy that had drawn them to communism before 1949 but now felt that the people speaking for those same ideals were not the regime but its liberal critics. The theme drew a wide following, well beyond the few who had launched the journal.

Another initial signer of the declaration on Internet rights was Wan Yanhai, an experienced activist for gay rights and AIDS prevention who in 1992 had opened an AIDS help hotline that the government charged with "agitating for human rights and homosexuality and supporting prostitutes."[35] In 1993 Wan was forced to close the hotline and resign as president of his group. Undeterred, in 1994 he founded the Love-Knowledge-Action Initiative to support AIDS victims. The group gained national and even international attention when it exposed the cover-up of a rapid spread of the HIV virus in Henan province. A government-sponsored project paid farmers to have their blood drawn, the plasma removed, and then the nonplasma residue injected back into them. The reinjections became contaminated with HIV, which then spread to hundreds of thousands of people. For more than a decade AIDS had been known in China as a terrifying illness, and now many unsuspecting people had contracted it. In August 2002, Wan's group published a booklet that summarized what had happened in Henan and explained how to prevent the further spread of HIV. For that Wan was detained "on suspicion of revealing state secrets." Xiaobo published an essay in response, "Is the Disappearance of Wan Yanhai an Arrest or a Kidnapping?"[36]

As Xiaobo's work spread wider, he met more and more regime critics who were "inside the system." The more he learned about them, the more his respect for them grew. In many cases their values were quite the same as those of critics "outside the system." They accepted certain compromises in order to stay inside, but they could be positioned to get more actual good done.

One of the remarkable friendships Xiaobo had with someone inside the system was with the once-prominent official Li Shenzhi. Li, born in 1923 and filled with communist idealism in his youth, fled to Mao Zedong's revolutionary base at Yan'an in the 1940s. Interested in international relations, he attended the Panmunjom talks at the end of the Korean War in 1951 and was rising in the Foreign Ministry until 1957, when Mao Zedong personally labeled him a "rightist" during the Anti-Rightist movement. Returning from disgrace after Mao died, Li accompanied Deng Xiaoping on Deng's historic visit to the United States in 1979. The next year he set up the Institute of American Studies at the Chinese Academy of Social Sciences and served as its first director. In 1989 he was vice president of the academy but resigned after the June Fourth massacre with the comment that he would "not serve as an official under bayonets." He turned his attention to writing and to nurturing younger scholars. In 1999, at the fiftieth anniversary of the founding of the People's Republic, he published an essay, "Bittersweet Harvests from Fifty Years," in which he openly repudiated the nearly three decades of Mao's rule and called for "reversing the verdict" on June Fourth. Xiaobo loved this essay and mentioned it often.

Through the early 2000s Xiaobo and Li Shenzhi exchanged e-mails and met several times. Li explained how he personally had traveled in a great circle: in the

1940s he had thirsted for democracy, so he joined the Communists, traveled with them for fifty years, ended far from his ideals, and now had circled back to pursue democracy again. The two argued over whether the language of Lu Xun or Hu Shi is easier for the common reader to grasp, Xiaobo claiming that Hu Shi's writing is clearer, Li Shenzhi that Lu Xun's is more passionate and therefore grabs people more deeply. When Li suddenly died of pneumonia in April 2003, Xiaobo wrote an article, "Honest Articulation of the Common Sense of Conscience," in which he called Li's passing "a major event in the intellectual world."[37] Published overseas, the article was republished inside China on a website called Thought and Opinion—a rare exception to the ban on publishing Xiaobo's work inside China.

The exception went further when the distinguished historian Ding Dong compiled a collection of people's memories of Li Shenzhi. Li had died at the height of a panic over the contagion of the SARS virus when people were afraid to leave home, making a public memorial service impossible. Instead Ding solicited written essays. He knew that no state-run publisher would accept such a "sensitive" topic directly, so he found a "book merchant" to produce the book. Ding asked Xiaobo's permission to include his article about Li Shenzhi in it. Xiaobo agreed, and the essay appeared without changes in a two-volume edited collection called *Remembering Li Shenzhi*. Its publication caused quite a stir. Most of the other contributors were "inside the system" intellectuals. Xiaobo's participation alongside them was a notable achievement—not only because it showed that he could get around the regime's ban, which was an interesting but relatively minor point (because the ban remained very effective in other media) but also because it signaled his solidarity with inside-the-system critics of the regime.

Despite these successes, the regime's own successes in continuing to repress society were keeping Xiaobo sober. In October and November 2002, he wrote essays about ways the regime was cowing the Chinese populace. One, "Unified Mass Taming," focuses on the remarkable capacity of people in China's lower classes to tolerate suffering and injustice.[38] Another, "The AWOL Spirits of Chinese Elites," argues that the regime could see in the 1990s that its survival depended on placating people at the top of society, especially in commerce, law, civil administration, and academe, so went to work using inducements of money and fame to buy these people off.[39] On the whole, this effort worked. By 2002 most elites had accepted the regime's emoluments-for-fealty bargain even if it created what Xiaobo called "empty seats." In the legal field, there was "an empty seat for conscience"; in the business world, "an empty seat for trust;" and in the universities, "an empty seat for critical thinking." Were people not embarrassed by the hypocrisy they were showing? They had to be, Xiaobo wrote. Just look at how they joked at dinner tables. They skewered the status quo with sarcasm and wine-induced zest, but the next day packed up their consciences and resumed their places in the system. People were lured so deeply into cynicism that many developed a kind of split consciousness.[40] This, for Xiaobo, was nearly as large a problem as the forcible repression outside.

14

Cascading Cases Build
a Movement

Beginning in late 2002 and extending through 2003, Xiaobo's new approach of working from the bottom up flourished as a number of dramatic "citizens' rights" cases appeared on the Internet. The public almost automatically sided with the victims, seeing their own conflicts with authority in the conflicts that others were reporting. Xiaobo followed the rights cases and joined—sometimes led—the popular outcry.

In October 2002 in Yan'an, the revered pre-revolutionary communist base in Shaanxi province, townspeople reported that two newlyweds, aged twenty-five and twenty-three, were watching a pornographic videotape at home. This broke no law, but the mood of a recent "strike hard" campaign against wayward behavior was still strong enough that a troop of police showed up one night at the couple's door to conduct a search. The husband, who made the mistake of offering a bit of physical resistance, was brought to the local police station, fined, and detained for fifteen days. Would that have happened, inquired an Internet wag, if the videotape had been a film about communist war victories? Jiang Xue, a reporter at *China Business News* in Xi'an, published the story and followed up assiduously for six months. The case sparked nationwide discussion in newspapers and Internet chat rooms. Jiang Xue's editors complained that they couldn't use their telephones because the lines were constantly jammed with incoming calls about the story. Political scientist Liu Junning wrote in *Southern Weekend* that "this way of infantilizing adults comes straight out of the paternalism of the political system."[1] There was an overwhelming consensus that the state had no business extending its reach inside a citizen's bedroll. More significantly, as Xiaobo pointed out, millions of people began to contemplate a theoretical question that had never before occurred to them: Where do the rights of the state end and my rights as a person begin? In the end the "offending" couple was awarded 29,137 yuan in reparation, and Jiang Xue at *China Business News* was awarded the *Southern Weekend* prize for "outstanding performance for media in the public service." Even Central Chinese Television went along, giving Jiang its "Chinese journalism star of the year" award.

In November 2002, Xiaobo made a new friend, He Depu, to whom he was introduced by the wife of an old friend and classmate, Xu Wenli. Xu had attended the same high school as Xiaobo in Changchun; he became an activist at Democracy Wall in 1978 and in 1998 was sentenced to thirteen years in prison for his work as a founding member of the Democracy Party of China. Xu's wife shared with Liu Xia the fate of living without imprisoned husbands, and the two women became close friends.

Xiaobo took an instant liking to He Depu, who was at the time preparing an open letter to the National People's Congress calling for "an end to one-party rule." Apparently for that bold act alone, he was sentenced to eight years in prison for "agitating to subvert state power." He's wife, Jia Jianying, attended her husband's sentencing and was in shock as she headed home. While still en route, she received a call from Xiaobo on her cell phone. "Come to our place," Xiaobo said. Jia did, and Liu Xia made dinner. Liu Xia seldom talked on such occasions, but she loved to cook for the wives of prisoners. Xiaobo informed the international press about what had happened and wrote an essay, "Protest the Communists' Sentencing of He Depu," in which he asked how a country that can send a human being into outer space can also fear a single gentle person like He.[2]

Xiaobo made a more momentous intervention in late 2002 when he sided with Liu Di, a student in the Psychology Department at Beijing Normal who was known on the Internet as "the stainless-steel rat." The Liu Di story had arisen two years earlier after a young man in Sichuan named Huang Qi inaugurated a "June Fourth Skyweb" to help look for people who were still missing from the 1989 massacre. Huang was arrested on June 3, 2000, and a firestorm of protest ensued on the Internet. Liu Di, owner of a mischievous intellect, posted several pieces supporting him, one of which was "Netizens in the Persimmon Oil Party Should Surrender to the Party and the State." "Persimmon oil" (*shiyou*) is a near homonym for "freedom" (*ziyou*), so everyone knew that "Persimmon Oil Party" meant "freedom party," i.e., the liberals. Liu Di suggested that all people who had ever posted on the Internet anything that supported the rights of Internet users should report en masse to police stations to turn themselves in as "Huang Qi elements." As her reputation for satire grew, she offered other tongue-in-cheek suggestions. People could, for example, hit the streets with mass parades in support of communism. This would get the attention of the authorities, she reasoned, because everyone knew that nothing frightened them more than large unauthorized gatherings—no matter the cause. Eventually the authorities had had enough of her. On November 8, 2002, she was charged with suspicion of "agitating to subvert state power." Did the authorities not recognize whimsical sarcasm when they saw it? Or were their minds subtle enough to perceive that ridicule of the state could indeed have undermining effects? This was hard to say, but Liu Di was arrested.

The arrest was highly upsetting to Liu Di's grandmother. Liu Di's mother had died when Liu Di was very young, and the little girl had been raised by her grandmother Liu Heng, who was eighty years old in 2002. Liu Heng was a legend in her own right. In the early 1950s she had been a reporter for the *People's Daily*. When Mao's Anti-Rightist Movement came in 1957, she was one of thirty-two people on the *People's Daily* staff—one of the chosen 5 percent—assigned the rightist labels informally known as "hats." But Liu Heng would not admit guilt. She was no "rightist." She was the only one at the *People's Daily* to refuse her hat. A few years later, when other rightists were "de-hatted"—meaning pardoned and allowed to resume work—Liu Heng could not accept de-hatting because she had never acknowledged a hat in the first place. Her political bosses tried to soften her stance but failed. She endured the rightist label until December 1978, when by central decree nearly all "rightists" were formally "exonerated" (*pingfan*). Exoneration was better than de-hatting because it was not a pardon for an offense; it was a certification that the original hatting had been a mistake.

Yet this intrepid heroine, when faced with the arrest of her granddaughter, became frantic with worry. When Xiaobo heard about the grand lady's distress, he took the initiative to call her and listened patiently as she related all the twists and turns of the story. During more than a year thereafter, Liu Heng called Xiaobo regularly, almost as if he were family, stressing time and again that her granddaughter was innocent. Xiaobo did what he could to comfort her and wrote a number of articles about her and Liu Di. Xiaobo had been fired from Beijing Normal University twelve years earlier and now had no formal connection with the school, but when he referred to Liu Di, Xu Wei, or other young people from Beijing Normal, he always used the affectionate term "schoolmate."

It was around this time that Xiaobo began using the term "human rights." Since the Mao years, the Chinese government had always attacked the term as a tool that the imperialist West was using in its attempt to overthrow socialism, and this distortion and superpoliticization of the concept made it more difficult than it should have been for the idea to spread in China. It was easier for the word "rights" alone to spread, and by the early 2000s it was used widely—far beyond the intellectual circles where it had originally appeared. Workers, farmers, retirees, petitioners, and others were increasingly aware of their rights and of the possibility of using media and the law to defend them. In January 2003, Xiaobo wrote an essay called "The Awakening of Human Rights Consciousness and Political Reform."[3] He was not afraid to append the adjective "human."

Cases like Liu Di's and the "pornography case" in Yan'an were beginning to clarify a way the Internet could be used to mobilize popular opinion and to push for change. Accounts of misbehavior by authorities and police could now be shared online, and popular reaction to such stories was so reliably on the side of victims that pressure could be put on wrongdoers, if only because they now had to answer to their superiors about embarrassing news.[4] In 2003 the frequency of such cases increased, and what was called a Rights Defense Movement took shape.

In February 2003, around the time of the lunar New Year, news of a "weird disease" spread from cities in the south. "Severe acute respiratory syndrome," or SARS, could be fatal. Doctors and nurses themselves were contracting it. People nationwide grew apprehensive. The government's first response to the bad news was to repress it. The second was to belittle the malady as nothing to worry about. Such reactions were standard, but in this case there was another reason for the obfuscation. Each year in March, the National People's Congress, with roughly 2,900 delegates, meets in Beijing to pass into formal law resolutions that the Communist Party has prepared. At the same time the Chinese People's Political Consultative Conference, consisting of about 2,200 members, exercises "democratic supervision" without voting on anything. Although often called a "rubber stamp" or "flower vases," the "two meetings" are occasion for great panoply. This year the coronation of the new president, Hu Jintao, and his associates was on the agenda. No one expected any surprises, but the symbolic weight of the matter had filled the air with tension.

In Guangzhou, just before the meetings, the *Southern Metropolitan Daily* reported that a local scientist named Zhong Nanshan had challenged the official account of the "weird disease" that the New China News Agency had published. Zhong said the disease was new, dangerous, and poorly understood. On March 14, the day the "two meetings" opened, *Southern Metropolitan* quoted a deputy director of the Ministry of Health saying that as yet there was no effective way to contain the disease. That drew a quick rebuttal from Zhang Dejiang, the Party secretary of Guangdong province, that later earned him notoriety: "The disease is not fearsome; what's fearsome is the media." Public opinion sided with *Southern Metropolitan*.

Xiaobo followed these events closely. In two articles that were very influential among liberals and supporters of the Rights Defense Movement, he argued that freedom of the press was "the key to political reform for the entire society."[5] The SARS case was an important test for journalists, he wrote. Everyone knows that if a medium goes too far and is crushed, more is lost than gained. But if the press does not persist in exposing wrongdoing, it fails in its mission. So where should the balance be struck?

Next, at a news conference on April 3, Zhang Wenkang, Minister of Health in the central government, gave false statistics on the number of SARS deaths in China. He claimed that the disease had "already been brought under control" and that it was "safe to work, live, and travel in China." Sitting at home, watching on television, a seventy-two-year-old physician named Jiang Yanyong, formerly head of general surgery at the People's Liberation Army Hospital in Beijing, was indignant. Just a few days earlier, at a conference of physicians from other PLA hospitals in China, Jiang had been listening to reports on the numbers of people who had contracted SARS and the numbers who had died from it. Those figures were far higher than what the Minister of Health was claiming.

Dr. Jiang sat down to write letters to the Ministry of Health, Central Chinese Television, and Phoenix Television, a station based in Hong Kong that had covered the Zhang Wenkang news conference. The letters got no response. But someone leaked one of them to *The Wall Street Journal* and *Time* magazine, and when those media approached Jiang he decided to answer their questions. The result was that on April 11 the World Health Organization, contradicting the Chinese government, declared China still to be "an epidemic area" for SARS. Only after April 20, when Zhang Wenkang and the mayor of Beijing, Meng Xuenong, took a fall for the regime and were dismissed, did the Chinese government launch an all-out effort to combat SARS.[6] (By the time the disease was controlled in China in summer 2003, there had been about 7,000 cases in China and Hong Kong and about 650 deaths.)

These events turned Dr. Jiang into a dissident. Like Ding Zilin of the Tiananmen Mothers, Yang Zili of the New Youth Study Association, and Falun Gong practitioners, and others, Jiang began with no thought of opposing the Communist Party but was pushed to that by the Party's own behavior. He had told the truth about SARS as a matter of conscience and professional responsibility. The authorities responded by accusing him of violating military discipline by talking to the foreign media. They put him under house arrest and banned his name from the media. He responded in turn by writing an open letter to China's state leaders recalling his experience on the night of June 3–4, 1989, when he was on duty as a surgeon at a Beijing hospital and tried to treat a shooting victim whose liver had been torn by shrapnel from a hollow-point bullet—the kind that by international agreement was illegal. Then he aligned himself with the Tiananmen Mothers.

Xiaobo visited the doctor often, and they became good friends. They watched soccer matches together—both were big fans of the World Cup. They cooperated in responding to pleas for help from the public. At "sensitive" times, they were forced apart—Xiaobo was put under house arrest while Dr. Jiang was "invited" (indeclinably) to go traveling outside Beijing. Xiaobo published essays about the doctor under titles like "Jiang Yanyong: Putting the Interests of the People First," "Jiang Yanyong Resists Dictatorship Single-Handedly," and "Protest the Persecution of the Nation's Conscience Jiang Yanyong."

While the SARS imbroglio was still raging, other rights cases popped up, like bamboo shoots after rain, as the popular idiom put it, and Xiaobo attended to them closely. A twenty-seven-year-old college graduate named Sun Zhigang, from Huanggang city in Hubei province, traveled to Guangzhou to take a job as an arts designer for a clothing company. On March 17, before he had had time to do his local registration in Guangzhou, police on the streets asked him for an ID. When they found that he had no local one, they brought him to a detention

FIGURE 14.1 With Wang Yi (standing, left), Teng Biao (standing, right), and Jiang Yanyong (seated), 2006.

Yu Jie

center under a program known as "custody and repatriation" designed to pick up vagrants who had come from the countryside and send them back home. After three days in the detention center, Sun was dead. The first official reports said he died of illness, but a reporter named Chen Feng at *Southern Metropolitan Daily*, who had noticed the story on an Internet thought page, Western Shrine Alley, did some investigating and found that Sun had been beaten to death. Police and detention-center guards both denied beating him, but the forensic evidence was unambiguous. How the beating started is unclear, but it seems likely that Sun angered his captors by objecting to his arbitrary detention. On April 25, *Southern Metropolitan* published a story called "On the Death of Detainee Sun Zhigang" that drew comments from across the nation. An uncle and brother of Sun, who lived in Guangzhou, got in touch with Professor Ai Xiaoming at Guangzhou's Sun Yat-sen University, and the professor organized a colloquium and then put the papers from it on the Internet. Her own paper was entitled "What Kind of System Is It That Incubates and Tolerates Such Sadism?" With that, the debate grew feverish and spread almost everywhere in China.

On May 14 three young legal scholars—Yu Jiang (Central China University of Science and Technology law school), Teng Biao (China University of Political Science and Law), and Xu Zhiyong (Beijing University of Posts and Telecommunications)—wrote an open letter to the Standing Committee of the National People's Congress arguing that "custody and repatriation" of the kind that netted Sun Zhigang was an illegal violation of the personal freedom of citizens and should be either reformed or eliminated. Nine days later, on May 23, five senior figures in the law field—He Weifang, Sheng Hong, Shen Kui, Xiao Han, and He Haibo—followed with another letter to the same Standing Committee. They asked for a special investigation into whether the system as exercised in the Sun Zhigang case violated the constitution. The media joined in pressing this question, and soon a major revision was announced. On June 20, Wen Jiabao, who had been premier of the State Council for only three months at that point, announced that the "Procedures for Custody and Repatriation of Vagrants and Beggars in Cities" was hereby abolished—to be replaced by a more kindly worded "Procedures for Assisting and Managing Vagrants and the Destitute in Cities." At the same time, punishments were announced for twenty-three people who had been involved in the abuse of Sun Zhigang. These victories infused the Rights Defense Movement with new hope. Xiaobo wrote: "An individual exercises a right . . . the media exposes the matter . . . popular opinion applies pressure . . . high officials notice . . . the media pursue and popular opinion gets stronger . . . the government makes a decision. This chain can be a master template for how an indigenous rights-support movement can bring systemic reform."[7]

The ferment around the Sun Zhigang case stimulated interest in other cases, including the date rape and murder case of Huang Jing. Huang was a music teacher in a primary school in the city of Xiangtan in Hunan province. On February 24, 2003, she was found dead on her bed, naked. Her body was bruised and scarred. Police at first ruled it a natural death due to heart failure, but the semen of her boyfriend was found at the scene, and an examination by the Nanjing Medical School contradicted the police report. But then important forensic evidence went missing.

Someone reported these facts to a website called Citizens' Rights Web, and the site manager, Li Jian, got in touch with Huang Jing's mother. Together they filed a lawsuit and organized a statement of support that several hundred people signed. Ai Xiaoming at Sun Yat-sen University wrote an article, "Date Rape and the Death of Huang Jing," and followed it with a documentary film about the case called *Heaven's Flower Garden*. On the other side, the Communications Administration in Beijing abruptly ordered Citizens' Rights Web to close. No reason was given, but apparently filing a court challenge to an official decision had not been welcome. When ordered to close, website managers normally complied but then reopened their site under a new registration. Li Jian decided not to do so; this was a battle he wanted to fight on principle. Xiaobo, eager to help and outraged at the government's action, went to his lawyer friend Li Jianqiang, who helped to file a lawsuit against the Communications Administration. The Xuanwu District Court in Beijing declined to accept the case, so Li appealed to the Beijing Intermediate People's Court, which likewise did nothing. It took more than four years, until December 8, 2007, for a final judgment on the Huang Jing case to emerge from the legal system. It said: "while Huang Jing was in a state of latent pathological change, [boyfriend] Jiang Junwu pursued unusual means of sexual activity that precipitated death." Jiang and Huang each bore 50 percent of the responsibility.[8] Li Jian had failed in court, but Xiaobo praised his methods. He had been right to sue, to appeal, and to publicize. This is what civil society advocacy in principle should do. It might or might not work but was the right course of action. It underscored a moral commonality between victims and the observing public.

Deeply immersed though he was in this kind of work, Xiaobo also took breaks. In March 2003, Ding Zilin and Jiang Peikun invited him and Liu Xia to visit their getaway home near Wuxi in Jiangsu province. They called their vacation spot "Lian's garden" to commemorate their dead son, Jielian. Xiaobo and Liu Xia accepted the invitation, and the two couples had much to talk about as they toured the scenic spots in Wuxi and nearby Suzhou. Ding Zilin remained Xiaobo's muse.

With four such politically radioactive people all in the same place, the regime arranged for ten or more police to accompany them everywhere they went. On the pretty islet on Lake Tai called Three-Mountain Island, as they were registering to stay in a hotel, they were surprised to learn that rooms in an adjacent hotel whose windows were directly across from theirs had already been occupied by police. The local people told them that the only pleasure boat on the island had been locked at its wharf twenty-four hours earlier, apparently due to the authorities' fear that the four major criminals might try to use it to flee.

During this trip, Ding Zilin and Jiang Peikun entrusted Xiaobo with a solemn duty. They asked that when they died, he take their ashes, mix them with the ashes of their deceased son, and spread them across a quiet surface of Lake Tai near Three-Mountain Island. Xiaobo agreed, but it was not fated to be. Jiang Peikun died in 2015, when Ding Zilin was still alive and could spread his ashes herself. Then Xiaobo himself died in 2017, while Ding Zilin was still alive.

Back in the trenches, in June 2003, another startling citizens' rights story suddenly appeared in the semiofficial paper *Chengdu Commerce*. Police in Chengdu had gone to the home of a drug user and taken her against her will to a rehabilitation center. She had resisted, complaining stoutly that her three-year-old daughter would be at home with no one to care for her. The police removed the mother anyway, and three days later the child, named Li Siyi, died of starvation. The story brought a huge outcry on the Internet. The first concrete consequence was that the reporter at *Chengdu Commerce* who had covered it was suspended for two years for misbehavior. Xiaobo was angry beyond words. Nothing incensed him more than to see completely innocent and defenseless people be victimized. In an essay, "The Death of Three-Year-Old Li Siyi Should Impale Our Souls," he wrote:

> *Who* has the right to disregard life in this way? What kind of a state—or nation, or people—is qualified to stand back and ignore the horrid death of little Siyi? No one! Not her parents, not the all-powerful civil administration, not the media who pretend to be society's ethical guardians, and not a numb and indifferent populace! *No one* has the right to be so beastly and cold! Anyone who had a role in little Siyi's death is a criminal; anyone who turns a back on her aggrieved soul is an accomplice in crime.[9]

In part because of the public pressure that Xiaobo and others aroused, a court in Chengdu did take action. The deputy chief of the police station whose crew had abandoned the little girl was sentenced to three years in prison. Another police-man got a two-year sentence. With this case Xiaobo had become virtually the unofficial scribe for the Rights Defense Movement.

A case that came to light in September 2003, involved bias against carriers of the hepatitis B virus, which Xiaobo himself carried and which led eventually to the liver cancer that took his life in 2017. The case also had an important national impact. A young man in Anhui took exams to qualify for the civil service and passed, but when he applied for a job he was rejected because he carried hepatitis B. Rejection for this reason had always been standard, but in the new age of "sup-porting rights," he decided to bring the matter to court. A famous professor at the Sichuan University law school, Zhou Wei, who had successfully argued cases of "height discrimination," announced in the press that he would take the young man's case pro bono. They claimed "discrimination against hepatitis B carriers," and they won. The press reported the result, and a tremendous nationwide response ensued. About 120 million people in China carried the hepatitis B virus at the time, so the base of those who might complain was broad.[10] Eventually a website called Liver and Gall at One [an idiom for unreserved trust] published "A Suggestion to Call Upon the Thirty-One Province-Level Governments in the Nation to Launch Investigations Into Whether Restrictions on the Hiring of Carriers of Hepatitis B Violate the Constitution and to Strengthen the Legal Rights of Carriers of Hepatitis B." Many people signed. The next year a number of provincial and municipal governments around the country revised their hir-ing criteria.

Also in September 2003, Xiaobo began writing about Sun Dawu, a wealthy farmer-entrepreneur whom he had known for several months. Sun owned a chicken farm in Hebei province and later branched out into pork, beef, and grapes until it grew into a 100-million-yuan business that he called the Dawu Farm and Husbandry Group. Sun built an all-new village, including a school, hospital, library, and nursing home, and about 1,500 people lived in it. For some reason, though, he had trouble getting bank loans. This may have been because he offered no bribes. But there were other reasons for the regime not to like him: he liked to go to Beijing to talk with liberal intellectuals such as the economist Mao Yushi and the eminent legal scholar Jiang Ping, and he published pieces by liberal intel-lectuals on his website. Unable to get loans, he decided to raise money by open-ing his own credit union. He offered higher interest rates than the banks did, so funds came in. But then in May 2003, something snapped within the regime. Someone decided that Sun Dawu must be stopped. He was arrested, charged with "illegal fundraising" (although his credit union had been entirely legal), fined thir-teen million yuan, and sentenced to three years in prison. People in the Rights

Defense Movement took his side, publicizing the case and providing legal help. Under public pressure, the regime released him after six months. (But in November 2020, the harsh regime of Xi Jinping rearrested Sun, charged him with illegal fundraising, encroaching on state farmland, and "picking quarrels and provoking trouble," and sentenced him to eighteen years in prison.)

It shows Xiaobo's view of human equality that he was not at all cowed by having a fabulously wealthy friend. On one visit to the Dawu Farm, Xiaobo noticed signs at the roadsides that said "Quotations from Dawu." This reminded him of the Mao quotes of years past and he bluntly said so, in the presence of both Sun and his other guests.

"You're using your thoughts to wash other people's brains, Dawu. It doesn't matter that this is your own farm and you are the total boss here. It's not right."

Dawu seemed unconvinced. He said it was part of "the enterprise culture."

That only further irritated Xiaobo: "Mao Zedong still lives deep in the minds of us Chinese. We should struggle to get him out of there."

Some heads nodded among the listeners. Sun conceded that Xiaobo, even though he wasn't very good at protecting the face of a host, had a point.

Around this time, in part because of the example of Sun Dawu, property rights became a topic of discussion in the Rights Defense Movement. Liberal thinkers were aware that private ownership of property had been important in the founding of democratic societies elsewhere in the world and were asking to "put private property into the constitution." Xiaobo concurred, but warned at the same time that a serious problem of "capitalism by bandits and their hangers-on" needed vigilance. For years, people with political power had used it to gain access to state-owned resources (not just land but raw materials, factories, transportation, and more) and had channeled these to their private companies, where they made huge unearned profits. To sanction "privatization" would be to anoint this plunder as legal. For this reason many critics, including "new left" intellectuals, opposed the constitutional amendment. Liberal intellectuals were split on the issue. No one liked the plunder, but some, especially the professional economists, felt that the guarantee of private property was so key to a transition to democracy that the wealthy might be offered a one-time "amnesty"; others, including Xiaobo, felt that the issue of social justice had to take precedence and the companies that had been built on plunder should be dismantled through the legal system. This change should not be done by force, however. Xiaobo favored "compromise and gradual progress toward a goal of societal transition."[11]

Abstract debate gave way to a crush of events in fall 2003. Du Daobin, a civil servant in the provincial government in Hubei, in early 2003 had led a protest of the way Liu Di (the stainless-steel rat) had been arrested and charged with subversion. He wrote an "Open Letter to Members of the National People's Congress and the Political Consultative Conference on the Case of Liu Di" and followed this up with a statement, "We Are Willing to Join Liu Di in Jail," that more than three hundred people signed.

On October 28, Du was apprehended right off a street in Yingcheng, Hubei. Simultaneously seven police went to his home, entered it before the startled eyes of his wife, Huang Chunrong, and began rummaging. Huang picked up the telephone and called Xiaobo. Neither she nor her husband had ever met him—she was just going on the recommendation of friends. She did not know how to use a computer, had not contacted any media, and understood little of what her husband had gotten himself into. Like others whom Xiaobo had helped, it seemed all she could do was shout into the telephone, "What am I going to *do*?!" The couple's twelve-year-old son was also at home. Xiaobo listened, rapidly taking notes on what she was telling him. Then, as he was about to speak, the phone went dead. He tried the telephone function on his computer, but that too had been cut. Two days later he finally was able to reconnect with Huang.

Police had been warning her to keep quiet and had been backing their words with threats. But Huang did want to speak out, and she asked Xiaobo's help in publicizing what she knew of her husband's disappearance. In the early hours of October 31, Xiaobo posted a piece on the Internet, "We Must Strongly Denounce the Arrest of Du Daobin by the Public Security Bureau in the Xiaogan District in Hubei."[12] Consciously defying what he well knew to be the regime's prohibitions on informing the outside world of political news, Xiaobo informed PEN International and then gathered signatures from PEN chairs in twenty-four countries around the world. The chair of PEN International, Jiri Grusa, signed, as did Eugene Schoulgin, the chair of the Writers in Prison Committee at PEN. Nobel Prize in Literature winners Nadine Gordimer from South Africa and Ōe Kenzaburō from Japan both signed, as did Goran Malmqvist, the distinguished Swedish Sinologist and member of the prize committee. Prominent Sinologists from Europe and the United States signed. This international response led to much stronger support for Du Daobin inside China, where people became less afraid to speak out.

Within days, two open letters appeared. One, "A Letter to Premier Wen Jiabao on the Case of the Internet Writer Du Daobin's Receipt of Criminal Punishment for His Words," was signed by Xiaobo, Wang Lixiong, and other dissidents who were "outside the system." More than six hundred others quickly joined. The second letter, from intellectuals "inside the system" including He

Weifang, Liu Junning, Xu Youyu, and eventually hundreds of others, was "A Declaration on the Detention of the Writer Du Daobin by Police in Hubei." After that Wang Yi, a young teacher at the Management School of Chengdu University in Sichuan—who ran a popular website called Teahouse for Any Talk until the regime closed it March 2002 —inaugurated a name list of people who were "Willing to Join Liu Di and Du Daobin in Jail." Wang further inspired his Internet followers by preparing a little booklet on how to retain a lawyer and what legal moves to make in the event of detention by police. (A decade later, Wang was pastor of the Early Rain Covenant Church, one of the largest non-state-approved churches in China, and in December 2019, he was sentenced to nine years in prison for subversion of state power.)

Xiaobo visited Ding Zilin and her husband, who had not yet heard about these activities, and came back prepared to write a piece called "Ding Zilin Also Wants to Accompany Du Daobin, Liu Di, and Yang Zili in Jail."[13] The news of Ding's position caused morale in the movement to soar. Three weeks later Huang Chunrong telephoned Xiaobo to thank him, because by then she had received more than 10,000 yuan in donations from good-hearted strangers who wanted to support her husband. Happy at the news, Xiaobo was also elated to see the difference in Huang Chunrong. A frightened, distraught spouse, struggling to be semi-articulate, had turned into a person who spoke with clarity and confidence. Xiaobo introduced Huang to his lawyer friend Li Jianqiang, and Li took her case.

In October 2003, Xiaobo was elected president of Independent Chinese PEN, an international group of Chinese writers, poets, scholars, and publishers founded by the poets Huang Beiling and Meng Lang in July 2001 under the mantle of PEN International. At its founding, Chinese PEN had only thirty-one members. The state-sponsored Chinese Writers Association, which had more than seven thousand members, dwarfed it. But unlike the official group, Chinese PEN was fiercely protective of free expression. Xiaobo, who was barred from exiting China, and Liu Binyan, who was barred from entering, were both founding members. Geographically dispersed, the group did all its voting online. Liu Binyan was elected the first president and Liu Xiaobo the second.[14] Xiaobo gave himself two warnings as he took on the role: one, "Better to do concrete good than to make high-flown pronouncements," and two, "To love freedom is to love life and to love other people; to love authority is to love oneself."[15] The first activity under Xiaobo's leadership was to press the Du Daobin case. The effort brought increased visibility to both Du and PEN.

Chinese PEN set up a committee to monitor the cases of all writers known to be imprisoned in China, whether PEN members or not. The committee issued appeals and stayed in touch with prisoners' families. Xiaobo, because of his rich experience in this kind of work, headed the effort. Chinese PEN's charter states that it is not a political organization, but to the regime, anyone who paid attention to imprisoned writers was a "hostile force," or at a minimum, highly "sensitive."

Meanwhile PEN's membership grew steadily. Of the thirty-one original members in 2001, only two, Xiaobo and Liu Xia, lived on the mainland. Before becoming president Xiaobo had persuaded Yu Jie, Ren Bumei, and several other friends to join. By 2005, there were 140 members, more than half of whom lived on the mainland. In 2007 the number was 220 members and included many prominent Chinese critics of the regime, both inside China and abroad. The senior dissident Chen Ziming joined, as did the legal scholar He Weifang, the prominent Shanghai dramatist Sha Yexin (whose satiric play *What If I Really Were?* had rocked the country in 1979), the journalist Gao Yu (sent to prison in 1989, 1993, and 2014 even as she was winning major international journalism awards), and Jiang Qisheng, a leader of the student dialogue delegation in 1989, imprisoned after the massacre and again in 1999 for conducting a candlelight memorial for the massacre victims, which the government called "agitating to subvert state power."

The authorities were watching. A writer on the mainland who contemplated joining PEN had to give the matter careful thought, because to join was to signal to the regime that one had shifted loyalty from the state-sponsored system and was now looking in a different direction. But Xiaobo continued reaching out to people, including those he had not seen for some time. One was Liu Ning, who had been a student at Beijing Normal in 1989 and was among the last to leave Tiananmen Square in the morning of June 4. Liu Ning remembered Xiaobo's pleas that he and others put down their bottles, clubs, and whatever other weapons they had, lest a mistake trigger a massacre. He had always felt grateful to Xiaobo for sticking with the students to the end. Now, fifteen years later, as he was meeting Xiaobo in person for the first time, he brought with him three treasured books: two by Xiaobo—*Aesthetics and Human Freedom* and *The Fog of Metaphysics*—and a third, a mordant keepsake, which was the government's denunciation called *Liu Xiaobo: Who He Is and What He Has Done.* Xiaobo signed all three books, adding notes that read, respectively, "Thanks for keeping it all these years," "The days of long hair are gone," and "Fifteen years!"[16]

An interesting challenge to Xiaobo's and PEN's broad-mindedness came when the playwright Zhang Guangtian, whose play *Che Guevara* was a commercial hit at the time, applied for PEN membership. The play trumpeted a romantic revolutionary myth about the Marxist guerilla Guevara even though, by then, the theme was long outdated in China. Xiaobo and Liu Xia went to see the play and found it disgusting. Xiaobo called it a "hate-filled, bloodthirsty, ear-splitting rant" and thought that it showed only how producers were making money by "using the commercial methods of capitalism to stir fervor for proletarian revolution and using attacks on the bourgeoisie to earn money from ordinary people."[17] Many of Xiaobo's friends saw Zhang Guangtian as a neo-Maoist. So should he be allowed to join PEN? The question went to PEN's nine-member executive committee. After the vote split four to four, it came to Xiaobo, as president, to cast the deciding vote. Xiaobo voted "yes" and Zhang Guangtian was in.[18]

The thought pages that had appeared on the Internet beginning in 1999–2000 grew steadily more important in the immediately ensuing years. Wang Yi, in Sichuan, wrote especially eloquent political and cultural essays for Teahouse for Any Talk, which he managed with some friends, but when their efforts brought severe threats from the regime, Wang eventually concluded that he would need to resign. In January 2002 he did so, after which Xiaobo wrote an essay, "The Resignation of Webpage Manager Wang Yi and What It Means."[19] The setback was only temporary, however. In February 2002 Liu Junning launched a new thought page called Forum for Constitutional Governance, for which he invited Wang Yi and his friend Chen Yongmiao, who had also worked on Teahouse for Any Talk, to be managers. And soon there were similar thought pages running in parallel: A Night of Unsound Sleep managed by Ren Bumei, Spring Thunder Action by Wen Kejian, and Freedom and Democracy by Ye Du. Xiaobo mentored all of these younger people, both online and in person. They looked to him for his experience and his indestructible independence of mind. Ye Du's Freedom and Democracy was shut down forty-seven times, but that did not stop him from registering it a forty-eighth time. Xiaobo admired his pluck. The three characters "Liu Xiaobo" were banned from the Internet, but Xiaobo sent contributions to Ye Du under the pen name Little Shrimp on the Water Surface. Whenever any thought page was closed or its manager harassed, Xiaobo made as loud a fuss as he could.

Thought pages increasingly became the backbone of resistance politics. The young lawyer Xu Zhiyong, who had helped to bring the Sun Zhigang case to light, broached his early thoughts about that case on a thought page at Peking University called Citizens' Life. Xu used the page as a sort of petri dish in which to try his notions out before jumping into the real world. He did the same for the Sun Dawu case, as well as for the idea that he himself might stand for election to the People's Congress of the Haidian District in Beijing, where Peking University is located. The high concentration of intellectuals in that district made the gambit thinkable. Xu did run, and he won. That feat had been achieved once before, in the same district, by Hu Ping, the ardent advocate of freedom of speech at Democracy Wall. That was in 1980, more than two decades earlier.

Thought pages sometimes led to books. Wang Yi self-published a book called *So Beautiful That It Startled Party Central*, for which Xiaobo wrote a preface, "Wang Yi Has Startled Me," praising Wang's incisive and witty language. Ren Bumei wrote a book called *Catastrophism*, in which he critiqued Chinese culture from the vantage of "theological liberalism." Ren published it on the Internet in installments, which he sent to Xiaobo, who read them conscientiously but in the end did not know what to say. He found the book's theoretical assumptions and logical connections odd, but he did not want to discourage his young friend. Eventually the two published a long, serious dialogue on the matter. Xiaobo also wrote a preface for Yu Jie's book *Refusing Mendacity* that could be published only overseas because Yu Jie too had been blacklisted.

The online intellectual ferment gave rise to a variety of offline salons, workshops, and book clubs. These included the Du Fu Thatched Cottage in Chengdu run by Wang Yi and Ran Yunfei; the Lawn Salon at Peking University run by Guo Yushan; and the "economics salon" run by Wen Kejian's Spring Bud Action group in Hangzhou. In Beijing Zhang Dajun convened what he called a "twice-monthly chat salon" to which he invited liberal scholars like Liu Junning, Cui Weiping, and Xu Youyu to speak. The salon met at the Royal Garden restaurant at Houhai in the city's center, but it got a bit too much "concerned care" from the authorities there, so Zhang resorted to the guerilla tactic of "fire a shot at one place then move to another." He changed location every time, and the "care" had trouble keeping up.

As the liberal thought pages flourished, it became much easier to gather names in support of statements and open letters. Xiaobo was gratified to see new names constantly appearing, outnumbering the familiar ones. He was happy too that the practice of listing names in order of importance was disappearing. The famous names were now just scattered within long lists of others. To Xiaobo, this was only one of several signs that "the human rights movement is expanding from elite culture into popular and general culture."[20] People from many parts of society were involved. Complaints, rights cases, and rights-support activities—some political, some not—kept popping up. The events were not linked and there was no master organization; but there was commonality in that all were responding within a shared new atmosphere. The regime had its hands full trying to repress all of them at once. It could not behead the movement because the movement had no head. It did have arms, though, in the growing ranks of rights lawyers. Teng Biao, Xu Zhiyong, Gao Zhisheng, and Chen Guangcheng were among the famous names, but there were hundreds of others as well. People paid special attention to rights cases. When news spread on the Internet that a court session on one of them was about to take place, crowds would attend to support the victim.

By the end of 2003 Xiaobo was feeling good. Thanks to the well-publicized matters of SARS, Sun Zhigang, little Siyi, the hepatitis case, the Sun Dawu case, and others, the year had seen important advances in the awareness of rights in society. A useful pattern had emerged: find an injustice, publicize it, then wait for popular opinion to force the government to make changes. It was especially hopeful to see how interlocking events could achieve momentum: Liu Di spoke out for Huang Qi, who was remembering June Fourth; when Liu Di was arrested Du Daobin announced that he would "accompany Liu Di in jail"; after that a long list of others declared they would "accompany Du Daobin in jail." Meanwhile, outside jail, increasingly large crowds showed up on behalf of victims in rights cases. In November, Sun Dawu and Liu Di were released on parole agreements, and Xiaobo saw Liu Di's release in particular as a result of popular pressure on the regime. The victory was nearly as important as the Sun Zhigang case, he felt. Society seemed to have reached a stage where the government, however crudely, was sharing power with voices of protesters. If so, that was a significant step forward and an opening that perhaps could be pressed further.

In an essay, "Civil Society Grows in a Harsh Environment," Xiaobo wrote at the end of November 2003:

> As long as people can continue to see how the cause of justice attracts popular support, the Rights Defense Movement will thrive. No longer will idealistic human rights activities have to be done furtively, in the shadows; they can be out in the open. They need not spring only from fleeting hatreds but can work for durable, long-term progress. They will not pursue grandiose blueprints that call for huge changes overnight but will build gradual progress from real cases that involve the way the system actually works. People will not be crestfallen when the ruling regime moves backward but always maintain an optimistic attitude toward the growing strength of civil society.[21]

The concept of "buildup" grew in Xiaobo's thinking. As rights cases appeared one after another, their cumulative effect would be to institutionalize the place of popular opinion in the political landscape, and that would entail a reduction in the space for the opinions of dictators. "The gradual buildup of new ways of thinking and of doing things," he wrote, "not only can lead eventually to a new political system but also can assure a smooth transition in getting there."[22]

The regime's attitude toward the rising Rights Defense Movement shifted from time to time, unpredictably. When the new president, Hu Jintao, and his group took power in March 2003, they apparently wanted to slow the momentum of the Rights Defense Movement but were unsure whether crackdown or appeasement was the better way to do it. Grants of parole for Sun Dawu and Liu Di in November 2003 were signs of a soft approach, and Xiaobo was hoping that Du Daobin would be treated similarly. On December 28, 2003, when authorities in Hubei province indicted Du for "the crime of agitating to subvert state power," the news struck Xiaobo like a bolt of lightning and set him to organizing yet another round of maximally loud online protests. (The day was, by chance, his forty-eighth birthday.) Rights advocates from both inside and outside the system, who had signed separate protests when Du was arrested in October, now were sufficiently indignant to ignore that distinction and came together with one voice. A single open letter was drafted and signed by 102 prominent people; after three days, 400 more had signed. They included veterans of political prison or detention (Ding Zilin, Bao Zunxin, Gao Yu, Jiang Qisheng, and others); independent writers (Wang Lixiong, Ran Yunfei, Xiao Shu, Murong Xuecun, and others); liberal website managers (Ye Du, Ren Bumei, Wen Kejian, and others); people from the emerging group of rights lawyers (Pu Zhiqiang, Teng Biao, Zhu Jiuhu, and others); and professors and senior editors (Mao Yushi, He Weifang, Liu Junning, Wu Si, Cui Weiping, Hao Jian, and more). There were many new names as well, including those of Zhang Yihe, author of the famous memoir *The Past Is Not Just Smoke*, about the persecution of "rightists" in the 1950s, and the senior poet Liu Shahe, then seventy-three years of age, who himself had been a persecuted rightist. The impressive depth and breadth of the list had much to do with Xiaobo's charisma and unflagging energy. Although the new custom of not ordering names according to prestige was observed, Xiaobo's name still appeared at the top.

Xiaobo joined with Wang Yi and Yu Jie to write and publicize "A Call for a Legal Explanation of 'the Crime of Agitating to Subvert State Power.'" They cited article 35 of China's constitution on the right of free speech of Chinese citizens, the "International Covenant on Economic, Social and Cultural Rights," and the "International Covenant on Civil and Political Rights." They invoked "The Johannesburg Principles on National Security, Freedom of Expression and Access to Information" (1995), in which it is stated that "the peaceful exercise of the right to freedom of expression shall not be considered a threat to national security or subjected to any restrictions or penalties." They insisted that "the manner in which Du Daobin wrote articles was peaceful; he wrote only on the Internet. The content of Du Daobin's articles was peaceful as well; in none of the articles listed by the Hubei police did he advocate or agitate for violence."[23]

But the Du Daobin indictment was the beginning of a turn by the Hu Jintao regime, showing its teeth toward the Rights Defense Movement. In early 2004 the *Southern Metropolitan Daily* was targeted. The newspaper had been a headache for the Hu leadership during 2003. It had carried the SARS story and broken the Sun Zhigang story, and had doggedly pursued both. By year's end Hu apparently had had enough. In January the Guangdong tax bureau, at the behest of the Public Security offices in Guangzhou city, who clearly would not have moved without orders from Beijing, dispatched agents to break into the financial office at *Southern Metropolitan* and, bypassing all legal formalities, examined its records and detained more than ten of its personnel, including the chief editor, Cheng Yizhong. The authorities alleged "economic crimes" for which Yu Huafeng, the newspaper's general manager, eventually was sentenced to twelve years in prison and Li Minying, a member of the editorial board, received eleven years. After loud protests, these sentences were reduced on appeal to eight years and six, and Cheng Yizhong, who had been detained in the raid, was released. Xiaobo wrote a trilogy of articles on the whole sorry matter that he called "How the Rights-Support Movement Views 'the *Southern Metropolitan* Case,'" "A Ruling That Blasphemes Legal Justice," and "A Ruling That Obstructs Reform in Media and Buries Conscience in Reporting." In his view, there could be no clearer example of using criminal charges for political purposes.

The harsh side of the Hu regime appeared again on March 28, 2004, when, without warning, police suddenly took Ding Zilin, Zhang Xianling, and a third leader of the Tiananmen Mothers, Huang Jinping (who had lost her husband in the massacre), from their homes. Ding's husband, Jiang Peikun, was allowed to stay at home, but police searched the couple's apartment and put him under house arrest. When Xiaobo heard the news he moved directly to notify the international press. Then he sat down and wrote: "Three people who were robbed of their dearest relatives fifteen years ago now have been robbed of their freedom as well. Their crime? It was to stand up on the spots where their loved ones were killed, to face down terror, and to bear witness. Through tears, they stood up in places where they knew it was not permitted to stand."[24]

Around this time, Ding Zilin asked Xiaobo why he had not chosen to pursue a scholarly career. His breadth of learning and sharp analytic gifts could have made him really stand out, she told him. Xiaobo answered that after a certain point in his life, he just couldn't change. Human rights work was too important. "Responsibility binds me now," he said. Ding wrote that she had seen the government persecute countless young people, but "the one who causes me the most constant and intense worry is Liu Xiaobo."[25]

As Hu Jintao's repression pushed forward, however, it stuttered with a few minor retreats as well. On February 14, a court in Hubei sent the indictment of Du Daobin back to Public Security, saying that more evidence was necessary. No one supposed that this was the decision of an independent judge, because that was out of the question in such a high-profile case. Xiaobo's friends wondered whether it might be a bow to the immense roar of protest against the indictment. On April 20 Du was re-indicted and on June 11 sentenced to "three years delayed by four," a formula that means a person is free for four years but watched, and then, if behavior has been "good," excused, and if not, then imprisoned for three years. This sentence was identical to the one given to Sun Dawu seven months earlier, but in Du's case it was a more encouraging sign because his crime was purely political, whereas Sun's had been an ambiguous blend of the economic and the political. Du's sentence, being lighter than expected, felt something like a victory for Xiaobo and the Rights Defense Movement. Their pressure had almost certainly made a difference. (In the end, after the four years' delay, the authorities locked up Du Daobin for the three years after all; during his probation he had been, they said, "unrepentant, unmanageable, and in violation of rules." He was finally released from prison on December 8, 2010.)

The Du Daobin case had helped to bring liberals "inside the system" and "outside the system" under the same flag. Whether for that reason or another, in early 2004 a number of inside-the-system people suddenly began speaking out on the issue of free speech. They seemed to streak from nowhere, like meteors across a night sky. Zhan Jiang, a professor in the Journalism Department at the China Youth University of Political Studies in Beijing, wrote a one-person open letter to Zhang Dejiang, the Communist Party secretary for Guangdong province, deploring the outrageous persecution of the leaders at *Southern Metropolitan Daily*. Jiao Guobiao, an associate professor in the Department of Journalism and Communications at Peking University, wrote an article, "Suppress the Propaganda Department," in which he listed fourteen ways that department "murders the constitution." It generated a deluge of online commentary.

Next, Lu Yuegang, a senior reporter at *China Youth News*, the mass-circulation newspaper of the Communist Youth League, wrote an open letter to Zhao Yong, the league's general secretary, protesting something Zhao had said at a meeting at *China Youth News* on May 24, 2004. Zhao had warned the assembled reporters and editors that they must not use "a spirit of idealism" to run their newspaper. The correct spirit, he explained, was Party policy, and he punctuated his point with a rhyme: "Anybody still want to disobey? Resign right now and be on your way!"[26] Lu Yuegang was an old friend of Xiaobo's. They had met while both were writing for Ding Ling's journal *China* in 1985–86, and both had attended the national conference in September 1986 on "Ten Years of Literature in the New Era" (discussed in chapter 6). Now, seeing that Lu Yuegang had directly challenged a Party secretary of the Youth League, Xiaobo sat down to write a long article in support of his friend. He wrote: "People inside the system, when they are strong, courageous, and open in their thinking, earn the respect of people both inside the system and outside it. By breaking down prohibitions inside the system, they continually expand the space for expression there and hence promote the principle of free expression in society as a whole."[27] Not long thereafter, Lu Yuegang and his colleague Li Datong were suspended from their positions and their popular column, "Freezing Point," was closed down. Xiaobo wrote seven articles about the matter in quick succession: "Remember Freezing Point and Its Assassins," "Taking Stock of the Freezing Point Affair—Great Journalists Versus Tiny Bureaucrats," "What on Earth Is the Propaganda Department?," and four others. In the process of doing some fact-checking with Lu Yuegang, Xiaobo learned that fifteen years earlier, at the Tiananmen demonstrations, Lu had been on the verge of publishing Xiaobo's June 2 "Hunger Strike Declaration" in the *China Youth News*. What an earthquake that would have caused!

In September 2004, Xiaobo wrote a long article, "Dissenting Views Within the System Are Silent No Longer."[28] Voices from inside the system sometimes commanded more moral authority than ones from outside, he observed, because the regime could not say, "That person is an outsider." Insiders also had closer access to the dirt within the system and therefore more credibility in explaining its details. Senior figures inside, such as those who wrote for *China Through the Ages*, could afford to be especially frank because their revolutionary gravitas protected them. Xiaobo presented the example of the very senior and sharp-tongued Li Rui: former secretary to Mao Zedong, former deputy minister of the standing committee of the Central Organization Department, member of the Communist Party earlier than the current top leader Hu Jintao was, and so on. Could the regime tell *him* to shut up? If he went on and on about Mao's cruelty and idiosyncrasies, well—who could say it wasn't so? In Xiaobo's view the strength of the dissent from elderly insiders in 2004 exceeded anything that dissenting intellectuals of the 1980s could have imagined. "If 2003 was 'upholding-popular-rights year,'" he wrote, "then 2004 was 'dissent-from-within-the-system year.'"[29]

The power of dissenters inside the system so impressed Xiaobo that it led him to muse on whether one of them might merit a Nobel Peace Prize. He rarely mentioned that prize and had no idea that it would someday affect him personally. He wrote:

> To send a famous inside-the-system dissenter to prison would be to consummate that person's moral character in the eyes of the public. The heavier the sentence, the higher the standing would be. From the government's point of view, a Nobel Peace Prize would do more harm than good. As the highest moral accolade the world has to offer, it would deliver a two-pronged message: affirmation of the

dissenter and censure of the dictatorial government. If the government held a Nobel Peace Prize winner in prison it would be squandering its political capital in the eyes of the world and pronouncing its own moral death sentence. It would, moreover, be cementing the credentials of an opposition leader.[30]

As if teasing himself for his wild speculation, Xiaobo commented that "of course it would not be easy"—even for a dictatorship—to create such a scene. He did not imagine that the daydream would indeed come true and that the prize winner would die in prison.

It was also in September 2004 that the Beijing Communications Administration issued an order to close down an especially lively electronic bulletin board at Peking University. Students had wryly called it The Mess (*yitahutu* in Chinese, punning on famous campus fixtures—the pagoda [*yita*], the Nameless Lake [*hu*], and the library [*tu*]). After it was closed, He Weifang, Peking University's preeminent legal scholar, wrote an open letter to the university president pleading that he resist the government's order, but the president did not. Xiaobo, inveterate defender of all online thought pages, wrote a piece called "He Weifang, Defender of Civilized Common Sense."[31] The essay was the beginning of a durable friendship between Xiaobo and He Weifang.

Later that autumn, He Weifang's name was banned from all mention in the media. This happened not just because of The Mess, but because the Hu Jintao regime ended its waffling on liberalism and decided on a general crackdown. The names of Wang Yi, Yu Jie, Liu Junning, Mao Yushi, and many others were banned at the same time. The crackdown may well have been related to the fact that, at a meeting of the Central Committee of the Communist Party in September, Hu Jintao had secured the position of Chair of the Military Commission, which he had long sought. The first sign of his more belligerent approach was a startling comment he made at that same Central Committee meeting: in ideological matters, the Party should learn from Cuba and North Korea. A first reaction of many people was to find this comment funny. When they realized Hu was not joking, a second reaction was to think: *impossible.* Society had come so far in the last quarter century that to turn toward a Cuban or North Korean model just would not work. Nonetheless, Hu and the other men behind the tall red walls began taking steps in that direction.

The political tightening worried Xiaobo and his friends for many reasons, one of which was how to proceed with the Freedom in Writing Prize that Chinese PEN was scheduled to award that fall. The prize had been established in 2002; this would be its second award ceremony, which by rights should be a large public event.

China already had literary prizes, the most famous being the Mao Dun Prize, named after the famous Chinese fiction writer and Communist Party stalwart Shen Yanbing, who wrote in the 1920s through 1940s under the pen name Mao Dun. But that prize was state sponsored and decidedly not for free writing of the kind Chinese PEN wanted to honor. Nominees for the Freedom in Writing Prize did not have to be "outside the system"; writers inside were eligible so long as they met the standards of writing both freely and well. The first recipient of the prize was Wang Lixiong, whose novel *Yellow Peril* is a political allegory depicting a bleak China of the future, beset with crises at home and great-power struggles abroad. Published in 1991, when the cultural environment was still numb in the aftermath of June Fourth, *Yellow Peril* was written under the pen name Baomi ("keep the secret") and sparked considerable excitement as it was passed around furtively.

Wang Lixiong and Xiaobo were old friends. Wang had once moved Xiaobo to tears by giving a jar of caviar to Liu Xia to carry to Xiaobo while he was in *laojiao* at Dalian. In 2001, when Wang announced publicly that he was withdrawing from the state-sponsored Chinese Writers Association, Xiaobo felt a new excitement about his old friend and decided to write an essay about him. Wang could have resigned from the Chinese Writers Association quietly but chose not to. His public announcement entailed considerable risk. Wang was also the first intellectual in post-Mao China to speak out vigorously for Tibetans, Uyghurs, and others of China's ethnic minorities. He was married to Woeser, a major Tibetan poet. He was also a founding member of Friends of Nature, China's first NGO concerned for the environment.

Chinese PEN designed strict rules for nominating and voting on the Freedom in Writing Prize. The rules were followed, and the 2004 prize went to Zhang Yihe, a brilliant writer "inside the system." (The reason for highlighting the rules is that the award to Zhang was sharply controversial—precisely because she was "inside the system". It was important to Xiaobo that the rules ruled.) This decision pleased Xiaobo, whose inclination, here as in other activities, was to reach beyond the circle of known "dissidents" and into society broadly. The prize seemed a golden opportunity to spread the ideal of free writing. But the selection of Zhang Yihe was controversial. She was retired from the Theater Research Institute of the Chinese National Academy of Arts, and all of her publications were at state presses, where they had been subjected to censorship to which she had acceded. The censorship had been minor, but some PEN members argued that to accept censorship is wrong in principle and that a person this far inside the system should not be chosen. Others, while supporting her, feared that she might decline the prize as "too sensitive." But in the end the offer was made and Zhang Yihe accepted.

Political "sensitivity" did not matter to her, in part because she had already made herself considerably sensitive by signing several open letters and statements.

Born in 1942, she was an expert on Chinese opera. Her father, Zhang Bojun, was active in the 1940s in founding two of the "eight democratic parties" that were given symbolic "flower vase" roles in the Communist Party's ruling structure after 1949. The democratic parties were powerless, but Zhang Bojun as an individual was appointed at the outset of the new regime to be Minister of Transport and president of the *Guangming Daily* newspaper. His daughter until age fifteen lived within a comfortable culture of her parents and their friends and acquaintances—newspapermen, lawyers, Peking opera aficionados, political commentators, and others—who had been part of the elite before 1949. In early 1957, when Mao Zedong called on intellectuals to express their frank views, Zhang Bojun made the mistake of proposing that China create a bicameral legislature. A few months later Mao named him "the number one rightist in China," and he never had a public role again. He died in 1969 during the Cultural Revolution, during which Yihe was named an "active counterrevolutionary" and sent to prison for ten years. She shared cells with thieves, murderers, and other criminals—as well as with prisoners of conscience and lesbians. (Being lesbian was grounds for a prison sentence.) Yihe gave birth to a daughter while in prison. Her memoir, *The Past Is Not Just Smoke*,[32] depicts the people in her life before political disaster struck and evokes their urbane civility with nostalgia and affection. Its point is that that past may be gone but is "not just smoke." To readers schooled in Communist education, the book was revelatory in a dramatic way.

The awards ceremony took place on October 30, 2004, in a northern suburb of Beijing. About sixty people attended, which made it the largest gathering Xiaobo had been part of since 1989. It was a who's who of Chinese resisters of authoritarianism over several generations. Zhang Yihe represented those who had been driven from public view in 1957. Xu Xiao, an editor at *Today*, the independent literary journal that had appeared at Democracy Wall in the late 1970s, was present. So was Bao Zunxin, who had been chief editor of the Walking Toward the Future book series in the 1980s. Lu Yuegang, who had openly challenged the leader of the Communist Youth League, and Jiao Guobiao, who had attacked the Propaganda Department, were there. Wu Si, whose journal *China Through the Ages* allowed elderly communists to bemoan today's communism, was present. Liang Xiaoyan, freshly fired from her university job for helping to make a film about Tiananmen, was there—smiling in spite of her recent fate. Pu Zhiqiang, the rights lawyer whose brilliant eloquence in court struck fear into the hearts of prosecutors, was there; so was Wang Lixiong, winner of the inaugural prize. Wang Yi and Liao Yiwu traveled all the way from Sichuan. Yu Jie and Yu

FIGURE 14.2 At the Freedom in Writing awards ceremony, fall 2004. Sitting around the table, left to right: Wang Kang, Ding Dong, Xing Xiaoqun, Zhang Boshu, Wu Si

Zhang Yu

Shicun, two up-and-coming PEN activists, organized a committee to make the arrangements for the ceremony; they found and decorated the rustic courtyard where it took place. The banner they made, in white characters arranged horizontally on a red background, read: "Ceremony for the Second Awarding of the Freedom in Writing Prize of Independent Chinese PEN." Attendees joked that "today's cow ghosts and snake spirits [Mao's epithet for intellectuals during the Cultural Revolution] have all gathered in one place."

In his talk at the ceremony, Xiaobo said that the damage inflicted in 1957 by the purge of 500,000 intellectuals (roughly the number who were persecuted, banished, or otherwise ruined during the Anti-Rightist Movement) could not be measured by numbers alone. The nation had been beheaded in 1957. It lost its independent thinking and creative spirit and fell under a system that, in essence, was the same one that constricted everyone in 2004. The literary prize they were awarding today, he said, lay outside that system. Zhang Yihe's writing restored the dignity of the Chinese language and kept it alive. Amid Xiaobo's eloquence, which his stuttering seemed only to enhance, someone on the dais observed that since 1989 Xiaobo had been prohibited from addressing groups larger than thirty. Someone in the audience yelled, "Let him talk longer! He needs it!" The crowning moment of the session came when Zhang Yihe herself spoke and told how, one rainy night in the Cultural Revolution era, she watched the burial of the corpse of one of her prison cellmates. Xiaobo's eyes moistened, as did many others'.[33]

After the award ceremony, the PEN organizers were relieved that it had gone well. The authorities had permitted it. Later, though, the name Zhang Yihe was added to those banned from appearance in print.

Soon PEN was clashing with the regime over another matter. On November 24, 2004, police in Changsha, Hunan province, arrested Shi Tao, a newspaper editor and PEN member, and took him from his home. The preceding April, as the fifteenth anniversary of the June Fourth massacre was approaching, Shi Tao and others received instructions from political higher-ups that only standard, centrally approved language could be used in writing about it. Indignant, Shi Tao forwarded the directive by Yahoo! e-mail to several friends, including to a prodemocracy website in New York. When government authorities discovered this disclosure, they asked Yahoo! for the identity of the sender, Yahoo! complied, and the police grabbed Shi Tao. Chinese PEN immediately issued an "Emergency Statement on the Arrest of Our Member Shi Tao." It detailed Shi Tao's credentials and achievements and publicized a threat that police had made against his wife: that she would suffer unspecified consequences if she publicized anything.

Xiaobo, anticipating that Shi Tao would be charged with leaking state secrets, published an essay on December 6, "Shi Tao Has No Secrets."[34] It showed how Shi Tao had consistently been the opposite of secretive: he had supported Du Daobin openly and had called for transparency about June Fourth. On December 14, Shi Tao was indeed charged with "the crime of illegally sending state secrets abroad." Respect for him within the Rights Defense Movement skyrocketed. Shi Tao concluded that he and Xiaobo saw things so similarly that, before he headed to prison, he telephoned Xiaobo and said that he needn't check before adding the name Shi Tao to public declarations and appeals that he might organize while Shi Tao was incarcerated. When Shi Tao's mother visited him behind bars, he counseled her, "If there's a problem, go to Bo."[35]

Also in December 2004, Xiaobo, Yu Jie, and Zhang Zuhua were working on a "report on China's human rights." Somehow the authorities got wind of the project. Around 5:00 p.m. on December 13, Xu Youyu and Xiaobo were chatting on the telephone about various things when Xiaobo suddenly said, "Hold on, somebody's knocking on the door," and put the phone down. After about sixty seconds Xu could hear in the background a stout voice saying, "We are the Public

Security Bureau of Beijing City, and we are here to carry out an order to search your home!" The voice was so crisp, so precisely articulated, and spoken in such standard Mandarin that Xu at first thought he was hearing the broadcast of a television drama from a set that had been left on. But this was real life—which became obvious when the "broadcast" ceased as quickly as it had begun, and Xiaobo did not return to the phone. Then the phone went dead. Xu redialed but couldn't get through. *We have news!* he told himself. *I'll have to report it.* He called Yu Jie, who called others. Within half an hour Xu was beset by requests from the foreign media to confirm the story. An hour later the police picked up Yu Jie too.

This raid, the harshest treatment the regime had dealt Xiaobo since his release from *laojiao* five years earlier, took him by surprise. About a dozen policemen edged into the little apartment. After their chief showed a search warrant for the home and a summons for Xiaobo, the police searched the place top to bottom, taking photos and videos of nearly everything. They left after about three and a half hours, carrying with them Xiaobo's computer, his floppy disks (used for data storage in those days), and some documents. They brought Xiaobo to the local police station and subjected him to intense interrogation until about 2:00 a.m. The questions were mostly about articles he had written. They showed him five or six examples and asked him to confess that he was the author. Then they brought him home but made it clear that he remained under house arrest. Liu Xia was not summoned to the police station, but two policewomen stayed with her throughout, and one of their duties was to inform her that she was not permitted to be in touch with people "in the outside world."

News of Xiaobo's detention triggered a flurry of outcry. As soon as he got home he received a steady stream of supportive phone calls from friends, acquaintances, and even strangers. The next day Wang Yi, Liao Yiwu, Yu Shicun, and others gathered signatures for an open protest. Independent Chinese PEN issued an appeal. Professors Ding Zilin and Jiang Peikun wrote an open letter addressed to Party General Secretary Hu Jintao and Premier of the State Council Wen Jiabao asking why Public Security would "come down so hard on a couple of armchair critics [Xiaobo and Yu Jie] who lack the brawn to truss a chicken." The phone calls became less frequent over the next few days but then suddenly, on December 21, a new barrage began. Reporters Without Borders had named Xiaobo recipient of its 2004 Press Freedom Award. Xiaobo had known in advance that he would be getting this award, so the news itself was not surprising. But the rush of warmth that he felt while he was kept at home under twenty-four-hour surveillance was exhilarating.

As he endured his personal kerfuffle, Xiaobo remained outraged at what Yahoo! had done to Shi Tao. He wrote "An Open Letter to Yahoo! CEO Jerry

Yang on the Shi Tao Affair," in which he charged that Yang's self-defense of saying "business is business" in reality amounted to "politics is business." It was just one more example of the fungibility of money and power.[36] Typically attentive to detail, Xiaobo noticed that Shi Tao and Jerry Yang, who was from Taiwan, were both thirty-seven years old. "You and Shi Tao have your ages in common," he wrote, "but nothing else." Xiaobo vowed never again to use a Yahoo! product and asked his readers on the Internet to join him in the boycott—unless, he added, Jerry Yang apologized to Shi Tao and to his family and paid reparations. Xiaobo's call for a boycott was translated into English and attracted support in the Western world.

Shi Tao was not Yahoo!'s only victim. A young man named Wang Xiaoning from Shenyang in Liaoning province had written articles asking for democratic reforms and an end to one-party dictatorship. Yahoo! delivered Wang's identity to state security, and he was sentenced to ten years in prison. Eventually Yahoo! was exposed and stoutly denounced in international opinion. On the defensive, the company agreed to pay Shi Tao's and Wang Xiaoning's families $3.2 million each and further, to provide about $17 million to establish a Yahoo! Human Rights Fund to support others who might be detained or persecuted for expressing views on the Chinese Internet.[37]

These experiences during 2001–2004 led Xiaobo, in stages, to conceive and refine a philosophy of what a Rights Defense Movement should be and how it should operate.

15

An Intellectual Transition

During the winter of 2004–05 police followed Xiaobo wherever he went. His friends, defiant in not minding, invited him out to eat almost daily. Police would loiter at the doors of the restaurants they visited and sometimes come in and sit down at a nearby table. This had no effect on the way Xiaobo and his friends chatted and joked. If the police were listening, fine, they seemed to say. Those young cops might learn something.

Moved by the support he was getting, Xiaobo wrote an essay about it, "Warmth from Society Amid a Freeze in Politics." It contains these words: "The authoritarian rule at the top in China today shows no sign of a spring that might warm a person's heart. But terror politics, however cold, cannot freeze the moral spring that arrives from below, from civil society."[1] He called the support he was receiving "stove fires in the dark winter." "Stove fires" meant people's free will, which continued to burn and even to spread, despite intimidation. "For me," he wrote, "these fires are both protection and encouragement. They are also a call to responsibility." The change in Xiaobo from the 1980s, when he saw himself as an isolated heroic figure, is striking. He now saw himself as deeply embedded in a community with shared values that included people he knew and people he did not know. They were a borderless group.

If they were his "stove fires," some of them saw him, in turn, as their "torch"—a steady flame that burned as if it would never run out of fuel. Followers also likened themselves to swimmers who watched Xiaobo swim out into the sea's deep water, beyond the shark nets, and decided to go out a bit farther themselves. The Hungarian writer Miklos Haraszti, in *The Velvet Prison*, observes that political pioneers have both "vanguard" and "rear guard" functions. Vanguards explore forward, but an equally important function is to inspire the rear guard, whose continual filling of the space behind the vanguard consolidates the progress it has made and provides the safety of numbers. Under a regime like China's that uses fear to maintain pressure, the role of people in the rear guard is crucial.

For several years Xiaobo had been moving closer to a realization that a future political transition in China would need to come from deep within society, not from elite idealists. The failure of the democracy movement in 1989 showed that to confront people at the top of the regime with stentorian principles does not work. The gesture may be beautiful, but the concrete results are often zero—or perhaps even harmful. Another reason was that after 1989, it was fairly clear that people at the top were no longer listening. From 1978 to 1989, advocates of democracy could at least imagine themselves in dialogue with the top. In 1978, when Wei Jingsheng called for democracy as a "fifth modernization," he was clearly echoing the "four modernizations" that Deng Xiaoping had named, and in that sense was in dialogue with Deng. Hu Yaobang, who from 1981 to 1987 was formally the highest-ranking person in the Communist Party of China, and Zhao Ziyang, who was in that position from 1987 to 1989, were both known as people who wanted to see a more open China and were at least sometimes willing to listen to suggestions from below. For example, writers in the Chinese Writers Association had long wanted to elect their own leaders, and in 1985 Hu Yaobang allowed them to do so for the first time (and, as it turned out, only time, because Deng had a different view). Push and pull between "reformists" and "conservatives" in the government lasted throughout the 1980s, and democracy advocates in society spent considerable time following events and rooting for the reformists. When students in the Tiananmen protests of 1989 called for "dialogue" with the top leaders, their demand was a long shot, to be sure, but no one found the idea outlandish. Appeal to high officials seemed normal and reasonable.

The 1989 massacre changed all that. No longer was there dialogue, direct or indirect, between society and the top, and news of jockeying between liberal and conservative officials was no longer heard. Those power rivalries seemed to have dissolved into a consensus that the business of officials was to focus on personal and family enrichment. In any case, the liberal officials upon whom people below might pin hopes were no longer there. Zhao Ziyang was under house arrest; Hu Yaobang had died; other reformist officials were either tightly monitored or in exile. Explicit dissidents—Wei Jingsheng, Su Xiaokang, Fang Lizhi, and others—were in either prison or exile. Who now would dare to stand up and criticize the regime or to form even the appearance of an organization that might challenge it? The Chinese idiom that "the bird that sticks its neck out gets its head blown off" had new relevance.

With the rise of the Rights Defense Movement in the early 2000s, the goal of a political transition remained very much alive, but the need to work from the bottom up was clear. Xiaobo began looking around—to Eastern Europe, to May Fourth, to Christian philosophers, and elsewhere—for reference and inspiration. Eastern Europe was attractive because there, after all, were people with experience in coping with repressive communist regimes. Vaclav Havel from Czechoslovakia and Adam Michnik from Poland became especially valuable resources after Cui Weiping translated a collection of Havel's works and followed it with a translation of Michnik's *Toward a Civil Society*.

Havel and Michnik both grounded their thinking in acceptance of the brute fact that the communist political systems in their countries were entrenched and backed by a strong foreign power in Moscow. Hence it made little sense to confront those systems directly; it was much better to look for starting points in the crevices of society, away from the centers of power, in the personal dignity of individuals and the associations of like-minded people. Havel and Michnik both showed how this approach could work. "Charter 77" in Czechoslovakia and the Solidarity labor union in Poland were two of its results.

Havel advised his fellow citizens to try to set aside the smothering power at the top of society and seek to "live in truth" in daily life, on the ground, where there was space "to approach life differently." When people maintain their personal dignity in daily life, they undermine the power of the controlling state and gradually hollow it out—and the hollowing eventually makes systemic change more possible. Chinese readers of Havel were heartened to learn that in Czechoslovakia, something as simple as the assertion of a rock 'n' roll group's right to sing eventually produced regime collapse. Similarly, Michnik asked his fellow resisters in Poland to speak directly to the public, not to the rulers of the state; to abandon the jargon of the state and speak in everyday language; to seek rights, not power; and to aim at building a society, not at toppling a regime. Any person, in any location, could begin such work.

Of course no state-run press in China could publish books by Havel or Michnik, but Cui Weiping's translations spread widely on the Internet and had a major influence on the Rights Defense Movement. A focus on daily life, common sense, decentered efforts, and gradual progress became a trend in the liberal camp of Chinese intellectuals. Xiaobo used Havel's and Michnik's ideas in his own writing. He urged his compatriots "to live an honest life in dignity" (from Havel) and to "start at the margins and permeate toward the center" (from Michnik).[2]

Looking back at May Fourth, intellectuals took new interest in the gradualist reformers of the day, especially Hu Shi, who studied at Columbia University in the late 1910s with the American pragmatist philosopher John Dewey and was hugely influential at the time in his advocacy of writing the Chinese language in a modern, Western-influenced mode. Hu advocated democracy for China but favored a gradual, "drop by drop" approach. He was China's ambassador to the United States from 1938 to 1942, president of Peking University from 1946 to 1948, and in 1949 followed the Nationalist government to Taiwan. Mao Zedong denounced him harshly in the 1950s, and intellectuals on the mainland were obliged to ignore him as long as Mao was alive. Beginning in the 1990s, though, as his liberal ideals and gradualist reformism were making increasingly good sense for China, his reputation saw a major resurgence.

In 1996, when the historian Zhu Xueqin compared the "British and American roads to democracy" with the more violent German and French ones, he used a chess metaphor to explain his preference for a gradualist approach like Hu Shi's: "it might be ten years before you first say 'check,' but you do not let a day pass without moving pawns."[3] At Tiananmen in 1989, Xiaobo wrote, the hunger strike had been a reckless move, a rush to say "check" too soon. The students had challenged the tiger, and it had eaten them. Wu Si, the editor of *China Through the Ages*, raised the question of whether the idea of "rights" might be needlessly hard to spread in China because its standard Chinese translation, *quanli* or "power advantage," seemed too foreign, too aggressive. Would not *quanfen*, "power portion," be better? *Fen* has deep roots in Chinese language and is natural in daily usage. *Wo de fen* is easily understood as "my (rightful) part."

For Xiaobo, the changing attitudes among liberal intellectuals coincided with a growing awareness that the middle and the bottom of Chinese society were very much alive. They were not inert "masses" or dull people who needed to be taught what their "rightful parts" of things might be. In an article, "Labor Protests and Political Reform in China," written in May 2002,[4] Xiaobo observed that the locations of protest demonstrations in China were no longer the major cities but remote areas, and the demands of the protesters had shifted as well—from abstract political concepts to immediate questions of food, shelter, and survival. The protesters were overwhelmingly people who were on the losing end of the ever-growing split between rich and poor that the new cutthroat economy was creating. Many were farmers; others were workers in state-owned enterprises.

Xiaobo became interested in new protests by farmers. There had already been a certain tradition of such protests. Farmers in Xiaogang Village in 1978 had independently set up the "household responsibility system" that Deng Xiaoping later appropriated as his own "reform" and allowed to spread to the whole country. (The system was revolutionary because it broke the pattern of the "people's communes," instituted in the late 1950s, by which crops from farmland belonged to the state and were redistributed to farmers according to formulae created by the state.) In 1980, farmers in Yishan county in Guangxi experimented with free election of their village leaders, and again the more liberal-minded leaders in Beijing reacted positively. In November 1987, a meeting of the Sixth National People's Congress passed a Law on the Organization of Village Committees that called for the economic independence of Chinese villages and made it possible for more grassroots activities in villages to move forward. After the 1989 massacre, just when the intellectual spirit in the elite was pressed to a low point, political ferment in Chinese villages continued and increased. Xiaobo could sense this after he emerged from the *laojiao* camp in 1999. In 2001–02 he visited villages in Hebei, Anhui, Guizhou, Sichuan, and elsewhere to learn more.

In 2001, out in a field that belonged to a village called Nining (Muddy) in Anhui province, Xiaobo talked with a farmer who had led some village protests. The man did not want to give his name, but he showed Xiaobo a plan for local self-rule that he had designed. It included a chart of interlocking rights and responsibilities of government offices at the county, township, and village levels. Xiaobo was startled to realize how much more sophisticated this farmer's plan was than anything he had ever seen from an urban intellectual. The farmer had invented a conceptual distinction between "officials' grain" and "people's grain." The idea was that officials could eat people's grain so long as they were doing things for the people. The plan also called for establishing village councils to oversee how well local officials were doing their jobs and to monitor the performance of the county government. The ultimate goal was to establish a national autonomous association of farmers that would supervise central authorities, watching the effects their policies had on villages. The farmer explained all this to Xiaobo and then asked, "If this comes true, will we farmers still be ranked below the city people? Will the household registry system still bind us unmovably to the countryside?"[5] (The household registry system fixes every person's legal residence at a certain address. Unless one finds a way to change the registration, which is not easy, one cannot legally live elsewhere.)

In a 2003 essay, Xiaobo wrote about how officials in Renshou county in Sichuan for many years levied arbitrary and illegal fees on local farmers until one of them, Zhang De'an, led a group to the county government offices to insist, once and for all, that the procedure stop.[6] Xiaobo saw Zhang De'an as a "new hero" in the farmers' movement. The regime always did its best to keep such activities from spreading to other places. But Xiaobo thought it possible that, through "gradual permeation," the activities might someday merge.

In another piece in spring 2003, Xiaobo argued that independence and equality for Chinese farmers would not be possible until they—not the state—owned the land that they tilled, the household registry system was abolished or revised, and the Communist Party entirely withdrew from local elections. The central government's Law on the Organization of Village Committees did not allow final authority to village elections; Party officials above the village level could reject the results.[7]

Workers in large state-owned industries were a parallel case but had different roots. During the Mao years, workers were theoretically the "leading class" in society and heavy-industry workers were the primary examples, but competition in the post-Mao years had caused some lumbering giants of the planned economy to decline and to lay off workers. Worker pensions shrank drastically because of inflation. Falling from honor to poverty, workers felt not only wronged but also betrayed. On March 1, 2002, more than 100,000 workers in Daqing, Liaoyang, and Fushun—major centers of heavy industry in China's northeast—protested in the streets and announced the formation of a provisional independent labor union. They elected representatives to negotiate with the government.

Also in early 2002, workers at an iron alloys foundry in Liaoyang city, Liaoning province, organized a "provisional alliance of laid-off workers in Liaoyang" and elected a worker named Yao Fuxin to be its spokesman. The group sent a delegation to Beijing to expose the deep-rooted corruption at its factory and to complain about the management's underpaying of both wages and workers' severance packages when they were laid off. In March, Yao led demonstrations at government offices in Liaoyang. Authorities arrested him on March 17, and the next day 40,000 workers from more than twenty factories took to the streets demanding his release. Xiaobo, writing about these events in February 2003, called Yao "a new hero for workers" just as Zhang De'an had been for farmers.[8] But in May the regime found Yao guilty of "agitation to subvert state power" and gave him a sentence of seven years in prison, which he served.

As Xiaobo continued hearing about these protests by workers and farmers, he realized that they were much more common than he had thought. The locus of protest in Chinese society had moved. Bringing this insight together with what he had learned from Havel, Michnik, Hu Shi, and others, he began a deep rethinking about the foundations for political reform in China. It was not just intellectual gadflies whose views diverged from the regime's. Many, likely most, ordinary people had different views as well; their criticisms were not political in the same sense as those of the intellectuals. Ordinary people were preoccupied with daily-life human values—livelihood, health, family, fairness, respect—and were indignant when these were violated. They definitely saw themselves as separate from the officials who ruled them. Officials were something like the weather—they were always present, and you had to cope with them, but they were not the same as you.

Xiaobo was gradually adopting the term *minjian,* literally "within the people," to label the exciting new viewpoint he was coming to appreciate. *Minjian* is
a clear concept in Chinese, but not easy to translate. "Popular" comes close. To
the regime, the term means "everything that lies outside the governing system,"
and in this sense is akin to "civil society" in Western parlance. Among people who
are proud to be *minjian,* it also has a clear connotation of "independent." Xiaobo
embraced the term and began to use it as both a noun and an adjective. He referred
to *minjian* views, *minjian* values, *minjian* autonomy, *minjian* forces, and *minjian*
reason. He wrote six articles, published in the first six months of 2003 in *Beijing
Spring,* that traced the rise of the Rights Defense Movement and developed an
ever-deeper analysis of *minjian.*[9]

Xiaobo felt strongly that the progress of China could be measured *only* by
advances at the *minjian* level. China's ruling elite—with foreign analysts in tow—
paid far too much attention to the ins and outs of politics in Zhongnanhai, as if
those were the driving forces in society, but they often were not. This view was
seriously inaccurate.[10] The post-Mao reforms sprang much less from visions
invented at the top than from concessions that the top had to make in order to
stay in control.

Truth telling was at the heart of *minjian* culture. It was what activists in a variety of fields—petitioners, environmentalists, advocates for AIDS victims, people whose houses were condemned to make way for developers, and others—had
been doing for some time. They insisted on telling unwelcome truths. But Xiaobo,
like Havel and Michnik, expanded the principle to ordinary people in daily life.
Anyone—young or old, aggrieved or not, inside the system or outside—was doing
good *minjian* practice whenever she or he stepped outside the regime's accustomed
language to speak plain truth about actual things. This was happening more and
more in the early 2000s. It meant that people could believe one another more than
before and that a speaker of truths could rely more than before on the assumption that a sympathetic audience would be listening. In one essay Xiaobo called
the change "a market depreciation of officialdom and market rise of civil society."[11]
He saw "official talk" losing credibility to "unofficial talk" both in society and
on the Internet.

With this trend, ethical standards different from the regime's were emerging.
Increasingly, Xiaobo wrote, "power resides with officials but moral conscience
with society." Intellectuals, whom the regime sometimes still labeled as "bourgeois liberal elements," were now viewed more as "society's conscience," and books
that the regime banned were for that very reason more sought after. A "popular
moral conscience" focused more on "rights." Moral awareness was not necessarily connected with political dissidence or overarching concepts of democracy, but

it did observe a clear divide between rulers and ruled. Xiaobo correlated this divide with certain other "huge rifts": between ruling power and political legitimacy, between a forced appearance of stability on the surface and social crises underneath, and between authority wielded in the name of the public and the actual public good.[12]

Xiaobo deplored the "huge rifts" but saw them also as opportunities for the Rights Defense Movement. "The rulers will never voluntarily surrender power," he wrote, but the "governing system" can change, and the extent to which it might change "depends importantly on whether *minjian* pressure is strong enough and can maintain itself long enough."[13] The pressure did not have to be organized: "People have their own positions in society and their own agendas, so of course they can and should choose methods that are appropriate for themselves. So long as what they are doing presses toward the same general transition in society, the combined effect of their various efforts will inevitably be greater than that of anyone acting alone."[14] Decentered, unplanned, and not explicitly political, *minjian* activity nevertheless does move the society toward a foundation for constitutional government: "When people feel free to pursue their individual interests and when pursuit of those interests and the diversity in values that the pursuit generates come to be accepted in society, then the *minjian* resources for the growth of constitutional government will be at hand and the social conditions for political change will be mature."[15] What is not planned as a political movement will in the end have functioned as one: "The power that diversification of society generates inevitably will challenge the monopolistic political structure, and the more diversification advances the stronger and more urgent popular demands for political change will be."[16]

In these observations Xiaobo was writing primarily as an analyst, describing processes as they might unfold. But he wrote as well from the viewpoint of an activist, reflecting on what tactics he and his friends should use. He felt that they should avoid rashness and look to progress in increments. In the May Fourth era Hu Shi had advocated "drop by drop" change as the only reasonable way to alter something as huge and entrenched as China's Confucian tradition. That was in the absence of threats from a harsh national government like the Communist dictatorship today, so now it was all the more important to move forward in small steps.

The best course, he thought, was to stake out modest advances, tap popular support for them, use the pressure of public opinion to induce authorities to tolerate them, at least temporarily, and then try to hold the positions until everyone concerned got used to them and they began to solidify as norms. If the authorities did push back, it was best to make a temporary retreat and wait for a later opportunity to advance again. To confront the authorities would be to risk a crackdown that could destroy the tentative progress and even endanger other gains. The essence of this approach was not timidity but wisdom. It was a better bet in the long term.[17] Xiaobo thought of the editors at the little newspapers and the online thought pages of the early 2000s as important examples of how to proceed, even if only "a centimeter at a time."[18]

Three principles that went hand in hand with this incrementalism were nonviolence, openness, and minimal organization. Xiaobo took nonviolence not only as a moral principle but also as the only rational way to engage a cruel and heavily armed adversary. His thoughts on nonviolence had first arisen during the 1989 Tiananmen movement, had drawn much from the Tiananmen Mothers in the 1990s, and had matured during his stay in the *laojiao* camp, where he read about Christian nonviolence, especially Augustine on the use of conscience to resist unjust law. He wrote in 2006: "people have no choice but to deal with tyranny and the suffering that it causes, [but] can respond to hate with love, to prejudice with tolerance, to arrogance with humility, to degradation with dignity, and to violence with reason. Through the power of sincerity and goodwill, victims can take a bold initiative: they can invite victimizers to come home to the rules of reason, peace, and compassion."[19] The "power of sincerity" depended on openness, an element that had special power precisely because it contrasted so sharply with the secretive culture of the regime, which used its opacity to try to make people cower, self-censor, and hide.[20] Openness between one citizen and another could feed a culture of living in truth and build trust. Moreover, it was perhaps the best answer to the regime's opacity. Xiaobo called this "using openness to overcome fear."[21] He admired Martin Luther King Jr.'s famous "Letter from Birmingham Jail," part of which he paraphrased as "one who breaks an unjust law must do so openly, lovingly, and with a willingness to accept the penalty."[22]

Xiaobo was gratified that the Rights Defense Movement was drawing increased numbers of participants but recommended that it continue to have no charter and no administrative structure. A formal organization would immediately make it a target of the regime. Perhaps because the Chinese Communists had themselves emerged from small but tightly organized beginnings, they appreciated why organization was so important. In the work units of the People's Republic, "organization departments" were the core of power.

The movement did have natural "communities" that could, Xiaobo felt, coalesce into organizations if a better time in China were someday to arrive. There were the "communities of the dissidents, the journalists, the scholars, the lawyers, the legal rights activists, the grassroots rights activists, the entrepreneurs, even of the private bookstore owners." They "interacted" through websites, open letters, lectures, and seminars. The result was "an unofficial organization that had no organizational form."[23]

As Xiaobo moved toward his new philosophy of gradualism and dispersion of power, he changed his earlier views about the importance of outstanding heroes—people like Lin Zhao, Yu Luoke, Vaclav Havel, Jesus Christ, Mohandas Gandhi, Martin Luther King Jr., and Dietrich Bonhoeffer. These were all still "moral models," but given current conditions in China, he warned against looking to heroes to lead movements. "We shouldn't expect imposing or charismatic figures to appear," he wrote.[24]

Within the movement, arguments continued over whether activists should be "inside the system" or "outside." Insiders were sometimes afraid of the political taint of associating with outsiders, and outsiders sometimes felt insiders might not be fully trustworthy. Insiders thought outsiders might be competing to establish heroic reputations; outsiders thought insiders might be inured to their privileges and thus not fully independent. People sometimes kept distance from the other side even if their ideas were the same. Xiaobo regretted this rift and consistently did what he could to bridge it.

In 2006 he wrote an elegant article, "To Change a Regime by Changing a Society," in which he pulled together most of his ideas about nonviolent resistance.[25] When he was sentenced to eleven years in prison in 2009, the essay was one of six that prosecutors singled out to illustrate his criminality. It is unlikely that anyone near the top of the regime, where this decision was made, appreciated the remarkable political thought that had gone into it. The phrase "change a regime" on its face may have appeared ghastly to them. The essay concludes with a list of six principles on which the Rights Defense Movement can be effective in transforming Chinese society from the bottom up:

1. Short of attempting to take over political power, the nonviolent Rights Defense Movement can work to expand civil society and thereby provide people with space in which to live in dignity. The movement can help people to change the ways they see their place in society, i.e., no longer to accept living in ignorance and timidity, hardly better than slaves. Wherever the social control of the dictatorship is weak, the Rights Defense Movement can use nonviolent resistance to shrink the space that the government controls and to increase the price that it must pay to maintain its domination within that space. Popular power can grow an inch every time official power is obliged to retreat an inch.

2. Without pursuing a grand program of total societal transformation, the Rights Defense Movement can concentrate on putting freedom into practice in daily life. By changing the ways people think and express themselves in their

everyday dealings with authorities—especially through the growing numbers of rights-defense cases—the movement can foster ethics in society, bring people together, and help people figure out how to cope. The overarching authoritarian structure can remain unchanged while the Rights Defense Movement operates inside its belly, inside countless small environments. For example, the reason senior news reporters Lu Yuegang and Li Datong at *China Youth News* recently were able to defy the state's propaganda system had a lot to do with the health of the small environment at their own newspaper.

3. No matter how strong the freedom-denying power of the regime and its apparatus becomes, each individual person can still attempt to view him- or herself as a free person, i.e., to live an honest life in dignity. In any society governed by dictators, if people who pursue freedom state and practice this ideal publicly, and if they can find ways to act within their immediate daily contexts without fear, then ordinary daily life can become a force that undermines the system of enslavement. If you yourself believe that you have a human conscience and are willing to follow it, then expose your conscience to the sunlight of public opinion and let it shine there for all people to see, especially for the dictators to see.

4. In insisting on the basic principles of liberalism, we must practice tolerance and support plurality of opinion. When people who engage in high-profile confrontation with the regime hear about people who are making different choices, perhaps pursuing matters in more low-key ways, the high-profile people should view the efforts of the low-key people not as errors but as contributions complementary to their own. People who are more confrontational are not necessarily great heroes who are therefore in a position to assign moral blame to others. This kind of aggressive moral blame is different from the regime's aggressive political blame but still far from the kind of tolerance that liberalism calls for. The decision by one person to pay a heavy price for the ideals he or she has chosen to pursue is insufficient grounds to demand that any other person make a similar sacrifice.

5. Regardless of whether a person is working inside or outside the system, or working to change things from the top down or from the bottom up, we should promote everyone's freedom of speech. Even words and actions that are couched in the styles of officialdom, so long as they do not harm the Rights Defense Movement or free speech among the people, should be viewed as potentially positive contributions to our society's transition and should have our full respect. People who favor top-down change should maintain healthy respect for those working from the bottom up. The whole project of finding a way to a successful transition to democracy will be easier if the advocates of "top down" and "bottom up" approach each other as equals and with respect. This sort of tolerance in no way

implies tacit compromise with tyranny or an acceptance of relativism. The Rights Defense Movement should maintain a non-negotiable position opposing all the government's techniques of forcible repression in whatever form, be it by intimidating people, buying them off, forcing them to express agreement, firing them, blacklisting them, or arresting them and charging them with crimes. None of this should be tolerated in the slightest.

6.   We must face squarely, with no illusions, the fact that the dictatorship will be with us for some time. We must do what we can to empower ordinary people rather than pinning hopes on the emergence of an enlightened ruler from within the regime. In the push and pull between the ruling authority and civil society, official policies will change from time to time, but our own unchanging priority must always be to encourage and support the Rights Defense Movement and to protect the independence of civil society. Especially when sycophants are so many and people who dare to speak against harsh government are so few, we must commit ourselves to criticizing and opposing the dictatorial regime from our position outside its system. When the official attitude is rigid, we should force it to soften; when it is soft, we should pursue the opportunity to expand civil society. While welcoming any enlightened decision that comes out of the system, we must maintain our "outside" position and make no change in our own standards.

In sum, China's road to a free society is going to depend on gradual improvements from the bottom up. It is hard to see any prospect of a top-down democratic transition of the kind Chiang Ching-kuo brought to Taiwan. Change from the bottom up will depend on the growing self-awareness among the people, popular rights-defense actions, and the autonomous, protracted, and ever-expanding pressures that this awareness and these actions place upon the regime. In a nutshell, rather than seek radical change of the regime, flawed though its legitimacy is, and then expect that the abrupt change will lead to a remolding of society, people who are pushing for a free and democratic China should concentrate on gradual change in society and expect that this will eventually force a change in regime.

Xiaobo's thinking about goals and tactics for the Rights Defense Movement was focused on life in China, but during the same years he thought about international questions as well. He took controversial positions and drew criticisms that were sometimes fair, sometimes not. On March 3, 2003, he wrote an essay supporting the invasion of Iraq by the American and British militaries. The Beijing government was quick to paint him as a U.S. lackey, and intellectuals on China's "new left" piled on. But to see Xiaobo as enamored of either war or imperialism is simply wrong. His views on the Middle East originated in the shock of

9/11. Despite his reputation for unfailing eloquence, that disaster left him temporarily inarticulate. "Hideous! Unimaginable!" he wrote. Then:

> This is hard to put into words. My only thought is to donate blood to the victims. I want to sign up with the antiterrorists. . . . I want to turn my life into a rescue ladder that unfolds from the sky and reaches down toward those people trapped in the upper stories [of the twin towers] crying for help. I want those despairing innocents to see beyond the thick smoke that blocks them from the sunlight and to see the blue skies over Manhattan again![26]

Looking at 9/11, Xiaobo did not see politics, nationality, or East and West. He saw victims. He saw people taking losses they could not recoup. He used the same lenses to look at China.

The next day, September 12, Bao Zunxin, Xiaobo, and twelve others wrote an open letter to the American people saying that "This is not a clash of cultures or a battle of nations; it is evil attacking life, freedom, and peace. It is an inhuman crime inflicted on ordinary innocent people . . . it is insane murder. . . . As we gaze through our tears at the smoldering ruins, we feel only empathy—that our own family has been lost and that our civilization is in peril."[27] Echoing John Kennedy's famous pronouncement in Berlin in 1963, "Ich bin ein Berliner," Xiaobo and his friends ended with, "Tonight, we are all Americans." Liu Xia seldom signed Xiaobo's statements and open letters, but she signed this one.

Xiaobo and his friends had not thought much about Iraq until the American and British governments drew the world's attention to it. They saw Saddam Hussein as a political cousin of the dictators who dominated them in China. Silencing opponents? Secret police? Disappearances? Political prisons? Murders? They knew what an unfettered dictator could do.[28] Life in China had given them a strong foundation for empathy with Iraqi victims. People who grew up in free societies might not so easily feel this way, but to Xiaobo and his friends it was visceral. A blow against Saddam was not only right in principle but also satisfying vicariously. In 2003 Vaclav Havel, Adam Michnik, and others from Eastern Europe also supported the effort to topple Saddam. They too needed no instruction in how tyranny feels.

In a group of articles written in late 2005 and early 2006, Xiaobo criticized the West, especially its romantic socialists on the left, for not seeing dictators for what they are. How could Western intellectuals in the 1930s have been enamored of Stalin? Why, also in the 1930s, did the free nations of Britain and France compromise so easily with the dictatorial machines in Germany and Italy? After World War II, why did the free countries, the United States and Britain, concede so much to the autocratic Soviets? In the 1960s and 1970s, how could leading European intellectuals catch "Mao Zedong fever," and how could it have had such staying power?[29] One anecdote from a Vaclav Havel essay written in 1984 left a deep impression: a young French student had approached Havel and told him "with a sincere glow in his eyes, that the Gulag was a tax paid for the ideals of socialism and that Solzhenitsyn is just a personally embittered man."[30] No amount of clear evidence from places as diverse as the Soviet Union, Eastern Europe, China, North Korea, Vietnam, and Cuba could alter the opinion of Western disciples of socialist theory. The intellectual mirage of ideal communism was impervious to decay.

To Xiaobo, the claim of the romantic left in the West that they were speaking for ordinary people—the downtrodden, underdogs, "the masses"—was especially galling. In fact, they were doing the very opposite: siding with those who oppressed underdogs. He could understand that they went to the Soviet Union and China with blinders on—put there by the host regimes—and therefore might not have known about things like political executions or world record-setting famines. But it was clear that at least sometimes, they did know yet remained silent. The allure of a romantic ideology, comfortably enjoyed inside the salons of free societies, distant from actual suffering, was apparently too strong to resist. Xiaobo names George Bernard Shaw, Romain Rolland, and Lion Feuchtwanger, among others, as part of the romantic left. Characteristically, he names himself as well. He blames himself for praising Sartre during his "dark horse" years in the late 1980s. Sartre had visited both the Soviet Union and China in the 1950s and had come back praising their communist governments. To Sartre this might have felt like supporting the subaltern—two "socialist" governments that the West treated as pariahs—but, Xiaobo wrote, those governments only made cynical use of Sartre's pronouncements by using them to show to their own oppressed people that communism had "friends all around the world" and this was one more reason everyone should be content and thankful.[31]

People on China's "new left"—Wang Shaoguang, Cui Zhiyuan, Wang Hui, and others—were often at odds with Xiaobo and the liberals. They agreed in deploring China's huge and ever-growing gap between rich and poor and the corruption and crony capitalism that led to it, but the two groups differed on what to do about these conditions. The liberals favored constitutional government and democracy; the new left favored a move back toward Mao—or, more precisely, toward a rosified view of Mao as seen from a distance. Xiaobo wondered how anyone who knew better could do so. What drew the new left to join the romantic Marxists of the West? Why be "Eastern students" of Western academic trends if it meant looking past the painful realities of one's own society? Why abandon clear language for the impenetrable jargon Western academics were using? To Xiaobo the most unmoored of the new left Chinese intellectuals were the ones who lived in the West, enjoying its freedoms and comforts while concentrating their criticisms on Western civilization, the very "angels that were protecting them." They knew that Western academics and the Beijing government both approved of what they were saying, and that gave them, in a material sense, the best of both worlds. Why should they think any deeper? Xiaobo could only part company with them.[32]

Some on the new left blamed Xiaobo for endorsing the American government's deception of the world on the question of whether Saddam Hussein had weapons of mass destruction. The charge is unfair, however; Xiaobo did not know about the deception when he wrote his anti-Saddam articles, around the time when 77 percent of the U.S. Senate (including future Democratic presidential candidates) voted for the Iraq war. When American politicians on the scene could not see the problem in advance, it is unfair to expect Xiaobo, in Beijing, to have seen it.

Xiaobo's growing sympathy for underdogs appeared again in September 2004 when he learned that 326 people, more than half of them children, had died in the breaking of the siege of a school in the town of Beslan in North Ossetia in Russia. He wrote that "after the night of 9/4, I am a Russian."[33] His feelings of solidarity with victims, especially innocent and defenseless ones, undergirded his embrace of universal human rights.

16

Stability Maintenance

After Xiaobo's six-hour interrogation on the night of December 13–14, 2004, he was put under house arrest until December 31, when, at midnight, his minders withdrew, declaring "the new year." The words did not sound like a new year's wish, however, and the reason they were delivered at precisely 12:00 is likely that the Ministry of Public Security's Department of Protection of Domestic Security, commonly referred to as *guobao* (state protection), had not yet issued orders on what to do with Xiaobo beginning at 0:01 a.m. on January 1. No one doubted that his monitoring, which had begun the moment he left the *laojiao* camp, should continue, but police always needed formal instructions before doing anything.

The unit that monitored Xiaobo had been around since May 2000, when the central government created a "Small Group to Lead Work in Maintaining [Political] Stability." In the months that followed, "stability offices" were set up at every level of government, right down to rural villages and to neighborhood committees in cities. Two years later, in 2002, the Chinese term *weiwen* (support stability) first appeared in the *People's Daily*. This mirrored the term *weiquan* (support rights) that the Rights Defense Movement was using.

During the early 2000s Xiaobo had seen many examples of *weiwen* being applied to *weiquan* people—Yang Zili, Xu Wei, Liu Di, Du Daobin, Sun Dawu, and many others—including, of course, himself. But the well-known cases were still only a tiny corner of what the system was suppressing. The bulk of *weiwen* work was to handle "masses incidents." In Communist jargon, "masses" means "people below"—the ones who are ruled. There don't even have to be a large number of them in order for the word "masses" to apply. "Masses incidents" include rallies, demonstrations, marches, sit-ins, strikes, traffic blocking, building seizures, road blockages, and so on, carried out by farmers, workers, miners, petitioners, and others. If a masses incident is large enough that police are needed to suppress it, the public security bureaucracy keeps a record of it. In 1993 there were about 8,700 masses incidents in China, and by 2005 that number had risen tenfold to more than 85,000 annually, or more than 200 per day.[1] The Ministry of Public Security stopped publishing statistics after 2005.

Weiwen included the entire system of police, courts, jails, labor camps, and related apparatus, including the *guobao* surveillance system that watched Xiaobo. (The term *guobao* refers both to workers in the system and to the system itself.) The duty of *guobao* is to *shanggang* (stand sentry). This is a military metaphor. In wartime, *gang* is a mound of earth that a scout climbs up onto (*shang*) to get the best view of enemies approaching from any side. It is implicit in the metaphor that regime critics like Xiaobo are enemies who need to be monitored twenty-four hours a day—from "above," as it were. The intensity increases when important meetings or important foreigners are nearby, "sensitive" anniversaries arrive, or anything else puts the regime's nerves on edge. In extreme cases an "alarm" is announced and monitoring becomes supertight.

Guobao have two basic functions: monitoring people when they are at home and following them when they go out. For Xiaobo, the monitoring was more irritating than the following. Two *guobao* were permanently assigned to him, and part of their job was to keep him apprised of what their superiors expected (which usually meant what activities he should not attend) and to issue him warnings if he disobeyed. The little reception station outside Xiaobo and Liu Xia's building was converted into an informal police station. From a glass window in its side, police could observe everyone who entered or left the building.

When political times were sensitive, between four and eight additional police were assigned to Xiaobo, and when "necessary" they would enter his building and sit in its first-floor corridor or even go up to the fifth floor and sit outside Xiaobo and Xia's apartment door, ready to block Xiaobo if he tried to exit. In such times no visitors of any kind, including Xia's apolitical friends, were allowed in. The telephone and computer connections to the outside were cut. Sometimes the blockage was only one way: Xiaobo and Xia could make telephone calls out, but no calls could come in. (The main point was to make it hard for international journalists to get comments on events.) Telephone and e-mail messages in both directions were monitored. It often happened that when Xiaobo arranged by telephone or e-mail to meet with someone, a policeman would come bounding up from the reception station to warn him not to meet or talk with that very person. This response was almost automatic if the conversation had been with an international journalist or anyone from an embassy.

The *guobao* duty to follow commences as soon as the watched person leaves home. There are two kinds of following, "covert" and "overt," and they operate on different principles. In covert following, the watched person is supposed to have no idea he or she is being watched. The goal is to gather information on where a person goes, whom he or she associates with, and, if possible, what is said. In overt following—which became much more common beginning in the 1990s—police make obvious what they are doing. The intention is to intimidate the target—to let the person know that they are being watched all the time and should be careful.

Neither Xiaobo nor Liu Xia drove a car, but they did hire taxis and ride in friends' cars, and when that happened police vehicles were reliably right behind. Sometimes a motorcycle followed too. Motorcycles could, presumably, be more nimble if there were a chase. Sometimes the *guobao* compelled Xiaobo to ride in their police car. They didn't charge him, but that was little comfort. When they arrived at a destination, if it was the home of a friend, the police would sit in their cars or outside the door of the building; if it was a restaurant, they would often come in and sit at a nearby table, ordering their own pot of tea or whatever.

Xiaobo did not write much about his adventures with *guobao*, but he had great fun telling stories about them. One story, from 2006, was about going to see the renowned artist Ai Weiwei at a restaurant in Beijing that Ai and some of friends owned and that Ai had playfully named Qu nar? (Where ya goin'?). Xiaobo arrived in a police car. Ai recalled seeing the car stop at the door and Xiaobo get out, with two cops following, and thinking, *Pretty nifty!*[2] That was before the police started giving Ai his own close surveillance.

One night Xiaobo and Liu Xia went to Wang Shuo's home for dinner. They were having trouble finding a taxi, and the night was cold, so they decided to take public bus number 830 across town. This created a problem for the *guobao* who had to follow them. Their team that night had an Audi, a Volkswagen Santana, and a motorcycle at their disposal, but they were supposed to follow a public bus. When the bus reached a stop, two unmarked cars queued up behind it. At the next stop, they queued again. The bus driver noticed and was irritated. He jumped from his seat and went back to pound on the Audi and yell, "Hanh?! A road as wide as this and you have nowhere to drive but on my tail?" He hopped back into his seat, drove to the next stop, and noticed the cars still tailing and again pulling up behind him, so hopped out again and went back to scream at them again. This delayed the bus along its route. But it was not the role of *guobao* to second-guess orders from above.

The *guobao* watching Xiaobo's residence sometimes continued their vigil even if they knew he was out of town. They were to watch his residence until they were ordered not to. At the end of 2001, Xiaobo and Liu Xia moved from Wanshou Road to their new apartment at Seven Sages Village. In February 2002, George W. Bush came to Beijing, and extra police details were assigned to watch Xiaobo. They stood sentry at Wanshou Road, apparently not knowing that the family had moved. As it happened, Xiaobo and Liu Xia had allowed friends to live in their Wanshou apartment, and the friends had invited two young nannies to live there too. The police, startled by the presence of strangers, brought the nannies into the police station and interrogated them at length about Liu Xiaobo—whom they had never heard of.

Guobao are fundamentally different from thought police like the ones who worked on Xiaobo's psychology when he entered Qincheng Prison. *Guobao* give orders, watch, obstruct, and report, but do not try to get inside the heads of the people they are assigned to. Many are not very well educated and would be poorly qualified to argue with intellectuals on topics like constitutionalism even if they were to try. They sometimes develop casual, even cordial relationships with the people they watch. Their pay is modest at best, and they sometimes open up to the people they watch about their problems with money or work schedules. The watched sometimes sympathize, and *guobao* sometimes express respect, even admiration, for the watched. Xiaobo got to know some of his *guobao* fairly well. He once observed that after all, he spent more time in their company than with some of his friends. When the political pressure was relatively mild, he and his *guobao* could negotiate compromises. On one occasion an especially exciting soccer match was to be broadcast on television, and one of Xiaobo's *guobao* wanted to go home to watch. He asked if Xiaobo could agree to stay home voluntarily that night and not cause any trouble so that he, the *guobao*, could have the night off. Xiaobo was a soccer fan. He understood. "Sure, go home," he said.

Guobao often need to switch back and forth between two different attitudes toward the people they watch. In one role they chat and joke; in another they *shanggang*. The two ways of thinking correspond to two different registers of *guobao* language. Most of the time, in speaking with their charges, they use ordinary language. But when they need to put on their police hat and represent the Communist Party, they revert to a hard, official-sounding voice. Xiaobo liked to challenge police by asking them to show their IDs. He knew that this would oblige them to switch to official jargon language, but Xiaobo, who had plenty of experience with that, knew that he could out-talk them there.

"To restrict the personal freedom of a citizen without legal authority is illegal," he would say.

The answers were always something like: "These are orders from our superiors. We are carrying out orders. We have no choice."

"Who are your superiors?" Xiaobo would ask. "There must be someone who gives the order, no?"

This parry often stymied the *guobao*. They had nothing to say and would change the subject. Xiaobo would stop too. To press further might elicit nervous outbursts like "Don't tell us about the law!" or some other imperative whose purpose was to remind Xiaobo who would have the upper hand if push were to come to shove. "We *are* the law" was implied.

A common device that *guobao* use in "justifying" their interventions is to say that they are "caring for" or "protecting" the watched person. In 2005 the French embassy was planning a send-off party for Paul Jean-Ortiz, a French diplomat who was leaving Beijing for a post in Hanoi. Xiaobo was invited to the party. A swarm of plainclothes police blocked him in the corridor of his building as he set out.

"You can't go," they told him.

"Why not?"

"Jean-Ortiz is number two in the embassy—a high position—and people from our country's Foreign Ministry will be there. If you were to run into them at the party, that would not be so good."

Xiaobo persisted. Exactly what would "not be so good"? Why should the attendance of someone else mean that his invitation was not valid? But reasoning at that level was beside the point. The government did not want Xiaobo to be there and did not want to say so, so it employed the far-fetched elocution of protecting everyone, including Xiaobo himself.

Particular events like a diplomatic party could bring limits to the freedom of particular dissidents. Meanwhile, at a more general level, there were shifts in how all dissidents were treated depending on broader political conditions.

For example, on January 17, 2005, Xiaobo arose late. This was normal. He usually worked late at night and into early mornings. When he pushed his door open he found several *guobao* squatting right outside, in the corridor. The police would not explain why. Xiaobo went back inside, opened his computer, and saw that Zhao Ziyang, the former General Secretary of the Communist Party who had been purged for being too soft on the student protesters at Tiananmen in 1989, had died at 7:00 a.m.

Within a few days in spring 1989, Zhao had fallen from highest-ranking Party leader to permanent house arrest in an elegant old Beijing courtyard. The address was no. 6 Fuqiang (wealth and power) Alley. Armed soldiers stood sentry at the door around the clock, and rolls of barbed wire were arrayed atop the compound wall. No unapproved person was allowed in. Only family and a very few former subordinates and friends from his hometown could see him. He spent his time reading, reflecting, and keeping notes that later were published as *Prisoner of the*

State: The Secret Journal of Premier Zhao Ziyang.[3] His star rose in public opinion during his fifteen years of house arrest, especially after people could see more clearly the corruption that had brought huge unearned wealth to other elite Communist families during those years.

Aware of Zhao's improving reputation, the regime saw his death as a danger. History had its lessons. On April 5, 1976, a large demonstration had taken place after the passing of Premier Zhou Enlai three months earlier. Zhou, although no liberal, was widely seen as far more humane than Mao Zedong. In spring 1989 the Tiananmen demonstrations also had been sparked by the death of a top leader for whom the public had warm feelings: Hu Yaobang, who had been Zhao's partner in reform. Might Zhao's passing trigger demonstrations too? To the regime, the possibility apparently was frightening. At least sentry work, if not something heavier, was imperative.

Zhao Ziyang's family set up a mourning altar inside their home and persuaded the authorities to allow visitors to enter and offer tributes. Fuqiang Alley was packed with so many overt plainclothes police that any visitor had to know his or her presence was being noted. Nevertheless, many came. On January 19 more than a thousand appeared. Xiaobo and other "sensitive" people, including Ding Zilin and Jiang Peikun, were blocked at home. Liu Xia was allowed out but followed constantly as she went to the market and to have a meal with her parents. Xiaobo could make telephone calls, but they kept getting cut off. He noticed that the regime seemed to have new technology. Whenever a sensitive term like "June Fourth" was pronounced on the phone, it went dead—automatically!—and he had to redial.

Xiaobo's tight house arrest for the Zhao Ziyang death lasted twelve days. During that time two police cars were always parked inside the courtyard of his apartment building, about ten yards away from the door. Five or six police were always on duty. The other residents of the compound found the police presence strange and were relieved when they learned that the purpose was only to monitor Xiaobo. After Zhao's memorial service on January 29 the police reinforcements disappeared.

Although the regime could not have known it, to oblige Xiaobo to stay home for twelve consecutive days might have been counterproductive to their own interests, because during those days he produced twelve articles, nine of which were about Zhao Ziyang. The weightiest, "The Sorrows of Zhao Ziyang and Hu Yaobang," was a piece Xiaobo had started in 2001 and had been struggling with on and off ever since, trying to get it just right.[4] The others bore titles like "Better to Break Through the Murk Than to Wait for the Dawn," "Remember Ziyang," and "The Miracles Wrought by Zhao Ziyang."[5]

FIGURE 16.1 Liu Xiaobo, Ding Zilin, and Jiang Peikun in 2005.

Zhao Tingjie

The burst of writing productivity was stimulated in part by a barrage of requests from editors in Hong Kong, the United States, and elsewhere who were eager to know what he thought of Zhao Ziyang. Even in normal times, though, Xiaobo wrote incessantly. He sometimes got a sore back from sitting at a computer too long and needed massages from Liu Xia to recover. He wrote brilliantly, on a wide variety of topics in politics, history, literature, and philosophy both East and West, but not all his essays are of the same quality. Some were rushed, and he sometimes borrowed from things he had written before.

Essays that appeared in a flurry were not necessarily the more superficial ones. Xiaobo mulled large questions and sometimes wrote about them years later. When editors asked Xiaobo for instant analyses of Zhao Ziyang, he drew from a deep well. He had been coming to the view that the regime's "reform and opening" policy had harbored an ambiguity right from its beginning in 1978. Was the original goal to pave the way for a more democratic political system or to offer concessions aimed at preserving the authoritarian system? The divergence between Zhao Ziyang and Deng Xiaoping in spring 1989 was an outgrowth of that very question. Zhao was more tolerant of the student protesters not just from principles of kindness but also because he thought they were going in the right direction. Deng did not. Zhao welcomed the popular outrage over corruption in 1989 not just because corruption is a bad thing but because the outrage itself was helping to push the society in the right direction.

Xiaobo's retrospection on Hu Yaobang was also taking a turn in the early 2000s. When Hu died in 1989 Xiaobo had thought that to make such a big fuss over the death of a "heroic" Communist leader reflected a servile mindset. But fifteen years later, he saw Hu Yaobang as someone who all along had wanted to bring fundamental political change to China. In the late 1970s, Hu's campaign to "reverse verdicts" on political victims of Mao had been not just humanitarian relief but a blow against the Maoist system of political stigmatization itself; his support for Democracy Wall was actually a courageous claim that the political system should be making room for public dissent; and his advocacy of a "publications law" for China was aimed at institutionalizing the right of free speech. In short, Xiaobo's twelve articles in twelve days after Zhao Ziyang died were feeding from aquifers in which ruminations such as these had long been flowing.

In the months after Zhao Ziyang's passing, Xiaobo's elbow room for action swelled and shrank like an accordion as unrelated events in society came and went. The contraction triggered by Zhao's death was followed by an expansion with the arrival on February 9 of Spring Festival, China's premier holiday, when many Chinese people go home. Xiaobo was allowed to visit friends and go to the home of Liu Xia's parents. State television at the time was broadcasting a drama, *The Great Emperor of Han* (referring to Han Wudi, 156–87 BCE), that carried not-so-subtle comparisons to the great potentates of the present. Xiaobo was incensed. This was nothing but great-power chauvinism, fed to the viewing public in the form of saccharine pseudo-history. He wrote a few articles about it, in one of which he pointed out that Han Wudi had castrated the historian Sima Qian for daring to write unbiased history. The television drama, Xiaobo wrote, amounted to spiritual self-castration.

The accordion closed on Xiaobo again in early March, not because of his broadside against Han Wudi but because the annual "two meetings" of China's on-paper legislatures were arriving. While five thousand delegates were again gathering to approve everything the Communist Party was doing, the people who had honest differences of opinion with the government—he and others—were confined to house arrest "so that the meetings would go smoothly." The regime found itself stretched thin, because by then there were too many "dangerous elements" and not enough staff to do the watching. To bridge the gap, the authorities began hiring rural migrants who had come to the city looking for work. Paid about 100 yuan per person per day, six or seven of them were assigned to each "dangerous element." They had virtually no idea whom they were watching or why and for that reason were not very efficient; but there were so many of them that it remained quite impossible for any dangerous element to think of slipping past them. They were not assigned to Xiaobo, because he was superdangerous among the dangerous. For him, only regular police would do.

The two meetings ended on March 16. The weather was warming and spring was in the air. But the accordion did not pull a bit open again right away. Condoleezza Rice, the new American secretary of state, was on a six-nation tour of Asia and set to arrive in Beijing on March 20. A special police detachment showed up at Xiaobo's door that morning; the chief explained that he and the others would be staying about three days while this important foreign political figure was in town. So Xiaobo wrote an article asking why, whenever a high-ranking U.S. or European politician or human rights official showed up or there was a meeting of Asian nations, he had to be immobilized. Did the authorities suppose that dissidents had some kind of supernatural power enabling them to stand outside the Great Hall of the People and control talk that went on inside it? The Rice visit came shortly after Western countries and the UN had finally made some progress in pressing China's authorities to release, or at least to acknowledge they were holding, fifty-six political prisoners. So why had the regime begun marching in the opposite direction—doing more detentions—during Rice's visit? That fact, in Xiaobo's view, showed not only the hypocrisy of the Chinese authorities but also how Western governments were willing to set aside their self-presentations as human rights defenders when the commercial interests of their business communities were at stake. Since China was a vast potential market, other countries did not want to risk embarrassing "the Chinese." France and Germany had recently urged the European Union to cancel its ban on arms sales to the Chinese government, Xiaobo noted.[6]

For the two months between late March, when Condoleezza Rice left, and late May, when the supersensitive anniversary of June Fourth was approaching, the political atmosphere warmed. Xiaobo had a bit more freedom, and his friends took the opportunity to see as much of him as they could. On April 23, a group that included Hao Jian, Cui Weiping, Liu Di (the stainless-steel rat) and others invited Xiaobo for a trout lunch in Changping, north of Beijing. Spirits were high and no conversation topic was off limits. After lunch, strolling and chatting in the fine weather, the group seemingly lost track of where they were wandering until they found themselves near the gate of Qincheng Prison. They decided not to go in, but Xiaobo and Liu Di, both of whom had served time inside, posed, giggling, for a photo on the outside. The group then moved on as Xiaobo mocked himself. "Look at me," he said, "either inside a prison or walking a road that leads to one."

His friends laughed, but then counseled him not to crack jokes like that. "It's bad luck." A bit too close to not being a joke.

House arrests of dissidents on anniversaries of the June Fourth massacre normally last about two weeks, from a week before June 4 to a week after. For round-number anniversaries—tenth, twentieth, etc.—the span is wider and the monitoring closer. 2005 was not a round-number year, but "normal care" for June Fourth activists like Xiaobo and Ding Zilin—as well as for anyone in the Tiananmen Mothers group; anyone who had spoken publicly of losing family, suffering wounds, or having seen certain things on the night of June 3–4, 1989; and any intellectual who had recently expressed in public an opinion different from the government's—was forced confinement at home. Telephone lines were tapped and were set to reject incoming calls.

The regime sometimes brought dissidents on "required vacations" to get them out of Beijing at sensitive times, but Xiaobo and Liu Xia were never afforded this special treatment. When they did travel outside the capital, a surveillance net followed. In summer 2005, when Liu Lu, a friend in Qingdao, Shandong province, invited them for a visit, the first move of the Qingdao police was to negotiate in advance with Liu Lu: if he would guarantee that Liu Xiaobo gave no university lectures and didn't get in touch with any democracy movement people, they would promise not to give any trouble.[7] The agreement was made, but the police still watched Xiaobo and Liu Xia continuously, even when they went out to the seacoast at 2:00 or 3:00 a.m. Liu Xia had made grotesque dolls with pained, grimacing faces that she liked to place upon the craggy rocks on the shore. It was her way of expressing her inner feelings.

On trips with more than one destination, police in the several cities would hand Xiaobo and Liu Xia from one to another like a baton in a relay. By tapping phones the police knew their itinerary and which trains they would be taking. It was all very mechanical. The police teams left one another alone.

In October 2006, Xiaobo and Liu Xia toured the lower Yangzi River area. They stopped first in Hangzhou, where they visited Wen Kejian, a young man they had met on the Internet three years earlier and found very impressive. Wen, a brilliant high school student from the nearby city of Yiwu, went to college in Shanghai, studied international trade, and found work that brought him on trips to Southeast Asia and Hong Kong. There he discovered uncensored Chinese books and magazines and loved them. He attended a June Fourth anniversary observance in Victoria Park in Hong Kong—famous for always having the largest annual memorial of the massacre—and his eyes opened to a whole new way of seeing recent Chinese history. Back in China he began to write incisive commentary for the independent website Teahouse for Any Talk and later opened his own site, Spring Thunder Action. He joined Chinese PEN when Xiaobo took over as president in 2003, and whenever he went to Beijing, made a point of visiting Xiaobo and Zhang Zuhua. He regarded them as the leaders in the elder generation of China's democracy pioneers.

Xiaobo and Liu Xia had a fine time with Wen Kejian in Zhejiang, but the group noticed that a car with Jiangxi license plates (not local ones) kept following them. One day they went to Qiandao (thousand island) Lake to ride in a speedboat. Wen Kejian's son came along. The boat they rented was, by chance, the last one available that day, and this created a problem for the trailing *guobao*. They consulted. Then their leader walked over to Wen Kejian and asked if a "representative" of his group could ride along in the speedboat. Wen asked Xiaobo's view, Xiaobo said fine, and so the boat sped off carrying three adults, one child, and one representative. After the ride Wen brought his group to a rural eatery where they had lunch, a large Qiandao fish plus a dish of pumpkin shreds. The latter was a local specialty so delicious that they asked for a second order. When Wen Kejian went to pay the bill, the manager told him it had already been paid by the people at the other table. The *guobao* may have calculated that this was fair compensation for the representative's boat ride. Xiaobo remarked that Zhejiang *guobao* obviously had bigger budgets than Beijing *guobao* did. On the drive back to Hangzhou, Wen got lost and couldn't find the entrance to the superhighway. He pulled to the side of the road, walked back to the tailing *guobao* car, and asked, "How about if you guys lead, instead of always following?" The police car led, and everybody got home.

Xiaobo collected such anecdotes and used them to entertain friends, but at a more serious level he found the *guobao* culture disgusting and offensive. How expensive it must be: so many people hired, so much equipment purchased. What a waste of public funds! To watch him alone must be costing many hundreds of thousands of yuan annually. Even worse was the egregious violation of human rights. At one point Xiaobo overheard his *guobao* comment that by now Xiaobo must be coming to accept the surveillance as "normal." Xiaobo flared. "There is no way I will ever accept this uncivilized practice of not treating people as people!"[8] To become accustomed to it was one thing, to accept it as "normal" quite another.

When Chinese officials said things like "human rights in China are better than in the United States," Xiaobo shot back with counterexamples drawn from the rich repertoire of his personal experience. On February 14, 2006, after Liu Zhengrong, an Internet-control official at China's State Council, said the Chinese government was managing the Internet in "the standard international way," Xiaobo used a search for his own name to refute the assertion. "Liu Xiaobo" on Google outside China yielded 528,000 results. On Google.cn it got only 21,000 and on Yahoo.cn 22,900. Baidu.com, China's largest search engine, offered the message "We're sorry. No items related to 'Liu Xiaobo' have been found." Xiaobo pointed out that there were quite a few Liu Xiaobos in China. Could Baidu not find even one of them?[9] In its use of such techniques the regime had, in fact, manufactured a semimystical persona for Xiaobo. People had heard of him, but his cyber-invisibility created the impression of an occult maestro who could accomplish things while out of sight.

The problem of computer security for dissidents was getting worse. The government not only tapped e-mail but also began phishing to try to monitor or even control personal computers. When Skype appeared in 2003, Xiaobo asked friends to teach him how to use it. He took the Skype name LLX, meaning Liu Lao Xia, "old knight-errant Liu"—the same name he had used when he published his dialogues with Wang Shuo. He hoped that Skype would be safer than e-mail but did not know. One never knew.

In November 2006, he joined Zhang Zuhua and Cai Chu (a Chinese poet living in the United States and former vice chair of Chinese PEN) in registering the online magazine *Democratic China* in Alabama as a nonprofit organization. They received a grant from the U.S. National Endowment for Democracy to support the effort. The masthead read "freedom, democracy, human rights, rule of law, and constitutional government." The magazine was open about its goals of strengthening civil society in China and pressing for a transition to democracy. Such a stance of course carried risks for people like Xiaobo and Zhang Zuhua who remained inside China, so they decided not to list those two names as editors. The editors' names were given as Cai Chu and He Lu (What road?), a joint pen name for Xiaobo and Zhang Zuhua.

In his writings in *Democratic China* and elsewhere, Xiaobo frequently used the term *ducai*, "dictatorship," to describe the Chinese government. Other writers used *zhuanzheng*, "exclusive government—authoritarianism" or *zhuanzhi*, "exclusive rule—autocracy," which suggested more continuity with China's premodern government than *ducai,* which was more modern. The Communist Party called the imperial system "feudal *zhuanzhi,*" and intellectuals in the 1980s, including Xiaobo, conceived democratization as the process of breaking out of *zhuanzhi* and leaving it behind. In the late 1990s, the term *jiquanzhuyi,* "extreme-powerism," which has been translated as "totalitarianism," began to appear. It seemed a good choice when importing the ideas of Eastern Europeans like Havel and Michnik or of writers like Hannah Arendt in referring to the German Nazi regime. Havel's "post-totalitarianism" entered the lexicon as well, as *houjiquanzhuyi* in Chinese. Depending on context, all of these words—and Xiaobo did use them all—might be translated as "dictatorship." But Xiaobo had a special preference for *ducai,* which focuses on the single person at the top and carries a flavor of "tyranny" or "despotism." People in the regime cannot have liked the term, which can mean both dictatorship as a system and the dictator who heads it.

Chinese people who were old enough to remember the 1940s could remember how the Communist Party used the modern word *ducai* to criticize the Nationalist government it was seeking to overthrow. In case they did not remember and for the many people who were too young to remember, a reporter named Chen Min, who wrote for the *Southern Weekend* under the pen name Xiao Shu, published a book in 1999 called *Harbingers of History: The Solemn Promises of Fifty Years Ago,* presenting more than a hundred articles from *Liberation Daily, New China Daily,* and other communist newspapers of the 1940s attacking the Nationalists as *ducai* and saying what China needs is democracy.[10] "Oppose dictatorship and bring democracy" was a platform on which the Communists in that era successfully attracted educated people to their cause.[11] One of the pieces reprinted in Xiao Shu's book, a 1946 editorial in *New China Daily* called "One-Party Dictatorship Brings Disaster Everywhere," left an especially deep impression among liberal intellectuals in the early 2000s.[12]

In the war of words in the 1940s, Nationalist newspapers were already calling the Communists dictators. Mao Zedong, instead of rejecting the label, embraced it publicly. On June 30, 1949, in commemoration of the 28th anniversary of the founding of the Communist Party of China, Mao wrote:

> You are right, dear gentlemen, to call us dictators. That's what we are. The experience that the Chinese people have accumulated over the past few decades tells us we must pursue a people's democratic authoritarianism [*zhuanzheng*], or call it a people's democratic dictatorship [*ducai*], if you like; in any case, the point is to deprive the reactionaries of their right to speak and to let the people alone have that right.[13]

This passage from Mao became well known among supporters of the Rights Defense Movement. Li Shenzhi cites it in his powerful article "Bittersweet Harvests from Fifty Years,"[14] which showed how freedom of speech had been much better under the Nationalists than it was under the Communists and invited comparison of the corruption in the Nationalist days with the immeasurably greater corruption that currently beset China. Although Xiaobo used the term *ducai* as early as 1988,[15] he used it much more after reading Li Shenzhi's article, and he used it considerably more than other regime critics did.

It seems clear that he favored the term to underscore the dramatic irony that Xiao Shu and Li Shenzhi had exposed. But another reason may have been that *ducai* has shallow roots in the Chinese language and so might better suggest a new kind of horror. *Zhuanzhi* recalls imperial China and suggests that "we have seen this before." A *zhuanzhi* ruler fits into cultural patterns. But a *ducai* ruler is from the twentieth century; he has no traditional precedents and therefore, in a sense, no limits and can rewrite the rules. Xiaobo felt that calling China's rulers *ducai* drew a sharper line between the aggressive regime and the society it was bullying.

His views that Mao Zedong was a *ducai* and that the Communist political system had not fundamentally changed since Mao entailed the view that his successors were *ducai* as well. He stood by that implication and used the *ducai* label consistently for Deng Xiaoping, Jiang Zemin, and Hu Jintao. When Hu visited France in January 2004, he wrote a piece, "Chirac Panders to the Dictator," in which he refers to Hu as "head of the Communist dictatorship." In April 2006, when Hu visited the United States, Xiaobo produced a train of articles following the *ducai* from stop to stop.

As *ducai* recurred in his writing, it morphed into an adjective. There was *ducai* power, a *ducai* regime, a *ducai* system, *ducai* methods, and so on. In the first half of 2005, Xiaobo wrote a series of seven articles on "Communist extremism" showing how, in its degree of inhumanity, the Chinese Communist regime "far exceeds other kinds of dictatorial regimes."[16] In certain ways its inhumanity should rank even below slave society. Slaves at least were able to live as they served their masters, but at the height of Maoist extremism in China, it was "a primary goal to exterminate the thinking, the livelihood, and the physical well-being of the entire part of the population that was labeled 'class enemies.'"[17]

In October 2005 China's State Council released a "white paper," "Building Democratic Politics in China," in which it proposed to begin with "inner-Party democracy." Xiaobo was furious, but it took him a number of weeks to compose a rebuttal, which finally appeared in January 2006 under the title "Can It Be That Chinese People Qualify Only to Live Under Inner-Party Democracy?"[18] The piece shows how, from Mao through Hu, "the power in government to initiate actions and to decide questions has been held exclusively in the hands of dictators." The word *ducai* appears eight times, and the dictators since Mao are named. Xiaobo was breaking several taboos by writing this way, and he knew it. When the article was published in Taiwan, the regime made no effort to answer it. But when Xiaobo was sentenced to prison for state subversion in 2009, this essay was a featured piece of evidence.

Xiaobo was fascinated by how tenacious China's dictatorship could be amid a society that in some ways was shifting so rapidly. The changes, especially in the cities, were obvious. Skyscrapers, high-speed rail systems, modern hotels, luxury consumerism, and more appeared with rapidity that made jaws drop around the world. At the same time, though, the country remained the world's greatest dictatorship. Beneath its eye-catching twenty-first-century appearance, a moldering nineteenth-century political system, quite unsuited to the modern world, endured.[19] Xiaobo called the paradoxical result "crippled reform" and wrote about how it burdened the nation with four dilemmas:

1. Monopoly management of large enterprises pulls in an opposite direction from market economics.
2. Privatization and emphasis on efficiency pull in an opposite direction from the needs of social justice.
3. Rapid growth of the economy goes hand in hand with rapid growth of corruption.
4. Diversity in society and centralization of political power pull in opposite directions.

Xiaobo stoutly rejected the view that problems like crony capitalism and the glaring wealth gap were inevitable consequences of the economic transition that China was going through. People pointed out that similar problems had attended the rise of capitalism in the West. But Xiaobo argued that China's major economic issues, including these four dilemmas, "arose from the systemic imbalance between a strong state and a weak society."[20] The problems could be ameliorated by a reversal in that imbalance. China's market reforms were born within a system where political power determined who got what, so were distorted from the very beginning. The original accumulation of capital in the West had led to corruption and wealth gaps, but nothing like the grotesque spectacle China was seeing.[21]

The stark contrast between the gleaming exterior and the corrupt core of China's cities had a parallel, in Xiaobo's analysis, with the suave exteriors that

Chinese officials presented and the thoughts that actually occupied their minds. In an essay, "Why Foreigners Can't Understand Chinese Communist Officials," he drew attention to the kinds of people the regime recruited for its middle- and high-level posts. The optimal recruit was a person who had studied in the West, or at least at a Chinese school that used Western curricula. The person had to know English or another foreign language and "should be a person who can switch back and forth easily not only between two languages but between two modes of behavior so that Westerners will not see the level that lies below the surface—the level where they are doing the Party's work, or perhaps pursuing their own private interests, while maintaining fluent language and an urbane bearing on the surface."[22] Foreigners could not understand such people because they had no way of measuring the distance between the surface and the substratum. They did not know what the substratum contained and might not even be aware that it existed.

Hu Jintao, China's top leader from 2002 to 2012, gave many people the impression of a relatively weak leader who was just trying to get through his terms as chief without any major collapses. A fad spread among Chinese intellectuals to describe him as "passing the flower to drumbeat." This referred to a game that resembles "musical chairs" in the West: people sit in a circle and pass a flower, or bouquet, while someone who isn't watching them beats a drum. When the drummer chooses abruptly to stop, whoever is holding the flower at that point drops out. Hu Jintao's only hope, it was said, was not to be the one holding the flower when the regime, for whatever reason, nosedived. Hu inaugurated a system at the top of "collective leadership" by which the nine members of the Party's Politburo, its highest ruling group, each took responsibility for one area of governance (economy, military, foreign relations, etc.) and, so long as no major crisis arose, had final say within that area. To describe this situation, Xiaobo began using the term "oligarchic dictatorship": "The strongman era in which one supreme authority stands above all the bureaucracies is closing, and a new arrangement, in which oligarchs bargain with one another at the top, is arriving. The Politburo is no longer the private chamber of the top dictator but a gaming room in which the competing interests of oligarchs create the limits on the powers of each."[23] In the power game at the top, Xiaobo showed, one oligarch could challenge another by attacking one of their underlings, avoiding direct confrontation. Direct attack would rock the boat of the whole system, and everyone had an interest in avoiding *that* outcome. In the end, "the oligarchic dictatorship forbids the appearance of anything, be it inside the regime or outside, that might threaten overall stability."[24]

For several years Xiaobo had been honing his understanding of the essential nature of China's dictatorship but had written little about it. In early 2006, he decided to address the topic conscientiously and produced a series of articles whose titles are a fair indication of their content:

"A Latter-Day Dictatorship Is Brilliant at Calculating Its Interests" (March 2, 2006)

"The Many Sides of the Chinese Communist Dictatorship" (March 13, 2006)

"The Civilized World Versus the Chinese Communist Dictatorship" (March 15, 2006)

"The Rise of the Chinese Communists and the New World Order" (March 31, 2006)

"Hu Jintao Meets George Bush: No Material Concessions Can Outweigh Their Incompatible Systems" (April 15, 2006)

"The Negative Effects of the Rise of a Dictatorship on Democracy in the World" (April 21, 2006)

"The Constantly Morphing Chinese Communist Dictatorship" (June 7, 2006)

"From a Revolutionary Party to a Party of Material Interests" (August 14, 2006)

"Behind the Rise of a Great Power" (December 27, 2006)

"The Decline of the Chinese Communist Oligarchic Dictatorship" (February 13, 2007)

"The Seventeenth Party Congress in View of the New Characteristics of the Communist Chinese Dictatorship" (July 31, 2007)

"Flexible Responses to the West from the Communist Chinese Dictatorship" (December 10, 2007)

Xiaobo's consistent view was that, from the 1940s to the present, the Communist Party had changed fundamentally from pursuit of revolution and idealism to pursuit of private interests and material values: "The dictatorship is the same, but the inspiration is gone. Practicality has replaced ideals. A mode of governance that puts calculation of interests higher than anything else has replaced political mobilization that was based in utopian enthusiasm. The methods of the dictatorship in calculating its political capital are growing increasingly more clever and fine-tuned."[25] The utility of the Communist Party in the present day, he held, was that it allowed people to use public power to pursue private benefit. What the national government called "Party and state interests" increasingly were "hollow things," because the real interests in play were those of different bureaucracies or localities and, ultimately, different families and individuals. Well-placed persons and families got the lion's share of the booty. Xiaobo cited the case of Li Peng, China's premier at the time of June Fourth, whose family later gained control of China's major public electricity service and, through a number of complicated steps, managed to convert it into their own private company. People began to call it sarcastically "Li family *dian*," where *dian* was a pun meaning both "electricity" (电) and "shop" (店). Li Peng's daughter Li Xiaolin became known as "the electric queen." Jiang Zemin's son Jiang Mianheng got into the information technology business early and, with help from his father's connections, became "big boss man." In 1985 Deng Xiaoping had proclaimed the development strategy of "letting some of the people get rich first," and now the slogan had become protection for the offspring of the superelite to seize and divide up major state resources. China's "high growth" was overwhelmingly in property that now belonged to the superelite. About 95 percent of Chinese competed on a playing field slanted against them and were heavily subsidizing the harvests that the elite were reaping.[26]

How can it be, Xiaobo asks in one article on this question, that a regime that so brazenly plunders an entire society can stay on top of it and maintain at least the appearance of order? He reviews the ways the regime buys off elites—in government, commerce, academe, and elsewhere—by offering tickets to the upper class in return for quiescence. He also reviews in detail how power holders weaponize the law: A can attack B for crime X not because of crime X but because A for other reasons wants to attack B. "Rule of law" becomes the outer garment for rule by persons. In a context where normal professional or commercial work almost requires that the rule of law be broken, potentially lethal blackmail quietly becomes pervasive. Business people give bribes because one has to in order to get certain things done; they avoid taxes because everyone else, including their competition, avoids taxes. Bureaucrats use the power of office for personal advantage; it's what bureaucrats do. Intellectuals are paid to speak and to write, and most of their statements are not judged to be "incorrect," but who knows when, and for what reason, they might be? Under the letter of the law broadly conceived, nearly everyone is guilty. But which individuals will be punished? A gray cloud constantly looms. A multimillionaire this week might be a penniless criminal the next; a movie star today could be in prison next month. No one is secure. The best defense is to stay in line.[27]

In the same article Xiaobo analyzes the ways the regime stifles criticism of itself. Mao Zedong had used noisy, society-wide campaigns for this purpose. Now the regime's techniques are quieter and more targeted. Sparks of dissent are snuffed out as soon as they appear. The ways dissidents are watched, followed, and isolated, their phones tapped and their computers undermined, resemble the methods of the East German Stasi more than those of Mao. But different from both, police now "invite people to tea," counsel them, and pretend to be their friends. They do not preach ideology, as in the past, but focus on the material livelihood of their targets. "You're very talented," police once counseled Wen Kejian. "Look! Your friends are driving Benzes. You could be too." The police pretend to be looking for a better route through life for the dissident and sketch ways to help make it happen. (This is not, of course, the approach of the regime-hired thugs who beat dissidents up. The thugs do not carry the police label. In the regime's language game, they are "someone else.") When dissidents prove incorrigible, the regime pulls out its big guns. It cannot risk that a dissident might attract a following inside China, so prison and forced exile become the options. Forced exile is preferable. It looks better to the international community and, inside China, takes a toll on the moral standing of the dissident (because, as some see it, the true hero stays and fights at whatever cost). The dissidents who remain in China, whether in prison or outside, are kept as tightly sealed from the public as possible. They might be famous internationally, but inside China are "famous" only within a small group.[28]

The rights lawyer Chen Guangcheng, Xiaobo wrote, was a good example of how the regime bottled up incorrigible dissidents. Chen, from a poor farming family in Shandong, lost his eyesight to disease in infancy. Yet bright and irrepressible, he went to schools for the blind and eventually earned a medical degree. He got into human rights work when he noticed that families of the disabled, including his family, were being taxed in ways that the law said they should not be. He brought a petition on this issue all the way to Beijing and won. Gifted with a prodigious memory, he decided to take up law by asking people to read law books to him; then he began to use the law to defend the disabled, poor farmers, and, in cases in 2005 that made him internationally famous, women in his home area of Linyi in Shandong who were victims of methods— forced abortions, arbitrary arrests of relatives, exorbitant fines, and harassment— that local officials were using to enforce the government's policies on limitation of family size.

Chen's success in exposing abuses made him a target for a variety of abusers. On September 6, 2005, while he was staying temporarily in Beijing, officials abducted him and took him to his home village of Dongshigu in Shandong, where he and his family were put under house arrest. The authorities stationed police cars and uniformed officers on the road to his village and hired about one hundred local people to watch him, in shifts, around the clock. He and his lawyers were beaten several times, without even the pretense of legality. A legal case against Chen did follow, though, and on August 24, 2006, he was found guilty of "intentionally damaging property and gathering crowds to disturb transport order" and sentenced to four years and three months in prison. He served the full term and was sent to house arrest afterward. In 2012 he made what seemed a miraculous escape from house arrest, found his way to Beijing with the help of friends, and from there left for the United States, where he has lived safely ever since, but has lost the enchanted following he had had in China.

Xiaobo wrote about many aspects of Chen's story—the injustice, brutality, and utter departure from reason and law. He also estimated its costs. The one hundred local people whose job it was to watch Chen during his house arrest were each paid 50 to 100 yuan per day. His arrest began in September 2005 and ended in March 2006, when he was put into a detention center. So just the cost of paying watchers for those six months came to more than a million yuan. He was held under house arrest again from September 2010 until April 2012. In addition there were all the other costs of the regular police, their cars, the Beijing kidnapping, the tapping of telephones and e-mail, the courts, the beating of supporters and lawyers, and gentler things, like barring Chen's young daughter, Chen Kesi, from going to school. And more. How much, in all, was literally incalculable.

Hu Jintao's ten years at the top in China, from 2002 to 2012, can be thought of as the "decade of *weiwen*." The timid man who hoped not to be holding the flower when the drumbeat stopped did what he could to nip any sign of disturbance in the bud. Xiaobo noticed that he got considerably more police "care" under Hu Jintao than under his predecessor Jiang Zemin. It is hard to estimate the astronomical costs of *weiwen* under Hu, but some of the publicly available government figures show increases during his years of one or even two orders of magnitude. That was when *weiwen* expenses came to exceed even the national defense budget.

17

Observing the World, Growing at Home

While "stability maintenance" was the top priority of the Hu Jintao regime inside China, Xiaobo argued in 2006, "buying friendship" became its first principle in its approach to the world.[1] The Communist Party did not seek to export communism, as under Mao. (It didn't even take communism in an economic sense seriously at home.) Its business model was a crony capitalism that allowed China's power elite to cooperate with foreign capital to exploit China's low-wage labor force. The workers in the new manufacturing boom were largely migrants from the countryside who worked long hours without help from independent labor unions, a free press, or impartial independent courts. They were kept in line by the regime's rules and its police. Western countries and corporations were not ideological opponents of Hu's regime so much as its partners, and sometimes its rivals, in the pursuit of wealth and power. Hu could be flexible with Western countries—cooperating here, opposing there, as the power interests of his regime needed. Western governments, under pressure from their business communities, were willing to appease a dictatorship if there was money to make. Xiaobo cringed to see politicians from democracies stand arm in arm with Chinese dictators.[2]

Whenever top leaders of the regime went abroad there was great pomp on the surface, but underneath, Xiaobo could see, the real purpose on the Chinese side was to buy friends. He called the foreign visits "bank card-swiping tours," and the transaction sums were mind-boggling. After the June 4, 1989, massacre, France had been the Western country with the best record of denouncing the killings and aiding the victims, but when President Hu Jintao went to France in 2004 he card-swiped four billion euros of business; when Premier Wen Jiabao followed in 2005 he card-swiped another 8.3 billion euros for 150 Airbus A320s and signed fifteen other deals with France in finance, rail, energy, and science. Favors of this size were returned by the French government in the form of softened voices, even silence, on China's human rights. In September 2007, the German Chancellor Angela Merkel angered Beijing by receiving the Dalai Lama. Two months later, when French President Nicolas Sarkozy visited Beijing, the regime came up with another 20 billion euros in commercial contracts for him. Xiaobo summed up the contrast as "punishing the candid Merkel and rewarding the slippery Sarkozy."[3]

Xiaobo paid special attention to state relations between China and the United States. He was shocked when he learned that George H.W. Bush, just two weeks after the June Fourth massacre, had violated his own ban on "high-level exchanges" with the dictators by secretly—very secretly!—dispatching two envoys to Beijing "as friends to resume our important dialogue." When the next President Bush, George W., was about to arrive in China in 2002, Xiaobo, fearing that he might go the way of his father, wrote a piece called "Let's Hope Bush, Jr. Shows Self-Respect."[4]

By 2005, however, when "Bush, Jr." made his second presidential visit to China, Xiaobo had arrived at the view that the Chinese and American governments might cooperate on specific issues but at a deeper level would always remain opposed because their systems and their fundamental values were just too different. He was aware that the appetite of Western business for low-wage Chinese labor was a major reason for the West's desire to trade with China. He also understood the U.S. hope that bringing China into the globalizing world would soften the regime because economic progress would naturally lead to demands from Chinese people for democratization. But he was not optimistic that this strategy would work and in January 2006 wrote a piece predicting that the world's leading democracy and the world's largest dictatorship would eventually come to loggerheads.[5]

Xiaobo liked to point out how the Hu Jintao regime, while denouncing the Americans for predicting "peaceful evolution" in China, tried hard to give the impression of peaceful cooperation with American business. In 2006, on the eve of Hu Jintao's visit to the United States, the regime got the visit off to a good start by announcing an order for $16.2 billion in U.S. goods. Americans had been complaining about theft of intellectual property in technical fields, and it was no accident that Hu made Seattle his first stop. He delivered a powerful statement at Microsoft about the sanctity of intellectual property and afterward went to Bill Gates's home for dinner. In Washington, people were concerned about China's government-fixed currency exchange rate, so Hu pledged to make the rate more flexible. Hu and his people kept the focus of the visit on money and markets and safely away from questions about human rights or universal values. Xiaobo wrote: "When America's Boeing company wants to sell more airplanes, of course it lobbies the American government to make concessions to the Chinese Communists; when Yahoo!, Microsoft, Google, and other big Internet companies want to increase their share of China's rapidly growing Internet market, they care not a whit for universal values and the human rights side of American foreign policy."[6] The Hu regime, even while performing its curious dances with the world's great democracies, was doing what it could to aid petty despots around the globe (whom they recognized, while not saying so, as their own kind). He wrote:

> The Chinese Communist regime has replaced the former Soviet Union as the blood-transfusion machine for tinhorn dictators. For years it has offered financial aid to rulers in North Korea, Cuba, and Burma in amounts sufficient to neutralize most of the effects of Western sanctions and to help tyrants struggle along on their wobbly legs. The Chinese Communists have signed numerous agreements on energy and other major projects with the notoriously malodorous regimes in Sudan, Syria, Zimbabwe, and elsewhere. They have begun to use promises of huge investments to attract regimes in South America who show signs of leaning their way. They have used cooperation on energy to forge alliances with Iran and other anti-American countries in the Middle East. They recently concluded an agreement with Iran by which China not only buys Iranian petroleum and natural gas but will invest 100 billion U.S. dollars to develop the Yadavaran oil field in Iran. It is the largest trade agreement Iran has ever signed with anyone. The Chinese Communists have also joined with the increasingly dictatorial Putin regime in Russia to help the clerics in Iran oppose the West on the question of developing nuclear weapons.[7]

The same essay concludes that:

> The only way, finally, to rid the world of the pernicious effects of the rise of the Communist Chinese dictatorship, the biggest in the world, is to help the Chinese people to transition to a free and democratic nation. China is an indispensable key to the larger project of helping the entire world move toward democracy. If China were free, other countries could follow much more easily. While the huge Chinese population remains captive, the Chinese dictators can continue to eat away at all of human civilization. That's why the dissolution of dictatorship in China should be a high priority not only for the Chinese people but also for people everywhere.

The last thing that Hu Jintao wanted, while swiping his bank card around the world, displaying smiles in front of credulous Western politicians, dining with a Microsoft chief, and so on, was a pesky dissident following his movements and articulating a different version of what he was up to. If Hu and his people noticed, they gave no signs at the time, but Xiaobo's most prominent article on the topic, "The Negative Effects on the World of the Rise of a Dictatorship," was one of the six cited three years later at his trial for "subversion of the state."

Chinese Communist rule had always rested in part on an ideology, a set of values that the public could believe in and safely assume that others believed in too. In the 1950s this was socialism. Slogans like "build a new China" and "serve the people" were widely embraced. Twenty years later, though, Mao Zedong's body blows to China—the Great Leap Forward famine and the Cultural Revolution— had destroyed the credibility of socialism as anything more than a language game. Reform and opening in the 1980s had briefly revived the hope for a "new era," but progress was uneven and the June Fourth massacre extinguished that flicker entirely. By the 1990s the regime was searching for something else to substitute and hit upon a primitive kind of nationalism as the best alternative. Using media, education, and the threat of punishment of gainsayers, the regime cast the new nationalism as "mainstream thought," to build support for the Communist Party and to be an antidote to the appeal of the West. Xiaobo was among the first to notice this problem and wrote about it with merciless candor.

He wrote that it was no fault of his fellow Chinese that they had been left in the 1990s with little to believe in. Their thirst for public values was legitimate, and the rousing new nationalism did have its appeal. Moreover, it was contagious. He knew that if he criticized supernationalism he would be asking for a backlash, but he did it anyway. And sure enough, zealots on the Internet were soon crying "Traitor!" "Turncoat!" and "Sell-out!" Xiaobo's friends were concerned for him until they noticed that the vitriol seemed not to bother him. If anything, it was simply confirmation that his analysis had been correct.

In June 2006 he collected his articles on nationalism and published them as a book, *Single-Blade Poison Sword: A Critique of Contemporary Chinese Nationalism*.[8] It would be the last book he would publish before going to prison for the rest of his life. The flyleaf carried a quote from him: "I have never felt the term 'patriotism,' in times of peace, to be worthy of exaltation. The people who huddle under its banner are either scheming politicians or flaming idiots." The book opens by reviewing how China's textbooks stress the country's humiliation during the century 1850 to 1950, when it was both backward and victimized by Western powers and Japan. Xiaobo argues that the feeling of victimhood reached the point of life-and-death fear and eventually generated a powerful urge for reprisal; that urge, in turn, needed the illusion of an outside threat even after actual outside threats were no longer present. In recent times, he continues—when China has grown strong but is not under attack—the reprisal urge manifests as a provocative posture on the international stage and violent language on the Internet.[9] Online hooting is triggered by incidents—some real, some imagined—between China and either the United States or Japan, or incidents that concern Taiwan or Hong Kong. The young supernationalists do not look seriously at the debased conditions they and their fellow citizens endure in China. They look only at their outside opponents: they oppose America, Japan, Taiwan independence, Dalai Lama splittism, and so on. Their superconfident emotion leaves no room to reflect on whether there might be such things as universal values or whether equality among nations might be a good idea.

The regime, having stimulated the nationalist mood, is happy to see its expression flourish even if it includes threats of violence. Whatever the language, it is the effects that matter: to increase support for the regime and to decrease it for the universal values that pull in a different direction. Xiaobo noticed that both the regime and the zealots had two levels: a surface level and another beneath it. China's power elite denounces the West but sends its excess money and its college-bound children there; young zealots might throw eggs at the U.S. embassy during the day (after the U.S.-China air collision over Hainan island in April 2001) but go home to study for the TOEFL (Test of English as a Foreign Language) in the evening.

In 2005, street protests against Japan broke out in several Chinese cities. People were objecting that Japanese textbooks did not look squarely at the facts of Japan's invasion of China in World War II. Xiaobo investigated some of these protests and wrote an article called "Anti-Japan Tempests on Demand."[10] He found that many of the demonstrations, although described in state media as autonomous, had in fact been planned and managed by the authorities. Student protesters had been ferried to the sites in government-supplied buses. When it was time to get back into the buses and return to campus, they were ready to go. The government handed out sheets of "background information" to foreign reporters and allowed them easy access to the scene, while holding Chinese reporters back and telling them they could publish only brief notices that used state-approved language. In other words, the world should know that the Chinese people were very angry at Japan, but the Chinese people should not get the impression that street demonstrations were legitimate. Xiaobo writes in summary that only two kinds of street demonstrations are allowed in China: the gleaming uniformed marches on National Day and the "patriotic demonstrations" like the current ones against Japan, whose participants wear ordinary clothes and might throw stones or overturn cars. The two kinds of demonstration look very different but are both offspring of the regime.

State-sponsored athletics, Xiaobo found, were another arena where nationalism was encouraged. From 2001, when Beijing won the bid to host the 2008 Summer Olympic Games, until 2008 when the Games took place, the regime's propaganda machine ran at full speed to generate patriotism, make it a dominant issue in public consciousness, and associate the accumulated glory with the government. Alternative views were repressed; the goal was to manufacture a unified China that spoke in one voice. The message was projected abroad too, in an effort to rosify the regime's image and raise its prestige. Xiaobo observed that "when a dictatorship hosts a major international competition, it is impossible that it not be political."[11]

The costs of the Games, paid without the approval of the populace from whom the money came, were enormous. The building of elegant stadia and facilities was only the beginning. There were also the vast expenses of preparing athletes to win as many gold medals as possible. In the early twenty-first century the Chinese state was still using the techniques established in the Soviet Union: athletic activities that prepared for international competitions were a monopoly of the state; "athletic committees" at all levels of government controlled resources; the state "took care of" all athletes and coaches; and it was an important political goal to win as many international accolades as possible. It was clear in China between 2001 and 2008 that the number of gold medals at the Olympics would be viewed as a measure of the strength of the state and the vitality of its people. Cost was no concern.

When the time came, the focus of the state media in China was not on athletics, health, or the Olympic spirit, but on a great-power dream. All eyes were on gold medals. National pride was supposed to be at stake, but in Xiaobo's analysis, *national* self-respect was precisely what was missing. The state, in its quest for glory, cared for the Olympic athletes, but how much did it care for the physical health of China's ordinary citizens? When the Games were over, Xiaobo did some calculations. China had spent more than any other country, but the area of athletic fields available to the Chinese public came to 0.006 square meters per capita. Most people could exercise only in parks or at roadsides. Of the 600,000 athletic fields and stadia in China, fewer than 7 percent were open to the public, and all of those were in cities. The concepts of "farmer" and "exercise facility" existed in two different worlds.[12]

The Olympic athletes themselves were making huge sacrifices:

Gold medal obsession obliges China's athletes to pay enormous prices in personal dignity and human relations. For the sake of Olympic gold, they enter government-run sports schools beginning even in childhood, live in special dormitories, are completely cut off from the outside world, and submit to training that is almost military in nature. They not only lose their freedom but must make sacrifices in love and affection as well. Even the love between a mother and daughter cannot be spared. Xian Dongmei, winner of the gold in judo, was the only mother on China's Olympic team. In order to train for the Games, she had to leave her eighteen-month-old daughter and didn't see her for an entire year. Cao Lei, who won the gold in weightlifting, was sealed off even from the news of his mother's death and did not attend her funeral. Chen Yibing, the gymnast who won the gold in the flying rings, was candid in an interview: "You have no control over your own life. The coach is always right there with you. Someone is always watching you, even the physicians and the cooks in the cafeteria. You've got no choice: you have to submit to the training."

The coercion in the centralized sports machine exacts another price from China's athletes: their health. Prospective Olympic divers are selected for training as young as five or six, even though health professionals know that to start diving at this age, before the eyes have fully developed, can do permanent harm. The force of impact when a diver enters the water is enough to damage a child's retina. Gold medalist Guo Jingjing, who had been recruited for the diving team at age six, has sustained serious eye damage. His vision is now so bad that he has trouble making out the diving board and could go blind at any time.[13]

In July 2007 the Beijing Olympic Committee announced "One World, One Dream" as the slogan for the 2008 Summer Games. In response, Xiaobo and Ding Zilin, on August 7, announced an appeal, open for others to sign, that they called "One World, One Dream, Equal Human Rights: Our Appeal and Our Proposals to the Beijing Olympic Committee." The statement affirmed some progress the government had made in human rights—for example, abolishing the "detention and repatriation" system in 2003 and writing the words "the state respects and guarantees human rights" into China's 2004 constitution. But it was hard to specify anything that the government had actually done about human rights. On the contrary, there had been a severe tightening on freedom of expression and of the press, increasingly blatant violations of the rights and interests of the poor and the vulnerable, and intensified repression of human rights defenders. The government and its officials had, for example, used "preparation for the Olympics" as a pretext for tearing down people's housing without their consent. A premise for the existence of "one world" must be respect for the human rights of all the world's people, including Chinese people. For that reason, the idea of "human rights" had to be incorporated into the Beijing Olympics. Xiaobo and Ding Zilin did not use the words "dictator" or "dictatorship"; Xiaobo was aware that, although he personally might prefer calling a spade a spade, he should take care when writing a draft for others who might not be ready to take the same risk.

The appeal drew signatures from prominent figures who were new to joining in such statements. The writer Dai Qing, who had negotiated with students at Tiananmen in 1989 and counseled them not to do a hunger strike—but afterward was sent to Qincheng Prison for seven months anyway—was ready to sign. So was Bao Tong, a top aide to Zhao Ziyang when Zhao served as Party general secretary in the 1980s. Bao chaired an elite group that Zhao had set up called the Research Institute on Reform of the Political System. When the prodemocracy demonstrations came in spring 1989, Bao stood with Zhao in opposing the use of force against protesters and for that was detained and sent to Qincheng Prison on May 28, 1989, even before the shooting began. Bao was the highest-ranking Communist official to be arrested in the spring events. (Zhao Ziyang's detention at home, although very tight, did not involve legal arrest.) Bao was sentenced to seven years in prison for "revealing state secrets" and "counterrevolutionary agitation" and when released in 1996 remained under strict surveillance. He never saw Zhao Ziyang again.

High-ranking though he was, Bao Tong had a personal relationship with Xiaobo. In 1986 at a meeting of the System Reform Institute, before they had met in person, someone criticized Xiaobo by name and Bao Tong came to his defense. He said he had read some of Xiaobo's essays and thought the young man was just trying to figure things out—there was no need to make a political case out of anything.[14] During Bao's strict surveillance after 2006, Xiaobo, imagining that Bao might be feeling lonely and bored, started calling him on the telephone. Bao's home was only a fifteen-minute walk from Xiaobo's, so one day Xiaobo and Liu Xia went to see him. Five or six guards at the gate of the building blocked them. Bao came out of the house, though, could see what was going on, and silently mouthed the words "Tomorrow at two, at McDonald's." The next day, at a McDonald's located between their two homes, the two did meet—each followed by his comet tail of plainclothes watchers. From then on they met like this every month, but switched from McDonald's to one of Xiaobo's favorite teahouses.

A writer from Wuhan named Hu Fayun was another of Xiaobo's important new allies. Hu had become famous in 2005 for his novel *Ruyan@SARS.come* (Such Is This World@SARS.come).[15] Set against the background of the SARS crisis of 2003, the novel is a trenchant retrospective on the Communist revolution and an examination of the fate of Chinese intellectuals in the present day.

Some are willing to face the history of the People's Republic honestly while others make cynical accommodations with their consciences. The book was a hit on the Chinese Internet until the regime repressed it. *Asia Weekly* named it one of the "ten best novels in Chinese in 2006," while the regime's General Administration of Press and Publication listed it, without explanation, as one of the "books in violation of regulations in 2006."

Hu Fayun sent Xiaobo an e-mail within hours of the appearance of the "One World, One Dream, Equal Human Rights" appeal, saying he would like to sign. Xiaobo, already a fan of Hu's famous novel, admired his daring and wrote: "Mr. Hu Fayun's novel *Ruyan* is an ingenious breakthrough in the world of Chinese letters since June Fourth. His readiness to sign the Olympics human rights appeal is his self-introduction to the public sphere. More and more people in their various fields are breaking into new territory in public. As they do, an independent public sphere for intellectuals will flourish in China."[16] Befriending Hu was an example of Xiaobo's determination to grow the rights movement by reaching deeper into the cultural world.

Yet another ally whom Xiaobo secured was the brilliant and energetic rights lawyer Gao Zhisheng. Gao had been well known since 2003 for his defense of the right of citizens in Shaanxi province to dig their own oil wells. That right had been recognized in the early years of "reform and opening," and when the provincial government abruptly withdrew it, people protested. Gao took the case of a man named Feng Bingxian, who had been criminally charged for representing individual well owners. The case was seen as a key test of the extent to which non-state enterprises could get legal protection in China. In the end the state had its way and Feng Bingxian was sentenced to three years in prison, but Gao Zhisheng's reputation as an intrepid attorney had been secured. He and his colleagues at the Beijing law firm Zhisheng Legal Associates took other cases of rights defense. They didn't always win, but they always fought hard.

Gao's most famous case arose in Guangdong province in 2005, after residents of a village called Taishi discovered that one of their officials had been highly corrupt. On September 26, Gao Zhisheng and six other rights lawyers organized a "Taishi Village Legal Consultancy." A bright lawyer from Zhisheng Legal Associates named Guo Feixiong went to help. Eventually four hundred villagers signed a petition to remove the corrupt official from office, and the immediate result was that about a dozen of the *protesters* were arrested, Guo Feixiong among them. Incensed, a villager named Feng Qiusheng decided to use the law to fight back. He organized a group to study the government's Law on Village Committees of the People's Republic of China. One day he climbed atop a pile of broken stones in the village and read the law aloud, item by item, to the cheers of listening villagers. On September 14, the *Southern Daily* (a branch of the *People's Daily*) ran a laudatory story about Feng expounding "democracy on a rock pile." Some elderly women in the village, afraid that the financial records showing the corruption might be removed from the village government offices, occupied those offices around the clock. Again, though, the local potentates "won." They called in police, recaptured the offices, beat a few people bloody, and arrested about a dozen, including the rock-pile lecturer Feng Qiusheng.

The international press discovered the Taishi Village story and began to follow it. This put pressure on local officials, and for a few days there was a standoff that saw various people being detained and released as if through a revolving door. Professor Ai Xiaoming in nearby Guangzhou stepped forward to support the villagers. Xiaobo wrote articles with titles like "Remember the Names of the Suppressors at Taishi Village" and "Who Really Won in Taishi Village?" Guo Feixiong, who had been detained on September 13, was finally released on December 27, "without charges." The Taishi villagers had made a valuable contribution by exposing problems in rural China and showing why the regime's advertised notion of "village democracy" was largely puffery. Their effort to rid themselves of a corrupt official had failed but still could be viewed, along with other cases in China at the time, as "useful failure."

Gao Zhisheng also defended cases for Falun Gong, which was perhaps the most provocative thing a lawyer could do at the time. In fall 2005, he wrote three open letters to Hu Jintao and Wen Jiabao complaining about the government's cruel repression of Falun Gong, including torture of its members. The Beijing Bureau of Justice answered on November 4, 2005, by shutting down Gao's law firm for one year. Two days later, Xiaobo published an essay, "The Lesson of Lawyer Gao Zhisheng," in which he pointed out that only four years earlier, in 2001, Chinese Central Television and the Ministry of Justice had jointly named Gao one of "the top ten high-honor lawyers" in the country.[17] Now he had become a thorn in the authorities' sides, and "in the stand-off between lawyer Gao and the vast dictatorial system arrayed against him, vile and dark official power reveals nothing but the panic of a regime that fears decline; in trenchant contrast, the punishment that lawyer Gao is accepting for the sake of freedom of belief and the dignity of lawyers shows the unruffled calm of a person guided by conscience."[18] At the end of 2005, *Asia Weekly* in Hong Kong named "China's rights lawyers" as the collective recipient of its Outstanding Person of the Year award. In an accompanying article, Gao and his colleague Guo Feixiong were named along with Xu Zhiyong, Teng Biao, Mo Shaoping, Pu Zhiqiang, Chen Guangcheng, and seven others.[19]

After his release from detention, Guo Feixiong wrote about how he had been treated, including a detailed account of being subjected to sleep deprivation. Plain-clothes police continued to follow him everywhere. On February 3, 2006, he tried to take a photo of them, only to have them bring him to a police station for ten hours—and then, in the early hours of February 4, give him a severe beating before letting him go. Learning of these events, Gao Zhisheng announced a "relay hunger strike to oppose persecution and uphold rights" (called a "relay" because some people took over fasting as others left off).

These audacious moves—the open letters and the hunger strike—drew wide attention. Gao's tactics went beyond what others in the Rights Defense Movement were doing and raised fears in some circles that they might provoke a government crackdown that would set the movement back. For Ding Zilin the tactic of hunger striking brought spring 1989 to mind and made her fear another life-and-death confrontation. On February 23, she wrote in an open letter to Gao Zhisheng, "Rights cases need to be resolved through legal channels. I must say I find it strange how ready you are to step out of your legal role and turn to political action. You are mixing legal work with activist work. In my view, it is a mistake to politicize legal work. It exposes rights lawyers to too much risk. . . . Space for freedom is pushed open inch by inch, and citizens' rights accumulate slowly, drop by drop."[20] The next day Gao replied to Ding in an open letter of his own. He explained that he saw his relay strike as moderate: no person's fasting would exceed forty-eight hours, there was no restriction on drinking water, and no one had to leave home. It was not a "mass movement." Gao expressed his tremendous respect for Ding Zilin but disagreed with her view that he had compromised his role as lawyer—a role he treasured as much as life itself—for the sake of activism. The regime had forced his hand, he wrote, and had used illegal means to do it.

Gao and Ding left the matter there, content to show that people in the movement could hold different views and express them in perfect civility.

The debate between "radical" and "moderate" approaches to resistance continued, however, and grew into what Xiaobo two years later called some "malignant disputes." He warned his friends in the movement that their rivalries risked becoming as bad as those inside the Communist Party.[21]

The incident that most exacerbated the radical-moderate split happened during May 2006. On May 1, an American NGO called ChinaAid, which specialized in protecting persecuted Chinese Christians and rights lawyers, posted on its website that "several famous Chinese dissident writers and rights-defense lawyers will be meeting in Washington, D.C., for a summit on 'The Condition of Freedom in China.'"[22] The notice listed Yu Jie, Wang Yi, Guo Feixiong, and rights lawyer Li Baiguang as planning to attend. Three others had been invited—lawyers Gao Zhisheng and Zhang Xingshui, and scholar Fan Yafeng—but the Chinese government had blocked them from leaving China.

In the morning of May 2, the four who had arrived in Washington—Yu, Wang, Guo, and Li—went to the Hudson Institute, a prestigious Washington think tank, to give talks. Everything so far was fine, at least on the surface. But then, on May 11, a controversial meeting with President George W. Bush took place at the White House. Yu Jie, Wang Yi, and Li Baiguang attended, as did Vice President Dick Cheney, National Security Adviser Stephen Hadley, a few other American officials, and Bob Fu, a minister from ChinaAid. The meeting had been scheduled for half an hour but lasted a full hour. A White House staff person who asked to remain anonymous revealed that the Chinese embassy had delivered a diplomatic note in advance of the meeting, asking Bush to cancel it.[23] The regime banned the Chinese state media from reporting the meeting, but news of it seeped into China anyway on the Internet, and democracy activists inside China were thrilled.

Then, on May 18, Guo Feixiong posted a piece on the Internet complaining that he had been wrongly excluded from the Bush meeting. In Guo's telling, on May 8, a few hours after it was known that Bush would meet with the Chinese visitors, Wang Yi, Yu Jie, Bob Fu, and one other, all Christians, embraced, prayed together, and reached the conclusion that Guo Feixiong should not attend the meeting. They informed him only afterward. Guo wrote that Wang Yi had explained, "You do politics; you're in the democracy movement. I do protection of religious freedom, which is something different, so I couldn't approve that you be there."[24] Guo Feixiong, like Gao Zhisheng, was in the "radical" wing of the rights movement; Yu Jie and Wang Yi were in the "moderate" wing.

Guo's Internet post elicited some fierce reactions both inside and outside China. Because it happened in Washington, D.C., the scandal got the nickname "Block-Guo-gate." Yu Jie wrote a "Declaration on the Matter of the Meeting with President Bush" that said:

> Wang Yi and I began with a clear conception of the nature of the meeting—that it should be on religious freedom—and we delivered that opinion to the White House in advance. We would come together with President Bush as brothers in the faith, and discussion would consist of lovely exchange between Christian and Christian. . . . If the meeting were to be "president meets with democracy movement people," then we were prepared to send our regrets.[25]

Wang Yi issued a statement confirming Yu Jie's. The notice of the meeting on the White House web page, however, quoted a State Department news release that said "President George W. Bush meets with Chinese Human Rights activists."

Xiaobo's initial opinion of the events was to regret what Yu Jie and Wang Yi had done. The opposition movement in China was still in a fragile, embryonic state, and this was no time to be getting into spats. He did not want to speak publicly, fearing that that would only add fuel to flames, but the issue fell into his lap anyway because Yu Jie and Wang Yi were both officers in Chinese PEN and Xiaobo was its president. Some people saw Yu and Wang as Xiaobo's right and left hands, and a few even suspected that Xiaobo was an instigator of Block-Guo-gate. He later faulted himself for not speaking out sooner. He had opted to wait for Yu and Wang to return to China and then spoke to them privately. At Xiaobo's urging the two wrote a letter of apology to the members of Chinese PEN. But that did not settle the matter. Some people resigned from PEN. Others signed a statement demanding that Yu Jie and Wang Yi relinquish their official positions in PEN.

Chinese dissidents by nature are strong-willed people. One does not take on a behemoth government if one is not. When they see something they think is wrong they often can't let it go; they reason on principle and pursue details with intensity, sometimes without regard to the costs they are imposing on themselves and others. The same uncompromising approach used on an adversary is sometimes directed at "one's own" in a democracy movement. Indeed, small wrongs that happen right next to a person sometimes sting more sharply, and produce more fiery reactions, than do large wrongs done at a distance. Derogatory terms pop up. A radical might categorize a moderate as "capitulationist"; a moderate might say to a radical, "You're behaving like a little Communist!" Because the government uses undercover agents, almost anyone can accuse almost anyone else of being a "spy." The suspicion that anyone—at least conceivably—might be a spy can have a corrosive effect on a whole movement.

On August 15, while Block-Guo-gate was still raging, Gao Zhisheng was arrested in China. Xiaobo and Ding Zilin wrote another open statement and invited people to join. The statement reviewed the major rights cases that Gao had worked on, emphasizing his defense of the much-persecuted Falun Gong, and demanded that the authorities guarantee respect for Gao's rights in prison. Many signed. Some felt that the statement was too gentle, and this difference of opinion threatened to widen the radical-moderate split, which in some ways was becoming a divide between people overseas and people inside China. Some overseas thought that violent methods and regime overthrow should not be ruled out.

Such views appeared on a website called Free China Forum, where, on August 24, Xiaobo posted a response titled "Let's Hope That Support of Rights Inside China Stays Away from Calls for Violence or Coups d'Etat." It began: "No matter how it is intended, the actual impact of political grandstanding or advocacy of violence or coups d'etat by people outside China is only to worsen conditions for rights work inside China. If people inside China are influenced by calls to move toward violence or coups d'etat, the dangers will be very real indeed."[26] A few days later Xiaobo expanded this comment into an article, "Answering Gao Han's Advice to People in China That Rashness Is the Better Part of Valor."[27] Gao Han was a veteran dissident and a member of Chinese PEN. He had been imprisoned in the 1970s as an "active counterrevolutionary" and had lived in exile since 1991. During Block-Guo-gate, he called Xiaobo a "moderate" and challenged him by saying that if the moderates did not have the radicals out in front taking the heat, moderates would get hit much harder. Xiaobo answered: "As I write here, it is 3:00 a.m., and a policeman still stands downstairs at the door to my building. And that is only one of the many crude limitations on my personal freedom."[28] Xiaobo noted how people sometimes make an unexamined assumption that a more radical position is morally superior just because it is more radical. That assumption is just as wrong, he said, as the one that people resisting from inside China are morally superior to ones who went into exile.

His essay, written at 3:00 a.m., calls on all sides to let go of claims of automatic moral superiority. He describes his own decision to remain in China as arising "not from a feeling of heroism but from a need to repent and to atone before the lost souls of June Fourth." As for exile:

> It is often the only option a person reasonably has. For some, it comes after many years in prison. When a person accepts exile, he or she escapes the blanket of fear one lives under in China but then faces a whole new set of problems—how to adjust, how to finance oneself, how to continue with one's work—that in some ways can be even more burdensome than the problems one leaves behind. Some exiles, moreover, are people who paid huge personal prices in China before they left. No one has the right to challenge their moral credentials.[29]

With equal fervor, he urges exiles to understand the risks that people inside China are taking and to be careful not to make things worse. They should consult with people on the inside before doing anything flamboyant. They should practice what Xiaobo came to call "responsible ethics," which meant: "[first,] to seek in any action to minimize the risk to which others in the movement will be exposed; second, to try to achieve concrete and effective results even if they are modest gains and less than one would have hoped. In this way the expansion of rights among the people can be built gradually, step by step and solidly."

Xiaobo continued to get criticism, especially from exiles, for his gradualist approach. The internal logic of going fast versus going slow seemed to work against him. Since the goal of both was to be rid of the dreadful dictatorial system, why wouldn't going faster be better? The burden of proof seemed to fall to the side that would go slower. Xiaobo felt that some of his critics outside China, although they did understand that political risks could bring suffering to people, did not grasp the point that rash action could bring tentative progress crashing down before it could solidify.

Activism in society was maturing during 2006 and 2007 in ways that gave Xiaobo reason for hope. Social media and the semiofficial press were having an ameliorative effect: by exposing stories that the state-run press normally would not touch, they were forcing the state media to address those stories as well, or lose credibility. When stories of official wrongdoing surfaced, the guilty were sometimes obliged to change their ways and even apologize or provide reparations—not from remorse for what they had done but from fear that their bureaucratic superiors would hold them responsible for "trouble" below. The best news that any subordinate in China's ruling bureaucracy can give a superior is "No news here; everything is stable." (If there is trouble, the local official looks bad and his superior looks bad too, before *his* superior.) These leveraged changes in the state press and the accountability of officials were two concrete benefits of the gradualist, bottom-up approach of the Rights Defense Movement.

Xiaobo saw another, more long-term reason for preferring the gradualist approach. He saw it as reducing the risk of violence during a future transition out of dictatorship, whenever that might come. Popular frustration and anger had been building. The regime itself clearly knew about this tension, or it would not invest so much time and money in *weiwen*. An unanticipated event could be a spark that ignited an explosion, and the resulting violence could be ugly. Xiaobo often told friends, and in several essays wrote, that the best hope for avoiding "transitional violence" was to soften the interface between regime and citizens. He wanted to see the emergence of a "flexible political space" within a "nonviolent legal order."[30] One way to create such a space, he felt, was to use political humor.

In a remarkable essay on the topic,[31] he summarizes two very different views among people in the opposition movement on whether political jokes are helpful in bringing political change. One side argued that they do harm, because "something that debunks the sacred and subverts authority but goes no further is only destructive" and might lead to "a moral wasteland." Besides, political jokes sometimes function as mere safety valves that release people's anger innocuously and therefore actually assist the regime in its *weiwen* work. On the other side of the argument, though, people pointed out that political jokes reach deep into society. Jokes about corruption reach as far as corruption itself—meaning virtually everywhere—and undermine the government's blanket claims to "correctness." Political humor was an important and widespread form of popular resistance in the Soviet Union and Eastern Europe before the great changeovers occurred in those places.

In early 2006 Xiaobo was inclined toward the first of these views,[32] but by September he had migrated to the second. He argued that laughing at officials had the additional virtue that it was a gentle technique—a way of humanizing the opposition even while opposing it. It should follow that:

> If and when a political collapse or major transition occurs, the fact that political humor has already been around for a number of years will likely ease the transition. In China political jokes have already been making it clear that the legitimacy of the dictatorship is unsustainable; this means that an end, when it comes, will not be so much of a shock. People will be able to take it more or less in stride, and this will have the benefit of reducing anxieties and lessening the likelihood that people will attempt violent revenge. Because jokes had been letting them blow off some of their anger all along, they will have less pent-up anger to disperse. And in addition to all that, the positive values that have underlain political jokes (satire of what is wrong implies that something else is right) will be available for use after the transition.[33]

In the same essay Xiaobo expresses his admiration of Milan Kundera and his novel *The Joke*. He asks whether a society like Czechoslovakia's in the 1970s, or China's in the 2000s, is more in need of Kundera with his gentle, quiet undermining approach or Vaclav Havel with his clear and spirited public exposition of principles. He answers that it is best to have both: "Truth telling and joking have worked hand in hand to dismantle post-totalitarian dictatorships. Both are crucial. Without the truth tellers, there would be no open expression of popular resistance or of moral courage; without the jokesters, the words of the truth tellers would fall on barren ground." The rise of civil society was affording a precious opportunity, but it was also opening uncharted territory. What should the Rights Defense Movement do next? There seemed a need to shift gears, but what should change and what must not? Such questions drew him into deep reflection, especially on what his personal principles should be.

He read a book by Qin Geng that had a considerable impact on him. Qin was a member of PEN who, like Xiaobo, had been sent to prison after the June Fourth massacre. After his release Qin found it hard to write about either the massacre or his prison life—he was afraid of the effects it might have on his young daughter. In 2002 he finally produced a memoir, *China's First Crime: A Record of My Happy Life in Prison.* The book uses a jocular tone throughout. "My positive feelings in prison had nothing to do with the prison environment," he wrote. "They came entirely from inside me."[34] Qin asked Xiaobo to write a preface and Xiaobo, impressed with Qin's approach, agreed. He called it "The Laughter of a Free Man Behind Bars" and took it as an opportunity to do some merciless self-analysis.

Xiaobo was already known for the view, which he had written a year earlier, that "the prison of the dictator is the first step toward true freedom."[35] Now he asked if that step might in a sense be selfish. Do people who go to prison for the cause of democracy feel that they are the unluckiest people in the world—or the luckiest? Is there a danger of feeling one's prison record is evidence of moral superiority, and a temptation, therefore, to exaggerate one's suffering and slip into an odd sort of narcissism? Could suffering make a person haughty, or even feed a hatred complex?

Qin Geng, in Xiaobo's view, was a model of how to avoid such perils. Qin saw going to prison in a dictatorship as no big deal. For people who had made the decision to live in truth, going to prison was like taking a required course in school. In Xiaobo's words:

> Just as workers should do their labor correctly, just as farmers should plant the earth on time, and just as students should learn their lessons properly, democracy advocates living in dictatorship need to do their prison time.... Your choice of occupation is your own. You are free to choose, as most people do, to keep quiet and out of prison. But if you do make the choice to speak out, then you should calmly accept whatever comes with it. You shouldn't go swearing at the gods or railing at other people about it, and it should be irrelevant to you whether social respect or a good reputation comes to you as a result. You certainly shouldn't think that going to jail earns you moral capital that society is duty-bound to repay. If accolades do come your way, it is your duty to stay clear-headed and to avoid inebriation with fame. Prisoners of conscience in Chinese prisons are neither oddballs nor mystic heroes but simply another kind of commoner. They are people who insist on human dignity and have the courage to seek freedom, but other than that are like everybody else. They have passions, desires, foibles—the gamut of human traits.[36]

As he had done several times earlier in his life, he is examining, censuring, and counseling himself here. He is also dredging his psychological history—from his early fixation on heroes to his deep remorse over his "repentance" in Qincheng Prison—and is wondering if he has been selfish. He seems aware that someday he might be in prison again and therefore perhaps should coach himself on how to do it right. He had chosen an unusual path in life, but at bottom was an ordinary human being. And ordinary human beings, whether inside prisons or outside, share the fundamental human condition. If he had showed weakness in prison the first time, that too was normal. Next time (should it come), he had to measure himself by his own standards, not let external factors make him feel either superior or inferior to others.

> Yes, prison is a disaster. . . . But what does one do? Moan to the heavens? Wail and implore? Such action might make you feel a bit better, but it accomplishes nothing. If you withdraw into an attitude of enmity, you only trap yourself in your own web. . . . You might garner a few cheap plaudits, but that's it. No, the best answer to terror from the outside is to overcome the fear that dwells within. You can avoid that fear by replacing self-inflation with a plain outlook, replacing dejection with inspiration, replacing pessimism with optimism, turning your predicament into a test of character, and using your willpower to reject the insults that are thrust upon you. You adhere to human dignity and to hope.[37]

It was also around this time that Jiri Grusa, the president of International PEN, published a book of his poems in Chinese translation and asked Xiaobo to write a preface. Grusa was an avant garde poet and Czech dissident who was banned from publishing in Czechoslovakia after the Prague Spring of 1968 and then became a construction worker. In 1977 he joined other Czech dissidents in the Charter 77 movement. After the Velvet Revolution of 1989, Grusa served the new democratic government of Czechoslovakia as minister of education as well as ambassador to Germany and to Austria. Xiaobo, inspired by Grusa's experience but still deep in his own musings on dissidence and prison, wrote a preface called "The Humility of Resisters":

> I find in the words and deeds [of resisters] evidence not only of the evils of dictatorship but also of the soul-searching of dictatorship's victims. Resisters of tyrannies are not only its victims but sometimes its enablers. We put conscience and courage into our resistance, but also must insist on rationality and responsible ethics. Tactics in the struggle of a resistance movement must strike a balance

between moral ideals and practical results, between pursuing what ought to be done and achieving what can be done.[38]

Xiaobo endorses Grusa's principle that civilized politics avoids stark oppositions—the idea that if something is not true, it is a lie; that if you're not a friend, you're automatically an enemy; or that as long as a person opposes the dictatorship, he or she of course is faultless.[39]

Xiaobo was beginning to view all of the divisions within the Rights Defense Movement—radical versus moderate, inside or outside the system, prison veteran or not—as undesirable. The central problem of the dictatorship must transcend all such distinctions. The focus should be on concrete projects, and all hands should be on deck. He wrote: "For the opposition and rights-support groups inside China, self-examination and self-reconstruction are now the most urgent tasks. The first task in self-reconstruction should be to cultivate responsible ethics, and the goal of those ethics should be to make civil society's opposition to dictatorship ever more humane."[40]

One reason for Xiaobo's continuously high regard for the Tiananmen Mothers during these years was that that group was always careful to put its work into the context of seeking, eventually, a nonviolent democratic transition. For them, he wrote:

> Solving the June Fourth problem is not just a matter of "reversing verdicts" on people whom the government judged unfairly, making reparations to people who were hurt, or purging society of the thinking that led to June Fourth. It is also a question of reducing to a minimum the upset and harm that can come to society during a transition and thereby handing to a new democratic government a social order that it can work with more easily than it could with a society wracked by upset and harm.[41]

Further endorsing the Tiananmen Mothers, he wrote on the anniversary of June Fourth in 2007:

> Solving the June Fourth problem should increase the likelihood of a peaceful transition, because in order to achieve reconciliation in society we need to start by tolerating our adversaries and getting rid of hatred. The stand of the Tiananmen Mothers is to reject illusions that immediate regime change is possible; to reject calls for eye-for-eye, tooth-for-tooth retribution; and to reject any kind of clever power-grabbing scheme. Past questions about perpetrators and

victims should be handled as much as possible by avoiding confrontation and by softening feelings of enmity. The opposition movement should be able to show itself to be more rational and more capable of compromise than the dictatorship is.[42]

In an essay aimed at showing "responsibility ethics" in a living example, Xiaobo focused on the veteran rights lawyer Zhang Sizhi, who, in Xiaobo's view, had gotten such ethics exactly right. Eighty years old in 2007, Zhang was an exemplar for Mo Shaoping, Pu Zhiqiang, Teng Biao, Li Heping, and others in the younger generation of brilliant rights lawyers. Beginning in the early 1990s Zhang had argued cases for Wei Jingsheng, Wang Juntao, Bao Tong, Gao Yu, Liu Di, the New Youth Study Association, and others who had been accused of political crimes. He never got an acquittal for any of them. But that did not mean he "lost," in Xiaobo's view. Zhang used the stage of law court to bring the universal values of human rights off paper and into living debate. Gently, rationally, and in the end powerfully, he obliged the regime to face the implications of its claim to uphold human rights. His exposure of the gap between rights on paper and rights in action was powerful because of the regime's strong need to pretend: it claimed to run a "people's" court in a "People's Republic," reported in a *"People's Daily,"* and so on. It could not accuse Zhang of subverting the state because the tools he used were the state's own words.[43] Zhang's argumentation was a splendid example of what Xiaobo meant by "pressing officialdom into a constricted position," and Zhang's character was a model of what Xiaobo was seeking:

> The greatest lessons that Mr. Zhang Sizhi's career in human rights law can hold for people in our opposition movement today are these: in an era when cynicism is rife, to maintain faith in human goodness, and in the face of nearly total despair at the state of affairs, to remain optimistic, tenacious, and clear-headed about the cause of freedom. These traits are far more valuable than any temporary outburst of passion or any illusion that overnight change can happen. Rationality and responsibility are far more important than flamboyant cursing or contests of who can be more daring.[44]

In December 2007, in an interview with a reporter from the U.S.-based Chinese-language website Participation, Xiaobo stressed that "a political transition in China will be a lengthy, complex, and gradual process."[45] He reviewed his gradualist approach and then added three new points:

1. Any person, including any leader, must follow agreed-upon rules; rules cannot be casually revised as one goes. No matter how great an injustice might be or how intense one's feelings, in a democracy no personal feelings are adequate reason to break rules.

2. In events involving large numbers of people, activists must understand the relationship between their personal interests and the public interest. Pride in one's activism is a legitimate personal interest; without such an incentive, a movement would dwindle or perhaps never begin. But personal goals should never take precedence over advancing the public interest. Activists should realize that maximization of the public interest is the most solid base they have for maximizing their own sense of accomplishment.

3. When an opposition movement suffers a defeat, activists should have the courage to examine their actions for weaknesses and try to avoid repeating mistakes. It is cowardly to blame everything on the iniquity of dictators. The iniquity is there, to be sure, but that factor is a constant. To point to it as the reason for all of one's failures is sophistry. If the political culture of our opposition movement does not encourage self-reflection and continual improvement, then hopes for a political transition will be even more tenuous. Our ability to reflect on our own work might be even more important than our work of criticizing the powers of officials.

These were principles that Xiaobo was recommending for the Rights Defense Movement, but they can also be read as criticism of the Communist Party of China in its origins. The Party had begun as a small group with millenarian ideals and a preconceived system that it applied to society from the top down. The fit was sometimes difficult and eventually was disastrous, and might have worked better if the young Communist zealots had listened better to society. Even before a democratic transition was in sight, Xiaobo was worrying over what its founding approach would be. It would need to be radically different from the Communists' approach.

Throughout 2007, an increasing number of revelations of official malfeasance, on the Internet and in the semiofficial press, led to a greater willingness of victims to speak out. After there was a noticeable rise in the size of crowds at demonstrations, 2007 came to be called "public opinion year." People were coming out to protest events that had not affected them personally. They protested out of sympathy for the abused, but also from something more. Having suffered abuse themselves, they were protesting their own cases vicariously. In reporting on crowd size, police were instructed to include a category called "people whose direct interests have not been harmed."[46] When rights cases appeared on the Internet, they served as lessons for the public on how the law worked (or was supposed to work) and how rights were (or at least ought to have been) protected. The word "accountability" entered public discourse. As an aware citizenry became more prominent, the contrast between it and officialdom grew sharper. Xiaobo's prediction in 2003 that "power will rest with officialdom, moral judgment with society" was coming true. Society was approaching a level where it could nearly hold its own with officialdom. Both optimism and apprehension were in the air. Talk of a "political transition" increased, but there was virtually no consensus on how it might happen.

18

The Gathering Storm

During 2007, as Xiaobo was trying to refine his thinking about "responsible ethics" in the Rights Defense Movement, some dramatic events arose in a way that seemed almost to be tests for his new thinking.

The first of these was the "black kilns" scandal. In May 2007, parents of missing children in Henan province reported their anxiety to journalists at a local television station. For several years the kidnapping of children had been on the rise nationwide, and there were rumors specifically that operators of brick kilns in Shanxi province were abducting people to do forced labor. Reporters from Henan television went undercover to Shanxi and found that indeed there was a major problem. Human traffickers had lured children from places like railroad stations in Henan and transported them to kiln operators in Shanxi. Once on site the children were sealed from communication with the outside and did hard physical labor that caused injury, sometimes crippling injury.

The story broke, and China was shocked. The international press reported on it, a government investigation followed, and during June and July 570 people, 69 of them children, were freed from what everyone agreed were conditions of slavery. President Hu Jintao and Premier Wen Jiabao issued a spate of directives and Xiaobo wrote a spate of articles—eight in all—with titles like "The Black Kilns Child Labor Story Lays Bare the Dereliction of Duty and the Cold Heart of the Dictatorial System" and "Don't Try to Tell Me the Black Kilns Child Labor Story 'Surprised' Hu and Wen!" In the hardest-hitting of Xiaobo's pieces, "A Deeper Look Into Why Child Slavery in China's 'Black Kilns' Could Happen," he argues that the Shanxi outrages were no anomaly.[1] They arose from conditions either created or exacerbated by China's dictatorial system. Since rumors of the child labor had been circulating for many months, the first question, Xiaobo wrote, was "Why wasn't it exposed and dealt with earlier?" "The truth is that in China the underworld and officialdom have interpenetrated and fused. Criminal elements have become officialized as officials have become criminalized. Underworld chiefs are invited to be members of the National People's Congress or the People's Political Consultative Conference, in return for which officials rely on the underworld to help keep society pacified." Another question was, "How could the regime be so coldhearted?"

> The reason is not that the human beings within the system are all coldhearted. The problem is the cruelty of the authoritarian system itself. This kind of system cannot adapt to respect life or to uphold human rights. A ruling group that makes maintenance of its monopoly on power its first priority can never turn around and put the lives of people—even children—in a higher position. In the end it is because the system does not treat people as human beings that such hair-raising atrocities can come about. Authoritarian power is as cold as ice. It obliges people to focus on power and power alone, and this makes feelings of human warmth impossible.

Hu Jintao and the other top leaders were accustomed to reading only praise of themselves and their system or, if criticisms did reach their desks, seeing them wrapped in layers of padding. Xiaobo's unapologetic exposure of actualities cannot have pleased them. This article on the black kilns was another of the six offered at his 2009 trial as evidence of his crimes.

A second startling occurrence was a spate of "strolling" protests. On June 1, 2007, which is "Children's Day" in China, a protest appeared in the city of Xiamen in Fujian province. Citizens were opposing the construction of a plant near the city's center that would produce p-Xylene, a toxic chemical used in the production of polymers. The demonstrators, aware that public protests organized by anyone other than the Communist Party were punishable, called their activity "strolling." Between eight and ten thousand people just happened to be out strolling at the same time. They were orderly and peaceful. Some did go so far as to hold up banners: "No PX, save Xiamen"; "Saving Xiamen Is Everyone's Duty"; and others. Many wore yellow ribbons, one a gas mask. They strolled to the government offices building, where a man named Lian Yue, a low-profile organizer (avoiding the danger of being high-profile), wrote a list of his "opinions" that circulated among the strollers: "First, don't be afraid ... If you feel comfortable doing this, tell your family, friends, neighbors, and colleagues what we are doing ... If you are not afraid, tell people in [the nearby cities of] Zhangzhou and

Quanzhou, because they face similar dangers . . . You don't have to do anything especially brave . . . If you just take these little steps you will have done your part to keep Xiamen alive."[2] In the end the strollers won. The government was obliged to move the p-Xylene plant farther from population centers. *Southern Weekend* gave one of its year-end prizes to "the people of Xiamen." The event was almost a model of what Xiaobo thought opposition activities should look like.

Then there was the "tiger" scandal. On October 12, 2007, a story about a tiger swept the country on the Internet. The Department of Forestry in Shaanxi province had held a press conference to announce that a hunter named Zhou Zhenglong had photographed a South China tiger—an endangered species—in the wild. Zhou received a reward of 20,000 yuan, and the region was being designated a South China tiger preserve. Three days later, though, someone posted on the Internet a list of six suspicious points about the photograph and invited others to contribute opinions. The response was overwhelming. A fake tiger, it turned out, was far more interesting than a real one. Experts in fields like zoology, botany, photography, and mathematics joined in, as did Henry Lee, a world-famous Chinese American forensic scientist. New developments rolled in every day, and popular knowledge of both tigers and digital cameras grew considerably.

The matter was fascinating in part because of its political ambiguity. From one viewpoint, it was not political at all. From another, though, much of the popular interest in the case came from measuring the distance between reality and something that the government had announced to be true. That interest only increased as the doubters began to win the contest. On February 4, 2008, the Department of Forestry in Shaanxi province retracted its claim and issued a public apology. To Xiaobo, this was a demonstration of how a peaceful transition out of dictatorship might happen. When the government's credibility declines to a point where people no longer believe anything it says, a door opens.

Other major events were of a more personal nature for Xiaobo. On October 28, 2007, his dear friend Bao Zunxin died of a cerebral hemorrhage. Bao was eighteen years older than Xiaobo, but the two had been close. In the late 1980s Bao had impressed Xiaobo by publishing "enlightenment" books, but after the 1989 massacre certain actions of the regime brought the two together. Both were sent to Qincheng Prison, where they were put in neighboring cells. They went to court on the same day to face charges of "agitating for counterrevolution" and left prison on the same day in 1991. Both then joined with others in an attempt to resuscitate the resistance.

After Xiaobo was sent to the *laojiao* camp in 1996, Bao was especially solicitous of Liu Xia. At least once a month, he visited her and took her wherever she wished to go for a day. She often chose bookshops. Liu Xia enjoyed browsing among books and bought many, some for herself and some to carry to Xiaobo in the camp. The gallant Mr. Bao always insisted on the privilege of carrying the heavy load of books. Then he invited her to a restaurant for dinner and would not let her go until he had seen her and her books safely into a taxi. Occasionally she chose to go to a hairdresser instead of a bookstore. In that case, he would wait for her at the doorway, smoking and reading, until the hair was all set.

In October 1999 when Xiaobo was released from *laojiao*, his first meal in his regained freedom was at the apartment of Bao and his wife. They ate fish-head hotpot, and Bao cracked a joke. "For three years," he said, "when I ate dinners with your young lady we consumed one bottle each of white liquor. Now you come along, and you don't drink, so it's a bit awkward."

"All right," Xiaobo answered, "from now on you just invite Liu Xia. I'll stay away in order not to wreck the atmosphere!" Both Liu Xia and Xiaobo referred to Bao Zunxin using the intimate nickname Bao Bao.

As of August 2007, when Bao signed Xiaobo and Ding Zilin's appeal, "One World, One Dream, Equal Human Rights," he appeared to be in fine health. When the stroke came in October, doctors did a quick operation, but Bao emerged from it gravely ill. On the afternoon of the day he died, his wife called from the hospital to say the end appeared near. Xiaobo and Zhang Zuhua rushed to the hospital to find Bao indeed at the brink. Their arrival seemed to spark a modest resurgence in his health, however. He could not speak, but when he saw friends his pulse rose from twenty to fifty-six beats per minute and his blood pressure increased from an abnormally low level. Bao's wife interpreted these minor "miracles" to his friends' presence. Had it stimulated one last effort to stay in this world? With Bao's condition seeming stable, the family advised Xiaobo that he could leave and come back the next day.

But Bao died less than half an hour after Xiaobo had left. Xiaobo rushed back to the hospital room and later wrote about that last encounter:

> Bao Bao, never while you were alive have I come this close to you physically. I bend my waist and for the first time put my cheek against yours. I put my ear to your chest, listening for a beating heart. But your hands and feet are cold; your face is cold. . . . We knew each other, at first, only from a distance. Later, as friends, our hearts grew closer than those of most relatives. Your talent and your ability filled a person with admiration; your obstinacy and backbone commanded a person's respect; and your sincerity and fidelity inspired confidence in what you said. But these admirable qualities were not what made me and Liu Xia feel close to you. What made us feel close, more than anything, were your

care and your warmth, your childlike transparency, your father-like love, and even your weaknesses.[3]

Xiaobo moved quickly to set up a committee for Bao's funeral. He was fighting a bad cold but was determined to plan an occasion that would be proper and respectable in every way. He and his friends prepared a large number of wreaths, elegiac couplets, and commemorative booklets. Xiaobo took overall responsibility for arrangements, no matter how large or small, but assigned himself "public relations" in particular. The senior editor Xu Xiao took responsibility for setting up the mourning hall and choosing the music. A number of out-of-town friends traveled to Beijing to say good-bye to this distinguished teacher of democracy.

Part of the "public relations" job was to obviate harassment by the police. The authorities knew there would be no way to stop the funeral, but they warned Xiaobo not to create "political incidents." Xiaobo answered that if they promised not to interfere, there would be no incidents. The police agreed but then, within hours, on orders from above, were already breaking their word. The funeral was scheduled for November 3, and on the evening of November 2 about two dozen of Bao's friends received police notices to stay at home the next day.

The event was to take place in the Beijing Dongjiao Funeral Parlor at 11:00 a.m. At 8:20, four police sedans and two police minibuses filled with uniformed police entered the funeral parlor parking lot—not through the main entrance but through a smaller entrance at the rear. In addition, plainclothes police were wandering around the parking lot on foot.

Funeral parlors in Beijing normally give the bereaved as much time as they need to set up a mourning hall, but when Xiaobo arrived early the doors of the Dongjiao Funeral Parlor were locked. He and Xu Xiao went to the managers to complain. It took extended argument, sometimes heated, to get the doors open so that Xu Xiao's logistics team could rush in to set up the wreaths. Xiaobo inspected every item to be sure it was placed correctly and that the names on the couplet ribbons were not obscured.

As he was checking the names on the ribbons against a list of people who had purchased them, to be sure that none was missing, Xiaobo got word that several of Bao's political friends were being prevented from attending. Lawyers Mo Shaoping and Pu Zhiqiang, the Tiananmen student leader Jiang Qisheng, and others had been blocked at the doors of their residences. Others had been removed to police stations. Xiaobo and members of Bao Zunxin's family went to the chief of the police detachment on the scene and argued vehemently. Xiaobo knew that these officers were not the ones who had ordered the blocking, but that did not prevent him from expressing his view that the police as a whole lacked humanity.

Next he learned that two others—the stainless-steel rat Liu Di and Li Hai, who had compiled the list of the names of ordinary Beijing citizens who had been locked up after June Fourth—had made it as far as the gate of the funeral parlor but then were abducted into a police car and driven away. Qi Zhiyong, who had lost a leg in the June Fourth massacre, was detained and interrogated "on suspicion of agitating to subvert state power." Others blocked from attending were Zhang Xianling from the Tiananmen Mothers, historian Chen Ziming and his wife, the Chinese PEN book-prize winner Wang Lixiong, and political scientist Liu Junning. In all, about one hundred were blocked.

About three hundred did get inside, where Xiaobo presided. The main eulogy was delivered by eighty-two-year-old Yu Haocheng, the founding director of the Masses Publishing House, which specialized in "antispy" stories that in the 1950s were used as training materials for Chinese police. During the Cultural Revolution, Yu was sent to Qincheng Prison as a counterrevolutionary, held there in solitary confinement, and denied reading materials. He maintained his sanity only by reciting Tang poems that he had memorized as a boy. In his speech, Yu

FIGURE 18.1 Speaking at the funeral of Bao Zunxin. Standing at the right are Yu Haocheng and Zhang Zuhua.

Xu Xiao

highlighted Bao Zunxin's prodigious output in the later 1980s, when, in addition to the "enlightenment books," his own writings on democracy inspired a generation.

For Xiaobo, the tension and anguish were almost unbearable: the death of a friend, collective mourning by a distinguished assembly, and pressure from police converged in his mind like storm waves. He watched as a journalist entered to take photos, was pulled aside by police, and had his camera confiscated. When he saw another plainclothes policeman come forward and try to walk away with the materials on Bao's life—letters, photos, and so on—that his friends had compiled, something snapped inside Xiaobo. He strode to a position face to face with the policeman, pointed a finger at him, and bellowed. He picked something up and smashed it to the floor. Friends rushed forward to restrain him in a bear hug. The policeman, realizing that his assignment to confiscate Bao's life records would not be easy, backed off. Xiaobo's friend Xu Youyu said he had never seen Xiaobo so enraged.

A few days later Xiaobo organized a symposium on Bao Zunxin's thought. It was scheduled for the evening of November 24 and was to be a small, informal affair, where people who knew Bao well would reflect on his intellectual contributions. When the day came, though, Xiaobo was blocked at his door. Others reached the meeting, but fifteen minutes into it, the lights went out. They called an electrician, but he couldn't find anything that needed repair.

The Chinese government opened 2008 by calling it "Olympics Year." The entire city of Beijing was festooned with Chinese-style red lanterns and slogan-bedecked red banners celebrating the approach of the Games. Images of five little mascot dolls, called in English the "Olympic Friendlies," appeared everywhere—always grinning, sometimes dancing, even carved into stone cliffs in the western suburbs. For the regime, the opportunity to elevate its international image required a thoroughgoing facelift for Beijing. The city's appearance could be preemptive rebuttal to accusations about income inequality or abuse of power, and for the most part the tactic worked. After the summer of 2008, the "China Dream" had a bit more credibility in the eyes of foreigners than it had had before.

Leaders of the world's democracies hoped that Beijing's hosting of the Olympics would pull it more into the mainstream of international practice in human rights. The Chinese rulers were aware of this and knew that their reputation was at stake. Repression of Beijing society had been increasing in the years leading up to the Games (tight control was necessary in order to do all the cosmetic work), but in late 2006 the authorities realized that they needed to present a façade of attending to human rights as well. The Chinese idiom "tight within, relaxed outside" captured the policy well.

To show the "relaxed" side, the regime opened a "human rights exhibition" in Beijing on November 17, 2006. It highlighted some United Nations documents and a Chinese government "white paper" on human rights. Then, two weeks later, on December 1, the State Council announced Order no. 477: Regulations on Interviews by Foreign Journalists During the Beijing Olympics and the Preparatory Period. It promised a suspension of restrictions on foreign journalists, and authorities made sure the veneer of relaxation was presented to the international press.

The simultaneous but unannounced "tightening within," however, was much stronger than the outer relaxation. Strict rules were laid down to avoid dirty air. Factories in the suburbs closed, autos were allowed only on alternate days, and clouds were seeded to bring rain. The streets had to look clean and green. Lawns were watered, shrubs planted, and even some sidewalks were painted green so that from a passing motorcar, they might look like lawn. It was forbidden to hang clothes out to dry in places where foreigners might see them. People on the street had to look good too. The approximately 300,000 migrant workers, who could not afford to dress well and whom the regime sometimes referred to as the "low end" population, were asked to stay home or leave the city. If they declined, police came visiting to force them out. Water and electricity were sometimes cut off from whole city blocks to make staying at home difficult.[4] Young women selected for being pretty and virtually the same height were trained to be "ceremony girls" at the Games. The training included standing for periods of time with books on their heads and a sheet of paper clenched between their knees to form and habituate good posture. One way to train them in a pleasant smile that showed "six to eight teeth" was to have them clench a chopstick in the mouth.[5]

For Xiaobo, the new Order 477 brought opportunities. Item 6 stated that in order for a foreign journalist to do an interview, "only the permission of the interviewee and the work unit is required." Xiaobo immediately became a test case for this rule. He had no work unit, so all a journalist needed in order to talk to him was his personal okay—which was no problem! His friends teased that he had become "Mr. Go-to Guy" for the international press. His *guobao*, whose job it was to seem relaxed on the outside but be tight on the inside, counseled him, warned him, and *pleaded* with him not to accept interviews, but Xiaobo didn't listen. The unintended consequence of a government edict had brought Xiaobo new freedom, and he was going to use it, even if doing so could add to the list of his "offenses" in a post-Olympics crackdown. He not only took risks but also was willing to stand at the front line, hazarding his safety to spare others. His friends began to count on him to do this.

Beyond Order 477, there were other external signs of political relaxation. The name of the disgraced Zhao Ziyang, banned from print since 1989, now appeared occasionally, and pressure on the Tiananmen Mothers let up a bit. Ding Zilin and Jiang Peikun, who had tried on June 3 of every year since 1989 to visit Muxidi, where their son Jielian was murdered, always had been blocked. Sometimes they had even been forced to stay at home, with their telephone and Internet connections cut. But on June 3 in 2006 and 2007 they were allowed out. *Guobao* watched them constantly, but they could go to Muxidi. There were also some prisoner releases. On February 5, 2008, Ching Cheong, a Hong Kong journalist who was serving a five-year prison sentence on espionage charges, was released two years early. Three days after that Yu Huafeng, former deputy chief editor of *Southern Metropolitan Daily*, who had been serving an eight-year prison sentence, was released after having served only four. No one could discern any rational pattern; the choices of these particular cases may have sprung from private connections inside the regime. But each time a political prisoner was released, the government made sure the international press knew about it. Xiaobo and others called the releases a "human rights show."

On December 27, 2007, "tightness within" penetrated to the surface again when a young human rights activist named Hu Jia was detained on subversion charges. (The choice of date illustrates the regime's recurrent tactic of arresting and trying dissidents during Western holidays when foreign journalists tend to be occupied elsewhere. Hu Jia was a perennial dissident who, with equal "reason," could have been nabbed at any time.) Hu had been a fifteen-year-old high school student when he saw the Tiananmen massacre with his own eyes. It so shocked him that he turned vegetarian and eventually Buddhist. His political activism began with environmental protection and moved later to advocacy for AIDS victims, families of June Fourth victims, and farmers whose land was being confiscated. Xiaobo and Zhang Zuhua organized an open letter on Hu Jia's detention and published it on January 7, 2008. In March Hu Jia was sentenced to three and a half years in prison.

A national emergency seized China in January 2008 when a huge blizzard caused problems for many millions of Chinese headed home for the Lunar New Year. In recent years travel at the New Year had grown unusually heavy because industrialization in the cities had drawn hundreds of millions of workers away from farms and into urban factories. When many went home at once, rail stations became extremely crowded. This year, on top of the normal congestion, the freakish blizzard was bringing snow and cold beyond what anyone could remember in the provinces of Guizhou, Hunan, Hubei, and Anhui. Even the normally milder provinces of Guangdong, Guangxi, and Yunnan had snow. It damaged crops and blocked roads. Railway stations became insufferably crowded. A few people died in stampedes. The pretty face of the country shown in Olympic propaganda masked a churning chaos of suffering.

For Xiaobo and his friends, the blizzard crisis was not just bad weather but a symptom of deeper social problems—two in particular. They were sensitive issues, but now, with the government needing to remain tolerant, at least on the surface, there was perhaps an opportunity to air them.

One issue was that organizations in civil society in other countries that could offer aid during crises did not exist in China. Other societies had charities, churches, civic clubs, and the like. In China, where the state crushes all organizations except its own, there are no such independent groups. When a disaster strikes, the state is the only party that can act, and if the state fails, then everyone is helpless. "The Communist regime," Xiaobo wrote, "not only does immense harm of its own but sucks out all of the social space in which charity might operate."[6]

The other issue that lurked beneath the blizzard disaster was the urban household registration system that the Communist government had established in 1958. This system gave every resident of a city the privileges of a legal address, legal employment, access to schools and hospitals, coupons for rationed goods, and more—and none of this to nonresidents. Rural people were prohibited from moving to the cities and had no rights if they did. When hundreds of millions of "farmer workers" arrived in the 1990s to work in construction, manufacturing, sanitation, household service, and other menial jobs, they were allowed to live as second-class citizens without rights to schools or hospitals and under perpetual threat of forcible return to the countryside. Chinese society had come to resemble both India's caste system in the way it affixed permanent unequal labels upon people and South Africa's apartheid system in the way it enforced the geographical separation of unequal populations.

On February 15, 2008, Xiaobo and some friends decided to gather signatures for a petition to the annual "two meetings" scheduled for the following month in Beijing. They labeled it "Immediately Abolish the System of Segregation Between City and Countryside and Make the Term 'Farmer Worker' a Thing of the Past." They collected two lists of signatures, of people inside China and of others in exile. On the domestic list Xiaobo signed first, and the next two names were Ding Zilin and Jiang Peikun. The two names topping the exile list were Hu Ping and Wang Dan. It was a bold move to put Xiaobo's name and Hu Ping's in parallel. Hu had cowritten two open letters with Xiaobo in spring 1989 that had become the main basis for the regime's charge that Xiaobo worked for "overseas counterrevolutionary organizations." Wang Dan, for his part, had been number one on the government's list of wanted students following the June Fourth massacre. Even though nineteen years had passed, to put one's name in parallel with those two—and to do it on such a major issue, in the "sensitive" days right before the "two meetings"—was dangerous.

The regime's pre-Olympics tightening showed again on March 6, when state security agents in Beijing, offering no reason, abducted the famous human rights lawyer Teng Biao as he was walking home from work. They placed a hood on him, forced him into a black sedan that had no license plates, held him for forty-one hours (he did not know where), and then let him go. The incident raised a question in Xiaobo's mind. Why would the regime opt for such a crude technique—and use it on a famous rights lawyer, of all people? And right when it was seeking acceptance on the world stage? Xiaobo wrote an essay trying to imagine the regime's point of view. "When the dictators can't see any enemies they get even more fidgety. Especially when they are getting ready to place laurels upon their own heads, they live in round-the-clock apprehension. During the day they see gray clouds; at night they are awakened by nightmares."[7] As the Olympics approached, the government seemed to have decided to take no chances and to seal off any possible dissent.

A few days after Teng Biao's abduction, a serious disturbance arose in Tibet. Early March is always a sensitive time in Lhasa, capital of Tibet, because of the anniversary of the uprising of 1959, when thousands of Tibetans surrounded the Norbulingka Palace in Lhasa to protect the Dalai Lama from the Chinese military and were forcibly repressed. In the afternoon of March 10, 2008, three hundred or more monks came out of Drepung Monastery and walked down the hillside on which it rested shouting "We demand religious freedom!" and "Don't let too many Han [Chinese] people into Tibet!" Military police blocked and then beat them. Government authorities closed their monastery and two others. Four days later, on March 14, resentment that had built during the previous days (and months and years) finally burst forth. Several thousand Tibetans took to the streets in protest. They ransacked stores owned by Han or Muslim Chinese, set fires, and smashed cars. Authorities later announced that thirteen people, mostly Han Chinese, had been killed. They produced a video showing how all of the fault lay with the Tibetans, who were rioters and hooligans, and rebroadcast it inveterately on nationwide television. But the international press was watching as well and reporting a different story. That other story was a heavy blow to the authorities' efforts to project a pre-Olympics image of a society that was all sweetness and light. The authorities clamped down even harder, especially in Tibet but elsewhere too, in an effort to prevent other embarrassing episodes.

From his high school days at Boulder Village High School in Horqin Right
Front Banner, Xiaobo had felt a natural sympathy with China's national minorities. He had shared classrooms with Mongolian, Manchu, Daur, Uyghur, and
other minority children, and they all had enjoyed a beautiful natural environment. This and his preference for siding with underdogs made it natural that he
would sympathize with the Tibetans in 2008. He had become especially concerned with Tibetan problems in 2004 when the Tibetan poet Woeser, wife of
his friend Wang Lixiong, published a book of essays called *Notes from Tibet*. The
book sold well and quickly needed a second printing, but then was suddenly
banned. The authorities demanded that Woeser write a self-criticism or pay the
price for refusing—which was loss of job, government housing, and government
benefits. Woeser chose the losses. When Xiaobo heard this story he immediately
sat down and wrote an article, "Woeser's Faith and the Communists' Atheism."
He praised her defense of human dignity and pledged to stand with her no matter what.

Ethnic questions have always been among the most politically radioactive in
Communist China. Xiaobo's support for Woeser—however plain from the point
of view of human rights—was a rare and perilous move that even others in the
Rights Defense Movement were leery of making. A slightly misspoken phrase
could cause the police to move against a person "on suspicion of the crime of splitting the country." Wang Lixiong was a veteran in taking such risks. He had been
arrested in 1999 for doing field research in Xinjiang, home of the Uyghur minority, but did not let this daunt him. In 2002, while Tibetan Buddhists were being
given death sentences, he and Xiaobo appealed to halt the execution of one of
them, the Living Buddha of Garze Prefecture in Sichuan. Their effort failed; the
Living Buddha was put to death in 2003. The smallest of comforts in their failure was that it marked the first time in Communist Chinese history that Han
intellectuals had spoken out for a persecuted Chinese minority.

Now, in 2008, Xiaobo and Wang Lixiong released an open letter on March 22
listing "Twelve Opinions on How to Handle the Situation in Tibet." It called for
the government to cease its one-sided reports, because these only worsened ethnic antagonisms and increased tensions. It called for an investigation both of the
Tibetans who had been responsible for the rioting and of the Han Chinese who
had fabricated reports to mislead public opinion. It further called for conscientious reflection on how to avoid problems in the future and, most importantly,
for a fundamental reconsideration of the national minorities policies that had so
obviously failed.[8] But when Xiaobo set out in search of others to sign the open
letter, he found progress difficult. Minority rights had never been a high priority
for Han activists.

One exception was Chang Ping, an influential commentator at *Southern Metropolitan News*, who published a commentary after the March 14 events, "Tibet: Nationalist Sentiment and the Truth." He criticized the Chinese government for its false reporting on Tibet, saying this only fed Han chauvinism. The piece sparked fevered controversy. Many people agreed with Chang Ping, but there were vociferous "patriotic" voices on the other side, and the government not surprisingly sided with the latter. By 2010 Chang Ping was forced to resign at *Southern Metropolitan*. He eventually fled to exile in Germany, where he wrote on China for Deutsche Welle.

After his and Wang Lixiong's open letter, Xiaobo wrote three more articles on Tibet in spring 2008: "The Tibet Crisis Is a Failure of the Materialist Dictatorship" (March 28);[9] "So Long as Chinese Have No Freedom, Tibet Will Have No Autonomy" (April 10);[10] and "My View of the Communists' Opening the Door to Negotiations" (April 27).[11] In these he argues that the "ethnic problem" between Han people and Tibetans is not as fundamental as the political problem that they share: both groups live under a dictatorship that has brought them suffering in demonstrably similar ways. Freedom for both Tibetans and Chinese, if it comes, will come on the same day. Meanwhile, Han Chinese should look at the Tibet issue as involving the whole of society, not just the government. All Chinese should show respect for Tibetan culture, and a good first step in that direction would be to welcome "the spirit of the snowy region," the Dalai Lama, back home. In an essay written on November 5, 2008, the day after Barack Obama was elected president of the United States, Xiaobo reflects on the ability of a democracy to choose a minority citizen as its president.[12] Borrowing a joke from Wang Lixiong, he wonders in the essay if the Chinese Communists "could invite the Dalai Lama back to China to serve as our nation's president, *our* Barack Obama. Such a move would make the best use of the Dalai Lama's stature in the world as well as in Tibet"—where he, like none other, might mollify Tibetan extremists. Moreover, it could

> bring into play a spirit of tolerance among Han Chinese.... With [the Dalai Lama's] worldwide prestige, he could do a huge amount to improve China's image and to gain international support for ways to handle China's ethnic conflicts.... In the Tibetan government-in-exile in Dharamsala, India, he has an excellent track record in implementing experiments in democracy similar to those of Chiang Ching-kuo in Taiwan in the 1980s. Such experiments could serve as models for the political transition of China as a whole.

It was a joke, but made a number of very serious points.

Despite the regime's tightening in early 2008, Xiaobo and a number of his political friends—Teng Biao, Liang Xiaoyan, Cui Weiping, Fan Yafeng, Zhou Duo, and others—attended a series of seminars between late March and mid-May on the topic of "reconciliation." Qiu Yueshou, a Chinese Australian scholar, and Wang Guangze, who did media work in China, founded the group, which they called Brains for Reconciliation in China. They recruited Chen Ziming to take the intellectual lead. The group rejected violence but also did not want to wait for a political deus ex machina to appear, because none was in sight. Moreover, no such savior could solve the larger problem, which the group saw as civil discourse: the question of how the Chinese could rise from the moral ruins the Communists had left behind to create a culture of dignified fellow citizens.

The regime harassed the group as they tried to find a restaurant where they could hold meetings, but the first session, on the topic "Conflict and Reconciliation," eventually did take place on March 29, 2008. Chen Ziming brought along three documents that he thought best articulated the case for reconciliation. One of them was the "The June Second Hunger Strike Declaration" that Xiaobo had drafted in 1989. He read several passages from it aloud.

Not everyone in the group agreed that reconciliation was the right path, when the regime was acting so crudely and arbitrarily. Chen Ziming answered that no matter how badly the other side behaved, the group should cultivate civility on their side. Xiaobo was equally direct: "If the authorities reject reconciliation, we should stress it all the more. We don't have the access to violence or the huge organizations that they have. We have only ethics. If we don't stress ethics, what can we stress?"[13] Others pointed out that some people had already paid heavy prices for their ethics. Was it not hard to ask them to "reconcile" with the people who had inflicted the suffering? Xiaobo had personal credibility on this question because he had been incarcerated three times. He answered that they had to rise above personal situations and take a more detached view:

> We need to look at society as a whole and observe how it has been advancing step by step, how the influences of our movement have gradually been pressing change upon the governing system. . . . As long as we remain committed to the morality of our ideals and continue to do the things that we believe we ought to do, there is no reason to despair for this country of ours. If the regime does not propose reconciliation, why does that mean our side cannot? It is not something that will come in a day or two. We need to keep pressing it. Look how long it took to get them to accept the term "human rights." It was first put to them in the 1980s, and it took until the next century to get into their constitution. But it did get there.[14]

For Xiaobo, "reconciliation" was more than a political program; it had become an approach to life in general. He observed it especially when interacting with police. He avoided language that would anger them, explaining:

> It takes special mettle and patience to remain civil even while absorbing the physical and verbal abuse that police dole out. It does no good to trade blows or curses with them. If you fire back by calling them dogs, it only reminds them that dogs bite people, and they will bite you. We need to remember when we look at police that if you mentally strip away their uniforms they are just people—ordinary people—whose morality, on average, is neither above nor below the norm. If they try to goad you into anger with insults, a civilized response from you will frustrate them and maybe even touch the humanity that is inside them.[15]

This was the first time anyone in China's opposition movement had made the proposal to reach out to the human nature that dwelled inside police. But Xiaobo's friends received the idea well. It was a radical negation of Mao Zedong's doctrine that there is no human nature but only "class natures" of different warring classes.

Xiaobo's view struck Zhou Duo with considerable force. Zhou pointed out that in Nazi Germany one part of the population was set aside, on ethnic grounds, as not human, and in Mao's China a similar thing was done on political grounds. On no grounds, he argued, could the group or anyone else tolerate any assumption that certain humans lack humanity. But this task was not easy. It would require a thorough overhaul of the political culture.

Chen Ziming raised the question whether the group needed a slogan or a formal statement of purpose. Xiaobo was skeptical. To try to put into concrete words an overarching statement that everyone could agree to would be difficult. The very question "Are we opponents or reconcilers?" was controversial. It would be better, Xiaobo said, to focus on specific projects: Can we aim to end *laojiao* and all "labor reform," or to abolish item no. 105 in the criminal code where "agitation to subvert state power" is listed as a crime?[16] At this level people could easily agree.

As the group wrestled with these questions, Mother Nature intervened. On May 12, 2008, an earthquake of 8.2 on the Richter scale struck in Wenchuan county in Sichuan province. Houses collapsed over a wide area. In some places landslides engulfed entire villages. Some people were buried even before they understood what was happening. Damage to rail lines and supply systems for water, electricity, and postal service made rescue efforts extremely difficult. Eventually the government announced the toll: 69,227 people killed, 374,644 injured, 17,923 missing.[17] The most heart-rending stories and images were of children's school buildings that had collapsed. Reports said that 5,300 primary school students had been lost. Photos of dead children still wearing their scarves and backpacks appeared on the Internet, as did photos of school buildings lying in ruins right next to other buildings that were still standing. Investigations revealed that the collapsed schools had been shoddily constructed. Inferior materials had been used, and corruption was the reason for it. The schools were derided as "beancurd-dreg" buildings. People's grief became laced with anger.

Traditionally, the Communist Party's policy on reporting disasters was to allow only a few journalists to visit the stricken site and require that the "trend" in their reporting be to show how heroic the rescue efforts were, not how bad the disaster was. Following the great Tangshan earthquake of 1976, in which about 300,000 people died, foreign journalists were barred from the area for fully seven years. In 2008, though—after the Olympics-related order no. 477 about increased freedom for foreign reporters—the policy had to be different. Foreign journalists and relief agencies were allowed into the Sichuan disaster area. China's Premier Wen Jiabao paid a visit to Wenchuan and won popular approval by appearing on television to show his concern.

The earthquake brought an unusual opportunity to activists in the Rights Defense Movement. Now they could be responsible citizens in ways other than opposing the political regime. Always before, the government had blocked citizens' efforts at disaster relief; Xiaobo had written criticisms on this very point.[18] But this time the tide of popular sympathy was so strong that blocking was not an option. More than three hundred relief groups and about three million volunteers showed up in the disaster areas. They reached everywhere—not only heavily hit areas but lightly affected ones as well, including remote mountain sites to which state-sponsored relief never came near. They offered everything from first aid to comfort counseling, and they supplied things like baby formula, paper diapers, tampons, and other items that state aid was not providing. They picked through rubble looking for survivors, lined up to donate blood, and played games with children inside tents at their schools. They exercised new dimensions in the concept of "citizen." Not only did citizens have rights before a government; they also had duties toward one another.

Many people wanted to donate money but did not trust government-run organizations, including the Chinese Red Cross. Perceiving a need, Luo Yonghao, manager of the web page Bullog, one of China's hottest at the time, announced that the site would receive disaster-relief donations and account for their use rigorously. Bullog had an excellent reputation in the rights movement because for two years it had been publishing China's best bloggers (Ai Weiwei, Han Han,

Liang Wendao, Lian Yue, Chang Ping, and others) and had shown integrity whenever confrontations with authorities had arisen. It had broadcast in real time the PX "strolling" demonstrations in Xiamen and had refused to back off from reporting the "black kiln" story in Shanxi. So it was not surprising that people responded confidently to its offer to accept donations for Wenchuan.

More than two million yuan came in. Han Han, the very popular author of short, politically charged blog posts, headed for Sichuan together with Luo Yong-hao, and they drove an off-road vehicle into the disaster areas to distribute relief supplies. They videotaped what they were doing and put all receipts and invoices— right down to the brand names of the bottled water they were handing out— onto the Internet at Bullog. Every penny was accounted for. They did this in part to thank contributors and to maintain their trust, but also in part to present a contrast to the black holes into which donations to government offices disappeared. Xiaobo wrote an essay, "Society's Splendor in a Great Earthquake," in which he explained why, seeing the popular outpouring of sympathy and support for the earthquake victims, he was now more confident than ever that hopes for China's future were best placed in *minjian* society—in energies that came from below.[19]

The dreadful earthquake allowed Xiaobo a respite, however fleeting, from his feelings of alienation from China's governing regime. When the State Council announced on May 18 that the next three days, May 19 through 21, would be national days of mourning for the victims, Xiaobo was moved. May 19 was the victims' seventh day in death, and it was a Chinese tradition to mark "day seven." In the morning, the national flag was lowered in respect. At 2:28 in the afternoon, everyone in the country was to observe three minutes of silence, while cars, trains, and ships sounded their horns and warning sirens wailed. As he watched these events on television, Xiaobo found that "the national flag stimulated feelings of respect in me for the first time."[20] It was also the first time since 1949 that the flag had been lowered to honor ordinary people. Xiaobo remained, as earlier in life, vulnerable to emotional surges. He wrote:

> I wept as I watched the flag go down. They were tears of gratitude: the souls of tens of thousands who had died in the great quake were getting a bit of comfort. But the far greater numbers of ordinary folk who had died during the last fifty years in human-caused disasters such as the Great Leap Forward, the Cultural Revolution, and the June Fourth massacre still hadn't received any national comfort. If we say that lowering the flag for the victims of a great natural disaster shows for the first time that state power is drawing closer to human life, human

nature, and popular opinion, then, when it finally is lowered for victims of human-caused disasters, we will be witnessing for the first time how state power is coming home to the universal values of human rights. It will also be a sign that China is moving toward freedom and democracy.[21]

The departed souls of June Fourth, hovering over him since 1990, were still hovering.

That year Xiaobo's annual poem for the June Fourth victims was called "Children · Mothers · Spring: For the Website of the Tiananmen Mothers." It contained these lines:

> Every night
> The lost souls can touch the Mothers' vault of heaven
> Like a child conceived in October
> Listening to its mother's heart beat[22]

On the sensitive date of June 3, a writers' group in China that called itself the Beijing Research Institute on Contemporary Chinese Language awarded Xiaobo its 2008 Prize for Contributions to Contemporary Chinese, to "honor his constructive and insightful use of words to move China toward freedom and democracy." The tribute recalled Xiaobo's past as a "dark horse" in the late 1980s and noted marked changes in both his writing and his deportment, from a brash "heavenly steed, racing across the sky" to a "mild, compassionate, reserved, and quietly tenacious" person in the present. It continued:

> He has moved beyond the roles of "combatant," "anti-establishment writer," and "dissident intellectual" and has concentrated on the actual conditions of society and the complexities that a democratic transition involves. He begins within the limits of the system as it exists today and works to use law, administrative process, and the pressure of public opinion to achieve realization of the rights of individual citizens and, step by step, practical changes that aim at maximizing public interest and helping society to advance.[23]

This was the first and only time Xiaobo received an award from inside China. It originated in the circle of friends who worked with him and reflected their shared high opinion of his character. Their decision to make the award on the eve of June Fourth was acknowledgment of the powerful spiritual bond that they knew he felt with the massacre victims. It touched Xiaobo deeply that his friends were so aware of this point. There was no award ceremony—there couldn't be—because *guobao* were confining Xiaobo at home during those very sensitive days. But he wrote a statement of thanks and used it, once again, to lay bare deep thoughts about his own inadequacies. Xiaobo evokes the tone of Lu Xun's prose poems collected in *Wild Grass*:

> As a survivor of the massacre—for nineteen years now!—no matter how hard I try to compensate, to find a route to dignity, to be an adequate person, to be worthy of the lost souls of those young, their dark eyes still peer down on me and I still live in shame. . . . About death, nothing that I say or write or do can ever equal the last glimpse that those lost souls took in the moment before they died, or ever equal a Tiananmen mother, with white hair, clutching a photo of her murdered child. The piercing intensity of those lost souls peering down puts a survivor like me on moral trial; the tomorrow that the white-haired mother beckons is an unending inspiration in a survivor like me. . . . As I accept [the award] and express my thanks for it, I should think of it not as a commendation for the past but as a warning for the future. . . . Wild grass grows from the soil of a wasteland; my Chinese language grows from beyond the grave.[24]

On the evening of June 4, Xiaobo and Liu Xia left their apartment to go to Liu Xia's parents' home for dinner. At the door to their building, police blocked their way and invited Xiaobo to come with them for a chat. When he refused, they manhandled him into their little police station in the courtyard. Xiaobo let his friends know about the incident, and that very evening Ding Zilin, Jiang Peikun, Jiang Qisheng, Zhang Zuhua, Liao Yiwu, and the stainless-steel rat wrote an open letter denouncing the use of force against Xiaobo. "For nineteen years [since the massacre]," they wrote, "Mr. Liu Xiaobo has adhered unfailingly to nonviolence and rational resistance in both theory and practice; he has tirelessly called upon his fellow citizens not to answer violence with violence and to use tolerant dialogue to dispel hatreds."[25]

Xiaobo's counsel of nonviolence had been clear in his advice to farmers in Taishi village three years earlier. He had praised them for their "Gandhian" principles, in particular these three:

1. When encountering a condition that conscience finds to be intolerably unjust, people by all means must rise in opposition and must persist in their opposition to the end even if there are repeated failures along the way and even if great personal risk is involved.

2. Once one begins in nonviolence, the principle of nonviolence must be maintained even if the other side uses violent repression or persecution by unjust law.

3. People can earn dignity and freedom by answering the regime's ability to create suffering with their own capacity to tolerate suffering and by using their spiritual power to withstand the physical violence of the regime.[26]

The teaching of nonviolence to Chinese protesters might seem a superfluous task, because unarmed civilians ought to know that a physical confrontation with a huge and heavily armed state is futile. However, during those years, ordinary citizens were sometimes resorting to violence. On July 1, 2008, for example, a young man named Yang Jia walked into a police station in the Zhabei district in Shanghai, killed six police with a knife, and injured four others. July 1 is the anniversary of the founding of the Communist Party of China in 1921. Leaders dress in military regalia for the occasion and make lengthy speeches that are broadcast on television. News of the Yang Jia incident spread widely on the Internet, and a hubbub of comment ensued.

The trouble had originated nine months earlier, on October 5, 2007, when Yang Jia, who was from Beijing, was in Shanghai as a tourist and rented a bicycle. Unfortunately the bicycle lacked the required license plate. Police stopped Yang, confronted him about the violation, and then brought him to the local police station in the Zhabei district, where they interrogated him for six hours. As he complained about this treatment, five or six policemen beat him. He returned to Beijing the next day but fired verbal broadsides in letters and e-mail to the Public Security offices both in Zhabei and at the municipal level in Shanghai. Apparently he made a good case, because Shanghai officials twice sent people to Beijing to negotiate with him. They offered him 300 yuan in reparation but refused to acknowledge any wrongdoing. Yang Jia insisted on the admission of wrongdoing and refused the money even as the offer rose, in stages, to 1,500 yuan. That was the background for July 1, when Yang went back to Shanghai and to the Zhabei police station with eight Molotov cocktails. His plan was to slip past the guard who stood outside, but the guard confronted him and became the first victim of murder by knife. Yang then went inside to assault the others.

Xiaobo had been noting for several years how popular respect for officialdom in China was declining as civic consciousness was rising. For the more extreme voices on the Internet, anyone who wore a state uniform, including the six police whom Yang Jia killed, represented the state. Therefore, Yang was "a hero," "a chivalric knight," and "one brave dude" for attacking not human beings but the state. Meanwhile the regime only made things worse. The very evening of the killings, it detained Yang Jia's mother, Wang Jingmei, brought her to a police station, and "disappeared" her. On October 5, 2007, during three of the six hours when Yang Jia was being roughed up by the Zhabei police, she had been on the telephone with her son. That made her obviously an important witness to what happened.

Eventually it emerged that the police had brought the mother to an insane asylum. She was held 173 days and released only after her son had been executed. As an asylum inmate, she had not been allowed to attend her son's trial. In court Yang Jia was represented by a state-appointed lawyer who happened also to be the legal adviser of the Zhabei district government. This lawyer presented a "letter of retention" from the mother, but no one could ever confirm that she had understood herself to be retaining him or had wanted to do so. The trial was first set for July 29 but, "for necessary reasons," was postponed. Those reasons clearly had something to do with the Olympic Games that were to open on August 8; the last thing the authorities could have wanted was a popular outcry over a politically fraught trial right then. The delay was no surprise to people accustomed to seeing political power trump law. The famous artist Ai Weiwei had written more than ten blog posts about the Yang Jia matter. He compared Yang to Sun Zhigang in the way both had been abducted and beaten and, without condoning murder, said he could understand Yang's anger: "Stalwarts like Yang Jia and Sun Zhigang stood up for the downtrodden. Their names can never be removed from the annals of those who have initiated change. They looked the purveyors of disgusting filth in the eye and didn't back down."[27] Ai also wrote about the astonishing disappearance of Yang's mother and said that the whole affair pointed to a need for a thorough revamping of China's legal system. His comments sparked quick and wide support on the Internet.

On August 24, right after the Olympics closed, the No. 2 Intermediate Court in Shanghai tried Yang Jia's case and sentenced him to death. Yang appealed, but the lower court's ruling was upheld. On October 20, Ai Weiwei announced a "Citizens' Proposal to Grant Clemency to Mr. Yang Jia." He gathered 44 names, and soon more than 4,000 had signed. Many of Xiaobo's friends—Zhang Zuhua, Liao Yiwu, and others—were among them.

Xiaobo did not sign. He completely supported Ai Weiwei's efforts to expose what had happened in the case and could understand Yang Jia's outburst. The pattern was one he had seen before: the regime abuses an ordinary citizen; the citizen finds no possibility of help from officials or the courts; all doors are closed; with nowhere to turn, he or she goes outside the system for escape or revenge. "When six police died," Xiaobo wrote, "it was a direct result of Yang

Jia's violent attack and an indirect result of the injustice in our legal system and the tyranny of our political system."[28]

Still, while Xiaobo saw Yang Jia as a victim of the system, he could not see him as a hero. Yang Jia's actions had focused Xiaobo's thinking on a topic he had long been struggling with: how—*by what methods*—could a transition to democracy happen in China? In the second half of July he wrote ten articles on the Yang Jia matter with titles that included "When a Murderer Becomes a Hero," "The Shanghai Police Cannot Bottle up the Truth of the Yang Jia Case," "The Violent Rule of the Regime and the Violent Revenge of Yang Jia," and "The Yang Jia Kind of Revenge Is Primitive Justice." He knew the articles would cast him as an opponent of the powerful surge of support for Yang Jia on the Internet. People there would denounce him as severely as the regime did. But this was who he was, so he went ahead.

He pointed out that Yang Jia differed from others who had lashed out because he was not under immediate threat at the moment when he chose violence. But his main point was:

> Yang Jia is not a hero because he ended the lives of six people. In my view a life is a life—there is no fundamental distinction between a policeman's and a citizen's. We cannot say that a police uniform is sufficient cause to execute the person who wears it. Even if it could be established that one of the six who died was in the group that had beaten Yang Jia, the crime would not be commensurate with the punishment.[29]

To some of Xiaobo's critics, saying that a policeman's life deserved the same respect as an ordinary citizen's was anathema. Xiaobo saw two possible causes for this. One was that the incident was a one-time release of anger at a system that in normal times forced its tyranny upon people and offered no other way out. The other was the survival in contemporary Chinese culture of the heroic "knight-errant" tradition like that found in the classic novel *Water Margin*, where "officials oppressed and people revolted" and "heroes of the green forests" who had been "pressed to the limit" fought back. In 1998 *Water Margin* had been dramatized on Chinese television in forty-three episodes, repeatedly intoning the theme song, "Act when action is needed and rampage across the realm!" In Xiaobo's view the series confused righteous action with simple pillage. Behind the quest for justice, which he supported, crouched a hate mentality, which he opposed. That mentality came close to revering vigilante violence and to viewing murder as heroism.[30]

Xiaobo began noticing a phenomenon that he called the "antagonism of the disinterested." In Chinese tradition, he noted, "every grievance has a cause, every debt a debtor,"[31] which meant that, to attain proper revenge, the offended party must find and punish exactly the person who committed the offense. In antagonism of the disinterested, however, person A expresses anger at person B not because B has harmed A but because B is *the kind of* person who has harmed A. Yang Jia killed people who were in the same *category* as those who beat him up. The countless voices on the Internet that praised him also illustrated a form of antagonism of the disinterested because they, although having no personal stake in the events, no doubt had suffered bullying by people who were in the same category as those who had bullied Yang Jia. Xiaobo had many other examples. On June 28, 2008, just two days before Yang Jia's rampage, the rape and murder of a young woman in Weng'an county in Guizhou province had brought tens of thousands of people from the surrounding areas to protest the unjust way officials were handling the case. "Why such huge crowds?" Xiaobo asked in an essay about the events.[32] The people were strangers to the victim's family, but they were hardly strangers to the kind of abuse the family was enduring. In government reports they "did not understand the facts" and "were riled by agitators." In fact, Xiaobo wrote, they were expressing deep resentment that had accumulated from many years of abuse they had experienced in their own lives.

To the regime, a large crowd of protesters like that was the worst of nightmares. It was a challenge to the regime's pretense that everything was always basically fine. Regime opponents often watched such events hoping that this time a straw would break a camel's back. Xiaobo did not take that view, though. He conceived the issue much more broadly. It meant little to hammer on the point that the regime is evil and needs to be replaced; of course that was so. What needed attention was the deeper question of how to do a political transition. The method the Communists used of knocking everything down and starting over was out of the question, and it was still further out of the question to imagine building a democracy in a rarefied space separated from China's actual conditions. Those conditions included Communist rule, so ending that rule and building a Chinese democracy inevitably would have to be two facets of the same process.

A key to the transition, as Vaclav Havel had taught, would be to cultivate civility in society. It worried Xiaobo to see even supporters of the Rights Defense Movement show remnants of premodern thinking, as when cheering Yang Jia as a *Water Margin* sort of hero. A major culture shift was a very tall order, of course; it would need to start before and would certainly last beyond the departure of the Communist system. But it needed to start somewhere.

Xiaobo laid out six reasons a gradual transition would be preferable to quicker, violent change:

1. Every earlier political transition in China, including that of the Communists, was done by violence. Rulers who win by violence go on to rule by violence. We don't want a transition to another violent regime.

2. If our governing system cannot respect human dignity, guarantee rights, and prevent state power from infringing on individual freedom, then we will remain basically in barbarism, in a place where the vigilante heroism of a Yang Jia comes at the price of loss of life on both sides and achieves, at most, only a primitive justice.

3. The cost of violent transition in both lives and money is extremely high. I am not speaking here only of vigilante violence. I mean also the violence that occurs within the law of the regime.

4. Given the current conditions of the Chinese regime and of the populace it rules, the possibility of success of a violent revolution is zero. Large-scale organization in civil society is impossible, and there are few funds for such an effort.

5. To continue with a policy that condones violence will spark violent incidents in the short run, cause the regime to redouble its use of political terror, and thereby weaken the already too-weak Rights Defense Movement. Conditions for progress in civil society will move from bad to worse.

6. A healthy legal system must be built on the assent of the people. For that, people first must believe in the law. It is easy to pass laws and to set up an enforcement system, but not so easy to earn the willingness of citizens to take the system as their own. In today's China, obedience of the law is not based at all on willing assent. Law is entirely a top-down instrument to enforce the will of the dictatorship. People obey not from an inner acceptance of the law but only from fear of punishment by it.[33]

Item 6 on this list may have been the most profound. In premodern Chinese political culture, as in Maoist culture, the assumption of inequality among people of different political status was so engrained that "equality before the law" was almost impossible to conceive. In asking his compatriots to learn to "take the law as their own," Xiaobo was calling for a crucial but very difficult change.

Through August and September 2008, Xiaobo felt that progress was becoming increasingly visible. Pressure from below was forcing the regime to make adjustments in its policies, sometimes from a defensive position. In the wake of the Weng'an and Yang Jia events, for example, there were new guidelines on how the police should deal with people they picked up on the streets or at demonstrations. They were warned to stay within published regulations and that if they were to use excessive force, they would be subject to dismissal. Xiaobo used the new standards to make his point that there are other ways than violence or hateful speech—ways that are more effective and less destructive—to express grievances or moral outrage. Hatred, he wrote, is but an "elementary stage" in human feelings.[34] He recalled for readers what he had written in the June 2 Hunger Strike Declaration at Tiananmen and added, "I still believe today, nineteen years later, in the spread of democracy in China through peaceful means . . . we must not let hatred or violence poison our minds or the process of China's democratization."[35]

19
Charter 08

On December 9, 2008, a statement called Charter 08, sent electronically from Beijing, appeared on Chinese-language websites in the United States and in English translation in *The New York Review of Books*. News of this flashed through media across the world. A careful statement of political ideals ranging from free speech to constitutional government to education to environmental protection, it can be seen as an indirect consequence of the bloody suppression at Tiananmen in 1989. For many Chinese, the moral authority of the Communist Party of China had slipped to virtually zero. The political idealists of the 1980s had given up on all rulers of the state; some had stepped "outside the system" and others had left the country. Those who remained now regarded the system as a mere machine, a dead shell worthy of neither their ideals nor their trust. The regime began offering them money making and shallow nationalism as things to believe in, but for moral or political ideals they could only look elsewhere.

Chinese citizens who covered their alienation with a patina of conformity were far more numerous than the regime ever wanted to admit. Resisters were not just students and intellectuals but ordinary people in many reaches of society. Controlling nearly all material resources, the regime worked hard to maintain tranquility on the surface, but the fit between the surface and the human struggles below was never very good. The Rights Defense Movement of the early and mid 2000s, with its welter of cases in a variety of fields, and the daily average of more than two hundred "masses incidents" of protest were evidence enough of discontent in society's innards.

Privately, intellectuals began to explore how they might reposition themselves. For some, Vaclav Havel and other Eastern Europeans were helpful. In Havel's famous essay "The Power of the Powerless," he writes that authoritarianism and normal human life begin from opposite points. Life begins from the self, authoritarianism from a system that controls all selves. Mao Zedong teaches that for revolutionaries, "life is resistance." Havel says no, life is life. It can include resistance but is always more than that. This new way of thinking became increasingly attractive to young people in China in the years after Tiananmen. To them it said one can take one's own situation and judgment as the starting point in life, no longer needing to look upward to an authority. Then, as people choose norms and ideals for themselves, they will discover natural affinities that can be the basis for new community and solidarity. The Internet became a big help in bringing people together. Feelings of isolation were far less common than before.

The influence of Eastern Europe and of Havel in particular is evident in the name of Charter 08. It is an echo of Charter 77, the "citizens' initiative" that appeared in Prague in 1977 a year after a group of young Czech citizens who called themselves "the plastic people of the universe" were arrested—and some imprisoned—for singing songs of which their government disapproved. To Vaclav Havel and others—philosopher Jan Patocka, actor Pavel Landovsky, literary critic Ludvik Vaculik, and Jiri Hajek, a former minister of education and of foreign affairs—the arrests of the plastic people represented an unacceptable threat to freedom. On January 6, 1977, they unveiled Charter 77, signed by 241 people from a variety of fields: writers, actors, professors, workers, and the discontent young; there were both members and nonmembers of the Communist Party and both Catholics and Protestants. Eventually more than a thousand people signed. The charter's position was that the Czechoslovak government, following the Helsinki Accords of 1975, had signed two international human rights covenants—one on "civil and political rights" and another on "economic, social, and cultural rights"— but had not implemented them. In freedoms of speech, publication, religion, and movement, and in respect for privacy, the authorities had gone in the opposite direction.

The authors of Charter 77 knew that they were expressing authentic and widespread sentiment, yet were careful to stay within certain bounds. They could remember—from Hungary in 1956 and from their own country in 1968—that posing political threats to satellite regimes of the Soviet Union could bring dreadful consequences. Charter 77 did eventually play an important role in the collapse of communism in Czechoslovakia, but it did not begin with that as a stated goal.

Like Charter 77, Charter 08 was originally signed by people from a range of social backgrounds. Lawyers, workers, farmers, professors, writers, journalists, business owners, environmental activists, retired Communist high officials, seasoned dissidents, grassroots activists, and members of the Tiananmen Mothers—303 people in all—signed before it was published. It differed considerably from Charter 77 in content, though. It was much broader, addressing democracy, constitutionalism, juridical independence, education, welfare, the environment, land ownership, and more. Although generally mild in its wording, it could be seen as a call for a new government. The difference between the two charters—one minimalist, the other expansive—can be understood by comparing their places in the opposition movements they accompanied. In Czechoslovakia, Charter 77 was the spark for a movement that followed. In China, Charter 08 was an outgrowth of a movement that had been building for nearly a decade. The difference can also be seen in how the two groups saw their relations with the larger society. Havel felt a need for "modesty." The Charter 08 activists saw themselves as leaders.

The earliest proposal for a charter in China came from Wen Kejian in Hangzhou. Wen had got to know Zhang Zuhua, eventually the main figure in Charter 08, when Zhang began managing some prodemocracy columns on Wen's website, Spring Thunder Action, in 2002. By temperament, Zhang was reserved and scholarly. During the Rights Defense Movement, when many of his friends were gaining reputations for speaking out on public issues, he stayed in the background. He sponsored some petitions but was never very well known until the Charter 08 project arrived. Wen Kejian was a regular petition signer, and trust between the two eventually reached a point where Wen authorized Zhang to add his name to petitions without prior consultation. Wen met Liu Xiaobo online in 2003, and mutual respect between them also grew quickly.

Wen brought important resources to the charter project: from his study of law at Zhejiang University, a sharp grasp of legal thinking, and from his work in the import-export business, a wide range of social contacts. A charter project occurred to him because, as he talked with the many people he knew, he often heard them say, "Yes, yes, yes, we know . . . but what are you going to *do* about it? What's the solution?" The question set Wen to thinking about the value of an overall vision statement that people in society might identify with.

The Rights Defense Movement had an inherent weakness, Wen felt. It depended too much on particular cases: the SARS case, the Liu Di case, the Sun Zhigang case, and so on. Each case had wider importance because it represented a principle (freedom of speech, freedom from arbitrary arrest, and others), and the nationwide support that poured in came because of the *principle* involved, not just the case itself. The movement did not highlight principles adequately and did not show how they were interrelated. Constituencies had grown up in parallel, as it were: rights lawyers wanted legal reform, journalists sought press freedom, economists wanted better markets, public intellectuals were interested in constitutions and civil society. What the movement needed, Wen reasoned, was an overarching statement of political principles that could subsume various interests, hold constant through time, and be a vision for all of society.

To put out a vision statement under the jealous scrutiny of the Communist Party of China would, Wen knew, be a delicate matter. Seven years earlier, in June 1998, a few of Wen's fellow provincials from Zhejiang had used the occasion of U.S. President Bill Clinton's visit to China to announce the formation of a Democracy Party of China, whose watchword was "End One-Party Dictatorship, Establish Democratic Government." People began to join. But "end one-party rule" was (and still is) the lethal third rail of Chinese Communist politics. Within days Wang Youcai and other leaders of the Democracy Party were rounded up and given prison sentences of nine to thirteen years. It was a ticklish challenge, therefore, to put out a broadly based statement of principles without the authors looking like a "party."

But Wen went ahead. He shared his idea with a small group of friends in Zhejiang, and they encouraged him. In August 2005, he brought the idea to Beijing and shared it with Xiaobo, Zhang Zuhua, Liu Junning, and several others. He heard three different reactions: go for it!; I'm not opposed; and better not.

Xiaobo was in the third category and gave three reasons for his skepticism: a text of such breadth would have to be put in abstract language and so might seem empty and lacking in new thought; similar things had been tried in the past and had never really made a difference (here Xiaobo was referring to an initiative by Qin Yongmin in 1993 and one by Yan Jiaqi in 1994);[1] and the time was not ripe for such an effort. It would be wiser, Xiaobo felt, to wait until many people were calling for a political transition, after which a statement could be drafted and implemented virtually overnight. Wen Kejian listened but was not persuaded. The earlier attempts that Xiaobo mentioned had not been well crafted; some of their provisions had been too frail and needed strengthening. Moreover, postponing the writing of a vision statement until the eve of a crisis would leave little time to form a broad consensus about it. A statement that was ready in advance could set the agenda for a transition.

Zhang Zuhua encouraged Wen more than Xiaobo had. Zhang agreed with Xiaobo that it was far too early to speak of forming a political party, but a public statement of principles, he thought, was a good idea. He had studied the transitions to democracy in South Korea and Taiwan and felt that the current situation in China, with the rise of the Internet and the emergence of the Rights Defense Movement, closely resembled the "outside the Party" stage (from the mid-1970s to the mid-1980s) of the movement toward democracy in Taiwan. In

Taiwan, "Party" referred to the Nationalist Party and its one-party rule, while *dangwai*, "outside the party," allowed space for activism for various causes: farmers' rights, environmental protection, food safety, gender equality, students' rights, and others. As Zhang saw it, the foundation that these activities laid made it possible, in the second half of 1986, to organize the political party that came to be called the Democratic Progressive Party. So for him, Wen Kejian's proposal offered a hope that the cacophony of rights activities in China might be brought under the common umbrella of support for democracy. In that case, Zhang wrote, the task became "to write a statement that articulates the broadest possible consensus, so that democracy advocates, human rights defenders, and intellectual liberals in the far-flung corners of China can be brought together into a strong and unified force."[2] Zhang Zuhua's views drew support from a number of others, especially an articulate friend named Wang Debang. Wang had entered the Philosophy Department of Beijing Normal University in 1985, around the time when Xiaobo was electrifying packed classrooms with his eloquent lectures on aesthetics and freedom. At Tiananmen in 1989, Wang was a member of Beijing Normal's "dialogue delegation" to talk to the government. After graduation he wrote criticisms of the regime that led several times to house arrest and police raids on his home. Supporting Zhang Zuhua and Wen Kejian, he argued that the Rights Defense Movement had reached a bottleneck:

> Most of our activity is tied to particular times and places. Rights-support work has become a project of chasing madly from one crisis to the next in search of temporary fixes. Unless the problems that cause the emergencies are addressed systemically, the flare-ups will only become more numerous and difficult. Unless we do it on purpose, rights-support work will not move up to the level of the political system or the reconstruction of values. Our work will not have any cumulative effect and will not reach the goal that rights be protected before they are violated. The authorities will just come in with their steamroller and crush whatever ad hoc advances we make.[3]

Liu Junning was at first dubious about the charter idea but later, after testing out some phrases in his own mind, began to warm to it. He told Zhang Zuhua that he hoped its language could resemble that of the U.S. Declaration of Independence—concise, comprehensive, high-minded. The analogy did not entirely persuade Zhang, but it did lead him to conceive the charter "not only as a statement of principles for today's democracy movement but also as the basis of a constitution for a democratic China of the future. . . . [It could be] a broad outline and basic indication of direction that people could think about, and it could be a contingency plan for an emergency."[4]

A lively discussion ensued about what to call the document. A "declaration"? An "open statement?" The word "charter" enjoyed the precedents of Charter 77 in Czechoslovakia and an Asian Human Rights Charter that had been announced in Kwangju, South Korea, in 1998. For the scholarly Zhang Zuhua, there was further reason. In the West, the word reached back to the British Magna Carta of 1215, and in China, the characters *xian* 宪 and *zhang* 章, which make up the compound that means "charter" in modern Chinese, appear in juxtaposition in the ancient *Book of Rites* to mean "imitate" or "learn from."[5] This chance confluence of East and West charmed him. For the time being, before any decision was reached, the drafters called it simply their "text" (*wenben*). This was partly defensive. The nondescript label made it seem perhaps academic or lacking a clear goal—not something the regime might feel it needed to nip in the bud.

Zhang Zuhua did most of the initial drafting of the charter and in late 2005 had produced just over 10,000 characters gathered under the four headings of politics, economy, society, and culture. Not feeling fully confident in the area of economics, he handed most of that section to Wen Kejian. For similar reasons he handed parts of the politics section to Liu Junning, but Liu, an academic, produced language that Zhang found arcane and in need of restating more plainly. In other parts of his draft Zhang drew heavily on documents from the democratic transition in Taiwan, especially from the pamphlets of presidential campaigns of the Democratic Progressive Party in the late 1990s. These included "Give Taiwan a Chance," the party's platform in the presidential campaign of 1995–1996; "We Should Live Better," its program for 1998; and seven volumes of "A New Road for a New Century: Chen Shuibian's Blueprint for the Nation" in 2000. Zhang bore in mind that some of the Taiwan programs could not be copied directly in China because Taiwan was so much smaller.

Xiaobo did not participate in the drafting. When Zhang Zuhua was finished with his first draft, he gave a copy to Xiaobo, who took it home to read. When Liu Xia saw what he was reading, she said, "You will be the one arrested—you alone, no one else—and the person doing the prison visits will be me alone."[6] She reminded him of the desolation of prison life and commented that she herself was not as young as she once was. Her ordeal of traveling thirty-eight times to Xiaobo's labor camp from 1996 to 1999 had taken a toll on her both mentally and physically. Xiaobo knew this. Liu Xia's warnings weighed on him.

Another factor that weighed on him was the lesson he had drawn from *minjian* experience. Hadn't he concluded that resistance must be bottom-up and gradual if it is to be long-lasting and solid? And that going too fast can induce crackdowns that shatter tentative progress before it solidifies? Was now the time to be confronting the regime?

Accordingly, while Xiaobo's friends continued to debate the charter through 2006, 2007, and the first half of 2008, Xiaobo himself kept a distance. Wen Kejian traveled from Hangzhou to Beijing about three or four times a year, carrying with him the views of his friends in Hangzhou. He regularly urged Xiaobo to get more involved. Xiaobo told Liu Xia that he planned only to sign—nothing more than that.[7] He did no drafting but sometimes commented on the drafts of others. In 2006 Xiaobo, Zhang Zuhua, and their spouses were part of a once-a-week badminton group. Zuhua came to rely on the fact that he could discuss things with Xiaobo during badminton.

In early 2006 Zhang began collecting signatures. By June he had thirty-six, including senior figures like Yu Haocheng, Bao Zunxin, Zhang Xianyang (a seventy-year-old liberal philosopher in the Chinese Academy of Social Sciences), Ding Zilin, and Jiang Peikun. Zhang was thinking of releasing the charter in 2006 on December 10, International Human Rights Day. He had the idea of organizing one hundred writers to publish one hundred articles supporting the charter on that day. Ding Zilin and Jiang Peikun agreed to this. They knew they might be punished for doing so. But what is life for?, they asked themselves. It's better to go ahead. Others felt that conditions were not yet ripe and that it would be better to wait. The advocates of waiting prevailed.

A year later, on June 16, 2007, an unplanned but important meeting took place at a retreat where Ding Zilin and Jiang Peikun were staying on the outskirts of Beijing. It happened because Yang Jianli, a prodemocracy activist and founder of the 21st Century Foundation in the United States, had just been released from prison. Five years earlier, the regime had barred Yang from entering China (despite his being a Chinese citizen), but he had decided to come home anyway. When the authorities found him inside China, they sentenced him to five years in prison for "entering the country illegally" (although he had come on his valid Chinese passport) and for "spying." When he was released in April 2007, he wanted to go pay his respects to professors Ding Zilin and Jiang Peikun. The two welcomed him and invited Xiaobo, Zhang Zuhua, Jiang Qisheng, Bao Zunxin, Mo Shaoping, and a few others to join. Zhang Zuhua brought photocopies of drafts of the charter with him, and spirited discussion ensued.

What the charter would say on the topic of land ownership became especially controversial. In 1955, after Mao Zedong ordered full collectivization of agriculture, all farmland belonged to the state. After Mao died, a major reform returned land to farmers to cultivate for themselves, but the state still owned it and could confiscate it at any time. "The state" meant the Party, and at local levels it referred to the interest coteries that the Party-state had become: local strongmen. In the charter, a draft proposal to privatize farmland was aimed at breaking this choke-hold so that farmers could make their own economic decisions and fairly reap the benefits of their labor. Xiaobo supported the reform and had written several arti-cles excoriating the Maoist system of land ownership. He argued that Mao had *not* ended landlordism in China but had simply reduced the number of landlords to one—the Communist Party. Others in the discussion argued against privati-zation of land, however. They feared that it could lead to aggregation of power in the hands of minorities and thus to social inequality. History contained clear les-sons about this danger.

Another thorny question that arose was whether and how to mention the words "Chinese federation." This involved the delicate matter of how to envision Tibetans, Uyghurs, and other minorities in the future of China, as well as the dangerous issue of how to use any label for the national polity other than The People's Republic of China. The authorities would view a proposed name change as an existential question. In the end, everyone agreed that drafting should con-tinue, in separate topical categories, to await a unifying editing later. For now, nothing would be put in public.

In early 2008 the question of when to release the charter arose again. One pro-posal was to do it on the opening day of the Olympics, August 8. Another was to do it on December 10, International Human Rights Day. A third was to wait for June 4, 2009, the twentieth anniversary of the 1989 massacre. In June 2008, when Zhang Zuhua, Wen Kejian, and Wang Debang visited the United States and dis-cussed the timing question with overseas activists, a consensus emerged against August 8 as the release date. World attention would be focused on the Olympics, and the charter would get less notice than it deserved.

In September Zuhua sent the latest version of the charter to Xiaobo by Skype. Xiaobo had no quarrel with any of the content but still doubted that the time was ripe for such a major move. He also found the writing a bit tedious—too abstract and wordy. He thought that doing something else, like an open letter on human rights that focused on a concrete issue, would be better. For example, the Chinese authorities in 1998 had signed the International Covenant on Civil and Political Rights, but now, ten years later, still had not ratified it. This meant that citizens of China still could not formally hold the regime to account for vio-lating the covenant. An open letter bearing important signatures might, Xiaobo thought, get that ratification done. This would be a smarter move right now than trying to push the bulky charter.

A few days later Zuhua reached Xiaobo by Skype again and used his considerable knowledge of history to argue for announcing the charter on December 10. That day would be the sixtieth anniversary of the passage in Paris of the United Nations' Universal Declaration of Human Rights, which a (Nationalist) Chinese diplomat, Zhang Pengchun, had participated in drafting. December 2008 was also the thirtieth anniversary of the "opening and reform" policy of the Deng Xiaoping era; the lives of countless people, including Xiaobo, were changed by what happened then. Moreover, it was the hundredth anniversary of constitutionalism in China, because in August 1908 the Qing dynasty had unveiled its Imperial Constitutional Outline (Qinding xianfa dagang) that established a "constitutional monarchy" in China. What could be a better year, Zuhua argued, for presenting a comprehensive political statement from civil society? He further pleaded with Xiaobo to help gather signatures from influential people both inside and outside the system; no one could match Xiaobo on that front. Xiaobo began to feel moved: here were friends of his, pushing forward in a way that he would not personally have chosen, but still, they were sincere and their goals were good. In the Rights Defense Movement, wasn't it a principle that everyone does what he or she can, without any commanders-in-chief? Maybe he should pitch in.

Ding Zilin and Jiang Peikun supported the charter strongly but thought the quality of the writing was uneven. It needed a good editing. Bao Zunxin, shortly before he died in 2007, had frankly told his good friend Zhang Zuhua that Zhang's writing style was wooden. It would need more power and elegance to attract readers. The conscientious Zuhua took this advice and was ready to find an editor. Since he also needed help soliciting signatures, the two professors, Ding and Jiang, thought it would be great if Xiaobo signed on for both tasks. They were spending September that year at their retreat in Wuxi, from where Ding Zilin regularly Skyped to Xiaobo, pressing him to say yes. Nineteen years after the June Fourth massacre, Xiaobo still felt obsessed by that traumatic event. How could he say no to the founder of the Tiananmen Mothers? So he agreed to edit and to solicit signatures.[8] (After Xiaobo's eleven-year prison sentence was handed down in December 2009, Ding Zilin sent Liu Xia a text message saying that she would not have pressured him to work on the charter if she had known the regime would be so harsh.)

Xiaobo continued to feel that June 4, 2009, the twentieth anniversary of the massacre, would be the best day to release the charter. To associate the rise of civil society in recent years with the horrid injustice of the massacre and its aftermath might be the most powerful statement the charter could make. Neither he nor Ding Zilin nor anyone else had imagined twenty years ago that well into the twenty-first century the surviving victims of the massacre, including family members, would still be silenced and ostracized—treated as if they were the per-petrators, not the victims, of the outrage. That pained Xiaobo intensely. He had commented to friends several times that he wanted to do something big at the twentieth anniversary, even if it cost him another trip to prison. Liu Xia was well aware of his obsession with the massacre, and her own fixation on it was not much less. The "lost souls" haunted them both. Her idea of what to do was to organize friends all across China to fax orders of flowers to the Tiananmen Moth-ers. Meanwhile, she managed to resign herself to Xiaobo's change of heart about working on the charter. "He couldn't stand aside any longer," she told an inter-viewer. "There was no other way than to join the battle. From then on I said nothing."[9]

Xiaobo himself thought about the safety issue. Living under twenty-four-hour surveillance, there was no way to ignore it, and his *guobao* kept giving him remind-ers. Xiaobo had fairly good relations with his *guobao*. In the past, when political issues loomed, they passed him warnings that came from their superiors, and together they figured out what to do. In mid-September, for example, the *guobao* gave him some preemptive advice on how to do the 2008 Chinese PEN writing awards ceremony: don't put up a banner in public, as he had last time; do it inside someone's home, and keep the number of participants down. They were frankly telling him: "If you cooperate this far, we are authorized to leave you alone." Such a pattern was hardly freedom, but it did reduce the foreboding sense of not know-ing what to expect. Sometimes the police delivered their warnings in actions, not words. In November 2004, for example, when Xiaobo, Zhang Zuhua, and Yu Jie wanted to release their report on human rights, all three of them, separately, were arrested and brought to police stations for one-night stays. That was a non-verbal way of saying "Stop." Because of precedents like these, Xiaobo felt he could count on advance signals from the police as the charter issue went forward.

In late September, Xiaobo Skyped to Zhang Yu, secretary-general of Chinese PEN, who was in Sweden at the time. Xiaobo told Zhang that Order No. 477 about freedom for foreign journalists remained in place and that he was planning an international news conference for December 9, 2008, at which he would announce the "cooperative project" (i.e., the charter), which would be released the next day. Zhang Yu, from his role with PEN, was especially sensitive to risk. He pointed to some risky language in the draft, such as "nationalization of the army." (The People's Liberation Army belonged—and still belongs—to the Communist Party, not the nation.) To this Xiaobo replied that sixty people had already signed the charter and that it would be hard to get approvals from all of them and unfair to make changes they didn't approve.[10] Zhang further asked if there were any way that Xiaobo could avoid being viewed as the leader of the charter movement. It would be better if the cooperative project did not appear to have a leader whom the regime could arrest in an effort to behead the movement. Xiaobo explained how loyalty to friends and the immense moral prestige of Ding Zilin had swayed him to take on certain tasks.[11] Now, in late September, he was on Skype with Zhang Zuhua nearly every evening discussing text revisions.

The first section of the charter addresses the last hundred or so years of Chinese history—how the country has struggled to modernize, has suffered terribly under both invasion and violent revolution, and has learned lessons. Then it states bluntly why the charter is necessary: "The decline of the current system has reached the point where change is no longer optional."[12] The charter's second section presents terse reviews of basic concepts: "freedom," "human rights," "equality," "republicanism," "democracy," "constitutional rule," and others. The third section, the longest, was the most difficult to reach consensus on. It is a list of political and social goals: "Revision of the Constitution," "Separation of Powers," "An Independent Judiciary," "Urban-Rural Equity," "Protection of the Environment," and about twenty-five others. Xiaobo, feeling strongly that economy of expression would make the document stronger, proposed cuts and combinations that, with Zhang Zuhua's approval, eventually reduced the number of topics from about thirty to twenty-one.

The line-to-line language of the charter was something of a jumble before Xiaobo's editing. It had been the product of many minds and hands, all of which he respected, but it needed rewriting in a unified voice and with better precision and professional accuracy. *The Blackwell Encyclopedia of Political Science* had been published in 2002 in Chinese translation, and Xiaobo relied on it to be sure that technical terms were used correctly. He also looked at the Chinese constitution, relevant parts of the criminal code, and documents from the CCP's Thirteenth National Congress to be sure that word choices were appropriate. He even looked at volume four of *Selections from Mao Zedong* for Mao's word choices on "nationalizing the army."[13] His goal was to find terms that would fit China's customary language habits but also not seem out of place in the modern world.

He sought to soften the language of the draft so that more people could feel comfortable signing it. He hoped that people inside the system, perhaps high-ranking in it, might be moved to sign. So he replaced phrases like "trample human rights" with "harm human rights" and dropped "dictatorship" (which he personally preferred) in favor of phrases like "comprehensive Party rule" and "one-party rule."

On October 31, Xiaobo's friend Jiang Qisheng, who had joined the project late, sent Xiaobo an e-mail with a provocative proposal. He wanted to add the words "we must abolish the special privilege of one party to monopolize power."

Everyone knew that this was a key issue—the elephant in the room. Dared they say it? Jiang's formulation was not as radical as it could have been. He was not saying "abolish the Communist Party." He was saying the Communist Party could exist, like others, and rule, like others, if and when it won elections. The point was that it could not *monopolize* power. After discussion, this phrase did go into the charter and was likely an important reason the men behind the tall red walls of Zhongnanhai so loathed the document.

Zhang Zuhua and Wen Kejian did most of the initial solicitation of signatures. Zhang headed a group called Chinese Human Rights Defenders, whose members signed readily. Wen gathered signatures from his Hangzhou group, which included some professors from Zhejiang University and some former members of the Democracy Party. Prominent members of Independent Chinese PEN, including Wang Yi, Yu Jie, Liu Di, and others, also signed quickly. These were low-hanging fruit. Xiaobo's mission was to use his broad social contacts to reach influential people beyond the familiar circles. Of the 303 original signatures, he secured about 70.

He approached about two-thirds of them by e-mail, the other third in person. For safety, he avoided mentioning the project on the telephone, which he used only to make appointments for personal meetings. His caution differed from Vaclav Havel's approach. According to his friends, Havel loved to argue and harangue on the telephone, and thereby must have supplied a gold mine of information to the police. He seemed almost not to mind their listening in. *You want to know what I'm doing and why I'm doing it? Good! You might learn something!* In a similar spirit Fang Lizhi joked in spring 1989 that he wasn't too concerned that his telephone was tapped: "I've been trying for years to get them to listen to me; if this is how they want to do it, fine!" Xiaobo avoided the telephone to protect others; his attitude toward sharing his views openly was the same as Havel's and Fang's.

One of the first people from whom Xiaobo sought a signature was Bao Tong. The two had been meeting about once a month for tea, but Xiaobo, not wanting to wait for the next tea date, set out one September morning to look for Bao in Yuyuantan Park in western Beijing. He knew that Bao went there very early every morning to do tai-ch'i exercises. Xiaobo was a late riser, but he got up at dawn that day and scoured Yuyuantan's more than 300 acres until he found Bao. The older man was astonished: "You found me *here*?" An agitated Xiaobo pulled some crumpled papers from his pocket and stuttered, "You . . . you have to . . . have to check this over for us; you . . . you have to sign." Bao so trusted Xiaobo that he agreed to sign after only a cursory reading. His only advice was, "Keep it as simple as possible; it doesn't have to be complex." Bao requested that his name not be listed at the top. "Keep it out of the top ten," he said. Xiaobo put it at number eleven. Over the next two months, Xiaobo and Zhang Zuhua continued to consult Bao on wording issues.

When Xiaobo approached the philosopher Xu Youyu he found Xu a bit skeptical. He felt that such measures should be reserved for times of crisis—do them too often and they lose their punch. Xiaobo parried that the release of this document would, in fact, be at a very special time: the sixtieth anniversary of the UN's International Declaration of Human Rights. Awareness of human rights was still weak in China, Xiaobo argued; this would be a consciousness-raising exercise, a way to help Chinese people become more aware of universal values as understood in the international world.[14] The document itself would be called either "A Declaration of Human Rights" or "Charter 08." Xiaobo handed the working draft to Xu and asked him to take it home, read it slowly, and then decide. Xu did take it home, applied his philosopher's eye to it, liked it, and signed. He noted that he saw nothing in it that broke existing Chinese law and offered a few handwritten edits.

Xiaobo continued to seek signatures in October and accelerated his pace in November. He had done this kind of work for open letters before, but there was an important difference this time: the text was not fixed; it was a "manuscript for discussion." The advantage of this method was that signers could offer corrections and suggestions, many of which were good. The disadvantage was that the text would change slightly after people had signed it. Hence trust was imperative. Xiaobo always tried to meet minds and establish enough trust that signers would not be bothered by small emendations. He did check back with people if he and Zuhua were considering substantive changes. (The ideal solution, having two or three hundred people in one room to discuss and agree all at once, was out of the question.)

Xiaobo asked Xu Youyu to come along when he went to solicit signatures from Hao Jian and Cui Weiping, two professors at the Beijing Film Academy. Cui, who had translated Vaclav Havel into Chinese, admired Havel's Charter 77 for its rigorous focus on human rights issues and social problems, leaving broad address of political structure for another day. This was smart, she felt. It made progress without incurring the risk of annihilation. Charter 08, by contrast, seemed a bit grandiose. After thinking it over she signed, though. "I needed that feeling of solidarity, that I was sharing everything—thought, danger, responsibility, destiny—with friends."[15]

Another method that Xiaobo used to collect signatures was to sit in the main room of the All Saints Book Grove and wait for friends to walk in looking for books. The bookstore manager, Liu Suli, whom Xiaobo had met during the

Tiananmen movement and again at Qincheng Prison, was happy to help. The distinguished legal scholar He Weifang, after a number of serious dialogues with Xiaobo at the bookstore, also agreed to sign.

Others whom Xiaobo recruited in person included veteran journalists Gao Yu and Li Datong; art critic Li Xianting; social activist Liang Xiaoyan; rights lawyer Teng Biao; historian Zhang Ming; and the artist brothers Gao Shensheng and Gao Qiangsheng. These people were not fringe figures in their fields. Their decisions to sign the charter did put them in one sense at the fringes—within a small percentage of people who dared to make such a move. But the act of signing also brought them deeper and wider respect. Xiaobo also got a signature from Zha Jianying, a Chinese writer based in New York who was visiting Beijing at the time, and even from ninety-year-old Li Pu, a former deputy chief of the New China News Agency.

For some who signed the charter, it was a milestone in their personal progress toward identifying with the Rights Defense Movement. Feng Qiusheng, the farmer in Taishi village in Guangdong province who became briefly famous for preaching "democracy on a rock pile," signed. He had become aware that justice at the grassroots cannot be gained at the grassroots alone.

Some people viewed as likely to sign the charter chose not to. Liu Suli, the cooperative manager of the All Saints Book Grove, was so in step with the chartrists that the regime at one point suspected he was their leader. But he declined to sign, even after many arguments with Xiaobo, because he thought the charter lacked an international perspective and didn't like its "enlightenment" rhetoric. Another who resisted signing was Xu Liangying, a distinguished physicist who had been punished as a "rightist" in 1957 and been expelled from the Communist Party in the 1980s after delivering an "incorrect" speech commemorating the thirtieth anniversary of Albert Einstein's death. In the 1990s Xu sponsored an open letter asking for human rights and tolerance and was gradually moving closer to a dissident position. When he saw the charter draft, though, he warned that the word "charter" was dangerous: it would get people arrested. Jiang Qisheng, himself a physicist and very respectful of Xu, responded that when people in disparate fields want to forge a common statement of ideals, "charter" is a good word to use. But Professor Xu still declined—and in the end his fears proved accurate. The Communist Party of China does not allow anyone, even if they are much smaller and weaker, to stand in parity with it.

Qin Hui, the famous liberal historian at Tsinghua University, also chose not to sign. He was disappointed that the charter made no mention of a welfare system. He also said that what China needed at the time was a vigorous debate about democracy, not one more signing of names. Hu Shigen, a veteran democracy advocate, declined because he thought the charter did not show enough sympathy for the poor.

Even as he worked to gather signatures, Xiaobo continued to feel that the best time to release the charter might be at the twentieth anniversary of the June Fourth massacre. Zhang Zuhua disagreed, and he and Xiaobo continued to debate the point through the first half of November. Zhang pointed to the possibility, which both of them recognized, that Xiaobo might be detained during the 2009 anniversary, and if so, it would of course be better to release the charter at the end of 2008. If Xiaobo were free in June 2009, they could do something else at that time.[16] Xiaobo had already been in touch with friends in more than twenty cities about tentative plans to unfurl June Fourth commemoration banners at a preset time on June 4, 2009.[17] All this considered, he decided to drop his opposition and agreed that the charter should be announced on December 10.

It was always in the back of Xiaobo's mind that he might be imprisoned again. During November he mentioned twice to Jiang Qisheng that he might end up behind bars sometime between then and the anniversary of the massacre in June 2009. By then, Xiaobo had largely outgrown the psychological need to atone that had burdened him after his "repentance" in Qincheng Prison in 1990. His second incarceration (eight months at the Fragrant Hills courtyard) and his third (three years in *laojiao*) had helped him to get past those feelings. Now he felt no strong need to go to prison—but also felt no particular fear of doing so. What he wanted most was to help the Rights Defense Movement. He would not let fear of prison get in the way of that. He could accept risk and could even accept it on behalf of others. His only caveat was to protect Liu Xia as much as possible. In her presence he tried to behave as if there were no imminent threat. When the two talked about a possible return to prison, it was only to recognize that it might happen next year, at the twentieth anniversary of the massacre. That prospect alone was enough to keep Liu Xia constantly worried.

The decision finally to name the document "Charter 08" was made on November 14, 2008. Ai Xiaoming, a professor and documentary filmmaker, had come to Beijing, and at a midday meal with Xiaobo, Zhang Zuhua, Jiang Qisheng, Yu Jie, and six or seven others, the group reached a consensus that "Charter 08" was the best name. It was terse and easy to remember, and echoed "Charter 77."[18] It meant, of course, that the idea of waiting until June 4, 2009, had been discarded.

Toward the end of November, Xiaobo continued his pursuit of signatures, via e-mail, to places outside Beijing. On November 27 he sent "Charter 08: Draft for Consideration" to Shanghai, to the famous dramatist Sha Yexin and to Zhao Dagong of Independent Chinese PEN. When Sha and Zhao had dinner that night, Xiaobo called them to ask their views. The next day he sent Sha Yexin this text message: "Here in Beijing many of our friends, including me, see you as the exception to the famous cynicism of Shanghai intellectuals. You long ago stepped off the utilitarian treadmill to live in your own world of clarity and conscience. I have always felt a connection with you, have a deep trust in you, and hope I can have your support."[19] Sha signed. Xiaobo sent the charter to Sichuan, to the poet Liu Shahe, who studied it with great care. He wrote questions to Xiaobo and the two e-mailed back and forth at length. In the end Liu Shahe also signed, as did his wife, the writer Wu Maohua.

In the last two weeks before Charter 08 was to be unveiled, so many suggestions for revisions were coming in that editing became something of a headache. Gu Chuan, a volunteer at Chinese Human Rights Defenders, offered language on education, saying that it should be free of politics. Zhang Lun, a scholar living in exile in France since 1989, sent in language about environmental protection. Zhao Changqing from Xi'an, a former political prisoner and member of PEN, said the charter should have a "Conclusion" and drafted one. Zhang Zuhua handled all these suggestions and others.

With new voices continually entering, problems kept coming up in keeping the document consistent. The questions were not just technical; they were sometimes political and tactical as well. Should repression of Falun Gong be addressed by name in the charter? Or was repression of "popular religious activities" better, to reduce people's fears about signing? An especially complex issue was what word to use to describe the regime. Autocratic? Dictatorial? Totalitarian? Neo-totalitarian? Crony capitalist? All such terms had their rationales, and people had their habits. Was it even possible to agree on a single word? After much discussion, "authoritarian" (*weiquan* 威权) was chosen. This was not ideal, because it was also the term used for rule in Taiwan and South Korea before the democratic transitions in those places, and those two regimes were much less brutal than that of the Chinese Communists. But the mild *weiquan* was a least common denominator; no one would shy away from the charter because the word was too strong.

In late November Zhang Zuhua held a Skype conference with Wen Kejian, Zhao Changqing, Wang Debang, and others. The group decided on some wording changes in the charter, many of which were cosmetic but one of which, about the troublesome "federation" question, proved fateful. It had been controversial all along. How should the charter refer to Taiwan, Hong Kong, and Macao—and, more subtly, minority areas like Tibet and Xinjiang that the regime called "autonomous" even though they were not? From mid-November the charter draft had referred to "a Chinese political community," but people regarded that as only a placeholder for a better phrase yet to be determined. At the Skype conference

Zhao Changqing argued that "a Chinese political community" was fine in spirit but would not accord with what Chinese people thought the name of a country should sound like. Zhao favored "a Chinese federated republic." After discussion, Zhang Zuhua accepted that phrase but thought it should be expanded to "a Chinese federated republic in a democratic constitutional framework." The header for the point in the charter is: "*Lianbang gonghe* 联邦共和 Federated Republic[anism]."

There was considerable fear that the regime would be inordinately affronted by the phrase. The Communist Party of China has always been fastidious, not to say paranoid, about the political naming of things. "Federated Republic of China" was likely too close to "People's Republic of China"—in vocabulary, in form, and even in rhythm. Some chartrists feared that Hu Jintao, precisely because of his weak profile as a leader, might be especially fearful of "losing the rivers and mountains"—a cliché that meant the regime's national legitimacy. There must have been much discussion behind closed doors; in any case, both the "federated republic" phrase and the one about "canceling the special privilege of one party to monopolize governance" were featured a year later in the legal indictment that sent Xiaobo to prison with his eleven-year sentence.

One problem with including these two dangerous phrases in the charter was that they were added after some people had already signed, when it was not easy to get approvals for additions. The phrase about one-party monopoly was added early enough that many (but not all) signers could be reached. The "federated republic" phrase was added on November 29, after 291 people had already signed and when the planned release date was only 11 days away. Chen Ziming, for one, thought the addition was a mistake, although he expressed his criticisms gently.[20] Some of Xiaobo's friends thought that Zhang Zuhua should not have added the phrase without involving Xiaobo in the debate. Xiaobo, who from the beginning had doubted that conditions were ripe for a confrontation with the regime, might well have argued against it.

On November 29, 2008, Zhang Zuhua left for Germany to accompany Zhang Sizhi as he traveled to receive the Petra Kelly Prize for "outstanding achievements in respecting human rights." Rights lawyers Pu Zhiqiang, Zhang Xingshui, and Ma Gangquan were also on that trip, and Zhang Zuhua used the occasion to persuade all of them, including Zhang Sizhi himself, to sign Charter 08. Wu Si, editor of *China Through the Ages*, was along but declined to sign. He feared the consequences for his magazine.

The Charter 08 activists had not set up a "spokesperson lineup" as the Charter 77 people in Czechoslovakia had done. Within the Charter 77 group, three names were put in order—a spokesperson, a backup, and a backup to the backup, in case disappearances began. For Charter 08, Zhang Zuhua and Liu Xiaobo worked as co-chiefs. When Zuhua set out for Germany, editing fell to Xiaobo. Besides making routine edits, Xiaobo devised punchy four-character labels for each of the items in part 2 of the charter, "What We Advocate": *chengxiang ping-deng* (urban-rural equality), *zongjiao ziyou* (religious freedom), *shehui baozhang* (social guarantees), and so on. Xiaobo also took over sending text alterations to California to Perry Link, whom Zuhua had commissioned in mid-November to translate the charter into English. Xiaobo appended a note to the end of the text: "This charter accepts signatures from the public—please use your real name or commonly used pen name and give your location and occupation." Two electronic mailboxes were offered for people to do so. Xiaobo also had to decide the order in which to list the signatories. Where should he put his own name? He had been mulling this question for some time. He was willing to put it first, which would increase his vulnerability to political punishment. In the end, though, friends persuaded him to follow the Chinese custom of listing revered elders first. He reserved fifteen spots for elders and listed his name sixteenth, Zhang Zuhua's seventeenth.

Meanwhile, the atmosphere was growing tense. On December 4, Wen Kejian in Hangzhou received a phone call from the chief of the city's *guobao* instructing him not to go out for the next few days. They wanted to come over to talk with him immediately. With that intimidating signal, Wen Kejian left home, went straight to the airport, and bought a ticket to Shenzhen. He planned to go to Hong Kong for a few days but didn't make it. Police blocked him at the Hong Kong border.

Early in the morning on December 5, Xiaobo placed a Skype call to Sweden to talk with Zhang Yu from Chinese PEN. He wanted to consult about options in case a crackdown came. Xiaobo told Zhang that the police had withdrawn their promise of two months earlier that Chinese PEN's annual award ceremony could go ahead as planned. They also had warned him not to talk with foreign journalists. Zhang Yu pressed him on the latter point.

ZHANG YU: So are you still planning to hold a press conference to announce the charter?

XIAOBO: It looks like we can't. They might even start picking us up in the next few days.

ZHANG YU: Have they asked you anything about the charter?

XIAOBO: No. They just warn me not to do anything.

ZHANG YU: Right! . . . I heard today that people were starting to be warned not to sign things.

XIAOBO: I've heard that too. But the *guobao* still haven't said a thing to me.

ZHANG YU: That might be bad news. They might be lying low, preparing a trap for you and not wanting to tip you off.

XIAOBO: Quite possible.[21]

Xiaobo went on to spell out three things that he hoped Zhang Yu would follow up on if indeed he were detained. One was the question of where to publish the charter. Xiaobo thought of *Democratic China*, the web magazine for which he was co-editor, even though he felt guilty about putting friends there at risk. The second concern was the English translation. The third was to continue pressing his long-term campaign to nominate the Tiananmen Mothers for the Nobel Peace Prize. In 2002 he and Fang Lizhi had gathered materials to support the case, but now six years had passed and they would need to do an update.

On December 7, Zhang Zuhua returned from Germany. After the airplane landed, while his group was still inside the airport, Zuhua signed a power of attorney agreement with Pu Zhiqiang so that Pu could act for him if he were arrested. Soon Xiaobo was on Skype with Zuhua to tell him that Charter 08 with 300 signatures was all ready to send to Cai Chu at *Democratic China*. "Fine," Zuhua said, and off it went. Xiaobo told Cai Chu that if anything should happen to him before December 10, Cai Chu should publish the charter ad as planned.

There was one other task that Xiaobo wanted to get done before anything happened to him: to go see Jiang Peikun, who was recovering from a stroke in the Beijing No. 3 Hospital. Jiang could barely talk, and Ding Zilin did not want him to receive visitors, but Xiaobo insisted and Ding relented. In the afternoon of December 7 Xiaobo and Liu Xia made their visit and stayed nearly an hour, during which Xiaobo told Jiang and Ding all about revising Charter 08 and whose signatures had been secured. Jiang kept nodding his head in approval. As Xiaobo and Xia were leaving the ward, Xiaobo turned to Ding Zilin to say that Charter 08 was now pretty much a done deal and he would be turning his attention to the project of nominating the Tiananmen Mothers for the Nobel Peace Prize. He was already mobilizing international China scholars to support the effort. It was the most important item on his agenda for the upcoming observance of the twentieth anniversary of the June Fourth massacre.

During those same days in early December Liu Xia was busy preparing to move her and Xiaobo's household from Seven Sages Village, where they had lived for seven years, to her parents' apartment at building no. 9, south courtyard, Yuyuantan South Road. The parents' apartment was lovely, but it was on the fifth floor of a building that had no elevator. The burden of climbing stairs had been a main reason the elderly parents had decided to move elsewhere and let their daughter and son-in-law take over their apartment. They had always liked Xiaobo, and he liked them. He found much more in common with them than with his own parents.

When Xiaobo awoke on December 8 at the Seven Sages address, he noticed that the police detail outside their building had been beefed up. Liu Xia had hired a craftsman to install kitchen cabinets at the Yuyuantan address and remembers, during a coffee break that day with the worker, sighing and saying, "We'll just have to see in the next couple of days whether we can get by."[22] In the afternoon, she and Xiaobo went out to the nearby All-China Supermarket to buy household items for the new apartment. A crush of police followed, monitoring their every move. Some were *guobao* whom they knew well, but on that day the expressions on their familiar faces were tense. Liu Xia felt spooked and said so; Xiaobo told her to relax, but she didn't. This is different, she said. They went home, and around 5:00 p.m. Xiaobo called Jiang Qisheng on Skype. He told Jiang there were a lot of policemen milling around outside his building and wanted to know if things were the same at Jiang's building.

"No," Jiang answered, "at least not last time I looked."

"What do you think is going on?" Xiaobo asked.

"Probably has to do with International Human Rights Day the day after tomorrow."

"That's my guess too. Anyway it's their own business. Let 'em go."[23]

Both men knew something was up, perhaps something dangerous.

About 8:00 p.m., Xiaobo was on Skype with Zhang Zuhua and Wen Kejian. They all thought the regime was preparing to act but did not expect anything too severe. Perhaps a detention for a while, or something like that. Xiaobo repeated an offer he had made before to Wen Kejian: "If they grab you, you can blame everything on me." He didn't want to see a young man like Wen lose his freedom.

At 11:00 p.m. a hand pounded on Xiaobo's and Liu Xia's door. Xiaobo got up from his computer and said to Liu Xia, "Quick, the telephone!" Liu Xia normally didn't use the phone. She just stared at Xiaobo for a moment, then said, "Let's open the door, Xiaobo."[24]

Outside was a bevy of police. They showed Xiaobo a summons and asked him to sign it. The line that read "charged with _____" was left blank. The police could not fill in the blank, so Xiaobo refused to sign. The police argued the point and Xiaobo argued back.

Debate was futile, though. The police blindfolded Xiaobo and dragged him from the apartment.[25] A dozen or so stayed behind to search. They confiscated his computer, all his letters, and any books they could find that were published underground or in Taiwan or Hong Kong. They stayed about eleven hours, until around noon the next day.

Zhang Zuhua was taken from his home about the same time on the same night, but the legal rubrics under which the two friends were detained differed slightly. For Zhang it was *chuanhuan* 传唤, "summons," a status that by law cannot extend beyond twelve hours. He was released to go home the next day but kept under tight house arrest afterward. His telephone line was not blocked and he could accept interviews. The rubric for Xiaobo was *juchuan* 拘传, "coercive summons," which is the same as *chuanhuan* except that it is done forcibly. *Juchuan* also cannot extend beyond twelve hours, so the next day the category of Xiaobo's detention was changed to *jianshi juzhu* 监视居住, a form of house arrest normally translated as "residential supervision" even though the supervision need not be at the detained person's residence. *Jianshi juzhu* required that Xiaobo be served with papers, and that meant he had the opportunity to write down "I deny the charge of agitating to subvert state power."

On Zhang Zuhua's summons, the "charged with" blank was filled with "suspicion of agitating to subvert state power." Most of the police questions during his interrogation were about Charter 08, especially about the last two months of its production. The police held the charter before Zhang and asked him to acknowledge that it was his work. He did, although he noticed that the copy they were holding was two months out of date.

By then Zhang had already sent the final version of the charter to Renée Xia, overseas director of Chinese Human Rights Defenders. (Zhang's version differed slightly from the one Xiaobo had sent to Cai Chu on December 7.) About 9:00 a.m. Beijing time on December 9, while Xiaobo and Zhang Zuhua were in custody, people from Chinese Human Rights Defenders both inside and outside China (Wen Kejian, Wang Debang, Renée Xia, and Zhang Lun) held an emergency Skype meeting about what to do. They would protest the arbitrary detention of Liu and Zhang, of course. But then what? Should they release the charter now, or wait a day to release it as planned, on December 10, International Human Rights Day? The consensus was to release it immediately, and the reason was practical: the regime obviously had begun its crackdown. Its next step might well be to forbid release of the charter. If it were released now, no one could be punished for defying a ban. The other option would be not to release it at all, but that was unthinkable.

About 11:00 a.m. on December 9, after the police had allowed Zhang Zuhua to go home, he and Renée Xia talked by telephone, and Zhang agreed with the decision to release the charter immediately. Zhang Lun sent it to the websites of *Duowei* news and *Boxun* news, where it appeared almost simultaneously with its posting on the Chinese Human Rights Defenders site. Perry Link sent the English translation to *The New York Review of Books,* on whose website it appeared the same day.

The regime went ahead with its program to expunge the charter from every kind of public view in China and to try to intimidate anyone who had had any connection with it. Xiaobo disappeared and remained incommunicado. Liu Xia knew nothing of his whereabouts until January 1, 2009, when she was driven to a restaurant to which he was driven separately—hooded—for a New Year's Day meal, following which they each were driven back "home."

20

The World Watches a Prison

In Oslo, the announcement came in the late morning of October 8, 2010: "The Norwegian Nobel Committee has decided to award the Nobel Peace Prize for 2010 to Liu Xiaobo for his long and nonviolent struggle for fundamental human rights in China."

At Jinzhou Prison in Liaoning province in China, thousands of miles away, it was 5:00 p.m. and Xiaobo, unaware of the announcement in Oslo, was passing the end of a routine day. Liu Xia reasoned that the Chinese authorities also must have been unaware of the decision until it was announced, because her phone went dead shortly after 5:00 p.m. even though she had been able to use it as late as 4:30 the same day. By 5:30, a crowd of foreign journalists carrying all kinds of cameras had gathered outside her apartment building, but police barred her from meeting with any of them.

Staff at Jinzhou Prison told Xiaobo the news of his award the next day, October 9. They also informed him that Liu Xia would come to the prison to see him on the 10th. That was a Sunday, when the prison normally did not allow visitors, but Beijing ordered the prison to make an exception. There was international opinion to fear if a visit were not allowed, and besides, the 260-mile trip to Liaoning would get Liu Xia out of the capital where international journalists were constantly demanding to see her. This time, though, she would not travel by rail. She would be escorted all the way in a police car. From then on, every trip to the prison would be by police car.

When she saw Xiaobo, his first comments were, "This prize is for all the lost souls of June Fourth; they are the ones who gave their lives for the spirit of peace, freedom, democracy, and nonviolence." She reported that Xiaobo wept as he pronounced the words "lost souls." In his mind, the June Fourth massacre always weighed the most. He hoped that this world-famous prize would lead people everywhere to think again of those fellow human beings now buried under the earth, forever unable to speak for themselves.

Xiaobo knew there was no way he could travel to Oslo to receive the prize. If he were to "confess guilt," the regime would likely let him go—but how could he possibly do that? He would leave prison with dignity or not leave at all. He asked Liu Xia to go to Oslo for him and take with her the "Final Statement" that he had not been allowed to finish reading at his trial. That could be his acceptance speech. She should be sure to read the lines about herself that the statement contained. Liu Xia felt awkward about the request, since those lines were so effusive in their praise, but she agreed.

The two talked about Xiaobo's health. At their previous meeting at the end of September, he had told her that a recent physical exam had found "stomach ulcers" and also had reached an "indeterminate diagnosis of hepatitis B." If the diagnosis had been "determinate," authorities would have been obliged to grant medical parole, and in that event he would be out of prison and free to move about—perhaps even to Oslo. This thought was in Liu Xia's mind but not, she knew, in his. Xiaobo would fear that the regime would bar him from returning to China once he was out. He would not accept such a risk for anything, not even the glory of a Nobel Prize ceremony.

At the end of their meeting Liu Xia presented Xiaobo with a dozen or so books that she had brought for him. One was *Nine Stories* by J. D. Salinger, in a bilingual edition with facing pages in Chinese and English. Xiaobo wanted to use his prison time to learn English. Their whole meeting lasted about an hour. The authorities videotaped it from start to finish.

2010 marked the second time in the history of the Nobel Peace Prize since its founding in 1895 that the award went to an imprisoned person. Carl von Ossietzky, winner of the 1935 prize, was the first. Ossietzky was a journalist who had begun reporting as early as 1926 on secret German rearmament after World War I—first of its army, and then by the creation of an air force. The actions were in clear violation of the Treaty of Versailles. Ossietzky wrote a piece in 1931 that confronted the rise of Hitler: How spiritually impoverished must a nation be, he asked, to see this scoundrel as a leader who offers something worth pursuing?[1] On February 28, 1933, the day after the Reichstag fire that followed the accession of Hitler to Germany's chancellorship, secret police arrested Ossietzky at his home. He was sent to concentration camps and prisons, where he suffered heart disease and contracted tuberculosis. Albert Einstein, Thomas Mann, and others pushed for the Nobel Peace Prize for Ossietzky, and in 1936 he was awarded the prize for 1935. The decision so enraged Hitler that he demanded that the

Reichstag pass a law forbidding *any* German citizen from going to Oslo to collect the prize. Ossietzky died in 1938, in a hospital but still in police custody, at age forty-eight. The parallels between Xiaobo and Ossietzky are many.

In China's state-controlled media, the first response to Xiaobo's prize was immaculate silence. Media managers knew they had to wait to hear from the top exactly which words to use. Searches for "Liu Xiaobo" or "Nobel Peace Prize" on Baidu, China's largest Internet search engine, yielded this: "The search result might not accord with relevant laws, regulations, or policies and cannot be shown." But this roadblock did not stop millions of Chinese from using VPNs to "jump the Great Firewall" and browse the international Internet. Within twenty-four hours of the Nobel announcement, the Chinese-language website at Human Rights Watch got more hits from mainland China than it had gotten during the entire preceding year.

At 7:00 p.m., two hours after the Nobel announcement, there was still no mention of it on state-run television. Finally, at 8:00 p.m., on the news program *Time and Space in the East*, an official statement from the New China News Agency appeared: "On October 8, Ma Zhaoxu, spokesperson for the Ministry of Foreign Affairs, stated that the Nobel Committee's giving of the Nobel Peace Prize to Liu Xiaobo completely betrays the goals of the prize and is a profound insult to it." The next day *Global Times*, a tabloid satellite of *People's Daily*, published an editorial, "The Nobel Peace Prize Vandalizes Its Own Brand Again," that said: "This prize once again puts itself in opposition to the Chinese people and to the Chinese project of reform and opening [and shows] the Chinese people the arrogance of Western ideology." "Once again" was a reference to the award of the 1989 Peace Prize to the Dalai Lama.

For Xiaobo's friends and supporters, the news from Oslo released a surge of joy whose ebullience is hard to overstate. As a reply to years of Chinese government bullying, nothing could have been more satisfying than this prize. Friends streamed from their homes, raised wine cups toward the sky, and headed toward restaurants, aiming mirthfully to *fànzuì*, a pun on "food and drinking" 饭醉 and "commit crime" 犯罪. At Peking University and Shandong University fireworks erupted; police noted the outbreaks as "origin undetermined." Wei Qiang, a student at the Central Academy of Fine Arts, walked around his campus handing out leaflets on the life of Liu Xiaobo. The rights lawyer Xu Zhiyong organized twenty-some friends and colleagues to wear yellow ribbons and go to the Earth Altar Park in Beijing, hold up signs to celebrate the prize, and explain to passersby what the excitement was about.

The celebrators were aware that their activity could be repressed at any time. At one party in a Beijing restaurant, eight or nine police cars carrying about thirty police showed up, apprehended the revelers, and separated them by bringing them to different police stations.

Xu Youyu wrote a "Declaration on the Award of the Nobel Peace Prize to Liu Xiaobo" and posted it on the Internet where others could sign. It said that Xiaobo's fame was fully deserved because it grew from his learning and his integrity. In both theory and practice, he had given the Chinese people a model of how to solve political and social conflicts. Xiaobo's old friend Zhou Duo and his college classmates Xu Jingya and Wang Xiaoni were among those who signed on.

After Liu Xia returned to Beijing from her October 10 visit with Xiaobo, police pressure on her escalated markedly. Agents mustered nearer to her door than before and followed her everywhere she went. Even stepping out to buy vegetables precipitated "accompaniment." Visitors from foreign embassies and journalists from Hong Kong or overseas who came to see her were blocked. She bought a new cell phone and the police destroyed it.

It was soon obvious that there was no way she could go to Oslo on December 10. Instead she drew up a list of 140 Chinese people she wanted to invite to the award ceremony. Consulting with friends, she chose people from different stages of Xiaobo's life who had known him in different ways—through politics, literature, art, education, or otherwise. None of this mattered, though, because Liu Xia was transparent about her list, the regime knew who was on it, and every person on it was barred from leaving China for a period of three months, for any reason. The regime apparently feared that people would leave on pretexts and then head for Oslo. In some cases, even the spouses and children of the listed people were blocked.

Hundreds of Xiaobo's friends and supporters who were already outside China could not be stopped, though, and many appeared at Oslo's City Hall on December 10.

It was cold that day, but the impending ceremony seemed to radiate a warmth. A man whom Oslo was calling a laureate and Beijing a criminal was about to be honored. All countries with embassies in Norway were invited to send representatives, and the Chinese government called for a boycott. In the end, forty-five embassies sent representatives, while nineteen—including Russia, Pakistan, Cuba, Saudi Arabia, Iraq, and Vietnam—stayed away. From the United States, House Speaker Nancy Pelosi attended, as did Representatives David Wu of Oregon and Christopher Smith of New Jersey.[2] The Polish dissident Adam Michnik, from whose writings Xiaobo had drawn much inspiration, was there.

The hall was decked in fresh flowers and the ceremony was exquisite. After the king and queen of Norway arrived to preside, the award presentation speech was delivered by Thorbjørn Jagland, who was chair of the prize committee, a former prime minister of Norway, and at the time secretary-general of the Council of Europe. A few minutes into his speech, he said: "We regret that the laureate is not present here today. He is in isolation in a prison in northeast China. . . . This fact alone shows that the award was necessary and appropriate." When he had finished reading these words the audience of about a thousand people interrupted with applause. The applause continued for about thirty seconds and then, when it seemed that the time had come for it to recede, suddenly took on a second life. It continued on and on, then turned into a standing ovation lasting three or four minutes. Jagland's face seemed to show relief. After the ceremony, in a news interview, he said that he understood the prolonged applause not only as powerful support for Liu Xiaobo but also as an endorsement of the controversial decision that his five-person committee had made.

In the remainder of his speech Jagland stressed the close connections among human rights, democracy, and peace. He reviewed the other four occasions in Nobel history when a Peace laureate could not travel to Oslo: Ossietzky in 1936; Andrei Sakharov, who in 1975 was not allowed to leave the USSR; Lech Walesa, who in 1983 feared that he would be barred from reentering Poland if he traveled to Oslo; and Aung Sang Suu Kyi, who in 1991 was under house arrest in Burma. Even so, each of the latter three was able to send a family member to collect the prize. Only Ossietzky and now Liu Xiaobo were denied even that.

Jagland stressed that his committee had great respect for the Chinese nation and admired its recent economic growth. He observed that support of dissidents makes countries stronger, not weaker. The United States had become a stronger nation because of the work of the Nobel Peace laureate Martin Luther King, Jr. The Chinese authorities were mistaken to view people like Liu Xiaobo as enemies, and the harsh sentence given him a year earlier only enhanced his prestige as an international symbol of human rights.

Following Jagland's speech the Norwegian actress Liv Ullman read the full text of Xiaobo's "I Have No Enemies: My Final Statement" that he had wanted to read at his trial but could not finish because of the four-minute limit imposed by the judge. Ullman's reading took about twenty-five minutes. She held the audience in rapt silence when she read a passage in which Xiaobo pays tribute to Liu Xia:

> If one were to ask what my most fortunate experience of the past twenty years has been, I would need to say that it has been the selfless love that I have received from my wife, Liu Xia. She was not allowed to come to court to hear me today, yet I feel a need to address her directly, so will: I feel confident, my dear one, that there cannot possibly be any change in your love for me. For several years now,

as I have been in and out of prison, external factors have forced bitterness upon our love, and yet, as I look back, the love still seems boundless. I have been held in tangible prisons, and you have waited for me within the intangible prison of the heart. Your love has been like sunlight that leaps over high walls and shines through iron windows, that caresses every inch of my skin and warms every cell of my body. It has bolstered my inner equanimity while I try to stay clear-headed and high-minded; it has infused every minute of my stays in prisons with meaning. My love for you, on the other hand, is burdened by my feelings of guilt and apology. These are so heavy that they sometimes seem to make me stagger. I am like a stone on a barren plain, whipped by fierce winds and driving rain, so cold that no one dares touch me. Yet my love is rock solid and sharp. It can pierce any barrier. Even were I ground to powder, still would I use my ashes to embrace you.

Armed with your love, dear one, I can face the sentence that I am about to receive with peace in my heart, with no regrets for the choices that I have made, and filled with optimism for tomorrow. I look forward to the day when our country will be a land of free expression: a country where the words of each citizen will get equal respect; a country where different values, ideas, beliefs, and political views can compete with one another even as they peacefully coexist; a country where expression of both majority and minority views will be secure, and, in particular, where political views that differ from those of the people in power will be fully respected and protected; a country where all political views will be spread out beneath the sun for citizens to choose among, and every citizen will be able to express views without the slightest of fears; a country where it will be impossible to suffer persecution for expressing a political view. I hope that I will be the last victim in China's long record of literary inquisitions and that from now on, no one will be sent to prison because of words.

The reading was followed by songs from a Norwegian children's choir. Xiaobo had told Liu Xia at their meeting at Jinzhou Prison on October 10 that he hoped that children could participate in the ceremony. Jagland, unable to hand the Nobel diploma and medal to Liu Xiaobo or to Liu Xia, placed both upon the empty chair where Xiaobo was supposed to have been sitting.

After the ceremony, a number of Xiaobo's overseas friends shared their impressions. Su Xiaokang, who had known Xiaobo since the 1989 democracy demonstrations, saluted Norway. "The big democracies—America, Britain, France, Germany—all know what democracy is but won't stand up to Beijing's contempt for human rights. Now a little country does a big thing." Renée Xia commented that her friend Liu Xiaobo's empty chair, while regrettable, was in part a good thing: "To us, that empty chair is not the least bit surprising. *Of course* Beijing treats its critics that way. This is wholly normal. If the rest of the world is startled, then good; maybe surprise can be the first step to better understanding of how things actually are." *Kong yizi*, "empty chair," became a symbol for Xiaobo's prize. Eventually the authorities had to ban the phrase from the Internet.

Fang Lizhi overheard Renée Xia's comment about the empty chair and added, with his characteristic wit, that China's rulers should feel satisfaction that they finally had aroused the attention of the Nobel Committee: "All those earlier atrocities—during the Anti-Rightist Movement, the Great Leap famine, the Cultural Revolution, the Beijing massacre—weren't enough to earn a Nobel Prize for a Chinese citizen. But now the world is starting to care what happens in China. It's a sign that China has become a 'big country,' and that's what Beijing has always said it wants, right?" Jimmy Lai, a media mogul in Hong Kong who became famous in 2020 for resisting Beijing's assault on Hong Kong's civil liberties and went to prison for doing so, referred to Mao Zedong's famous line from 1949 that "the Chinese people have stood up." Lai said, "No, in fact we did not stand up then. But now it could happen. Now people can see that 'China' in the twenty-first century can be something much bigger and better than the Communist Party."

Others were not so optimistic. Hu Ping, Xiaobo's old friend from New York, thought that recent history had taught China's rulers that repression does in fact pay: "As they see it, the strategy works. The formula 'money + violence' works. It helps us stay on top. We know what the world means by 'human rights and democracy,' but why should we go in that direction? Aren't we getting stronger and richer all the time? Twenty years ago the West wasn't afraid of us, but now they have to be. Why should we change what works?" Hu recalled something that Xiaobo had said to him two decades earlier. "We are lucky," Hu recalled Liu as saying, "to live in this time and this place—China. It might be difficult for us, but at least we do have a chance to make a very, very large difference. Most people in their lifetimes do not have this kind of opportunity."

For Xiaobo's friends in the Rights Defense Movement in China, the Nobel award ceremony brought another round of repression. On December 9, plainclothes police nabbed Zhang Zuhua from a Beijing sidewalk and brought him in a car with curtained windows to a Public Security guesthouse, where they held him incommunicado until December 12. Others in the movement were similarly quarantined. Fearing groups, as they always did, the authorities put each person in a different location. Their conditions varied widely. Zhang Zuhua was held in a drab room that had no electric lighting. Cui Weiping was given a room in what seemed like a four- or five-star hotel, where she was able to watch a rebroadcast of the Nobel award ceremony on CNN—hardly what the police had intended. On

February 19, 2011, Teng Biao was kidnapped again (as he had been in 2008, before the Olympics) and held for seventy days at a secret location where he was beaten and deprived of sleep.

For the Chinese authorities, punishing Chinese citizens was necessary but insufficient retaliation. Norway too had to be punished. Beijing had recently granted citizens of European Union nations the privilege of entering China for seventy-two hours without visas, but Norwegians were denied that. Exporters of Norwegian salmon to China also began to complain that their shipments were being held up by Chinese food safety inspectors in ways they had never seen before. In one case an entire shipment was rejected and fish were left to rot on a wharf.

At Jinzhou Prison, Xiaobo's material life improved after the Nobel Prize. The authorities apparently were afraid that Liu Xia or someone else might report to the world on how her famous husband was doing. In any case, Xiaobo was given a single-room cell and better food. In the past, he had been given the rice-and-vegetable mix that was supplied to all prisoners. Now his vegetables were laid on a bed of rice, and there were more of them. The prison even supplied him with a microwave oven that he could use to reheat food. But his stomachaches persisted, especially when seasons changed.

Although the prison wardens treated Xiaobo a bit better materially, they were even stricter in preventing any possibility of contact with the outside world. He was not allowed to talk with his lawyers. His parents' home was off limits even though it was nearby and his father, Liu Ling, remained a loyal Communist. He could write no letters to his parents. When the Nobel Prize was announced in October, and again in the days before and after the award ceremony in December, the parents, inside their own home, were not allowed to make telephone calls to anyone. Xiaobo's brothers, Xiaoguang, Xiaoxuan, and Xiaohui, were allowed to go to the prison to see him once per year on condition that they went together, as a group of three.

In Beijing, Liu Xia's house arrest became ever tighter. The number of police assigned to watch the door of her apartment building grew to more than twenty; they observed a rotating schedule that kept about eight of them on duty around the clock. At one point two policewomen moved directly into her apartment. On the ground floor of the building, two military cots were placed at the sides of the corridor, leaving only a narrow passageway through which people could pass single file. Residents of the building not only were inconvenienced but also began to feel that they too were being watched. Liu Xia could make telephone calls only to her parents' home and could receive no incoming calls. She was let out two hours per week to go to her parents' home but barred from seeing anyone else.

When she was outside, police accompanied her at every step. They stopped providing the outside world with information about her, including whether she was making her monthly trips to see Xiaobo. Her letters did not reach him, and she received no letters back.

Beginning in June 2011, she was able to see him according to the old schedule—the pre-Nobel pattern of monthly visits. She was not allowed to tell him about her own difficult conditions in Beijing. The most she could risk was gentle, indirect suggestion, such as "I am going through almost the same as what you are."

Their postprize meetings were different in several ways. Before the prize she had traveled on her own, and friends could accompany her on the journey. Now she could travel only by police car, without friends. Formerly she had sat across a table from Xiaobo, but now the two were separated by soundproof glass and could speak only through a telephone as prison guards stood by. Formerly a good-bye hug was permitted; now, no. Formerly they could talk about friends or events in society as long as they steered clear of "sensitive" topics; now topics were strictly limited to family. To violate the rule was to end the conversation. This happened once after the Chinese writer Mo Yan won the Nobel Prize for literature. When Liu Xia uttered the two syllables "Mo Yan," the telephone went dead.

Exchange of letters between husband and wife had been allowed before the Nobel Prize but was not afterward. All of their letters were confiscated. Liu Xia said she was sure Xiaobo was still writing letters, and it is hard to imagine that he was not. During his three years in the labor camp at Dalian, he had never stopped writing—not only letters but also reading notes, essays, and poems. It is also hard to imagine that he was not writing his annual poems for the lost souls of the June Fourth massacre.

At the Dalian labor camp Liu Xia had been able to bring medicines to Xiaobo. At Jinzhou this was prohibited. She continued bringing him books, but now they seldom reached him. In the past, prison officials would check the books and then let them through. Now they were either confiscated or returned to her to carry back to Beijing. The wardens asked her, instead, to present lists of books that she would like him to see. They would get them for him. This sometimes worked, but it could take up to six months.[3]

On September 12, 2011, Xiaobo's father, Liu Ling, died of liver cancer at age eighty. A week later, at the traditional marking of the "first seven" days in death, police allowed Xiaobo's eldest brother, Xiaoguang, to pick up Xiaobo from the prison and drive him to Dalian to bow at his father's mourning site and pay last respects. Xiaobo had never gotten along with his father, and they had chosen very different paths in life. We can only imagine what he might have been thinking. When news of his brief release from prison became known on the outside, a journalist tried to interview Xiaoxuan about it. Xiaoxuan said only, "It is hard to narrate how long Liu Xiaobo stopped at home or what he did."[4] This was a euphemism for "I am not at liberty to say."

When Xi Jinping ascended to the top of the Communist Party of China in November 2012, some Nobel laureates from around the world wanted to see whether he would be more lenient than his predecessor Hu Jintao. On December 4, they announced an open letter urging that Xi release Liu Xiaobo, who was the only Nobel laureate in any field currently in prison. The letter also called for the release of Liu Xia from house arrest. It was signed by the Dalai Lama; Bishop Desmond Tutu; the American writer Toni Morrison; the current year's joint winner of the Prize for Medicine, John Gurdon; and 130 others. It warned that to restrict freedom of thought is to endanger all fields of inquiry: "Across all disciplines, the distinguishing feature which led to our recognition as Nobel Laureates is that we have embraced the power of our intellectual freedom and creative inspiration to do our part to advance the human condition. . . . No government can restrict freedom of thought and association without having a negative effect on . . . important human innovation."[5] The letter got no response.

The world got an unanticipated glimpse into Liu Xia's life two days later, on December 6, 2012, when Associated Press reporter Isolda Morillo was able to go as far as the door of Liu Xia's apartment. This happened because the guards were rotating shifts for the noon meal and temporarily left no one in charge of blocking journalists. When Morillo knocked, Liu Xia came to the door, was startled to see a foreign journalist, and began trembling and sobbing uncontrollably. She was able to tell Morillo this much: she had television in her apartment but no Internet or telephone. She could go out once a week to buy vegetables and to see her parents. The police escorted her once a month to visit Xiaobo. She had given much thought over the years to what it might be like to be married to a dissident, but how could she ever have guessed that her husband's getting a Nobel Prize would mean that she could not leave her apartment?[6]

December 28, 2012, was Xiaobo's fifty-seventh birthday. Around 9:00 p.m. a number of his friends—Xu Youyu, Hao Jian, Hu Jia, Liu Di, and others—encouraged by the contact Morillo had been able to make, gathered in front of Liu Xia's apartment building and called out her name. Hearing them, she pushed open a window and answered. *Guobao* rushed to try to quell the visitors, and, as a discussion between them and the visitors heated up, Liu Xia came downstairs and pushed the door open from the inside. The visitors then lifted the *guobao* out of the way, entered, and followed Liu Xia up to her fifth-floor apartment. Hugs and tears of joy filled the room. At the same time, Liu Xia sensed danger. She pulled Xu Youyu aside and, through sobs, whispered something about hidden surveillance cameras. Xu couldn't hear clearly, but her point seemed to be that she was afraid that the push through the door and up the stairs might trigger punishment. Accordingly, after only about three minutes, the friends left.[7] This was the only occasion during the nearly eight years of Liu Xia's house arrest when she saw "political" friends, as the regime called them.

In spring 2013, the Jinzhou Prison authorities allowed some books on Christian philosophy, in which Liu Xia and Xiaobo had recently developed a shared interest, to get through to Xiaobo. In April they also let pass a new book, published just a year earlier: *The Red Wheel in Reverse: Reminiscences by Russian Intellectuals* by Jin Yan, a Chinese historian of the Soviet Union and Eastern Europe. The book title is inspired by Aleksandr Solzhenitsyn's cycle of novels called *The Red Wheel* about how the Soviet Union emerged from World War I. Solzhenitsyn conceived the "wheel" as a huge, inhuman, irrational, unstoppable force. Millions of ordinary people were caught up in its turning. Jin's book shows how, beginning in the 1860s, certain Russian intellectuals, in the name of overthrowing czarist rule, went "among the people" to organize. They were cruelly repressed. This made them all the more convinced that their cause was noble, and that led to their embrace of radical Bolshevism. Repressed again for that reason, they turned ever more radical and eventually to violent revolution. Jin saw her analysis as done "in reverse" because she could now examine the first turnings of the big wheel with the benefit of knowing the harm that it had done in the long run. The book was drawing wide attention among intellectuals in China. Perhaps it got past the prison censors because it discussed events of more than a century earlier, or because it was set in a foreign land. In any case the censors, who normally were not especially well-educated people, had missed its obvious contemporary relevance.

Some improvements appeared in Xiaobo's living conditions in 2013 and 2014. They were for Xiaobo only, not for all prisoners or even for other "thought prisoners." The wardens gave no reason, but the Nobel laureate in 2013 got a slightly larger cell and could watch a few more television channels than before. A solar water heater was installed on the roof of his building that made it possible, at least sometimes, for him to take hot showers. In 2014 he was assigned a small plot of land in the prison courtyard where he could grow vegetables—cucumbers, tomatoes, eggplants, and the like. Liu Xia said it "was for fun, mostly." Xiaobo sometimes brought his produce to the prison mess hall to share with others.[8]

Meanwhile, another nightmare was approaching. On March 9, 2012, the Public Security bureau in the Huairou district of Beijing detained Liu Xia's brother Liu Hui on "suspicion of the crime of swindling." A business partner named Zhao Juntian was detained around the same time, and a month later the two were formally arrested and charged with conspiring in 2010 to cheat three million yuan from Zhang Bing, the operator of a construction project.

The news shocked the Liu Hui family. Their understanding was that the money had been a legitimate commission, not swindled, and of course they wanted to find the best possible lawyer to defend Liu Hui. They thought immediately of Xiaobo's lawyer, Mo Shaoping, and sought him out. This alarmed the authorities. To involve Mo in the case might bring renewed attention, both national and international, to Xiaobo, and keeping him out of the news was a top regime priority. They went to Liu Hui's family with an offer: they would release Liu Hui on bail if the family would help keep the case out of the press and not bring in a famous lawyer.[9] Mo explained to the family that the offer to "release on bail" subtly created a time frame of one year (the normal duration of bail) during which the problem might melt away—as it would if, for example, the family were to return the disputed money and the government were to drop the criminal case against Liu Hui. The arrangement would naturally put increased pressure on the family to "behave well" politically. They considered the matter and agreed. On September 29, 2012, the Huairou Public Security Bureau released Liu Hui and Zhao Juntian on bail.

Four months later—on January 31, 2013—Liu Hui and Zhao Juntian were re-apprehended on the original charges. Was the reversal in part punishment for Liu Xia's disobedience in allowing Xu Youyu, Hao Jian, and others into her apartment a month earlier, on Xiaobo's birthday? Liu Hui and his family suspected this to be the case, and that put immense pressure on Liu Xia.

On March 12, 2013, the Huairou People's Procuratorate of Beijing City issued an indictment of Liu Hui and Zhao Juntian. It read in part:

> Legal investigations have revealed that defendants Liu Hui and Zhao Juntian, between July and September of 2010, falsely represented themselves as contracting for parts of the construction of the "Golden Palace Garden" project of Beijing Capital Realty, Inc. at no. 77 Guang'anmenwai South Road in the Western District of Beijing City, and after fraudulently earning the trust of the victim Zhang Bing, repeatedly swindled Zhang of amounts that totaled three million yuan. Defendant Zhao Juntian has returned 900,000 yuan of the lost funds.

The Liu Hui family felt that since the authorities had reneged on their part of the understanding, they needn't honor their part either, so they engaged Mo Shaoping to defend Liu Hui. On Mo's advice, Liu Hui placed 2.1 million of the disputed funds in escrow with the authorities. The 0.9 million returned by Zhao Juntian was similarly put in escrow. The money could be returned to Liu and Zhao if the court found them innocent or forwarded to Zhang Bing if it found them guilty.[10]

Liu Hui's trial took place on April 23, and Liu Xia was permitted to attend. Reporters were eager to see her, but she was kept away from them and managed only to shout two sentences as she left the court building: "I still am not free! If they tell you I am free, tell them that I am not!"

On June 9 the verdict on the swindling case was announced: "Convicted of the crime of swindling, defendant Liu Hui is sentenced to eleven years in prison, with political rights suspended for an additional two, and is fined 10,000 yuan." Mo Shaoping later said in an interview with the British Broadcasting Company that he had argued in court that the dispute over funds, which his client said were a legitimate commission, was a matter of civil law that had no place in criminal court. Mo also disclosed that the court had claimed Liu Hui's sentence had been "reduced" to eleven years because he had "voluntarily placed 2.1 million in escrow," whereas prosecutors had recommended twelve to fourteen years.[11] The money held in escrow was forwarded to Zhang Bing.

Liu Xia felt deeply indignant about the sentence. She saw the treatment of her brother as political persecution stemming from her husband's case. She now had "lost all faith" in the government. On June 12, she wrote an open letter to Xi Jinping and published it on the Twitter account of her lawyer, Shang Baojun. Liu Hui's sentence was "entirely unfair," she wrote, "and I doubt that judicial organs and the entire system of public authority are operating properly." She also spoke of her own plight: "Since October 2010, I have lost all of my personal freedom. I have been under house arrest. No one has told me the reason for this arrest. I've searched my imagination and can only conclude that, in this country, to be the wife of Liu Xiaobo must be some kind of 'crime.'"[12] Commenting on Xi Jinping's ideal that "the China dream" be realized in the life of every citizen, Liu Xia wrote, "I hope this China dream won't be bringing us citizens a 'China nightmare.'"

Liu Hui asked Mo Shaoping to appeal his sentence. At the same time, Liu Xia was asking Mo to prepare two other lawsuits: an appeal of the judgment of the appellate court on Xiaobo's case—Xiaobo never did accept the verdict and had mentioned several times that he wanted to appeal the case further; and a suit by Liu Xia herself against the Beijing Public Security Bureau for illegally confining her for three years. Lawyer Mo thus had three Liu family cases in his lap. On June 26, pressed by journalists, he said it would take time to prepare them, especially the Liu Xiaobo appeal. Pressed further, he acknowledged that the existence of the Liu Xiaobo appeal might indeed put pressure on the authorities to treat Liu Hui more leniently than they otherwise would.

On August 16, the appeal in the Liu Hui case was rejected. Liu Xia, who had been feeling ill, did not go to the court to hear the decision. The psychological burden of what was happening to her brother was taking an ever-heavier toll on her. She wrote to friends about carrying "two eleven-years" on her back. Moreover, with Liu Hui back in prison and unable to work, her parents were under financial pressure. Her health declined to a point where even her *guobao* were worried. She suffered depression and on many nights could sleep only by taking pills. She also felt that something was wrong with her heart. On December 3 she used the well-known blog of Zeng Jinyan, wife of the imprisoned filmmaker Hu Jia, to demand that the regime allow her to take salaried employment and seek medical treatment as she preferred, and to allow her and Xiaobo to see each other's letters.

Eventually Xiaobo's old friend Liu Suli, proprietor of the All Saints Book Grove, was able to mediate an understanding with Liu Xia's *guobao* that gave her a bit more freedom to see family and friends. In early 2014 she was allowed to go to a hospital for a physical exam. Another of Xiaobo's old friends, the truth-telling Dr. Jiang Yanyong, arranged for her to see physicians at Beijing's 301 army hospital for a comprehensive physical. She was also allowed to see friends from time to time. She had to submit a list of their names to her *guobao* in advance and could not see anyone who was even slightly "sensitive" politically, but she could visit with certain friends in art and culture circles. Her home telephone was reconnected, and although it obviously was monitored, both incoming and outgoing calls were possible. From time to time she was allowed out to go to bookstores under police accompaniment.

On May 17, 2014, she used Shang Baojun's Twitter account to make two declarations:

1. Some stories that my health is precarious have been circulating. They are not accurate. My health has rebounded very well. Doctors have said there is nothing wrong with my heart, and I am getting regular psychiatric care. I am on my way back to normal daily life and do not wish to be disturbed with these questions, but I do appreciate everyone's concerns!
2. We are temporarily suspending Liu Xiaobo's appeal case.[13]

She made no mention of the other lawsuit she had asked Mo Shaoping to prepare—her own suit against the Beijing Public Security Bureau. That one apparently was suspended as well. She did not give reasons.

On May 21, Liu Hui was granted medical parole and allowed to come home from prison. Around the same time, Beijing Public Security asked the Liu family lawyers to "promise to halt their involvement in the Liu Xiaobo appeal case and in matters related to his imprisonment," and the lawyers agreed.[14] Three years later, in a public interview with Radio Free Asia, Mo Shaoping acknowledged that a deal had been struck to release Liu Hui in return for dropping Liu Xiaobo's appeal: "Hadn't Liu Xia's younger brother been arrested? So we did an exchange that said we would no longer appeal the Liu Xiaobo case."[15] A year later, Mo explained that the deal originally had been his own idea.[16] He knew that Liu Xia and Liu Hui were close and that Liu Hui's conviction had been very hard on Liu Xia. A deal like this might be the only way to get Liu Hui out of prison. The authorities were amenable because there were advantages in it for them: it avoided news on a Liu Xiaobo appeal and also put pressure on Liu Xia to keep quiet. Mo recalled that around the middle of May 2014, Liu Xia called him to approve "suspending the appeal," and later the same day, that authorities called to say, "We agree to medical parole for Liu Hui." They added that Mo himself was to do no press interviews about the matter.

The regime's goal of keeping Liu Xia quiet had some effect. With Liu Hui's fate in mind, she had to be cautious in raising questions about Xiaobo's prison conditions (her lawyers, as noted above, had already agreed not to be involved). She did not pursue the prison clinic's finding of "indeterminate diagnosis of hepatitis B" and did not apply for medical parole for Xiaobo. She continued faithfully to visit him every month but was careful to report back nothing about his condition that might arouse concern. When friends asked, she would reply, "He's fine," or "He's doing fine—better than I am." She was careful to meet only with a small number of friends who kept their distance from politics. She avoided foreign journalists. She saw less of her lawyers, Mo Shaoping and Shang Baojun. Legally speaking, both she and Xiaobo had been checkmated.

Xiaobo, in prison, was unaware of Liu Hui's arrest, trial, or medical parole, and Liu Xia did not try to tell him. She feared being cut off if she did, and even if she succeeded the news would, she feared, only have further burdened his mind. The most she told him—and that only vaguely—was that Liu Hui could no longer do business.

On December 9, 2014, Liao Yiwu, in Germany, posted a paragraph from his old friend Xiaobo on his Facebook page. Liao noted that to protect people inside China, he could not reveal how the paragraph had gotten out of Jinzhou Prison and into his hands. It read: "I'm not doing badly. Since entering prison I haven't stopped reading or thinking. Study and reflection increases my confidence that I have no personal enemies. More than enough credit has fallen my way. Please direct the attention of the world to all those victims who aren't very well known—or not known at all." His statement that "I have no personal enemies" was a clear echo of his "I have no enemies" statement at trial and evidence that, after five years in Jinzhou Prison, he was maintaining his view that the enemy was a system, not the human beings who populated it.

From 2014 through 2016 Liu Xia sank ever more steadily into gloom. She wrote a poem in September 2016 that she called "Untitled—Following Tanikawa Shuntarō." Tanikawa, a Japanese poet born in 1931, had written a poem called "Untitled" that began:

> I'm weary
> Weary of my flesh
> Weary of tea bowls, flags, pigeons on the sidewalk
> Weary of long, soft hair
> Weary of the presentations of dawn and dusk . . .

Liu Xia's poem reads:

> I am weary
> I am weary of my white pills
> I am weary of smiling at you
> I am weary of toilets on the train
> I am weary of your reputation
> I am weary of my mental exhaustion
>
> I am weary
> I am weary of seeing all pathways blocked
> I am weary of the filthy sky
> I am weary of weeping
> I am weary of super-pure life
> I am weary of fake talk
>
> I am weary of plants dying
> I am weary of sleepless nights
> I am weary of my empty mailbox
> I am weary of all the scoldings
> I am weary of the months and years that pass wordlessly
> I am weary of the conspicuous scarlet letter on my body
> I am weary of cages
> My love
> I am weary[17]

Fearful of adding to Xiaobo's psychological strains, Liu Xia had long been reluctant to mention her weariness, let alone her clinical depression. Around the time she wrote this poem, though, her own burdens were becoming overwhelming: her father had died, her mother was nearing death, and the threat of Liu Hui's return to prison loomed still. She finally decided to open up to Xiaobo, and during a regular visit on March 30, 2017, she did. Depressed for seven years. Heart troubles. Her mother at the brink. Liu Hui's eleven-year sentence. (These dire reports did not violate prison rules because they all were about her own person and family.) The news shocked Xiaobo. He immediately felt guilty, seeing himself as the cause of Liu Xia's and Liu Hui's suffering. He would do anything for them now. But what?

This emotional breakthrough happened before either of them knew about the deadly cancer that was growing inside Xiaobo.

As early as November 1997, doctors at the Dalian labor camp had found "active hepatitis B virus" in Xiaobo's blood. His mother, who had also carried the virus, died of cirrhosis of the liver. His father had been seriously ill with hepatitis and had died of liver cancer. For all these reasons, Jinzhou Prison should have monitored the condition of his liver. When he lay dying, on June 28, 2017, the Justice Bureau of Shenyang city claimed that monitoring had been happening all along:

> Documents that the criminal Liu Xiaobo supplied to Jinzhou Prison upon entry show that he already had a medical history of hepatitis B. . . . After entry, he was given annual physical examinations and semiannual scheduled visits, and the prison has kept a complete medical file. Beginning in 2012, based on the physical examination results, he was also given screening tests for hepatitis and tumors, and all of the tests were negative.[18]

Xiaobo's first test for hepatitis B at Jinzhou Prison had shown the virus to be "indeterminate"—the same word that had been used at the labor camp—but that judgment was likely colored by the political need to keep him ineligible for medical parole. In any case, there was ample reason to monitor the matter and take precautions, because carrying the hepatitis B virus often leads to an active phase of the disease, which in turn often leads to liver cancer. The progression is not automatic; when it does happen, it takes time—time in which treatment can be effective.

The only bit of evidence to suggest that the prison hospital might actually have been monitoring Xiaobo's liver came in February 2017, when the Information Centre for Human Rights and Democracy, a group based in Hong Kong, reported that his brother Liu Xiaoguang had said that Xiaobo had had two CT scans during 2016.[19] There was no indication of why the scans were done or what the results were, but a CT scan is not part of a routine physical exam; if two were done within one year, someone must have known that there was something to be watched.

In April 2017, Cai Chu was able to reach Liu Xia by telephone from the United States and asked her, among other things, about Xiaobo's health. She said it was "Okay." She said the prison authorities had recently given him a complete physical but had not told her any results and, as far as she knew, had not told Xiaobo either.

It strains credulity to imagine that authorities who were so intensely vigilant in observing and measuring every thought that emerged from Xiaobo's brain could somehow not notice until the last moment that his liver had produced a lump more than four inches in diameter, about the size of a fist. If they were concealing what they knew about the tumor, they were doing so during the very months when specialists could have tried to control it. On July 7, 2017, Dr. Markus Büchler, a world authority on liver cancer, traveled from Germany to visit Xiaobo in the hospital when the end was near. It was clear, the doctor said, that the development of the cancer had gone on too long without medical attention. Did the prison people not know what was happening, or did they know and purposely do nothing? This was hard to say—it was probably something in between.[20]

If decisions were made about whether, when, and how to treat Xiaobo's liver condition, they were not necessarily made by physicians. Prison doctors ordered tests and interpreted results, but decisions on what actions to take, if any, were made by the political authorities to whom the doctors reported. Wei Jingsheng gave an interview shortly after Xiaobo's death in which he illustrated this pattern from his own prison experience. A doctor once told him informally that tests showed a minor problem with his heart and advised him to have his family send him a certain medication. A Public Security officer overheard the comment and scowled; the miscreant doctor was later dismissed from his position and reassigned to a remote clinic where no high-profile political prisoner would ever be sent.[21]

In early April 2017, Liu Xia, still knowing nothing of the cancer, was working on a plan to get her husband, her brother, and herself all out of China and to Germany, where their old friend Liao Yiwu lived, her depression might be relieved, and Liu Hui would certainly be safer than he was in China. The plan would mean that Xiaobo would need to relinquish his long-standing pledge to himself not to leave China. But after his shock of learning of Liu Xia's illness, Xiaobo was ready to agree and told her so. It would be his contribution to a cure for her.[22] On April 9, Liu Xia wrote a letter to the authorities:

In the past few years, for a number of reasons, my physical and mental condition has been pressed to a limit. My depression has never seen fundamental improvement. It keeps recurring. My doctors say a complete change in living environment would be best. . . . Xiaobo has agreed to accompany me in going abroad for treatment. . . . The German government has said it is more than ready to receive our family in Germany. . . . I appeal to you to let Liu Xiaobo, Liu Hui, and me go to Germany together to seek medical treatment and to live a low-profile life. I hope you will approve this application and forward it to the relevant officials.[23]

The letter got no response. One problem may have been that Liu Hui, who was out of prison on medical parole, was still legally a prisoner, and Chinese law does not allow current prisoners to leave the country. An exception would need to be made. But the regime would hardly be eager to make the exception and see him emigrate, given his obvious value as a hostage. Further, there was the question of whether the authorities would want to let Xiaobo out. In the 1990s, after the June Fourth massacre, the regime was happy to see dissidents leave the country because this was a way to subdue their influence inside China. Xiaobo was a Nobel Peace laureate and would have a larger-than-normal megaphone in the outside world for his criticisms of the regime.

Liu Xia persisted with her idea of emigration by pursuing it from the other end. On April 20, she wrote to Liao Yiwu in Berlin for his help, and Liao went immediately to work. He reached out to German officials including the office of Chancellor Angela Merkel, who had made it clear she would be willing to help.

On May 29, when Liu Xia set out for her regular monthly visit to Xiaobo, she was filled with hope. The two spoke, as usual, through a glass partition. Xiaobo said he remained willing to leave for Germany. When Liu Xia returned to Beijing, still unaware of his cancer, she reported to friends that his health seemed normal except that he might have been a bit thinner than before. A few days later the sky fell in. She got a phone call from the Jinzhou Prison asking her to come to see Xiaobo as soon as possible. She had never before been able to see him outside of scheduled visits. Now she was being summoned. Alarmed, she asked if Xiaobo was ill. The answer was no, but he "really wants to see you." So she left—by police car, as usual—for Jinzhou.

Urgent though the meeting was, they still spoke through a glass partition. Xiaobo told her that he had been running a high fever for two weeks, felt nauseated, and had no energy. To him it was an entirely new feeling, he said. The prison authorities had not brought him to an outside hospital. They notified her, as his wife, and his brother Xiaoguang, who was also on his way to the prison.

Liu Xia was told the diagnosis of cancer before Xiaobo was, and she was the one who gave him the news. He reacted calmly. He had seen from the cases of both his parents what the cruel and inexorable consequences of liver disease are like. He opted to decline treatment. "Just let it go," he said to Liu Xia. His lifetime of reading in philosophy and religion had equipped him with ways to maintain equanimity in the face of death. Liu Xia respected Xiaobo's decision but would not allow the doctors to abandon treatment. Aside from the very small hope that Xiaobo might survive, the hope of their getting out to Germany might also depend on it.

The next day Xiaobo was transferred from Jinzhou Prison to the First Hospital of China Medical University in Shenyang, 135 miles away. Liu Xia followed and found a nearby hotel. Shenyang is the capital of Liaoning province and its largest city. This hospital, the leading one in the area, had all the modern equipment. According to a report released a few days after Xiaobo's arrival, the hospital had invited the best tumor experts in China—from Beijing, Nanjing, and elsewhere—to come to Shenyang to join a team that agreed unanimously on a diagnosis of liver cancer that had metastasized throughout the body. Xiaobo was facing the last few days of his life.

For Xiaobo and his loved ones, the cancer now loomed like a great zombie, but for the political authorities, the announcement of Xiaobo's condition was a call to action. This was the time to "show concern" and, even more importantly, to broadcast the fact that great concern was being shown. The outside world would demand an explanation, and the story would have to be that the regime was shocked, animated, blameless. The twin goals were to isolate Xiaobo from the world and to advertise to the world that he was getting only the best of care.

Another parallel with Carl von Ossietzky emerges. In April 1936 the Nazi regime knew that Ossietzky, then in a concentration camp, was seriously ill with tuberculosis and other ailments. Authorities snapped into action, giving him all kinds of tests and keeping detailed records. Leaders of the secret police made personal reports on Ossietzky's health to Hitler's deputy Hermann Göring. In June 1936 Ossietzky was moved from the concentration camp to a hospital in Berlin, where he received meticulous care while still under Gestapo surveillance. In November 1936 people from the Nobel committee were able to reach him and present him with his prize. He died of tuberculosis on May 4, 1938, at another hospital, still under police watch. In their deaths too, the records of Ossietzky and Xiaobo were similar, although on balance, Ossietzky fared a bit better.

When Xiaobo arrived in Shenyang he still did not formally have medical parole, so could not leave the hospital. Liu Xia could visit him there, but prison rules still applied: twenty minutes maximum, and then she was shepherded out.

Police were everywhere—along the corridors, lining the walls inside Xiaobo's room, and at his bedside. The young policemen stared with numb, unblinking gazes. Liu Xia counted about twenty-five at any given time. No fewer would do, apparently, to protect the gigantic state from her gravely ill husband.

The news of Xiaobo's hospitalization reached the international media on June 26, when Xiaobo's lawyer Shang Baojun announced on Voice of America that Xiaobo had late-stage liver cancer and that the prison had decided on its own to grant him medical parole. ("On its own" was added to honor the lawyers' prior agreement not to be involved with questions of Xiaobo's prison conditions.) Also on June 26, the Liaoning Prison Administration Bureau posted this brief message on its website:

> The Liaoning provincial prisoner Liu Xiaobo has been diagnosed with liver cancer. In recent days the Prisons Management Bureau of Liaoning Province has approved the medical parole of Liu Xiaobo according to law. The First Hospital of China Medical University convened a small group of eight leading tumor experts from China who have determined a course of treatment, and Liu Xiaobo is currently being treated in accordance with that plan.[24]

Late that same night Xiaobo and Liu Xia's old friend, the poet Zhou Zhongling, posted on the Internet a video recording of Liu Xia in tears, telling the world that Xiaobo "is beyond treatment by surgery, radiation, or chemotherapy."[25] The post caused shock and disbelief among Xiaobo's friends and followers. How was it possible that his condition had become unsalvageable virtually overnight? A group of citizens' rights activists in Shenyang went to the hospital to try to visit Xiaobo but could not even get confirmation that he was there. Staff at Reception, Internal Medicine, and even in the Tumors Section checked computer monitors and said they could see no listing of a Liu Xiaobo. To the visitors, the only evidence that he was indeed inside the hospital was the swarm of police patrolling outside.

Liao Yiwu, still working hard in Berlin to make Xiaobo's travel to Germany possible, decided on June 27 to release on Twitter Liu Xia's message of April 20 in which she said that Xiaobo was willing to leave China. He felt he had to do this because Xiaobo's original resolve not to leave was well known. The news spread quickly, and the request to leave China took on special urgency because of the news of the cancer. Thirteen hundred people inside China, braving punishment, joined an appeal to "return to Liu Xiaobo his right of freedom." People who came to see him in the hospital were blocked. His status of "on medical parole" did not allow a loosening of the police net around him. He did not have a cell phone and was not allowed to use a hospital telephone. In short, he was still effectively in prison. Only Liu Xia, and sometimes Liu Hui, who arrived in Shenyang on July 3, were allowed to see him.

On June 28, the website of the Bureau of Justice of Shenyang City issued a statement: "On May 31, 2017, in a routine physical examination of Liu Xiaobo, Jinzhou Prison in Liaoning province discovered a suspicious symptom in the internal organs of his abdominal cavity and arranged immediately for him to leave prison for medical examination." The lie was blatant. The Shenyang hospital itself had records, transferred from Jinzhou, showing that Xiaobo had run a fever and complained of unusual pain in the chest as early as May 23.[26]

Also on June 28, an unusual video appeared on YouTube. About three minutes long, it showed Xiaobo's happy and healthy daily life inside Jinzhou Prison and clearly was intended to answer the worries and accusations of people outside the prison and outside China. No one could have made such a video without the blessings of the regime: the outdoor shots were from surveillance cameras on the prison walls, and the indoor shots could not possibly have been done by a prisoner. The video was not presented as an official product of the New China News Agency, however, but as something that had come from an unnamed person savvy enough to "jump the firewall" of official Internet censorship and post it on YouTube. The ruse of unofficial origins was likely designed to mislead foreign opinion. The outdoor shots show Xiaobo playing badminton, jogging in the prison courtyard, and shoveling snow with fellow inmates after a blizzard. The indoor shots show Xiaobo receiving routine medical care: blood-pressure measurement, height measurement, vision tests, and a dental exam. Some of the shots that show nonroutine health care—a chest X-ray, an ultrasound, a CT scan—seem aimed at heading off accusations about neglect of the liver cancer. Xiaobo is shown lying on an examination table, naked to the waist, answering a doctor's questions. None of the shots shows him visibly happy, but all show him in situations where nothing should make a person unhappy. There are shots of his leaving prison to go to his father's funeral, of him and Liu Xia talking through a glass partition, of him assuring her that his medical tests came out all right, and of him thanking medical staff in the prison for their care. Viewers who did not know about the "no enemies" philosophy that led him to respect even his prosecutors in court might think that his thanks in the video amounted to support for the system that was persecuting him. If so, the video was successful in its aims.

Politicians around the world—with Germany and the United States taking the lead—launched what they saw as a rescue effort. On June 29, diplomats from several Western countries met in Beijing with a Chinese vice minister of justice. The vice minister told them that Xiaobo was seriously ill and that it was "inadvisable" to move him long distances, and that he personally was not in a position to decide the question of Xiaobo's going abroad for treatment.

Meanwhile Xiaobo's supporters in China continued to demand that he be allowed to leave. Zeng Jinyan and Ye Du posted three photos on Twitter that showed Liu Xia and Xiaobo together in his hospital room. One showed her feeding him kiwi fruit with a spoon. Another showed them toasting each other with cups that sported images of bear cubs; this one seemed especially valuable because both were smiling. A third, which got the widest circulation, showed them in an embrace, each with skinny arms clutching the other in a way that made it seem one could almost hear the bones clacking. The photos had a big impact among Xiaobo's supporters around the world and especially with his close friends in China. Here were a husband and wife, wedged apart for nine years, smiling and hugging. The filmmaker Hu Jia offered an analysis of what one could learn about Xiaobo's health from the evidence of the photos. He took to Twitter to rebut the government's assertion that Xiaobo was unfit for air travel: "We see here that Liu Xiaobo can stand up, can walk, can sit. He can eat with his mouth, so is not entirely dependent on intravenous feeding. Liu Xia is with him. Add a medical team to assist, and there is no reason he could not do air travel." Liu Xia's close friend Gan Qi, who had helped Zhou Zhongling arrange Xiaobo's dialogues with Wang Shuo eighteen years earlier and was now chief editor at the Chinese University of Hong Kong Press, found the news of Xiaobo's illness hard to believe. She wanted, somehow, to hear the news straight from Xiaobo, and on June 27, via a recording on Liu Hui's cell phone, she got this oral reply: "Hey, it's been a long time! Don't worry about me. I'm an iron egg embryo and I've been through so much—this little matter is nothing to mention. I'll be fine, I'll stick it out to the end, for Liu Xia—." When he reached the words "for Liu Xia" he suddenly broke off and did not continue. It was very much in character that he wanted to tell people not to worry about him. The recording appears to be the last one of his voice.

At the time, Gan Qi was preparing to publish a collection of Liu Xia's artistic photographs tentatively entitled *Blind Spot: Accompanying Liu Xiaobo*, and she asked Xiaobo if he would contribute a preface commenting on Liu Xia's photographs, poems, and paintings. The next day she pressed him on the matter: "Will you do it?" Xiaobo answered by text using the kind of playful banter he often used with friends: "I'll do this bit of homework for you." Time passed, and Gan Qi, still waiting, pressed again: "I'm not going to get it?" The next day she heard back: "I'll do it."

A few days later, still with no manuscript, Gan Qi tried another tack. She proposed that Xiaobo simply say some words into a microphone; she would organize them into a written preface. But then the answer came back: "An old guy like me gets too short of breath—writing is better after all." On July 9 Gan Qi received three handwritten pages on paper that appeared to have been torn from an ordinary notebook. The characters were sometimes hard to discern, especially near the end, but the meaning was sharp and clear. Xiaobo's thinking was as meticulous and lively as usual.

The tone of the literary exchange between Xiaobo and Liu Xia had always been special. Their sentences often turned poetic, not to say a bit mystical and paradoxical. It was as if, when addressing each other, they turned their backs on the world. One of their recurrent little games concerned Liu Xia's standing "command" that Xiaobo praise her. In this, his final essay, Xiaobo wrote:

> My praise of you may in fact be an unpardonable poison: a dark desk lamp, and my first computer, which you gave to me—maybe it was a Pentium 586. That dumpy room of ours made my loving gaze feel a bit too crowded. You'll remember that little poem I wrote about my preposterous wife the Little Shrimp who went to the kitchen to make porridge for me and demanded that within the 360 seconds before she returned I produce an elegy to her more devastating than any the world has ever seen:[27]

FIGURE 20.1 Liu Xia and three photos, 2008

Liu Xia

Dusky lamp, dumpy room, peeling tea table
And Little Shrimp's preposterous command
The astonishment when a rock and a star first meet
In seamless, flawless union

From then on, praising you became my indelible fate, like the instinct of a polar
bear to enjoy hibernation within a boundless white void. . . .[28]

The essay was dated July 5, 2017. To the end, Xiaobo maintained his habit of dat-
ing each piece he wrote.

At the top of the first page of the essay were two lines unrelated to it. These
must have been the final two lines of a preceding essay in the copybook from
which the pages were torn. They read: "kill, a stiff, imprisoned body, to a person's
morality . . . the crime strangles the moral foundations of justice." It was dated
June 19, 2017. To judge from that fragment, the writing may have been his last
essay on political philosophy and, written twelve days after his admission to the
hospital, must have been done with clear knowledge that he had very little time
left. It may have extraordinary value, if it has not been destroyed.

On July 5 Xiaobo's health took an ominous nosedive, and the next day the
Shenyang hospital issued a statement on his condition. That step was highly
unusual. Normally such announcements are made only for state leaders; making
one in Xiaobo's case clearly had to do with the pressure of international opinion.
Still at pains to present itself as doing all the right things, the regime seemed also
to want to prepare public opinion for a death announcement. The hospital report
said that leading experts from across China had conferred on a diagnosis and
agreed that Liu Xiaobo's condition had become critical. Water in the abdomen
was increasing, liver function was declining, and thrombosis had appeared in the
left calf. The family had been notified.

On the same day, the President of China, Xi Jinping, arrived in Hamburg, Germany, for the twelfth summit of the leaders of the G-20 countries. There, Chancellor Angela Merkel asked this Western suit-wearing emperor of China to allow
the Nobel Peace Prize-winning Liu Xiaobo to come to Germany. Xi responded
that Liu was ill—too ill to travel—but then said he would welcome Western doctors to come see Liu in China.[29]

Very soon thereafter, Markus Büchler, an expert on liver cancer at the University of Heidelberg in Germany, and Joseph Herman, from the Anderson Cancer
Center at the University of Texas in the United States, received invitations to go
to Shenyang, and both went without delay. In Shenyang, Chinese doctors used a

FIGURE 20.2   In the Shenyang hospital, 2017

Liu Hui

FIGURE 20.3   Xiaobo's final sketch

Gan Qi

PowerPoint presentation to brief them thoroughly on Xiaobo's medical condition and the next day accompanied them to see the patient. Everyone agreed on the diagnosis of late-stage liver cancer. The Western doctors were impressed that Xiaobo was currently getting first-rate medical attention but were shown no clinical records of his condition year by year or month by month in the past.

Their visit with the patient lasted about half an hour. Xiaobo's voice was firm, and he was able to speak with them in English. (Apparently his efforts to learn English in prison had been somewhat successful.) He was aware that the number of his days in this world was dwindling. His only concern, he told the doctors, was for Liu Xia. He entreated them several times to get her out of China. He said he was willing to go with her, preferably to Germany. He did not mention Liu Hui. He gasped as he spoke; shortness of breath, the doctors said, was a symptom of his kind of cancer. Liu Xia was nearly frantic; she grabbed Dr. Büchler's arm so tightly that it was not easy for the doctor to pull free. On July 9, Drs. Büchler and Herman issued a joint statement that Xiaobo's condition would permit him to travel abroad for treatment, but this should be done very quickly. Clearly the end was near. Xiaobo's brothers Xiaoguang and Xiaoxuan were allowed into his hospital room to see him.

On July 10 the German embassy in Beijing issued a "Statement About Breach of Doctor-Patient Confidentiality by Certain Actors in the Case of Liu Xiaobo." It said:

[We feel] deep concern that certain authorities have evidently made audio and video surveillance recordings of the medical visit of Mr. Liu Xiaobo by a German doctor. These recordings were made against the expressed wishes of the German side, which were communicated in writing prior to the visit. It seems that these recordings are being leaked selectively to certain Chinese state media outlets. It seems that security organs are steering the process, not medical experts.[30]

On the same day, Xiaobo was moved into an intensive care unit. The hospital had begun releasing daily announcements on his condition on July 6, but on the 12th issued two reports, in the morning and the afternoon. The morning report said that every effort was being made to save Xiaobo, but liver function continued to decline. The afternoon report said that the decline was accelerating, and "The patient's breathing has become difficult and shows no marked improvement after delivery of oxygen at high dosage. Support of life depends on machine-assisted breathing. The family, apprised of this condition, has decided to decline further use of assisted breathing." The end of the report stated that while the patient was close to death, the hospital continued to exert full effort for him and the family had signed papers acknowledging all the details.

Xiaobo's head remained clear to the end. He asked Liu Xia to enjoy her life and expressed his thanks to all the doctors and nurses who had attended him.

On July 13 at 12:30 p.m. six relatives—wife, Liu Xia; brother-in-law, Liu Hui; and brothers Liu Xiaoguang and Liu Xiaoxuan and their wives—gathered at Xiaobo's bedside. As Xiaobo's consciousness slipped away, doctors asked the family if they should do a tracheotomy to assure continued breathing. Liu Xia found the suggestion upsetting, and the others agreed that tubes inserted at this point would serve no real purpose. It would be better just to let Xiaobo depart peacefully. The family watched in anguish as his breathing grew weaker and weaker and then as his heartbeat ceased. He died at 5:35 p.m. on July 13, 2017.

For the *guobao* assigned to Xiaobo, who were still on duty to prevent him from subverting state power, his final breath was the signal for their next duty. They entered his hospital room to take possession of his prison writings. Xiaobo had brought with him to the hospital many of the handwritten reading notes and essays that he had done in prison. They were stored at the head of his bed. Liu Xia tried to halt the confiscation—protesting and resisting as strongly as she could—but to no avail. Today the fate of the materials is known only to people within the Communist Party's Public Security system. The value of the materials can only be imagined.

The regime maintained its guard at the hospital for some time. Inside Xiaobo's family home in Dalian, his empty room was designated a military-protected area that unauthorized persons were forbidden to enter.

Those days were the most painful of Liu Xia's life. She felt with every step as if walking on the points of knives. The regime, using the threat of curtailing her brother's freedom, forced her to agree to the prompt disposal of her husband's physical remains and their quick burial at sea.

Around 6:30 a.m. on July 15, Liu Xiaobo's body was cremated at the Hunnan District Funeral Home in Shenyang. The same six relatives who were with him when he died attended a brief ceremony there, along with small crowd of others. None of the relatives knew who the others were.

When the cremation was finished, Liu Xia was presented with a box containing the ashes, which she clutched closely to her chest. The burial at sea happened that same afternoon. The regime preferred burial at sea because this method left no piece of earth at which loved ones or admirers might later assemble. Gatherings for Liu Xiaobo, dead or alive, were dangerous.

Xiaobo himself had never much liked the sea. In an essay in 1993 he poked fun at people who wanted to be buried there: "Many people instruct their relatives to cast their ashes into the sea after they die. Is this from capacious thinking? Or from an incurable longing for immortality? Struggling at the end to stay alive, do people think of the boundless sea as a receptacle for their hopes for an extension of life, for a place to continue their quest of wealth and fame?"[31] Typical of his self-interrogation, he then went on to ask why he felt as he did. Perhaps it was because the sea "is unfeeling, lacks love and sympathy, and is dangerous. . . . It is indifferent, cares about nothing, goes along with anything; its huge size and its suggestion of eternity do nothing to lessen its utter lack of scruple. . . . There are no fresh flowers or green grass around graves in the sea."[32] More than once in his writings, Xiaobo invoked a line from the Soviet poetess Marina Tsvetaeva: "The sea may be vast, but it cannot walk."[33]

FIGURE 20.4 A week after Liu Xiaobo's death, a group of friends, defying tight police surveillance, met to remember him. Front row (squatting), from left: Liu Di, Wang Zhihong, Jin Yan, Liang Xiaoyan, Wang Junxiu, Mao Yuyuan. Standing behind, from left: Wu Si, Liu Suli, Lü Pu, Mo Shaoping, Shang Baojun, Liu Junning, Liu Xingping, Mo Zhixu, Jiang Qisheng, Zhang Jie, Ma Shaofang, Qin Hui, Ding Xikui, Bi Yimin, Xu Xiao

Xu Xiao

There is no sign that the regime knew anything about these views of Xiaobo. Their reason for burying his ashes at sea was only to disperse them so that no one could honor their location.

After Xiaobo's death, the police continued to watch Liu Xia closely. She still could not interact with people freely. On July 12, 2018, she left for Germany.

Epilogue

The Legacy of Liu Xiaobo

Some of Liu Xiaobo's characteristics were easy to observe. He ate ravenously, cleaning communal plates as well as his own, yet never seemed to put on weight. He avoided drink because of an allergic reaction to alcohol, but he smoked his entire life, beginning at age ten. He was gregarious and formed close relationships with people of different social stations, of both sexes, and spanning a wide range of ages. He read voraciously in history, literature, and philosophy both Eastern and Western, both ancient and modern. His gift of a photographic memory served him well in impressing friends, including his first girlfriend in the early 1970s, and in delivering brilliant lectures that packed university auditoria in the mid- to late 1980s. He was a lifetime stutterer—but not when he was either angry or intently focused on delivering eloquence. He was basically monolingual, although he did have some exposure to Japanese in college and studied English intermittently, including during his final prison years.

Beneath the surface, his mind had two strong but countervailing tendencies that remained with him in one form or another throughout his life. He was fiercely independent, accepting only what his own brain had certified for him. Fads, authority, and peer pressure were barred. Yet he was constantly self-questioning and self-revising. *Am I right? Should I change?* Very few people of strong mind also have this second habit. Xiaobo did, but not because he set out to cultivate it. It was a natural part of him.

Some examples, first, of the strong-mindedness: he felt bored in first grade because his teacher's explanations were too simple—and he said so. In graduate school in 1984 he argued loudly with his M.A. thesis adviser because the two interpreted the literary theory of the Tang poet Sikong Tu differently. Later, as a dissident, he wrote barbed essays precisely on the "sensitive" topics that the regime had boxed off as politically radioactive: the Tiananmen Mothers, Falun Gong, Tibet, prisoners of conscience, and more. In 2006, when Chinese President Hu Jintao left China on an important tour of the United States, Xiaobo published articles, one after another, almost city by city on the tour, calling Hu a "dictator." It would be wrong to see this fusillade as Xiaobo's attempt to provoke Hu—who in any case would not read the articles. It was more a reminder to himself to refuse self-censorship stoutly by continually saying "no" when the stakes were highest.

Examples of his inner questioning and self-scrutiny: his early poem "Believe!," written when he was twenty-three years old, includes the words "heavy," "steel," "cold," "gunfire," "ghosts," and "death" along with the words "dawn," "cradle," "rose," "love," and "longings"—and both kinds of words are offered with gusto. He seems torn between two poles, focused on both but allied with neither. Ten years later, when he was thirty-three, as his book *Contemporary Chinese Politics and Chinese Intellectuals* was going to press, he abruptly concluded that one of its main premises was flawed. What to do? Try to halt production? Just let the matter go? He opted to write an epilogue undermining his own book's main argument.

His most soul-searching self-recalibration came in the early 1990s, after his release from Qincheng Prison. Tao Li had asked for a divorce while he was incarcerated, and he completely accepted her move. He had, in his own view, been a grossly irresponsible husband and father—disloyal to Tao Li romantically and stingy in finding time for his son. Moreover, the "confession" that authorities had extracted from him inside Qincheng had been craven. On both counts Xiaobo felt overwhelming guilt and a powerful urge to change and to atone. His unwavering loyalty to his second wife, Liu Xia, can be seen in part as an effort to compensate for his maltreatment of Tao Li. And his readiness to return to prison (three more incarcerations lay in his future at that point) came in part from a wish to purge the shame that he had brought upon himself inside Qincheng. He sometimes spoke as if he *belonged* back in prison. The thought seems actually to have given him courage.

In his Tiananmen memoir *Monologue of a Doomsday Survivor*, he notes the irony that China's Communist regime—stupidly, if viewed from a distance—creates the heroes that oppose it. He himself was an example. When he flew from New York on April 27, 1989, to join the protest movement in Beijing, he was expecting, based on his fame as a brilliant lecturer a year earlier, to be welcomed as a hero. But this did not happen. Burning new issues had surged to the fore in Beijing, and students now found him insufficiently radical. He, in turn, criticized them for their undemocratic practices and for poor hygiene on the square. He was, in short, much less than what the regime would soon send him to prison for being: a behind-the-scenes "black hand" manipulating the movement on behalf of counterrevolutionary forces in New York. Only after he got out of prison in the 1990s, discovered the Tiananmen Mothers, and grew very close to Ding Zilin did his identification with the massacre solidify. He and Ding Zilin became China's two most powerful symbols of June Fourth. He came to be seen both among freethinkers, who admired his stance, and the regime, which loathed it, as a sort of "Mr. June Fourth." The government watched him for the rest of his life, whether he was in prison or not.

The PRC avoids public mention of the massacre whenever possible and when this cannot be done, prefers words like "incident." The effort at minimization is undertaken precisely because the felt threat is inordinately large, even existential. Communist Party leaders fear that to admit responsibility for June Fourth could lead to the dissolution of their power. Could a government that runs the world's second-largest economy and its second-largest standing army really fall if it admitted a "historical mistake"? Probably not. But the rulers do have such fears, evident in their indefatigable efforts, even decades later, to eradicate *absolutely any* memory of June Fourth.

The absolutism of their approach is helpful in understanding Liu Xiaobo's work as a dissident. In CCP ideology the Party, axiomatically, is 100 percent correct. Individuals might "make mistakes." Even Mao Zedong, in the judgment of Deng Xiaoping in 1981, was "70 percent correct, 30 percent mistaken." But the Party itself was infallible by definition. This habit of thought was borrowed in part from the Soviet Union. In explaining why the Soviets had no choice but to exile Alexandr Solzhenitsyn—a single human being who had no ambition to hold any office—Vaclav Havel cut to the heart of the matter. Silencing Solzhenitsyn was

> a desperate attempt to plug up the wellspring of truth, a truth that might cause incalculable transformations in social consciousness [and] one day produce political debacles unpredictable in their consequences. . . . As long as [the regime] seals off hermetically the entire society, it appears to be made of stone. But the moment . . . a single person breaks the rules of the game, thus exposing it as a game, everything suddenly appears in another light.[1]

Havel makes an important point about as tersely as it can be made. Why do people look to a dissident loner like Solzhenitsyn in order to understand a mainstream? Why listen to someone who stands at the very fringe of a society in order to perceive its core? The act of accepting a position at the fringe is precisely what liberates a person to speak truthfully of the core. Conversely, if a person who is flowing within the mainstream suddenly decides to describe it truthfully and publicly, he or she will for that reason be shipped by the system to the fringe. This condition holds for dissidents worldwide—Solzhenitsyn, Havel, Liu Xiaobo, and many others.

That said, the environment for dissidents in the PRC has been even more forbidding than it was in the Soviet Union or Eastern Europe. Communist authoritarianism arrived in China against the backdrop of a long imperial tradition in which it was already quite clear that one could lose one's head for contradicting an emperor. On the question of regime legitimacy, "one view only" was already an iron rule. Mao Zedong's blistering politics pressed the dictatorship deeper into society, to its very grassroots—and then, to an extent unmatched by any tyranny in history, even into private minds. "Make revolution in the depths of your soul," Mao taught. Families sundered by political faction. Jiang Zemin and Hu Jintao were weak versions of Mao, but the system that they inherited, as they ruled over a vast populace still not fully recovered from the deep wounds that Mao had inflicted, left Chinese dissidents exposed to headwinds much stiffer than even what the intrepid Solzhenitsyn and Havel had had to face.

Chinese dissidents have made a variety of choices in the face of those headwinds. Some have dropped out of politics, some have opted for exile, and some have gone to work inside the regime. Working "inside the system" itself spans a wide spectrum. Lü Xiang, a student demonstrator at Tiananmen in 1989, now writes virulently proregime pieces for the *Global Times*, but many others have entered the establishment with the goal of improving it or at least mitigating its harm. Xiaobo always insisted that people who pushed for good inside the system should be viewed as confreres with those pushing outside. His own choice was to stay outside the system but inside China. It was his country, not just the regime's. If his decision meant that he would live in prison, then so be it. He would still be in China and intellectually free.

Xiaobo's general approach to other people changed radically between the end of the 1980s and the end of the 1990s. Friends who knew him from earlier times said that the man who emerged from the Dalian labor camp in 1999 was almost a different person. He had turned gentle, modest, nonconfrontational. In the camp he had spent time reading history, philosophy, and religion, especially Christianity, and had resumed writing poems, most of them "to Xia" or "for Xia," his beloved wife. His transformation was the fruit of a fully conscious and difficult struggle to retool his character. He saw himself and his generation as having grown

up on the "wolf's milk" of Maoist education, according to which the world is populated with enemies whom heroes must find, fight, subdue, and annihilate. Sympathy and love are not in that picture.

It was one thing to perceive this problem, quite another to solve it. Xiaobo
wrote that for him and perhaps others, the change needed to proceed "from the
bone marrow out" and "may take a lifetime."[2] Even pride in his own progress could
be dangerous, he felt, because such confidence about doing good can blind one
from seeing what one is actually doing. Four years after the June Fourth massacre, Xiaobo startled fellow dissidents by reflecting that in some ways they had all
been "defeated by our own righteousness." Does opposition to a horrid government guarantee that a person can do no wrong? Xiaobo had observed this non
sequitur at work in others and was determined to purge it from himself if at all
possible.

His starting point in seeking a new way to relate to others was to listen. (Mao
heroes did not listen; they knew the whole truth in advance.) He listened to the
views of people both inside and outside the system. He listened to society's
underdogs—petitioners, laid-off workers, Falun Gong, Tibetans, prisoners of
conscience, farmers whose land had been confiscated, and many others. He
became known as the first recourse for anyone in a political lurch who needed
help. He listened to women—Ding Zilin, Liu Xia, and (through memory) Tao
Li. No male in his life shaped him more than those three women.

Listening to people and understanding their problems became the foundation
for his activism in the Rights Defense Movement from 2002 to 2008. This movement's approach marked a sharp turn from the prodemocracy activism of the
1980s, which had aimed at urging top leaders to institute reform from the top
down—and had failed. In 1978 Wei Jingsheng had responded to Deng Xiaoping's Four Modernizations by proposing a "fifth"—democracy—and been sent
to prison for fourteen years. Through the middle and late 1980s, intellectuals often
rooted for high-ranking leaders of "liberal" tendency (Hu Yaobang, Hu Qili, Tian
Jiyun, Zhao Ziyang, Wen Jiabao, and others) whom they hoped would listen to
reason from below and who occasionally did. Social and political change could
be pursued by lobbying the top, people felt. As late as spring 1989, students were
demanding "dialogue" with state leaders.

The June Fourth massacre shattered all that. Shock and fear froze any impulse
to continue addressing the regime, and the "liberal" leaders the people might have
tried to engage no longer were there. Hu Yaobang had died, Zhao Ziyang was
under house arrest, and others were terrified of getting anywhere near liberalism.
People like Liu Xiaobo and his friends, battered but unwilling to give up, could
only look downward into society, rather than upward toward an elite, in pursuit

of their ideals. In retrospect it can be seen as fortuitous that this happened. The bottom-up approach turned out to be far more productive than dialogue with the top had ever been.

Something of a formula for grassroots activism emerged and produced a welter of successful results. We cannot call it a Liu Xiaobo formula because it arose from practice, not from anyone's blueprint, and many people helped to shape it. But Xiaobo was as much associated with it as anyone, and in our view it stands as his most important contribution to this world. It has eight identifiable steps. They are not strictly temporal; in actual instances they often intermingled.

1. *Look for actual people with actual problems.* The point is to avoid abstractions about "the people" that top-down theoretical approaches took in the past. If people somewhere are having problems with land seizures, heavy taxes, police brutality, water pollution, or whatever else, go there. Listen. Don't preach about democracy; just listen. In this way you will be able to connect with people, and from the start they will trust you as someone who understands.

2. *Publicize the issue.* The Internet was spreading quickly in the early 2000s and, for the first time in Communist China, made it possible for citizens to spread news to one another on a medium more advanced than the oral grapevine. Now possessing a "platform," ordinary people could begin to see that they agreed with one another much more than, in their previously atomized condition, they had realized. Your air is polluted? Ours too! You're protesting? We support you! In putting news of abuses on the Internet, protesters could be quite certain that reader support of them would be *overwhelming*—not just from human empathy (although that was present) but also because people elsewhere had suffered similarly. Their indignation was vicarious.

3. *Put pressure on local officials.* In an essay called "Imprisoning People for Words and the Power of Public Opinion," Xiaobo outlines six cases in which city or county officials repressed the truth telling of local people only to see themselves exposed and denounced on the Internet for doing so.[3] Embarrassed, they were obliged to apologize and in some cases pay fines. Their apologies did not come from feelings of regret about how they had treated the people below them. In China's bureaucratic system, what matters is only the opinion of one's superior. What superiors care about is that the masses at the bottom be quiescent. They want to report this happy fact to *their* superiors. Accordingly a provincial-level official will punish a county-level official if the masses in his or her area become restless. An activist on the Internet can exploit this mechanism.

4. *Oblige state media to improve.* Before the Internet, state-run media had no competition except word of mouth. The official version of an event could stand even if it were a house of cards, because it stood in a windless room. But after the

arrival of the Internet, when state media put out a story, for example, that a young man in a detention center had died "of illness" while a more credible report on the Internet detailed how police had beaten him to death, readers had little trouble deciding which source to believe.[4] Recognizing this problem, state media had to adjust and steer at least partway back toward the truth to recoup credibility. To omit stories that were already out on the Internet or to distort their truth too wildly did more harm than good to Communist Party power. The result was a balancing act that eventually led to a complex web of instructions. Xiao Qiang at Berkeley has compiled a large archive of these orders as "Directives of the Ministry of Truth." They show how editors at all levels in China are told whether or not to mention news item N and, if so, with what headline H and what font size F on what page P, and so on. For websites, the instruction is sometimes "You may post story S, but do not allow comment boxes." Though deplorable, the truth directives were at least an advance over the outright censorship that had been in place before.

5. *Watch for shared principles to emerge.* Popular indignation might appear unruly, as a visceral outpouring with little shape. But Liu Xiaobo found that people act on principles of right and wrong. Garden-variety values of what is fair or unfair survive within the Chinese cultural turf no matter how trampled it has been by the history of the CCP years. Denunciation of murder, rape, corruption, kidnapping, bullying, and lying has always been stout, but more "sophisticated" values, like freedom of speech, also are implicit in popular outcry. The Chinese people Xiaobo follows in his "Imprisoning People for Words" essay did not need Thomas Jefferson or Human Rights Watch to tell them that they should have freedom of speech. They needed only their local experience plus communication on the Internet to arrive at that conclusion. The theme of the last book Xiaobo wrote, *The Dawn of a Free China Lies in Civil Awakening,* is that the values that are implicit in daily life in China are sufficient to outlast and eventually to deconstruct an oppressive political regime.

6. *Based on shared principles, advocate rule changes.* When public consensus is achieved that certain practices are unfair, it is a natural next step to ask if a rule or law can be established to prevent recurrence. The record of the Rights Defense Movement was uneven in this regard. In 2003 the nationwide surge of indignation over how Sun Zhigang died eventually produced a national law that abolished the "custody and repatriation" practice under which police had arrested and beaten him. When a young man in Anhui was rejected for a civil service job because he carried the hepatitis B virus, the outcry on the Internet did not result in a national law but did produce a number of rule changes in local areas. Activists in the Huang Jing date-rape case basically failed to establish new rules,

although Xiaobo and others felt they had carried out the effort in exactly the right way.[5]

7. *Be gradual and nonviolent.* Violence against a huge and heavily armed opponent is unwise for obvious reasons, but Xiaobo had less obvious reasons, and they were well thought out. As Vaclav Havel had noticed in Czechoslovakia, there are fissures in any society, no matter how totalitarian, and inside them a citizen can be civil. Treating each other with dignity, people together can push upward and outward to expand the scope of a citizens' culture that contrasts with the harsh official culture, and can reach to people "inside the system"—why not? If the authorities lash back, citizens should not fight but retreat, wait a while, then reoccupy the lost ground, perhaps going a bit further. This strategy can win in the long run because the garden-variety moral values of the populace are on its side, not the side of the regime. Eventually citizens can "change a regime by changing a society," as Xiaobo put it in 2006. It is no accident that Xiaobo's essay of this title was a primary piece of criminal evidence at his final trial. The authorities, leery of *regime change* in any form, saw his point and feared it.

8. *Be leaderless.* Movements naturally have leaders, who supply ideas, organization, or perhaps charisma to their groups. In these senses Xiaobo was one of the leaders of the Rights Defense Movement. But a repressive regime has its own reasons for wanting an opposition movement to have a leader: removing that person can paralyze a movement, and punishing that person is an effective way to intimidate followers. These are the main reasons Xiaobo favored leaderlessness, or at least minimization of the leader's role. He thought it was splendid in 2001 when thirty-eight journalists at *Southern Weekend* protested the firing of liberal editors by sending in thirty-eight separate letters—in concert but not lockstep. He would have cheered Hong Kong people who took to the streets in 2019 to protest an extradition law aimed at allowing Hong Kong authorities to send people to the mainland for sentencing in the courts of the Communist regime. The demonstrators moved from one spot in the city to another "like water," under a slogan of "occupy, disrupt, disperse, repeat." The principle involved was not only a clever tactic; it was a democratic announcement: "We are a group; you cannot cut off our head because we all have heads." This was quite in the tradition of the Rights Defense Movement.

If Liu Xiaobo had abandoned the approach of pushing for democracy from the top down in favor of building it from the bottom up, why did he launch a top-down blueprint like Charter 08? Readers of this book will know that he did not launch Charter 08. He of course agreed with its principles but felt that the time was not yet ripe to broach a manifesto. In his view, the bottom-up Rights Defense Movement was doing well, and the democratization effort should move forward in that pattern. His own plans during fall 2008 were about activities to mark the upcoming twentieth anniversary of the June Fourth massacre in spring 2009. To challenge the regime at the theoretical level of the charter might trigger a crackdown that could set the whole Rights Defense Movement back. In September 2008 he did eventually join the Charter 08 effort, largely at the urging of Ding Zilin, whose moral authority for him was paramount. On October 10, 2010, when Liu Xia told Xiaobo of his Nobel Peace Prize, he said, "This prize is for the lost souls of June Fourth," not "This is for Charter 08," even though the charter and the prison sentence it brought him were the proximate causes for his getting the prize.

He knew in advance that someone would pay a price for Charter 08. Everyone involved knew. The regime, for its own purposes, would want to find a leader to punish. In the days leading up to announcement of the charter, Xiaobo made the remarkable decision to accept the label of "leader" despite his initial misgivings about the entire project. He told one of the young organizers to "blame everything on me" if the police came asking. The youngster obeyed and was spared punishment. During Xiaobo's own lengthy pretrial interrogations, he consistently misled police into believing that he alone had engineered production of the charter at every stage: drafting, revising, copyediting, and collecting signatures. His lawyers reported that when they visited him in jail he was eager to know if anyone other than him had been arrested for Charter 08 offenses and when he learned that none had, broke into a smile.

Why accept punishment—almost seek it—when an exculpatory path was available? We have noted earlier Xiaobo's remorse over his behavior in Qincheng Prison in 1990 and his urge to atone for it. In a sense he felt that prison was the place to atone. Beyond that, another of the elements in his native character may have been in play. Part of his lifelong habit of critical self-examination was a bent to protect others by "taking responsibility" for his mistakes. His epilogue to *Contemporary Chinese Politics and Chinese Intellectuals* is an example; he needed to take responsibility and protect his readers from his error. An earlier example, from his college years, is the incident in which he was caught cribbing from the homework of a fellow student in Japanese class. As the teacher was preparing to punish both students, Xiaobo stood up and said, "You should punish only me, not him." Here too he was protecting another by taking responsibility.

Liu Xiaobo's advocacy of nonviolence has led some to compare his thinking with that of Martin Luther King Jr. and Mohandas Gandhi, both of whom he admired and wrote about. But, working under conditions far more repressive than those King and Gandhi endured, Xiaobo had nothing resembling their public followings. His readiness to go to prison for political principle led other supporters to call him, wishfully, "China's Mandela." His from-the-grassroots-upward approach to political change owes much, as noted, to Vaclav Havel and Adam Michnik. Tenzin Gyatso, the 14th Dalai Lama, was among the first to congratulate Xiaobo on his Nobel Peace Prize, writing that Xiaobo's principles "moved and encouraged me greatly." Nobel Peace Prize winners who resembled Xiaobo in sacrificing their freedom as the price for hewing to principle included Andrei Sakharov (winner in 1975), Lech Walesa (1983), and Aung Sang Suu Kyi (1991). But the one who resembled Xiaobo most closely was the German Carl von Ossietzky (1935), whose challenges to Adolph Hitler eventually led to Ossietzky's death from disease in prison custody. The two had one other interesting point in common: not only did the regimes that oppressed them deny them permission to travel to Oslo to collect their prizes; the authorities barred even their family members from going in their place.

In mentioning people like Mandela, Havel, and Walesa, the question of pivots from dissidence to national power arises. Those three freedom fighters became presidents of their nations after liberation was achieved. Suu Kyi also came close, in title if not in power. Liu Xiaobo lacked any organization like the African National Congress, Poland's Solidarity Union, or Myanmar's National League for Democracy, and in China any such organization would have been obliterated if it had even begun to arise. Comparisons therefore must be limited to counterfactual speculation. It is difficult at present to imagine the shape of a post-CCP China; it is even more difficult to estimate what Liu Xiaobo's place in history might be if he could have lived to see it.

What we can do, tentatively, is to assess Liu Xiaobo's actual legacy in the context of the China we see today. First, we must acknowledge that Xiaobo's fears about promoting Charter 08 in fall 2008 were well founded. The regime's crackdown—which led to scrubbing the Internet, intimidating activists, harassing lawyers, and more—expanded to a scope that far exceeded repression of the charter itself. It brought a halt to the hopeful ferment that had been burgeoning within the Rights Defense Movement since 2002. When Xi Jinping moved to the top post in the regime in 2012, conditions grew even worse. Major repressive events that were visible from the outside—such as the systematic purge of rights lawyers in 2015, the herding of Uyghurs into reeducation camps in 2017, and the squashing of freedom in Hong Kong in 2020—told the story well but only in part. Activism disappeared from mainstream life as well. The Internet, where twenty years earlier popular indignation could rise up and bring social changes, now was inhabited—and sometimes, it seemed, dominated—by wisecracking "little pink" (*xiao fenhong*) youngsters whose only values seemed to be materialism and a kind of paper-thin jingoism. Liu Xiaobo's departed spirit would grieve.

After Xiaobo's trial in 2009 he became known for the title of his final statement: "I Have No Enemies." Would he maintain that stance today? He said at trial that even his prosecutors, Zhang Rongge and Pan Xueqing, were not his enemies. They worked within an evil system, but they themselves were not evil. Would Xiaobo say such a thing today about, for example, Xi Jinping? Given Xi's bland personality and modest talents, Xiaobo might indeed. The train of CCP victims since 1949 is long and multifarious, and Xiaobo would likely see the little pinks, who have embarrassed their country on the Internet by loudly cheering for Vladimir Putin, as part of that train even though they do not see themselves that way. As offenders they are clowns, but as victims they are no joke. How did their grasp of their own country's history come to be so warped? Who stimulated their nationalist juices to impel them past the better parts of their country's culture and straight to adolescent bravado? Are they "enemies"?

Ultranationalist sentiment in China today is a much larger problem than the little pinks. In certain ways it recalls the Cultural Revolution ideology fifty years ago. Mao taught in that era that the East wind was rising over the West wind and that China represented a new political model to offer to the world. Chinese people everywhere could identify with his New China and feel pride. He, Chairman of Everything, was the "core." After Mao died, the regime gave the decade 1966–76 the name "ten years of catastrophe" and blamed a "Gang of Four" for it. Chinese officials and intellectuals were virtually unanimous then that nothing like the Cultural Revolution could ever happen again. They spoke as if China had been inoculated. Years later, though, in 2006, Liu Xiaobo expressed some doubts. There might be "another catastrophe for the Chinese people," he wrote, "if the Communists succeed in once again leading China down a disastrously mistaken historical road."[6] Xiaobo was not writing about Xi Jinping, who in 2006 was Communist Party secretary in Zhejiang province. He was reasoning on general principles about how the CCP stimulates and then exploits Chinese nationalism—repeatedly and at whatever cost.

Is anything left of the Rights Defense Movement? It was forced to stand down after 2008, but its spirit survived. The very next year in Panyu, outside Guangzhou, citizens protested plans to build a large garbage incinerator in their neighborhood, and Liu Xiaobo would have applauded their tactics. They held up signs reading "We have no leaders" and "We have discipline, but no organization." A decade later, the same technique appeared in Hong Kong. In 2020 in Hohhot, Inner Mongolia, authorities closed a weekly magazine after it had published complaints about the removal of the Mongolian language from elementary schools. Editors at the magazine wrote a statement of protest and signed it by arranging their names in a circle, so that none would appear at the top.

The brilliance of the Rights Defense Movement was to see that the daily-life values of ordinary people are a moral bedrock that survives beneath all the storms of official language and demands that regularly descend from above. Slogans like "The Dalai Lama is a splittist!" come from above; concerns like "Can my child get medical care?" grow from below. The two kinds of values interface in daily life, and a person needs to deal with both. But the natures of the values, at root, are different. The official values are aimed to support the power of the regime; the home-grown values are aimed to help oneself and one's family. Liu Xiaobo showed rare political acumen when he decided, in the early 2000s, to stop hoping for change at the official level and work with the garden-variety values of ordinary people.

The contrast between regime-sponsored values and popular values remains pervasive and is sometimes very sharp. The winter Olympics in 2022, at the official level, were a spectacular honor for the ruling regime. Beijing had hosted the summer Olympics in 2008 and fourteen years later had followed with the winter Games. What glory! The great rejuvenation of China was on! According to the International Olympic Committee, an estimated 600 million Chinese watched the games between February 4 and February 20, 2022.

Meanwhile, beginning January 28, a story on the Chinese Internet attracted computer clicks in an even greater number—an estimated 1.9 billion. A woman living in a hovel in a village in Xuzhou, Jiangsu province, had been trafficked many years earlier and held as a sex slave who produced, over the years, eight children for her owner. Now she had been discovered with (literally!) an iron chain around her neck. Local officials put out a story trying to explain the outrage, but people on the Internet didn't buy it. The officials put out a second story, again largely in vain. After four such attempts to save some face, people still believed the nonofficial accounts. Indignation flooded the Internet all across China and reached to Chinese around the world. Liu Xiaobo, were he alive, would ask us to reflect on *why* the story spread. It was not because hundreds of millions of people knew this woman personally or had friends and family in Xuzhou and were worried for their safety. As Xiaobo showed in a number of his essays, Chinese people respond this way, both in demonstrations and on the Internet, in part from human empathy—a universal value that all people are born with—but, even more importantly, from an urge to express their own indignation. People who heard about the woman had seen bullying and exploitation in their own lives. The cases were seldom so severe, but the iron-chain woman symbolized a general malaise, a sense of endemic unfairness that many people felt. *Why are we enduring a society where things like this can happen?* What can be done about a bully culture? The option to participate within a deluge of public outcry, protected by the anonymity of being only one in a large crowd, could offer catharsis.

The contrast between popular laments over the iron-chain woman and the regime's triumphalism at the Winter Olympics is worth pondering in depth. Two very different kinds of values stood side by side in public view. Both had long-standing presences in society and both were expressed with verve. But one was politically constructed and aimed to enhance the power of the regime; the other grew from below, among people sorting through things and seeking common values. Xiaobo would be heartened, but not surprised, to see that the societal foundation he relied upon in the Rights Defense Movement remains very sturdy.

A Final Note from Wu Dazhi

P eople around the world who watch China, as I do, always hoping for the best, as I do, often look to established dissidents and their accustomed methods for the latest signs of hope. There is nothing wrong with this, but the lessons of recent decades in China, which my friend Liu Xiaobo came to learn as well as anyone, is that the Chinese people themselves are an endless source of energy and creativity, as unpredictable as they are unstoppable in their quest to build a free and dignified society. Keep watching for new faces. They will be coming.

Notes

ABBREVIATIONS

LXBQRQS Zheng Wang 郑旺 and Ji Kuai 季蒯. *Liu Xiaobo qiren qishi* 刘晓波其人其事 [Liu Xiaobo: Who he is and what he has done]. Beijing: Zhongguo qingnian chubanshe, 1989.

LXLXS Liu Xiaobo and Liu Xia, eds. *Liu Xiaobo Liu Xia Shixuan* 刘晓波刘霞诗选 [A selection of poems by Liu Xiaobo and Liu Xia]. Hong Kong: Xiafeier guoji chubanshe, 2000.

MXD Liu Xiaobo *Mori xingcunzhe de dubai* 末日幸存者的独白 [Monologues of a doomsday survivor]. Taipei: Zhongguo shibao chubanshe, 1992.

NENH Perry Link, Tienchi Martin-Liao, and Liu Xia, eds. *No Enemies, No Hatred: Selected Essays and Poems of Liu Xiaobo.* Cambridge, MA: Harvard University Press, 2012.

RYRQ *Ren yu renquan* 人与人权 [Human beings and human rights]. http://www.renyurenquan.org.

XXQCNM Wu Renhua 吴仁华. 天安门血腥清场内幕 *1989.6.4* [The inside story of the bloody clearing of Tiananmen Square, June 4, 1989]. Hong Kong: Yunchen chubanshe, 2014.

ZDZYZZ Liu Xiaobo. *Zhongguo dangdai zhengzhi yu Zhongguo zhishifenzi* 中国当代政治与中国知识分子 [Contemporary Chinese politics and Chinese intellectuals]. Taipei: Taiwan tangshan chubanshe 台湾唐山出版社, 1990.

1. ARREST, TRIAL, AND THE ROAD TO A NOBEL PRIZE

1. “不断蜕变的中共独裁” [The ceaselessly changing Chinese communist dictatorship] (July 30, 2006), *Minzhu Zhongguo*, August 2006, https://minzhuzhongguo.org/UploadCenter/mz_magazine/155issue/2006-7-31-5s.htm.
2. “余英时等海外华人学者就国内各界发布的<零八宪章>的声明” [Proclamation by Yu Yingshi and other overseas Chinese scholars on the release of Charter 08 by people in several fields in China]

in 自由荆冠: 刘晓波与诺贝尔和平奖 [A crown of thorns of freedom: Liu Xiaobo and the Nobel Peace Prize], ed. Chen Kuide 陈奎德 and Xia Ming 夏明 (Hong Kong: Chenzhong shuju 晨钟书局, 2010), 165; http://chinainperspective.com/artshow.aspx?ArtShow.aspx?AID=8544165.

3. "我们与刘晓波不可分割" in 自由荆冠, 169.

4. "Statement From His Holiness the Dalai Lama," Office of His Holiness the Dalai Lama, December 11, 2008, https://www.dalailama.com/news/2008/statement-from-his-holiness-the-dalai-lama.

5. Accessed April 26, 2020, https://www.cecc.gov/media-center/press-releases/cecc-recommends -action-on-charter-08-and-the-detention-of-liu-xiaobo.

6. *The Wall Street Journal*, December 19, 2008, https://www.wsj.com/articles/SB12296494466 5820499.

7. Hu Jintao 胡锦涛, "在纪念改革开放30周年大会讲话" [Talk at the assembly for the thirtieth anniversary of reform and opening], 中国新闻网 [China news net], December 18, 2008, http://www .chinanews.com/gn/news/2008/12-18/1492872.shtml.

8. The name apparently is borrowed from the title of William Morris's novel *News from Nowhere*, which had been translated into Chinese as 乌有乡消息.

9. Li Xiaorong 李晓蓉 and Zhang Zuhua 张祖桦, 零八宪章 [Charter 08] (Hong Kong: Kaifang chu-banshe, 2009), 233–304.

10. Interview of Liu Xia by Hao Jian 郝建, February 2009, accessed September 9, 2019, https:// www.youtube.com/watch?v=lFKxjClgMxE.

11. Radio France Internationale, "刘晓波被捕后首度会见律师" [Liu Xiaobo's first meeting with his lawyers after his arrest], accessed August 30, 2020, http://www1.rfi.fr/actucn/articles/114/article_14525.asp.

12. "我们愿与刘晓波共同承担责任" [We want to share responsibility with Liu Xiaobo] Charter 08 website, December 10, 2009, http://www.2008xianzhang.info/Messages/20091210.html.

13. Liu Xiaobo, "我的自辩" [My self-defense], Radio Free Asia, January 20, 2010, https://www.rfa.org /mandarin/yataibaodao/lxb-01202010122210.html; translated by Perry Link in *NENH*, 313–320.

14. Shang Baojun 尚宝军 and Ding Xikui 丁锡奎, "刘晓波案一审辩护词" [Statement of the defense in the initial trial of the case of Liu Xiaobo], *Boxun* news, December 2009, https://blog.boxun.com /hero/200912/xianzhang/294_1.shtml.

15. Mao Zedong 毛泽东, "湖南建设的根本问题: 湖南共和国" [The fundamental question in Hunan development: A republic of Hunan], September 3, 1920, and Mao Zedong, "反对统一" [Opposing unification], October 10, 1920, in 中共中央文献研究室 and 中共湖南省委毛泽东早期文稿 编辑组, ed., 毛泽东早期文稿 [Early manuscripts of Mao Zedong] (Hunan renmin chubanshe, 1990), 503– 506 and 530–534.

16. "中国共产党第二次代表大会宣言" [Declaration of the second representative assembly of the Communist Party of China], 1922, in 中央档案馆 [Central archives], ed., 中共中央文件选集 (1921–1925) [Selections of documents of Chinese Communist Party Central (1921–1925)] (Beijing: Zhonggong zhongyang dangxiao chubanshe, 1989), 115–116.

17. Liu Xiaobo, "我没有敌人: 我的最后陈述" [I have no enemies: My final statement], December 23, 2009. Translated by Perry Link in *NENH*, 321–322.

18. Ai Qing 艾青, "我爱这土地" [I love this land], November 17, 1938, https://www.qingshiwang.com /xinshishangxi/499.html.

19. Radio Free Asia Cantonese Service, "刘晓波被重判入狱十一年" [Liu Xiaobo receives a heavy sentence of eleven years in prison], accessed May 2, 2020, https://www.rfa.org/cantonese/news/china _verdict-12252009090257.html.

20. Supplied by Liu Xiaobo's lawyers to Shang baojun on January 28, 2010.

21. Radio Free Asia Cantonese Service, "刘晓波被重" [Liu Xiaobo receives a heavy sentence].

22. Cui Weiping 崔卫平, "138人关于刘晓波案的看法" [The views of 138 people on the Liu Xiaobo case], 北京之春 [Beijing spring], February 2010, http://beijingspring.com/bj2/2010/120/2010131151928.htm.

23. Ershi Zhonggong yuanlao 二十中共元老, "请中央纠正对刘晓波的违法错判" [Asking Party Central to correct its illegal and wrong conviction of Liu Xiaobo] *Mingbao*, February 1, 2010.

24. Project Syndicate, January 18, 2010, https://www.project-syndicate.org/commentary/a-chinese-champion-of-peace-and-freedom.

25. Kwame Anthony Appiah, "Nomination of Liu Xiaobo for the Nobel Peace Prize," January 29, 2010, Pen America, https://pen.org/kwame-anthony-appiahs-nomination-of-liu-xiaobo-for-the-nobel-peace-prize/.

26. "Herta Müller Recommends Liu Xiaobo for Nobel Peace Prize," Signandsight, August 2, 2010, http://www.signandsight.com/features/1988.html.

27. Liu Xia, Twitter, March 19, 2010.

28. Vaclav Havel, Dana Nemcova, and Vaclav Maly, "A Nobel Prize for a Chinese Dissident," *The New York Times,* September 20, 2010, https://www.nytimes.com/2010/09/21/opinion/21iht-edhavel.html.

29. Tania Branigan, "Nobel committee warned not to award peace prize to Chinese dissident," *The Guardian*, September 28, 2010, https://www.theguardian.com/world/2010/sep/28/nobel-peace-prize-liu-xiaobo.

30. "诺委会执行秘书: 中国判重刑坚定我们颁奖给刘晓波的决心" [Executive secretary of the Norwegian Nobel Committee: China's heavy sentence determined our resolve to award the prize to Liu Xiaobo], *Shijie ribao,* October 29, 2010, https://www.backchina.com/news/2010/10/29/111811.html.

2. REBEL IN EMBRYO

1. Czeslaw Milosz, *The Captive Mind* (New York: Knopf, 1953), 135.

2. Much of our description of Changchun here and below is from Feng Yan 冯艳, "人民大街每一个'曾用名'都是不可磨灭的历史" [The earlier names of People's Avenue are an indelible part of history], 新文化画报 [News pictorial] (Changchun), January 1, 2016, A04.

3. Liu Xiaobo, "樱花的中国劫难" [The cherry blossoms' China calamity], 民主中国 [Democratic China], April 11, 2006, https://minzhuzhongguo.org/UploadCenter/mz_magazine/152issue/2006_4_8_7s.htm.

4. 中国大学信息查询系统: 东北师范大学 [System for finding information on universities in China: Northeast Normal University], accessed July 4, 2020, http://www.gx211.com/collegemanage/content195_03.shtml.

5. Text message from Zhang Li, a nursery school classmate of Xiaobo's, September 15, 2018, courtesy of Yang Zhuo.

6. Zou Jin, text message to Wu Dazhi, September 2017.

7. "军事语言的拓新者—记大连陆军学院副教授刘伶" [A pioneer in military language: Associate professor Liu Ling at the Dalian Army College], 解放军报, February 17, 1987, 2.

8. "A Pioneer in Military Language," 2.

9. Adam Michnik, *Letters from Freedom: Post–Cold War Realities and Perspectives* (Berkeley and Los Angeles: University of California Press, 1998), 30.

10. Liu Xiaobo, "长达半个世纪的诗意—序《蔡楚诗选》" [Half a century of poetry: A preface to Cai Chu, *Collected Poems*], http://minzhuzhongguo.org/MainArtShow.aspx?AID=6421.

11. Liu Xiaobo, "按权力分配—毛时代的不平等（下）" [Distribution by power: Inequality in the Mao era (II)], accessed July 12, 2019, http://www.epochtimes.com/gb/4/1/14/n448307.htm.

12. Liu Lu 刘路, "刺穿黑暗的朝霞" [Bright morning clouds penetrating the darkness], accessed July 12, 2019, https://news.boxun.com/news/gb/intl/2008/12/200812281019.shtml.

13. Zhao Dagong 赵达功, "回忆与刘晓波二三事" [Remembering a few things about Liu Xiaobo], accessed July 12, 2019, http://minzhuzhongguo.org/MainArtShow.aspx?AID=97033.

14. Liu Xiaobo, "我从十一岁开始吸烟 —为"文革"三十年而作" [I began smoking at age eleven: Written for the thirtieth year of the "Cultural Revolution"], *Zhengming* 争鸣 [Contending], May 1996.

15. Jin Zhong 金钟, "文坛'黑马'刘晓波—刘晓波答记者问" [The "dark horse" of the literary scene: An interview with Liu Xiaobo], 解放月报 [Emancipation monthly] 12.

16. This and the next six paragraphs are from Liu Xiaobo, "我从十一岁开始吸烟—为'文革'三十年而作" [I began smoking at age eleven: Written for the thirtieth year of the "Cultural Revolution"], https://www.chinesepen.org/blog/archives/91622.

17. Liu Xiaobo, "作秀与戏子中国—从大陆传媒作秀谈起" [Shows and actors: starting from the shows in the mainland media], in 向良知说谎的民族 [A nation that lies to its conscience] (Taipei: Taiwan jieyou chubanshe, 2010), 30.

18. Jiang Dongping 姜东平, "长春武斗罹难者及墓地述略" [An account of the fatalities and graves from the armed struggle in Changchun], in 老照片 [Old photos]. 73 (2010).

19. Zhang Li 张荔, "我们是走下祭坛的一代" [We are the generation who came down off the sacrificial altar], accessed August 25, 2017, http://blog.sina.com.cn/s/blog_8e8adfa301017edr.html (later classified "secret" and removed).

20. *Quotations from Chairman Mao Tse-tung* (Peking: Foreign Languages Press, 1966), 21–22.

21. Liu Xiaobo, "从娃娃抓起的残忍—为文革三十五周年而作" [My cruelty began in infancy: Written for the thirty-fifth year of the Cultural Revolution], 民主中国 *Minzhu Zhongguo* 92 (April 2001), http://www.liu-xiaobo.org/blog/archives/5616.

22. Liu Xiaobo, "I Began Smoking at Age Eleven."

23. Liu Xiaobo, "I Began Smoking at Age Eleven."

24. Gan Qi, text message to Wu Dazhi, June 27, 2017.

3. PUPPY LOVE AND SERIOUS READING

1. "1969" at the web page of Northeast Normal University, accessed July 17, 2019, http://www.nenu.edu.cn/65/f1/c716a26097/page.htm.

2. 科右前旗人民政府 [Government of the Horqin Right Front Banner], "人口民族" [Population and nationality], accessed September 4, 2019, http://www.kyqq.gov.cn/kyqq/mlkyqq/rkmz40/index.html.

3. In PRC nomenclature, Inner Mongolia is not a province but an ethnic "autonomous area," like Xinjiang, Tibet, Ningxia, and Guangxi. In practice, the difference between provinces and autonomous areas is merely formal.

4. Song Yongyi 宋永毅, in 文革中"非正常死亡"了多少人? —读苏扬的《文革中中国农村的集体屠杀》 [How many "unnatural deaths" were there during the Cultural Revolution?: Reading Su Yang's *Collective Killings in China During the Cultural Revolution*] cites official statistics from Hao Weimin, 郝维民, 内蒙古自治区史 [A history of Inner Mongolia] （Nei Menggu chubanshe, 1991): in ten years of the Cultural Revolution, "more than 27,900 people were persecuted to death and more than 120,000 were injured by persecution." *Dongxiang* 动向, September 2011.

5. In an ancient myth, two lovers, a herd boy and a weaving girl, are banished to opposite sides of the Milky Way. Only on the seventh day of the seventh month of the lunar calendar are they allowed to meet, as magpies form a bridge over which they can cross.

6. Liu Xiaobo, *MXD*, 38.

7. Lao Sha 老沙, "文革记忆（三）" [Memories of the Cultural Revolution, III], accessed September 15, 2017, http://blog.sina.com.cn/s/blog_4aeb13ce0101tl7d.html.

8. Liu Xiaofeng 刘晓峰 and Bing Daowen 冰岛文, "狂人刘晓波" [The crazy Liu Xiaobo], in 大学生 [University students] 1989; republished in *LXBQRQS*.

9. Xiaobo's college classmates Zhang Xiaoyang, Zou Jin, Huo Yongling, and Gao Wenlong, group interview by Wu Dazhi, August 30, 2018. Gao related this story.

10. Liu Xiaobo, "在地狱的入口处—对马克思主义的再检讨" [At the entrance to hell: A re-examination of Marxism], 解放月报 [Emancipation monthly] 4 (1989): 86.

11. Liu Xiaofeng and Bing Daowen, "The Crazy Liu Xiaobo."

12. Liu Xiaobo, "启蒙之光照亮自由之路—狱中读康德《什么是启蒙？》" [The brightness of enlightenment illuminates the road to freedom: Reading Kant's "What Is Freedom?" in prison], 1998, https://www.chinesepen.org/blog/archives/92276.

13. Liu Xiaobo, "At the Entrance to Hell."

14. Jin Zhong, "文坛'黑马'刘晓波—刘晓波答记者问" [The "dark horse" of the literary scene: An interview with Liu Xiaobo], 解放月报 [Emancipation monthly] 12 (1988).

15. The descriptions here and in the following paragraph are from Tieshu 铁树 [Iron tree] (pseud.), "石寨公社的记忆" (一) (三) [Memories of Boulder Commune, (I) and (III)], accessed July 21, 2019, http://blog.sina.com.cn/s/blog_a2e4a6720101fqot.html and http://blog.sina.com.cn/s/blog_a2e4a6720101gtoe.html.

16. That Xiaobo did not return from Horqin Banner until fall 1973 is confirmed in an interview he gave to Zhang Min 张敏 of Radio Free Asia, January 3, 2001.

17. Liu Xiaoxuan, telephone interview by Wu Dazhi, August 18, 2018.

18. Liu Xiaobo, "用真话颠覆谎言制度：接受 '杰出民主人士奖'的答谢词" [Using truth to undermine a system built on lies: Statement of thanks in accepting the Outstanding Democracy Activist Award], 争鸣 [Contending] 6 (2003), https://blog.boxun.com/hero/liuxb/76_1.shtml; translated by Eva S. Chou in *NENH*, 292.

19. In 赤子心 [Pure hearts] 6 (1980).

4. COLLEGE YEARS, AND THE MASK OF MAO FALLS

1. Ling Zhijun 凌志军 and Ma Licheng 马立诚, "把印红宝书的纸拿去印考卷" [Taking paper for printing the precious red book and using it to print exam papers], in 呼喊：当今中国的五种声音 [Shouting: five kinds of voices from today's China] (Beijing: Renmin ribao chubanshe, 2011), 17.

2. Lao Yuan 老范, "202 室趣事(一) 唠了一宿嗑" [Anecdotes from room 202 (one): chatting a whole night away], accessed July 22, 2019, http://read.guanhuaju.com/sanwen/62/622189.html.

3. Wang Dongcheng, WeChat communication with Wu Dazhi and other friends, July 21, 2017.

4. Bao Tong 鲍彤, "刘晓波和他的政治主张" [Liu Xiaobo and what he stood for politically], accessed July 23, 2019, https://www.rfa.org/mandarin/pinglun/baotong/bt-07132017095549.html.

5. Liu Xiaobo 刘晓波 and Wang Shuo 王朔, 美人赠我蒙汗药 [A beauty gave me a knockout drug] (Wuhan: Changjiang wenyi chubanshe, 2000), 192.

6. Lu Xinhua 卢新华, "Shanghen" 伤痕 [Scar], *Wenhui Daily* (Shanghai), August 11, 1978.

7. Liu Xiaobo, "往俗里走和无灵魂 —文革后的大众文化与党文化" [Toward the vulgar, without a soul: Popular culture and Party culture since the Cultural Revolution], 中国之春 [China spring] 120 (May 1993).

8. Liu Xiaobo, "Toward the Vulgar, Without a Soul."

9. Liu Xiaobo, "Toward the Vulgar, Without a Soul."

10. Wen Yujie 温玉杰, "诗人的趣闻轶事" [Interesting stories and anecdotes about poets], accessed April 22, 2018, http://jida1977.blog.163.com/blog/static/17616823620110103484135s/.

11. Zhang Xiaoyang, e-mail to Wu Dazhi, September 19, 2017.

12. Zhang Xiaoyang, e-mail to Wu Dazhi, September 19, 2017.

13. Xu Jingya 徐敬亚, "魏大记者经典傻样" [Classic stupid appearances of great journalist Wei], accessed July 23, 2019, jida1977.blog.163.com/blog/static/176168236201182210382932s/.

14. Wei Haitian, interview by Wu Dazhi, Beijing, October 2018.

15. Cui Weiping 崔卫平, "138人关于刘晓波案的看法" [The views of 138 people on the Liu Xiaobo case], 北京之春 [Beijing spring], February 2010, http://beijingspring.com/bj2/2010/120/2010131151928.htm.

16. Liu Xiaobo, "危机，新时期文学面临危机" [Crisis, literature in the new era faces a crisis], 深圳青年报 [Shenzhen youth news], October 3, 1986.

17. Zhang Xiaoyang, e-mail to Wu Dazhi, September 23, 2017.

18. Zhonggong Liaoning shengwei "gongchandangyuan" zazhi she 中共辽宁省委《共产党员》杂志社, "敢为真理而奋斗" [Daring to struggle for truth], *People's Daily,* May 25, 1979.

19. Xiaobo's college classmates Zhang Xiaoyang, Zou Jin, Huo Yongling, and Gao Wenlong, group interview by Wu Dazhi, August 30, 2018. This story was from Zhang Xiaoyang.

20. Mu Qing 穆青, Guo Chaoren 郭超人 and Lu Fuwei 陆拂为, "历史的审判" [The judgment of history], 人民日报 [People's daily], January 27, 1981.

21. A full story is told in Lian Xi, *Blood Letters: The Untold Story of Lin Zhao* (New York: Basic Books, 2018).

22. Liu Xiaobo, "林昭用生命写就的遗言是当代中国仅存的自由之声," accessed July 24, 2019, https://blog.boxun.com/hero/liuxb/146_1.shtml.

23. Wang Chen 王晨 and Zhang Tianlai 张天来, "划破夜幕的陨星: 记思想解放的先驱遇罗克," *Guangming ribao,* July 21 and 22, 1981.

24. Liu Xiaobo, "遇罗克的亡灵仍在泣血: 写在文革35周年之际" [The departed soul of Yu Luoke is still weeping blood: Written on the thirty-fifth anniversary of the Cultural Revolution], accessed July 24, 2019, http://www.epochtimes.com/b5/1/5/15/n88610.htm; also Liu Xiaobo, "以由衷的谦卑向遇罗克致意: 纪念文革四十週年" [Saluting Yu Luoke in sincere humility: Marking the fortieth year after the Cultural Revolution], in 民主中国 *Minzhu Zhongguo,* May 16, 2001, http://minzhuzhongguo.org/filedata/153issue/2006-5-15-3s.htm.

25. Liu Xiaobo, "Saluting Yu Luoke in Sincere Humility."

26. Liu Xiaobo, interview by Hao Jian, October 2008.

27. Liu Xiaobo, "Saluting Yu Luoke in Sincere Humility."

28. Liu Xiaobo, "Saluting Yu Luoke in Sincere Humility."

29. Gao Ertai 高尔泰, "异化问题近观" [An up-close look at the problem of alienation], in 人是马克思主义的出发点 [People are the starting point of Marxism] (Beijing: Renmin chubanshe, 1981), 77.

30. Xu Jingya 徐敬亚, "1986: 那一场诗的疾风暴雨" [1986: That torrent of poetry], accessed July 25, 2020, http://www.eeo.com.cn/zt/ggkf30/zgssn/2007/07/09/75330.shtml.

31. Zou Jin, interview by Wu Dazhi, Beijing, August 30, 2018.

32. These are stanzas 4 and 5 of the seven-stanza poem as translated by Bonnie McDougall in Bei Dao, *The August Sleepwalker* (New York: New Directions, 1990), 33.

33. Gao Wenlong, one of Xiaobo's roommates at Jilin University, interview by Wu Dazhi, Beijing, August 30, 2018.

34. Wang Dongcheng, microblog communication to friends, July 21, 2020.

35. 北京师范大学刘晓波档案 [The file of Liu Xiaobo at Beijing Normal University]. "Repair a floor" here means literally to repair a floor. We do not know the story behind it.

5. AESTHETICS AND HUMAN FREEDOM

1. This and other details in this chapter about Xiaobo's relationship with Yang Jidong 杨济东 are from a telephone conversation between Wu Dazhi and Yang on August 25, 2018.

2. Weixin message from Wei Haitian to Wu Dazhi, October 5, 2018.

3. Zhong Zi'ao 钟子翱，刘勰论写作之道 [Liu Xie on the ways of writing] (Beijing: Changzheng chubanshe, 1984).

4. Liu Xiaobo, "司空图所说'诗味'的特殊内涵" [The special meaning of "poetic flavor" in the aesthetics of Sikong Tu], in "试论司空图'诗味说'的美学意义" [An inquiry into the aesthetic significance of Sikong Tu's "theory of aesthetic flavor"] (M.A. thesis), part I, 18. (Available in the library of Beijing Normal University.)

5. Liu Xiaobo, "The Special Meaning of 'Poetic Flavor' in the Aesthetics of Sikong Tu," 53.

6. Geremie Barmé 白杰明，"中国人的解放在自我觉醒—与个性派批评家刘晓波一席谈" [The liberation of Chinese people lies in self-awakening—a conversation with the individualist critic Liu Xiaobo], 解放月报 [Liberation monthly] 3 (1987): 64.

7. Liu Xiaobo, "我国古典美学的表述方法," [Classic modes of aesthetic expression in China], 百科知识 [Knowledge of every kind] 12 (1983): 20–22.

8. Liu Xiaobo, "Classic Modes of Aesthetic Expression in China," 4–8.

9. "艺术直觉初探" [A preliminary investigation of artistic intuition], 国际关系学院学报 [Journal of the institute of international relations] 2 (1984): 91–101.

10. "论庄子的自然全美观" [On universal natural aesthetics in Zhuangzi], 艺论稿 [Essays on art] 13 (1984): 96–111.

11. Personnel file of Liu Xiaobo, Beijing Normal University.

12. 马克思恩格斯全集 [The complete works of Marx and Engels] (Beijing: Renmin chubanshe, 1983), 53 vols.

13. Personnel file of Liu Xiaobo, Beijing Normal University.

14. In 名作欣赏 [Appreciating famous works] 3 (1985): 142–147.

15. Han Fudong 韩福东，"严打'双刃剑,'" [Strike hard against the "double-edged sword"], 南方都市报 [Southern metropolitan news], December 11, 2013, AA34.

16. Deng Xiaoping 邓小平，"党和国家领导制度的改革" [Reform of the leadership system of the party and the state], 人民日报 [People's daily], August 18, 1980.

17. It was called a "May fourth" movement because of its association with a student protest in Tiananmen Square on May 4, 1919, against the decision by Western powers after World War I to give control to China's Shandong peninsula, formerly controlled by Germany, to Japan instead of returning it to China.

18. Chen Xiaoya 陈小雅，八九民运史 [A history of the 1989 democracy movement] (Taipei: Fengyun shidai chuban gongsi, 1996), chapter 18, section 5.

19. Zhong Acheng 钟阿城，"棋王" [The chessmaster], 上海文学 [Shanghai literature] (July 1984): 15–35. Han Shaogong 韩少功, "爸爸爸" [Ba, ba, ba], 人民文学 [People's literature] 6 (1985).

20. Anecdotes shared in 2018 by a Beijing Normal classmate of Xiaobo's who asked not to be named.

21. Karl Marx and Friedrich Engels, "The German Ideology," in 马克思恩格斯选集 [Selections from Marx and Engels] (Beijing: Renmin chubanshe, 1966), 36.

22. Liu Xiaobo, "审美与人的自由" [Aesthetics and human freedom], 名作欣赏 [Appreciating famous works] 1 (1986): 63.

23. Liu Xiaobo, "Aesthetics and Human Freedom," 61.

24. Liu Xiaobo, "Aesthetics and Human Freedom," 58.

25. Liu Xiaobo, "赤身裸体，走向上帝" [Naked and exposed, moving toward God], 名作欣赏 [Appreciating famous works] 4 (1986): 20–25.

26. Liu Xiaobo, "表现与再现—中西审美意识的比较研究" [Appearance and reappearance: A comparative study of aesthetic consciousness East and West], in 东西方文化研究 [Cultural research East and West] (Zhengzhou: Henan renmin chubanshe, 1986), 96–111.

27. Liu Xiaobo, "冲突与和谐—中西审美意识的根本差异" [Conflict vs. harmony: The basic differences between Chinese and Western aesthetic consciousness], 北京师范大学学报 [The journal of Beijing Normal University] 4 (1986): 11–19.

28. Liu Xiaobo, "危机, 新时期文学面临危机" [Crisis, literature in the new era faces a crisis], 深圳青年报 [Shenzhen youth news], October 3, 1986, 3.

29. Liu Xiaobo, 无法回避的反思—由几篇知识分子题材的小说所想到的 [An unavoidable reappraisal: Thoughts on rereading some recent fiction about intellectuals], 中国 [China] 4 (1986): 103–111. Xiaobo's initial inclination for the title is evident in his brief self-description accompanying his article, 一种新的审美思潮—从徐星、陈村、刘索拉的三部作品谈起 [A new trend in aesthetics: On three pieces by Xu Xing, Chen Cun, and Liu Suola], 文学评论 [Literary criticism] 3 (1986): 35–43.

30. Xu Chi 徐迟, "哥德巴赫猜想" [The Goldbach conjecture], 人民文学 [People's literature] (January 1978).

31. Chen Rong 谌容, "人到中年" [At middle age], 收获 [Harvest] 1 (1980): 52–92.

32. The story that Liu Xiaobo has in mind here is 灵与肉 [Spirit and flesh], 朔方 [The north] (September 1980): 3–16, 48. Several of Zhang Xianliang's other works illustrate the same basic point but do not show precisely the same details.

33. Luo Gang 罗钢, "长歌当哭—怀念富仁" [A long song to be wept: Remembering Furen], 名作欣赏 [Appreciating famous works] 34 (2017): 39.

34. Wang Furen 王富仁, "中国反封建思想革命的一面镜子: 论 '呐喊,' '彷徨' 的思想意义" [A mirror for China's revolution against feudalism: On the intellectual significance of Outcry and Hesitation], 中国现代文学研究丛刊 [Studies on modern Chinese literature] (Beijing) 1 (1983): 1–29.

35. Wang Furen 王富仁, "A Mirror for China's Revolution Against Feudalism," 29. Wang eventually expanded this article to be his Ph.D. dissertation and in August 1986 published it as a book with Beijing Normal University Press.

36. Liu Xiaobo, "An Unavoidable Reappraisal."

37. Liu Xiaobo, "An Unavoidable Reappraisal," 106–107.

38. Liu Xiaobo, "A New Trend in Aesthetics."

39. For more on Ding Ling, see Yi-tsi Mei Feuerwerker, *Ding Ling's Fiction: Ideology and Narrative in Modern Chinese Literature* (Cambridge, MA: Harvard University Press, 1982).

40. Cui Weiping 崔卫平, "138人关于刘晓波案的看法" [The views of 138 people on the Liu Xiaobo case], 北京之春 [Beijing spring], February 2010, http://beijingspring.com/bj2/2010/120/2010131151928.htm.

41. Zou Jin, Weixin message to Wu Dazhi, September 15, 2017.

42. Imamichi Tomonobu 今道友信 et al., 美学的方法 [Methods of aesthetics], trans. Li Xinfeng 李心峰 and others (Beijing: Wenhua yishu chubanshe, 1990).

43. Sun Jin, a graduate school classmate of Liu Xiaobo's, e-mail to Wu Dazhi, August 8, 2017.

44. Xu Xing 徐星, "我所认识的刘晓波" [Liu Xiaobo as I have known him], accessed August 2, 2019, http://www.64memo.com/b5/1373.htm.

45. Guo Lijia 郭力家, Weixin to Wu Dazhi, November 5, 2017.

46. Personnel file of Liu Xiaobo, Beijing Normal University.

6. MUTINY! A DARK HORSE SOARS

1. Liu Zaifu 刘再复, "论新时期文学主潮: 在 '中国新时期文学十年学术讨论会' 上的发言内容提要 [On the main currents of literature in the new era: Summary of the content of my speech at the Scholarly Conference on Chinese Literature in Ten Years of the New Era], 文学评论 [Literary criticism] 10 (1986): 15.

2. Liu Zaifu, 性格组合论 [On composite character] (Shanghai: Wenyi chubanshe, 1986).

3. Linda Jaivin, *The Monkey and the Dragon* (Melbourne, Australia: Text Publishing, 2001), 226.

4. Li Jie 李劼, "回忆刘晓波" [Remembering Liu Xiaobo], accessed August 2, 2019, https://news.boxun .com/news/gb/pubvp/2010/01/201001301435.shtml.

5. Liu Xiaobo, "危机, 新时期文学面临危机" [Crisis, literature in the new era faces a crisis], 深圳青年报 [Shenzhen youth news], October 3, 1986, 3.

6. Liu Xiaobo, "Crisis," 3.

7. Deng Youmei 邓友梅, "烟壶" [Snuff bottles], 收获 [Harvest] 1 (1984).

8. Liu Xinwu 刘心武, "钟鼓楼" [Drum tower], 当代 [Contemporary times] 1 (1985).

9. Jia Pingwa 贾平凹 published an essay, "商州初录" [First records of Shangzhou], in the May 1983 issue of 钟山 *Zhongshan* magazine in Nanjing and followed that with a series of further essays and fiction on Shangzhou, including "商州又录" [Further records of Shangzhou, 1984], "商州再录" [Shangzhou records once more, 1984], and a novel, 商州 [Shangzhou] (1984).

10. Xiaobo does not say which work(s) by Liu Shaotang he has in mind, but "烟村四五家" [Four or five families of Smokey Village] (Shanghai wenyi chubanshe, 1985) is likely one.

11. Han Shaogong 韩少功, "爸爸爸" [Ba, ba, ba], 人民文学 [People's literature] 6 (1985).

12. Wang Anyi 王安忆, 小鲍庄 [Little Bao farmstead], 中国作家 [Chinese writers] 2 (1985); translated by Martha Avery as *Baotown* (New York: Norton, 1989).

13. Zhang Xinxin 张辛欣 and Sang Ye 桑烨, 北京人: 一百个中国人的自述 [Beijing people: One hundred Chinese in their own words] (Shanghai wenyi chubanshe, 1986).

14. Liu Xiaobo, "Crisis."

15. Liu Xiaobo, "Crisis."

16. Li Qingxi 李庆西, "开会记" [Notes on the meeting], 书城 [Book city] 10 (2009).

17. Xu Jingya, e-mail to Wu Dazhi, July 29, 2017.

18. These included: 批判哲学的批判 [A critique of critical philosophy] (1979); 中国近代思想史论 [A history of modern Chinese thought] (1979); 美的历程 [The path of beauty] (1981); 中国美学史 [A history of Chinese aesthetics] (1984); and 中国古代思想史论 [A history of ancient Chinese thought] (1984).

19. Liu Xiaobo, "与李泽厚对话: 感性·个人·我的选择" [A dialogue with Li Zehou: Sensibility, the individual, and my choice], 中国 [China] 10 (1986).

20. Li Zehou 李泽厚, "启蒙与救亡的双重变奏," 走向未来 [Going toward the future] 1 (August 1986); reprinted in 中国现代思想史论 [A history of modern Chinese thought] (Beijing: Dongfang chubanshe, 1987), 7–49.

21. Li Zehou 李泽厚, 美的历程 [The path of beauty] (Beijing: Wenwu chubanshe, 1981), 25.

22. Gao Ertai 高尔泰, "美的追求与人的解放" [Pursuing beauty and liberating humanity], 当代文艺思潮 [Trends in contemporary thought] 5 (1983): 70–72.

23. Liu Xiaobo, "A Dialogue with Li Zehou."

24. Liu Xiaobo, "A Dialogue with Li Zehou," 55.

25. Liu Xiaobo, "A Dialogue with Li Zehou," 55.

26. Liu Xiaobo, "A Dialogue with Li Zehou," 53.

27. Liu Xiaobo, "A Dialogue with Li Zehou," 53.

28. Liu Xiaobo, "A Dialogue with Li Zehou," 74.

29. Liu Xiaobo, "A Dialogue with Li Zehou," 62.

30. Liu Xiaobo, "A Dialogue with Li Zehou," 67.

31. Liu Xiaobo, "A Dialogue with Li Zehou," 74.

32. Liu Xiaobo, "把大陆民族主义梳理回八十年代" [Put mainland nationalism back into the 1980s], 民主中国 [Democratic China] 4 (2002). In 2002 Li Zehou agreed. "Culture fever in fact was borrowing culture to argue about politics," he wrote. See Li Zehou 李泽厚 and Chen Ming 陈明, "浮生论学: 李泽厚陈明2001年对谈录" [Study of a floating life: Record of a chat between Li Zehou and Chen Ming in 2001] (Beijing: Huaxia chubanshe, 2002), 123.

33. The text of *Heshang* 河殇 is by Su Xiaokang 苏晓康 and Wang Luxiang 王鲁湘 (Beijing: Xiandai chubanshe, 1988).

34. Wu Liang 吴亮, "刘晓波旋风" [Liu Xiaobo tornado], in "文坛掠影" [Flickers on the literary scene], a column in 文汇读书周报 [Wenhui reading weekly], November 29, 1986.

35. Tang Xiaodu 唐晓渡, "面对生存：困境和出路 —1986年冬与杨炼对话" [Facing survival: Predicaments and escape routes: a dialogue with Yang Lian in winter 1986], 知识分子 [Intellectuals] (Spring 1987), accessed September 28, 2017, http://blog.sina.com.cn/s/blog_48ecc3b70102e012.html.

36. Hao Jian 郝建, "'黑马''黑手'和文章好手刘晓波 ["Dark horse," "black hand," and skilled essayist Liu Xiaobo], 纵览中国 [China perspective], October 15, 2010; reprinted in 自由荆冠: 刘晓波与诺贝尔和平奖 [A crown of thorns of freedom: Liu Xiaobo and the Nobel Peace Prize], ed. Chen Kuide 陈奎德 and Xia Ming 夏明 (Hong Kong: Chenzhong shuju 晨钟书局, 2010).

37. Liu Xiaobo, "我看屈原" [My view of Qu Yuan], 关东文学 [Northeast literature] 12 (1987): 25–26.

38. Li Zehou 李泽厚, "我和八十年代" [The 1980s and me], 经济观察报 [Economic observer], June 9, 2008, 45.

39. Li's phrase in Chinese was 洛阳纸贵, "the price of paper has risen in Luoyang," an idiom based on a case in the Western Jin period, 1,800 years earlier, when popular demand for an article the emperor had praised grew strong enough to cause a shortage of paper in the city of Luoyang and a consequent rise in its price.

40. Cui Weiping 崔卫平, "138人关于刘晓波案的看法" [The views of 138 people on the Liu Xiaobo case], 北京之春 [Beijing spring] (February 2010), http://beijingspring.com/bj2/2010/120/2010131151928 .htm.

41. We have not been able to determine the precise date.

42. Cheng Yinghong 程映虹, "'两个刘晓波'和中国知识份子的转型" ["Two Liu Xiaobos" and the transition of Chinese intellectuals], in 自由荆冠: 刘晓波与诺贝尔和平奖 [A crown of thorns of freedom: Liu Xiaobo and the Nobel Peace Prize], ed. Chen Kuide and Xia Ming.

43. Liu Dong, Weixin message to Wu Dazhi, August 17, 2017.

44. Lecture on December 12, 1986. See *LXBQRQS* 90.

45. *LXBQRQS* 93.

46. Feng Congde 封从德, 六四日记 [June fourth diary] (Hong Kong: Suyuan shushe 溯源书社, 2014), 236.

47. Yu Shicun 余世存, 权力的实行方式: 晓波印象记 [Modes of wielding power: Impressions of Xiaobo], accessed August 5, 2019, https://www.chinesepen.org/old-posts/?p=19285.

48. Jin Zhong 金钟, "文坛'黑马'刘晓波—刘晓波答记者问" [The "dark horse" of the literary scene: An interview with Liu Xiaobo], 解放月报 [Emancipation monthly] 12 (1988).

49. Yisha 伊沙, "长篇访谈录 (一)" [Long interview with Yisha (one)], "诗生活"网站"伊沙专栏" [Special column on Yisha at the website "life of poetry"], accessed January 14, 2020, https://www.poemlife .com/index.php?mod=showart&id=54807&str=1268.

50. Mou Sen 牟森, "戏剧作为对抗—与自己有关" [Drama as opposition: Things related to myself], accessed August 8, 2020, http://gb.oversea.cnki.net/KCMS/detail/detail.aspx?filename=JBZZ 200411006&dbcode=CJFD&dbname=CJFD2004.

51. Tong Qingbing 童庆炳, "我所认识的刘晓波" [Liu Xiaobo as I have known him], in parts of 旧梦与 远山: 回忆录 [Old dreams and distant mountains: Reminiscences] (Beijing: Beijing daxue chubanshe, 2015) that were removed by censorship before publication.

52. Tong Qingbing, "Liu Xiaobo as I Have Known Him."

53. Zhuge shanren 诸葛山人, "最后100天: 中国青年报'两代知识分子对话录'始末记" [The final 100 days: The complete record of "a dialogue between two generations of intellectuals" at *China Youth News*]. Publication of the book was halted because of the massacre in 1989, and it has not been published since. Li Datong 李大同 supplied it to Wu Dazhi by e-mail on April 10, 2019. The material in the next twelve paragraphs is taken from it as well.

54. Tong Qingbing, "Liu Xiaobo as I Have Known Him."

55. Xing Xiaoqun 邢小群, "黄药眠和他的博士" [Huang Yaomian and his Ph.D.s], 小众群言, July 1, 2017, accessed January 14, 2020, http://www.liu-xiaobo.org/blog/archives/23636.

56. Liu Xiaobo, "喝狼奶最多, 消化也最好" [The more wolf milk you drink, the better you digest it], *RYRQ* (March 2006), accessed September 3, 2019. http://www.renyurenquan.org/ ren yu renquan _article@article_id=415.html.

57. Bai Jieming 白杰明 (Geremie Barmé), "中国人的解放在自我觉醒: 与个性派批评家刘晓波一席谈" [The liberation of Chinese lies in self-awakening: A chat with the individualism-school critic Liu Xiaobo], 解放月报 [Emancipation monthly] (March 1987): 64.

58. Jaivin, *The Monkey and the Dragon*, 113.

59. Jaivin, *The Monkey and the Dragon*, 225.

60. Liu Xiaobo, 选择的批判: 与李泽厚对话 [Critique of choices: A dialogue with Li Zehou] (Shanghai: Renmin chubanshe, 1988).

61. Liu Xiaobo, *Critique of Choices*, 10.

62. Liu Xiaobo, *Critique of Choices*, 30. Emphasis in original.

63. Kong Qingdong 孔庆东, "你别无选择吗?" [Have you no other choice?], 东方纪事[Eastern miscellany] 1 (1989).

64. Xia Zhongyi 夏中义, "选择的批判之批判" [A criticism of *Critique of Choices*], 学术月刊 [Scholarship monthly] 2 (1994): 79.

65. Liu Xiaobo, 形而上学的迷雾 [The fog of metaphysics] (Shanghai: People's Publishing House, 1989).

66. Liu Xiaobo, *The Fog of Metaphysics*, 2.

67. Liu Xiaobo, *The Fog of Metaphysics*, 5.

68. Liu Xiaobo, *The Fog of Metaphysics*, 71. Emphasis in the original.

69. Liu Xiaobo, *The Fog of Metaphysics*, 100–101.

70. Liu Xiaobo, *The Fog of Metaphysics*, 102. Emphasis in the original.

71. Yang Zhuo, a childhood friend of Liu Xiaobo's, interview by Wu Dazhi, September 18, 2018.

72. *LXLXS* 193; translated by Nicholas Admussen in *NENH*, 240–241.

73. Liu Xiaobo, *The Fog of Metaphysics*, 115.

74. Liu Xiaobo, *The Fog of Metaphysics*, 189.

75. Liu Xiaobo, *The Fog of Metaphysics*, 201.

76. Liu Xiaobo, *The Fog of Metaphysics*, 227.

77. Su Xiaokang 苏晓康, "刘晓波把激进煎熬成温和" [Liu Xiaobo turns radical torment into moderation], in 刘晓波纪念文集 [Liu Xiaobo commemorative collection], ed. Cai Chu 蔡楚 (Somerdale, NJ: Zhongguo minzhu zhuanxing yanjiusuo, 2017).

78. Wang Xuedian 王学典, "'八十年代'是怎样被'重构'的？" [How have "the 1980s" been "reconstructed"?], 开放时代 [Open times] 6 (2009).

79. Liu Xiaobo, "形而上学与中国文化" [Metaphysics and Chinese culture], 新启蒙 [New enlightenment] (Hunan jiaoyu chubanshe) 1 (1988): 74.

80. Liu Xiaobo, "网友的关切让我感到温暖: 致茉莉的一封信" [The concern of friends on the Internet makes me feel warm: A letter to Moli], accessed August 2, 2019, https://blog.boxun.com/hero/liuxb /41_1.shtml.

7. GODS AND DEMONS WRESTLE

1. Tong Qingbing, "序" [Preface] to Liu Xiaobo, 审美与人的自由 [Aesthetics and human freedom] (Beijing: Beijing shifandaxue chubanshe, 1988), 3.

2. Sun Jin, e-mail to Wu Dazhi, October 7, 2017.

3. Liu Xiaobo, *Aesthetics and Human Freedom*, 32.

4. Liu Xiaobo, *Aesthetics and Human Freedom*, 169.
5. Liu Xiaobo, *Aesthetics and Human Freedom*, 189.
6. Liu Xiaobo, *Aesthetics and Human Freedom*, 190.
7. Liu Xiaobo, *Aesthetics and Human Freedom*, 194.
8. Liu Xiaobo, *Aesthetics and Human Freedom*, 196.
9. Liu Xiaobo, *Aesthetics and Human Freedom*, 197.
10. Liu Xiaobo, *Aesthetics and Human Freedom*, 193.
11. Liu Xiaobo, *Aesthetics and Human Freedom*, 192.
12. Liu Xiaobo, *Aesthetics and Human Freedom*, 200.
13. Sun Jin, e-mail to Wu Dazhi, August 7, 2017.
14. See chapter 10, pp. 202 ff.
15. See chapter 6.
16. See chapter 5, pp. 104 ff.
17. Tong Qingbing, "我所认识的刘晓波" [Liu Xiaobo as I have known him], in parts of 旧梦与远山:回忆录 [Old dreams and distant mountains: Memoirs] (Beijing: Beijing daxue chubanshe, 2015).
18. Gao Ertai 高尔泰, "王元化先生" [Mr. Wang Yuanhua], 美文 [Aesthetic culture] 3 (2008): 48.
19. Tong Qingbing, "Liu Xiaobo as I Have Known Him."
20. Gao Ertai, "Mr. Wang Yuanhua," 48.
21. Gao Ertai, "Mr. Wang Yuanhua,"48.
22. Fang Lizhi, "奥斯陆四日四记" [Four notes on four days in Oslo], China News Digest online, accessed January 11, 2020, http://fang-lizhi.hxwk.org/2010/12/12/奥斯陆四日四记.
23. The Liu Xiaobo file at Beijing Normal University.
24. Liu Xiaobo, "我看审美" [My view of aesthetics], 文艺争鸣 (Literary controversies) 5 (1988): 4.
25. Liu Xiaobo, "My View of Aesthetics," 4–11.
26. Liu Xiaobo, "My View of Aesthetics," 6.
27. Liu Xiaobo, *Aesthetics and Human Freedom*, 200.
28. Liu Xiaobo, *ZDZYZZ*, 162. Epilogue translated by Stacey Mosher in *NENH*, 124.
29. *Xiyouji* 西游记 [Journey to the west], a classic sixteenth-century Chinese novel attributed to Wu Cheng'en 吳承恩 and translated in four volumes by Anthony Yu (Chicago: University of Chicago Press, 1980–84).
30. *MXD*, 245.
31. *MXD*, 146–147.
32. Yang Jidong, interview by Wu Dazhi, Taiyuan, Shanxi Province, August 25, 2018.
33. Tao Li 陶力, 紫式部和她的源氏物语 [Shikibu and her *Tale of Genji*] (Beijing: Beijing yuyanxueyuan chubanshe, 1994), 162.
34. Tao Li, *Shikibu and Her* Tale of Genji, 163.
35. Tao Li, *Shikibu and Her* Tale of Genji, 109–110.
36. Tao Li, *Shikibu and Her* Tale of Genji, 07.
37. *ZDZYZZ*, flyleaf.

8. OUT INTO THE WORLD

1. Bei Dao, *The August Skywalker*, tr. Bonnie S. McDougall (New York: New Directions, 1988). Bei Dao, *Waves*, tr. Bonnie S. McDougall (Hong Kong: Chinese University Press, 1985.
2. *MXD* 82.
3. Liu Xiaobo, "但愿香港永远是世界的自由港" [Let's hope Hong Kong will always be a free port in the world], in *LXBQRQS* 113.

4. Jin Zhong 金钟, "'文坛'黑马'刘晓波—刘晓波答记者问" [The "dark horse" of the literary scene: An interview with Liu Xiaobo], 解放月报 [Emancipation monthly] 12 (1988), http://www.liu-xiaobo .org/blog/archives/5229.

5. Liu Xiaobo, "混世魔王毛泽东" [Devil incarnate Mao Zedong], 解放月报 Emancipation monthly] (November 1988; reprinted August 1989).

6. Liu Xiaobo, "Let's Hope Hong Kong Will Always Be a Free Port in the World," 107.

7. Liu Xiaobo, "Let's Hope Hong Kong Will Always Be a Free Port in the World," 108.

8. Liu Xiaobo, "Let's Hope Hong Kong Will Always Be a Free Port in the World," 109.

9. Li Yi 李怡, "世界唔配有劉曉波" [The world doesn't deserve Liu Xiaobo], accessed September 5, 2019, http://nextplus.nextmedia.com/news/%E6%99%82%E4%BA%8B%E8%A6%81%E8%81%9E /20170714/530032.

10. Jin Zhong, "The 'Dark Horse' of the Literary Scene."

11. Liu Xiaobo, "我与《开放》结缘十九年" [My nineteen years of involvement with *Open Magazine*], *Kaifang* [Open] (January 2007).

12. Karl Marx, "The Future Results of British Rule in India," *New York Daily Tribune*, August 8, 1853; Liu Xiaobo, "Let's Hope Hong Kong Will Always Be a Free Port in the World."

13. Liu Xiaobo, "启蒙的悲剧—'五四'运动批判" [The tragedy of enlightenment: a critique of May Fourth], 中国之春 [China spring] 1 (1989), http://www.liu-xiaobo.org/blog/archives/5224.

14. Karl Marx, "The British Rule in India," *New York Daily Tribune*, June 25, 1853. Here "murder itself" appears to refer to the practice of *sati*, in which a widow throws herself onto her husband's funeral pyre.

15. Karl Marx, "The Future Results."

16. Liu Xiaobo, "The Tragedy of Enlightenment."

17. *LXBQRQS* 1.

18. Geremie Barmé, "Confession, Redemption, and Death: Liu Xiaobo and the Protest Movement of 1989," in *The Broken Mirror: China After Tiananmen*, ed. George Hicks (Chicago: St. James Press, 1990), 58.

19. *ZDZYZZ*.

20. *ZDZYZZ* 5.

21. *ZDZYZZ* 41.

22. Liu Xiaobo, "用真话颠覆谎言制度: 接受 '杰出民主人士奖'的答谢词" [Using truth to undermine a system built on lies: Statement of thanks in accepting the Outstanding Democracy Activist Award], 争鸣 [Contending] 6 (2003), accessed July 22, 2019, https://blog.boxun.com/hero/liuxb/76_1 .shtml; translated by Eva S. Chou in *NENH*, 293.

23. Liu Xiaobo, *MXD*, 76.

24. *MXD* 118.

25. *MXD* 118.

26. *ZDZYZZ* 31.

27. *ZDZYZZ* 32.

28. *ZDZYZZ* 32

29. *ZDZYZZ* 86.

30. *ZDZYZZ* 17.

31. *ZDZYZZ* 155.

32. *ZDZYZZ* 159.

33. *ZDZYZZ* 162.

34. He wrote a long article, "对马克思主义的再检讨" [A reexamination of Marxism], published in Hong Kong in 1989 in 解放月报 [Emancipation monthly] in three installments (no. 4, 86–87; no. 5, 87–88; no. 8, 55–58).

35. Liu Xiaobo, "两种不同的马克思主义" [Two different kinds of Marxism], 解放月报 [Emancipation monthly] 8 (1989): 56.

36. Bei Ling 贝岭, "别无选择: 记1989年前后的刘晓波" [No other choice: Remembering Liu Xiaobo in the years before and after 1989], 议报 [Discussion], June 19, 2010, http://www.yibaochina.com/article/display?articleId=612.

37. Bei Ling 贝岭, "刘晓波传" [A biography of Liu Xiaobo] (unpublished ms.), chapter 4.

38. *ZDZYZZ* 165.

39. *ZDZYZZ* 158.

40. Liu Xiaobo, "读胡平想起'民主墙一代'" [Reading Hu Ping and recalling "the Democracy Wall generation"], *RYRQ* (July 2006), accessed July 22, 2019, http://www.liu-xiaobo.org/blog/archives/7571.

41. Liu Xiaobo, "Reading Hu Ping and Recalling 'the Democracy Wall Generation.'"

42. *LXBQRQS* 1.

43. Hu Ping 胡平, "我和晓波的交往（上）" [My encounters with Xiaobo (part 1)], 北京之春 [Beijing spring], November 2010.

44. Ya Yi 亚衣, "中国民运需要职业的经营者: 采访陈军" [The Chinese democracy movement needs professional managers: An interview with Chen Jun], 北京之春 [Beijing spring], February 1997.

45. See "胡平、劉曉波、陳軍等十人共同發'改革建言'促中共反省糾正錯誤" [Hu Ping, Liu Xiaobo, Chen Jun, and seven others jointly publicize a "proposal for reform" urging the Chinese Communists to reflect on their mistakes and to correct them], *Ming Pao*, April 20, 1989.

46. Hu Ping 胡平, Liu Xiaobo, et al., "致全中国大学生的公开信" [An open letter to all college students in the country], in *LXBQRQS* 129–130.

47. *MXD* 74.

48. *MXD* 75.

49. Liu Xiaobo, "悲剧英雄的悲剧: 胡耀邦逝世现象评论之一" [I. The tragedy of a tragic hero]; "完善制度还是塑造完美领袖: 胡耀邦逝世现象评论之二" [II. Perfect a system—or merely create the image of a perfect leader?]; "中国民主化的目标与程序: 胡耀邦逝世现象评论之三" [III. The aims and procedures of Chinese democratization], published as a trio in 解放月报 [Emancipation monthly], May 1989.

50. Liu Xiaobo, from "II. Perfect a System," 33.

51. Liu Xiaobo, from "II. Perfect a System," 33.

9. IN TIANANMEN SQUARE

1. *MXD* 73–80.

2. Zhao Changqing 赵常青, "学生'黑手'在哪里？: 89学生领袖陈章宝采访录 [Where is the students' "black hand"?: An interview with student leader Chen Zhangbao], 民主中国 *Minzhu Zhongguo*, June 6, 2010, accessed July 22, 2019, http://minzhuzhongguo.org/MainArtShow.aspx?AID=14997.

3. *MXD* 87.

4. *MXD* 93.

5. "赵紫阳会见亚发银行理事会成员讲话" [Speech of Zhao Ziyang at the meeting of the members of the Asian Development Bank], *People's Daily*, May 5, 1989.

6. *MXD* 96.

7. Wuerkaixi 吾尔开希, "我的老师和朋友刘晓波" [My teacher and friend Liu Xiaobo], 开放 [Open] 10 (2010), http://www.open.com.hk/old_version/1011p60.html.

8. Zhou Duo 周舵, "血腥的黎明" [Bloody dawn], accessed October 21, 2019, https://blog.boxun.com/hero/200903/zhouduo/1_1.shtml.

9. *MXD* 107.

10. *MXD* 107.

11. *MXD* 112.

12. *MXD* 123.

13. *MXD* 123.

14. *MXD* 125–126.

15. *MXD* 135.

16. *MXD* 130.

17. *LXBQRQS* 132–136.

18. *LXBQRQS* 131.

19. *MXD* 165.

20. *MXD* 147.

21. *MXD* 180.

22. According to *MXD* 180, Xiaobo also mentioned Chai Ling and Feng Congde as candidates for the role. But Chai Ling and others remember that Xiaobo named Wuerkaixi alone.

23. *MXD* 182.

24. Zhang Min 张敏, "刘晓波访谈录" [Interview with Liu Xiaobo], Radio Free Asia, January 3, 2001, accessed July 22, 2019, https://docs.google.com/document/d/1sPWmhWRCx-PhMSckSio6FLL RlauACepot1y-sLwyf1w/edit.

25. *MXD* 192.

26. *MXD* 192.

27. Liu Xiaobo, Zhou Duo 周舵, Hou Dejian 侯德健, and Gao Xin 高新, "六二绝食宣言" [The June second hunger strike declaration], translated in *NENH*, 277–283. All the translations from the declaration that appear below are taken from this source.

28. *MXD* 199.

29. *MXD* 199.

30. Anqi 安琪, "在自由中寻求自由本身: 专访美国哈佛大学费正清中心访问学者高新" [Amid freedom looking for freedom itself: An interview with Gao Xin, a visiting scholar at the Fairbank Center at Harvard University], *Boxun* 百家争鸣, accessed February 6, 2020, https://blog.boxun.com/hero/anqi/48_1 .shtml.

31. Wang Juntao 王军涛, "刘晓波的坚持、率性与玩世不恭" [The persistence, rashness, and irreverence of Liu Xiaobo], *Boxun*, accessed February 6, 2020, http://www.boxun.com/news/gb/china/2010 /10/201010190627.shtml.

32. These descriptions are a paraphrase of *MXD* 205.

33. *XXQCNM* 97.

34. *MXD* 134

35. *ZDZYZZ* 107–131.

36. *MXD* 76–77.

37. *MXD* 215.

10. A "BLACK HAND" GOES TO PRISON, FEELS DEEP REMORSE

1. Zhang Liang (pseud.), comp., *The Tiananmen Papers*, ed. Andrew J. Nathan and Perry Link (New York: Public Affairs, 2001), 349–353.

2. *XXQCNM* 29.

3. Deguo Yachen ba jiu xue she 德国亚琛八九学社, ed., 回顾与反思—八九学运历史回顾与反思研讨会 记录 [Recollections and reflections: Proceedings of the conference on recollection and memory of the 1989 student movement (Paris, France, July 14–24, 1991)], quotation from Li Lu 李禄, "六三道 一夜" [The night of June 3] (Essen, Germany: Rhine PEN Association), 309; accessed February 7, 2020, http://www.tsquare.tv/chinese/archives/h5.html.

4. *XXQCNM* 96–97.

5. *XXQCNM* 98–100.

6. *XXQCNM* 238.

7. "北京市人民政府中国人民解放军戒严部队指挥部通告" [Notice of the headquarters of the martial law troops of the People's Liberation Army of the people's government of Beijing city], in *XXQCNM* 222.

8. *MXD* 227.

9. *MXD* 228.

10. Hou Dejian 侯德健, "六月四日撤离天安门广场时我的亲身经历" [My personal experiences at the time of withdrawing from Tiananmen Square on June 4], 香港经济日报, August 24, 1989, http://www .tiananmenduizhi.com/2015/08/blog-post 16,html.

11. Zhou Duo 周舵, "血腥的黎明" [Bloody dawn], accessed October 21, 2019, https://blog.boxun.com /hero/200903/zhouduo/1_1.shtml.

12. Liu Xiaobo's thinking as summarized in this and the following two paragraphs is from *MXD*, 223 and *XXQCNM* 249.

13. Qiu Yongsheng 邱永生, Huang Zhimin 黄智敏, Yi Jianru 易俭如, Zhang Baorui 张宝瑞, and Zhu Yu 朱玉, "和平撤离, 无人死亡:6月4日天安门广场清场当事人访谈录" [Peaceful withdrawal, no deaths: Interviews with witnesses to the clearing of Tiananmen Square on June Fourth], *Renmin ribao*, September 5, 1989, 5. This government account is consistent with Hou Dejian, "My Personal Experiences," and *XXQCNM* 250.

14. *The Gate of Heavenly Peace*, dir. the Long Bow group, Boston, MA, 1995, http://www.tsquare.tv /longbow/ at 2 hours, 41 minutes, 3–26 seconds.

15. *MXD* 229.

16. Hou Dejian, "My Personal Experiences."

17. *MXD* 230.

18. *MXD* 230–231.

19. *XXQCNM* 304.

20. *XXQCNM* 313.

21. Zhang Liang, comp., *The Tiananmen Papers*, 370.

22. Hou Dejian, "My Personal Experiences," and Zhou Duo, "Bloody Dawn."

23. Deguo Yachen ba jiu xue she 德国亚琛八九学社, ed., 回顾与反思 –八九学运历史回顾与反思研讨会记录 [Recollections and reflections: Proceedings of the conference on recollection and memory of the 1989 student movement (Paris, France, July 14–24, 1991)], quotation from Feng Congde 封从德 (Essen, Germany: Rhine PEN Association), 309; 5.4.1 口头表决 (voice vote), 318; also accessed February 7, 2020, at "The Gate of Heavenly Peace" http://www.tsquare.tv/chinese/archives/h5 .html; also "六四日记:广场上的共和国" [June Fourth Diary: The republic on the square] (Taipei: Suyuan shushe, 2013) 516–517.

24. *XXQCNM* 329.

25. *MXD* 233.

26. Press conference with Yuan Mu, spokesman for the State Council of China, Beijing, June 6, 1989, accessed February 23, 2020, https://www.youtube.com/watch?v=I5ijUcOsciQ.

27. *MXD* 241–242.

28. Zhang Liang, comp., *The Tiananmen Papers*, 349.

29. *MXD* 247.

30. Zhang Min 张敏, "刘晓波访谈录记者" [Interview with Liu Xiaobo], Radio Free Asia, January 3, 2001, accessed July 22, 2019, http://www.liu-xiaobo.org/blog/archives/5555.

31. "给廖亦武的信" [Letter to Liao Yiwu], Independent Chinese PEN Center, accessed February 23, 2020, https://blog.boxun.com/hero/liuxb; translated by Perry Link in *NENH*, 286.

32. Liao Yiwu, *For a Song and a Hundred Songs* (Boston and New York: Houghton Mifflin Harcourt, 2013), 81–89.

33. *MXD* 42.

34. *LXBQRQS* 9.

35. Chen Xitong 陈希同, "关于制止动乱和平息反革命暴乱的情况报告" [A report on stopping turmoil and pacifying the counterrevolutionary riot], 国务院公报 [State council gazette], accessed August 13, 2020, https://www.gov.cn/gongbao/shuju/1989/gwyb198911.pdf.

36. *XXQCNM* 257.

37. Claudia Rosett, "Lost in the Chinese Gulag," *The Wall Street Journal*, August 8, 1989.

38. This and the next two sentences are taken almost verbatim from Geremie Barmé, "Confession, Redemption, and Death: Liu Xiaobo and the Protest Movement of 1989," in *The Broken Mirror: China After Tiananmen*, ed. George Hicks (Chicago: St. James Press, 1990), 84–85.

39. Per Hovdenakk, Yngcar Lochen, Finn Carling, Ole Henrik Moe, Inger Sitter, and Paal-Helge Haugen, "授予刘晓波诺贝尔和平奖的建议" [A proposal to award the Nobel Peace Prize to Liu Xiaobo], 解放月报 [Emancipation monthly] 9 (1989): 77.

40. Linda Jaivin, *The Monkey and the Dragon* (Melbourne, Australia: Text Publishing, 2001), 329.

41. Xinhuashe 新华社, "侯德健谈"六·四"凌晨广场见闻" [Hou Dejian tells what he saw and heard in the early morning of "June Fourth"], accessed February 23, 2020, http://www.tiananmenduizhi.com /2015/08/blog-post.html.

42. *MXD* 33–34.

43. Qiu Yongsheng et al., "Peaceful Withdrawal, No Deaths," 5.

44. *MXD* 34.

45. *MXD* 35.

46. Wen Ping 闻平, "从民族虚无主义到卖国主义: 评刘晓波的资产阶级自由化谬论" [From nihilist to traitor: The bourgeois liberal absurdities of Liu Xiaobo], *Renmin ribao*, November 7, 1989, 1.

47. Sun Jin, e-mail to Wu Dazhi, August 1, 2017.

48. *MXD* 30,

49. Liu Xiaobo, "包包, 我们爱你: 为包遵信送行" [Baobao, we love you: Seeing off Bao Zunxin], November 25, 2007, *RYRQ* (December 2007), http://www.renyurenquan.org/ryrq_article@article_id=788.html.

50. *MXD* 35.

51. *MXD* 245–246.

52. See "Liu Xiaobo: L'homme qui a défié Pékin" [Liu Xiaobo: The man who defied Beijing], a film by Peter Haski (June 2019), Paris: IMBDPro, https://www.imdb.com/title/tt10528084.

53. *MXD* 36.

54. *MXD* 36–38.

55. Here Liu Xiaobo is quoting a line from himself that appeared in 中国人的解放在自我觉醒 [The liberation of the Chinese people will lie in their self-awakening], 九十年代 [The nineties], an interview with Geremie Barmé, March 1987.

56. *MXD* 44–45.

57. *MXD* 45.

58. *MXD* 21.

59. *MXD* 17.

60. *MXD* 21.

61. *MXD* 46.

11. PICKING UP AND STARTING OVER

1. This and the next two paragraphs are from *MXD* 17–18.

2. Tong Qingbing, "我所认识的刘晓波" [Liu Xiaobo as I have known him], in parts of 旧梦与远山:回忆录 [Old dreams and distant mountains] (Beijing: Beijing daxue chubanshe, 2015) that were removed by censorship before publication.

3. In George Hicks, ed., *The Broken Mirror: China After Tiananmen* (Chicago: St. James Press, 1990), 52–99.

4. *MXD* 54.

5. Ding Zilin 丁子霖 and Jiang Peikun 蒋培坤, "我们与晓波的相知、相识和相交（上）" [Our knowledge of, familiarity with, and relations with Xiaobo (part I)], accessed February 25, 2020, http://www .tiananmenmother.org/tiananmenmother/m100116001.htm.

6. Translated by Isaac P. Hsieh in *NENH* 13–15.

7. See Jeffrey Yang, tr., *June Fourth Elegies* (New York: Graywolf Press, 2012).

8. *MXD* 20.

9. Liu Xiaobo, "我没有敌人：我的最后陈述" [I have no enemies: My final statement], December 23, 2009, translated by Perry Link in *NENH* 321–322.

10. Liu Xiaobo, "我身体中的六四：六四十二周年祭" [June Fourth inside my body: On the twelfth anniversary of June Fourth], accessed February 25, 2020, https://blog.boxun.com/hero/liuxb/413_1 .shtml.

11. Yang Jidong, telephone conversation with Wu Dazhi, August 25, 2018.

12. Wei Haitian, electronic message to Wu Dazhi, October 8, 2018.

13. Wang Ya 王娅, "怀念" [Reminiscences], text message to Wu Dazhi, September 30, 2018.

14. *MXD* 19.

15. We feel it best not to publish her name. In later years she became a scholar and a representative to the Chinese People's Political Consultative Conference.

16. *MXD* 9

17. *MXD* 69.

18. *MXD* 83.

19. *MXD* 83–84.

20. *MXD* 190.

21. *MXD* 145.

22. *MXD* 89.

23. *MXD* 146.

24. Liu Xiaobo, "我们被我们的'正义'压倒" [We were defeated by our own "righteousness"], 联合报 [United daily news], June 4–5, 1993.

25. Liu Xiaobo, "We Were Defeated by Our Own 'Righteousness.'"

26. Liu Xiaobo, "We Were Defeated by Our Own 'Righteousness.'"

27. Liu Binyan 刘宾雁, "走出幻想(之四)" [Taking leave of illusion (no. 4)], 北京之春 [Beijing spring], April 1994.

28. Wang Ruowang 王若望, "关于八九民运反思：对刘晓波观点的质疑" [Reflections on the '89 democracy movement: Some doubts about the views of Liu Xiaobo], 探索 [Beijing spring], August 1993.

29. Ding Zilin and Jiang Peikun, "Our Knowledge of, Familiarity with, and Relations with Xiaobo (Part I)."

30. Wang Chaohua, interview by Wu Dazhi, January 21, 2018, Riverside, California.

31. Jianying Zha, "Servant of the State," *The New Yorker*, November 8, 2010.

32. *MXD* 25.

33. *MXD* 25–26.

34. *MXD* 24.

35. *MXD* 25.

36. *MXD* 60.

37. *MXD* 47.

38. *MXD* 59.

39. *MXD* 43, 196.

40. Liu Xiaobo, "往俗里走和无灵魂 —文革后的大众文化与党文化" [Toward the vulgar, without a soul: Popular culture and Party culture since the Cultural Revolution], 中国之春 [China spring] 120 (May 1993), http://chinesepen.org/Index.shtml. See also "情色狂欢: 中国商业文化批评之一" [Erotic carnival: A criticism of China's commercial culture], translated by Nicholas Admussen as "The Erotic Carnival in Recent Chinese History," in *NENH* 156.

41. Liu Xiaobo, "透视大陆人民的文化生活" [A look into the cultural life of people on the mainland], 中国时报周刊 [China times weekly], February 28, March 7, and March 14, 1993.

42. Liu Xiaobo, "A Look Into the Cultural Life of People on the Mainland," February 28, 1993, 71.

43. Liu Xiaobo, "王朔访谈录" [Transcript of an interview with Wang Shuo], *Zhengming*, January 1993.

44. In Hong Kong, Xiaobo wrote for the magazines 开放 [Open], 争鸣 [Contending], and 动向 [The trend], and newspapers including 信报 [Fidelity; official English title: *Economic Times*], 明报 [Bright], and 大公报 [Great public]; in Taiwan, for 苹果日报 [Apple daily], and in the United States, for 北京之春 [Beijing spring], edited by Hu Ping, and 民主中国 [Democratic China], edited by Su Xiaokang. He also wrote for overseas websites and online political journals including 观察 [Observe China], 新世纪 [The new century], 议报 [Discussion], 民主论坛 [Democracy forum; official English title: *Democratic China*], 大纪元 [The epoch times], and the Chinese-language website of the British Broadcasting Company.

45. Han Qing 含青, "独立作家刘晓波获汉语贡献奖" [Independent writer Liu Xiaobo receives the prize for contributions to the Chinese language], *Radio Free Asia*, accessed March 1, 2020, https://www .rfa.org/mandarin/yataibaodao/liuxiaobo-06042008104909.html.

46. Liu Xiaobo, "Toward the Vulgar, Without a Soul."

47. Vaclav Havel, *Open Letters: Selected Writings, 1965–1990* (London: Faber & Faber, 1991), 59.

48. Liu Xiaobo, "给胡平信, 1993年4月21日" [Letter to Hu Ping, April 21, 1993], 北京之春 [Beijing spring], December 2010.

49. Chen Jun 陈军, "刘晓波把入狱当成洗刷自己罪名的机会" [Liu Xiaobo uses an entry to prison to purge himself of his transgressions], accessed March 2, 2020 at https://www.boxun.com/news/gb /china/2010/10/201010160222.shtml.

50. Ya Yi 亚衣, "既入地狱, 就不抱怨黑暗: 采访刘晓波" [If you're going to hell, don't complain that it's dark], 中国之春 [Beijing spring], May 1993.

51. Ya Yi, "If You're Going to Hell."

52. Ya Yi, "If You're Going to Hell."

53. Linda Jaivin, "A Nobel Affair," *The Monthly*, December 2010–January 2011, https://www .themonthly.com.au/monthly-essays-linda-jaivin-nobel-affair-liu-xiaobo-2928.

54. Wei Hua 卫华, "大气子明" [The august Ziming], in 殉道者 [Martyrs], ed. Xu Xiao 徐晓 (New York: Mingjing chubanshe, 2014), 74–75.

55. Bao Zunxin 包遵信, Chen Xiaoping 陈小平, Liu Xiaobo, Wang Ruoshui 王若水, Chen Ziming 陈子明, Xu Wenli 徐文立, Zhou Duo 周舵, Wu Xuecan 吴学灿, Min Qi 闵琦, Sha Yuguang 沙裕光, Liao Yiwu 廖亦武, and Jin Cheng 金橙, "反腐建议书: 致八届人大三次会议" [A proposal for opposing corruption: To the Third Plenary Session of the Eighth National People's Congress], 北京之春 [Beijing spring], April 1995.

56. Bao Zunxin, Chen Xiaoping, Liu Xiaobo, et al., "废除收容审查, 保障人身自由: 致八届人大三次会议" [Abolish detention for investigation and protect personal freedom: To the Third Plenary Session of the Eighth National People's Congress], 北京之春 [Beijing spring], April 1995.

57. Liu Xiaobo and Chen Xiaoping, "汲取血的教训推进民主进程: '六四'六周年呼吁书" [Lessons written in blood press us toward democracy: An appeal on the sixth anniversary of "June Fourth"], 北京之春 [Beijing spring], July 1995.

58. Liu Xiaobo, "陈小平的挑战和呼吁: 有感于陈小平起诉中共驻纽约总领事馆" [The challenge and appeal of Chen Xiaoping: On Chen Xiaoping's lawsuit against the consulate general of the Chinese communists in New York], accessed March 4, 2020, http://www.boxun.com/news/gb/pubvp/2002/08/200208272313.shtml.

59. Liu Xiaobo, "我与互联网" [The Internet and me], *Minzhu Zhongguo* [Democratic China], February 18, 2006, accessed February 25, 2020, https://blog.boxun.com/hero/liuxb/513_1.shtml, translated by Louisa Chiang as "Long Live the Internet" in *NENH* 203–210.

60. Wang Ganchang 王淦昌 et al., "呼唤实现国内宽容" [Calling for the reality of tolerance inside the country], 北京之春 [Beijing spring], July 1995.

61. Liu Xiaobo, "Letter to Liao Yiwu," Independent Chinese PEN Center, accessed February 23, 2020, https://blog.boxun.com/hero/liuxb, translated by Perry Link in *NENH* 286.

62. The story is told in Liu Xiaobo, "The Internet and Me."

63. Ji Xianlin 季羡林, 牛棚杂记, translated by Chengxin Jiang as *The Cowshed: Memories of the Chinese Cultural Revolution* (New York: New York Review Books, 2006).

12. LOVE THAT JUMPS WALLS

1. Liu Xia, "一九八九年六月二日: 给晓波" [For Xiaobo on June 2, 1989], *LXLXS* 374–375.

2. Liu Xiaobo, "回忆: 给我们共同的岁月" [Reminiscences: For our shared past years], *LXLXS* 251–252.

3. After 1997, Central University of Finance and Economics.

4. This is an estimate. We have not been able to find Xiang's date of birth.

5. Liu Xiaobo, "给外公（模拟刘霞）: 给从未见过外公的刘霞" [For Grandfather (in the voice of Liu Xia): For Liu Xia, who never saw her maternal grandfather], *LXLXS* 153–159.

6. "向大光关于党政军警对付学运方式的几点建议致朱家骅" [A few suggestions from Xiang Daguang to Zhu Jiahua on the ways the Party, government, army, and police have handled the student movement], in 中华民国史档案资料汇编, 第五辑第三编, 政治第四册 [Volume 4, Group 3, compilation 5 of the collected materials of the historical archives of the Republic of China Political] (Nanjing: 江苏古籍出版社 [Jiangsu ancient-text publishing house], 1999), 161.

7. Liu Xiaobo, "狱中随笔之一" [Prison notes I], July 14, 1997, in 国际笔会独立中文作家笔会会刊试刊号 [Trial issue of the Bulletin of Independent Chinese Writers PEN of International PEN], chinaaffairs.org, http://www.chinaaffairs.org/gb/detail.asp?id=53424.

8. Ai Xiaoming, interview of Liu Xia, April 2, 2009, accessed February 25, 2020, https://www.peacehall.com/news/gb/china/2010/10/201010082129.shtml.

9. Ai Xiaoming, interview of Liu Xia, April 2009; Bei Ming, "刘霞的世界: 与刘霞碎语" [Liu Xia's world: Snippets with Liu Xia], *China News Digest*, November 2, 2010, http://hx.cnd.org/2010/11/02/%e5%8c%97%e6%98%8e%ef%bc%9a%e5%88%98%e9%9c%9e%e7%9a%84%e4%b8%96%e7%95%8c%e2%80%95%e2%80%95%e4%b8%8e%e5%88%98%e9%9c%9e%e7%a2%8e%e8%af%ad%ef%bc%88%e9%99%84%e7%85%a7%e7%89%87%ef%bc%89/.

10. Liu Xia, 一个词 [One word], *LXLXS*, June 28, 1995, 314.

11. Liu Xia, "给休斯" [For Hughes], *LXLXS*, July 1999, 338.

12. Liao Yiwu, preface to Liu Xia, *Empty Chairs* (New York: Graywolf Press, 2015), xii.

13. Zhou Zhongling 周忠陵, "为刘晓波刘霞诗集而作" [For Liu Xiaobo and Liu Xia's poetry collection], *LXLXS* 16.

14. *LXLXS*, December 1992, 376–377.

15. Zhou Zhongling 周忠陵, "For Liu Xiaobo and Liu Xia's Poetry Collection," *LXLXS* 17.

16. Liu Xiaobo, "五分钟的赞美: 给霞" [Praise in five minutes: For Xia], July 11, 1993, *LXLXS* 45–47.

17. Liu Xiaobo, "危险的欢乐: 给霞" [Dangerous merriment: For Xia], June 21, 1993, *LXLXS* 43–44.

18. Liu Xiaobo, "某天早晨: 给一个人去西藏的霞" [One morning: For Xia, who went to Tibet alone], July 14, 1993, LXLXS 48–50, translated by Nick Admussen in *NENH* 267–268.

19. No author cited, "六四前一帮人激动表态要回国, 只有刘晓波回去了" [Before June Fourth a bunch of people were excited about returning to China, but only Liu Xiaobo did it], *Voice of America*, July 1, 2017, https://www.wenxuecity.com/news/2017/07/01/6360644.html.

20. Bei Ming 北明, "刘霞的世界: 与刘霞碎语" [Liu Xia's world: Random talk with Liu Xia], *Boxun*, October 4, 2010, accessed February 25, 2020, http://blog.boxun.com/hero/201011/beiming/2_1.shtml.

21. Wen Yujie 温玉杰, "诗人的趣闻轶事" [Amusing anecdotes of a poet], accessed November 19, 2019, http://jida1977.blog.163.com/blog/static/1761682362011010034841355/.

22. Shao Jiang 邵江, "刘晓波的抵抗: 从民主墙到互联网" [Liu Xiaobo's resistance: From Democracy Wall to the Internet], *Minzhu Zhongguo*, October 27, 2017, accessed July 22, 2019, http://minzhuzhongguo.org/MainArtShow.aspx?AID=92245.

23. Radio Free Asia, interview with Liu Xiaobo, October 1999, rebroadcast July 14, 2017, https://www.rfa.org/mandarin/zhuanlan/butongdeshengyin/jkdv-07142017162411.html.

24. Liao Yiwu 廖亦武, "刘晓波得诺奖: 选自出逃回忆录" [Liu Xiaobo wins the Nobel Prize: Selections from *Reminiscences of Escape*], January 23 to February 5, 2015, 中国人权双周刊 [China human rights bimonthly] 149, accessed March 7, 2020, http://biweeklyarchive.hrichina.org/article/24869.html.

25. Liu Xiaobo, "九十年代中国的政治保守主义" [Political conservatism in China in the 1990s], 北京之春 [Beijing spring], December 1996.

26. Liu Xiaobo, "九十年代中国的极端民族主义" [Extreme nationalism in China in the 1990s], originally drafted in July 1996, 北京之春 [Beijing spring], January 1997.

27. Here and below, much of our description of Xiaobo's *laojiao* experience is taken from Liu Xiaobo, "我的人身自由在十几分钟内被剥夺: 写在劳改基金会主办'苏联的古拉格和中国的劳改'国际研讨会即将召开之际" [My personal freedom was taken from me within fifteen minutes: Written at the opening of the international conference on "The Soviet Gulag and the Chinese Laogai" organized by The Laogai Foundation], 观察 [Observe China], April 29, 2006, accessed July 22, 2019, https://blog.boxun.com/hero/2006/liuxb/8_1.shtml.

28. Liu Xiaobo, "For Grandfather [in the Voice of Liu Xia]: For Liu Xia, Who Never Saw Her Maternal Grandfather."

29. Lin Qing 林青, "海内外民运简讯" [Notes on the democracy movement at home and abroad], 北京之春 [Beijing spring], February 1997, http://beijingspring.com/bj2/1997/440/20031215172843.htm.

30. Lin Qing, "Notes on the Democracy Movement at Home and Abroad."

31. Lin Qing, "Notes on the Democracy Movement at Home and Abroad."

32. He Zongan, "刘晓波等待两年多领到了结婚证" [Liu Xiaobo gets a marriage license after more than two years of waiting], Voice of America CHINA/DISSIDENT, April 22, 1998, accessed July 22, 2019, http://liuxiaobo.net/archives/19248.

33. Jiang Weiping 姜维平, "刘晓波在大连坐牢的日子" [Liu Xiaobo's days in prison in Dalian], *Kaifang*, August 2009; also known on the Internet under the title "我所知道的刘晓波" [What I know about Liu Xiaobo].

34. Lin Qing, "Notes on the Democracy Movement at Home and Abroad."

35. Jiang Weiping, "Liu Xiaobo's Days in Prison in Dalian."

36. Guy Sorman, *The Empire of Lies: The Truth About China in the Twenty-First Century* (New York: Encounter Books, 2008), 45.

37. Hu Ping 胡平 "刘霞的一封旧信 —'还刘霞自由'活动致辞" [An old letter from Liu Xia: Talk at the function to "Give Liu Xia Her Freedom Back"] accessed March 9, 2020, http://www.chinainperspective.com/ArtShow.aspx?AID=24298. We have changed the order of some of the sentences.

38. Liu Xia, "这就是我们的生活: 在国际笔会东京纪念会上的录像讲话" [This is our life: Videotaped talk at the memorial meeting in Tokyo of PEN International], accessed March 8, 2020, https://www.youtube.com/watch?v=ljhzrV1IzH8 and http://www.liu-xiaobo.org/blog/archives/16601.

39. Liu Xia, "This Is Our Life."

40. Liu Xia, "This Is Our Life."

41. *LXLXS* 193–196; translated by Nick Admussen in *NENH* 240–241. The poems cited in the next few pages all appear and are easy to find in *LXLXS*.

42. Translated by Isaac P. Hsieh in *NENH* 242–244.

43. *LXLXS* 93–94.

44. *LXLXS* 124.

45. *LXLXS* 412–414.

46. Composed October 9, 1998; published in *LXLXS*; translated by Nick Admussen in *NENH* 284–285.

47. Liu Xiaobo, "卡米尔·克罗岱尔致刘霞 —给我的妻子" [From Camille Claudel to Liu Xia—for my wife], *LXLXS* 125.

48. Hao Jian, videotaped interview with Liu Xiaobo shortly before arrest in 2008, https://www.youtube.com/watch?v=ry5nbyvfquk.

49. Liu Xiaobo, "公民不服从运动在中国的前景" [The future in China of citizens' not obeying movements], *Boxun*, October 9, 2005, accessed July 22, 2019, https://blog.boxun.com/hero/liuxb/445_1.shtml.

50. Liu Xiaobo, "从娃娃抓起的残忍—为文革三十五周年而作" [My cruelty began in infancy: Written for the thirty-fifth year of the Cultural Revolution], 民主中国 [Democratic China] 92 (April 2001), accessed July 22, 2019, http://www.liu-xiaobo.org/blog/archives/5616.

51. Liu Xiaobo, "恐怖对人性的摧残: 狱中读*1957*年的夏季" [The ravages of terror on human nature: Reading *Summer 1957* in prison], 新世纪网, [New century web], March 14, 1999, accessed February 25, 2020, http://www.liu-xiaobo.org/blog/archives/5385.

52. Translated by Burton Watson as *Records of the Grand Historian* (New York: Columbia University Press, 1961).

53. Liu Xiaobo, "读汉代学术史略" [Reading *Outline History of the Han Dynasty*], May 4, 1999, 议报 [Discussion], March 8, 2002, accessed July 22, 2019, http://www.liu-xiaobo.org/blog/archives/5392.

54. Liu Xiaobo, "铁窗后的福音: 狱中读书笔记" [The gospel behind bars: Reading notes from prison], 议报 [Discussion] 18 (December 1, 2001), accessed July 22, 2019, http://www.liu-xiaobo.org/blog/archives/5310.

55. Liu Xiaobo, "面对恐怖和死亡的从容: 狱中重读狱中书简" [Equanimity in the face of terror and death: Rereading *Letters from Prison* in prison], August 31, 1998, 大纪元 [Epoch times], November 15, 2003, http://www.epochtimes.com/gb/3/11/15/n411566.htm.

56. Radio Free Asia, interview with Liu Xiaobo, October 1999.

13. IN THE SERVICE OF UNDERDOGS

1. Zhu Xueqin 朱学勤, "1998，自由主义学理的言说" [Talks on the principles of liberalism, 1998], 南方周末 [Southern weekend], December 25, 1998.

2. He Weifang 贺卫方, "复转军人进法院" [Old soldiers go to court], 南方周末, January 2, 1998.

3. Liu Junning 刘军宁, "统治者" [Rulers], 南方周末, December 29, 1999.

4. Lao Xia 老侠 and Wang Shuo 王朔, 美人赠我蒙汗药 [A beauty gave me a knockout drug] (Wuchang: Changjiang wenyichubanshe, 2000), 16.

5. Lao Xia and Wang Shuo, *A Beauty Gave Me a Knockout Drug*, 39.

6. Lao Xia and Wang Shuo, *A Beauty Gave Me a Knockout Drug*, 40.

7. Lao Xia and Wang Shuo, *A Beauty Gave Me a Knockout Drug*, 41–42.

8. "给廖亦武的信" [A letter to Liao Yiwu]; *NENH* 287–288.

9. Yu Jie 余杰, 刘晓波传 [Biography of Liu Xiaobo] (Hong Kong: New Century Publishing House, 2012).

10. Liu Xiaobo, "我与互联网" [The Internet and me], *Minzhu Zhongguo* [Democratic China], February 18, 2006, accessed July 22, 2019, https://blog.boxun.com/hero/liuxb/513_1.shtml; translated by Louisa Chiang as "Long Live the Internet" in *NENH* 203–210.

11. Liu Xiaobo, "The Internet and Me."

12. Liu Xiaobo, "请小布什自我珍重" [Respect yourself, please, Bush Jr.], 人民网 [People's web], February 14, 2002, accessed July 22, 2019, https://www.chineseopen.org/blog/archives/102088.

13. Liu Xiaobo, "迎接奥运, 释放政治犯" [Welcome the Olympics, release political prisoners] 苹果日报 [Apple daily], July 16, 2001.

14. Liu Xiaobo, "除夕夜, 记住那些破碎的家庭" [On New Year's eve, let's not forget the broken families], 观察 [Observe China], January 20, 2002, https://docs.google.com/document/d/17Ghprl5au J5eLJuktxvEqQ4CdxQwDYPK40kmQhhQTUs/edit.

15. Liu Xiaobo, "镇压下的辉煌" [Brilliance under repression], *Kaifang* [Open] 3 (2000), https://www .chineseopen.org/blog/archives/93087; "被扼杀两次的孩子" [Twice-strangled children], *Dajiyuan*, March 16, 2001, https://www.chineseopen.org/blog/archives/93099; "法轮功与价值多元化" [Falun Gong and diversity in values], *Dajiyuan*, December 28, 2002, http://www.epochtimes.com/gb/2 /12/20/n257716.htm; "迫害法轮功的新罪名" [The new crime of persecuting Falun Gong], *Minzhu Zhongguo*, January 10, 2003, "Democracy Forum," https://www.secretchina.com/news/gb/2003 /01/17/32330.html.

16. Liu Xiaobo, "法轮功与人权意识的普及" [Falun Gong and the spread of human rights consciousness] 大纪元, December 19, 2002; "在恐惧和利诱中学会无耻" [How terror and self-interest teach shamelessness] and "向良心说谎的民族" [A nation that lies to its conscience], both originally published in 2001, are collected in 向良心说谎的民族 [A nation that lies to its conscience] (Taipei: Taiwan jieyou chubanshe, 2002).

17. Liu Xiaobo, "来自坟墓的震撼: '六四' 十一周年祭'" [A jolt from the graves: Remembering the eleventh anniversary of "June Fourth"], accessed September 9, 2019, http://www.liu-xiaobo.org/blog /archives/5520.

18. An expanded version was published: Ding Zilin 丁子霖, 寻访六四受难者 [In search of the victims of June Fourth] (Hong Kong: Kaifang zazhishe, 2005).

19. Liu Xiaobo, "A Jolt from the Graves."

20. Liu Xiaobo, "A Jolt from the Graves."

21. Liu Xiaobo, "A Jolt from the Graves."

22. Liu Xiaobo, "倾听天安门母亲的声音" [Listen carefully to the voices of the Tiananmen Mothers].

23. Liu Xiaobo, "我认识的杨子立和路坤" [Yang Zili and Lu Kun as I have known them], accessed September 9, 2019, https://blog.boxun.com/hero/liuxb/9_1.shtml.

24. Mo Shaoping 莫少平, "徐伟、杨子立、靳海科、张宏海等人涉嫌颠覆国家政权罪案辩护词" [Legal defense of Xu Wei, Yang Zili, Jin Haike, Zhang Honghai, and others against criminal charges of subversion of state power], accessed September 9, 2019, https://www.boxun.com/news/gb/china /2003/11/200311120832.shtml.

25. Liu Xiaobo, "心牢中的女人" [A woman in a mental prison], written at home in Beijing, August 31, 2001, accessed July 22, 2019, http://www.liu-xiaobo.org/blog/archives/5864. In this essay Xiaobo refers to Xu Wei's girlfriend as Wang Ying 王英, but her name was Wang Li 王丽. We do not know whether this was a mistake or a protective measure.

26. Liu Xiaobo, "人权人士呼吁释放原新青年学会四君子" [Human rights people call for the release of the four gentlemen founders of the New Youth Study Association], accessed September 9, 2019, https://www.rfa.org/mandarin/yataibaodao/humanrights-20080122.html.

27. Liu Xiaobo, "灰色: 既生存又抗争" [In the gray area: Resisting while surviving], *Minzhu Zhongguo*, March 2002, accessed July 22, 2019, https://www.chinesepen.org/blog/archives/102099.

28. See Mo Li 茉莉, "報刊遭整肅, 中國知識界「有話要說」" [A newspaper is purged, but Chinese intellectuals 'have things to say'"], accessed March 12, 2021, https://www.secretchina.com/news/b5/2001/09/11/102900.html.

29. Fan Zhongyan 范仲淹, "Lingwu fu" 灵乌赋 [Ode to a spirited raven], https://so.gushiwen.cn/shiwenv_16535151d5b1.aspx.

30. "Stray Birds 49" (1916), https://sacred-texts.com/hin/tagore/strybrds.htm.

31. Liu Xiaobo, "In the Gray Area."

32. Liu Xiaobo, "In the Gray Area."

33. Liu Xiaobo, "In the Gray Area."

34. Liu Xiaobo, "In the Gray Area."

35. Wan Yanhai 万延海, "Shibanianqian de jintian, wo shoudao weisheng dangzu de chufen" 十八年前的今天, 我受到卫生党组的处分 [Eighteen years ago I was punished by the Party group for public health], May 11, 2011, accessed July 22, 2019, https://www.chinanews.co/news/gb/china/2011/05/201105110822.shtml.

36. Liu Xiaobo, "万延海失踪, 是被捕还是被绑架?" [Is the disappearance of Wan Yanhai an arrest or a kidnapping?], September 1, 2002, accessed July 22, 2019, http://www.liu-xiaobo.org/blog/archives/6141.

37. Liu Xiaobo, "诚实地说出常识的良知: 祭李慎之先生" [Honest articulation of the common sense of conscience: Commemorating Mr. Li Shenzhi], 民主论坛, June 10, 2003, accessed July 22, 2019, https://blog.boxun.com/hero/liuxb/79_2.shtml.

38. Liu Xiaobo, "一体化的大众驯服" [Unified mass taming], *Minzhu Zhongguo*, October 2002, https://www.chinesepen.org/blog/archives/108061.

39. Liu Xiaobo, "精神缺席的中国精英" [The AWOL spirits of Chinese elites], *Boxun*, November 8, 2002, accessed July 22, 2019, https://www.boxun.com/news/gb/pubvp/2002/11/200211080353.shtml.

40. Liu Xiaobo, "The AWOL Spirits of Chinese Elites."

14. CASCADING CASES BUILD A MOVEMENT

1. Liu Junning 刘军宁, "观'黄'事件的深层意义" [The deep meaning of the "watching pornography" incident], 南方周末 [Southern weekend], November 11, 2002.

2. Liu Xiaobo, "抗议中共审判何德普" [Protest the Communists' sentencing of He Depu], 大纪元 [Epoch times], October 17, 2003, http://www.epochtimes.com/gb/3/10/18/n395900.htm.

3. Liu Xiaobo, "人权意识的觉醒和政治改革" [The awakening of human rights consciousness and political reform], 北京之春 [Beijing spring], February 2003.

4. In February 2008, Xiaobo explained this technique and gave examples in an essay, "当代文字狱与民间舆论救济" [Contemporary literary prisons and help from public opinion], *RYRQ*, March 2008, translated by Louisa Chiang as "Imprisoning People for Words and the Power of Public Opinion" in *NENH* 211–220.

5. The two articles were "传媒的趋势与政治改革: 三论未来的自由中国在民间" [Media trends and political reform: The dawn of a free China lies in civil awakening, part III], 北京之春 [Beijing spring], March 2003; "大陆媒体民间化努力" [Efforts on the mainland to bring the media into civil society], BBC Chinese.com, April 16, 2003, http://news.bbc.co.uk/hi/chinese/china_news/newsid_2952000/29528191.stm. The quotation is from the former.

6. Matt Pottinger et al., "Outraged Surgeon Forces China to Swallow a Dose of the Truth," *The Wall Street Journal*, April 22, 2003.

7. Liu Xiaobo, "民间维权运动的胜利" [Victories for the popular rights movement], BBC Chinese.com, July 16, 2003, http://news.bbc.co.uk/chinese/simp/hi/newsid_3070000/newsid_3071100/3071189.stm.

8. No author cited, "湖南女教师裸死案终审裁定被告获判无罪" [The accused is judged to be not guilty in the final ruling in the case of the death of the naked Hunan schoolteacher], 长沙晚报 [Changsha evening news], December 8, 2007.

9. Liu Xiaobo, "三岁李思怡之死拷问灵魂" [The death of three-year-old Li Siyi should impale our souls], 观察 [Observe China], July 2003, accessed July 22, 2019, https://www.boxun.com/news/gb/yuanqing/2003/07/200307151247.shtml.

10. Wang Xin 王欣, ed., "反乙肝歧视: 不仅仅是1.2亿人的胜利" [Oppose bias against hepatitis B: It's more than just a victory for 120 million people], 人民网 [People's web], August 6, 2004, accessed July 22, 2019, http://www.people.com.cn/GB/shehui/1063/2691794.html.

11. Liu Xiaobo, "保护私产: 修宪与反修宪之争" [Protect private property: The controversy over constitutionalism], 民主中国 *Minzhu Zhongguo*, May 2003, accessed July 22, 2019, https://www.chinesepen.org/blog/archives/108734; republished in 未来的自由中国在民间 [The dawn of a free China lies in civil awakening] (Washington, D.C.: The Laogai Foundation, 2005), 171–186.

12. Liu Xiaobo, "强烈抗议湖北省孝感地区应城市公安局逮捕杜导斌" [Strongly denounce the arrest of Du Daobin by the Public Security Bureau in the Xiaogan district in Hubei], December 30, 2003, accessed July 22, 2019, http://www.liu-xiaobo.org/blog/archives/13224.

13. Liu Xiaobo, "'我也愿意陪杜导斌、刘荻、杨子立坐牢!' 丁子霖、蒋培坤夫妇关注杜导斌" ["We too are willing to go to jail with Du Daobin, Liu Di, and Yang Zili!": Ding Zilin and Jiang Peikun on Du Daobin], *Epoch Times*, November 4, 2003, http://www.epochtimes.com/gb/3/11/4/n405653.htm.

14. Zhang Yu 张裕, "刘晓波诺奖无敌" [Liu Xiaobo's Nobel Prize has no enemies], 民主中国 *Minzhu Zhongguo*, October 23, 2017, accessed July 22, 2019, http://minzhuzhongguo.org/MainArtShow.aspx?AID=92248.

15. Liu Xiaobo, "2003年担任独立中文笔会会长就职说明" [An explanation upon assuming the presidency on Independent Chinese PEN in 2003], published in an internal forum of Chinese PEN, accessed January 4, 2020, http://www.liu-xiaobo.org/blog/archives/8515.

16. Yu Shicun 余世存, "2004第二届自由写作奖颁奖侧记" [Notes from the sidelines at the awards ceremony for the second awarding of the Freedom in Writing Award], Chinese PEN online, accessed January 4, 2020, https://www.chinesepen.org/old-posts/?paged=70&author=1.

17. Liu Xiaobo, "被炒作的革命—透视切·格瓦拉现象" [Revolution hyped: Seeing through the "Che Guevara" phenomenon], accessed January 4, 2020, http://www.liu-xiaobo.org/blog/archives/5584.

18. Yu Jie 余杰, "我无罪: 刘晓波传" [I am innocent: A biography of Liu Xiaobo] (Hong Kong: Xin shiji chubanshe, 2012), 290–291.

19. Liu Xiaobo, "从版主王怡的辞职谈起" [The resignation of webpage manager Wang Yi and what it means], 民主中国 *Minzhu Zhongguo,* March 2002, accessed July 22, 2019, https://www.chinesepen.org/blog/archives/102094.

20. Liu Xiaobo, "The Awakening of Human Rights Consciousness and Political Reform."

21. Liu Xiaobo, "民间维权萧杀中成长 (下)" [Civil society grows in a harsh environment, part III], accessed January 4, 2020, http://www.epochtimes.com/gb/3/11/26/n418342.htm.

22. Liu Xiaobo, "但愿杜导斌是又一个刘荻" [Here's hoping Du Daobin is another Liu Di], 观察 [Observe China], February 12, 2004, https://www.chinesepen.org/blog/archives/109112.

23. Liu Xiaobo, Wang Yi 王怡, Yu Jie 余杰, et al., "要求对"煽动颠覆国家政权罪"作出司法解释的呼吁信" [A call for a legal explanation of "the crime of agitating to subvert state power"], February 1, 2004, 北京之春 [Beijing spring], March 2004, http://beijingspring.com/bj2/2004/200/2004227232136.htm.

24. Liu Xiaobo, "受难母亲的泪与爱: 献给被捕的丁子霖、张先玲、黄金平" [The tears and the love of distressed mothers: An offering to the arrested Ding Zilin, Zhang Xianling, and Huang Jinping], 大纪元 [Epoch times], March 31, 2004, https://www.epochtimes.com/b5/4/3/31/n497378.htm.

25. Ding Zilin and Jiang Peikun, "我们与晓波的相知、相识和相交（上）" [Our knowledge, familiarity, and relations with Xiaobo (part I)], accessed February 25, 2020, http://www.tiananmenmother.org /tiananmenmother/m100116001.htm.

26. In Chinese: 谁要是不想干，今天打报告就可以滚蛋。

27. Liu Xiaobo, "新闻良知蔑视小官僚面孔: 有感于中国青年报记者卢跃刚的公开信" [A journalist with a conscience shows contempt for the face of a minor functionary: An open letter on my feelings about the *China Youth News* journalist Lu Yuegang], 争鸣 [Contending], August 2004.

28. Liu Xiaobo, "体制内异见力量不再沉默" [Dissenting views within the system are silent no longer], 民主中国 *Minzhu Zhongguo*, October 2004, https://www.chinesepen.org/blog/archives/109346.

29. Liu Xiaobo, *The Dawn of a Free China Lies in Civil Awakening*, 357.

30. Liu Xiaobo, "Dissenting Views Within the System Are Silent No Longer," *Minzhu Zhongguo*, October 2004, reprinted in *The Dawn of a Free China Lies in Civil Awakening*, 381. This was not the first time Xiaobo mentioned the Nobel Peace Prize, however. In early 2002 he had made similar comments in "中国民间反对派的贫困—'六四'十三周年祭" [The poverty of the opposition in China: On the thirteenth anniversary of "June Fourth"], 民主中国 *Minzhu Zhongguo*, June 2002, https://www.chinesepen.org/blog/archives/103098.

31. Liu Xiaobo, "捍卫文明常识的贺卫方" [He Weifang, defender of civilized common sense], 大纪元 [Epoch times], September 24, 2004, http://www.epochtimes.com/gb/4/9/24/n670454.htm.

32. Zhang Yihe 章诒和, 往事并不如烟 [The past is not just smoke] (Beijing: Renmin wenxue chubanshe, 2004).

33. Yu Shicun, "Notes from the Sidelines at the Awards Ceremony for the Second Awarding of the Freedom in Writing Award."

34. Liu Xiaobo, "师涛没有秘密" [Shi Tao has no secrets], 大纪元 [Epoch times], accessed January 4, 2020, http://www.epochtimes.com/gb/4/12/6/n738499.htm.

35. Hu Ping 胡平, "从若干小事看刘晓波的人品" [A few small things that reveal Liu Xiaobo's character], Radio Free Asia, August 2, 2017, https://www.rfa.org/mandarin/pinglun/huping/hp -08022017142010.html.

36. Liu Xiaobo, "就师涛案致雅虎公司董事长杨致远的公开信" [An open letter to Yahoo! CEO Jerry Yang on the Shi Tao affair], 观察 [Observe China], 2005, accessed July 22, 2019, https://blog.boxun .com/hero/liuxb/444_1.shtml.

37. 观察网, "雅虎用户资料外泄愿增赔偿金至1.17亿美元 [Yahoo! is ready to increase its compensation for releasing subscribers' data to US$117,000,000], accessed August 24, 2020, https://www.guancha .cn/ChanJing/2019_04_11_497264.shtml.

15. AN INTELLECTUAL TRANSITION

1. Liu Xiaobo, "我的感激: 政治严寒中的民间温暖" [My gratitude: Warmth from society amid a freeze in politics], *Boxun,* January 2005, accessed July 22, 2019, https://blog.boxun.com/hero /liuxb/254_1.shtml.

2. Liu Xiaobo, "通过改变社会来改变政权" [To change a regime by changing a society], 观察 [Boxun], February 26, 2006, translated by Perry Link in *NENH* 26; and "民间权利意识在觉醒: 著名作家刘晓波谈中国独立民间社会当前的发展" [Awareness of rights is growing among the people: The famous writer Liu Xiaobo talks about current developments in independent society], interview by Yang Yi 杨逸, December 18, 2007, published in 参与 [Participation], December 19, 2007, accessed July 22, 2019, https://news.boxun.com/news/gb/china/2007/12/200712190609.shtml.

3. Zhu Xueqin 朱学勤, "让人为难的罗素" [The challenging Mr. Russell], 读书 [Reading], January 1996, 9.

4. Liu Xiaobo, 未来的民主中国在民间 [The dawn of a free China lies in civil awakening] (Washington, D.C.: The Laogai Foundation, 2005), 209, 216.

5. Liu Xiaobo, "村民自治的发展及其意义: 四论未来的自由中国在民间" [The growth of village self-rule and its significance: Free China dawning, no. 4], 北京之春 [Beijing spring], April 2003.

6. Liu Xiaobo, "民间的升值与政治民主化" [The rising value of civil society and political democratization], *Boxun*, February 2003, accessed July 22, 2019, https://blog.boxun.com/hero/liuxb/57_1.shtml.

7. Liu Xiaobo, "再论村民自治与党权退出: 六论未来的自由中国在民间" [A second discussion of village self-rule and the retreat of the Party: Free China dawning, no. 6], 北京之春 [Beijing spring], June 2003. See also "中国农民的土地宣言" [The land manifestoes of Chinese farmers], translated by A. E. Clark in *NENH* 30–36.

8. Liu Xiaobo, "The Rising Value of Civil Society and Political Democratization."

9. Re-published in Liu Xiaobo, *The Dawn of a Free China Lies in Civil Awakening*, 27–227.

10. Liu Xiaobo, "迷途知返的深层动力" [The underlying power of mending one's ways], *RYRQ*, February 2005, accessed January 5, 2020, https://www.chinesepen.org/blog/archives/109439.

11. Liu Xiaobo, "The Underlying Power of Mending One's Ways."

12. Liu Xiaobo, "The Underlying Power of Mending One's Ways."

13. Liu Xiaobo, "未来的自由中国在民间: 中国政改的有利条件" [The dawn of a free China lies in civil awakening: Opportune conditions for political reform in China], 北京之春 [Beijing spring], January 2003.

14. Liu Xiaobo, "灰色: 既生存又抗争" [In the gray area: Resisting while surviving], 民主中国 *Minzhu Zhongguo*, March 2002, https://www.chinesepen.org/blog/archives/102099.

15. Liu Xiaobo, *The Dawn of a Free China Lies in Civil Awakening*.

16. Liu Xiaobo, *The Dawn of a Free China Lies in Civil Awakening*.

17. Abridged from Liu Xiaobo, "民间觉醒时代的政治转型" [Political transition in the era of an awakening civil society], *RYRQ*, October 2005.

18. Liu Xiaobo, *The Dawn of a Free China Lies in Civil Awakening*, 320.

19. Liu Xiaobo, "通过改变社会来改变政权" [To change a regime by changing a society], 观察, February 26, 2006, translated by Perry Link in *NENH* 26.

20. Liu Xiaobo, *The Dawn of a Free China Lies in Civil Awakening*, 328.

21. Liu Xiaobo, *The Dawn of a Free China Lies in Civil Awakening*, 331.

22. Martin Luther King, "Letter from a Birmingham Jail," April 16, 1963; quoted in Liu Xiaobo, *The Dawn of a Free China Lies in Civil Awakening*, 332.

23. Yang Yi, "Awareness of Rights Is Growing Among the People."

24. Liu Xiaobo, "维权面对利益党的自我调整" [The rights movement faces self-correction by a party of private interests], 争鸣 [Contending], December 2006, accessed July 22, 2019, https://blog.boxun.com/hero/2006/liuxb/83_2.shtml.

25. Liu Xiaobo, "To Change a Regime by Changing a Society."

26. Liu Xiaobo, "我想为捍卫生命、和平与自由而战: 献给大灾难中的殉难者" [I want to fight to protect life, peace, and freedom: An offering to the victims of a great disaster], 民主论坛 [Democracy forum], September 2001, accessed July 22, 2019, http://www.liu-xiaobo.org/blog/archives/18024.

27. Bao Zunxin, Liu Xiaobo, Ren Bumei 任不寐, Liao Yiwu, Yu Jie, Xie Yong 谢泳, Liu Suli 刘苏里, Zhao Cheng 赵诚, Wang Tong 王童, Xiao Shu 笑蜀, Fan Baihua 樊百华, Xiao Han 萧瀚, Chen Weiwei 陈威威, and Liu Xia 刘霞, "致布希总统和美国人民" [To President Bush and the American people], 北京之春 [Beijing spring], October 2001.

28. Liu Xiaobo, "倒萨之战与联合国权威" [The war to topple Saddam and the authority of the United Nations], *Boxun*, March 18, 2003, accessed July 22, 2019, https://blog.boxun.com/hero/liuxb/65_1.shtml.

29. See the following articles, published under the general title "自由国家在二十世纪的四大失误" [The four big mistakes of the free countries in the twentieth century] but with the following subtitles:

"第一大错误：三十年代迷失于"斯大林热" [Big mistake number one: Lost in "Stalin fever" in the 1930s], 北京之春 [Beijing spring], November 2005.

"第二大错误：自由英法向极权德意的无原则妥协" [Big mistake number two: England and France, both free, make unprincipled compromises with the German and Italian dictatorships], 北京之春 [Beijing spring], November 29, 2005.

"第三大错误：自由美英向极权苏联的让步" [Big mistake number three: The United States and England, both free, make concessions to the Soviet dictatorship], 北京之春 [Beijing spring], January 2006.

"第四大错误：六、七十年代迷失于"毛泽东热" [Big mistake number four: Lost in "Mao Zedong fever" in the 1960s and 1970s], 北京之春 [Beijing spring], February 2006.

30. Vaclav Havel, "Politics and Conscience," in *Open Letters: Selected Writings, 1965–1990* (London: Faber & Faber, 1991), 266.

31. Referring to an article by Sartre called "我对新中国的观感," published in the *People's Daily* on November 2, 1955, Liu Xiaobo wrote "萨特说，反共产主义者是条狗" [Sartre says opponents of communism are dogs], 民主中国 *Minzhu Zhongguo*, November 3, 2005, accessed July 22, 2019, https://blog.boxun.com/hero/liuxb/470_1.shtml.

32. Liu Xiaobo, "'新左'的面具" [The masks of the "new left"], 观察 [Boxun], February 11, 2003, https://blog.boxun.com/hero/liuxb/55_1.shtml.

33. Liu Xiaobo, "记住被恐怖分子屠戮的孩子" [Remember the children slaughtered by the terrorists], 大纪元 [Epoch times], September 4, 2005, accessed September 9, 2019, https://blog.boxun.com/hero/liuxb/198_1.shtml.

16. STABILITY MAINTENANCE

1. Yu Jianrong 于建嵘, "Disturbance Incidents and Management Crisis in China," October, 2007; see Mainland Affairs Council, Republic of China, "Briefing Room," December 28, 2007, accessed September 9, 2019, https://www.mac.gov.tw/en/News_Content.aspx?n=C4319C691F14B564&sms=F6A174A7F58D9580&s=39DD131DFE110C04. See also Murray Scott Tanner, "Chinese Government Responses to Rising Social Unrest: Testimony Presented to the US-China Economic and Security Review Commission on April 14, 2005" (Rand Corporation, 2005), 2.

2. Zhang Zanbo 张赞波, "艾未未谈刘晓波他的价值不是拿诺贝尔奖" [Ai Weiwei discusses why the value of Liu Xiaobo is not in his winning the Nobel Prize], 报道者 [Reporter], October 17, 2017, https://www.twreporter.org/a/interview-ai-weiwei-3.

3. Zhao Ziyang 赵紫阳, 改革历程 [The course of reform] (Hong Kong: Xinshiji chubanshe, 2009). Translated by Bao Pu and published in English as *Prisoner of the State: The Secret Journal of Premier Zhao Ziyang* (New York: Simon and Schuster, 2009).

4. Liu Xiaobo, "悲情的赵紫阳和胡耀邦" [The sorrows of Zhao Ziyang and Hu Yaobang], 民主中国 [Democratic China], accessed March 14, 2020, http://minzhuzhongguo.org/filedata/137issue/137_3_tg1.htm.

5. Liu Xiaobo, "与其等待黎明 不如冲破黑暗" [Better to break through the murk than to wait for the dawn], 独立中文笔会 [Boxun], January 17, 2005, accessed July 22, 2019, https://blog.boxun.com/hero/liuxb/245_1.shtml; "记住紫阳" [Remember Ziyang] (January 18, 2005), 争鸣 [Contending],

February 2005, https://blog.boxun.com/hero/liuxb/259_1.shtml; and "赵紫阳创造的奇迹" [The miracles wrought by Zhao Ziyang] (January 19, 2005), 开放 [Open], February 2005.

6. Liu Xiaobo, "赖斯来了, 警察又上岗" [Rice arrives and the police go on guard again], 大纪元 [Epoch times], March 20, 2005, https://www.peacehall.com/news/gb/pubvp/2005/03/200503211715 .shtml.

7. Liu Lu 刘路, "刺穿黑暗的朝霞: 谨以此文献给晓波老师53岁生日" [Bright morning clouds break the darkness: Offering this essay to teacher Xiaobo on his 53rd birthday], *Boxun*, December 25, 2008, accessed September 9, 2019, https://blog.boxun.com/hero/200812/wmm/20_1.shtml.

8. Liu Xiaobo, "唐家璇的脸皮真够厚" [Tang Jiaxuan's skin is plenty thick], 民主中国 [Democratic China], November 17, 2005, accessed September 9, 2019, https://blog.boxun.com/hero/liuxb/463 _1.shtml.

9. Liu Xiaobo, "公开的谎言, 无耻的狡辩" [Public lies, shameless sophistry], 民主论坛 [Democracy forum], February 15, 2006, accessed September 9, 2019, https://blog.boxun.com/hero/liuxb/511_1 .shtml.

10. Xiao Shu 笑蜀, 历史的先声: 半个世纪前的庄严承诺 [Harbingers of history: The solemn promises of fifty years ago] (Shantou: Shantou daxue chubanshe, 1999).

11. Liu Xiaobo, "用谎言写就的悼词: 为拯救历史和恢复记忆而作" [Using lies to do a eulogy: Written in the cause of saving history and restoring memory], 中国之春 [China spring], August 3, 2001, accessed September 9, 2019, http://www.liu-xiaobo.org/blog/archives/5844.

12. "一党独裁, 遍地成灾" [One-party dictatorship brings disaster everywhere], 新华日报 [New China daily], March 30, 1946.

13. Mao Zedong 毛泽东, "论人民民主专政" [On the people's democratic dictatorship] (June 30, 1949), in 毛泽东选集 [Selected works of Mao Zedong], vol. 4 (Beijing: Renmin chubanshe, 1991), 1468–1482.

14. See chapter 13.

15. The term appears in "混世魔王毛泽东" [Devil incarnate Mao Zedong], 解放月报 [Emancipation monthly], November 1988; reprinted August 1989.

16. Liu Xiaobo, "共产极权是人类历史上最大的强盗: 四论共产极权为野蛮之最" [Communist authoritarianism is the greatest thief in human history: The extremes of communist authoritarianism's incivility, no. 4], 大纪元 [Epoch times], August 15, 2005, http://www.epochtimes.com/gb/5/8/16 /n1020087.htm.

17. Liu Xiaobo, "比奴隶制还要野蛮的共产极权: 论共产极权为野蛮之最之一" [Communist authoritarianism is the greatest thief in human history: The extremes of communist authoritarianism's incivility, no. 1], 大纪元 [Epoch times], July 11, 2005, https://www.epochtimes.com/b5/5/7/12 /n982777.htm.

18. Liu Xiaobo, "难道中国人只配接受党内民主?" [Can it be that Chinese people qualify only to live under inner-party democracy?], 观察 [Observe China], January 6, 2006, accessed September 9, 2019, https://blog.boxun.com/hero/liuxb/487_1.shtml.

19. Liu Xiaobo, "独裁者的道德狂妄" [The moral arrogance of dictators], 大纪元 [Epoch times], November 4, 2001, accessed September 9, 2019, http://www.liu-xiaobo.org/blog/archives/5917.

20. Liu Xiaobo, "跛足改革带来的统治危机" [The crisis in governance brought by crippled reform] (January 15, 2006), 争鸣 [Contending], February 2006.

21. Liu Xiaobo, "制度性的'为富不仁'" [A systemic version of "the rich cannot be moral"] (April 14, 2006), 争鸣 [Contending], May 2006.

22. Liu Xiaobo, "老外看不懂中共官僚" [Why foreigners can't understand Chinese Communist officials], 大纪元 [Epoch times], March 24, 2006, http://www.epochtimes.com/gb/6/3/24/n1264986.htm.

23. Liu Xiaobo, "不断蜕变的中共独裁" [The ceaselessly changing Chinese Communist dictatorship] (July 30, 2006), *Minzhu Zhongguo*, August 2006, accessed July 22, 2019, https://blog.boxun.com /hero/2006/liuxb/44_2.shtml.

24. Liu Xiaobo, "中共寡头独裁的衰败" [The decline of the Chinese Communist oligarchic dictatorship], 大纪元 [Epoch times], February 13, 2007, http://www.epochtimes.com/gb/7/2/16/n1624572.htm.

25. Liu Xiaobo, "The Ceaselessly Changing Chinese Communist Dictatorship."

26. Liu Xiaobo, "权贵家族与政治改革" [Families of the power elite and political reform], 中国之春 [China spring], March 20, 2001.

27. Liu Xiaobo, "多面的中共独裁" [The many sides of the Chinese communist dictatorship], 观察 [Observe China], March 13, 2006, accessed July 22, 2019, https://blog.boxun.com/hero/liuxb/525_1.shtml. Xiaobo had presaged this analysis in 2003 in "恶法治国及其受害者: 评孙大午非法融资案" [Bad law and its victims: On the Sun Dawu illegal finance case], *RYRQ*, September 2003, accessed July 22, 2019, http://www.renyurenquan.org/ren yu renquan_article@article_id=212.html.

28. Liu Xiaobo, "The Ceaselessly Changing Chinese Communist Dictatorship."

17. OBSERVING THE WORLD, GROWING AT HOME

1. Liu Xiaobo, "崩溃论与稳定论的互补" [The synergy of the theory of collapse and the theory of stability], 动向 [The trend], September 19, 2006, accessed July 22, 2019, https://www.boxun.com/news/gb/pubvp/2006/09/200609192042.shtml.

2. Liu Xiaobo, "不断蜕变的中共独裁" [The ceaselessly changing Chinese communist dictatorship] (July 30, 2006), *Minzhu Zhongguo*, August 2006, accessed July 22, 2019, https://blog.boxun.com/hero/2006/liuxb/44_2.shtml.

3. Liu Xiaobo, "独裁中共对自由西方的灵活应对" [The flexible responses to the free West by the dictatorial Chinese communists], BBC Chinese.com, December 10, 2007, http://news.bbc.co.uk/chinese/simp/hi/newsid_7130000/newsid_7136200/7136265.stm.

4. Liu Xiaobo, "请小布什自我珍重" [Let's hope Bush, Jr. shows self-respect], 人民网 [People's web], February 14, 2002, accessed July 22, 2019, https://www.chineseopen.org/blog/archives/102088.

5. Liu Xiaobo, "我看美国对中国的核心战略" [My view of America's core strategy toward China], *RYRQ*, January 2006, accessed July 22, 2019, https://blog.boxun.com/hero/liuxb/496_1.shtml.

6. Liu Xiaobo, "中共崛起对于世界民主化的负面效应" [The negative effects of the rise of the Chinese Communists on democratization in the world], BBC Chinese.com, May 3, 2006, http://news.bbc.co.uk/chinese/simp/hi/newsid_4960000/newsid_4969600/4969676.stm.

7. Liu Xiaobo, "独裁崛起对世界民主化的负面效应," April 21, 2006, accessed July 22, 2019, https://blog.boxun.com/hero/2006/liuxb/12_1.shtml (a different version of the article cited in the previous note).

8. Liu Xiaobo, 单刀毒剑: 中国民族主义批判 [Single-blade poison sword: A critique of contemporary Chinese nationalism] (Pasadena, CA: Boda chubanshe 博大出版, 2006).

9. Liu Xiaobo, "新世纪大陆爱国主义的转向" [The change in direction of mainland nationalism in the new century], BBC Chinese.com, June 19, 2002, http://news.bbc.co.uk/hi/chinese/china_news/newsid_2053000/20538561.stm.

10. Liu Xiaobo, "召之来挥之去的反日风潮" [Anti-Japan tempests on demand] (April 20, 2005), *RYRQ*, May 2005, accessed July 22, 2019, http://www.liu-xiaobo.org/blog/archives/7129.

11. Liu Xiaobo, "政治奥运 腐败奥运" [A political Olympics, a corrupt Olympics], 开放 [Open], September 2007.

12. Liu Xiaobo, "金牌崇拜与独裁民族主义" [The worship of gold medals and dictatorial nationalism], *RYRQ*, September 2008, accessed July 22, 2019, http://www.renyurenquan.org/ren tu renquan_article@article_id=986.html.

13. Liu Xiaobo, "中共奥运战略的金牌综合症" [The gold medal syndrome in the Olympics strategy of the Chinese Communists] (September 18, 2008), 争鸣 [Contending], September 2008;

translated by A. E. Clark in *NENH* as "The Communist Party's Olympic Gold Medal Syndrome," 245–256.

14. Bao Tong, interview by Cai Wenbin 蔡文彬, Beijing, summer 2018.

15. Hu Fayun 胡发云, *Ruyan@SARS.come* (Beijing: Zhongguo guoji guangbo chubanshe, 2006); translated by A. E. Clark as *Such Is This World@SARS.come* (Dobbs Ferry, NY: Ragged Banner Press, 2011).

16. Liu Xiaobo, "有感于著名作家胡发云支持四十人建议书" [My feelings on how the famed author Hu Fayun has supported the suggestions of the forty], 观察 [Observe China], republished in *Boxun*, August 8, 2007, accessed July 22, 2019, https://www.boxun.com/news/gb/pubvp/2007/08/20070808 0504.shtml.

17. Liu Xiaobo, "高智晟律师的启示" [The lesson of lawyer Gao Zhisheng], 民主中国 *Minzhu Zhongguo*, November 6, 2005, accessed July 22, 2019, https://blog.boxun.com/hero/liuxb/458_1.shtml.

18. Liu Xiaobo, "The Lesson of Lawyer Gao Zhisheng."

19. Ji Shuoming 纪硕鸣 and Wang Jianmin 王健民, "中国维权律师法制先锋" [Leaders in the rule of law among China's rights lawyers], 亚洲周刊 [Asia weekly] 19, no. 52 (December 25, 2005).

20. Ding Zilin, "致高智晟公开信：请回到维权的行列中来" [An open letter to Gao Zhisheng: Please return to the ranks of rights-support lawyers], *Boxun*, April 23, 2006, accessed July 22, 2019, https://boxun.com/news/gb/china/2006/02/200602232225.shtml.

21. Liu Xiaobo, "独裁制度对人的道德谋杀" [How a dictatorial system murders human morality], *RYRQ*, March 20, 2007, accessed July 22, 2019, http://www.renyurenquan.org/ren yu requan_article@article_id=634.html.

22. ChinaAid news, "中国自由状况高峰会本周在美国首府华盛顿召开；范亚峰，高智晟，张星水被当局阻挠出席" [Summit meeting on freedom in China to be held in Washington, the American capital: The regime blocks Fan Yafeng, Gao Zhisheng, and Zhang Xingshui from attending], accessed March 21, 2020, https://www.chinaaid.net/2006/05/blog-post_1.html.

23. Radio Free Asia Cantonese Service, "布什总统在白宫接见余杰，王怡和李柏光" [President Bush meets at the White House with Yu Jie, Wang Yi, and Li Baiguang], May 11, 2006, https://www.rfa.org/cantonese/news/us_china_humanrights-20060511.html.

24. [No author], "郭飞雄的紧急信与余杰的声明" [Guo Feixiong's urgent letter and Yu Jie's declaration], 大纪元 [Epoch times], May 20, 2006, http://www.epochtimes.com/gb/6/5/20/n1324527.htm.

25. "Guo Feixiong's Urgent Letter and Yu Jie's Declaration."

26. Liu Xiaobo, "希望国内维权远离境外的暴力或者政变煽动" [Let's hope that support of rights inside China stays away from calls for violence or coups d'etat], 自由中国论坛 [Free China forum], accessed March 22, 2020, https://blog.boxun.com/hero/2006/liuxb/53_1.shtml.

27. Liu Xiaobo, "回应呼吁国内 '见坏就上' 的高寒" [Answering Gao Han's advice to people in China that rashness is the better part of valor], 民主中国 *Minzhu Zhongguo*, August 28, 2006, accessed July 22, 2019, http://minzhuzhongguo.org/filedata/156issue/2006-8-28-3s.htm.

28. Liu Xiaobo, "Answering Gao Han's Advice to People in China That Rashness Is the Better Part of Valor."

29. Liu Xiaobo, "Answering Gao Han's Advice to People in China That Rashness Is the Better Part of Valor."

30. Liu Xiaobo, "跛足改革带来的统治危机" [The crisis in governance brought by crippled reform] (January 15, 2006), 争鸣 [Contending], February 2006, accessed July 22, 2019, https://blog.boxun.com/hero/liuxb/515_1.shtml.

31. Liu Xiaobo, "从王朔式调侃到胡戈式恶搞：兼论后极权独裁下的民间笑话政治" [From Wang Shuo's satire to Hu Ge's lampooning: And with consideration to the politics of popular jokes under post-authoritarian dictatorship] (September 18, 2006), *RYRQ*, October 2006, accessed September 9, 2019, https://blog.boxun.com/hero/2006/liuxb/71_2.shtml, translated by Teresa Zimmerman-Liu in *NENH*, 177–187.

32. Liu Xiaobo, "新年向中南海做鬼脸" [Making faces at Zhongnanhai on New Year's] (January 1, 2006), 民主中国 *Minzhu Zhongguo*, January 2006, accessed September 9, 2019, https://blog.boxun.com /hero/liuxb/485_1.shtml.

33. Liu Xiaobo, "From Wang Shuo's Satire to Hu Ge's Lampooning."

34. The quote is Liu Xiaobo's paraphrase of Qin Geng, not Qin's original words. Liu Xiaobo, "自由人 面对铁窗的微笑: 为秦耕中国第一罪: 我在监狱的快乐生活纪实 作序" [The laughter of a free man behind bars: A preface for Qin Geng's *China's First Crime: A Record of My Happy Life in Prison*] (October 12, 2006), 观察 [Observe China], November 13, 2006, accessed September 9, 2019, https:// blog.boxun.com/hero/2006/liuxb/81_2.shtml.

35. Liu Xiaobo, "独裁监狱是通向自由的第一道门槛: 为张林的言论自由辩护" [The dictator's prison is the first threshold on the route to freedom: In defense of Zhang Lin's freedom of speech], 大纪元 [Epoch times], June 19, 2005, http://www.epochtimes.com/gb/5/6/20/n959736.htm.

36. Liu Xiaobo, "The Laughter of a Free Man Behind Bars."

37. Liu Xiaobo, "The Laughter of a Free Man Behind Bars."

38. Liu Xiaobo, "反抗者的谦卑: 为格鲁沙诗文选作序" [The humility of resisters: A preface for Grusa's collection of poetry and essays], 观察 [Observe China], November 28, 2006, accessed September 9, 2019, https://blog.boxun.com/hero/2006/liuxb/87_1.shtml.

39. Liu Xiaobo, "The Humility of Resisters."

40. Liu Xiaobo, "How a Dictatorial System Murders Human Morality."

41. Liu Xiaobo, "天安门母亲的诉求与转型正义: '六四'十八周年祭" [The demands of the Tiananmen Mothers and transition justice: On the eighteenth anniversary of "June Fourth"] (May 21, 2007), *RYRQ*, June 2007, accessed September 9, 2019, http://www.renyurenquan.org/renyu renquan _article@article_id=660.html.

42. Liu Xiaobo, "The Demands of the Tiananmen Mothers and Transition Justice."

43. Liu Xiaobo, "责任伦理让勇气升华: 为张思之先生诞辰八十周年暨执业五十周年庆贺文集而作" [Responsible ethics increase courage: For The Congratulatory Collection for the Eightieth Birthday and the Fiftieth Anniversary of Entering his Profession of Mr. Zhang Sizhi], October 9, 2007, accessed September 9, 2019, https://blog.boxun.com/hero/2007/liuxb/71_1.shtml.

44. Liu Xiaobo, "Responsible Ethics Increase Courage."

45. Yang Yi 杨逸, "民间权利意识在觉醒: 著名作家刘晓波谈中国独立民间社会当前的发展" [Consciousness of people's rights is awakening: The famous writer Liu Xiaobo discusses the current situation of independent popular society in China], 参与 [Participation], December 19, 2007, accessed September 9, 2019, https://www.boxun.com/news/gb/china/2007/12/200712190609.shtml.

46. Liu Xiaobo, "'瓮安事件'的启示" [The significance of "the Weng'an incident"], 观察 [Observe China], June 30, 2008, accessed September 9, 2019, http://www.liu-xiaobo.org/blog/archives /8025, translated by Josephine Chiu-Duke in *NENH*, 107–113.

18. THE GATHERING STORM

1. Liu Xiaobo, "对黑窑童奴案的继续追问" [A deeper look into why child slavery in China's 'black kilns' could happen], *RYRQ* 8 (July 16, 2007), http://www.2008xianzhang.info/xiaobo/opaper6. html, translated by Perry Link in *NENH* 94–106.

2. Zeng Fanxu 曾繁旭 and Jiang Zhigao 蒋志高, "厦门市民与 PX 的 PK 战" [The PK war of Xiamen citizens with PX], 南方人物周刊 [Southern personage weekly], December 28, 2007, http://news.sina .com.cn/c/2007-12-28/173414624557.shtml.

3. Liu Xiaobo, "包包, 我们爱你: 为包遵信送行" [Baobao, we love you: Seeing off Bao Zunxin] (November 25, 2007), *RYRQ*, December 2007, accessed July 22, 2019, http://www.renyurenquan.org/ren yu renquan_article@article_id=788.html.

4. Zhou Xi 周西, "奥运安保扰民百姓寻求 '避运' 之道" [As Olympics security does its hassling, ordinary people seek routes of avoidance], *Radio France Internationale,* April 8, 2008, http://www1.rfi.fr /actucn/articles/104/article_8764.asp.

5. Li Ai 李艾, "北京奥运礼仪小姐咬筷子训练微笑" [Ceremony girls for the Beijing Olympics bite chopsticks to train for smiles], 北京时报 [Beijing times], January 10, 2008, news.ifeng.com/mainland /200801/0110_17_359244.shtml.

6. Liu Xiaobo, "垄断 '救灾' 正是独裁之灾" [Monopolizing "disaster relief" is one of the disasters of dictatorship], 苹果日报 [Apple daily], February 15, 2008.

7. Liu Xiaobo, "黑暗权力的颠狂: 有感于滕彪被绑架" [The dementia of dark power: Thoughts on the kidnapping of Teng Biao], 观察 [Observe China], March 8, 2008, accessed July 22, 2019, http:// blog.bnn.co/hero/200803/liuxb/3_1.shtml.

8. Wang Lixiong 王力雄, Liu Xiaobo, and twenty-seven others, "关于处理西藏局势的十二点意见" [Twelve opinions on how to handle the situation in Tibet], *Human Rights Watch,* March 21, 2008, https://www.hrw.org/zh-hans/news/2008/03/21/234189.

9. Liu Xiaobo, "西藏危机是唯物主义独裁的失败" [The Tibet crisis is the failure of the materialist dictatorship], BBC Chinese.com, accessed March 28, 2020, http://news.bbc.co.uk/chinese/simp/hi /newsid_7320000/newsid_7322300/7322376.stm.

10. Liu Xiaobo, "汉人无自由, 藏人无自治" [So long as Chinese have no freedom, Tibet will have no autonomy], 观察 [Observe China], April 11, 2008, accessed July 22, 2019, https://www.boxun.com /news/gb/pubvp/2008/04/200804120513.shtml, translated by Eva S. Chou in *NENH* 262–266.

11. Liu Xiaobo, "我看中共开启谈判大门" [My view of the Communists' opening the door to negotiations], 观察 [Observe China], accessed July 22, 2019, https://blog.boxun.com/hero/200804/liuxb/8_1.shtml.

12. Liu Xiaobo, "共和党对奥巴马当选的贡献" [The contribution of the Republican Party to Obama's election], 观察 [Observe China], 2008, https://www.chinesepen.org/old-posts/?p=16123, translated by Paul G. Pickowicz in *NENH* 270–274.

13. Quoted in Zhongguo hejie zhiku 中国和解智库, "'冲突与和解'主题座谈会纪要" [Written summary of the conference on "conflict and reconciliation"] (April 6, 2008), first published in 冲突与和解网 [Conflict and reconciliation web], accessed March 28, 2020, http://beijingspring.com/c7/xw/rqmy /20080406195302.htm.

14. Zhongguo hejie zhiku, "Written Summary of the Conference on 'Conflict and Reconciliation.'"

15. Zhongguo hejie zhiku, "Written Summary of the Conference on 'Conflict and Reconciliation.'"

16. Zhongguo hejie zhiku, "Written Summary of the Conference on 'Conflict and Reconciliation.'"

17. News Office of the China State Council, September 25, 2008.

18. Liu Xiaobo, "Monopolizing 'Disaster Relief' Is One of the Disasters of Dictatorship."

19. Liu Xiaobo, "大地震中的民间之光" [Society's splendor in a great earthquake], 观察 [Observe China], May 14, 2008, accessed July 22, 2019, https://blog.boxun.com/hero/200805/liuxb/2_1.shtml.

20. Liu Xiaobo, "今天国旗降下, 哪天国旗再降" [The national flag is lowered today; when will it next be lowered?], 观察 [Observe China], May 19, 2008, accessed July 22, 2019, https://blog.boxun.com /hero/200805/4_1.shtml.

21. Liu Xiaobo, "The National Flag Is Lowered Today; When Will It Next Be Lowered?"

22. Liu Xiaobo, "孩子·母亲·春天: 为'天安门母亲网站开通而作" [Children · mothers · spring: For the Website of the Tiananmen Mothers], 天安门母亲 [Tiananmen Mothers] website, May 2008, accessed July 22, 2019, https://blog.boxun.com/hero/200805/liuxb/5_1.shtml.

23. Liu Ning 刘柠, "刘晓波的微言大义" [The valor of Liu Xiaobo's small words], 民主中国 [Democratic China], June 2, 2008, accessed July 22, 2019, http://minzhuzhongguo.org/MainArtShow.aspx?AID =7105.

24. Liu Xiaobo, "从野草到荒原: '2008年度当代汉语贡献奖' 答谢辞" [From wild grass to a wasteland: Statement of thanks on receiving the "2008 award for contributions in the use of the Chinese language"], June 3, 2008, 观察 [Observe China], accessed July 22, 2019, https://blog.boxun.com/hero /200806/liuxb/2_1.shtml.

25. Jiang Qisheng 江棋生 and fourteen others, "六四夜，我们抗议警方对刘晓波先生施暴" [On the night of June Fourth, we protest the police violence against Mr. Liu Xiaobo], 独立中文笔会 [Independent Chinese PEN], accessed March 29, 2020, https://blog.boxun.com/hero/200806/jqsheng/1_1 .shtml.

26. Liu Xiaobo, "甘地式非暴力反抗的微缩中国版: 有感于太石村村民的接力绝食抗议" [A miniature Chinese version of Gandhi's nonviolence: Thoughts on the relay hunger strike resistance by the villagers of Taishi] (September 3, 2005), 民主中国 [Democratic China], September 5, 2005, accessed July 22, 2019, https://blog.boxun.com/hero/liuxb/426_1.shtml.

27. Ai Weiwei 艾未未, "一个孤僻的人" [An eccentric], 现实中国 [Actual China], August 3, 2003, accessed July 22, 2019, https://blog.boxun.com/hero/200808/yjlt/17_1.shtml.

28. Liu Xiaobo, "官权的暴力统治与杨佳的暴力复仇" [The violent rule of the authorities and the violent revenge of Yang Jia] (July 25, 2008), accessed September 9, 2019, *RYRQ*, August 2008, http:// www.renyurenquan.org/ren yu renquan_article@article_id=963.html.

29. Liu Xiaobo, "The Violent Rule of the Authorities and the Violent Revenge of Yang Jia."

30. Liu Xiaobo, "杨佳式暴力复仇仅仅是'原始正义'" [Violent revenge like Yang Jia's is only "primitive justice"] (August 21, 2008), 争鸣 [Contending], September 2008, accessed July 22, 2019, https:// blog.boxun.com/hero/200809/liuxb/1_1.shtml.

31. In Chinese, 冤有头，债有主.

32. Liu Xiaobo, "'瓮安事件'的启示" [The significance of "the Weng'an incident"], 观察 [Observe China], June 30, 2008, accessed July 22, 2019, http://www.liu-xiaobo.org/blog/archives/8025, translated by Josephine Chiu-Duke in *NENH* 107–113.

33. Liu Xiaobo, "Violent Revenge Like Yang Jia's Is Only 'Primitive Justice.'" The list of six reasons here is paraphrased for concision.

34. Liu Xiaobo, "The Violent Rule of the Authorities and the Violent Revenge of Yang Jia."

35. Liu Xiaobo, "The Violent Rule of the Authorities and the Violent Revenge of Yang Jia."

19. CHARTER 08

1. Qin Yongmin, a democracy activist from Hubei, in 1993 took the lead in writing a "Peace Constitution" that was the first programmatic statement by a political opposition group in China since 1949. Its key provision was "to establish and carry out, as soon as possible, a transition from a single-center to a multiple-center political system" (北京之春, August 2013). Qin was arrested within hours of announcing the document and sentenced to two years of labor education. A similar failed attempt happened in January 1994, when a group of Chinese democrats in the United States led by the political scientist Yan Jiaqi announced a "Constitution of the Federated Republic of China."

2. Zhang Zuhua 张祖桦, "自由之火，生生不息: 刘晓波的精神遗产" [Torch of freedom, fecundity without end: The spiritual legacy of Liu Xiaobo], 民主中国 *Minzhu Zhongguo*, December 7, 2017, accessed September 9, 2019, http://minzhuzhongguo.org/MainArtShow.aspx?AID=93267.

3. Wang Debang 王德邦, "提升全民维权的层次: 《零八宪章》的历史担当" [Raising the level of rights for all the people: A historic role for Charter 08], in 零八宪章 [Charter 08], ed. Li Xiaorong 李晓蓉 and Zhang Zuhua (Hong Kong: Kaifang chubanshe, 2009), 50–51.

4. Zhang Zuhua, "Torch of Freedom, Fecundity Without End."

5. "仲尼祖述尧舜,宪章文武" [Confucius succeeded Yao and Shun, and learned from King Wen and King Wu of Zhou], 礼记·中庸 [Book of rites, doctrine of the mean].

6. Ai Xiaoming 艾晓明, "让他回家，放了刘晓波！: 和刘霞的对话" [Release Liu Xiaobo and let him go home!: A dialogue with Liu Xia], April 2, 2009, accessed September 9, 2019, https://www.boxun .com/news/gb/china/2010/10/201010082129.shtml.

7. Ai Xiaoming, "Release Liu Xiaobo and Let Him Go Home!"

8. Ding Zilin and Jiang Peikun, "我们与晓波的相知、相识和相交（上）" [Our knowledge, familiarity, and relations with Xiaobo (part I)], accessed February 25, 2020, http://www.tiananmenmother.org /tiananmenmother/m100116001.htm.

9. Ai Xiaoming, "Release Liu Xiaobo and Let Him Go Home!"

10. Ai Xiaoming, "Release Liu Xiaobo and Let Him Go Home!"

11. Zhang Yu 张裕, "刘晓波、笔会和《零八宪章》的几个稿本（一）" [Liu Xiaobo, Chinese PEN, and the several texts of Charter 08], 民主中国 *Minzhu Zhongguo,* accessed December 15, 2022, http://liux-iaobo.info/blog/archives/37393.

12. "Charter 08," translated by Perry Link in *NENH* 303.

13. These details come from a record of police interrogation of Xiaobo, and it is possible that they are exaggerated or even fabricated. The police could have been trying to increase Xiaobo's culpability as an author of Charter 08.

14. Xu Youyu, "忆刘晓波见蒯大富" [Recalling an encounter between Liu Xiaobo and Kuai Dafu], 开放 [Open], March 2001.

15. Cui Weiping 崔卫平, "我为什么在宪章上签名" [Why I put my name on the charter], in Li Xiaorong and Zhang Zuhua, eds., 零八宪章 [Charter 08], section 2, 5–9.

16. Zhang Zuhua, interview by Wu Dazhi, Beijing, August 12, 2018.

17. Ma Shaofang, text message to Wu Dazhi, March 26, 2019.

18. Jiang Qisheng 江棋生, "坚毅前行是对于晓波最好的声援" [Determined movement forward is the best way to support Xiaobo], Radio Free Asia, December 14, 2008, accessed September 9, 2019, https://www.boxun.com/news/gb/china/2008/12/200812140915.shtml.

19. Sha Yexin 沙叶新, "诺奖眼中有状元" [The Nobel committee finds a number one], 开放 [Open], March 2011.

20. Chen Ziming 陈子明, "'零八宪章'运动的意义" [The significance of the "Charter 08" Movement], 新世纪 [The new century], December 10, 2009, http://www.2008xianzhang.info/Reviews /20091221%20chen-ziming.html.

21. Zhang Yu, "Liu Xiaobo, Chinese PEN, and the Several Texts of Charter 08."

22. Liu Xia, interview by Hao Jian, YouTube, accessed September 9, 2019, https://www.youtube.com /watch?v=lFKxjClgMxE.

23. Jiang Qisheng 江棋生, "公民之志不可夺也" [The will of citizens cannot be confiscated], *Radio Free Asia*, December 8, 2009, https://www.rfa.org/mandarin/pinglun/jiangqisheng/jqs-12082009135424 .html.

24. Liao Yiwu 廖亦武, "回应刘霞" [Answering Liu Xia], *Radio Free Asia,* December 8, 2009, http:// www.wrchina.org/archives/6616.

25. Liao Yiwu, "Answering Liu Xia."

20. THE WORLD WATCHES A PRISON

1. Quoted in Yang Kailiang 杨开亮, "奥西茨基：一个用思想撞击法西斯的殉道者：和平战士奥西茨基" [Ossietzky: A martyr who attacked fascism with thought: The peaceful warrior Ossietzky], 中国选举与治理网, [China elections and governance web], October 13, 2010, accessed September 9, 2019, http://www.liu-xiaobo.org/blog/archives/22225.

2. The descriptions of the ceremony here draw on Perry Link, "At the Nobel Ceremony: Liu Xiaobo's Empty Chair," *The New York Review of Books Daily*, December 13, 2010, https://www.nybooks.com /daily/2010/12/13/nobel-peace-prize-ceremony-liu-xiaobo/.

3. Liu Xia, interview by Perry Link, Berlin, November 1, 2018.

4. Radio France Internationale, "刘晓波曾被允许会见家人和短暂出狱为父奔丧" [Liu Xiaobo was permitted to exit prison and to visit briefly with family for the purpose of attending his father's funeral], October 4, 2011, http://www.rfi.fr/cn/中国/20111004-刘晓波曾被允许会见家人和短暂出狱为父奔丧.

5. Radio Free Asia, December 12, 2012, https://www.rfa.org/english/news/china/nobel-1204201 2075021.html.

6. Isolda Morillo and Alexa Olesen, "China Nobel Wife Speaks on Detention," Associated Press, December 6, 2012, https://news.yahoo.com/ap-exclusive-china-nobel-wife-speaks-detention -012905518.html; see also Deutsche Welle, "美联社记者成功探访被软禁两年的刘霞" [An Associated Press reporter succeeds in interviewing Liu Xia, who has been under house arrest for two years], December 6, 2012, https://www.dw.com/zh/美联社记者成功探访被软禁两年的刘霞/a-16431553-0; video recording of the encounter, accessed July 24, 2019, https://lihliiposterous.wordpress.com /2012/12/07/121206-icable.

7. Xu Youyu, "新年前夕的生日问候: 我们见到了刘霞" [A birthday greeting on the eve of the new year: We have met Liu Xia], *China in Perspective*, accessed August 16, 2019, http://www.chinainperspective.com/ArtShow.aspx?AID=191082013.

8. Liu Xia, interview by Perry Link, Berlin, November 1, 2018. Jiang Weiping 姜维平, "刘晓波狱中种菜" [Liu Xiaobo plants vegetables in prison], *China in Perspective*, accessed May 3, 2020, http://www.chinainperspective.com/ArtShow.aspx?AID=158798.

9. Mo Shaoping, WeChat message to Wu Dazhi, August 21, 2019.

10. Mo Shaoping, text message to Wu Dazhi, August 23, 2019.

11. BBC Chinese.com, "中国以欺诈罪判囚刘晓波妻弟刘晖11年" [China sentences Liu Hui, brother-in-law of Liu Xiaobo, to eleven years in prison on charges of swindling], June 10, 2013, https://www .bbc.com/zhongwen/simp/china/2013/06/130609_china_liu_inlaw_verdict.

12. Shang Baojun (@shangbaojun19), Twitter, 10:21 p.m., June 13, 2013, https://twitter.com /shangbaojun19/status/345410738787082240.

13. Shang Baojun (@shangbaojun19), Twitter, 5:01 p.m., May 17, 2014, https://twitter.com/search?q =shangbaojun19%20%E5%88%98%E9%9C%9E%E6%8E%88%E6%9D%83&src=typed_query &f=top.

14. Mo Shaoping, WeChat voice message to Wu Dazhi, July 1, 2019, states that "the promise was an exchange for Liu Hui's being released on medical parole." See also 苹果日报 [Apple daily], "諾獎得主劉曉波肝癌末期 保外就醫" [Nobel laureate Liu Xiaobo is sent to hospital for late-stage liver cancer], July 26, 2017; Deutsche Welle, "律师曝刘晓波患肝癌晚期 保外就医" [Lawyers reveal that Liu Xiaobo has late-stage liver cancer and is on medical parole], June 26, 2017, accessed September 9, 2019, http://news.dwnews.com/china/news/2017-06-26/59821986.html.

15. "Asia-Pacific Report," Radio Free Asia, "刘霞视频哭诉: 刘晓波已不能动手术, 不能放疗, 不能化疗" [A video of Liu Xia in tears: Liu Xiaobo is inoperable and cannot do radiation therapy or chemotherapy], June 26, 2017, https://www.rfa.org/mandarin/yataibaodao/renquanfazhi/yl-06262 017102404.html.

16. Mo Shaoping, interview by Wu Dazhi, Beijing, August 29, 2018.

17. Liao Yiwu 廖亦武, "刘晓波生日与刘霞近作" [Liu Xiaobo's birthday and recent works by Liu Xia], 民主中国 [Democratic China], December 28, 2016, accessed September 9, 2019, http://minzhu zhongguo.org/MainArtShow.aspx?AID=75760.

18. A message entitled 刘晓波正在住院接受治疗 [Liu Xiaobo is in hospital receiving treatment] appeared on the website of the Bureau of Justice of Shenyang Province on June 28 but was later taken down. The message is available elsewhere, for example on May 9, 2020, at https://blog.dwnews .com/post-959411.html and at http://www.sinovision.net/home/space/do/blog/uid/510514/id /315849.html.

19. "劉曉波做 CT 檢查 病況不明" [Liu Xiaobo undergoes CT scans, illness unclear]. 明报新闻网 [Ming Pao news net], February 5, 2017, accessed September 9, 2019, https://news.mingpao.com/pns /中國/article/20170205/s00013/1486230792401/劉曉波做 ct 檢查-病況.

20. Markus Büchler, Chair of Surgery, University of Heidelberg, interview by Perry Link, November 12, 2018.

21. "刘晓波过世，举世哀悼，中国人民不知道？" [Liu Xiaobo dies, the world mourns, and the Chinese people do not know?], Radio Free Asia, July 14, 2017, https://www.youtube.com/watch?v=AnyCwSzFap4.

22. Liao Yiwu, *Bullets and Opium: Real-Life Stories of China After the Tiananmen Square Massacre* (New York: Signal Press/Atria, 2019), 234.

23. He Pin 何频 (@MJTVHoPin), Twitter, June 28, 2017. See also Liao Yiwu (@liaoyiwu1), Twitter, 11:15 p.m., June 27, 2017, https://twitter.com/i/web/status/879946223360323585.

24. This notice, which appeared on the website of the Bureau of Prisons of Liaoning Province, was removed shortly after it was posted, but a screenshot of it was preserved on BBC Chinese.com, accessed August 16, 2020, https://www.bbc.com/zhongwen/simp/chinese-news-40413945.

25. Radio Free Asia, "A Video of Liu Xia in Tears: Liu Xiaobo Is Inoperable and Cannot Do Radiation Therapy or Chemotherapy."

26. First Hospital of China Medical University, Shenyang City, "Report on the Medical Condition of Liu Xiaobo," July 6, 2017, states that the fever and the complaints of chest pain came "two weeks prior to [the patient's] admission to our hospital on June 7, 2017." The report appeared on the hospital's web page, but later it and all reports on Liu Xiaobo were deleted. It still can be accessed at http://liuxiaobo.info/blog/archives/23897.

27. "Little Shrimp" (*xiaoxia*) is a pun on Little Xia, Xiaobo's familiar name for Liu Xia. "360 seconds" is apparently a mistake for five minutes—300 seconds—as Xiaobo originally recorded the incident. (See chapter 12.)

28. Zhang Jieping 張潔平, "劉曉波7月5日最後手稿全文披露，送給劉霞的最後禮物" [The complete text of Liu Xiaobo's final manuscript is revealed: His last gift to Liu Xia], 端传媒 [Initium media], accessed May 9, 2020, https://theinitium.com/article/20170714-mainland-liuxiaobo/.

29. This and the following two paragraphs are drawn from Marcus Büchler, interview by Perry Link, University of Heidelberg, November 12, 2018.

30. Embassy of the Republic of Germany to the People's Republic of China, "Statement About Breach of Doctor-Patient Confidentiality by Certain Actors in the Case of Liu Xiaobo (10.07.2017)," accessed May 9, 2020, https://china.diplo.de/cn-zh/aktuelles/erklaerungen/170710-statemvideolxb/1308808.

31. Liu Xiaobo, "只身面对大海" [Only my body facing the vast ocean], 倾向 [Tendency] 3–4 (1994).

32. Liu Xiaobo, "Only My Body Facing the Vast Ocean."

33. See for example 狱中随笔之一 [Prison notes I] (July 14, 1997), 国际笔会独立中文作家笔会会刊试刊号 [Trial issue of the Journal of Independent Chinese PEN], spring 2005, https://blog.boxun.com/hero/liuxb/295_1.shtml.

EPILOGUE: THE LEGACY OF LIU XIAOBO

1. Vaclav Havel, *Living in Truth*, ed. Jan Vladislav (London: Faber and Faber, 1989), 59.

2. "Using Truth to Undermine a System Built on Lies," translated by Eva S. Chou in *NENH* 293.

3. "Imprisoning People for Words and the Power of Public Opinion," translated by Louisa Chiang in *NENH* 211–220.

4. See the account of Sun Zhigang in chapter 14.

5. See chapter 14 for the three cases mentioned here.

6. "Behind the Rise of Great Powers," translated by Josephine Chiu-Duke in *NENH* 239.

Index

A Cheng, 96, 112

academic career of Liu Xiaobo, 126–27; experiences as visiting scholar overseas (1988), 153–74; Liu Xiaobo fired from Beijing Normal University, 221; public speaking engagements, 122–23, 145; reasons for abandoning, 324; rising fame and its consequences, 105–6, 109–35, 139, 145, 147, 149; self-appraisals, 89, 145; and studies of popular culture, 239–41; troubles with Education Commission, 126–27, 140, 141; visit to Australia and U.S. (1993), 242–44; and Wang Xuedian's views on Liu Xiaobo, 134. *See also* aesthetics; Beijing Normal University; graduate school, Liu Xiaobo in; Jilin University; literature, Chinese; publications and statements of Liu Xiaobo

accumulation theory, 116–18

activism, 280–345; activism "inside the system" vs. "outside the system," 303–4, 325–26, 343, 344, 475; and attitudes toward prison, 385–86; Brains for Reconciliation in China, 404–5; and Charter 08 (*see* Charter 08); and citizens' rights cases reported on the Internet, 306–33 (*see also specific cases under this heading*); comfort and aid for prisoners and their families, 297–99, 307, 317, 318, 331; and "constructive opposition," 245; and current conditions in China, 477–80; and "custody and repatriation" program, 312, 375, 474; and debate over "radical" and "moderate" approaches, 379–84; and discrimination against hepatitis B carriers, 315, 322, 474; dispute over "Block-Guo-gate," 380–81; Du Daobin case, 316–18, 322–25; and farmers' movement, 338–39; formula for effective activism, 473–75; foundations for Liu Xiaobo's activism, 148; and freedom of the press, 309–10; and freedom of speech, 325–26, 344–45; and gradual changes, 336–37, 339, 341–43, 345, 382–84, 388, 414, 475; He Depu case, 307; and HIV/AIDS, 302–3; in Hong Kong, 475, 478; Hu Jia case, 399; Huang Jing case, 313, 474; impact of social media, 309, 320–22, 383, 473–74 (*see also* Internet); and importance of listening, 472; and increased willingness of victims to speak out, 389–90; increasing participation in demonstrations, 389–90; and individual letter-writing, 300, 475; informal political group in Beijing, 244–48; Jiang Yanyong case, 310–11; Li Siyi case, 314–15, 322; Liu Di ("stainless-steel rat") case, 307–9, 323; Liu Xiaobo's increasing interest in the persecuted and forgotten, 288–89, 348; Liu Xiaobo's initial indifference to political protest, 128; Liu Xiaobo's recommendations for progress toward societal transformation, 341–45; Living Buddha of Garze Prefecture case, 402; low-key tactics, 299–301; mass demonstrations coordinated by the regime, 373–74; and masses incidents (strikes, demonstrations, etc.), 349–50, 389–90, 392–93, 407, 413, 416, 478 (*see also* protests); and media crackdown (2004), 323–25; and migrant worker rights, 312, 400–401, 474; and minimal organization/movements remaining leaderless, 341–43, 475; and *minjian* activity, 340–41; and minority rights, 402–3; need for activists to distinguish personal interests and the public interest, 389; and need for self-reflection, 387, 389; and need for vision statement for rights movement, 419 (*see also* Charter 08); and "nibbling at the system's edges," 299–300; and nonviolence (*see* nonviolence); and offline salons, workshops, and book clubs, 321; and open letter technique, 298, 423; and openness, 342; and political humor, 307–8,